Happy Birthday Rainer.
With all my love Oska 13/2/04

The LONDON
Compendium

The LONDON Compendium

Exploring the Hidden Metropolis

Ed Glinert

ALLEN LANE
an imprint of
PENGUIN BOOKS

ALLEN LANE

Published by the Penguin Group
Penguin Books Ltd, 80 Strand, London WC2R ORL, England
Penguin Putnam Inc., 375 Hudson Street, New York, New York 10014, USA
Penguin Books Australia Ltd, 250 Camberwell Road, Camberwell, Victoria 3124, Australia
Penguin Books Canada Ltd, 10 Alcorn Avenue, Toronto, Ontario, Canada M4V 3B2
Penguin Books India (P) Ltd, 11, Community Centre, Panchsheel Park, New Delhi – 110 017, India
Penguin Books (NZ) Ltd, Cnr Rosedale and Airborne Roads, Albany, Auckland, New Zealand
Penguin Books (South Africa) (Pty) Ltd, 24 Sturdee Avenue, Rosebank 2196, South Africa

Penguin Books Ltd, Registered Offices: 80 Strand, London WC2R ORL, England

www.penguin.com

First published 2003
1

Copyright © Ed Glinert, 2003

Grateful acknowledgement is made for permission to reproduce extracts from 'City' (1937), 'Middlesex' (1954), 'The Metropolitan Railway' (1954) and *Summoned by Bells* (1960) by John Betjeman. Reprinted by permission of the executors of the estate of John Betjeman and John Murray.

The moral right of the author has been asserted

Designed by Andrew Barker
Set in 9/11.25 pt PostScript Adobe Minion
Typeset by Rowland Phototypesetting Ltd, Bury St Edmunds, Suffolk
Printed in England by Clays Ltd, St Ives plc

ISBN 0–713–99688–9

For Katy and Marian

Contents

Acknowledgements

Without my agent, Faith Evans, and editor, Margaret Bluman, this book would not have been possible, and I cannot thank them enough for their guidance, hard work and help.

I would like to thank a number of people for providing information, inspiration and assistance: Celia Boggis, John Naughton, Tessa Fry, David Stone, Richard Aron, Simon Rose, Lucy Richmond, Nancy Hopkins, Tim Perry, Martin Morris, David Rich of Tower Hamlets archives, and the staff of the London Library.

Many thanks also to Cormach Moore and Andrea Vincenti.

In producing the book, Penguin's Nigel Wilcockson, Louise Ball (publicity), Elisabeth Merriman, Andrew Barker (design) and Paul Simonon (for the stunning cover).

Finally, I would like to thank Katy Walsh Glinert for listening so patiently while I read out to her vast chunks of the editorial, Marian Walsh for all her time, patience and care, and in particular John Nicholson and Peter Golds for all the wonderful stories, nuggets of information and ideas they gave me, month after month, without which this book would have been a considerably duller affair.

Foreword

Lord Macaulay, the great early-Victorian historian, claimed he had walked down every street in London. Sam Weller, according to Charles Dickens in *The Pickwick Papers*, had a knowledge of London that was 'extensive and peculiar'. Sherlock Holmes, according to his narrator, Dr Watson, had 'an exact knowledge of London'.

Although there are considerably more London streets now than there were in the nineteenth century, it was with these august gentlemen in mind that I walked across the capital – from Limehouse to Lambeth, from Sands Ends to Somers Town, from Whitehall to Whitechapel – also hoping to gain an 'extensive and peculiar' understanding of London, even if the 'exact knowledge' of Sherlock Holmes is unattainable, in researching *The London Compendium*.

The book attempts to unravel the mystery of London and relate its most interesting stories not in chronological order of events, through a haphazard list of themes and subjects, or in an A-Z format, but through the physical reality of the place: its areas, streets and buildings. This differentiates *The London Compendium* from countless numbers of other books on London – themed guides, directories, encyclopaedias and area histories – in that it not only contains considerable information on all the main topics that one would expect to find in a book of this size and scope – local history, politics, architecture, royal scandal, literature, espionage and the secret state, music, art, religious activity, immigration, crime, sleaze, football, transport, and so on – but sets out the information in a clear and easily accessible manner.

Let us see how this works in practice by taking a typical London street – Dean Street in Soho. A lively and welcoming West End thoroughfare, Dean Street is thronged with office workers and the occasional celebrity by day, revellers and partygoers at night, and tourists at the weekend straying between the shops of Oxford Street and the cafés of Old Compton Street. On the wall of No. 28 is a plaque commemorating the residency of Karl Marx during the 1850s. There is another plaque, to the considerably less well-known Dr Joseph Rogers, a Victorian-era health reformer, at No. 33. Neither plaque has room to reveal anything other than the name of the house's illustrious former occupant, and most London guidebooks say little about Dean Street other than a cursory mention of its restaurants and pubs or a brief summary of Marx's stay.

Yet Dean Street has a history that is characteristic of London and worth relating in detail. At No. 21, on the east side, once stood the Venetian ambassador's chapel where, in 1763, the seven-year-old Mozart played the harpsichord accompanied by his four-year-old sister. It was rebuilt in the 1860s as a school, converted into the West End Synagogue in 1944, and after that closed, in the late 1990s became the Soho Theatre. Almost next door is the Quo Vadis restaurant, opened by the Italian Peppino

Leoni, in 1926. For fourteen years Leoni worked hard to make his restaurant one of the finest in London. Then, in 1940, Italy joined the Second World War against the Allies. Leoni, to his chagrin, was interned as an enemy alien. He later recalled how walking to his cell he felt a 'sudden hatred for the police, for the British government which had issued the instructions for my internment, and for all forms of authority', having lived in the country for thirty-three years with no political or criminal blemish on his record. Released after the end of the war, Leoni returned to Soho and had to start afresh to re-establish the restaurant's reputation. Having done so, he was outraged when Westminster council decided to erect a blue plaque on the wall of the restaurant commemorating the one-time residency of Karl Marx in an apartment upstairs. 'My clientele is the very best rich people . . . nobility and royalty, and Marx was the person who wanted to get rid of them all,' Leoni wailed, to no avail.

That story leads us on to the tragic Soho stay of Marx himself. The founder of communism lived at 28 Dean Street, above the modern-day Quo Vadis restaurant, from 1850 to 1856 with his wife, Jenny, maid Lenchen, and a number of children, in what he described as 'an old hovel', with no toilet or running water. Three of the Marxes' children died while they lived here, although one who survived was Eleanor, his last child, known in her own right as a socialist campaigner and writer. Yet No. 28 was not Marx and his family's only Dean Street address. They had previously lodged at the now demolished No. 64, at a time when they were so badly in debt that Jenny went to Holland to beg money from her uncle, Lion Philips, one of the founders of the Philips electric company that now dominates the city of Eindhoven. But Philips, worried about the effect socialist activity, of the kind that Marx advocated, was having on his business, refused to make a loan, and when Jenny threatened that she and Karl would therefore have to emigrate to America he explained that such a move would be an excellent idea.

The history of Dean Street comes more up-to-date with stories relating to the long-running nightclub at No. 69, which during the early years of the twentieth century was the Gargoyle club, opened in 1925 by the Hon. David Tennant and his fiancée, the actress Hermione Baddeley. They spared no expense: Edwin Lutyens was hired as architect and Henri Matisse as designer, and attracted a membership that included the actors Noël Coward and Fred Astaire and the actress Tallulah Bankhead. During the Second World War some of the Gargoyle's luxurious scenery was sold off, but after the war it briefly reverted to being Soho's most prestigious nightspot, where swing bands played and men in white tuxedos, such as the spies Guy Burgess and Donald Maclean, bestrode the floor. By 1978 Steve Strange and Rusty Egan were running a successful disco here, playing records by David Bowie, Roxy Music and Kraftwerk, and its clientele went on to play a major role in the development of the New Romantic movement, typified by groups such as Culture Club, Depeche Mode and Spandau Ballet. The following year Don Ward opened the Comedy Store here, giving aspiring comics (one of whom was Alexei Sayle) the chance to prove they had the talent to perform live in front of a probably hostile crowd.

Opposite the former Gargoyle is the even more exotic Groucho club, where the nation's best-known journalists and media celebrities congregate. During the mid-1990s one could queue at the bar next to Salman Rushdie (it was the least likely place where he might succumb to the *fatwah*), shock artist Damien Hirst and the bass player from Blur. The Groucho still enjoys a fashionable reputation, as does the nearby French House pub, once a popular haunt for writers and artists, where Charles de Gaulle allegedly drew up his Free French call-to-arms during the Second World War. A few doors to the north is the Colony Club, where the artist Francis Bacon was once paid £10 a week to bring in rich customers and where Colin MacInnes, author of *Absolute Beginners*, liked to sit on sunny days with the curtains drawn 'gossiping one's life away'. And we must not to miss out the Golden Lion at No. 51, a gay pub since the 1920s, which was frequented in the 1970s by Dennis Nilsen, the mass murderer who killed at least seventeen men in the London suburbs around that time. It was here in November 1981 that he picked up Paul Nobbs, one of the few targets he failed to murder.

All wonderful tales, I am sure you will agree, as central to the story of London as the Changing of the Guard and the history of the Routemaster buses, and absent from other guidebooks. But instead of these stories being presented in a Soho chapter as continuous narrative, they appear in *The London Compendium* as entries in their own right, logically ordered to make life as easy as possible for the reader, whether they be a London enthusiast familiar with the capital's history, or a tourist who has never been to the capital before. The text for Dean Street simply begins at one end of the street, the Shaftesbury Avenue end, works its way up the west side, noting each place of interest in turn and telling its story, until Oxford Street is reached. Crossing the road it then works its way down the east side, repeating the process until reaching the end. The same system works for Dean Street's neighbours – Frith, Greek, Old Compton, Wardour streets, Soho Square, Carnaby Street, Golden Square, everywhere else in Soho and the West End. The rest of London – Portobello Road, Brick Lane, Euston Road, Cheyne Walk, Long Acre, Strand – is treated the same way.

Readers familiar with the Buildings of England series started by Nikolaus Pevsner, which takes each street in an area and analyses its architecture in detail, will realize that *The London Compendium* adopts a similar approach, but instead of dealing just with architecture, covers every possible subject of interest that might attract the curious

reader, giving as full and fascinating a history of the place as possible. So, for instance, on Portobello Road we deal with antique stores, the history of Virgin Records, the Electric Cinema, Martin Amis's *London Fields* and the one-time residency at No. 22 of George Orwell. On Brick Lane the subjects cover the market, Jewish immigration, the Ben Truman brewery, the Beigel Bake, Bloom's and the 1999 bomb.

The structure of the chapters is also easy to follow. First I have split London into the inner areas and the outer suburbs and then, rather than dividing up the city into arbitrary blocks, I have followed the postal district boundaries, as these letters and numbers appear on every street nameplate and can therefore guide visitors and tourists as well as locals. In inner London there are chapters on The City of London (EC1–4), Central London (EC1 areas outside the City, i.e. Clerkenwell, WC1 and WC2), The West End (W1) and Westminster/Whitehall (SW1). In outer London there are chapters on East London (E1 and onwards), North London (N1 etc.), North-west London (NW1 etc.), South-east London (SE1 etc.), South-west London (SW1 areas outside Westminster proper, which is mainly Belgravia, and so on) and West London (W2 etc). Between inner and outer London lies the section on the River Thames, so that the Thames runs in the middle of the book, as it does physically between north London and south London.

Within the area sections the postal districts are listed in numerical order (Kensington W8, North Kensington W10, Notting Hill W11), and within them the streets are listed alphabetically, unless the number of entries dictates dividing the area into more manageable smaller chunks, such as Chelsea village, Cheyne Walk, Hoxton and so on.

Another device adopted to help readers navigate their way through the book is the use of little arrows at the end of a number of entries guiding the reader to another page where they will find a story on a similar topic, individual or organization. Given that no one is likely to read *The London Compendium* from beginning to end these arrows provide a host of alternative routes through the book and allow the reader to glimpse something else of interest while looking for more information on a particular subject.

Of course in a book of this size there is not enough room to include every area (alas Mill Hill, Penge and Forest Gate have ended up on the cutting-room floor) or every wonderful story that could be told. So readers searching for the tale of the group of Italian anarchists who plotted the assassination of the fascist dictator Benito Mussolini in an Old Compton Street café, or for shocking details of the life led by Rolling Stones guitarist Brian Jones and actress Anita Pallenberg in their flat at 1 Courtfield Road, South Kensington – what Marianne Faithfull in her 1994 autobiography described as a 'veritable witches' coven of decadent illuminati, rock princelings and hip aristos . . . peeling paint, clothes, newspapers and magazines strewn everywhere' – will have to wait for now.

The City of London

The world's leading financial centre and home of the Bank of England, the Stock Exchange, ancient churches and medieval alleyways, the City of London occupies one square mile of land on the north bank of the Thames between the Temple and Tower Hill and is the oldest settlement in the capital. It was founded by the Romans by the Walbrook stream in AD 43 as Londinium (from Lyn-dun, fortified town by the lake, the latter occupying much of the land around the modern-day Fenchurch Street), whose 330 acres, roughly corresponding to the centre of the modern-day City, were enclosed by a wall that partly survives, particularly seen near the street known as London Wall.

The Romans also built a public hall, or basilica, near where Leadenhall Market now stands, an amphitheatre on the site of what became the Guildhall, a bridge near what is now London Bridge – the lowest convenient point where the river could be crossed – and roads leading to other settlements such as Camulodunum (Colchester) and Durovernum (Canterbury). Within a decade the town was a flourishing mercantile centre, as archaeological remains unearthed in December 2000 indicate, but Londinium was sacked in AD 61 after a rebellion of tribes led by the Norfolk warrior Boadicea and rebuilt soon after under Gaius Julinus Alpinus Classicianus, the Roman procurator. By the beginning of the second century Londinium was the capital of the Roman province that included Britain, but it fell in 410 when the Emperor Honorius refused pleas from British cities to help repel invaders and it was not until 604, when Ethelbert founded St Paul's on the site of the present-day building, that the Roman town was revived.

William the Conqueror founded the Tower at the east end of London in 1078, at a time when Norman barons were settling locally and building trade links with their home towns, and around a hundred years later London acquired its first mayor, Henry Fitz Ailwyn. London was granted 'ancient liberties and free customs, as well by land and by water' in the Magna Carta of 1215, and around this time many of the craft guilds that today survive as livery companies were established. London became a great commercial centre in the fifteenth century, home of successful stock companies such as the Muscovy Company (the world's first), founded in 1553 after an expedition made its way to the court of Ivan the Terrible in Russia; the Hudson Bay Company, which traded in furs; the Levant Company, which traded in the Middle East; and the largest of all, the East India Company. But in the following century London was beset by disasters such as the plague of 1665, in which around 100,000 people, about one-fifth of the City's population, died, and the Fire of London, which began in a bakery on Pudding Lane, to the north of London Bridge, on 2 September 1666 and destroyed seven-eighths of what is now the City.

Christopher Wren was put in charge of rebuilding London after the Fire and he proposed a grand scheme with streets radiating from scenic points and embankments along the Thames, intending to rebuild 'all the Parish Churches in such a manner as to be seen at the end of a Vista of Houses, and dispersed in such Distances from each other, as to appear neither too thick, nor thin in Prospect'. However, Wren was overruled by the authorities, who refused to redraw property boundaries that by then existed only in the ashes of the Fire and claimed his plans would cost too much money, and most of his suggestions were abandoned.

After the Fire most of London's wealthy inhabitants moved west, colonizing undeveloped areas in what is now Mayfair and Marylebone, but commercial power remained in what came to be known as the City, zealously preserved by the Corporation of London at the Guildhall and the livery companies in their hundred or so halls. The founding of the Bank of England in 1694 helped the City regain its prestige status and in the century after the Fire major civic buildings such as the Mansion House and the Bank of England were constructed.

By the end of the eighteenth century the power of the City of London was so great that all cargo-bearing ships coming to London had to unload in the heavily crowded Pool, to the east of where Tower Bridge now stands, and pay a tariff to the City.

As London spread, railways and new wide straight roads such as Queen Victoria Street were cut through the old slums, following campaigns against unsanitary conditions led by Charles Dickens and the journalist Henry Mayhew, and the City's population declined from 129,000 in 1851 to 50,000 in 1881 as the working class left for the developing inner suburbs such as Hackney. Although the twentieth century saw the City lose thousands more inhabitants, its streets devastated by Second World War bombing, and industries such as newspaper publishing depart *en masse*, the area has remained a financial stronghold and economic centre thanks to the ability of its biggest concerns such as the Bank of England and the Stock Exchange to adapt to changing circumstances and retain their independence from Westminster.

ALDERSGATE, EC1

The area of the City north of St Paul's Cathedral, Aldersgate is dominated by Smithfield meat market, the various buildings of St Bartholomew's Hospital (Bart's) and the winding alleyways between, protected in Roman and medieval times by Aldersgate (originally Ealdred's Gate).
● For EC1 entries outside the City see Clerkenwell, pp. 67–82.

(i) Holborn–Holborn Viaduct

Holborn

The brief stretch of road between Gray's Inn and Holborn Circus, which shares its name with that of the area to the south, commemorates the long-vanished Holbourne stream, a tributary of the River Fleet, and is marked by two nineteenth-century granite obelisks which stand either side of the road at its Gray's Inn Road junction at the site of Holborn Bars, medieval tollgates for traffic entering the City. In the eighteenth century the road was lined with coaching inns, including the **Dagger** – frequented by the Elizabethan playwright Ben Jonson and mentioned in his 1610 play *The Alchemist* – which was famous for its 'dagger frumety', a pie decorated with dagger shapes, and the **Bull and Gate**, a terminus for many of the stage-coaches running between London and northern towns, which is featured in Henry Fielding's *Tom Jones*. Henry Mayhew, in his 1861 review of the capital's poverty, *London Labour and the London Poor*, recalled how costermongers would surround coaches pulling into London at Holborn to sell travellers bread and fruit: 'In their hopes of sale they followed anyone a mile if encouraged, even by a few approving glances.' The inns were demolished after the growth of the railways in the mid nineteenth century made their prime purpose redundant and the road's only relic of the pre-industrial age is the late-sixteenth century Staple Inn, one of London's few surviving timber-faced buildings.

north side: Gray's Inn Road to Holborn Circus
Furnival's Inn, Holborn at Brook Street, north-east junction
An Inn of Chancery from 1383 to 1817, named after the Fournyvals who rode to the Crusades with Richard I and lived locally, it later was converted to apartments and was where Charles Dickens wrote *The Pickwick Papers* from 1834 to 1837. The new **Furnival's Inn** was itself demolished in 1897 when the Prudential building (now Holborn Bars) was extended on to the site.

Inns of Chancery

The nine Inns of Chancery (Barnard's Inn, Clement's Inn, Clifford's Inn, Furnival's Inn, Lyon's Inn, New Inn, Staple Inn, Strand Inn and Thavies' Inn) were institutions involved in running chancery law – law relating to public records and archives – that came to be used for training barristers for the Inns of Court (Gray's Inn, Lincoln's Inn and the Inner and Middle Temple). Each of the Inns was run as a miniature version of the Inns of Court, with a hall and chambers but no chapel, and by the nineteenth century their functions had mostly been assumed by the Law Society. They soon closed, and almost all the buildings were demolished towards the end of the century, although their names live on in the titles of nearby streets.

Prudential Assurance (Holborn Bars), Holborn at Brook Street, north-east junction
Alfred Waterhouse's grand Gothic office block in fiery-red brick and terracotta, one of twenty-seven similar Prudential complexes across the country, was built from 1899 to 1906 on land where the Pneumatic Despatch Company had opened a station for its mid-nineteenth-century underground railway. The railway ran from Holborn to Euston in tunnels only 4 ft high, passengers being obliged to lie in coffin-like

carriages, to their great discomfort, and was not a success, closing in 1874. The tunnels are now used for cables. In 1879 the Prudential Mutual Assurance, Investment and Loan Association Company, founded in 1848 and aimed at professionals, but persuaded by the government to provide penny policies to help poorer workers save for funerals, bought the land and commissioned Waterhouse to design a new headquarters in his distinctive 'Waterhouse slaughterhouse' style. The company moved out in the 1990s.

▶ Mount Pleasant underground post railway, p. 73.

Gamage's, Nos. 116–128, between Leather Lane and Hatton Garden
One of London's best-known twentieth-century stores, **Gamage's** was built in 1878 next to the **Black Bull**, one of Holborn's great coaching inns, featured by Charles Dickens in *Martin Chuzzlewit*, and was owned by draper Arthur Gamage, who hung a sign above the door proclaiming: 'Tall Oaks From Little Acorns Grow'. Gamage gradually bought up the surrounding properties to create a huge rambling store which specialized in toys, bikes and uniforms (it was the official outfitter to the Boy Scouts), and shoppers had much fun exploring the nooks, passageways and oddly shaped rooms until the store closed in 1972. Richard Seifert's British Telecom building covers the site, and below ground level is the citadel which stores De Beers's diamonds.

south side: Holborn Viaduct to Staple Inn
Daily Mirror (1961–90), Holborn at Holborn Circus
The *Daily Mirror*, founded in 1903 off Fleet Street, moved to Holborn Circus in the early 1960s, a time when the paper was the flagship of the world's biggest media organization, IPC, and run by Cecil Harmsworth King, nephew of the paper's founder, Alfred Harmsworth (Lord Northcliffe). King had inherited his uncle's strain of megalomania and unpredictability and in the summer of 1968, having been rebuffed by Lord Mountbatten, the army's recently retired

Chief of Defence Staff, over a plan to overthrow the Labour government and install a national government peopled by capable businessmen (such as himself), King turned to his own newspapers, splashing a vicious editorial in the *Mirror* calling for a new Labour leader and Prime Minister with an article headlined: 'Enough is Enough!'. It proved enough for the *Mirror* board, which promptly sacked King and replaced him with Hugh Cudlipp whom King, ironically, had sent to open negotiations with Mountbatten.

Cudlipp produced a paper that carefully balanced serious news against ephemera – coverage of the Vietnam War alongside light-hearted stories about the affairs of Princess Margaret, a campaign against drink-driving at Christmas next to a feature about the ever decreasing length of the mini-skirt – and nurtured a talented group of writers that could justly be described as the envy of Fleet Street: Keith Waterhouse, Marjorie Proops, Anne Robinson, Geoffrey Goodman, Paul Foot, Kingsley Amis, Paul Callan and Benny Green.

After Cudlipp retired in 1974 the paper's fortunes declined and management launched a futile and costly campaign of aping Rupert Murdoch's new *Sun*, which meant that quality, popular, left-of-centre journalism was replaced with increased coverage of the royal family and TV soaps on the dubious grounds that its readers no longer had the attention span to deal with anything other than the most flippant stories.

In July 1984 the *Mirror*'s owners, Reed, sold the group for £113.4 million to Robert Maxwell, the controversial millionaire socialist, and he turned the paper into his personal newsletter, contributing articles on the miners' strike under the pseudonym Charles Wilberforce, splashing stories about Robert Maxwell solving the miners' strike, Robert Maxwell meeting East European dignitaries and Robert Maxwell the football club owner who would 'save' Reading and Oxford by merging them, alongside interviews with civilians who had recently enjoyed the honour of meeting . . . Robert Maxwell. Although profits increased under Maxwell's stewardship, despite his predilection for raiding the group's pension fund, readers and respected writers deserted the paper, and by the time he died in mysterious circumstances in 1991 it had lost its credibility. In the 1990s the *Mirror* moved to the Isle of Dogs, where it has recently staged a renaissance.

► Birth of the *Daily Mirror*, p. 51; Fleet Street, p. 41, Lord Mountbatten's address, p. 402.

Staple Inn

London's only existing sixteenth-century domestic building, Staple Inn, whose façade precariously overhangs the roadway, was an Inn of Chancery built from 1545 to 1549, restored in 1886, reconstructed in 1937, and badly damaged by a bomb in 1944. It was later restored and rebuilt by the Prudential Insurance Company, and is now used by the Institute of Actuaries and various other companies. Old Holborn tobacco, originally produced in an alleyway on the north side of Holborn, used to feature images of Staple Inn on its packets.

► Inns of Chancery, p. 4.

Holborn Viaduct

A major feat of Victorian engineering, first proposed in the *Builder* in the 1840s and built in the 1860s to ease the traffic flow between the City and the West End, Holborn Viaduct spans the valley of the now culverted Fleet River and replaced Holborn Hill, on which Charles Dickens imagined a 'megalosaurus forty feet long or so, waddling like an elephantine lizard' in the opening page of *Bleak House*. The roadway's grand Romanesque name is complemented by much civic embellishment, including statues representing Agriculture, Commerce, Fine Arts and Science.

north side: Holborn Circus to Giltspur Street

De Beers, junction Holborn Viaduct and Charterhouse Street

The world's largest diamond company, producing about 43 per cent of the world's supply, De Beers was formed in 1888 during the diamond rush at Kimberley, South Africa, and named after the brothers who owned the land where prospecting took place. De Beers's marketing arm, the Central Selling Organization, has been based in London since its foundation, the gems mostly arriving by helicopter and being stored below ground.

► Hatton Garden, p. 72.

The Church of the Holy Sepulchre-without-Newgate

The largest parish church in the City, and the regimental church of the Royal Fusiliers, who hold their annual service here, Holy Sepulchre was founded in 1137, dedicated to St Edmund the Martyr, a king of East Anglia, and designed in a style similar to that of the Church of the Holy Sepulchre in Jerusalem. As its distance from the now demolished north-west gate of the City corresponded almost exactly with the distance of its Jerusalem namesake from the Sepulchre and Calvary, it became an appropriate starting point for the Crusaders setting off on their journey to the Holy Land to rescue the Holy Sepulchre from the Saracens. The church was destroyed in the Fire of London and rebuilt on its original foundations with some of the surviving medieval masonry, such as the stone basin in the west wall, which bears scorch marks from the blaze. There are memorials to Captain John Smith, early-seventeenth-century founder of the US state of Virginia, rescued from death by the Princess Pocahontas, who is buried in the south-west corner of the church and commemorated in one of the windows; the composer John Ireland, above which the closing bars of his song 'Sea Fever' are depicted; Dame Nellie Melba, the famous Australian singer; and Henry Wood, founder and conductor of the annual Promenade concerts, whose laurel wreath is taken to the Royal Albert Hall to adorn his bust during the Proms and is returned to the church at the end of the season.

south side: Old Bailey to Holborn Circus

𝔥𝔬𝔩𝔟𝔬𝔯𝔫 𝔙𝔦𝔞𝔡𝔲𝔠𝔱 𝔰𝔱𝔞𝔱𝔦𝔬𝔫, opposite Snow
Hill

The London, Chatham and Dover Railway
opened a station and hotel on the new
Holborn Viaduct in 1867 but the latter was a
commercial failure and was soon converted
into offices. The station closed in 1990 when
the tunnel under Snow Hill was reopened
and a new station, the clumsily named City
Thameslink, was built a little further to the
south to cater for trains running between
Bedford and Brighton.

City Temple, Holborn Viaduct at Shoe Lane

Built in 1874, City Temple became the
leading centre for Nonconformity in
nineteenth-century London and was run by
the Revd Joseph Parker, a radical firebrand
whose telegraphic address was simply
'Preacher, London', who attracted the
young Mahatma Gandhi to services. In the
1920s two of the first million-selling records,
Master Ernest Luff's 'O for the Wings of a
Dove' and the Temple choir's version of
Mendelssohn's 'Hear My Prayer', were
recorded at the church. Martin Luther
King Jnr spoke at City Temple about
racial tyranny in December 1964 before
going to Oslo to receive the Nobel Peace
Prize.

St Andrew

Rebuilt by Christopher Wren from 1684 to
1690 with a double-storeyed Portland stone
exterior to frame what is his largest parish
church, St Andrew was originally a wooden
Saxon church, first mentioned in 951, and
was where in 1808 the essayist William
Hazlitt was married, his best man, the
essayist Charles Lamb, having to be
restrained several times from bursting out
laughing.

The nineteenth-century Tory prime
minister Benjamin Disraeli, despite being
born Jewish, was baptized at St Andrew's in
July 1817 after an argument between his
father and the elders of Bevis Marks
Synagogue. When the surgeon William
Marsden found a woman dying on the
steps of the church in 1827 and could not
get her admitted to a hospital he opened a
new hospital at 16 Greville Street, off Hatton
Garden, the forerunner of what is now the
Royal Free Hospital in Hampstead.

St Andrew lost its graveyard when Holborn
Viaduct was built in the 1860s, and was
almost destroyed during the Second World
War, but it was restored as the church of the
London trade guilds and since 1991 has been
the headquarters of the Royal College of
Organists.

(ii) west of Little Britain (Smithfield)

Smithfield, best known for its meat market,
was originally Smooth Field, a swamp just
outside the City boundaries, where the
Romans buried their rubbish and their
dead, and where some 270 Protestants,
including John Rogers, vicar of the nearby
church of St Sepulchre, and John Aston,
who had been found eating pork during
Lent, were executed during the reign of
Mary Tudor (1553–8) while being forced to
face the west door of the church of
St Bartholomew-the-Great. During the 1665
Plague Smithfield was used as a mass burial
pit, and the following year the area escaped
the ravages of the Fire only thanks to the
ditch that separated it from the City and a
sudden change in the direction of the wind.
In 1715 Smithfield was one of three local
places chosen by the Jacobite rebels as a
rallying point if their putsch on London to
seize the throne for James II's Catholic son
was successful. After assembling at Smithfield the mob planned to march on the Bank
of England, set it on fire and kill some of the
chief magistrates, but their coup was unsuccessful. When the live cattle market was
removed from the City to Caledonian Road
in 1855 Smithfield became a meat market,
which continues to operate successfully, its
huge Victorian buildings dominating the
area.

Charterhouse Street

The street, which is named after Charterhouse School (based locally until 1872) and leads from Holborn Circus towards Smithfield meat market, is a relatively new road for the area, as can be determined from its straightness. At No. 115 is the Fox and Anchor, one of a number of local pubs with unusual licensing hours to cater for the nearby meat market workers, which is famed for its massive breakfasts.

south side

Smithfield meat market

The market for which the area is best known has stood here since 1174 and was originally a live cattle market, slaughtering and leather tanning not being tolerated in the centre of the City. Until 1855 trade climaxed on the Monday before Christmas when some 30,000 animals were crammed into the market prior to mass slaughtering, the ground 'covered nearly ankle-deep with filth and mire; a thick steam perpetually rising from the reeking bodies of the cattle', as Charles Dickens explained in *Oliver Twist*. When the sale of live cattle was moved to Caledonian Road (p. 326) Smithfield became purely a meat market, and new Italianate buildings, designed by Horace Jones with flamboyant corner turrets and imposing statuary, were erected. When a rocket fell on the market towards the end of the Second World War hundreds of people were queuing for their meat ration, many staff were trapped in the refrigerators, and 115 people lost their lives. In 1963 a poultry market was added on the site, and in the 1990s new health legislation wiped out the practice of lorries pulling up at any available gate, leaving the meat to be exposed to the elements and handled by large numbers of workers; now the vehicles back on to special sealed loading bays where the meat is placed on to a semi-automated rail system with the aid of a robot. The market deals with some 85,000 tons of produce – meat, poultry, cheese, pies – every year, with customers able to walk along the central avenues choosing from the goods on display, while constant refurbishment and renovation have made it one of the most up-to-date markets of its kind in Europe.

► Covent Garden market, p. 110.

Cock Lane

Now a forgotten side street, Cock Lane was the only place in medieval London where licensed prostitutes could solicit for trade and was where in 1688 John Bunyan, the author of *Pilgrim's Progress*, died from a fever caught during a heavy bout of rain. In 1762 there were reports that a girl at **No. 33** had seen a ghostly apparition of a late relative who had died of smallpox. Hundreds of people came to Cock Lane to find proof of the phenomenon, being greeted most amicably by the landlords of the local taverns. The girl was taken to the rectory of **St John's**, Clerkenwell, where she was visited by, among others, Dr Johnson, who decried her claims in 'An Account of the Imposture in Cock Lane'.

Giltspur Street

The fourteen-year-old Richard II met Wat Tyler and the other leaders of the Peasants' Revolt in Giltspur Street on 15 June 1381, promising to agree to the rebels' demands, which included a repeal of the Statute of Labourers that prevented workers changing jobs for better pay. However, during the negotiations William Walworth, Lord Mayor of London, lured away Tyler and stabbed him, and when the peasants' leader took refuge in St Bartholomew's church he was dragged out and beheaded. The Revolt later subsided.

Fortune of War, north junction with Cock Lane, west side

In the eighteenth century surgeons from St Bartholomew's Hospital used a room at the **Fortune of War** to inspect bodies snatched from graves that could be useful for their experiments. The pub was demolished in 1910 and on the façade of the current building, the furthest point north-west reached by the 1666 Great Fire of London and known as Pye Corner, is a cherub, a symbol of gluttony, the sin which supposedly led to divine retribution in the form of the Fire.

St Bartholomew's Hospital, east side
London's oldest hospital, popularly known as Bart's, was founded in 1123 by Rahere, jester to Henry I, who, according to legend, caught malaria on a pilgrimage to Rome and vowed to build a hospital and church dedicated to St Bartholomew if he survived. On his return to London Rahere petitioned the king for land in Smithfield to fulfil his pledge and in 1123 a small hospital opened as part of a priory which Henry vowed 'to defend and maintain even as my crown', patients arriving by boat on the Fleet River and disembarking at a specially constructed wharf.

The site was extended during the reign of Edward III (1327–77) when a church, St Bartholomew-the-Less, part of which still survives, was built, and though Henry VIII closed down the priory, he re-founded St Bartholomew's as a royal hospital in 1546 with governors, rather than monks, in charge, Smithfield residents being levied a rate to pay for the hospital's upkeep.

In 1730 James Gibbs, architect of St Martin-in-the-Fields church, was chosen to rebuild the hospital and funds were raised by public subscription and endowment. The clay for Gibbs's work was dug in Kent and fired in kilns just outside the City, slate was brought from Wales, timber came by ships from Norway, and stone was brought from Ralph Allen's quarries in Bath. The work took nearly thirty years and Gibbs's hospital, in the form of a quadrangle with four detached wings, opened in 1769 with room for 500 beds. Three of the four wings survive, the southern wing having been demolished in 1935, as does Gibbs's masterpiece, the Great Hall, its staircase decorated with Hogarth's first historical paintings, *The Good Samaritan* (1736) and *The Pool of Bethesda* (1736), which the locally born artist produced for free when he heard that the hospital wanted a foreigner, the Venetian Jacopo Amigoni, to carry out the work. There were further exten-

sions to the building at the end of the nineteenth century to cope with the greater number of patients. Physicians connected with the hospital include John of Gaddesden, court doctor in the early fourteenth century to Edward II, who treated smallpox victims by advising that the patient and all their surroundings be coloured red; Dr Rodrigo Lopez, who was accused of plotting to poison Elizabeth I and was hanged; and William Harvey, who discovered the circulation of the blood in 1615, in the face of colleagues' scepticism. Later members of staff include the cricketer W. G. Grace; Robert Bridges, poet laureate 1913–30; Edward Wilson, who died with Scott and Oates on the 1912 South Pole expedition; and, according to literary legend, Sherlock Holmes, who in *A Study in Scarlet* (1887) is introduced to Dr Watson for the first time at Bart's, where he is researching chemistry.

The government announced plans to close the hospital in 1992 but after a vociferous campaign of opposition from the London public there was a reprieve and it now specializes in cardiac and cancer care.

St Bartholomew-the-Less, east side
The hospital's parish church, which stands within the hospital's grounds, was founded c. 1184 and after surviving the Fire of London was rebuilt by George Dance the Younger in 1789 around the fifteenth century tower and vestry. Dance's timber quickly rotted and so the church had to be rebuilt again in 1825. A 1904 Act of Parliament allowed for the demolition of the church to extend the hospital but this was never carried out.

Newgate Street

Newgate Street is named after the 1135 gate, the main route west out of the City, which was used as a prison until a gaol was built on the site of the Old Bailey in the 1420s and was redesigned according to the terms of Dick Whittington's will in 1423, being demolished along with the other City gates in the 1760s. Until 1381, when slaughtering was banned from the City and removed to nearby Smithfield, it was also the site of the butchers' market known as the Shambles, which incorporated the Flesh Shambles at its western end and Bladder Street to the east. Over the centuries Newgate Street was also home to three long demolished institutions **Christ's Hospital**, founded by Edward VI as a charitable school for orphans and poor boys, **Greyfriars Monastery** and **Christ Church Newgate Street**, the tower and outer walls of which remain.

► Aldersgate, p. 4.

Newgate Prison, Newgate Street at Old Bailey, south side

The City's main prison for nearly 500 years, Newgate was built in 1423 with money left by three times Lord Mayor Dick Whittington, being nicknamed Whittington's Palace, and was where condemned prisoners were kept in a mass dungeon with one window and woken at midnight by twenty rings of a handbell before being given a long admonishment on sin.

Inmates included Sir Thomas Malory, who wrote 'Morte D'Arthur' while serving a term for murder from 1469 to 1470, and is believed to have died in the prison; Mary Frith (Moll Cutpurse), the seventeenth-century highwaywoman, who robbed General Fairfax, commander-in-chief of the Parliamentarian army during the Civil War, and used £2,000 of her ill-gotten loot to buy her way out of prison; and the writer Daniel Defoe, who was sent to Newgate in 1702 after publishing an anonymous satirical pamphlet, 'The Shortest Way with the Dissenters', which so cleverly sent up the views of High Church Tories that it was taken seriously as an attack on the Tories' opponents, and who put his Newgate experience to use for the prison scenes in *Moll Flanders* (1722).

Newgate was rebuilt after the Fire of London, but it continued to have a wretched reputation for overcrowding and unsanitary conditions – pigs were allowed to be kept within the walls – until the early

eighteenth century when the mass dungeon was replaced by fifteen new cells. On 30 August 1724 Jack Sheppard, the burglar and recidivist prison-breaker romanticized in John Gay's *The Beggar's Opera* (1728), escaped from Newgate dressed as a woman to avoid hanging, was recaptured on Finchley Common, and sent back to Newgate, where his execution was delayed. On 15 October Sheppard escaped from the strongest room in the prison, broke through six iron doors and reached the roof, where he decided to return to his cell to retrieve some blankets so that he could lower himself down the prison wall. Sheppard was eventually found drunk in a gin shop on Drury Lane and sent back to Newgate, where he was held down by 300 lbs of iron, and later executed at Tyburn.

George Dance Jr rebuilt Newgate in 1770, and ten years later it was attacked during the Gordon Riots, when demonstrators battered down cell doors with sledgehammers and pickaxes, released prisoners, and set fire to the building as crowds of onlookers cheered. Towards the end of the eighteenth century hangings moved from Tyburn, following pressure from Mayfair residents, and locals began charging spectators £10 to sit at a window overlooking the place of execution. Once the victim had been officially declared dead a black flag would be hoisted and the crowd would give three cheers; ironically in 1807 twenty-eight people died in a crush when the scaffolding fell as they tried to watch the hangings.

Those hanged here in the early nineteenth century included Arthur Thistlewood, leader of the Cato Street conspirators who planned to assassinate the British Cabinet. He went to the gallows sucking an orange on 1 May 1820 alongside fellow conspirator William Davidson, one of the first black people to feature in British political history, and before he died exclaimed: 'Albion is still in the chains of slavery. I quit it without regret.' In the early nineteenth century Elizabeth Fry, the prison reformer, began visiting Newgate amid much controversy over whether it was safe for a woman to enter the gaol and concern over the number of women prisoners who were being forced into prostitution. 'We long to burn her alive,' wrote Sydney Smith, the eccentric clergyman, 'examples of living virtue disturb our repose and give birth to distressing comparisons.' Fry's report to the House of Commons' Committee on Prisons resulted in several reforms, including the founding of a school for prisoners' children, who she noticed spoke in nothing other than oaths and curses, and the abolition of the flogging of women from 1820.

The last public hanging at Newgate took place on 26 May 1868 when Michael Barrett, who had taken part in the Fenian bombing of the Clerkenwell House of Detention (p. 74), went to the gallows, after which Newgate executions were held behind closed doors. In 1902 the prison was demolished and replaced by an enlarged Central Criminal Court and some of the artefacts were sold as gruesome relics. Lord George Gordon's cell fetched £5 and one of the prison doors was taken to Flask Walk, Hampstead, where it still stands.
► Old Bailey, p. 58.

Snow Hill
One of the City's few hills, Snow Hill, which winds eastwards from Farringdon Street south of Smithfield market, was home to the Saracen's Head (demolished 1868), a popular tavern used by Samuel Pepys and Jonathan Swift, and was where the eighteenth-century Mohock gang engaged in their practice of kidnapping elderly women and placing them in barrels which they rolled downhill to Newgate Street. The rebuilding in the 1980s of the railway tunnel under the hill enabled the Thameslink line to take trains north–south through London.

West Smithfield
In the Middle Ages the land now occupied by the roundabout at the eastern end of West Smithfield was an open space used for jousting, sports and executions.

William Wallace, the Scottish nationalist who was convicted of treason at Westminster Hall in 1305, was dragged alive through the streets to West Smithfield and there briefly hanged on the gallows, taken down, and allowed to recuperate for a few minutes before his intestines were ripped from his body in front of the crowd. Wallace's head and limbs were then removed and his body parts sent to different locations across the country, his head being stuck on a pole on London Bridge, his right arm displayed on Newcastle Bridge, his left arm exhibited in Berwick, his right leg displayed in Perth, and his left leg put on show in Aberdeen.

From 1133 to 1855 West Smithfield was the setting for the annual August **Bartholomew Fair**, a cloth fair held for three days around 24 August (St Bartholomew's Day), where the curiosities included a one-foot tall girl of sixteen, monkeys dancing on ropes, men fighting dogs and women fighting women. The atmosphere of the event was captured by Ben Jonson in his 1614 play of the same name, which follows the fortunes of the drunks and cut-throats at the event, and by the poet William Wordsworth who, in the seventh book of *The Prelude* (1805), complained about the 'anarchy and din' of the fair with its 'Albinos, painted Indians, Dwarfs, the Horse of knowledge, and the learned Pig'. In recent years the event has been revived as a late summer street festival, without the medieval paraphernalia.

(iii) Little Britain

Little Britain
Built on land owned by the Dukes of Brittany, the street began to attract printers in the late fifteenth century, following the success of William Caxton's pioneering printing press in Westminster, and before long was the most important place for publishing in London, being where Fleet Street's first daily newspaper, the *Daily Courant*, was printed in 1702. The three-year-old Samuel Johnson stayed here in 1712,

when his mother brought him to London to cure his skin disease, and thirteen years later Benjamin Franklin, the American scientist, took lodgings on Little Britain after arriving from the American colonies with a package supposedly containing letters of credit from the Governor of Pennsylvania to buy type fonts. When Franklin opened it up the letters were not there and so he found himself stranded in London penniless, eventually securing employment as a printer in the nearby church of St Bartholomew-the-Great. The street is now dominated by buildings associated with St Bartholomew's Hospital.

east side

St Bartholomew-the-Great Gatehouse
The gatehouse leading to the church of St Bartholomew-the-Great was built for Sir Philip Scudamore in the sixteenth century and was where Mary Tudor is believed to have feasted on chicken and red wine while watching Protestant martyrs burn at the stake. When the church was bombed by a Zeppelin in 1916 during the First World War tiles fell off revealing the Elizabethan half-timbering beneath.

St Bartholomew-the-Great
London's oldest parish church, where the local-born artist William Hogarth was baptized on 28 November 1697, was founded according to the wishes of Rahere, jester to Henry I, as part of the St Bartholomew Hospital and priory, and was where Wat Tyler, leader of the 1381 Peasants' Revolt, tried to take refuge from William Walworth, the Lord Mayor of London, but was dragged outside and beheaded. The church was originally 300 ft longer than it is today, but after Henry VIII dissolved the priory in October 1539 the nave was demolished, thus reducing it to its present-day size and leaving an open space in front of the entrance. After the Reformation parts of the church were used for commercial purposes, with a black-smith's forge, stable, school, hop store and printers setting up inside. Every Good Friday twenty-one poor widows over sixty years old are given a sum of money and a hot-cross bun placed on a gravestone in the churchyard.

(iv) east of Little Britain

Aldersgate Street
The street, with its small shops and offices on the west side and Barbican tower blocks on the east side, is named after the Roman **Ealdred's Gate**, which stood near the modern-day junction of Aldersgate Street at Long Lane and had residential quarters. In the sixteenth century these were occupied by John Day, who in 1549 introduced Anglo-Saxon type and italics to Britain and here printed an early copy of the Bible, the *Folio Bible*. James I entered London for the first time as king through Aldersgate in 1603, but by 1761 it was found to be causing traffic congestion and demolished. By that time Aldersgate Street was lined with smart houses but it gradually became commercialized and was heavily bombed during the second world war.

▶ Cripplegate, p. 15.

St Botolph, west side
A church founded in 1290 and dedicated to Botolph, patron saint of travellers, was rebuilt by Nathaniel Wright in 1788 and decorated with a plaster ceiling and an oak pulpit resting on a carved palm tree. A window depicts John Wesley, founder of Methodism, who experienced an evangelical conversion nearby in 1738.

Location of John Wesley's conversion, Aldersgate Street by Ironmongers' Hall, east side
John Wesley, the early-eighteenth-century preacher who founded Methodism, experienced an evangelical conversion near the present-day Ironmongers' Hall, on 24 May 1738, later writing how 'in the evening I went very unwillingly to a society in Aldersgate Street, where one was reading Luther's preface to the Epistle to the Romans. About a quarter before nine, while he was describing the change which God works in the heart through faith in Christ, I felt my heart strangely warmed. I felt I

did trust in Christ, Christ alone for salvation.'
► Wesley's Chapel, p. 82.

Bartholomew Close

A meandering alleyway to the east of St Bartholomew's Hospital, it was here in 1659 that the poet John Milton went into hiding from supporters of Charles II, looking to punish Milton for his support of the regicide of Charles I in 1649.

It was also where later that year the hangman of London publicly burned copies of Milton's anti-royalist tract *Defensio pro populo Anglicano*. William Hogarth, who became London's leading social commentator through his paintings and engravings, was born at 𝕹𝕠. 𝟻𝟾 on 10 November 1697, his Christian name being chosen in honour of the new king, William III. Bartholomew Close was one of the first streets in the capital to suffer an air attack, being hit during a Zeppelin raid during the First World War.
► William Hogarth in Leicester Square, p. 102.

Cloth Fair

Named in honour of the annual medieval festival 𝕭𝖆𝖗𝖙𝖍𝖔𝖑𝖔𝖒𝖊𝖜 𝕵𝖆𝖎𝖗 (p. 11), which was mainly a cloth fair, the street was home in the late seventeenth century to the publisher John Twyn, whose house was raided in October 1663 by Roger L'Estrange, Charles II's royal censor. L'Estrange seized all the documents Twyn had not managed to destroy and convicted him of publishing seditious material, the punishment being that Twyn be 'hanged by the neck, cut down before he was dead, shamefully mutilated, his entrails taken out' and his head cut off and disposed of 'at the pleasure of the king's majesty'. The sentence was carried out at Tyburn and sections of Twyn's body were later displayed at various city gates 'as an example to all men who advocate death or disobedience to such a monarch'.

John Betjeman, late-twentieth-century poet laureate, moved into No. 43 in 1955, enthusing about Smithfield's medieval street pattern where 'everything could be reached on foot, down alleys and passages'. He moved away in 1977, claiming that the noise of the articulated lorries using Smithfield market had become unbearable. Alongside the poet's former property, at Nos. 41 and 42, are two rare pre-Fire of London City buildings.

King Edward Street

Stinking Lane until 1843, on account of the stench of the nearby market where animals were slaughtered, it was home in the eighteenth century to the galleried coaching inn the 𝕭𝖚𝖑𝖑 𝖆𝖓𝖉 𝕸𝖔𝖚𝖙𝖍 (the name a corruption of Boulogne Mouth). Britain's first national mail coaches began their journeys here, and the building was later replaced by a post office on the roof of which the Italian inventor Guglielmo Marconi first transmitted wireless signals on 27 July 1896. As the Italian government had previously rejected his ideas, the Post Office and the Admiralty became Marconi's first sponsors. When a new post office was built here in 1905, part of the Romans' London wall was uncovered and preserved in the basement. The building later became the home of the National Postal Museum (outside is a statue of Rowland Hill, inventor of the Penny Post) and is now offices.
► John Logie Baird's early work on television, p. 197.

Middle Street

One of a number of tiny passages to the east of St Bartholomew's Hospital.
Hand and Shears, No. 1
A pub known to locals as the Fist and Clippers replaced a building where the medieval Court of *Pieds Poudres* (Dusty Feet) tried tailors accused of selling short measures of cloth. In the sixteenth century many of those attending 𝕭𝖆𝖗𝖙𝖍𝖔𝖑𝖔𝖒𝖊𝖜 𝕵𝖆𝖎𝖗 would meet here the night before festivities began for an evening of drunken debauchery during which local tailors, fuelled by copious amounts of ale, would rush out of the pub waving shears above their heads crying 'the proceedings shall begin'. The

following morning the Lord Mayor of London would announce the official opening of the fair outside the pub.
▶ **Bartholomew Fair**, p. 11.

St Martin's-le-Grand

A short stretch of road north of St Paul's tube station, it is named after the college and church of **St Martin's-le-Grand**, founded in 700, which offered sanctuary to thieves and debtors, but not traitors, and which featured a bell that in medieval times tolled the start of the City's evening curfew. The buildings were demolished in 1538, a time when, as the bishop Hugh Latimer noted, the street was a popular haunt of prostitutes and was filled with 'houses with walled gardens where men and women perform their filthie ceremonies'. While working in the General Post Office, which stood on the east side of the street in the early nineteenth century, the young Anthony Trollope invented the pillar-box, later capturing his experiences in his 1858 novel, *The Three Clerks*.

MOORGATE, EC2

The part of the City based around the busy traffic route of Moorgate, named after the long vanished Roman and medieval gate, it encompasses much of the City's financial centre, including the Bank of England and Stock Exchange, as well as the City's only residential estate, the Barbican.

(i) Barbican

The Barbican is a thirty-five-acre traffic-free estate of concrete tower blocks, some over 400 ft high and among the tallest in Europe. The City's only residential estate, it contains 2,113 flats housing some 6,500 people and is named after a local watchtower demolished by Henry III in 1267. The area was fashionable in the sixteenth and seventeenth centuries, when William Shakespeare and the poet John Milton were among the residents, and became commercialized in the nineteenth century when hundreds of rag trade workshops filled the side streets. After being heavily bombed in the Second World War the area remained neglected until 1956 when Duncan Sandys, Minister of Housing and Local Government, proposed building a housing estate, and soon after the City of London Corporation and the London County Council placed a compulsory purchase order on the area. Construction work followed over the next twenty years to the designs of Chamberlin, Powell and Bon, who opted for an estate of tower blocks built in brutalist concrete, a style that had become popularly reviled by the time the estate was completed in the 1970s.

A hostile, bleak and eerie place, with no obvious entrance or traditional streets, where movement is along a network of elevated walkways marked with yellow lines that connect major landmarks, the Barbican was detested by most Londoners as soon as it went up. Still more tolerated than admired, it is now something of an anomaly, a timepiece of early postwar utopian social planning of a kind that once threatened to devour large cities but was long ago abandoned. However, unlike almost all other similar estates, it is aimed at high earners, is run as a village community, contains cleverly arranged flats that mostly offer superb views, and is blessed with an excellent arts centre, a well-stocked and fascinating museum (the Museum of London), a tube station and copious underground parking – attributes that have attracted a number of well-known inhabitants, including former Tory minister Norman Tebbit and ex-miners' leader Arthur Scargill.

London Wall *Also see p. 21.*
Dominated by huge corporate office blocks and particularly lacking in character, given its antiquated sounding name, London Wall, which connects Aldersgate Street and Old Broad Street, is named after the Romans' two-mile wall of Kentish ragstone,

built in the second century to enclose their fort and 330-acre estate, small sections of which remain in place. The street was heavily bombed in the Second World War and in 1955, in its derelict state, was used to depict war-torn London in Michael Anderson's film of George Orwell's *1984*, in which it is festooned with 'Big Brother Is Watching You' posters. In the early 1960s planners chose London Wall as the location for an architectural experiment of building office blocks on two-storey podia in staggered arrangement, the roofs connected by bridges across the roadway to provide a traffic-free walkway for pedestrians, which was abandoned partly built.

Museum of London, London Wall at Aldersgate Street

Despite its concealed, barely accessible location at the edge of the Barbican, the museum is a popular facility that features a wide range of informative exhibitions on the history of the capital using reconstructed street scenes, changing displays on different aspects of London's history, and a vast collection of documents, pamphlets and books relating to the metropolis. The galleries divide London's history around major events such as the dissolution of the monasteries, the Fire and the two world wars, with the 2002-built World City Gallery tracing how London became the world's first metropolis.

Milton Street

Milton Street, which connects Chiswell Street and the Barbican, was formerly Grub Street, whose name came to be used as a metaphor for hack writing in the seventeenth century and whose inhabitants were derided by Alexander Pope in *The Dunciad* (1728) in the memorable couplet 'While pensive poets painful vigil keep / Sleepless themselves, to give their readers sleep'. Grub Street was renamed Milton Street in the 1830s, not after the poet, John, but after the landlord who owned most of the properties. Its buildings were demolished when the Barbican was built in the 1960s.

Silk Street

Barbican Arts Centre, south side

The Barbican, London's major arts centre, contains a cinema, art gallery, concert hall (home of the London Symphony Orchestra), library and two theatres which have been home to the Royal Shakespeare Company (RSC). It opened in 1982 with the RSC complaining about the small size of the Pit theatre, the orchestra moaning about the acoustics of the concert hall – the pianist Maurizio Pollini refused to play until 2,000 glass spheres which he claimed ruined the sound were removed from the ceiling – and members of the audience claiming that they had spent so long trying to find their way into the complex they had missed the opening of the performance. However, the complex's fortunes improved out of all expectations following the 1994 appointments of John Tusa as managing director and Graham Sheffield as artistic director. The acoustics were improved, innovative new work was commissioned, and with nearby areas such as Clerkenwell, Shoreditch and Spitalfields being reborn as residential centres the Barbican now has the benefit of a ready-made local audience willing to experience challenging works and concerts.

Wood Street

Cripplegate, north end of Wood Street

One of eight medieval gates at the edge of the City, **Cripplegate** took its name either from the Anglo-Saxon word for tunnel (*crepel*), from the cripples who begged in the vicinity, or from a cripples' hospital that once stood nearby, and was where in 1010 the body of King Edmund the Martyr was brought into London, resulting, it was said, in miracles, including the healing of the lame, being performed by the gate. In 1461 a victorious Henry VI, who outfought Warwick the Kingmaker at St Albans, arrived in London through **Cripplegate**, but his celebrations were curtailed when he heard that Warwick and the future Edward IV were about to re-enter the capital. Cripplegate was demolished in 1760.

► Moorgate, p. 18.

St Giles Cripplegate, north-west end of
Wood Street
The oldest building in the area, St Giles's
church was originally built by Alfune *c.* 1090
alongside the Jews' Garden, the only place in
England where Jews could then be buried,
and named in honour of the patron saint
of beggars and cripples. The church was
rebuilt after a fire in 1545 (ironically it
survived the 1666 Great Fire of London)
and was where in August 1620 Oliver Cromwell, then an unknown Huntingdon landowner, married Elizabeth Bourchier. The
poet John Milton, who worshipped at
St Giles and wrote much of his epic biblical
poem *Paradise Lost* (1667) locally, was
buried here in 1674. Around a hundred years
later his body was exhumed by workmen
who caused the collapse of one of the ribs
and knocked out some teeth, which they
kept as souvenirs. (There is now a life-size
statue of the poet near the pulpit.) St Giles
was almost entirely destroyed in the 1940
Blitz, with only the outer walls surviving,
and now incongruously stands in a
pedestrianized courtyard amid the Barbican
tower blocks.

(ii) south of the Barbican

Cheapside
Cheapside was London's main medieval
market (the word *'ceap'* being an ancient
term for market) until Henry III switched
the unloading of fish to Queenhithe – local
streets such as Bread Street and Milk Street
extend the connection – and was where the
Normans under William the Conqueror
fought with Londoners on 20 December
1066, two months after the Battle of Hastings, according to evidence discovered
during archaeological excavations in the late
twentieth century. Thomas à Becket, the
priest and chancellor to Henry II murdered
by the latter's knights in Canterbury
Cathedral in 1170, was born at the junction
of Cheapside and Ironmonger Lane in 1118.
Two years after his murder he was

canonized, becoming second in importance
only to St Paul as London's saint.

In 1290 Edward I built **Cheapside Cross**
at the corner of Cheapside and Wood Street
to commemorate the City resting-place of
the coffin containing the body of his queen,
Eleanor (other resting-places being named
accordingly Charing Cross and Waltham
Cross), decorating it with statues of the
Pope, the Madonna and Child, and the
Apostles. After being subjected to violent
attacks by the Puritans, the statue was
demolished in 1643. The church that stood
alongside, **St Peter Westcheap**, was
destroyed in the 1666 Fire and never rebuilt,
although its garden, which contains the
plane tree mentioned by William Wordsworth in his 1797 poem 'Poor Susan',
survives.

On St John's Night 1510 the nineteen-
year-old Henry VIII strolled along
Cheapside unrecognized, dressed as a
Yeoman of the Guard, and drank in some of
the local taverns until he spotted the Night
Watch and beat a retreat. The romantic poet
John Keats lived with his brothers at **No. 76**
in 1817 when he was working as a dresser at
Guy's Hospital and there wrote 'Ode on a
Grecian Urn'. Mrs Beeton, the Victorian
cookery writer, was born Isabella Mayson
on Cheapside in 1836.

Coleman Street
Coleman Street, just west of Moorgate, is
named after the occupation of its medieval
residents and was a Puritan stronghold in
the 1640s when five MPs whom Charles I
tried to arrest took refuge in a house here.
London's first public telephone exchange
opened at No. 36 in August 1879, resulting
in the Post Office, worried about the possible loss of revenue should the public switch
from writing to talking, successfully
lobbying Parliament to legislate against
telephone companies running wires under
or over private houses without the owners'
permission. The Post Office's stance
changed towards the end of the century
when it set up its own telephone company,

and by 1911 it had seen off nearly all its rivals, establishing a monopoly throughout England, except in Hull. The church of 𝔖𝔱 𝔖𝔱𝔢𝔭𝔥𝔢𝔫 at the south-western end of Coleman Street, where the romantic poet John Keats was buried in 1821, and which was destroyed in the Second World War, was reached from the pavement through what was known as 'The Gate of Judgement', a fearsome looking gate commemorating the Great Plague.

Gresham Street

Gresham Street, which connects Aldersgate Street and Moorgate, is named after Thomas Gresham, founder of the Royal Exchange, and is the location of Christopher Wren's handsome church, St Lawrence Jewry.
north side: Aldersgate Street to Coleman Street

St Anne and St Agnes

A church was first built on the site in 1137, rebuilt after a fire in 1548 and, after destruction in the Great Fire of 1666, redesigned by Christopher Wren from parts of the fourteenth-century tower. The church was damaged again in the Second World War and restored from 1963 to 1966 by Braddock and Martin-Smith. It is now used by Lutherans, with services in Swahili, Chinese and Amharic, as well as English.

St Lawrence Jewry, Gresham Street at Guildhall Yard

First built in 1136, the church was so named as it was built on the fringe of the Jewish ghetto, and even after the expulsion of the Jews from London in 1291 the suffix remained to distinguish the church from the 125 others in the City. St Lawrence Jewry burned down in the Fire of London, was rebuilt by Christopher Wren, and was reopened by Charles II in 1677. But after Second World War bombing all that remained were the walls, the tower and a painting of the martyrdom of St Lawrence by an unknown member of the North Italian School of the late sixteenth century, which survived unscathed. St Lawrence was later rebuilt by Cecil Brown to Wren's

design and it is now the official church of the Corporation of London.

Guildhall Yard

A small opening north of Gresham Street, Guildhall Yard leads to the Guildhall, the seat of the Corporation of London, and was the home of the medieval 𝔗𝔥𝔯𝔢𝔢 𝔗𝔲𝔫𝔰 𝔗𝔞𝔳𝔢𝔯𝔫 where General Monck, who brought Charles II to the throne in 1660 after eleven years of the Commonwealth, had his military headquarters. Remains of a Roman amphitheatre were found under Guildhall Yard in 2000.

Guildhall

The administrative headquarters of the Corporation of the City of London, the Square Mile's local authority, for over 800 years, Guildhall takes its name from its original role as the place where *geld* (money) was collected in taxes and was used in medieval times for trials, including those of Henry Howard, Earl of Surrey, who introduced blank verse into English poetry and was charged with treason in 1547; the nine-day queen, Lady Jane Grey, and her husband, Lord Guildford Dudley, six years later; and Henry Garnet, one of the Gunpowder Plot conspirators, in 1606. The Polish composer Frederic Chopin gave his last public performance at a Guildhall concert in aid of Polish exiles from the rebellion of 1848 that year. At the end of the century Guildhall was the setting for meetings of the newly formed London County Council, the first local authority directly elected by Londoners, which moved to County Hall in 1922. The building is also now used for the presentation of the Booker Prize, the best-known literary prize in Britain.
➤ County Hall, p. 387.

Ironmonger Lane

At the north-eastern end of Cheapside is Ironmonger Lane where pots, pans, cutlery and fire implements were made to service the adjacent medieval poultry market and where the Mercers' Hall now stands, the Mercers Company being first in order of precedence among the City livery companies, a status which carries considerable civic prestige.

City livery companies

The 102 City livery companies, successors of the medieval guilds formed by merchants to protect their skills and trades, evolved as 'friendly' societies responsible for training apprentices and setting wages but were fiercely competitive, their rivalry occasionally spilling over into violence (the Fishmongers and Skinners fought a pitched battle in 1340). Their economic powers waned when limited companies were created and they now enjoy a mostly ceremonial purpose, organizing functions and banquets, performing charitable works, and meeting in the various livery halls that can be found throughout the City such as the Apothecaries' Hall on Blackfriars Lane and the Drapers' Hall on Throgmorton Street. Guild members, also known as liverymen, choose the Sheriffs and Lord Mayor of the City of London (not to be confused with the capital-wide elected mayor of London), a mostly ceremonial figure. The livery companies are ranked in an order of precedence based loosely on their date of incorporation, with the Mercers (dealers in fine cloth) being first and the Grocers second.

Moorgate

A major traffic route leading to the Bank of England and lined with huge office blocks containing accountancy firms, bankers and insurance agents, Moorgate is named after the medieval City gate that led to the Fens, which was rebuilt in 1672 to allow soldiers to pass through with their pikes upright and demolished in 1762 when the stones were used to secure London Bridge, then in danger of being washed away by the tides.
► Bishopsgate, p. 24.

Soviet Spy Centre (1920s), No. 49, west side
The Soviet Union ran a spy ring from No. 49 in the 1920s under the guise of the All-Russian Co-Operative Society (Arcos) which was mostly ignored by the British authorities until the Soviet government tried to capitalize on political unrest caused by the 1926 General Strike and sent financial donations to British trade unions, including £250,000 to the strike committee. When the news leaked out the Trades Union Congress demanded that all money be returned to the Russians immediately and the British government decided to halt Arcos's activities. Prime Minister Stanley Baldwin ordered a raid, and on 12 May 1927 fifty Special Branch officers left Scotland Yard, travelled together by tube as inconspicuously as possible and, after being met at Moorgate station by around a hundred uniformed Corporation of London uniformed police officers, raided the building. There they found managers rushing downstairs to seal the steel door that led to the room in which staff were busily shoving incriminating documents into the fire. The officers forced entry and managed to retrieve some 250,000 papers, as well as crates of rifles which they took away in two truck loads, but much of the information turned out, inevitably, to be of questionable value, typified by, as Nigel West revealed in his book *MI5*, descriptions of party members along the lines of: 'Adams. Stoker. A good orator but a bad stoker and a slacker. The other stokers do his work for him. Deserted in Odessa.'
► Russian Tea Rooms, p. 424.

Old Jewry

The street's name recalls the large local medieval Jewish community which grew after William the Conqueror invited the Jewish merchants of Rouen to settle in London in the eleventh century so that they could take charge of lending money at interest, even to the Norman and Angevin kings, Christians being barred from doing so. The ghetto was subjected to various privations over the next 200 years, including the killing of an ailing man as part of a blood libel in 1130 and accusations of ritual murder in 1224 after it was alleged that gashes found on the body of a dead child were in the form of Hebrew characters.

In 1232 Henry III closed London's main synagogue on the pretext that the chanting could be heard in a neighbouring church, and thirty years later the area was beset by violence when hundreds of Jews were murdered after a Jew supposedly charged a gentile too much interest. In 1291 Edward I expelled the Jews from England and seized their property, selling it for considerable gain. The pioneering printer William Caxton lived in a house on Old Jewry that had previously been a synagogue from 1438 to 1446. The street is the fictitious address of Jonathan Swift's Lemuel Gulliver, hero of *Gulliver's Travels* (1726). No trace of medieval Old Jewry remains.

► Jewry Street community of sixteenth-century Jews, p. 36.

(iii) east of Moorgate

Liverpool Street

The street, best known for its railway terminus, has no connections with the northern city but is named after Lord Liverpool, early-nineteenth-century prime minister.

north side: Eldon Street to Bishopsgate
Broad Street station, Liverpool Street at Sun Street Passage
Built in 1865 as the City terminus of the East & West India Docks & Birmingham Junction Railway; a line that opened in September 1850 to take goods unloaded at the various east London docks to the Midlands, it had become the third busiest passenger terminus in London by the end of the century, being used by trains on the North London Line, a popular suburban route that brought clerks living in the suburbs into the City and whose western end reached Richmond. In the 1980s the authorities decided that **Broad Street station** had outlived its usefulness and after it closed in 1984 it was demolished to make way for an office block.

Liverpool Street station

The terminus for the Great Eastern Railway was built on land that had been the burial ground for the Royal Bethlehem Hospital (Bedlam) and opened in 1874 to replace the Bishopsgate terminus, half a mile north. With the railway now enjoying a City outlet, the owners encouraged clerks and bankers to move out of central London to the growing north-eastern suburbs served by the line, such as Walthamstow, journeying on what the poet John Betjeman later described as 'extraordinary, cramped and uncomfortable Great Eastern carriages drawn out above the East End housetops to wide acres of Essex suburb'.

In 1894 Liverpool Street was extended to accommodate trains bound for the east coast, becoming the biggest station in London, a mass of grey brick tempered by the occasional moulded cherub and other baroque flourish encasing a warren of platforms, bridges and secret corners, with the attached Great Eastern Hotel, famed for its Louis XVI-styled ironwork staircase, being for decades the City's only hotel. The station had its character ripped out when it was rebuilt in the late 1980s as part of the Broadgate Centre.

CIRCLE LINE

Created in 1884 after Joseph Paxton's plans to encase a railway in glass – The Great Victorian Way – fell through, the Circle Line, originally known as the Inner Circle, links most of London's main railway termini and is formed entirely of other lines – the Metropolitan, Hammersmith and City and District lines – apart from two tiny sections of track: just south of Aldgate and just west of Gloucester Road.

Paddington The western terminus of London's first underground, the Metropolitan Railway, opened as Bishop's Road on 9 January 1863.

Edgware Road The station is dwarfed by the Marylebone Flyover, which connects Marylebone Road with the Westway.

Baker Street Rebuilt from 1911 to 1933 as London Underground's flagship station with attached offices and a luxury block of flats.

Great Portland Street It opened as Portland Road on the first underground line in January 1863.

Euston Square The first shaft for London's first underground line was sunk here in 1860. The station opened three years later as Gower Street.

King's Cross The original station was situated a few hundred yards to the east of the present site. Its disused platforms can still be seen from Circle/Metropolitan/Hammersmith and City line trains.

Farringdon The site was chosen for the eastern terminus of London's first underground line, which opened in January 1863, due to the proximity of Smithfield market.

Barbican The Dynamiters, who blew up a train passing through Paddington in 1883, took revenge for the seven-year sentence given to one of their members in April 1897 by leaving a bomb at this station (then Aldersgate Street) that killed one man. The demolition of the original booking hall and roof in 1955 inspired John Betjeman's poem 'Monody on the Death of Aldersgate Street Station'. It became Barbican in 1968.

Moorgate Named after the old medieval gate rather than the area, which in the 1860s, when the station was built, was known as Moorfields.

Liverpool Street One of only two stations on the network, the other being Sloane Square, which as late as the 1980s had a platform bar.

Aldgate The station is built on the site of the 'terrible [Plague] pit' that Daniel Defoe described in *A Journal of the Plague Year* in which more than 1,000 people were buried in two weeks in 1665.

Tower Hill Named after the hill on which prisoners used to be executed.

Monument The only station on the underground connected to another (Bank) by escalator.

Cannon Street The last station to be built on the Circle Line (in 1884).

Mansion House The station was originally intended as a vast junction of all planned London underground lines, but the scheme was later aborted and the downgraded station given an erroneous name, the Mansion House, home of the Lord Mayor, being situated some distance to the east by Bank station.

Blackfriars The underground outlet for what was in the early twentieth century an important London railway terminus known as St Paul's.

Temple When it opened in the 1860s the station sported a roof promenade, but it was shut soon after, having become a haunt of prostitutes.

Embankment Built on the site of Warren's Blacking Factory where Charles Dickens worked as a boy, it opened as Charing Cross in 1909.

Westminster When work on the station began in the 1860s engineers had to ensure that the foundations of Westminster Abbey did not fall into the gully.

St James's Park Rebuilt by the underground's greatest architect, Charles Holden, in the late 1920s, with a surrounding office block, whose façade was decorated with statues by Jacob Epstein and Henry Moore, and which was then the tallest building in London.

Victoria In the 1948 Ealing comedy *Passport to Pimlico* tube trains leaving the station are halted at the border with Pimlico which has declared UDI from Britain.

Sloane Square The River Westbourne is conveyed above the station platforms in a large, visible pipe.

South Kensington The station was planned in the late nineteenth century as the capital's terminus for the London and South Wales Railway, a line that was never built.

Gloucester Road Sherlock Holmes wanders along the tracks leading to the station while investigating a murder in the Arthur Conan Doyle short story 'The Bruce-Partington Plans'.

High Street Kensington Originally called Kensington, the station was redesigned in 1905 with commercial considerations uppermost; passengers could walk straight from the booking hall into Ponting's, Derry & Tom's and Barker's, which owned all three stores and ran special trains to bring customers to their sales.

Notting Hill Gate Opened on the Hammersmith & City railway in 1864.

Bayswater Walter Sickert's 1916 work *Queen's Road, Bayswater, Station* was one of the first paintings with a London underground theme and shows a seated figure awaiting a train underneath an advert for Whiteley's store near a sign for Queen's Road (Bayswater), the station's original name.

London Wall *Also see p. 14.*

Bethlem Royal Hospital (1676–1815), east of Circus Place

> Of Bedlam beggars, who, with roaring voices / Strike in their numb'd and morti-fied bare arms / Pins, wooden pricks, nailes, sprigs of rosemary . . . – *King Lear*, William Shakespeare (1605)

Also known as Bedlam, for many years Britain's only national hospital for the insane, it was founded in Bishopsgate in 1247 as the Priory of St Mary Bethlehem, to which a hospital was added in 1329, and was where the practice of chaining violent and unstable prisoners began fifty years later. After the priory was dissolved in 1547, the hospital was refounded as a lunatic asylum, moving here in 1675, the entrance framed by two large stone statues, 'Raving Madness and Melancholy Madness', which were

designed by Caius Cibber using a soldier from Cromwell's New Model Army as his model and which were described by William Wordsworth in *The Prelude* as 'those carved maniacs at the gates'. By the end of the century the hospital had become a tourist attraction, with visitors inspecting the caged prisoners much as they would animals at a zoo, a practice that continued until 1770. One inmate subjected to such treatment was Nathaniel Lee, the seventeenth-century play-wright and actor, who once asked a visitor to leap off the roof with him to 'immortalise ourselves' but was convinced it would be more immortalizing to leap up on to the roof, thereby being saved from instant death. In 1815 the hospital moved to a site in Lambeth which now houses the Imperial War Museum.

► Imperial War Museum, p. 385.

All Hallows London Wall, No. 83

The church, first built by the Roman wall in the twelfth century, was repaired in the fifteenth century and was where from 1474 to 1494 the hermit Simon the Anker was confined to a cell, writing 'The Fruyte of Redempcyon', one of the first books ever printed, produced by Wynkyn de Worde in 1514. The church escaped the Fire of London and was rebuilt by George Dance the Younger, for whom it was his first com-mission, between 1765 and 1767. Damaged during the Second World War, All Hallows was rebuilt between 1960 and 1962 by David Nye as offices for the Council for the Care of Churches. No services are now held inside.

Threadneedle Street

Home of the Bank of England – the 'Old Lady of Threadneedle Street', as first described by the eighteenth-century play-wright Richard Brinsley Sheridan – Threadneedle Street is named after the City's Needlemakers' Company, which traditionally sported three needles in their civic arms. The first London omnibus service ran from here to the Yorkshire Stingo inn, Paddington, in 1829.

Bank of England, north side

England's most important financial institution and the world's first privately owned, national central bank, the Bank of England was founded in 1694 by two City merchants, William Paterson and Michael Godfrey, to help the King, William III, raise money for the war against an expansionist France. It was incorporated on 27 July 1694 at Mercers' Hall, off Cheapside, moving later that year to Grocers' Hall on Princes Street where, according to Daniel Defoe, 'No place in the world [had] so much business done with so much ease', and then to Threadneedle Street in 1734. The public was invited to invest in the new bank, subscriptions totalling £1.2 million forming the initial capital stock, and in 1706 the Bank began to act as the direct agent for the Exchequer, managing the nation's accounts, making loans to the government, arranging the coinage, taking deposits and issuing notes, practices which created the idea of 'imaginary money' – a store of assets that couldn't be counted in terms of coinage but could be used to drive the economy.

Things did not always go well. During the failed 1745 Jacobite uprising there were fears of a run on the bank as investors panicked about the security of their assets and managers paid out to those who demanded their money in sixpences, only just having enough. At the end of the century, following the outbreak of the Napoleonic Wars, there were further runs on the Bank, caused by a false alarm that the French had landed in Wales. As the war with France proceeded, the wealthy began hoarding their money rather than depositing it with the Bank, and demanded their cash.

The Bank's coinage dwindled to only £1 million, forcing the government to issue Spanish notes and coins seized from captured ships, and, for the first time, £1 and £5 notes appeared, meaning that the currency was no longer worth its weight in metal. Detractors argued that the national currency could be maintained at its proper value only by limiting the amount of notes in circulation (a view now known as monetarism), leading the pamphleteer William Cobbett to comment: 'The Bank is blamed for putting out paper and causing high prices; and blamed at the same time for not putting out paper to accommodate merchants and keep them from breaking. It cannot be to blame for both and indeed is blameable for neither. It is the fellows that put out the paper and then break that do the mischief.'

By the mid nineteenth century the Bank had a monopoly on issuing notes, and the 1844 Bank Charter Act ensured that the Bank's capital of £14 million was backed by gold coin or bullion, an arrangement that led to a long period of price stability. During this time the coinage was linked to the gold standard, but this was suspended during the First World War, and reintroduced only in 1925 after impassioned campaigning by the governor, Montagu Norman, although not with the full approval of the Chancellor of the Exchequer, Winston Churchill, who complained: 'I'm lost and reduced to groping.' Unemployment then rose past the 1 million mark, as Churchill had feared, and in 1931, one of the worst years in the bank's history, during which the German economy collapsed, gold losses briefly averaged £2½ million a day, the Bank dropped the gold standard for good, and the country's gold reserves were transferred to the Treasury.

The Labour government of the late 1940s nationalized the Bank, which became the Treasury's debt manager and adviser, and monetary targets, introduced in 1976 to curb inflation, became a guide to political policy during Margaret Thatcher's premiership, leading to lower inflation and higher unemployment, amid considerable public controversy. The Bank's main modern-day functions are to design and issue banknotes, store gold, and, as the government's banker, manage the national debt.

► Montagu Norman's alliances with Hitler, p. 438.

Throgmorton Street

Throgmorton is a corruption of Throckmorton, Nicholas Throckmorton being
Elizabeth I's ambassador to France and Scotland. In the mid sixteenth century the street
was home to the incorrigible Thomas Cromwell, Master of the King's Jewels, Lord Privy
Seal, Vicar General, Earl of Essex and
favourite of Henry VIII, whose power and
unpredictability were such that he evicted
the inhabitants of a row of local cottages,
built himself a mansion on the site, and
then, unsatisfied with his acquisition, seized
the gardens of his neighbours. Cromwell
was executed after a disagreement with the
king in 1540, and the following year his property was bought by the Drapers' Company
to be used as their hall. General Monck
based his campaign to restore Charles II to
the throne in the hall in 1660 and the
building was rebuilt following damage in
the 1666 Fire of London and a fire of 1772.
Throgmorton Street is now the home of
the dour brutalist tower that houses the
Stock Exchange. Opposite, on its
northern side, the street is lined with
elegant shops.

Stock Exchange, No. 2, south side
London's major trading floor, a market
place that deals in share trading, government bonds, debentures, insurance and
commodities, the Stock Exchange is where
stockbrokers compete against each other in
share trading. It was formed by traders who
met at the Royal Exchange (p. 29) and
behaved in such a rowdy fashion the
building's owners forced them out, which
led them to set up on their own, opening
premises in 1773 on the corner of Threadneedle Street and Sweetings Alley.

The Stock Exchange moved to the present
site in the early nineteenth century and
installed a system whereby trading was
divided between jobbers and stockbrokers.
Jobbers dominated the trading floor, buying
and selling shares for stockbrokers, making
money through the difference between what
stockbrokers were prepared to pay for
shares and the price at which they were
bought and sold, and stockbrokers made
money from commissions earned from
buying and selling shares to the outside
world at large.

The London Stock Exchange began
playing a major role in financing the first
industrial companies, eclipsing its main
rival, Amsterdam, in the mid nineteenth
century, and introducing the innovation of
telegraphic tickertape, running at six words
per minute, to help business in 1872. A
major blow came in the financial crash of
1931 when the Exchange lost most of its
overseas business, while after the Second
World War there were fears that the Labour
government would nationalize the institution. Although this was averted, the Stock
Exchange was hampered by exchange
controls that prevented British residents
from buying non-Sterling securities until
1979 when the Thatcher government introduced deregulation. This allowed outside
corporations to own member firms, abolished minimum levels of commission and
resulted in the functions of jobbers and
brokers being merged.

The so-called 'Big Bang' of 27 October
1986 saw the Exchange become a private
limited company, with individual members
no longer having voting rights, profits used
for financing developments by the
Exchange, rather than being distributed to
shareholders, and trading conducted on
computer and telephone, rather than in
person. With the financial world dominated
by takeovers, mergers, salary hikes and
acquisitions, a worldwide stockmarket crash
occurred on Black Monday, 19 October 1987,
when the City lost £94 billion.
► Royal Exchange, p. 29.

Tokenhouse Yard

Off Lothbury is Tokenhouse Yard, site of
the office where in 1635 Lord Maltravers
became the sole issuer of tokens, small coins
which shopkeepers handed to customers as
change until halfpenny and farthing coins
were introduced. London traders were
outraged when Maltravers successfully asked

Charles I for permission to run the trade as a monopoly, for previously each trader produced their own coins, which could be used only at the issuing shop. Tokens were officially withdrawn from circulation in 1672 on the introduction of low denominational coins.

(iv) Bishopsgate and east

Bishopsgate

Part of the main north–south road at the eastern side of the City, Bishopsgate was named after the **Bishop's Gate** that stood by present-day Camomile Street and was the major route out of the City towards Hertfordshire. It is dominated on the west side by Liverpool Street station and the 1990s Broadgate development, and on the east side by a number of narrow antiquated passageways that provide glimpses of a mostly vanished City of cramped rooms and small shops.

west side: Cornhill to Norton Folgate
South Sea Company, corner with Threadneedle Street
One of the most spectacular financial crashes in London history befell the **South Sea Company**, formed in 1711 to trade with Spanish America and provide the region with slaves, after a bill was passed in 1720 allowing people who were owed portions of the national debt by the government to exchange their claims for shares in company stock. The directors of the **South Sea Company** took on around three-fifths of the national debt – £9 million – resulting in considerable speculation in company stock, with shares rising in value from £100 to £1,000 and speculators trying to win finance for impossible projects. When the bubble burst in September 1720 many investors were ruined. Isaac Newton, the leading English scientist of the era, had sold £7,000-worth of stock the previous April at 100 per cent profit but had then unwisely re-entered the market and lost £20,000, which led him to comment: 'I can calculate the motions of the heavenly bodies, but not the madness of

people.' Some of those found guilty were thrown in the Tower. The Postmaster-General, James Craggs the Elder, who was blamed for the fiasco, killed himself shortly before his trial.

➤ Baring Brothers collapse, p. 25.

The Muggletonians

Lodowick Muggleton, a Bishopsgate-born tailor, claimed in 1651 that God had appointed him and his cousin, John Reeve, as the Two Last Witnesses, as foretold in the verse in the Book of Revelations, which warns: 'I will give power unto my two witnesses and they shall prophesy one thousand two hundred and threescore days clothed in sackcloth'. Muggleton and Reeve formed a sect, the Muggletonians, whose major tenets were that:
1. God and the man Jesus Christ are synonymous expressions.
2. The devil and human reason are synonymous.
3. The soul dies and rises again with the body.
4. Heaven is a place above the stars.
5. At present hell is nowhere, but this earth, darkened after the last judgement, will be hell.
6. Angels are the only beings of pure reason.
Reeve died in 1658, and Muggleton in 1698, after which their teachings were handed down family to family. But as followers did not believe in converting outsiders the sect slowly died out. For instance, in 1697 nearly 250 people attended Muggleton's funeral, but the list of believers in 1803 showed there were just over 100 members, and around 100 years later only seventeen attended the monthly meeting. An article in the *Times Literary Supplement* in 1974 unearthed a handful of believers in Kent, and by 1979 it was thought there were only two remaining Muggletonians.

➤ Joanna Southcott and Richard Brothers, millennial prophets, p. 152 and p. 153.

St Botolph without Bishopsgate, opposite Houndsditch

The Norman church of 1212 was replaced in 1572 and the building, despite surviving the Great Fire, was demolished in 1724 and rebuilt by George Dance the Elder. John Betjeman recounted in his 1937 collection of poems, *Continual Dew*, how he used to sit down in the churchyard and wait 'for the spirit of my grandfather / Toddling along from the Barbican'. Though largely spared from Second World War bombing, the church was damaged in 1992 by the IRA bomb that destroyed the nearby Baltic Exchange.

White Hart, Nos. 119–121

Many of those making long journeys to visit inmates at the **Bethlem Asylum** (Bedlam), which stood nearby from 1676, used to stay overnight at the White Hart until the practice of visiting inmates ceased in 1770, resulting in the White Hart's losing much of its trade. The pub has since been rebuilt.

London Tavern, No. 123

Now rebuilt as the George bar and restaurant, the **London Tavern** was the setting in the eighteenth and nineteenth centuries for many lavish functions connected with the docks and a popular meeting place for radicals, where in 1849 the free trade campaigners John Bright and Richard Cobden set up the National Freehold Society (subsequently the National Building Society) to campaign for universal male suffrage. In Charles Dickens's *Nicholas Nickleby* the United Metropolitan Hot Muffin and Crumpet Baking and Punctual Delivery Company meet here.

Liverpool Street station

See Liverpool Street, p. 19.

east side: Norton Folgate to Leadenhall Street

Dirty Dick's, Nos. 202–204

'Dirty Dick' was the nickname of Nathaniel Bentley, a local nineteenth-century ironmonger who preserved the unused wedding breakfast that was left over when his fiancée died on the eve of their marriage and spent the rest of his life in squalor. When Bentley died the landlord of the pub that stood on this site bought the contents of his shop and house, including what remained of the wedding breakfast, as well as the bodies of Bentley's dead cats, which were displayed here until the 1980s.

Bishopsgate, Bishopsgate at Camomile Street

The Roman gate that stood here led to Ermine Street, the road to Lincoln and York, and was rebuilt in the seventh century by Eorconweald, Bishop of London, whose successors received one stick from every cart of wood passing through. It was demolished in 1760.

▶ Aldgate, p. 30.

St Ethelburga-the-Virgin within Bishopsgate

An exquisite thirteenth-century church, named after the seventh-century abbess of Barking, it was where Henry Hudson, the explorer who opened up vast swathes of North America to Europeans, and his crew took communion in 1607 before leaving on their ill-fated expedition to find the Northwest Passage. The church escaped the Fire of London and Second World War destruction but was almost entirely destroyed by an IRA bomb in 1993. Since then various schemes have been proposed for rebuilding it, including the innovative idea of leaving the ruins unrestored behind a glass wall, a plan rejected in favour of a proposal to rebuild the church as a Centre for Reconciliation and Peace. Past rectors include John Larke, who was hanged, drawn and quartered after refusing to accept Henry VIII's Oath of Supremacy that made the king head of the Church of England.

Baring Brothers, No. 8

London's oldest merchant bank, brought down by the activities of a rogue trader in 1995, was founded as an import and export agency by John and Francis Baring in 1762 and soon became an important independent merchant bank, underwriting marine insurance and helping William Pitt the Younger finance the Napoleonic Wars.

Barings was celebrated by Lord Byron in 'Don Juan' ('Who keeps the world both old and new, in pain / Or pleasure? Who makes politicians run gibber all? / The shade of Bonaparte's double daring / Jew Rothschild and his fellow, Christian Baring'), and such was its power that it was said that a man in Boston could not buy a cargo of tea in Canton without getting credit from Messrs Matheson (a rival) or Messrs Baring.

In the nineteenth century Barings began to speculate in English, French, Russian and Austrian stocks, Panama bonds and American railroad shares, raising $500 million in loans to the United States and Canadian governments. But at the end of the century Edmund Baring (Lord Revelstoke) took a gamble in Argentina that spectacularly backfired, underwriting a £2 million share issue by the Buenos Aires Water Supply and Drainage Company and sending the money abroad before selling the shares, which he was subsequently unable to shift. Barings had insufficient funds to pay the huge debt, but City powerbrokers reasoned that if the bank collapsed it would drag down with it too many firms and confidence in the Square Mile would be shattered. So in November 1890 a consortium led by the Governor of the Bank of England bailed it out, resulting in the bank's being reconstituted as Baring Brothers & Co. Ltd and Revelstoke ruined.

Around 100 years later a trader, Nick Leeson, working out of Barings' Singapore office, lost $1.3 billion after a gamble that the Japanese stock exchange would rise went awry. Leeson blamed management in London for the débâcle, they in turn blamed him, but he was arrested and held for nine months in a Frankfurt prison before being extradited to Singapore where he was given a six-and-a-half-year sentence. The bank collapsed and the parts that were salvageable were subsumed into the ING corporation in the late 1990s.

▶ BCCI banking scandal, p. 32.

FENCHURCH, EC3

The eastern end of the City, which includes Houndsditch, Leadenhall Street, Fenchurch Street and Eastcheap and is one of the least populated areas in London, was built on the marshy or fenny ground (hence the name, Fenchurch) by the banks of the long-vanished Langbourn stream. At the eastern end was 𝕬𝖑𝖉𝖌𝖆𝖙𝖊, the Romans' eastern gate into Londinium from Essex, remembered in the road and tube station of the same name. The streets around Fenchurch Street station, which stands in the centre of EC3, are dominated by finance houses such as Lloyd's of London and some of the most desirable office locations in the City, particularly those on cobbled St Helen's Place, off Bishopsgate.

(i) around Cornhill

Castle Court
George and Vulture
The tavern that has stood here, south of Cornhill, since 1175 was rebuilt after the Fire of London, and again in the early nineteenth century, and has been patronized by writers such as Jonathan Swift and Charles Dickens (it features in *The Pickwick Papers* and is decorated with pictures relating to the novel). In the eighteenth century the George and Vulture was home to the Hellfire Club, an aristocratic drinking and womanizing club which flirted with Masonic ritual, the occult and Satanism and was led by a group of wealthy playboys that included Sir Francis Dashwood, who as a young man had attended a Black Mass in France and made contact with Masonic societies in Italy whose members had been excommunicated by the Pope. Dashwood was later Chancellor of the Exchequer and Postmaster-General to George III.

Change Alley
In 1669 Thomas Garraway, who introduced into England tea, a drink he claimed to be

the 'cure of all disorders', opened 𝕲𝖆𝖗𝖗𝖆𝖜𝖆𝖞'𝖘, which became the City's leading eighteenth-century maritime auction house and in the nineteenth century an estate agent's and drugs store, earning a mention in Charles Dickens's *Pickwick Papers* and *Little Dorrit*. It closed in 1872 and was demolished soon after. Martin's Bank now stands on the site.

➤ **𝕵𝖊𝖗𝖚𝖘𝖆𝖑𝖊𝖒 𝖈𝖔𝖋𝖋𝖊𝖊 𝖍𝖔𝖚𝖘𝖊**, Cowper's Court, below.

Cornhill

Settlements were established on Cornhill, the highest point in the City, overlooking the River Walbrook, following the Roman invasion of AD 43, and some twenty years later Roman London, having been sacked by Boadicea in AD 60, was refounded here. Cornhill later became the location of the pillory and was where the author Daniel Defoe was placed in 1703 for writing a seditious pamphlet about the government. The street, which connects Bank tube with the southern end of Bishopsgate, features much elegant nineteenth-century architecture and two of the City's most imposing churches – St Peter upon Cornhill and St Michael.

south side: Gracechurch Street to Bank tube
St Peter upon Cornhill
The oldest place of Christian worship in London, the church was founded by Lucius, Britain's first Christian king, *c.* 179 and was rebuilt by Christopher Wren after the 1666 Fire of London. Above the entrance are three forbidding-looking figures installed in anger by the architect who erected the adjacent Victorian office block but was prevented by the Church authorities from encroaching on church land. Home in the late fourteenth century to the Guild of St Peter, which was established by members of the Worshipful Company of Fishmongers, it is now a Christian Aid centre.
St Michael
The first church on the site, built *c.* 1055, burned down in the Fire of London and was redesigned by Christopher Wren, the work

being completed by Nicholas Hawksmoor, who modelled it on his own Magdalen College tower in Oxford. William Boyce, the eighteenth-century composer of choral music, was organist here for thirty-two years. In Charles Dickens's *A Christmas Carol* its gruff old bell was 'always peeping down at Scrooge out of a Gothic window in the wall'.

No. 32
A carved panel on the street door features a number of reliefs relating to local historical scenes, including an 1847 meeting that took place at Smith and Elder's publishers, which was then based here, between the Victorian authors Charlotte Brontë and William Thackeray.

Cowper's Court

Traders who dealt with India met in the 1770s at the **𝕵𝖊𝖗𝖚𝖘𝖆𝖑𝖊𝖒 𝖈𝖔𝖋𝖋𝖊𝖊 𝖍𝖔𝖚𝖘𝖊** on Cowper's Court, off Cornhill, to discuss business, and for many years the Jerusalem rivalled Lloyd's as a centre of maritime commerce. In the nineteenth century metal traders, obliged to move out of the Royal Exchange to discuss their affairs, met there, establishing the 'tradition of the ring', during which merchants with metal to sell would draw a circle on the floor with sawdust and call out 'Change', at which point all those wishing to trade would assemble around the circle and make their bids.

➤ **𝕭𝖔𝖜𝖒𝖆𝖓'𝖘 𝖈𝖔𝖋𝖋𝖊𝖊 𝖍𝖔𝖚𝖘𝖊**, St Michael's Alley, p. 29.

Gracechurch Street

A street of handsome nineteenth-century banks and grand offices, south of Bishopsgate, named after the church of **𝕾𝖙 𝕭𝖊𝖓𝖊𝖙 𝕲𝖗𝖆𝖘𝖘** (demolished 1868), Gracechurch Street stands on the site of a huge Roman forum and basilica, whose existence was uncovered during excavation work in the 1950s.
Leadenhall market, east side
An exquisite collection of Victorian market buildings, dating from 1881, Leadenhall market stands on the site of a Roman

basilica and was first opened in the four-teenth century for the sale of poultry, cheese and butter. The market was destroyed in the Fire of London but was rebuilt and enlarged to sell leather, wool and meat. It now contains a variety of shops, bars and restaurants, and much preserved period architecture, but is spoiled by an excess of faux Victoriana.

► Smithfield meat market, p. 8.

Lombard Street

Once the Jews, the City's moneylenders, had been expelled from England in 1290, Venetians and Lombardians, who had first arrived in London during the mid-thirteenth-century reign of Henry III to collect taxes due to the Pope, took up the same role, later introducing into England double-entry book-keeping, *doppia scrittura*, which had been invented by a fifteenth-century Italian monk. The Lombardians' power base was challenged by the opening of the first Exchange in 1565. They responded by increasing their banking rates, which failed to win back custom. In 1692 Lloyd's Insurance moved from (Great) Tower Street to Lombard Street, and began publishing *Lloyd's News*, the forerunner of *Lloyd's List and Shipping Gazette*, here four years later. By the nineteenth century the street contained the headquarters of a number of major banks, including Barclay's and Martin's, and was described by Walter Bagehot, editor of the *Economist*, as 'the greatest combination of economical power and economical delicacy that the world has ever seen'. It is still one of the most pres-tigious streets for finance companies in the City.

St Edmund the King, north side at George Yard

Originally St Edmund Grasschurch, on account of the nearby herb market, the church is dedicated to the East Anglian king shot by Danes for refusing to renounce Christianity. Christopher Wren redesigned the building after the Fire and work was completed by Robert Hooke in 1690. It was one of the few City churches to be damaged during the First World War.

St Mary Woolnoth of the Nativity, south side at King William Street

Nicholas Hawksmoor's only City church, built 1716–17 and one of London's best-loved examples of the English Baroque, is named after the Saxon noble Wulfnoth and occupies a site first used as a place of worship in 1273. The church was damaged, but not destroyed, in the 1666 Fire of London, and Christopher Wren performed basic remedial work, but by the time the Fifty New Churches Act of 1711 was passed it was derelict. Hawksmoor, who was appointed architect for a new church on the site, discovered the remains of an ancient temple while laying the foundations and decided to install a cornice of a Roman temple dedicated to Mars Vindicator inside the new building. Also inside is a memorial to the slave trader John Newton, 'once an infedil and libertine [but] preserved, restored, pardoned and appointed to preach the faith he had long laboured to destroy', who worked on the slave run between Africa and America, later became church rector, and wrote the hymn 'How Sweet the Name of Jesus Sounds'. The church was targeted for demolition during the tube building programme of the 1890s, but such was the public outcry the City and South London Railway was obliged to change its mind and underpin the church's foundations when constructing the new station nearby. The tube company also bought the crypt, for £340,000, money which went on building thirty new churches in the London suburbs. The church is featured in T. S. Eliot's *The Waste Land* and Peter Ackroyd's 1985 mystery novel *Hawksmoor*.

► Christchurch Spitalfields, p. 285.

Royal Exchange Buildings

A stretch of pavement named after the adjacent Royal Exchange, it is where in 1851 Paul Julius Reuter (born Israel Beer Josaphat), having moved from Belgium, where he used pigeons to take news of the closing prices on the Brussels Bourse to Aachen in a tiny silk bag tied under a wing, set up a news agency (at No. 1) to gather information from the local financial centres and sell it to investors. Reuter believed that those who wanted to keep abreast of political and social developments that might affect their assets would pay well for information and approached *The Times* for a commission. When they turned him down he went to the *Morning Advertiser*, who engaged him after he promised to deliver news free for a fortnight while the editor made up his mind. Within seven years Reuter was supplying information to a host of London newspapers including the *Morning Star*, *Daily News*, *Morning Post* and the initially dismissive *Times*. Once the company was established it moved to Fleet Street, becoming the world's best-known news agency.

Royal Exchange (1565–1939), Threadneedle Street at Royal Exchange Buildings

> There is no Place in the Town which I so love to frequent as the Royal Exchange. I am wonderfully delighted to see such a Body of Men thriving in their own private Fortunes, and at the same time promoting the Public Stock – *The Spectator*, Joseph Addison (1711)

Impressed by the Antwerp Bourse, where the English Merchant Adventurers had set up office, Thomas Gresham, an Elizabethan merchant who owned a shop in Lombard Street at the Sign of the Grasshopper, founded the Exchange in 1565 for tradesmen to meet and discuss business. Gresham's building was festooned with grasshopper symbols adapted from the family crest and inside there were passageways with names such as Grocers' Walk, Silkmen's Walk and Druggists' Walk, trade becoming so vibrant that the writer Thomas Dekker, Shakespeare's contemporary, noted how when walking in the Exchange 'a man is put in mind of Babel, there is such confusion of languages'.

Following a visit by Elizabeth I in January 1570 the Exchange became the Royal

Exchange, one of the buildings from where new kings and queens were officially announced, but it soon declined in status and became a refuge for tramps and prostitutes. After it was destroyed in the 1666 Fire Christopher Wren planned a building which would be the focus of the new City, but the scheme was abandoned along with most of his proposals. A new Exchange was designed instead by Edward Jarman, the City Surveyor, which opened in 1669 and grew to contain, as William Pyne noted in his 1806 *Microcosm of London*, 'the Lord Mayor's court-office, the Royal Exchange assurance office, the merchant seamen's office, Lloyd's subscription coffee-houses, counting houses for merchants and underwriters . . . and [outlets] for stockbrokers, lottery office keepers and various retail traders', until it too was destroyed by fire, in 1838.

The current Exchange, readily identifiable by its giant portico of eight Corinthian columns, designed by William Tite in 1842, continued functioning until 1939 when trading ceased and the premises were taken over by the Guardian Royal Exchange Assurance Company. The building was redeveloped within Tite's frame as a luxurious shopping centre at the end of the twentieth century, with outlets for Paul Smith and Prada among others.

▶ Stock Exchange, p. 23.

St Michael's Alley

London's first coffee house, **Bowman's**, was opened on St Michael's Alley in 1652 by Pasqua Rosee, a Turk, and Christopher Bowman, and was where at the end of the decade Charles II's supporters prepared for his return to the throne. Ironically, in 1675, fifteen years after taking the throne, Charles tried to ban coffee houses such as **Bowman's** on the grounds that they were places where 'the disaffected meet and spread scandalous reports concerning the conduct of his Majesty and his Ministers'. Charles was supported by a group of City women who, the previous year, had presented the king with a petition against coffee, 'representing to public consideration the grand inconveniences accruing to their sex from the excessive use of the dying and enfeebling liquor'. The king's attempt to close the establishments failed, the order was rescinded within days, and by the beginning of the eighteenth century there were more than 1,000 coffee houses in London and twenty-six between Cornhill and Threadneedle Street alone. The 𝕴𝕒𝕞𝕒𝕚𝕔𝕒 𝖈𝖔𝖋𝖋𝖊𝖊 𝖍𝖔𝖚𝖘𝖊 (since rebuilt as the Jamaica Wine House) replaced 𝕭𝖔𝖜𝖒𝖆𝖓'𝖘 in the 1670s. The coffee houses died out during the nineteenth century.

(ii) north of Fenchurch Street

Aldgate
Originally Ealdgate ('the old gate'), a Roman gate at the start of the route leading from the City to Colchester, the Roman capital, its gatehouse included apartments. Here, the poet Geoffrey Chaucer lived rent-free, in return for allowing troops use of the fortification in time of attack, from 1374 to 1385 while engaged in customs duties for the government at the nearby Port of London, and wrote a number of works including *Troilus and Criseyde* (1385). The surrounding area suffered considerable hardship during the 1665 Plague and as Daniel Defoe noted in *A Journal of the Plague Year* (1722): 'There was no parish in or about London where [the plague] raged with such violence as in . . . Aldgate.' The gate was demolished in 1761 and Aldgate, the road named after the gate, became heavily commercialized, attracting in the nineteenth century shops associated with the local clothing trade that were mostly staffed by Jewish immigrants from eastern Europe. Although some clothing shops remain the industry has now moved east and is run by Bangladeshis. At the junction of Aldgate, Fenchurch Street and Leadenhall Street is Aldgate Pump, which ceased being used for dispensing water in 1876 when locals complained about the unusual taste. The stream that fed the well was examined, and it was discovered that the water passed through a graveyard *en route* to Aldgate and had been contaminated by human remains.
▶ Temple Bar, p. 42.

Bevis Marks
Bevis Marks is a corruption of 'Buries Marks', the burial limits of land once owned by the abbots of Bury St Edmunds. The road of the same name, sandwiched between Camomile Street and Duke's Place, is best known for the long-standing Spanish and Portuguese Synagogue.

Spanish and Portuguese Synagogue, west junction with Heneage Lane

London's most famous synagogue, the oldest in Britain, was built on the site of the Abbot of Bury St Edmunds's town house in 1701 for the large influx of Jews with roots in the Iberian peninsula who had been officially allowed to return to England by Oliver Cromwell in 1655, nearly 400 years after Edward I had expelled the Jews from England. When the building was planned the City authorities insisted that the entrance be installed on the side street, Heneage Lane, as they were worried about the reaction of non-Jewish locals to the sight of a synagogue being built. The architect chosen for the project was a Quaker, Joseph Avis, who had worked on the Fleet Street church of St Bride's, and his simple brick building with a galleried interior, which provided a template for synagogue designers for the next century, has barely been altered since.

The synagogue's register of births includes Benjamin D'Israeli (later Disraeli), from 1804. However, the future Tory prime minister was also baptized at St Andrew's, Holborn, taken there by his father after a row with the synagogue authorities, the baptism later allowing Disraeli to become a Member of Parliament and therefore prime minister. Seat No. 354, occupied in the early nineteenth century by the stockbroker Sir Moses Montefiore (1784–1885), brother-in-law of the Rothschild *paterfamilias* Nathan Mayer, is roped off and can be used

only by Montefiore's descendants or the Lord Mayor of London. Services are still held in Portuguese, as well as in Hebrew.
► 𝕲𝖗𝖊𝖆𝖙 𝕾𝖞𝖓𝖆𝖌𝖔𝖌𝖚𝖊, below.

Duke's Place

Duke's Place was named after Thomas Howard, Duke of Norfolk, who was beheaded in 1572, and built on the site of the medieval Augustinian Priory of 𝕳𝖔𝖑𝖞 𝕿𝖗𝖎𝖓𝖎𝖙𝖞, 𝕬𝖑𝖉𝖌𝖆𝖙𝖊. It was home to the 𝕲𝖗𝖊𝖆𝖙 𝕾𝖞𝖓𝖆𝖌𝖔𝖌𝖚𝖊, the seat of the Chief Rabbi, from the 1690s until it was destroyed in the Second World War, which was visited in the early nineteenth century by Leigh Hunt, publisher of the poets Keats and Shelley, who 'took pleasure in witnessing the semi-catholic pomp of their service, and in hearing their fine singing; not without something of as constant astonishment at their wearing their hats'. In the nineteenth century Duke's Place was almost entirely occupied by Jews of northern European ancestry (Ashkenazim) and lined with Jewish shops, as Henry Mayhew noted in *London Labour and the London Poor*. Duke's Place has since been entirely rebuilt and bears no trace of its Jewish history.
► Old Jewry, p. 18.

Great St Helen's

William Shakespeare is believed to have lived on the alleyway leading from Bishopsgate to the church of St Helen in 1598, although there is no proof that the Shakespeare concerned was the playwright.
St Helen Bishopsgate
Emperor Constantine, the first Christian emperor of Rome, had links with the original church built on the site in the fourth century, which was joined *c.* 1204 by a Benedictine nunnery, and although the nunnery was dissolved in 1538 the nuns' church, St Helen Bishopsgate, surprisingly survives, tucked away to the east of the modern corporate blocks of Bishopsgate. It features the finest collection of monuments of any City church, including a memorial to Shakespeare who is believed to have lived locally, as well as some unusual medieval features such as a hagioscope (squint) which allowed the nuns to see the altar without entering the church. John Wesley, the founder of Methodism, spoke here in 1768 shortly before his epiphany, but only once, for although he noted that his heart 'was so enlarged to declare the love of God to all that were oppressed by the Devil', he was told afterwards: 'Sir, you must preach here no more.' The church was damaged by the IRA bomb that destroyed nearby St Ethelburga in 1992 and restored by Quinlan Terry.

Houndsditch

A major road leading from Liverpool Street to Aldgate, named after the ditch in which people left their dead dogs in medieval times and which was filled in *c.* 1590, it was where in 1866 Dr Thomas Barnardo, a trainee missionary, found eleven boys sleeping huddled together in the gutter. Subsequently he began raising money to establish a home for destitute boys, which he founded soon after in Stepney as the first of the Barnardo's homes. In the nineteenth century the street was dominated by clothing industry sweatshops, their conditions so gruesome that Charles Kingsley, the novelist and clergyman best known for *The Water Babies* (1863), railed: 'What is flogging or hanging to the slavery, starvation, waste of life, year-long imprisonment in dungeons narrower and fouler than those of the Inquisition, which goes on among thousands of free English clothesmakers at this day?' The street is now dominated by characterless office blocks, and many premises in the side streets are still involved in the less glamorous end of the clothing trade.
► Dr Barnardo in Stepney, p. 292.

Leadenhall Street

An important City artery, linking Bishopsgate and Aldgate, for centuries it attracted prestigious institutions such as the East India Company, which was established here in 1600, and Lloyd's of London (now based to the south on Lime Street).

The Houndsditch murders

During the weekend of 17–18 December 1910 a gang of Latvian anarchists killed three policemen who disturbed them in the early stages of a raid on a jeweller's shop at 119 Houndsditch. The ten-strong gang included Fritz Svaars, who was on the run after robbing a bank in America, and George Gardstein, who used to walk in the middle of the road to avoid arrest by policemen or 'Tsarist agents lurking in doorways'. They chose the Houndsditch shop after being told it contained jewels belonging to the hated Tsar of Russia, which, if expropriated, would raise funds all the sweeter to use for their political escapades. To facilitate their heist the gang rented a room in 𝕰𝖝𝖈𝖍𝖆𝖓𝖌𝖊 𝕭𝖚𝖎𝖑𝖉𝖎𝖓𝖌𝖘, Cutler Street, at the rear of No. 119, and planned digging a tunnel to the shop over the weekend. But neighbours, who heard their hammering, alerted police, and when officers went to check what they thought was a routine burglary they were fired on by members of the gang. Three policemen were killed and Gardstein was accidentally shot by one of his own men as a dying policeman pulled him down to use as a shield from the bullets. The gang escaped to a safe house in Mile End where a doctor was asked to come and heal a man 'accidentally shot by a friend', and the doctor eventually called the police, who found Gardstein dead and a woman frantically throwing papers into the fire. When police realized that they might have stumbled on the Houndsditch gang they mounted a huge search to find the rest of the villains, putting up posters in English and Yiddish across the East End asking for information. Meanwhile, some of the gang were holed up at 100 Sidney Street, Stepney, and when police discovered the hideout a few weeks later it became the setting for a well-documented siege.

► The Sidney Street siege, p. 303.

north side: Bishopsgate to Aldgate

Bank of Credit and Commerce International (BCCI), No. 100

The most discredited bank in the world in the late twentieth century, BCCI, which had its London headquarters here, went bust in 1991 with debts of around $12 billion, almost bankrupting a number of councils across Britain and thousands of Asian businessmen. Twenty years previously BCCI had been created by Agha Hasan Abedi, who persuaded the Bank of America to deal with him as a means of gaining influence in the Middle East. During the seventies it grew into a huge corporation, with 400 branches in seventy countries, 14,000 staff worldwide, assets of $20 billion worldwide and issues of credit cards featuring the sign of the zodiac. But BCCI had also grown too quickly, from four UK offices in 1973 to forty-five offices by 1977, and it escaped the level of supervision afforded to its rivals by basing its holding company in Luxembourg, where it had no branches, registering in the Cayman Islands, where again it had no branches, and conducting most of its global business from its Leadenhall Street offices in London. The Bank of England therefore considered it to be a foreign bank, based in Luxembourg and the Grand Caymans, and thus the responsibility of regulators in those countries.

Although the Bank of England admitted early on that BCCI was 'the most difficult bank we have to deal with', no action was taken until 1988, when it became apparent that it was involved with the financing of terrorism and the laundering of drug money. On 5 July 1991 banking regulators swooped on BCCI's offices in seven countries, including Britain, and froze its assets, to the horror of thousands of small businessmen and thirty British local authorities who had taken advantage of its generous credit terms. The precipitous closure meant that innumerable financial transactions were left incomplete, and when news of the drama unfolded many branches were surrounded by desperate investors anxious to withdraw their savings, to no avail. The subsequent investigation into BCCI, run from an office in Finsbury Square, was the biggest and most complex financial investigation ever witnessed in the City. Scarcely credible stories of corruption and brutality soon emerged – BCCI had helped the CIA fund illegal arms sales to Iran, Iraq and Afghanistan, and maintained accounts for Saddam Hussein, the PLO, Mossad (the Israeli secret service) and various terrorist groups, Left and Right, as well as the governments of China, Libya and Syria. By the beginning of the twenty-first century the BCCI scandal had failed to reach a conclusion, although accountants and lawyers had managed to salvage around $7 billion of the bank's $12 billion losses.

► Baring Brothers' collapse, p. 25.

St Katharine Cree

St Katherine de Christchurch at Aldgate in medieval times, it was rebuilt in 1504 and again in 1630, on that occasion to the strictures of William Laud, Bishop of London, an enthusiast of ceremonies and the spiritual aspects of Christianity. One of only eight City churches to survive the 1666 Fire, its tower dates from 1504, making it some 200 years older than most City spires. John Wesley, founder of Methodism, spoke here in 1768, shortly before his epiphany, but was told afterwards that he was no longer welcome to preach. Every 17 October the Lion Sermon is read, commemorating the deliverance of Sir John Gayer, Lord Mayor of London in 1646, from a lion in the Arabian desert.

south side: Fenchurch Street to Gracechurch Street

𝕰𝖆𝖘𝖙 𝕴𝖓𝖉𝖎𝖆 𝕳𝖔𝖚𝖘𝖊, junction with Lime Street The East India Company, which became the City's most powerful company, was established here in 1600 to challenge the Dutch–Portuguese monopoly of the spice trade in the Orient, and gained its first foothold in the East some ten years later when it seized control of the nutmeg-producing island of Puloroon, a feat that so impressed James I

that, on hearing the news, he styled himself 'King of England, Scotland, Ireland, France . . . and Puloroon'. After tussling with the Dutch, Portuguese and French for control of trade routes in the area over the next 100 years, the company began to establish itself as a major force, opening up Hong Kong and Singapore to the West, introducing tea to Britain, spices to the West Indies, opium to China, porcelain to Russia and coffee to Arabia and establishing trading posts in Madras and Calcutta. Meanwhile, the East India Company faced competition and opposition at home. In 1694 Parliament passed legislation which enabled *all* British firms to trade with the subcontinent, and when even this resulted in little change to the company's dominant position throughout the eighteenth century the prime minister, William Pitt, convinced Parliament to accept a new India Bill, which weakened the power of the Company. Despite having become the largest single commercial enterprise the world had ever seen, trading for a fifth of the world's population, the East India Company lost commercial and political power, saw its monopoly broken in 1813, and from 1834 simply became a managing agency for the British government in India, a role that ended with the Indian Mutiny of 1858. Four years later the company headquarters on Leadenhall Street were demolished, Lloyd's taking over the site.

► East India Docks, p. 264.

Lime Street

Lloyd's of London

An incorporated society of private insurers and one of the world's best-known companies, occupying Richard Rogers's equally well-known building of 1986, Lloyd's was begun in the 1860s by Edward Lloyd, who opened a coffee house on Tower Street and encouraged patrons connected with shipping to visit and exchange news. By the eighteenth century runners were scurrying back and forth between the coffee house and the docks gathering the latest information, and before long shipowners were coming to Lloyd's to fill in forms listing the details of their proposed voyage – the route, intended ports of call, and value of the cargo – with speculators announcing how much they were willing to pay for insurance. Other investors, meanwhile, would decide how much they were willing to risk in exchange for the premium, writing their names on the shipowner's slip under the relevant information (hence the term 'underwriter'), with the thrill of accruing large profits offset by the risk of incurring unlimited liability.

In 1760 the first Lloyd's Register of Ships was published and nine years later a new branch was opened in Pope's Head Alley, off Cornhill, the first of several different City addresses where business could be discussed more formally. The company sealed its reputation as a symbol of trust following the 1906 San Francisco earthquake, when Cuthbert Evan Heath, a leading broker and underwriter, telegraphed instructions to his California representatives to pay all claims to Lloyd's customers in full, immediately, whatever the terms of their policies. Twelve years later the sinking of the *Titanic* cost Lloyd's underwriters more than $1 million, but decades of success followed until the end of the twentieth century when a series of cataclysmic events – asbestos poisoning, hurricanes, maritime disasters such as the *Exxon Valdez* oil spill – resulted in $12.4 billion in losses, losses exacerbated by the 2001 World Trade Center destruction.

Some Lloyd's 'Names' (those who had pledged a large sum to join a syndicate) refused to meet the losses, saying they had been cheated by those with inside information; the company's solution was to offer the 34,000 Names a $5 billion package that would cut their losses in return for an agreement to end all litigation.

● In 1986 Lloyd's moved into Richard Rogers's glamorous hi-tech tower, festooned with exposed pipes, ducts and lifts in the style of his Pompidou Centre in France. The design, though seen by many as a gimmick, has clever financial advantages, allowing repair work to take place without incurring the usual expensive costs of burrowing into the building's fabric.

Mitre Square
One of the City's lesser known squares, it marks the site of the cloisters of the 𝔓𝔯𝔦𝔬𝔯𝔶 𝔬𝔣 𝔱𝔥𝔢 𝔥𝔬𝔩𝔶 𝔗𝔯𝔦𝔫𝔦𝔱𝔶, founded in 1108 by Mathilda of Scotland.

Location of the fifth Jack the Ripper murder, south-east corner
Catherine Eddowes, an occasional prostitute, became Jack the Ripper's fifth victim, murdered in Mitre Square just before 2 a.m. on 30 September 1888, shortly after Elizabeth Stride had become the fourth victim. Only a few hours previously, Eddowes had been arrested on Aldgate High Street for being drunk and running along the road imitating a fire engine, and after being released she went looking for a client. At 1.30 a.m. Eddowes was seen talking to a man but twenty minutes later she was dead. Witnesses who were called to the inquest gave what remains the only description of the Ripper, as wearing a tweed jacket, deerstalker cap and red neckerchief.
► Location of the sixth Jack the Ripper murder, p. 286.

Mitre Street
Mitre Street, to the west of Aldgate, a row of shabby workshops and offices, was the location of a factory where the South London Richardson gang ran a 'long firm' fraud in 1962, initially buying luxury goods, such as silk stockings, on credit, paying the bills well within the expected time to build a trustworthy reputation, and buying new stock on credit, which again was paid off quickly. Once this process had occurred several times, and the firm had gained a reputation as prompt and reliable payers, the stock was removed so that the warehouse could be set on fire and a claim lodged with insurers for the 'destroyed' goods. But when the Richardsons' explosives expert carried out his task, the conflagration was greater than expected and the building exploded, taking with it a

gas mains, which caused fires and explosions in nearby shops and led to the entire street and a neighbouring factory catching light. Twenty-seven fire engines were called out to quell the flames; the gang made around a quarter of a million pounds profit from the insurance claim.

▶ The Richardsons in South London, p. 378.

St Mary Axe

The street is named after the church of **St Mary Axe**, demolished in the late sixteenth century and properly known as St Mary the Virgin and St Ursula and the Eleven Thousand Virgins. It took its name from the legend of the English princess who went on a journey to Germany with 11,000 handmaidens and met a bloody end from Attila the Hun, who killed them with three axes, one of which was later stored in the church.

east side: Houndsditch to Leadenhall Street
Baltic Exchange, Nos. 14–20
Merchants working the Baltic routes founded the Baltic Exchange as a centre for freight distribution and chartering (where cargoes were found for ships and ships for cargoes) in May 1744 in a Threadneedle Street coffee house that was soon renamed the Virginia and Baltick Coffee House. In 1903 the company moved into an ornate Portland Stone headquarters on St Mary Axe that was badly damaged by an IRA bomb on 10 April 1992 which left only the brick shell of the grand hall. Controversy dogged plans to redevelop the site, with Norman Foster's forty-one-storey tower for the Swiss Re insurance company – the so-called 'erotic gherkin' – winning planning permission in 2001 and dominating the skyline by 2003.

St Andrew Undershaft
The first church on the site, St Andrew Cornhill, was built *c.* 1147 and because of the tall maypole erected alongside every spring became known as St Andrew Under the Shaft, or St Andrew Undershaft. On 1 May 1517 the seasonal festivities were marred by a riot against immigrants and foreign goods,

which led to fourteen locals being hanged for inciting the destruction of foreigners' homes, and when in 1549 the curate of the nearby church of St Katharine Cree declared that the maypole was idolatrous locals arrived with axes to chop it down. John Stow, the pioneering historian, was buried inside in 1605 and is commemorated with a marble monument. Its hand holds a quill pen replaced every year by the Lord Mayor, who gives the old pen to the child who has written the best essay on the capital. The west window features English monarchs and heraldic decorations.

St Helen's Place
A cobbled courtyard lined with ornate office blocks, St Helen's Place is also home to a hall run by the Leathersellers' Company, founded *c.* 1370 by a group of leather merchant sellers who petitioned the Court of Aldermen to regulate against the sale of artificial leather. The hall is a near perfect 38 ft cube and was restored in 1959 after Second World War bombing.

(iii) Fenchurch Street and south

Byward Street
Byward refers to the byword, or password, given out at night at the nearby Tower of London.

All Hallows Barking
Founded in 675 by Eorconweald, Bishop of London, on land owned by Barking Abbey, the church is supposedly the burial place of Richard the Lionheart's heart and was where in January 1650 twenty-seven barrels of gunpowder stored on the premises accidentally exploded, blowing up around fifty houses and killing a large number of people. The diarist Samuel Pepys climbed to the top of the church on Wednesday 5 September 1666 during the Fire of London and there 'saw the saddest sight of desolation that I ever saw' – the charred remains of much of the City. Two important figures from early American history have connections with the church: William Penn, who went on to

found Pennsylvania, was born on Tower Hill in 1644 and baptized in All Hallows; and John Quincy Adams became the sixth President of the USA in 1825, twenty-eight years after he married here. The Christian charity Toc H moved its headquarters to the church in 1922. Although Second World War bombing left only the tower, walls and a few monuments undamaged, a Saxon doorway containing Roman tiles and the remains of a Roman pavement were uncovered and can be seen in the Crypt. The church was rebuilt in 1949 and a new pulpit from the bombed 𝕾𝖙 𝕾𝖜𝖎𝖙𝖍𝖎𝖓 𝕷𝖔𝖓𝖉𝖔𝖓 𝕾𝖙𝖔𝖓𝖊 inserted.

Fenchurch Street
A busy traffic route connecting the centre of the City with the East End, Fenchurch Street is best known for the railway terminus of the same name and in late medieval times was the home of the 𝕶𝖎𝖓𝖌'𝖘 𝕳𝖊𝖆𝖉 𝕿𝖆𝖛𝖊𝖗𝖓 (at the junction with Mark Lane), where Princess Elizabeth (later Elizabeth I) enjoyed a meal of pork and peas on 10 May 1554 after being released from the Tower, having been imprisoned there by Mary Tudor for being a threat to the latter's place on the throne; it was renamed the Queen's Head after she was crowned in 1558. Fountain House near Cullum Street on the north side, designed by W. H. Rogers in the mid-1950s, was the first of London's many slab office blocks built on a podium.
► Fenchurch Street station, p. 38.

Fish Street Hill
Until London Bridge was repositioned Fish Street Hill was the main route connecting the bridge with Gracechurch Street.
The Monument, Fish Street Hill at Monument Street
A memorial to the Great Fire of 1666, the Monument, designed by Christopher Wren and Robert Hooke in 1671–7, is the tallest stone column in the world at 205 ft, its height being the same as the distance between it and the baker's shop on nearby Pudding Lane where the Fire started, and is topped with a vase of flames but not the

intended statue of Charles II as the king refused the honour, telling Wren: 'I didn't start the Fire.' Because of a seventeenth-century conspiracy theory which held that the Fire was started deliberately by Catholics to purge the City of sin, its inscription was altered in 1681 to read: 'But Popish frenzy, which wrought such horrors, is not yet quenched', which led the Catholic poet Alexander Pope to note in 'To Lord Bathurst' (1735) how 'London's column, pointing at the skies / Like a tall bully, lifts the head and lies'. The 'Popish' reference was removed in 1831.

Jewry Street
The street was the home in the sixteenth century of the first Jews allowed to live in London since Edward I expelled the Jews from England in 1291, its number including Rodrigo Lopez, physician to Elizabeth I, who was accused of being implicated in a plot to poison the queen and on whom Shakespeare partly based Shylock. The Jewish immigrants had come mostly from Spain and Portugal, where they had acquired the insulting name *marannos* (Spanish for swine), due to their practice of hanging pigs outside their homes to show they were good *conversos* (converts to Catholicism), and where they had formed secret congregations. They were officially allowed back in England in the 1650s by Oliver Cromwell, Lord Protector, who, as a Puritan – the strain of Christianity which was then the most powerful – believed in a literal application of the Bible and respect for Jews and negotiated with the Amsterdam rabbi, Menasseh Ben Israel, author of *The Hope of Israel*, a book that propounded the idea that the American Indians were the descendants of the lost ten tribes.
► Spanish and Portuguese Synagogue, Bevis Marks, p. 30.

Lower Thames Street
A major traffic route, Lower Thames Street was once home to Billingsgate market and the 𝕮𝖔𝖆𝖑 𝕰𝖝𝖈𝖍𝖆𝖓𝖌𝖊, a cast-iron building of 1849 whose demolition was universally

condemned, particularly by John Betjeman who praised its 'great domed interior' as 'one of the very best in the City'.

south side: Tower end to London Bridge end

Custom House, opposite St Dunstan's Hill

The custom house built here in 1275 to raise duty on goods imported into London by river was where the poet Geoffrey Chaucer worked as Controller of export tax on wool in the 1370s. It was destroyed by fire in 1559, and after its replacement burned down just over a hundred years later, during the Fire of London, the government commissioned Christopher Wren to design a new structure. This in turn was severely damaged by an accidental gunpowder explosion in 1714, being rebuilt by Thomas Ripley in 1717–25. The present building, designed by David Laing and built between 1813 and 1817, now accommodates offices.

Billingsgate market (1016–1982), opposite St Mary at Hill

A market for food and wine (and later fish) that had been brought into London by boat opened here in 1016, and after the 1415 Battle of Agincourt the porters began wearing hats modelled on the leather helmets worn by Henry V's archers. Those that worked here in the twentieth century included the writer George Orwell, in the early 1930s, and the Kray twins, Reggie (as a trainee salesman) and Ronnie (as an 'empties boy', scouring the market for empty fish boxes) in the early 1950s. The market moved to the Isle of Dogs in 1982 after 900 years in the City, while the building, designed by Horace Jones in the French Renaissance style in the 1870s, has since been renovated into offices.

St Magnus the Martyr, opposite Pudding Lane

St Magnus was a Norwegian earl murdered by his cousin in 1110 and the church named after him has stood on the site for over 1,000 years, being rebuilt between 1671 and 1676 after the Fire of London by Christopher Wren, who used a Jesuit church in Antwerp as his model. Until the resiting of London Bridge in the nineteenth century, the church stood at the bridge's northern approach and

was known as St Magnus ad pontem. Miles Coverdale, who worked with William Tyndale on the first English translation of the Bible, was rector here in the sixteenth century and, though originally buried in 𝕾𝖙 𝕭𝖆𝖗𝖙𝖍𝖔𝖑𝖔𝖒𝖊𝖜=𝖇𝖞=𝖙𝖍𝖊=𝕰𝖝𝖈𝖍𝖆𝖓𝖌𝖊, his body was moved to St Magnus after the latter was demolished in 1841. T. S. Eliot featured the church in his epic 1922 poem *The Waste Land*.

Pudding Lane

The Great Fire of London began in Farryner's baker's shop on this small turning near London Bridge on 2 September 1666, quickly spreading along the street and setting fire to large parts of the City, or, as the anonymous ballad 'London Mourning in Ashes' recalled it, 'swallow'd Fishstreet hill, and straight / it lick'd up Lombardstreet / Down Cannon-street in blazing State / it flew with flaming feet'. The fire was not taken seriously at first, the mayor, Sir Thomas Bloodworth, dismissing it with a curt 'Pish! A woman might piss it out!', but the month had been dry and the flames soon spread around the wharves, fuelled by their wood and coal, and along the narrow streets, raging for five days and destroying seven-eighths of the City, including St Paul's, the Guildhall, Custom House, the Royal Exchange, eighty-seven churches and nearly 15,000 homes, the last embers still smouldering the following March. There were claims that the Fire was started by Papists and that Frenchmen had been seen throwing fireballs into houses, and one Huguenot who 'confessed' to starting the blaze was hanged at Tyburn, while the Dutch saw the conflagration as a judgement on English arrogance, showing the country that 'God is the only master of the elements, by punishing her, as Lucifer was punished, with the torments of fire'. Parliament, however, officially split the blame, claiming that the Fire was 'due to the hand of God upon us, a great wind and a season so very dry'.

Railway Place
Fenchurch Street station
Built in 1841 for the London and Blackwall
Railway Company to replace the original
terminus situated a little further east, it was
served by trains that were wound into the
station by cable until 1854 when the station
was extended for a new company, the
London, Tilbury and Southend Railway, and
steam trains were introduced. Fenchurch
Street is the only London terminus that does
not cater for express trains and the only one
without a tube station of the same name,
although Tower Hill station is located only a
few hundred yards to the south. Nevertheless the line running east from the station
offers the most stimulating view of any
London railway line, encompassing the East
End slums, two Nicholas Hawksmoor
churches and a number of industrialized
waterways, diverging at Barking where the
northern section makes its way through
nondescript flatlands to Southend and the
southern part through the mostly desolate
stretches of the Thames estuary to Tilbury.
► Cannon Street station, p. 64.

Seething Lane
'Seething' refers to the Anglo-Saxon word
for chaff rather than to boiling liquids and
the lane was where Sir Francis Walsingham,
Elizabeth I's minister and spy, died in 1590
and where Samuel Pepys was allocated a
Navy house when he was appointed Clerk of
the Acts in 1660 following the Restoration of
the monarchy. Pepys was still living here
when the Fire of London began on
2 September 1666 and he was awoken at
three in the morning by a maid to see a red
glow from his bedroom window. Not
particularly alarmed, Pepys returned to
sleep, and the next day being a Sunday woke
late to hear the maid informing him that the
Fire had now destroyed 300 houses and was
still raging. He took a boat on to the
Thames to gauge the true extent of the blaze
and quickly made for Whitehall where he
relayed the news to King Charles. Every 24
June a red rose is presented to the Lord

Mayor of London at Mansion House as rent
for a bridge built across Seething Lane in the
fourteenth century.
► Samuel Pepys's Diary, p. 222.

St Olave's, Seething Lane at Hart Street
The church is named after King Olaf of
Norway who fought with Ethelred the
Unready in the Battle of London Bridge in
1014 and was canonized soon after his death.
The diarist Samuel Pepys and his wife, Elizabeth, who lived locally, are buried here; the
bust of Pepys's wife in the nave was sited so
that Pepys could see it from his pew.
St Olave's was Charles Dickens's favourite
City church – he described it as his 'best
beloved churchyard, the churchyard of
ghastly grim, its ferocious strong spiked iron
gate like a jail ornamented with skulls and
cross bones', in 'Uncommercial Traveller:
City of the Absent'.

FLEET STREET | ST PAUL'S, EC4

The oldest section of the City, being close to
the pre-Roman settlements around Ludgate,
it comprises the City's most important
religious building, St Paul's Cathedral, and
its most famous street, Fleet Street, which,
until the end of the twentieth century, was
the home of the British newspaper industry.

(i) north of Fleet Street

A small area which grew after the 1666 Fire
of London, when the population was forced
out of the streets further east that had been
most affected by the blaze, it is characterized
by the street pattern of the period – mostly
dark alleyways with period names such as
Hen and Chickens Court and Wine Office
Court. During Fleet Street's heyday as the
centre of the British newspaper industry the
area was filled with small workshops for
associated trades such as stationers, printers,
bookbinders, ink sellers, engravers and type-
writer repairers. It is now dominated by

offices connected with law, finance and accountancy, the most famous local building being the museum to Dr Johnson on Gough Square.

Fetter Lane

Fetter probably stems from the Old French '*faitor*', meaning lawyer, and residents of Fetter Lane have included the seventeenth-century poet John Dryden; the political thinkers Thomas Hobbes and Tom Paine; and, fictionally, Lemuel Gulliver, hero of Jonathan Swift's *Gulliver's Travels* (1726). In the sixteenth century the street was known for its pawnbrokers, as Ben Jonson noted in *Every Man Out of His Humour*, and in November 1789 the first major discussion in London of the recent French Revolution took place at Fetter Lane's Moravian chapel with the Dissenting minister Dr Richard Price announcing: 'The times are auspicious, Tremble all ye oppressors of the world', which led Edmund Burke to respond with his *Reflections on the Revolution in France* (1790), in which he argued that British radicals ought not to copy their French counterparts. The statue of the late eighteenth-century political agitator John Wilkes (p. 76) at the corner of Fetter Lane and New Fetter Lane, captures the subject's squint and is said to be the only cross-eyed statue in London.

west side: Fleet Street to Holborn
Daily Mirror (1920–61), Geraldine House, Fetter Lane at Rolls Buildings, north side
The *Daily Mirror*, founded in 1903 by Alfred Harmsworth (p. 51), moved to offices north of Fleet Street in 1924. Although it soon became the first newspaper in the world to sell more than a million copies, it declined in importance under the stewardship of the late owner's brother, Lord Rothermere, whose journalistic acumen could not match his commercial skills and who flirted with Fascism, writing articles for the paper in favour of the British Union of Fascists ('the Blackshirts') in 1934.

At the end of the decade, with sales down to 734,000, Harry Bartholomew took over as managing director and made ingenious improvements in production as well as shaping editorial content according to the tabloid Holy Trinity of sex, crime and sport. Bartholomew also added a strong measure of campaigning journalism, the paper becoming increasingly left wing, and sales doubled in three years.

During the Second World War the *Mirror* took up the cause of the common soldier and housewife under the banner 'Forward with the People', reflecting the broadly socialist thinking that propelled the Labour Party to power in 1945, and by 1949 sales had topped 4 million. Soon after, Cecil Harmsworth King, the founder's nephew, forced out Bartholomew and took over as chairman, improving the quality of the *Mirror* with striking headlines, punchy stories, enticing pictures and unusual front pages, such as that for 17 May 1960, addressed to the Soviet premier, Nikita Khrushchev, which read: 'Mr K!, (If you will pardon an olde English phrase) DON'T BE SO BLOODY RUDE. P.S. Who do you think you are? Stalin?' King also expanded the *Mirror* Group into a powerful new conglomeration, the International Publishing Corporation (IPC), and in 1961 the *Mirror* moved to new lavish headquarters on Holborn Circus.
▶ **Daily Mirror**, Holborn Circus, p. 5.

Gough Square

Only Dr Johnson's house remains out of the original buildings on Gough Square, built by wool merchant Richard Gough, those demolished including No. 3, home in Johnson's day of a surgeon who once brought home with him the body of a man hanged at Tyburn, which had been sold to him for medical purposes. When a maid, unable to resist a peek, approached the 'corpse', it came to life. The surgeon cleaned up the man, who seemed to be none the worse for his ordeal, and arranged for him to be sent to America, where he made a fortune which he bequeathed to his saviour.

Dr Johnson's address (1748–58) / Dr Johnson's House, No. 17

Dr Samuel Johnson, the great scholar and wit, moved into this large brick house – a rare eighteenth-century survival for the area – in 1748 after drawing up his plan for a Dictionary in which he aimed to 'preserve the purity, and ascertain the meaning of our English idiom'. Johnson calculated that it would take him three years to compile the Dictionary, and when a friend, Dr Adams, told him that forty members of the French Academy had taken forty years to compile theirs he replied: 'Let me see; forty times forty is sixteen hundred. As is three to sixteen hundred, so is the proportion of an Englishman to a Frenchman.' In fact it took Johnson nine years of work in Gough Square's attic, where he was joined by six, mostly Scottish, clerks, who toiled standing up, to complete the 2,300-page manuscript. When the messenger who carried the last sheet to the publishers returned, Johnson asked him: 'Well, what did he say?' The messenger replied: 'Sir, he said "Thank God, I have done with him." ' The *Dictionary* was published in April 1755 as two volumes, described by Johnson, not too elegantly, as 'a dictionary by which the pronunciation of our language may be fixed, and its attainment facilitated; by which its purity may be preserved, its use ascertained, and its duration lengthened.' When it was suggested to Johnson that perhaps he had not realized the enormity of the undertaking he replied: 'I knew very well what I was undertaking – and very well how to do it – and have done it very well.'

Johnson moved away when the Dictionary was finished and the house later became a hotel, being bought by Lord Northcliffe in 1910. It is now a museum which contains a number of the doctor's personal artefacts, a first edition copy of the *Dictionary* and his 'gout' chair from the Olde Cock Tavern, designed to ease the weight from the legs.

Shoe Lane

Daily Express (1900–33), No. 23, south of St Bride Street

The *Daily Express*, founded in 1900 by Arthur Pearson, was bailed out financially in 1916 by the wealthy Canadian businessman and Conservative MP William Maxwell Aitken, who immediately began campaigning vigorously against the Coalition government of Herbert Asquith in favour of his rival, David Lloyd George; when the latter took over as prime minister in 1916 he was ennobled as Lord Beaverbrook and given a place in the wartime Cabinet. Irrepressible, unpredictable and inconsistent ('nothing is so bad as consistency', he once claimed) and dazzled with his own power, Beaverbrook soon became the major newspaper magnate in Britain, hiring writers of the calibre of Arnold Bennett and Evelyn Waugh who was sacked after two months but later put his experience to use in writing his 1938 Fleet Street novel, *Scoop*, taking Lord Beaverbrook as his model for Lord Copper. He even formed a political party, the new United Empire Party, in February 1930, to promote what he called his Empire Crusade of protectionist tariffs in favour of goods produced by countries in the British Empire. The *Daily Express* moved to a new site on Fleet Street in 1933.

► *Daily Express*, Fleet Street, p. 44.

Wine Office Court

Licences for the sale of wine were formerly issued from this court off Fleet Street.

Ye Old Cheshire Cheese, Wine Office Court at Fleet Street

One of London's oldest and most popular pubs, the Cheshire Cheese, described by Arthur Ransome in *Bohemia in London* as 'the dirty-fronted, low browed tavern with stone flasks in the window', was where Augustus Sala, the nineteenth-century man of letters, noted how 'the waiters are always furious . . . How could it be otherwise when on the waiter's soul there lies the perpetual sense of injury caused by the savoury odour of steaks; of cheese bubbling in tiny tins; of floury potatoes and fragrant green peas; of cool salads, and cooler tankards of bitter beer without being able to spare the time to consume them in comfort?'

The first new building to be erected locally after the Fire of London, it was named after the cheese that replaced the Suffolk brand as London's most popular around that time and its decor, dominated by oak beams and low ceilings, has changed little since the seventeenth century, as emphasized by the sawdust which the landlord liberally sprinkles on the floor. The establishment has long been popular with tourists attracted by its lengthy literary history, which dates back to Dr Johnson, who may have drunk here in the eighteenth century and who is commemorated by a plaque on what is claimed to be his seat in the ground-floor restaurant. At the end of the century the pub was home to the Rhymers' Club of poets, whose number included W. B. Yeats and who came here to recite their poetry aloud to each other, and early in the twentieth century it was regularly visited by the novelist G. K. Chesterton, who would dress up as Dr Johnson at the Cheshire Cheese's period costume dinners dedicated to the Dictionary compiler. Around the same time the Cheshire Cheese was home to a parrot whose language shocked even the local newspapermen and whose death in 1926, at the reputed age of forty, was marked by obituaries in many publications. Since the departure of Fleet Street's journalists to east London the pub has attracted a broader range of patrons.

(ii) Fleet Street

Fleet Street

A major east–west route through the City, Fleet Street is still synonymous with the British newspaper industry, even though few newspaper offices are left. Its status as a centre for printing dates back to 1500 when William Caxton's assistant, Wynandus van Woerden (better known as Wynkyn de

Worde), opened a printing shop at the sign of the Sun on Shoe Lane and there produced some 800 works over the next thirty-five years.

Being halfway between the finance houses of the City and the royal courts and Parliament of Westminster, as well as being close to Somerset House, where until 1855 newspapers had to be stamped individually, the area was convenient for publishers and writers, the first formal local publication being Benjamin Harris's *The Domestick Intelligence*, a pro-Whig, Protestant journal which was launched on 7 July 1679. A month later, a rival appeared with, confusingly, the same name. Each derided the other as an impostor, but the latter was forced to make a change and publish as *The Protestant (Domestick) Intelligence*. Censorship laws were eased in 1693 – anyone was now free to publish what they liked, provided they took the consequences – and on 11 March 1702 Fleet Street's first newspaper, the *Daily Courant*, appeared, published for 'E. Mallett against the Ditch at Fleet Bridge [Ludgate Circus]', having no competitor until the advent of the *Daily Post* in 1719. The first Sunday papers appeared in 1780, and the following century, with the advent of rail travel, the abolition of taxes on adverts in 1853, the removal of stamp duty in 1855 and paper duty in 1861 and the passing of the Education Act of 1870, the newspaper industry grew apace, helped by the introduction of new rotary presses which increased the speed of production and new linotype machines which could quickly produce bulky papers.

By the late nineteenth century most of the present-day national papers were based on or around Fleet Street, although ironically few dailies were based on the street itself, which instead was dominated by the London offices of provincial titles. The industry continued to thrive, tempered by wartime paper rationing, until the 1970s when proprietors began to clash ever more vociferously with the leaders of the various print unions. These bodies, who had their

origins in Elizabethan guilds and secret societies, set strict demarcation lines for the
various tasks needed in bringing out a newspaper, devised their own elaborate hier-
archies, headed by the grandly named
'Imperial Father', which ensured that jobs
were handed not to the most capable
prospective employees but to favoured
friends and those with family ties, and were
responsible for an arcane pay structure that
included 'fat' payments – wages paid for
work which though not undertaken might
have been.

During the 1970s the number of strikes
began to increase steadily, and in 1978–9
The Times failed to appear for almost a year,
the most severe industrial action in British
newspaper history, during which time it
recorded losses of £40 million. Change,
which was inevitable, came courtesy of an
outsider, the Australian tycoon Rupert
Murdoch, who had briefly worked as a sub-
editor at the *Daily Express* on Fleet Street in
the 1950s before returning to Australia to
take over the business built up by his father,
Sir Keith Murdoch, and on moving to
London in the late 1960s bought the *News of
the World* and the *Sun*. Realizing that the
inevitable arrival of computer technology
would replace most of the traditional
printing jobs, after months of secret planning Murdoch moved production of his
four titles, *The Times, Sunday Times, Sun*
and *News of the World*, to a new non-
unionized plant at Wapping in January 1986
amid considerable union opposition.
Within a few years all his rivals had
embraced new technology and had vacated
their Fleet Street area locations (mostly for
Docklands) to break up the print unions
and their traditional power structures.
Nowadays Fleet Street no longer has a newspaper industry (the name is still used as a
catch-all term for the press) and has little to
distinguish it from other busy City streets
other than the crushing weight of its own
history.

north side: Temple Bar to Ludgate Circus
Temple Bar, junction Fleet Street and Strand
The City's western gateway, originally a
chain tied between two posts, became a gate
with a prison above in 1351. It was rebuilt by
Christopher Wren in the 1670s, by which
time it had become the setting for the
pillory, where the heads of those executed
were displayed, with spyglasses hired out to
morbid onlookers at halfpenny a look.
Wren's Temple Bar was removed in 1878
and taken to Theobalds Park, Hertfordshire
(there are plans to return it to the City at
Paternoster Square, by St Paul's Cathedral)
and replaced by Horace Jones's 1880
memorial containing Charles Birch's bronze
griffin. According to custom Temple Bar is
the only place where the monarch can enter
the City of London, being obliged to beg
permission from the Lord Mayor of London
who presents the sovereign with the City's
Pearl Sword. Once the monarch has entered
the City Temple Bar is ceremonially closed.
St Dunstan-in-the-West, Fleet Street at Hen
and Chickens Court

> Strike me ugly, if I should not find as
> much pleasure in choosing my mistress
> by the information of a lamp under the
> clock of St Dunstan's – *The Vicar of Wake-
> field*, Oliver Goldsmith (1766)

The church, best known for its unusual
clock, was founded *c.* 1185 as St Dunstan's
Over Against the Temple, and from 1278 was
known as St Dunstan in the *West* to differentiate it from St Dunstan in the *East* in
Stepney. William Tyndale, whose transla-
tions of the New Testament from the Greek
provided the basis for the King James Bible,
preached here in 1523, and a hundred years
later the poet and cleric John Donne was
rector. *The Compleat Angler*, the pioneering
work on fishing by Izaak Walton, who held
the posts of scavenger, questman (pigeon
shooter) and sidesman for the church, was
first published on the church's press in 1653.
The church's clock, the first in London to be
marked with minutes, was erected in 1671 as
a thanksgiving from parishioners relieved
that the church had been spared by the Fire

of London. It features two burly figures, Gog and Magog, originally known as Gogmagog (an Ancient Briton) and Corineus (a Trojan invader), symbolizing warriors destroyed *c.* 1000 BC by Brutus the Trojan, founder of London according to some legends, which were paraded in medieval pageants. Over the years the name of Corineus passed into disuse and the two giants were rechristened by a split in the name of the other. In 1825 the clock was bought by the Marquess of Hertford for his Regent's Park villa but was returned to the church by the newspaper magnate Lord Rothermere in 1935.

Sweeney Todd's barber shop, No. 186
Sweeney Todd, the so-called 'demon barber of Fleet Street' is believed to have robbed and murdered more than 150 customers in his Fleet Street shop at **No. 186** towards the end of the eighteenth century, thereby making him one of the biggest serial killers in British history. However, few historians have been able to agree on even the most basic details surrounding his identity and existence and the main support for the story now comes from Peter Haining, who in a 1993 biography claimed that Todd, imprisoned in Newgate for petty theft, vowed to avenge himself on mankind and after his release in 1785 established himself as a barber at 186 Fleet Street under the sign 'Easy shaving for a penny – as good as you will find any'. The legend of his misdeeds probably arose from an article in the *Daily Courant* (Fleet Street's first newspaper) of 14 April 1785 about a 'horrid murder committed in Fleet Street on the person of a young gentleman from the country while on a visit to relatives in London who fell into conversation with a man in the clothing of a barber' who, after an argument, 'took from his clothing a razor and slit the throat of the young man'. In subsequent murders, so the story goes, Todd terrorized his victims in his shop with a cut-throat razor while they sat in a revolving chair poised over a trapdoor to the cellars into which they were dropped once dead. According to Haining, the shop

was connected by tunnel with a building on nearby Bell Yard where Todd's lover, Margery Lovett, cooked the flesh of the victims in meat pies. Todd's first name has since been enshrined in London lore as cockney rhyming slang for the Flying Squad, Scotland Yard's elite crime-busting force.

No. 166
Thomas Paine's *The Rights of Man*, the well-known radical work that claimed 'all men are born equal and with equal natural right', was printed at J. S. Jordan's shop at No. 166 in 1791 after an agreement that Paine remove one sentence – 'Everything in the English Government appears to me the reverse of what it ought to be, and of what it is said to be'. The first run of 10,000 sold out almost overnight, and over the next two years the book sold an astonishing 2 million copies in Britain, America and France.

Ye Olde Cheshire Cheese, Fleet Street at Wine Office Court
See Wine Office Court, above, p. 40.

Daily Telegraph (1862–1987), No. 135
The *Daily Telegraph*, founded in 1855 on the Strand (p. 127), moved to Fleet Street in 1862 and within a few years was the biggest-selling newspaper in the world. It was also one of the world's most faithful employers, for John le Sage, who was appointed editor in 1885, was still in charge in 1923 at the age of eighty-three, unable to use the phone and obliged to hand reporters their assignments by hand. And not only did the paper have an editor in his eighties, it had no news editor or news desk, was put together at night by six journalists who worked in silence in a comfortable room furnished with horsehair sofas, and was staffed with an unknown number of ancient men dressed in green baize aprons who seemed to serve no apparent purpose except to creep fastidiously from room to room. With sales down to 84,000 by 1927, the paper was bought by the Berry brothers, William (later Lord Camrose) and Gomer (Lord Kemsley), who also owned the *Sunday Times*, and in halving the *Telegraph*'s price to 1d saw circulation pass the half million mark.

When the Second World War broke out staff reacted quickly. Clare Hollingworth, foreign affairs correspondent, was immediately dispatched to Poland and after watching Hitler's tanks roll into Katowice gave one of the earliest first-hand accounts of the conflict. (Fifty years later, aged seventy-nine, she shinned up a lamppost in Peking to gain a good vantage point in reporting on the trouble in Tiananmen Square.)

In 1954 Lord Camrose died and was succeeded by his second son, Michael Berry, Lord Hartwell, who maintained a stifling in-house style that constrained the paper in such bumptious absurdity that when Elizabeth Taylor visited the UK and stepped off the plane at Heathrow airport announcing she 'felt like a million dollars', the *Telegraph* reported her as saying 'I feel like a million dollars (£357,000)'. Hartwell's most difficult moment in charge came in 1973 when the *Sunday Telegraph* deputy editor, Peregrine Worsthorne, asked by a BBC interviewer about a story linking the Tory politician Anthony Lambton with a call-girl, replied live on air that he didn't think the British people would 'give a fuck'. No. 135 Fleet Street was in turmoil, wondering how to react to this horrific incident, and when the night editor phoned Hartwell, disturbing him in the middle of an important dinner party to read him the story, there was a pregnant pause at the other end of the line before Hartwell replied: 'Three paragraphs, middle page, below the fold, but no fucking in the paper please.'

The Berry family remained owners until the 1980s, by which time the paper was enmeshed in the kind of chaos that had greeted their forefathers' arrival in 1928, having become, according to Stephen Glover, who later co-founded the *Independent*, a 'monument to laziness and general shirking, a temple to restrictive practices and stone age labour relations'. As the Berrys could not afford to modernize the paper, they sold the title in December 1985 to the Canadian Conrad Black, who revived the *Telegraph* with the appointment of Max Hastings as editor and moved the two titles from Fleet Street to the Isle of Dogs.

Daily Express (**1933–89**), No. 127

In 1933 the *Daily Express* moved into a vast glass and vitrolite palace designed by Owen Williams, the engineer who had worked on Wembley Stadium, where the lights could be seen shining all night, giving the impression that the newspaper was in a permanent state of indefatigable production. Williams's building upstaged the *Daily Telegraph*'s new Fleet Street headquarters at No. 135, and its construction saw the paper's owner, the irrepressible Canadian magnate Lord Beaverbrook, launch an ambitious sales boosting scheme, distributing to registered readers 10,000 pairs of silk stockings and other items of clothing. This led Malcolm Muggeridge to comment in his book *The Thirties* that 'a whole Welsh family could be clothed from head to foot for the price of eight weeks' reading', and resulted in sales of 2 million copies of the *Express* a day, then the highest sales of any newspaper in the world. By the time Beaverbrook died in 1964, the paper was selling in excess of 4 million copies a day, but Beaverbrook's son, the playboy and war hero Sir Max Aitken, was unable to maintain his father's high standards and oversaw the beginning of what one-time editor Robert Edwards called 'years of bad editing and hopeless leadership'. In 1977 the Express group was sold for £14.6m to Victor Matthews's Trafalgar House company, owners of the London Ritz and the *QE II*, but while the *Express*'s long-standing rival, the *Daily Mail*, went from strength to strength, the *Express* declined further, continuing to search desperately and unsuccessfully for readers through a succession of uninspired owners and nondescript editors. The last national daily to be published in Fleet Street, it moved on 17 November 1989 a few hundred yards south-east, across Blackfriars Bridge, instead of joining the exodus to east London, after which the building was abandoned, thieves ripping out the chromium serpent handrails in the entrance hall, and lay empty until 2000 when it was renovated into offices.

Anderton's Hotel (1880s), No. 126
The first meeting of what became the Football League took place at **Anderton's Hotel** on 22 March 1888, having been called by William McGregor, a Birmingham businessman, who wrote to a number of professional football clubs including the previous two winners of the FA Cup, Aston Villa and Blackburn Rovers, suggesting that 'ten or twelve of the most prominent clubs in England combine to arrange home and away fixtures each season'. A month later the decision was ratified at the Royal Hotel, Manchester, and in September the first League season began with twelve teams all from the North or the Midlands: Accrington, Aston Villa, Blackburn Rovers, Bolton Wanderers, Burnley, Derby County, Everton, Notts County, Preston North End, Stoke City, West Bromwich Albion and Wolverhampton Wanderers. In February 1892 the leading southern clubs met at **Anderton's** to form their own league, the Southern League, and twelve clubs, including Woolwich Arsenal, were elected, Tottenham Hotspur coming bottom of the poll with only one vote.

south side: Ludgate Circus to Temple Bar
Punch Tavern, No. 99
In 1841 the founders of *Punch* magazine used to meet in the tavern. It now sports period tiles and ornate mirrors and the walls are decorated with appropriate nineteenth-century memorabilia, including a gilded Mr Punch, the grinning portraits of Mr and Mrs Punch, old-fashioned framed cartoons, and pages from the magazine.

Reuters, Nos. 82–85
Reuter's news agency, founded by Paul Julius Reuter in 1849 and established in the City two years later, moved to new Fleet Street headquarters, designed by Edwin Lutyens, in 1939. Later in the year, the government put pressure on the company to serve British interests during the war by restructuring itself as a private company owned by the British provincial and national press, but Reuters refused to accept the proposal and established a trust to safeguard its independence. In 1964 the agency pioneered the use of computers to transmit financial data internationally and launched Monitor Money Rates Service, an electronic market place for foreign exchange, in 1973. It became a publicly quoted company on the London Stock Exchange in 1984.
► Reuters' first London base, p. 28.

No. 55a
Louis Rothman took the lease of a shop at 55a Fleet Street in the 1890s and sat there late into the night hand-rolling cigarettes to sell the following day to journalists. Within ten years business was so good Rothman was able to move to a luxury showroom on Pall Mall.

No. 55
No. 55 marks the furthest west the 1666 Fire of London advanced.

El Vino, No. 47
The major local bar in the great days of Fleet Street, the front door of which, according to the veteran journalist Keith Waterhouse, 'looks like a small Dublin pub, the back room like a working tea shop', El Vino's was for long the bastion of the most snobbish writers, such as the novelist G. K. Chesterton and the essayist Hilaire Belloc at the beginning of the twentieth century, and the journalist Auberon Waugh at the end of the century. Charles Wintour, editor of the *Evening Standard* in the 1960s, once put in an appearance to impress his staff but unwittingly chose the day when the recidivist prison escaper Alfie Hinds staged one of his innumerable breakouts. When the story broke in a rival publication the *Standard*'s owner, Lord Beaverbrook, furious that his paper had been beaten to the story, phoned the office to put matters right and, shocked to discover that Wintour was in El Vino, phoned the wine bar and told his editor sharply: 'Mr Wintour, may I give you a piece of advice? Mr Wintour, my advice to you is this. You will not find Alfred Hinds in El Vino's public house. Good day to you,

Mr Wintour.' With its bedrock clientele now departed and its great days seemingly over, El Vino's has undergone some degree of modernization: women are no longer obliged to sit down and be waited upon, but they must still wear a skirt, while men must sport a tie and jacket.

Hoare's Bank, No. 37

The only remaining independent bank in London, it was founded in 1672 by goldsmith Richard Hoare and since 1690 has been located at what was then the sign of the Golden Bottle and is now 37 Fleet Street (rebuilt 1827). It was here on 11 July 1676 that one of the first ever cheques was written: 'Mr. Hoare . . . Pray pay to the bearer hereof Mr. Witt Morgan fifty-four pounds ten shillings and ten pence and take his receipt for the same. Your loving friend, Will Hale, for Mr. Richard Hoare, at the Golden Bottle in Cheapside.'

Prince Henry's Room, No. 17

Built in the 1610s as a tavern, the Prince's Arms, it was named after Henry, Prince of Wales, James I's sickly eldest son, who died from typhoid on 12 November 1612 aged only eighteen, despite the best efforts of the era's leading physicians who tried to cure his fever by applying the flesh of newly killed cocks and pigeons to his weak frame. When the prince's condition continued to deteriorate they administered a medicine of 'pearl, musk, hartshorn, bezoarstone, mint, borage, gentian, mace, sugar, aloes and spirits of wine' devised by Sir Walter Ralegh, but this too failed to work. The building later housed Mrs Salmon's Waxworks, at the Sign of the Trout, as mentioned by Charles Dickens in *David Copperfield*, and by 1870 was a barber's. Now an exhibition centre, its first-floor room houses a permanent exhibition display on the diarist Samuel Pepys, who may have patronized the tavern in the seventeenth century.

The Devil's Tavern, No. 2

The tavern, with its sign of the devil's nose being tweaked by pincers, was home to the sixteenth-century Apollo Club ('Welcome all who lead or follow / To the oracle of Apollo'), one of London's first literary groups, founded by the playwright Ben Jonson. Later patrons included the poet Alexander Pope and the Dictionary-compiler Dr Johnson, who once described the landlord of the time, Sim Wadlow, as 'the king of stinkers'. The first newspaper proprietors met at the tavern in the 1720s. The building was demolished in the 1770s.

Child & Co., No. 1

Britain's oldest bank, founded following a merger of two goldsmiths' shops in 1661, moved to Fleet Street in 1673. Five years later the poet John Dryden deposited £50 here as a reward for anyone who could give him information on the thugs who had beaten him in Rose Alley, Covent Garden. It later transpired that the assailants were in the pay of the Earl of Rochester, who wrongly believed that Dryden had written an essay satirizing him and the king. The bank remained a small concern throughout the nineteenth century, with profits of just £49,490 in 1845, but its proximity to the Inns of Court and Chancery attracted a number of wealthy customers. In 1923 the owner, the Earl of Jersey, sold the firm to Glyn, Mills, Currie, Holt & Co. and in 1939 Glyn's was acquired by the Royal Bank of Scotland. Charles Dickens portrayed it as Tellson's Bank, 'very small, very dark, very ugly, very incommodious', in *A Tale of Two Cities* (1859).

(iii) The Temple

The Temple

Those bricky towers, the which on Thames broad aged back doth ride / wherein the studious lawyers have their bowers / And whilom wont the Templar knights to bide – *Prothalamion*, Edmund Spenser (1596)

The Inner and Middle Temple, two of London's four Inns of Court, where lawyers live and work, or, as William Wordsworth put it in *The Prelude*, 'Look out on waters, walks and gardens green', take their names from the Knights Templar, a body of French warrior monks founded in 1118 as the Pauperes Commilitones Christi et Templi Solomoni ('the Poor Fellow-Soldiers of Christ and of the Temple of Solomon') to protect pilgrims travelling to the Holy Land. Answerable to the Pope, and identifiable by their white tunics emblazoned with a red cross, the Knights Templar turned to banking and property development. In 1162 they acquired the land where the Temple now stands, then just beyond the City boundary, and built a church, known as the New Temple, a monastery, halls and chambers of residence, which were home in 1215 to King John when the barons forced him to sign the Magna Carta.

The Knights Templar's power and wealth attracted envy from many in authority, such as Philip the Fair of France, who accused them, unjustly, of blasphemy and sodomy, and persuaded the Vatican to suppress the order. In 1312 the Pope decreed that the Knights Templar be abolished and their buildings and furnishings handed to their rivals, the Knights Hospitallers (the Order of St John of Jerusalem), who leased what is now the Temple to lawyers for use as a hostel. The Hospitallers' possessions were seized by the Crown in 1539 and in 1609 James I granted the estate to the Benchers of the two local Inns, the Inner and Middle Temple, on the condition that they maintained the Temple Church and its services in perpetuity. In the nineteenth century membership was widened to include law students from overseas and from 1919 women were admitted, the first woman barrister (Ivy Williams) being called to the bar by the Inner Temple in 1922.

A maze of courtyards, the Temple does not lend itself to easy exploration. The Middle Temple is based on and to the west of Middle Temple Lane, its lampposts, railings and doorways being decorated with the image of a lamb. Past members include the Elizabethan courtier Sir Walter Ralegh, the diarist John Evelyn, the playwright William Congreve and the novelists Henry Fielding, William Makepeace Thackeray and John Buchan. The Inner Temple lies further east and its sites are decorated with the winged horse, Pegasus. Past members include Dr Johnson's biographer James Boswell, the playwright Richard Brinsley Sheridan, the librettist W. S. Gilbert, *Dracula* author Bram Stoker and the Indian leaders Mahatma Gandhi and Jawaharlal Nehru. There are helpful maps on the walls (one by the porch on Middle Temple Lane and one by Carpmael Buildings), marked with sites of mostly literary interest.

Inner Temple Lane
Temple Church
The first Gothic church to be built in London, erected between 1160 and 1185 in the style of the Church of the Sepulchre in Jerusalem, and consecrated by Heraclius, the Patriarch of Jerusalem, in 1185, Temple Church was where in the thirteenth century initiation rites welcoming newcomers into the order of the Knights Templar, the warrior monks after whom the Temple is named, took place. Despite escaping the Great Fire, the church was refurbished in the late seventeenth century by Christopher Wren, who inserted box pews (removed in 1842), and was severely damaged by the last raid of the 1941 Blitz. The north window bears the crest of the Middle Temple (the Holy Lamb and Flag), the south window that of the Inner Temple (Pegasus, the winged horse) and a recess in the south wall contains a Purbeck marble effigy of Bishop Sylvester, thirteenth-century Bishop of Carlisle, who was killed when he fell off his horse in London in 1255, and was buried in the Temple. A door in the north-west corner of the choir leads to the Penitential Cell, where knights who had disobeyed the Master or broken Temple rules were imprisoned and in some cases starved to death. Those buried in the church include the sixteenth-century lawyer Edmund Plowden, who never left the Temple's precincts in the three years he was studying

for the Bar, later became treasurer of the Middle Temple and was responsible for building Middle Temple Hall. Plowden coined the phrase 'the case is altered' while defending a priest accused of holding an illegal mass, when on being told that the man was an *agent provocateur* he exclaimed: 'The case is altered; no priest, no mass.'

Middle Temple Lane

Middle Temple Lane, which originally ran down from Fleet Street to the river, divides the Inner Temple from the Middle Temple. **Middle Temple Hall**, Middle Temple Lane at Fountain Court

Built between 1563 and 1573, the hall soon became a regular venue for plays and masques and on 2 February 1601 was where the première of Shakespeare's *Twelfth Night*, possibly staged by the playwright's own company, took place before Elizabeth I. The event was noted by John Manningham, a member of the Temple, who wrote in his diary: 'Feb 2 at our feast we had a play called *Twelfth Night* or *What you Will*, much like the *Comedy of Errors* . . . A good practise is it to make the steward believe his Lady widdowe was in Love with him by coun-terfayting a lettre, as from his Lady, in general termes, telling him what shee liked best in him and prescribing his gesture in smiling his apparraile etc. And then when he came to practise, making him beleeve they took him to be mad.'

A number of long-standing Temple traditions are associated with the hall. In the past a card marked with a topic for discussion would be placed beside the salt cellar, the details kept from the diners until after the meal, when two junior barristers would argue from opposing sides, while lawyers must sign the roll on the battered-looking hall table given to the Inn by Sir Francis Drake and formerly part of the furnishings on his ship, *The Golden Hind*. A crest on the Chancellor's window, which contains three deer on a burnt-orange back-ground pertaining to former member Josephus Jekyll, near to a blue and yellow

shield belonging to Robertus Hyde, gave the nineteenth-century novelist Robert Louis Stevenson the surnames of his two famous characters in the horror tale *Dr Jekyll and Mr Hyde*. The hall's double hammerbeam roof survived Second World War bombing and although the carved screen, which separates the hall from the service area, was badly damaged, fragments that had been collected while it was being restored were pieced together with cuttings taken from a sixteenth-century oak barn.

(iv) Alsatia

The land lying between the Temple and Blackfriars offered sanctuary to those on the run from persecution in the Middle Ages but degenerated into lawlessness in the 1550s once Edward VI had abandoned Bridewell, the palace his father, Henry VIII, built here. With neither the Temple nor the City ready to take responsibility for the place, and the police force of the time, the night watch, abandoning the streets, it became one of the most violent enclaves of the capital, nick-named 'Alsatia' in mock honour of Alsace, the disputed land between France and Germany. Alsatia soon attracted an assort-ment of criminals and those on the run such as the writer Daniel Defoe who in 1692, after writing seditious material, took refuge here after spotting 'wanted' posters of himself in Fleet Street taverns complete with descrip-tion ('a middle sized, spare man . . . a hook nose, a sharp chin, grey eyes and a large mole near his mouth') and details of a reward for those who brought him to justice.

The repugnant atmosphere of the area was captured in a number of works, particu-larly Thomas Shadwell's *The Squire of Alsatia* (1688), which was written in a thieves' argot incomprehensible without translation, and Walter Scott's later novel *The Fortunes of Nigel* (1822), but in 1697 Alsatia's independence was abolished and slowly the area assumed the identity of its neighbours as a bustling part of the City.

The word 'alsatia' continued to be used to denote run-down neighbourhoods until the advent of the term 'slum' some time around 1880.

Villains and con-men of Elizabethan Alsatia

Alsatia had a variety of esoteric terms to describe local villains and characters including:

Abram men or **Tom o' Bedlams** Thieves who pretended to be mad and would wear ribbons or a fox tail.

Anglers Thieves who used a fishing rod with a hook to lift goods at night through open windows.

Dommerars Men who pretended to be mutes.

Fencing cullies Receivers of stolen goods.

Fraters Men who pretended to be collecting money for a hospital.

Patricios or **stroller's priests** Those who performed mock marriage ceremonies, often joining couples over a dead horse.

Polliards or **clapperdogeons** Beggars who preyed on people's sympathy by working with children, not usually their own.

Priggers or **prancers** Horse-thieves who went around with a saddle and bridle in case they should spot an untied horse, which they would steal and disguise by changing the colour of its coat or adding new marks.

Quire birds Those who escaped hanging by turning informer on their fellows.

Rufflers Beggars who pretended to be wounded soldiers.

Strowling morts Old women who pretended to be widows.

Toppin cove The hangman.

Upright man The gang leader.

Whip Jack A sailor who begged with a woman he claimed to have saved from a shipwreck.

In the late nineteenth century the City authorities established a freehold estate in the area, which made it attractive to companies wanting to build new offices, and over the next few years, the *Evening News*,

Daily Mail, Daily Mirror, News of the World, News Chronicle and *Observer* opened offices here, making Alsatia the centre of Britain's twentieth-century newspaper industry until Rupert Murdoch moved his titles to Wapping in 1986. With the departure of the whirr of the presses, the shouts of the newspaper workers, and the to-ing and fro-ing of the journalists the area lost its character and now awaits a new identity.

Bouverie Street

Built in 1799, and named after landlords the Pleydell-Bouveries, the street contained Fleet Street's first print works, built for the Scot James Moyes in 1824, and became one of the great centres of the British newspaper industry in the nineteenth and twentieth centuries, with offices for the *Daily News, Punch, News Chronicle, Daily Mirror, News of the World* and *Sun*.

east side: Fleet Street to Tudor Street
𝕹𝖊𝖜𝖘 𝖔𝖋 𝖙𝖍𝖊 𝖂𝖔𝖗𝖑𝖉 (1892–1986), Nos. 30–32
The most commercially successful British newspaper of the twentieth century, which at one point was selling 8 million copies, the *News of the World* owed its success to Emsley Carr (editor 1891–1941), who installed the banner 'all human life is here' under the title and developed the tabloid strategy of preaching conservative morals amid a stream of soft porn, titillation and sensation, a format which has endured into the twenty-first century among much of the popular press.

At the end of the 1960s the title was put up for sale, and when it looked likely that the new buyer would be the Labour politician and businessman Robert Maxwell, the editor, Stafford Somerfield, attacked the latter's Czech origins and announced that the paper was 'as British as roast beef and Yorkshire pudding'. He nevertheless sold the title to the Australian Rupert Murdoch who relentlessly maintained the paper's sensationalist edge, coining the catchphrase 'No one ever went broke underestimating the public taste' to explain his approach. Murdoch moved the title to Wapping along with his other papers in 1986 (p. 42). Under the site of the former *News of the World* building, which was renovated at the beginning of the twenty-first century, are remains of a crypt from the Carmelites' long vanished fifteenth-century Whitefriars monastery.

𝔖𝔲𝔫 (1969–86), No. 30

Britain's biggest-selling daily newspaper arose out of the demise of the Labour movement paper, the *Daily Herald*, which closed in 1964 and was relaunched as the *Sun*, with the front-page boast that it was 'born of the age we live in'. The *Sun* failed to keep up with its main rival, the *Mirror*, whose sales at 5 million were then five times larger, until it was bought in 1969 by the Australian Rupert Murdoch, who relaunched it as a sensationalist tabloid with a heady blend of sport, titillation, base patriotism and vicarious excitement. Murdoch's *coup de grâce* was Page 3, and its daily picture of a near-naked female provoked a fascinating argument with the *Mirror* over the vital question of whether such pictures should feature nipples, the *Sun* printing nipples brazenly, the *Mirror*, with one eye on its colleagues in the Labour movement, the other on the expanding market for sleaze, opting for a compromise: that nipples would only be shown 'where relevant'.

In 1981 Kelvin McKenzie became editor. He had won his sub-editing spurs at the *New York Post* by headlining a story about the discovery of a decapitated corpse in a sleazy hostelry 'Headless Body in Topless Bar', and he continued to originate memorable headlines, most notably 'Gotcha' on 3 May 1982 following the sinking of the Argentine ship *General Belgrano*, which was later pulled in favour of 'Did 1200 Argies Drown?' when *Sun* executives realized the enormity of the event. By the beginning of the 1980s the *Sun*'s Bouverie Street building had become so run down it was barely usable, with cockroaches and mice gathered around the old copper tea urn, tramps wandering around the works and sleeping among the piles of paper, and the noise from the presses louder than the permitted

level of 100 decibels. Murdoch solved the problem by moving the *Sun* and his other national titles to a new plant in Wapping amid much controversy in 1986.

▶ Murdoch titles at Wapping, p. 299.

Bridewell Place
𝔅𝔯𝔦𝔡𝔢𝔴𝔢𝔩𝔩 𝔓𝔞𝔩𝔞𝔠𝔢

Henry VIII built a royal palace by the Thames and Fleet River between 1515 and 1520, naming it Bridewell after the nearby well dedicated to St Bride. It was here in 1528 that the king discussed his proposed divorce from Catherine of Aragon with the Pope's representatives and held a number of meetings relating to the English Church's break with Rome. After Henry's death Edward VI granted **𝔅𝔯𝔦𝔡𝔢𝔴𝔢𝔩𝔩 𝔓𝔞𝔩𝔞𝔠𝔢** to the City authorities and it became a workhouse for vagrants and beggars and a house of correction-cum-prison for petty offenders, the name soon becoming a generic term for similar institutions. In 1855 inmates were transferred to Holloway and all the buildings, apart from the 1802 gateway on New Bridge Street, were demolished.

● Bridewell was the setting for two well-known paintings: Holbein's *The Ambassadors* (1533) and one of the scenes in William Hogarth's *The Harlot's Progress* (1732).

Carmelite Street

The monks of the local monastery Whitefriars, the buildings of which dominated the area from the thirteenth century, were also known as Carmelites. During the twentieth century Carmelite Street was dominated by newspaper offices, particularly those of the *Daily Mail* and its stablemates.

west side: Victoria Embankment to Tudor Street

𝔇𝔞𝔦𝔩𝔶 𝔐𝔞𝔦𝔩 (1897–1927), Carmelite House, south-west junction with Tallis Street

The *Daily Mail*, Britain's first mass appeal newspaper, was founded on 4 May 1896 by Alfred Harmsworth (later Lord Northcliffe), a Napoleon-obsessed megalomaniac with an unerring eye for producing mass-market publications, with what was then a revolutionary format of short, snappy paragraphs, opinion columns, sports coverage and concise parliamentary reports. It was the first paper to offer advertisers a rate per thousand sales, the first to have audited circulation figures (a sure method of attracting advertisers) and caused a revelation in the staid Fleet Street market. Businessmen and salesmen who did not have the leisure time that gentlemen had to spend with a newspaper could now keep abreast of the news quickly, and the *Mail* was selling a million copies a day by the end of the year, despite the derision of the Prime Minister, Lord Salisbury, who blasted it as 'a journal produced by office boys for office boys'. After Harmsworth died in 1922, his brother, Harold (Lord Rothermere), took over and two years later pulled off one of the greatest scams in newspaper history, the so-called 'Zinoviev Letter', which unfolded on 25 October 1924, four days before the general election, when the *Mail* ran a sensational headline: 'Civil War Plot By Socialists' Masters. Moscow Order to Our Reds. Great Plot Disclosed Yesterday', above a story about how the Foreign Office had gained possession of a 'Very Secret' letter written by Grigory Zinoviev, head of the Communist International, urging British Communists to 'strain every nerve' to press the Labour Party into ratifying a treaty between Russia and Britain preparing for revolution. The letter appeared to be genuine and not just the *Mail*, but the *Daily Express*, *Times* and *Telegraph* united to condemn Labour as Trojan horses who would be usurped by their Soviet paymasters within days of retaining office. Only the Labour-supporting *Daily Herald* warned that the letter might be a forgery, and indeed it was, faked by a group of White Russians to discredit the Soviet Union, but it helped the Conservatives win the election. The *Daily Mail* moved to Tudor Street in 1927.

▶ *Daily Mail* in Tudor Street, p. 52; bizarre death of Alfred Harmsworth (Lord Northcliffe), p. 206.

Daily Mirror (1903–05), No. 2, south-west junction with Tudor Street
Alfred Harmsworth (later Lord Northcliffe), owner of the *Daily Mail* (see above), launched the *Daily Mirror* on 2 November 1903 as 'the first newspaper for gentlewomen'. The paper was not only aimed at women, but written by women and edited by a woman (Mary Howarth), and copies of the first issue were published with the free, womanly gift of . . . a mirror. News was condensed to a few brief paragraphs and for those readers who lacked the necessary attention span these snippets were complemented by a 'Today's News at a Glance' box of single-sentence captions. The *Mirror* was a spectacular failure, sales slipping from a daily 265,000 to 25,000 within three months. Inevitably Harmsworth blamed the women ('women can't write and don't want to read', he thundered), replacing Mary Howarth with Hamilton Fyfe (a man), who sacked the women and relaunched the *Mirror* in January 1904 as the *Daily Illustrated Mirror*. The new paper was staffed by photojournalists who were rushed to hotspots such as the battleground of the Russo-Japanese War to take pictures which they would then despatch to London, no matter how trying the circumstances. In January 1905 the paper moved to new premises on nearby Whitefriars Street (p. 53).

St Bride's Avenue
St Bride
Known as the journalists' church, St Bride stands on a pagan site of worship dedicated some 2,000 years ago to Brigit or Brighde, the Celtic goddess of healing, childbirth and fire, and in the sixth century a church dedicated to St Bridget, an Irish saint, was built on the same plot, later rebuilt by the Danes and Normans, and used in 1210 by King John for convening one of the first Parliaments. William Vyner, warden of the Fleet Prison, rebuilt the church in the Perpendicular style in the fifteenth century and in 1670 Christopher Wren added the famous steeple, then London's tallest at 234 ft, which

inspired a Ludgate Hill baker to create the first tiered wedding cake.

After St Bride was heavily bombed on 30 December 1940 items from the church's ancient past were found, including a small section of tessellated pavement, now preserved in the crypt alongside an exhibition on the history of the church and local printing industry. In January 1986 the rector held an all-night vigil for those who wanted to pray for the future of Fleet Street as a newspaper centre, and despite the exodus of local newspapers to east London the church has retained nominal links with the industry. Those buried here include Wynkyn de Worde, William Caxton's assistant, who brought the first printing press with movable type to Fleet Street in 1500, and the diarist Samuel Pepys, who was baptized here in 1633 (the font survives) and thirty-one years later was obliged to bribe the gravedigger to 'jostle together' bodies so that he could make room for his late brother, Tom.

Tudor Street

When Alsatia was at its most lawless in the seventeenth century, lawyers from the Temple tried to protect themselves from the area's unruly inhabitants by bricking up the Tudor Street entrance to the Temple, but locals tore down the barrier as soon as the mason had put the last touches to it. For much of the twentieth century Tudor Street was one of a number of local streets dominated by the newspaper industry, with offices at various times for the *Daily Mail*, *Observer*, *Pall Mall Gazette*, the *Westminster Gazette* and *Reynolds News*.

Daily Mail (1927–89), Northcliffe House, north-west junction with Whitefriars Street
When the *Daily Mail* moved into Northcliffe House in the late 1920s it was owned by Harold Harmsworth (Lord Rothermere), a financier with little journalistic flair but a knack for making grand gestures. Envious of the status of Lord Beaverbrook, the *Daily Express* owner who had served in the British Cabinet during the First World War, Rother-

mere attempted to become a magnate-statesman himself, but made the mistake of trying to hold the Conservative Party leader, Stanley Baldwin, to ransom by pledging the paper's support only if Baldwin discussed party policy with him and consulted him on Cabinet appointments. When Baldwin refused to comply, Rothermere wrote an unsigned editorial denouncing Baldwin as unfit to lead the Conservatives and the latter responded with a speech in which he railed against press lords who aimed at 'power without responsibility – the prerogative of the harlot throughout the ages', words written for him by Rudyard Kipling. Unfazed, Rothermere directed his attentions to the rising phenomenon of fascism, which by the early thirties had become a political force in Britain, writing an editorial on 8 January 1934 headlined 'Hurrah for the Blackshirts' (Oswald Mosley's British Union of Fascists). Rothermere withdrew support after violence broke out at a Blackshirts' rally at Olympia in June 1934, which led him to send a telegram to his correspondent in Berlin stating: 'The Blackshirts are in the wash and the colour is running very fast.' Rothermere died, conveniently, critics said, in 1940 at the outset of the Second World War and the paper remained a spent force until its revival in the 1970s under the editorship of David English.

Whitefriars Street

The Carmelite **Whitefriars Monastery**, founded locally in 1241 and named after the white mantle friars wore over their brown habit, covered much of the land on the west bank of the Fleet and was one of the few local buildings left untouched by the mob during the 1381 Peasants' Revolt, such was the friars' popularity. The monastery was shut down in the 1530s and though there are no visible remains some sections survive below street level, including a crypt from around 1420 under the former *News of the World* building on the east side of Bouverie Street. Thomas Tompion, known as the 'father of English watchmaking', who

supplied barometers and sundials to William III, had his shop at the northern end of Whitefriars Street in the seventeenth century.
Daily Mirror (1905–20), No. 12, west side
The *Daily Mirror*, founded on Carmelite Street as a paper for women in 1903 (p. 51), moved two years later to Whitefriars Street, where it was relaunched as a picture-led populist paper with strong news content. The paper was heavily criticized in May 1910 for showing a picture of the late Edward VII lying in state, and debate raged over whether the media was intruding into private grief, until it was revealed that the king's consort, Queen Alexandra, had herself given the paper, her favourite, permission. The following year pictures taken at the Investiture of the Prince of Wales at Caernarvon Castle were thrown from the castle wall, caught in a blanket, and rushed to London by motor-cycle so that the *Mirror* could beat rivals to the presses. The *Mirror*'s proprietor, Alfred Harmsworth, sold the paper to his brother Harold (Lord Rothermere) in 1914, by which time its circulation had topped 1 million. Six years later it moved to Fetter Lane (p. 39).

(v) Blackfriars

The area, which lies south of Ludgate Hill, is named after the Blackfriars' Dominican monastery of 1221 to 1538 and became a fashionable suburb of the City in the seventeenth century when residents included the playwright Ben Jonson, the artist Anthony Van Dyck and William Shakespeare, who is believed to have moved into a house on Ireland Yard in 1612. Despite modern redevelopment and Second World War bombing Blackfriars has retained much of its medieval street pattern of small, twisting lanes.

Ireland Yard
William Shakespeare is believed to have moved to the street in 1612 to be near Richard Burbage's theatre (see below), where he acted.

Blackfriars Monastery
The Dominican monastery of Blackfriars, founded in 1221 in Shoe Lane, north of Fleet Street, moved here in 1278 and was used as a meeting place by Parliament in 1311 and a storehouse for state records the following decade. It was here in 1382 that the Archbishop of Canterbury's council met to denounce John Wycliffe's religious doctrines and translation of the Bible into English, and when the City was rocked by an earthquake as the hearing began Wycliffe, understandably, claimed the event as a sign of God's discontent with the council's decisions while the council, with equal confidence, took it as a sign of the Lord's displeasure with Wycliffe and found against him.

A 1529 court held at Blackfriars heard the divorce proceedings between Catherine of Aragon and Henry VIII, and after Henry spoke the queen threw herself at his feet, begging for mercy, with the plea: 'Alas! Sir, how have I offended you? This twenty years I have been your true wife and more, and by me ye have had children, although it hath pleased God to call them out of this world,' thereby neatly encapsulating Henry's main problem with Catherine – her inability to provide him with a male heir. Henry's marriage to Catherine was later declared to be 'utterly void and annulled' – but without Rome's blessing – which led to the break from the Church of Rome in 1533.

Blackfriars Monastery was dissolved in 1538, most of the buildings being demolished soon after, and at the end of the century the surviving sections were used as a playhouse, where Shakespeare's company, the King's Players, acted, and which was closed by the Puritans in 1642. Apart from a fragment of the original wall in Ireland Yard, all remaining traces of the monastery perished in the Fire of London, but excavations in 1890 uncovered an arcade, which was taken to Selsdon Park, Croydon, and in 1925 part of the choir, which was moved to St Dominic's Priory, Haverstock Hill.

► Shakespeare in Bankside, p. 376.

Queen Victoria Street *Also see p. 65*

A relatively new road for the City, as can be seen from its straight route which uncompromisingly cuts through the older lanes of Blackfriars, it was built from 1867 to 1871 to cover the newly built District Line.

north side

The Black Friar, No. 174

An excessively decorated art nouveau pub, designed by H. Fuller Clark (1904–6), and built on the site of the 𝔅lackfriars 𝔐onastery, it contains a statue of a large laughing friar above the main door and walls clad in green and red marble which are covered with illustrations of monks and friars singing carols and playing instruments.

𝔗he 𝔗imes (1785–1974), Printing House Square, west of St Andrew's Hill

> One of the greatest powers in the world. I don't know anything which has more power, except perhaps the Mississippi –
> Abraham Lincoln (1861)

Britain's most famous newspaper began publishing on 1 January 1785 as the *Daily Universal Register*, a business information sheet run by John Walter, a coal merchant. It became *The Times* three years later, soon being at the forefront of new advances in newspaper production such as the introduction of logotype, which allowed whole words rather than individual letters to be pre-set, and in 1814 becoming the first paper to use a steam press.

The Times's best-known writer of that period was Henry Crabb Robinson, said to be the first foreign correspondent (he was sent to Germany in 1807), and its first professional editor was Thomas Barnes, who occupied the chair from 1817 to 1841, took a cudgel with him when completing an edition in case, he claimed, he was 'set upon by Tory thugs', and called for the people to 'petition, ay, thunder for reform', thereby inadvertently giving the paper its long-term soubriquet, 'The Thunderer'.

In 1872 the founder's grandson, John Walter III, who had taken over the paper, designed new premises, incorporating a vast pediment on the Queen Victoria Street frontage, the spandrel of which contained a clock and *The Times* crest and motto, but by the end of the century the paper had run into financial difficulties, with circulation down to 40,000. Negotiations soon began between its owners and a mysterious 'Mr X', and to the amazement of the newspaper industry, the latter turned out to be Alfred Harmsworth, founder of the populist *Daily Mail* and *Daily Mirror*, owner of *Comic Cuts*, *Home Chat* and other cheap periodicals, and then the most successful proprietor in the land. Harmsworth bought into the title for £320,000 amid considerable outcry – the Liberal politician David Lloyd George remarked how in Europe people believed *The Times* to have a 'semi official character and to be inspired by the British Government. Not everyone knew that it was a threepenny edition of the *Daily Mail*' – and ignoring its sobriety and aloof arrogance sought to transform it in his own populist manner, increasing pagination, reducing the price, cutting back staff numbers and introducing an offbeat fourth editorial, a books page and fashion articles, despite opposition from the paper's shadowy senior editorial figures, the so-called 'Black Friars'. Sales rose dramatically.

When Harmsworth died in 1922 John Jacob Astor, whose brother William Waldorf had bought the *Observer* from Harmsworth in 1911, outbid Lord Rothermere, Harmsworth's brother, for the title. In 1966 Astor's son, Gavin, faced with a circulation challenge from rival 'heavyweights', the *Telegraph* and *Guardian*, shocked the world by including news ('London to be new H.Q. for Nato'), rather than advertisements, on the front page. Sales soared, production costs rose, but advertising and circulation revenue declined – it was calculated that the paper was losing 6d on every sale – and after nearly fifty years in charge the Astors were replaced by the dynamic elderly Canadian Roy Thomson, who had introduced the Yellow Pages telephone directories to Britain and who already owned the *Sunday Times*. *The Times* moved to Gray's Inn Road in 1974 and then to Wapping in 1986. Printing House Square was redeveloped at the beginning of the twenty-first century.

Observer (1969–88), No. 160

The *Observer*, Britain's oldest Sunday newspaper, founded on the Strand in 1711, moved to a site by *The Times*'s office in 1969 and, under the stewardship of David Astor (proprietor–editor, 1948–75), continued as a crusading weekly at the forefront of a host of liberal campaigns. By the 1970s the paper was beset by losses of £750,000 a year and was put up for sale, but when Rupert Murdoch, owner of the *Sun* and *News of the World*, emerged as the likely buyer, Clive James, the paper's television correspondent, claimed that selling the *Observer* to Murdoch would be like giving your beautiful seventeen-year-old daughter to a gorilla. Just when it looked as if Murdoch would be successful, a previously unmentioned company, the Atlantic Richfield Corporation, bought the title, appointing a new editor, Donald Trelford, with John Cole, later a well-known TV political correspondent famed for his impenetrable Belfast accent, as his deputy. In 1981 a new owner emerged in the shape of Lonrho, long-running investors in Africa, whom, ten years previously, prime minister Edward Heath had described as the 'unacceptable face of British capitalism' on account of its attempt to avoid tax. Lonrho was run by the mysterious 'Tiny' Rowland, the German-born Rowland Walter Fuhrhop, who had joined the Hitler youth movement in the 1930s. When the company completed the purchase the Monopolies and Mergers Commission ruled that six independent directors had to be placed on the board. Over the next decade the *Observer*'s status as an organ of detached sobriety and independent analysis was compromised by countless wrangles between the editorial team and Rowland over coverage of Africa, where Lonrho had many financial interests, and the latter's obsession with buying the Harrods store, a battle he lost to Mohamed

Al-Fayed. The paper has since regained its reputation by becoming part of the *Guardian* Media group.

St Andrew by the Wardrobe

Originally the church of St Andre de Castello, named after the nearby palace of **Baynard Castle**, it was built in the thirteenth century and renamed in 1361 after the Crown Wardrobe where ceremonial clothes were stored. The church was destroyed in the Great Fire of 1666 and redesigned by Christopher Wren, who opted for a plain brick rectangle, and was partly destroyed during the Second World War, being rebuilt by Marshall Sisson in 1959 to 1961 to Wren's design. The window in the west gallery contains a memorial to Shakespeare carved in oak and limewood, and the church has antique fittings taken from other London churches destroyed in the last war, including a pulpit from the demolished **St Matthew Friday Street**.

Faraday House, west of Godliman Street

A nine-storey telephone exchange built in the 1940s on the site of the demolished College of Advocates and Doctors of Law (Doctors' Commons), Faraday House originally contained the international exchange for overseas calls and during the Second World War most of London's strategic communications ran through cables between here, St Martin's-le-Grand post office, and the Holborn exchange. Underneath Faraday House there remains a junction of tunnels built by successive governments during the second half of the twentieth century to house civil servants and dignitaries in the event of a 'manageable' nuclear war.

► British Telecom Tower (former Post Office Tower), p. 146.

College of Arms

Founded by Richard III in 1484, the college is officially the Corporation of Kings, Heralds and Pursuivants of Arms. In medieval times heralds were in charge of announcing and organizing jousting tournaments and were recognized by the arms on their shields and the crests on their helmets;

nowadays they have mostly ceremonial duties during events such as the State Opening of Parliament, state funerals and the monarch's coronation.

(vi) around St Paul's

The area between Newgate Street and Ludgate Hill is dominated by St Paul's Cathedral and the Central Criminal Court (Old Bailey).

Amen Court

The court's unusual name honours the prayers of nearby St Paul's and contains the late-seventeenth-century houses of the cathedral's canons. The Campaign for Nuclear Disarmament (CND) was formed in the Amen Court flat of John Collins, canon of St Paul's Cathedral, in January 1958, its aim being to persuade the British people that Britain should 'renounce unconditionally the use or production of nuclear weapons and to refuse to allow their use by others in her defence'. The founding meeting was attended by Labour MPs Michael Foot and Denis Healey, and support soon followed from playwrights John Osborne and Arnold Wesker, actresses Flora Robson and Edith Evans, and the composers Benjamin Britten and Michael Tippett, with the philosopher–mathematician Bertrand Russell appointed honorary president. The organization's first public meeting was held at Central Hall, Westminster, on 17 February 1958.
➤ Central Hall, Westminster, p. 230.

Farringdon Street

Built on the course of the River Fleet in 1737, when the waterway was arched over, it was named after William de Farringdone, a thirteenth-century goldsmith, and is now part of the main traffic route between King's Cross and Blackfriars Bridge.
east side: Holborn Viaduct to Ludgate Circus
Congregational Memorial Hall, No. 14
The first ever meeting of the Labour Party was held in the **Congregational Memorial**

Hall on 27 February 1900 following a decision made by members of the Trades Union Congress to form a 'distinct Labour group in parliament who should have their own whips and agree upon their policy, which must embrace a readiness to cooperate with any party which for the time being may be engaged in promoting legislation in the direct interests of labour'. The committee's first secretary was James Ramsay MacDonald (later the first Labour prime minister) and the fifteen candidates put forward for the 1900 general election between them won 62,698 votes with two, Keir Hardie and Richard Bell, elected. In 1926 the General Strike was organized – unsuccessfully – from the hall and later that year the world's first table tennis championship was held there, the men dressing in a variety of costumes – long trousers, shorts, pullovers, plain suits and even ties – the women in long dresses; participants were forbidden to leave the hall without special permission.

Oswald Mosley's British Union of Fascists held its first meeting here in October 1932, but after Mosley used the phrase 'three warriors of class war all from Jerusalem' in a speech Israel Sieff, the Jewish owner of Marks and Spencer, withdrew his support for the party. Scuffles took place in the street outside the hall following the meeting, something that became a regular outcome at fascist meetings throughout the decade. Unabashed at the outcome of the Second World War, fascists held their first formal postwar meeting here on 15 November 1947 with delegates from more than fifty organizations urging Mosley, who had been imprisoned during the war, to return to politics. The hall was demolished in 1969 and rebuilt on the site as part of Caroone House.
Fleet Prison, between Fleet Lane and Ludgate Hill
The first purpose-built prison in London, the Fleet opened here *c.* 1170 on what was then a small island in the Fleet River that flooded when it rained and was used mostly for debtors, who were obliged to pay for the

irons that shackled them. The money raised went to the Keeper, who, according to a hereditary principle, was always a member of the Leveland family, and abuse of the system was common, with some prisoners going missing for several days at a time, if bothering to return at all. During the Peasants' Revolt of 1381 rioters broke in and set the prisoners free, but 400 years later when the prison was attacked and opened during the Gordon Riots many prisoners refused to leave – they felt that life was easier inside the prison than outside. The best-known Fleet prisoners included the poet John Donne, incarcerated in 1601 after being convicted of marrying a minor, and John Cleland, who spent his time writing the risqué *Memoirs of a Woman of Pleasure* (1748), better known as *Fanny Hill*, one of the first pornographic novels. The prison was pulled down in 1846.

► Marshalsea Gaol, pp. 382–3.

Fleet Lane

The lane recalls the now culverted Fleet River, which flows from Hampstead and Highgate into the Thames at Blackfriars and formed the Romans' western London boundary. In the Middle Ages its waters were thought to have therapeutic qualities and entrepreneurs opened pleasure gardens and taverns along parts of the route. But in the City the river remained an open sewer, running red with the blood of animals slaughtered at Smithfield market, and, as Jonathan Swift noted in *A Description of a City Shower*, full of 'Sweepings from Butchers' Stalls, Dung, Guts and Blood, / Drown'd Puppies, stinking Sprats, all drench'd in Mud, / Dead Cats and Turnip-Tops [which came] tumbling down the Flood'. The communities that grew along its southern banks were among the poorest, dirtiest, unhealthiest and most criminal in the capital, and after the Fire of London in 1666 Christopher Wren proposed converting the river into an ornamental canal. In 1731 it was arched over between Holborn Viaduct and Ludgate Circus to

create Farringdon Street and in 1766 the remainder of the river's City route was culverted to become a sewer. The northern stretches continued to be moved underground as London grew and the only remaining visible parts are Highgate Ponds. A 1996 scheme launched by Clerkenwell residents to open up the river again was not taken up by the authorities.

Ludgate Hill

According to London legend Brutus, grandson of the Trojan king Aeneas, a direct descendant of the Hebrew tribe founder, Judah, built a city, New Troy, on Ludgate Hill *c.* 1100 BC, which was rebuilt in the year 113 BC by Lud and renamed Caerlud (the city of Lud), a name later corrupted to Caerlundein, Londinium, and simply London.

north side: Ludgate Circus to St Paul's Churchyard

Ludgate, immediately west of St Martin-within-Ludgate

The gate is believed to have been built in 66 BC by King Lud, who is buried underneath the entrance, but it is also possible that the origin of the name was 'Flodgate', the gate having been constructed to prevent the Fleet from flooding the City. William de Jumieges, the eleventh-century French historian, claimed that William the Conqueror entered London in December 1066, two months after the Battle of Hastings, through **Ludgate**, which had been opened by collaborators, but that Londoners fought back and William took control of the town only after much bloodshed. The gate was rebuilt in 1215, probably using material taken from the houses of rich Jews who had been expelled from the City, for when **Ludgate** was again rebuilt in the early seventeenth century Hebrew inscriptions were found on some of the stones. In 1377 it was converted into a debtors' prison, some of whose inmates came voluntarily to flee from their creditors. The prisoners were let loose as the Fire swept through the City in September 1666. **Ludgate** was demolished in 1760.

St Martin-within-Ludgate, east of Old
Bailey
The origins of the church, whose earliest
records date back to 1138, are shrouded in
confusion and have been unreliably attributed to the seventh-century Welsh hero
Cadwallader. The church burned down in
the Great Fire and was rebuilt by Christopher Wren with an elegant lead tower.
The font is decorated with the transliterated
Greek palindrome *Niyon anomhma mh
monan oyin* ('Cleanse my sin and not just
my face').

Old Bailey
The street is synonymous with the Central
Criminal Court, which is based by its junction with Newgate Street.
Magpie and Stump, No. 18, west side
A chop-house and tavern with a long
history, the Magpie and Stump was the
closest public house to Newgate Prison and
was originally known as the Magpie, the
'Stump' suffix added in mock honour of the
headless victims executed at the prison.
Before the Newgate executions were
removed from the public arena in 1868, spectators would pay £10 to gain a good view of
events from the first floor of the house. In
recent years the rebuilt pub has featured
regularly in the television series *Rumpole of
the Bailey*.
Central Criminal Court, Old Bailey at
Newgate Street, east side
Britain's most famous law courts, which
opened in 1907 to replace those that joined
Newgate Prison, have been the setting for
many of the most famous criminal cases of
the last 100 years.
● The first major murder trial held at the
Old Bailey was in 1907 when the unfortunate **Horace Rayner** was accused of
murdering the wealthy grocer William
Whiteley at his Westbourne Grove premises.
Rayner was arrested at the scene of the
crime and in his pockets was found a note
which read: 'To all whom it may concern
William Whiteley is my father and has
brought upon himself and me a double

fatality by reason of his own refusal of a
request perfectly reasonable, R.I.P.' Twenty-
seven years previously Whiteley had impregnated a girl who gave birth to a son she
named Horace and whom she brought up
with her husband, George Rayner,
Whiteley's friend. Rayner later told the boy:
'Any time you're in trouble, go and see your
real father, William Whiteley', and when
Horace Rayner eventually did so a bemused
Whiteley, by then seventy-five, suggested he
went abroad, resulting in Horace shooting
Whiteley dead and wounding himself. At
the trial Rayner pleaded insanity, but
although the jury convicted him on the
basis of the words 'double fatality' in the
note, considerable public sympathy led
180,000 people to petition the Home Secretary to protest against the hanging of a
penniless son wronged by a rich father, and
Rayner was eventually released.
● **Arnold Leese**, rabid anti-Semite and
founder of the Imperial Fascist League, who
derided Oswald Mosley's British Union of
Fascists as 'kosher fascists' on discovering
that the grandfather of Oswald Mosley's
wife, Cynthia, was Jewish, was tried for
seditious libel and inciting a public mischief
at the courts in 1936 after describing Jewish
slaughter of animals as ritual murder. Leese,
who believed that Christianity was part of a
Jewish plot to undermine the virility of the
Nordic races, carried out his own defence,
on the predictable grounds that all lawyers
are in the pay of Jews, and although
acquitted of seditious libel was found guilty
of 'inciting a public mischief by rendering
His Majesty's subjects of the Jewish faith
liable to suspicion, affront and boycott'. He
refused to pay his fine and was sentenced to
six months in Wandsworth Prison.
● At the end of the Second World War
William Joyce (Lord Haw Haw) was tried
for high treason – broadcasting anti-British
propaganda over the wireless from Germany
in a contrived aristocratic voice mocking
Winston Churchill that earned him the
name 'Lord Haw Haw'. In 1945 Joyce was
arrested near the Germany–Denmark

border and brought back to Britain, but the start of the trial was delayed by wrangling over his nationality, for though Joyce owned a British passport he claimed he had been born in Ireland. He was found guilty, taken to Wandsworth Gaol, and hanged there in January 1946.

● Osteopath **Stephen Ward** was tried in July 1963 for living off immoral earnings in a case that made the society call-girls Christine Keeler and Mandy Rice-Davies household names and brought about the resignation of the Secretary of State for War, John Profumo, who had lied about having an affair with Keeler (see Marylebone, p. 157). When Rice-Davies was told by Lord Astor's counsel that Lord Astor categorically denied her allegation that she had had sex with him she famously replied: 'Well he would, wouldn't he', a phrase which now appears in the *Oxford Dictionary of Quotations*. Ward committed suicide a day before he was found guilty in his absence, leaving behind fourteen suicide notes.

● **The Kray twins**, Reggie and Ronnie, planned the daring murder of a witness who was due to appear in court in February 1968 through an associate who wanted to prove his worth to the Krays' organization. The man would take into the court an attaché case containing a hypodermic needle and syringe filled with cyanide attached to a small brass ring which, when pulled, would push the needle out, and jab the witness with it as he walked by. The victim would die of poisoning five minutes later, by which time the assailant would have escaped. The plan failed on the relevant day when the witness did not walk through the designated spot, the Krays unaware at the time that they had been set up by a man working for Scotland Yard's undercover team that was investigating their criminal activities. Within months the Krays were themselves in court at the Old Bailey on various charges including murdering two fellow gangsters, George Cornell and Jack 'The Hat' McVitie, and on 8 March 1969 they were sentenced to life imprisonment for the two murders with

the recommendation that they served 'not less than thirty years'.

● On 30 May 1972 the trial of the **Angry Brigade**, anarcho anti-capitalists modelled on Germany's Baader-Meinhof gang and the USA's Weathermen, began with eight suspects – James Greenfield, Anna Mendleson, John Barker, Hilary Creek, Stuart Christie, Christopher Bott, Angela Weir and Kate McLean – known as the Stoke Newington Eight, after the area where they were caught, accused of placing a series of bombs at various locations around Britain. The trial became the twentieth-century's longest for a political case, the jury being shown 688 items including a Beretta sub-machine gun and an 'unidentified substance found at the foot of a tree in the garden'. Although there were claims that evidence had been planted and that the defendants had been forced into making incriminating statements, Greenfield, Mendleson, Barker and Creek were found guilty, receiving ten years each.

● In October 1983 civil servant **Dennis Nilsen** went on trial as 'the killer of the century' and was sentenced to life with a stipulation that he serve a minimum of twenty-five years on six counts of murder and two of attempted murder, after prob-ably killing twice that number in Crickle-wood and Muswell Hill in the late 1970s and early 1980s. The victims were mostly homo-sexuals whom Nilsen had picked up in West End bars, taken home and strangled, burying their bodies under the floorboards. As astonishing as Nilsen's catalogue of crimes was his cool, unfussed manner. When the lawyer asked him why he had killed the men, he replied: 'I was hoping you could tell me that.'

● In July 2000 **David Copeland**, a loner who bore a grudge against immigrants and homo-sexuals and whose house was decorated with Nazi posters, was jailed for life for planting a bomb that killed three people in the Admiral Duncan pub in Soho. Copeland had also left a bomb near Brixton station, which exploded but caused only minor injuries, and one outside a Brick Lane curry house, which went off on a Saturday, the day that Copeland wrongly assumed would be the area's most busy. Copeland pleaded not guilty, declaring he was a righteous messenger from God, but was convicted.

▶ Royal Courts of Justice, p. 128.

Paternoster Row

The capital's major publishing and book-selling area in the fifteenth century, Paternoster Row was also renowned for its taverns and coffee houses, such as the **Chapter coffee house**, where the ill-fated late eighteenth-century teenage poet Thomas Chatterton knew 'all the geniuses', as he claimed in a letter to his mother, and which the novelist Elizabeth Gaskell described as having the appearance of a 'dwelling-house, two hundred years old or so, such as one sometimes sees in ancient country towns'. Corinthian Casuals, Britain's best-known amateur football team, were founded in an office on Paternoster Row in 1882 and in the early years of international football their players dominated the England team, contributing fifty-two of the eighty-eight players awarded caps between 1883 and 1890. The Corinthians even fielded the full England side twice, in 1894 and 1895, but declined as a force once professionalism took hold. Paternoster Row was devastated by enemy bombing during the Second World War, when some 6 million volumes of books stored here were destroyed.

Paternoster Square

Home of the Newgate meat market until 1869, Paternoster Square was destroyed in one of the worst Second World War bombing raids and redeveloped in the 1960s in an uncompromising brutalist style, courtesy of Trehearne, Preston and Partners, that had few supporters, especially once it was realized that the tallest building, although only 205 ft high, partially blocked the view of St Paul's Cathedral from Parliament Hill. By the beginning of the twenty-first century the square was again being redeveloped.

St Paul's Churchyard

Martyrs were executed outside St Paul's Cathedral in medieval times, the five main conspirators of the 1606 Gunpowder Plot, including Guy Fawkes, being hanged, drawn and quartered in St Paul's Churchyard for plotting to kill James I and 500 MPs. St Paul's Churchyard was also a centre for second-hand bookselling and a major publishing area, where Shakespeare's *Sonnets* and *Hamlet*, and Mary Wollstonecraft's *A Vindication of the Rights of Women* (1792) were first published. The original St Paul's School, which was founded here by John Colet in 1509, was the largest school in England, the number of pupils (153) being the same as the number of fishes caught in the gospel story. St Paul's School moved to Hammersmith in 1884 and is now in Barnes. Four London Masonic lodges met at the **Goose and Gridiron Ale House** in St Paul's Churchyard on 24 June 1717 to form the world's first Grand Lodge. A rival, claiming greater antiquity, was formed in London thirty-four years later and for sixty years the two Grand Lodges co-existed before merging in 1813 to form the United Grand Lodge of England. George Williams and a group of eleven other men established the Young Men's Christian Association above a draper's shop in St Paul's Churchyard in 1844 'with the view of uniting and directing the efforts of Christian young men for the spiritual welfare of their fellows in the various departments of commercial life'. Before long other branches were formed, first in London and then throughout the world.

Paul's Cross

Paul's Cross, a wooden pulpit, stood in front of St Paul's Cathedral until the Puritans pulled it down in 1643 and was where papal bulls and royal proclamations were made until the fourteenth century. A preacher by the name of Beal stirred up the crowd so passionately on May Day 1517 that riots broke out across London, the crowd turning on merchants from Flanders and the Baltic on what later came to be called

Evil May Day. On 12 May 1521 an unusual book, *The Defence of the Seven Sacraments*, was unveiled at Paul's Cross. The volume, supposedly written by Henry VIII, the jousting, hunting, non-bookish king, set out Catholic arguments against the new Protestant creed being propounded by Martin Luther in Germany, and though few believed that Henry was capable of such a feat, evidence shows that the king was indeed the author of the work which was dedicated to the Pope, earning Henry the title 'Defender of the Faith'. Although Henry is now best known for propagating the schism which led to England's break from the Church of Rome, and the accompanying violent dissolution of the monasteries so that he could divorce Catherine of Aragon and marry Anne Boleyn, he himself never rejected Catholicism *per se*, just the authority of Rome.

St Paul's Cathedral

Britain's major cathedral, the setting for state occasions and one of the capital's leading tourist attractions, was founded in 604 by Ethelbert, King of Kent, and Mellitus, Bishop of the East Saxons, and built of wood. Rebuilt in stone by Bishop Erkenwald in 675 after a fire, it was destroyed by Vikings in the ninth century, and when its replacement, which lasted from 962 to 1087, also burned down, Maurice, Bishop of London, chose to build a new, grand cathedral on a larger scale than anything witnessed outside central Europe.

Work on this Norman cathedral, now referred to as Old St Paul's, took place throughout the first half of the thirteenth century, being finished in 1240. Eighteen years later the Norman choir was extended and the length of the church increased to 1,600 ft, making it the largest cathedral in Europe after Seville and Milan, with its spire at 489 ft, completed in 1315, the tallest ever built. During the Reformation of the sixteenth century the High Altar was pulled down and replaced by a plain table, many of the tombs were destroyed, the reredos was smashed to pieces, and St Paul's became

more of a social centre than a church. The nave, Paul's Walk, was used as a market for selling groceries and animals, delivery boys cut through to avoid traffic, and prostitutes touted for business, although in 1554 the authorities did at least try to ban 'the leading of mules and horses' through the building.

Inigo Jones, appointed King's Surveyor in 1628, oversaw further rebuilding, basing his design on Palladio's portico of the Temple of Venus in Rome, and demolished the adjoining houses and shops, but during the Civil War of the 1640s the Parliamentarians took away the scaffolding encasing the south transept, which duly collapsed, and set up a cavalry barracks in the nave, while Oliver Cromwell even toyed with the idea of selling off the cathedral to the Jewish community for use as a synagogue. Meanwhile its collection of holy relics, helpful in attracting gifts from pilgrims, continued to be sold off, the supply seemingly inexhaustible, for the authorities were still selling portions of the Virgin Mary's milk and the hand of St John 150 years later.

In August 1666 a commission set up to examine the state of the building hired as architect Christopher Wren, who proposed rebuilding it with a 'Noble cupola, a forme of Church-building, not as yet known in England, but of wonderful grace'. A few weeks later the Fire of London destroyed much of the City, including St Paul's, and after the Fire the site lay untouched for eighteen months. Wren was asked to rebuild the cathedral, the authorities levying a special tax on London coal to pay for the new building, and though the foundation stone was laid in 1675 it was not until 1697 that the first service could be held. Parliament declared the new cathedral finished in 1711, when Wren was seventy-nine, and the work was heralded by many as the finest example of Renaissance architecture in Britain, characteristic of the new-found freedoms architects were able to express following the austerity of Puritan life under Oliver Cromwell. Wren's cathedral has been

St Paul's glossary

All Souls chapel Dedicated in 1925 to Lord Kitchener of Khartoum, who was killed during the First World War.

American Memorial Chapel Formerly the Jesus Chapel, where in 1951 General Eisenhower presented to the cathedral the Roll of Honour, a list of 28,000 US citizens based in Britain who died in the Second World War.

Balustrade Added in 1718 against Wren's wishes.

Chapel of the Modern Martyrs The chapel commemorates Anglican martyrs of the last 150 years, their names recorded in a book locked in a marble casket, and is reserved for private prayer.

Chapel of St Dunstan The 1778 chandelier which hangs here was taken from the church of 𝔖𝔱 𝔐𝔦𝔩𝔡𝔯𝔢𝔡 𝔓𝔬𝔲𝔩𝔱𝔯𝔶, demolished in 1872.

Choir The carvings on the stalls are by Grinling Gibbons and the wrought ironwork, including the choir screens, by Jean Tijou, a Huguenot refugee.

Clock tower The clock, Big Tom, is 16 ft in diameter, with 10 ft-long hands and contains a 17-tonne bell, Great Paul, which is rung for five minutes every day at 1 p.m.

Crypt Those buried in the crypt, which stretches underneath the entire ground level, include Christopher Wren (who died in 1723), Lord Nelson (1805) and the Duke of Wellington (1852). The crypt's outer walls are those of Old St Paul's, which

burned down in the Fire of London, and in medieval times the space was occupied by another church, 𝔖𝔱 𝔍𝔞𝔦𝔱𝔥'𝔰 𝔲𝔫𝔡𝔢𝔯 𝔖𝔱 𝔓𝔞𝔲𝔩'𝔰, the parish church for the community that lived in Paternoster Row and Paternoster Square, its location marked by a brass strip. During the 1666 Fire of London parishioners left their books and documents in St Faith's, mistakenly assuming they would be safe against the flames, but lost everything.

Dimensions The cathedral is 510 ft long, 460 ft wide, and 365 ft high.

Dome The second biggest in the world, after St Peter's, Rome, its design was changed many times by Wren, a tribute to whom can be read on the paving beneath: 'Lector, si monumentum requiris, circumspice' – 'Reader, if you seek his monument, look around'.

Exterior St Paul's is built in Portland stone.

Marriages In 1501 Prince Arthur, eldest son of Henry VII and heir to the throne, married Catherine of Aragon in the cathedral amid great splendour, but the marriage was probably never consummated, despite Arthur's boast to an aide to 'bring me a cup of ale, for I have been this night in the midst of Spain', and a year later the prince was dead. Catherine then married Arthur's brother, Henry VIII. In 1981 the marriage of Prince Charles and Lady Diana Spencer took place here.

Nave The nave is 40 ft wide and 89 ft high.

altered little since and remarkably avoided Second World War damage, despite the devastation met by much of the City.

(vii) around Cannon Street

Cannon Street runs from St Paul's Cathedral to Monument tube, a feeder for a host of small, quiet streets where the less glamorous parts of the City's commercial life take place in an area that is now almost completely non-residential.

Bow Lane

Originally Cordwainer Street, on account of the local shoemakers, and now one of the City's most pleasant streets, with its picturesque shop-fronts, it is home to the well-known church of St Mary-le-Bow and the older, but lesser-known, St Mary Aldermary.

St Mary-le-Bow, west side

The most famous of the City's thirty-nine churches, St Mary-le-Bow is enshrined in two London legends: that of Dick Whittington, who in Highgate sometime in the late fourteenth century heard in the sound

North Aisle Contains memorials to Lord Melbourne (prime minister 1834–41); Lord Leighton, the late-nineteenth-century painter; the Duke of Wellington; and General Gordon of Khartoum.

North Choir Aisle A statue of Dr Johnson has the Dictionary-compiler dressed incongruously as an ancient Greek.

North Transept and Chapel Bombed in the Second World War and restored, it contains a life-size terracotta statue of the Virgin and Child designed by the Portuguese Josefina de Vasconcelos and is festooned with the colours of the Middlesex Regiment.

South Aisle Here can be found the 259 steps leading to the Whispering Gallery.

South Choir Aisle A statue of John Donne in a niche has the metaphysical poet, who was Dean of St Paul's from 1621 to 1631, wrapped in a shroud, standing on an urn awaiting his own resurrection. It was the only St Paul's memorial to survive the 1666 Fire of London. Alongside is a piece of stone from Solomon's Temple in Jerusalem.

South Transept There are memorials to Captain Scott, who died trying to find the South Pole in 1912; the painter J. M. W. Turner; and Admiral Nelson.

Towers They were added by Christopher Wren in 1707 when he was seventy-five.

West door It is opened only on special occasions.

Whispering Gallery The acoustics enable whispers to echo around the dome.

St Mary Aldermary to the south), was erected *c.* 1080 on marshy land riddled with underground streams and had to be reinforced with stone bow arches, hence its later name, St Mary-le-Bow, originally *Sancta Maria de Arcubus*. William Longbeard, a radical orator, took sanctuary in the church in 1196 after speaking out against the greed of the wealthy and the paying of a special tax to free Richard I from imprisonment in Europe. After Archbishop Hubert instructed that the church be set on fire Longbeard fled. But he was captured and stabbed to death, taken to the gallows in Smithfield and hanged on a gibbet as a warning to others thinking of publicly denouncing the king.

Christopher Wren rebuilt the church after the Fire of London, modelling it on the Basilica of Maxentius in Rome, with the grand doorway at the foot of the tower based on the work by François Mansart in the Hotel de Conti, Paris. The church was bombed again in the 1940s Blitz after which only the outer walls and steeple were left undamaged. The bells were recast using the original metal and sounded again for the first time in 1964.

● In 1991 Dr Malcolm Hough of the Meteorological Office used weather and wind data to show that before the invention of motorized vehicles the church's bells could have been heard across central London and in suburbs such as Highgate.

of its bells a call to return to London and after a remarkable change of fortune became Lord Mayor of London three times; and that only those born within the sound of the church's bells are true cockneys – the word is a corruption of the Middle English *cockeney*, or cock's egg, the misshapen eggs laid by young hens – a term first applied to those born in the City of London by rural dwellers, who felt themselves to be sturdier and purer.

The first church to be built on this site, St Mary New Church (the old church was

Cannon Street

Cannon Street, one of the City's main southern routes, which links St Paul's Cathedral with London Bridge, is a corruption of Candelwrithe Street, a name commemorating the candle makers who worked here from the twelfth century, and was where Samuel Pepys, during the Fire of London, met the Lord Mayor, who cried out to him: 'Lord! What can I do? I have been pulling down houses, but the fire overtakes us faster than we can do it.' The street became a major commercial artery after the building of the railway station of the same name in the 1860s.

London Stone, No. 111, north side

> At length he sat on London Stone and heard Jerusalem's voice – *Jerusalem*, William Blake (1820)

London Stone, a block of Clipsham limestone embodied in the wall of 111 Cannon Street, and previously in the wall of 𝔖𝔱 𝔖𝔴𝔦𝔱𝔥𝔦𝔫'𝔰 church on the same site, may have been either a Roman milestone for all British distances, the sacred pagan centre of the town, or even the ancient stone from which King Arthur pulled Excalibur. In medieval times it was used as a totem for the City's safety, where crowds used to assemble to discuss important issues of the day and hear proclamations and new laws, and was where the Kent rebel Jack Cade, who in 1450 led a band of men into the City to demonstrate against what they saw as bad government and legal injustice, stopped to tap the ancient monument as a show of strength. Cade set up his headquarters at the White Hart in Southwark while planning to seize control of the capital, but was routed after a few days when Londoners tired of the rebellion. Shakespeare dramatized Cade's arrival in *Henry VI Part II* (1591) in which the rebel stops at London Stone and orders the 'pissing-conduit [the poor people's well] run nothing but claret wine this first year of our reign'.

Cannon Street station, south side

The station was built between 1865 and 1867 by John Hawkshaw for the South Eastern Railway on the site where in the first century AD the Roman governor of London had his palace. Here, in 1157, the Hanseatic League of German and Scandinavian countries built a trading headquarters, the Steelyard, that faced considerable local prejudice until Edward II threatened to imprison for one year and one day anyone who offended the foreign visitors. Cannon Street station was originally fronted by the ℭ𝔞𝔫𝔫𝔬𝔫 𝔖𝔱𝔯𝔢𝔢𝔱 ℌ𝔬𝔱𝔢𝔩, designed by E. M. Barry in 1867, where on 31 July 1920 the British Communist Party was

founded, three years after the Russian Revolution, from a hotch-potch of socialist organizations including the Socialist Prohibition Fellowship which wanted to suppress the production of alcoholic drinks. The Soviet Union leader, Lenin, who granted the British communists £55,000 of state funds (just over £1 million in early twenty-first-century prices), sent the conference a message in the form of a pamphlet entitled 'Left Wing Communism – An Infantile Disorder' which urged the BCP to seek affiliation to the Labour Party, a plea the conference rejected. In 1931 Oswald Mosley launched his short-lived New Party at the same venue, and a year later closed it down to found the British Union of Fascists. The hotel was converted to offices in 1931 and destroyed in the Second World War when the station itself was badly damaged. Hawkshaw's arched roof was removed in the 1960s when the station was remodelled to incorporate pedestrian walkways and a precinct.

Clement's Lane
St Clement Eastcheap

A church was built in the eleventh century and dedicated to Clement, the third Bishop of Rome, who was cast into the sea chained to an anchor. After being destroyed in the Great Fire it was rebuilt by Christopher Wren from 1683 to 1687 in an intimate style, being only 64 ft long and 40 ft wide. The St Clement of the nursery rhyme 'Oranges and Lemons' is probably this church, rather than St Clement Danes, as it was closer to the wharf where cargoes of citrus fruits were unloaded.

Mansion House Place
Mansion House

Mansion House, the official residence of the Lord Mayor of London, the nominal head of the City, and not to be confused with the newly created political mayor of London, was designed by George Dance the Elder and built in 1753 on the site of the Stock Market. As one of the City's major strategic buildings, Mansion House has attracted the

Oranges and Lemons

The verses of the well-known nursery rhyme 'Oranges and Lemons' were originally sung to imitate the sound of the bells of the various City churches which, according to the song, rang the following sounds:

Aldgate (St Botolph, Aldgate High Street) 'Old Father Baldpate.'

Bow (St Mary-le-Bow, Cheapside) 'I'm sure I don't know.'

Old Bailey 'When will you pay me?'

St Anne's (Gresham Street) 'Kettles and pans.'

St Clement's (St Clement Eastcheap) 'Oranges and lemons.'

St Giles (St Giles Cripplegate, Wood Street) 'Brickbats and tiles.'

St Helen's (Bishopsgate) 'You owe me ten shillings.'

St John's (St John the Evangelist, Friday Street) 'Pokers and tongs.'

St Catherine's (St Katherine Coleman, Fenchurch Street) 'Maids in white aprons.'

St Marg'ret's (New Fish Street Hill) 'Bull's eyes and targets'.

St Martin's (St Martin Ongar, Martin Lane) 'You owe me five farthings.'

St Peter's (St Peter Westcheap, Cheapside) 'Pancake and fritters.'

Shoreditch (St Leonard's, Shoreditch High Street) 'When I grow rich.'

Stepney (St Dunstan and All Saints, Stepney High Street) 'Pray, when will that be?'

Whitechapel (St Mary, Whitechapel High Street) 'Two sticks and an apple.'

ire of various groups of demonstrators over the years. In 1768 supporters of the popular orator John Wilkes, celebrating the latter's election as MP, broke the windows when they noticed they were not lit, and twelve years later the building was damaged during the anti-Catholic Gordon Riots. Had the Cato Street Conspirators been successful in their attempt to kill the entire British Cabinet in 1820, the heads of Cabinet ministers Lord Castlereagh and Lord Sidmouth would have been displayed on pikes on the steps of Mansion House. Various City ceremonies take place at Mansion House, including the Butchers' Company's annual presentation to the Lord Mayor of London of a boar's head to mark the ancient payment for land on which they cleaned their beasts' entrails and the Fruiterers' Company's annual tribute of a selection of fruit in memory of the Fruit Meters, which were tolls on fruit entering the City.

➤ Guildhall, p. 17.

Queen Victoria Street *Also see p. 54*

St Nicholas Cole Abbey, north side

Records for the church date back to 1144, a charter from 1272 referring to the church as 'Sci Nichi retro fishtrate' (St Nick's behind Fish Street), but the name is something of a misnomer, given that there never was an abbey nor a Nicholas Cole, and results from a nearby coldharbour, or shelter. When the Catholic Mary Tudor took the throne in 1553 she introduced a ruling that all married clergy were automatically divorced, which led Thomas Sowdley, the church's priest, to sell his wife to a butcher, after which he was nicknamed the Parson Chicken and pelted with chamber pots and eggs. St Nicholas was the first church to be rebuilt by Christopher Wren after the Fire, and after being destroyed on Sunday 11 May 1941 in a Second World War raid in which more than 3,000 were killed it was restored to Wren's designs. In the 1951 Ealing comedy *The Lavender Hill Mob* the gold bullion robbery takes place just outside the church, a scene which captures the devastation caused by the Blitz, showing St Nicholas without glass in the windows, roof or spire. In 1982 the Church of England leased St Nicholas to the Free Church of Scotland and many artefacts were transferred to the Blackfriars church of St Andrew-by-the-Wardrobe.

Temple of Mithras, No. 11, south side

A Roman temple to the light god, Mithras, 60 ft long and 26 ft wide and built by the Walbrook stream, was discovered in 1954 when the ground was excavated in preparation for the building of an office block, Bucklersbury House, on the site, and the artefacts taken to the Museum of London. Knowledge of the worship of Mithras – which began in Persia in the first century BC, was available only to men and was carried out in specially constructed caves, *Mithraea*, one of which was created in London near the site now occupied by Mansion House – is limited due to the extreme secrecy surrounding the cult.

Central London

CLERKENWELL | FINSBURY, EC1

Although there were busy trades in Clerkenwell, and working jewellers by scores, it was a purer place, with farm-houses nearer to it than many modern Londoners would readily believe, and lovers' walks at no great distance, which turned into squalid courts – *Barnaby Rudge*, Charles Dickens (1841)

Clerkenwell, London's first suburb, grew in medieval times on the slightly raised ground to the north of the City by the east bank of the River Fleet and took its name from the *Fons Clericorum*, or Clerks' Well, on Farringdon Lane, a glimpse of which can be seen behind the façade at 14 Farringdon Lane. To the east, between Sadler's Wells and Shoreditch, what is now Finsbury was a fen, but in Clerkenwell springs, spas and archery grounds abounded. By the four-teenth century Clerkenwell was home to three great religious institutions – the Priory of the Knights of St John, the Augustinian nunnery of St Mary (both founded *c.* 1140) and the Charterhouse Priory (1371), all of which were dissolved by Henry VIII during the Reformation.

After the 1666 Fire of London many of those who had been made homeless in the City fled to the area, making living conditions difficult. In the eighteenth century Clerkenwell was colonized by Huguenots (French Protestants fleeing persecution), who opened workshops to capitalize on their skills in making watches, locks and jewellery, and these trades flourished alongside the more traditional saddle-making and leather work, which were banned from the City. At that time the local landscape was dominated by the Fleet River, which ran along the course of what is now Farringdon Road, and was little more than an open sewer. The average local life expectancy was twenty-two years, and the district was so violent, even clergy had to be escorted by the police.

Many of the worst slums were wiped out when the eastern end of the first underground line, the Metropolitan Railway, was built in the Fleet valley between 1859 and 1863, a story recounted by Arnold Bennett in his 1923 novel *Riceyman Steps*, in which he referred, albeit slightly with tongue-in-cheek, to the 'great metropolitan industrial district of Clerkenwell'. By this time Clerkenwell was heavily associated with radical politics and publishing: the Russian agitator and future Soviet leader V. I. Lenin produced his Bolshevik newspaper, *Iskra*, at what is now the Marx Memorial Library on Clerkenwell Green in 1903 and the communist daily *Morning Star* operated from offices on Farringdon Road in the mid twentieth century near where the *Guardian* and *Observer* are now based. Meanwhile, the local council, Finsbury, built a reputation as one of the most radical and progressive in the metropolis, opening free libraries and the pioneering Finsbury Health Centre in 1938, but was abolished during local government reorganization in 1965.

Clerkenwell's population, which peaked at 65,000 in 1861, declined through housing reforms and Second World War bombing but, even though many of the better houses were bombed, the area's traditional street pattern was left intact and major landmarks and turnings, such as Clerkenwell Green, the nearby church of St James, the twisting Clerkenwell Close and Myddelton Square, remained to attract recent generations. Clerkenwell's revival, which would have seemed unlikely in the 1960s but is now taken for granted, began in the late 1970s when media companies, advertising agencies, restaurant owners and City workers, tired of commuting into central London from afar, began seeking out the abandoned workshops and factories, buoyed by the village charm that could be found away from the main roads, and made the area into what is now one of the most sought after in central London.

(i) Little Italy

In the eighteenth century, before the Fleet River was culverted, the area around Hatton Garden was one of the most overcrowded and unhygienic in London: a warren of courts, alleyways and passages, often connected by planks between windows and over ditches, where strangers were robbed and occasionally killed, their bodies being dropped from trapdoors into the river, and was where Charles Dickens set Fagin's Den in *Oliver Twist*.

Following the Napoleonic Wars of the early nineteenth century Italian immigrants moved here, their community run according to a hierarchical system that involved a *padrone* being in charge of the new arrivals and handing out rooms and jobs in return for a portion of the immigrants' wages.

Many of the Italians were craftsmen, picture-framers and watchmakers, who set up workshops around Hatton Garden (now the centre of London's jewellery trade, although with little Italian presence), while the poorer ones became ice-cream vendors or knife sharpeners, living in cramped tenements on Leather Lane. Slum clearance of the late nineteenth century cleaned up the area, and Italian immigration died out after the fascist regime of Benito Mussolini imposed a restriction on emigration in 1927.

There are still traces of an Italian presence around the church of St Peter on Clerkenwell Road while elsewhere, particularly around the Hatton Garden jewellery district, the uncontrived liveliness and lack of sophistication has helped create one of central London's most appealing districts.

● Little Italy occupies the area between Mount Pleasant and Holborn, west of Farringdon Road.

Bleeding Heart Yard

Bleeding Heart Yard . . . a place much changed in feature and in fortune, yet with some relish of ancient greatness about it – *Little Dorrit*, Charles Dickens (1857)

A well-concealed dingy courtyard, south of Greville Street, whose unusual name dates back to a myth that grew up around the fate of Lady Elizabeth Hatton, who in 1626 supposedly danced here with the devil and was found the next morning dead, her heart still pumping blood.

Brooke Street

The street, which leads north from Holborn, stands on the site of **Brooke House**, a mansion built in 1536 by the Earl of Bath as Bath House and renamed by Elizabeth I's Chancellor of the Exchequer, the poet Fulke Greville (Lord Brooke), who was murdered in the house by his manservant when the latter discovered he had been left out of Greville's will. Oliver Cromwell entertained the French government at Brooke House in 1656 when he ruled the country as Lord Protector and the house was demolished twenty years later. William Friese-Greene gave the first ever demonstration of moving pictures on his kinematograph in his laboratory at **No. 20** in 1889.

west side: Holborn to Dorrington Street
Thomas Chatterton's address (1770), **No. 39**

Chatterton, the romantic poet described by John Keats as 'the purest writer in the English language', died at **39 Brooke Street** (demolished 1880) at the age of seventeen from a fatal dose of arsenic which he took in a fit of depression induced by a publisher's rejection of his poems (some believe he was taking the mineral to alleviate venereal disease). After his death, poems which he claimed had been written by Thomas Rowley, a fifteenth-century monk, were found among his papers, published in 1777, and hailed as masterpieces. But when the scholar Thomas Tyrwhitt proved that the poems could not have been written by the monk, as they used grammatical constructions unknown at that time, it appeared as if they must have been written by Chatterton, who then became fêted as a poetic genius and doomed romantic figure. In 1856 Henry Wallis painted *The Death of Chatterton* in the room in which the poet had died, the novelist and poet George Meredith posing as Chatterton. Peter Ackroyd's 1987 novel, entitled simply *Chatterton*, interweaves Chatterton's life with that of a modern-day aspiring writer, Charles Wychwood. A branch of Barclays Bank now stands on the site.

► Keats House, Hampstead, p. 364.

William Friese-Greene's workshop, **No. 20**
William Friese-Greene invented the kinematograph (Greek for 'motion writing'), a camera that could take a series of photographs on a roll of film moving behind a shutter, in his laboratory at **20 Brooke Street** in January 1889, and used it to make a film showing 'leisurely pedestrians, open-topped buses and hansom-cabs with trotting horses' in Hyde Park. Although Friese-Greene was the first person to witness moving pictures on a screen, his camera was too slow to be of practical use (it could not take shots quickly enough for animation) and he gave no public performances of his moving pictures, which is why credit for the

invention has gone instead to Thomas Edison, who produced a more sophisticated machine. Friese-Greene later pioneered stereoscopic and colour cinematography but did not have the technical knowledge to develop his ideas commercially, and despite taking out seventy-eight patents between 1889 and 1921, none was developed commercially, resulting in a number of experts dismissing him as a charlatan. He was honoured by John Boulting in the 1951 film *The Magic Box*.

▶ John Logie Baird's pioneering television work, p. 197.

Clerkenwell Road
Originally Liquorpond Street, it was upgraded from a lane in 1879 when scores of tiny alleyways and crumbling tenements were demolished.

St Peter, west of Herbal Hill
London's main Italian church, also known as the Chiesa Italiana di San Pietro, designed by John Bryson and based on the basilica of St Cristogona in Trastevere, Rome, opened in 1863 and was for nearly a hundred years the religious and social centre of the large local Italian community. It is now used by a congregation that has moved far from Clerkenwell, and on the first Sunday after 16 July every year there is a service based around the feast of Our Lady of Mount Carmel, after which a lively procession makes its way through the local streets.

▶ The London Oratory of St Philip Neri, p. 421.

Coldbath Square
Barely noticeable as a square, and occupying a squalid location opposite the huge Mount Pleasant post office, it marks the site of the Cold Bath Fields where, in 1697, Walter Baynes found a cold spring and bottled a water 'famed for the curing compulsion, creeping fevers, dropsy, disorders of the spleen, deafness . . . and most nerval disorders'. In 1737 Eustace Budgell, a resident of the square and barrister in the Inner Temple, who had lost three-quarters of his fortune in the South Sea Bubble crash and was later disgraced in contesting a will, left his house in Coldbath Square, took a boat out on the Thames, and having filled his pockets with stones jumped in the water half-way across and drowned. In 1794 the **Middlesex House of Correction**, also known as Coldbath Prison, was built here, ruining the square's residential status. The prison was often used for those suspected of insurrection against the state, but its best-known incumbent was John Williams, the prime suspect for the 1811 Ratcliff Highway Murders, who committed suicide in gaol before he could be brought to trial. Some experts believe there was no case against Williams and that he was murdered in prison to end the investigation. The prison closed in 1877 and the square was all but eradicated for the construction of Rosebery Avenue.

▶ Ratcliff Highway murders, pp. 298–9.

Ely Court
The Olde Mitre
A tavern founded in 1546 for the staff of the adjacent **Ely Palace**, medieval home of the Bishops of Ely, its opening and closing times were set by magistrates in Ely, Cambridgeshire, until the liberalization of the licensing laws in the 1980s, and technically the police were not allowed to enter unless invited to do so. Elizabeth I supposedly once danced around the cherry tree preserved in the corner of the bar.

Ely Place
A well-preserved terrace of Georgian houses built in 1770 on the site of the medieval **Ely Palace**, it was guarded by men in top hats and frock coats until the 1980s. Between Nos. 9 and 10 a narrow court leads to the Olde Mitre pub, while at its northern end a high wall acts as a social and physical boundary between the elegance of the street and the shabbiness of Bleeding Heart Yard (p. 70).

Ely Palace

A medieval palace owned by the Bishops of Ely – the garden was noted for its strawberries, as mentioned by Shakespeare in *Richard III* – it was where John of Gaunt, son of Edward III and mentor of the poet Geoffrey Chaucer, effectively ruled England in the 1370s. It was also where Henry VIII, according to the London chronicler John Stow, hosted a five-day feast in May 1531 for which the menu included '24 great beefs, 100 fat muttons, 51 veals, 34 porks, 91 pigs, 10 dozen capons, 14 dozen cocks, 37 dozen pigeons, 14 dozen swans and 340 dozen larks'. In 1576 Elizabeth I ordered the Bishop of Ely to rent out some of the buildings to Christopher Hatton, a favoured courtier, and the palace was later demolished with only the chapel, now the church of St Etheldreda's, remaining (see below).
➤ **Whitehall Palace**, p. 233.

St Etheldreda, west side

St Etheldreda is the oldest Catholic church in England and the only surviving building from the medieval **Ely Palace**, of which it was the chapel. Parts of the church date from 1290 and along with some of the chapels of Westminster Abbey are the only examples of Edward I era architecture to survive in London. During the Reformation the chapel became a Protestant place of worship. Fortunate to escape the Fire of London in 1666, it was renamed in honour of Etheldreda, seventh-century abbess of Ely. It became a Welsh chapel in 1833 and returned to the Catholic fold in 1874 when it was bought by the Rosminian Fathers. The huge west window, completed in 1964, commemorates the English martyrs of the Tudor period.

Greville Street

Greville Street, named after Elizabeth I's Chancellor of the Exchequer, the poet Fulke Greville, is a ramshackle street off Farringdon Road at the edge of London's jewellery trade, best known for its twenty-four-hour kosher-styled café, the Knosherie, opened in 1999 by Michael Bloom after the East End branch of Bloom's restaurant closed.
➤ Bloom's in the East End, p. 304.

Hatton Garden

A shabby, lively street at the centre of London's jewellery trade, it is named after Sir Christopher Hatton, late-sixteenth-century Master of the Game at the Inner Temple, who met Elizabeth I at the theatre and became one of the queen's favourites, being appointed Vice-Chamberlain in 1577 and Lord Keeper of the Great Seal in 1587. During the eighteenth century Hatton Garden was a desirable residential street, but in the nineteenth century jewellers, silversmiths and goldsmiths opened small workshops near the luxurious houses and by the end of the century the smart houses had all been demolished and the entire street had come to be dominated by traders.

Because of the riches on display Hatton Garden has long been a target for criminals. In the early years of the twentieth century hustlers would go into a jeweller's shop with a £100 ring they were trying to sell, refuse to accept the shopkeeper's offer, no matter how large, but return a few seconds later having changed their mind and now willing to sell. If the shopkeeper failed to examine the ring again he would find himself handing over a large sum for an imitation paste copy the crook had exchanged outside for the real ring. In 1919 the Soviet Union's trade commissar Leonid Krasin, who was later in charge of embalming Lenin's body, and Leon Trotsky's brother-in-law, Lev Kamenev, a member of the Soviet Politburo, sold £40,000-worth of diamonds and platinum they had smuggled into Britain in Hatton Garden, intending to use the proceeds to bankroll the labour newspaper, the *Daily Herald*. When the details emerged in the conservative *Morning Post*, the *Herald* claimed it had known nothing of the scam and returned the money to the Soviets.
➤ *Daily Herald*, p. 115.

Leather Lane

One of London's oldest, if not more auspicious, markets, its name relates not to the sale of leather but to the French word *leveroun* (greyhound), believed to be the name of a local inn. It was home in the nineteenth century to organ-grinders, beggars and thieves and the location of public baths where those with venereal disease would sweat in a tub and try to cure themselves by taking mercury, often in harmful doses. Richard Trevithick built Britain's first steam coach at 𝔍𝔢𝔩𝔱𝔬𝔫'𝔰 𝔠𝔬𝔞𝔠𝔥𝔴𝔬𝔯𝔨𝔰, which stood at No. 36, in 1802, the vehicle making the first ever journey by a machine using its own power, ten miles from here to Paddington and back, during which time it went out of control and caused some damage.

► Petticoat Lane market, p. 289.

Mount Pleasant

Mount Pleasant post office
Opened in 1877 on the site of Cold Bath Fields, it was rebuilt from 1913 to 1917 to incorporate the Post Office's underground electric railway system, which runs from Paddington to Whitechapel via Wimpole Street post office, Drury Lane, Mount Pleasant, St Martin's-le-Grand and Liverpool Street station using automatic, driverless trains which travel at around 35 mph and carry half a ton of letters. The tunnel was used as a shelter during the First World War and was where the Elgin Marbles were stored during the Second World War.

► Elgin Marbles at the British Museum, p. 90.

Saffron Hill

Once the main north–south route through the area but now a minor road, Saffron Hill, named after the herb that grew here in medieval times, was the centre of Italian life in London in the nineteenth century. At No. 1 is the Diamond Trading Company, which handles the sale of gems for the De Beers group, brought in by helicopters that land on the roof.

The Sabini gang

Saffron Hill in the 1920s and 1930s was home to the Sabini gang, then London's most feared criminal organization, headed by Darby Sabini, on whom Graham Greene based the gangster Colleoni in *Brighton Rock*, assisted by brothers Fred, Joseph, Harry-Boy and George. Like the later Krays, the Sabinis were excellent boxers in their youth, but could not maintain the discipline required to become successful professionals, and in the 1920s swapped the ring for ringside security, emerging as a serious underworld force after Darby Sabini broke the jaw of a rival gangster, Monkey Benneyworth, when the latter deliberately tore the barmaid's dress in the Griffin pub on Saffron Hill. The Sabinis began to organize crime and protection at south-east racetracks, where they would surround bookmakers, standing sideways so that the hammers in their pockets could be seen, and prevent punters from placing bets until the bookmaker had paid the required premium. Their 'protection' involved hiring out stools at a grossly inflated price to on-course bookmakers or taking round pails and sponges which bookmakers would be obliged to use to clean their blackboards after each race, again for a price, wiping the odds at an inconvenient moment of the racing if the bookmaker refused to pay up. The Sabinis, whose members promised not to swear or drink alcohol under the age of twenty, expanded in the 1930s so that their number included Jews and second generation Sicilians, none of whom spoke Italian, but after older members of the family were interned as enemy aliens at the outbreak of the Second World War their reign collapsed.

► The Krays, p. 310; the Richardsons, p. 378.

(ii) Clerkenwell Green area

The centre of Clerkenwell village, home of the eighteenth-century church of St James, the Green features a number of enticing alleyways leading off at odd angles.

Clerkenwell Close

A winding medieval lane built in the grounds of 𝔖𝔱 𝔐𝔞𝔯𝔶'𝔰 ℜ𝔲𝔫𝔫𝔢𝔯𝔶, it was lined with elegant villas in the sixteenth century and residents later included Thomas Challoner, friend of Oliver Cromwell, in whose house the Parliamentarian leader stayed at the outbreak of the English Civil War of the 1640s. These properties fell into decay when the wealthy moved west at the end of the following century, and were mostly divided into flats or converted to workshops, being demolished in the nineteenth century when space in Clerkenwell became greatly sought. A rare survival is the pair of late-eighteenth-century converted houses at Nos. 47–48. Council plans in 1951 to demolish the lane and replace it with a school and car park were thwarted. The feminist magazine *Spare Rib* was launched at No. 27 in 1972.

east side: Corporation Row to Clerkenwell Green

House of Detention (nineteenth century), north of Sans Walk

A prison built in 1845 on the site of the seventeenth-century Clerkenwell Bridewell, it was where in December 1867 a group of Fenians (Irish nationalists) attempted to help some jailed associates escape by detonating a beer barrel full of explosives outside the prison wall. Although the police in Dublin had warned the Metropolitan Police that there would be an attempt to spring the Fenians from Clerkenwell, few precautions were taken and a constable who saw a group of men drag a barrel to the prison wall, light a fuse, and drag the barrel away as it smouldered and fizzled out failed to report the incident to his superiors. Two days later, the feat was repeated by three men and one woman who hauled a 30-gallon cask containing more than 500 lbs of gunpowder to Clerkenwell Close and asked a girl playing in the street to fetch a match. In the blast six people (including the girl) died and

another 120 were injured. The Fenian ringleader, Michael Barrett, was hanged at Newgate a year later in what was London's last public execution.

The prison closed in the 1890s and the buildings were converted into the Hugh Myddelton School, which was opened by Edward, Prince of Wales, the first time a member of the royal family had performed such a ceremony. Some 2,000 children attended the school, such was the density of the local population, many enticed by the offer of free school meals. Only the primary school, to the west in Bowling Green Lane, is now in use, the other buildings functioning as a further education college. A network of tunnels and dungeons from the prison days, which were used as air-raid shelters during the Second World War, and briefly opened as a museum in the 1990s, remains underneath.

St James, north of Clerkenwell Green
The church, which stands in one of the most glorious settings in London, is all that remains of the medieval Augustinian nunnery of 𝔖𝔱 𝔐𝔞𝔯𝔶, founded by Jordan de Briset in 1140 on fourteen acres of land by the Clerks' Well, dissolved by Henry VIII in 1539, when it was the twelfth richest monastery in England, and demolished in 1780. Twelve years later James Carr rebuilt the church in a baroque style, described by John Summerson in Georgian London as 'a belated imitation of a Wren steeple', with colonial-style box pews at the back for church officers.

Clerkenwell Green

> Last Sunday evening I spent on Clerkenwell Green – a great assembly place for radical meetings – George Gissing, letter to his sister (1887)

Clerkenwell's village green, its appearance more like that of a continental piazza than a London square, was the medieval setting for the parish clerks' mystery plays and was where rebels from the North camped out during the 1381 Peasants' Revolt before destroying the nearby priory of St John. In the nineteenth century the Green became a popular setting for political demonstrations, and was where William Cobbett, author of *Rural Rides* (1830), spoke against the Corn Laws in February 1826. During the Chartist agitation of 1842 the prime minister, Robert Peel, banned public meetings from taking place here, but the Green later came to be used for rallies again: in 1867 to protest against the proposed hanging of three Fenians; in 1871 in support of the Paris Commune; and, most famously of all, on 13 November 1887, when Annie Besant and William Morris addressed a large crowd in favour of the right to assembly and marched to Trafalgar Square where a riot that became known as Bloody Sunday took place. The world's first May Day march left from Clerkenwell Green in 1890 and annual May Day marches still do so. Since the 1980s revival of Clerkenwell the Green has become a popular location for companies and smart restaurants, although plans outlined in October 2001 may yet see it shorn of its character with unsuitable new development.

Marx Memorial Library, No. 37a, north side

A socialist library containing some 100,000 books, pamphlets, tracts and publications, its collection includes the first published English translation of Marx and Engels's *Communist Manifesto*, the suffragettes' *Votes for Women* and William Morris's *Commonweal*. It is housed in what was built as a Welsh charity school in 1738 and from 1872 was home to the London Patriotic Club, a radical organization co-founded by John Stuart Mill that, unusually for the time, was open to women. In 1893 the premises were bought by the designer and socialist extraordinaire William Morris for the Twentieth Century Press, one of Britain's first left-wing print works, which produced the weekly journal *Justice* ('The Organ of the Social Democracy'). In 1902 the Russian revolutionary V. I. Lenin, who had just arrived in London, came here to produce his revolutionary communist paper, *Iskra* (The Spark), on a printing press that still survives

and in a room so cramped that, according to the Russian, 'there was no room for another chair'.

Iskra, which was bankrolled by the millionaire manufacturer Savva Morozov, moved to Geneva in April 1903, and after the Twentieth Century Press left Clerkenwell in 1922 the building was used by a variety of businesses until 1933 when, on the fiftieth anniversary of Marx's death, a conference held here led to the founding of the Marx Memorial Library, such a venture being chosen because at the time the Nazis in Germany were burning books. The building was saved from demolition in the 1960s after a campaign involving the poet John Betjeman that led to the discovery of tunnels in the basement that are linked with the former Sessions House on the west side of the Green and the now-demolished 𝕹𝖊𝖜𝖌𝖆𝖙𝖊 𝕻𝖗𝖎𝖘𝖔𝖓, and were once part of the medieval St Mary's nunnery.

► Marx's burial place, Highgate Cemetery, p. 335; Lenin's Bloomsbury haunts, p. 92.

Farringdon Lane

A street off Clerkenwell Green flanked by the deep ditch of the Metropolitan Railway, it once formed the embankment of the Fleet River.

The Clerks' Well, Nos. 14–16

The well which gave the area its name and was filled with 'excellent springs, the water of which is sweet, clear and salubrious', according to William Fitzstephen, secretary to the twelfth-century martyr Thomas à Becket, is visible through the window of 14–16 Farringdon Lane, although access is limited. The well went into disuse through pollution in the nineteenth century and was lost, but was rediscovered in 1924. The socialist magazine *New Statesman* had its offices here in the mid-1980s.

Farringdon Road

The road, originally Victoria Street, was cut through the area's worst slums along the course of the culverted Fleet River in 1845–6 and soon began to attract printers and publishers, the only surviving examples of which are the *Guardian* and *Observer* newspapers at Nos. 119–141. It soon became a major road, part of the main route linking King's Cross and Blackfriars Bridge, and was renamed Farringdon Road in 1863.

Guardian / Observer, Nos. 119–141, west side

The *Guardian*, Britain's only left-leaning national daily broadsheet, was founded in Manchester in 1821 as the *Manchester Guardian* and was published weekly until 1855 when Stamp Duty was abolished, after which it became a daily. C. P. Scott, editor and owner for fifty-seven years from 1872, originated the famous slogan that has long been the paper's guiding principle – 'Comment is free, facts are sacred' – and his son and successor, John Russell Scott, transferred ownership of the paper to a trust to protect his father's principles. The *Guardian* left Manchester in the 1960s to raise its profile, but in doing so lost its unique status as a national paper with a northern, rather than a metropolitan, perspective, and has survived financially not through sales but, ironically, through the subsidies of its illiberal stablemate, the *Manchester Evening News*.

In 1988 the *Guardian* underwent a costly and only partially successful redesign and in the 1990s many features were transferred from the main broadsheet edition to an increasingly downmarket tabloid section. However, improvement in its news section and the publication of a series of high-profile investigations into sleaze within the 1990s Tory government, in particular the behaviour of Tory MPs Neil Hamilton and Jonathan Aitken, saw the paper gain new credibility, especially after the latter, who vowed to fight the *Guardian* armed only with 'the simple sword of truth and the trusty shield of British fair play', not only lost his case but was convicted of perjury and sent to jail. Given the similarities between the *Guardian* and the *Observer* since the Second World War, a merger long seemed likely and this finally took place in 1993, a deal which meant that the liberal Left now had a Sunday voice.

► Early days of the *Observer*, p. 126.

St John's Square
Barely noticeable as a square and straddling both sides of the busy Clerkenwell Road,

---

Wilkes and liberty

John Wilkes, the best-known radical politician of eighteenth-century London, was born in St John's Square in 1725 and after becoming a country squire joined the Hell-Fire Club that met in the ruins of St Mary's Abbey at Medmenham for 'tasteful' orgies. When a fellow member, the Earl of Sandwich, warned Wilkes that he would die either of the pox or on the gallows, the latter memorably replied: 'That depends, my lord, whether I embrace your mistress or your principles.' In 1762 Wilkes published the first issue of his satirical journal, *The North Briton*, named in mock honour of the government's publication *The Briton*, and after attacking political corruption in Issue 45 (in April 1763) he was arrested on charges of seditious libel and sent to the Tower. Wilkes won his appeal and as the self-styled leader of the people against tyrannical government was cheered back to his Westminster home by crowds chanting 'For Wilkes and Liberty'. When in 1768 Wilkes entered Parliament as member for Middlesex his supporters chalked 'No. 45' (in honour of the offending volume) on various London buildings and on the soles of the Austrian ambassador's boots. Six years later he introduced a bill 'for the just and equal Representation of the People of England in Parliament', and later supported the independence claims of the American colonists (there are a number of American towns named after him), but his popularity waned after the 1780 Gordon Riots when in a desperate bid to reassert public order he ordered troops to fire on the crowd. Wilkes died in 1797.

► The Gordon Riots, p. 125.

St John's Square marks the site of the medieval 𝔓𝔯𝔦𝔬𝔯𝔶 𝔬𝔣 𝔖𝔱 𝔍𝔬𝔥𝔫, dissolved by Henry VIII in the mid sixteenth century. A number of aristocrats, including the Earls of Carlisle and Essex and the Bishop of Durham, built lavish properties here after the Fire of London. John Wilkes, the colourful eighteenth-century politician, was born here in 1725. The square declined after Clerkenwell Road was cut through its centre in 1879.

𝔓𝔯𝔦𝔬𝔯𝔶 𝔬𝔣 𝔖𝔱 𝔍𝔬𝔥𝔫, north side
A medieval priory founded in 1144 by Jordan de Briset, a local landowner, St John's was for centuries one of the most powerful institutions north of the City. It was here in 1185 that Heraclius, Patriarch of Jerusalem, met Henry II to urge England to join his war against the Turks and on being rebutted exclaimed: 'We come to seek a king, not money, for every corner of the world sends us money but not one a prince. Here is my head; treat me if you like as you did your brother [Thomas à Becket]; it matters little to me whether I die by your orders or in Syria by the hands of infidels, for you are worse than a Saracen', thereby bringing the meeting to an untimely end. Dick Whittington was given lodgings at St John's on arriving in London penniless in 1368, and thirteen years later the leaders of the Peasants' Revolt attacked and sacked the priory as it was the working address of Sir Robert Hales, 'Bob the Robber', the Lord Treasurer of England, who collected the hated poll tax. The priory was rebuilt, but after it was shut down in 1540 during the Reformation members fled to Malta, which remained the headquarters of the Knights of St John until Napoleon conquered the island in 1798. The former priory buildings were used as offices by the Master of Revels, who licensed plays, until the seventeenth century when they were mostly demolished, leaving only the Church of St John (see below) and the imposing gateway south of Clerkenwell Road (p. 79).

The Grand Priory Church of the Order of St John, east side
Modelled on the Church of the Holy Sepulchre in Jerusalem, and consecrated in 1185 by Heraclius, Patriarch of Jerusalem, who was in England to raise funds for the war against the Turks, the church is one of only two remaining structures of the medieval Priory of St John and its crypt is one of the few surviving Norman structures in London. In 1550 the Duke of Somerset, Protector of Edward VI, blew up the church and used the stone to build the first Somerset House on the Strand, the surviving crypt serving as a wine cellar for the next hundred years. When the graveyard was cleaned out in 1894 the cost of the work, which included scraping out human remains three feet deep, was passed on to ratepayers who took the council to court and lost. Since 1931 the church has been used by the charitable Order of St John.

(iii) Farringdon

The area south of Clerkenwell Road is dominated by the railway lines around Farringdon station and the buildings of Charterhouse, the former monastery and public school.

Charterhouse Square
The most dramatic-looking of London squares, thanks to its curious five-sided design, the buildings of Charterhouse and a collection of properties dating from the last four centuries.

Charterhouse, north side
An intriguing mixture of Tudor, Georgian and Victorian buildings, now mostly used by St Bartholomew's Hospital as a medical college, Charterhouse began in 1348 as a priory outside the City's jurisdiction. It was built on land used as a burial ground for some 40,000 victims of the Black Death, with twenty-four cells for monks living in solitary confinement and water piped down to the site from the hills around Barnsbury. The priory was closed down in 1535 when

John Houghton, the prior, and three monks who refused to accept Henry VIII as head of the Church and were accused of high treason, led away on a cart, dragged upside down through the streets to Tyburn gallows, and there half-hanged, disembowelled, and relieved of at least one limb each. One of Houghton's arms was then fastened to the outer gate of Charterhouse as a warning to others.

Elizabeth I used the premises to prepare for her Coronation in 1558, spending five days at Charterhouse as the crowds gathered outside, and it was also here that a later owner, Thomas Howard, Duke of Norfolk, plotted with Ridolfi, agent of King Philip of Spain, to overthrow Elizabeth and replace her with Mary Queen of Scots. In 1611 the property was sold to the mining magnate Thomas Sutton, reputedly the richest man in England, who played a prominent role in saving England from the Spanish Armada and was Ben Jonson's model for the venal Volpone, the title character of his 1605 play of the same name. In his will Sutton left funds to convert the buildings into a hospice for eighty military pensioners and a school for forty boys. The school opened as Charterhouse, famous alumni including Joseph Addison, who founded the *Spectator* (in the 1680s); John Wesley, founder of Methodism (1714–20); and William Makepeace Thackeray (1822–8), who was propositioned by a fellow pupil within five minutes of arriving on his first day and later lampooned Charterhouse as Slaughterhouse in *Vanity Fair* (1848) and more sympathetically as Greyfriars in *The Newcomes* (1855).

By the early nineteenth century the surrounding area had become so unpleasant that a tunnel connecting the school with the pupils' boarding house was built for the safety of pupils. The school moved to Surrey in 1872 and Merchant Taylors' school took over the site, moving in 1933 when the medical college for the nearby St Bartholomew's Hospital took the eastern portion. Charterhouse was bombed in May 1941 and the Elizabethan staircase where the Duke of

Norfolk was arrested was destroyed. Rebuilding uncovered parts of the original monastery, including one of the monks' cells and the Elizabethan Great Chamber, which was expertly restored. Charterhouse is now mostly offices for St Bartholomew's Hospital and home to a number of hospice pensioners.

Cowcross Street

Cattle en route to Smithfield market crossed the River Fleet at this point until 1855 when the market stopped using live animals. Eight years later Farringdon Street station (now Farringdon) opened here.

north side: Farringdon Road to St John Street

Farringdon station

Opened with brass bands and a banquet on 9 January 1863 as Farringdon Street, the eastern terminus of the Metropolitan Railway, the world's first underground line, the site was chosen because of the proximity of Smithfield market, with the western terminus at Praed Street (now Paddington). The line had been first planned in the 1840s as an attempt to solve the growing traffic problems in the capital, where the population had doubled since the start of the century, and the intention was for it to link the three London railway termini of Paddington, Euston and King's Cross (St Pancras not then having been built).

As the technology to encase a line in a tunnel well below ground level had not yet been developed, Charles Pearson, Solicitor to the City of London, MP for Lambeth and the main inspiration for the line, advocated a 'cut and cover' system of lines lying in shallow ditches that were occasionally open and occasionally covered. It took fourteen years to raise the money to build the line, and it was not until 1860 that the first shaft was sunk – in Euston Square. Building work involved not only constructing huge chasms in the roads, and diverting sewers and gas and water mains, but also protecting the line from the Westbourne, Tyburn and Fleet rivers, the latter bursting through a number of times. For the vehicles ordinary steam engines were unsuitable, as people would suffocate, but Pearson's suggestion that the trains be hauled by pulleys was rejected. Eventually, the engineer, John Fowler, advocated diverting the smoke and steam through exhaust ducts as the trains emerged from the tunnels.

The line was an immediate success and was soon carrying 12 million passengers, being extended to Moorgate the following year. Later extensions saw the line subsumed into the labyrinthine Metropolitan Line, the western section of which is now known as the Hammersmith and City Line.
▶ Metropolitan Line, p. 370.

St John's Lane
A road of great antiquity, it still contains much period charm, largely on account of the presence of the medieval St John's Gate at its northern end.
St John's Gate, north end
A gatehouse of Kentish ragstone, built in 1504, and one of the oldest structures in London, it was originally part of the Priory of St John of Jerusalem, which was sacked during the dissolution of the monasteries in the 1530s. In the sixteenth century it was adapted for commercial use and later incorporated a tavern run by Richard Hogarth, father of the eighteenth-century artist William, in which patrons had to speak in Latin, but which unsurprisingly flopped. It was also home of the *Gentleman's Magazine*, one of whose staff in the 1730s was Dr Johnson. The St John Ambulance Brigade was founded here in 1877. The gatehouse is home to the British Order of St John and contains a museum and library relating to the history of the Order.
▶ Priory of St John, p. 77.

St John Street
The main street leading from Smithfield to the Angel was until the mid nineteenth century the last leg of the journey for cattle and sheep being taken from the farms of Middlesex and Hertfordshire to the Smithfield livestock market and later became the home of scores of dingy workshops and offices. It now contains a number of smart restaurants and bars that have opened since the gentrification of the area in the 1990s.

(iv) Finsbury

The land north of Clerkenwell Green was a fen belonging to St Paul's Cathedral which was drained in the seventeenth century when gravel was laid down and houses built around the London terminus of the New River, the canal cut through from Hertfordshire to bring water to the capital. Much of the land was covered with cheap housing, but nearer Pentonville Road handsome houses were erected for the middle class, which are now among the most sought-out properties in central London.

The Borough of Finsbury that was created for the built-up community in 1900 was the most radical in London during the twentieth century until its abolition in 1965, when it was subsumed into Islington. It was responsible for the pioneering Finsbury Health Centre.

Exmouth Market
Baynes Row, where the clown Joseph Grimaldi grew up, was renamed Exmouth Street in honour of Admiral Pellew, Lord Exmouth, in 1818 and Exmouth Market in 1939, but little of the market remains now, save for one or two stalls by the Rosebery Avenue junction. At No. 70 is the London Spa pub, which is built on the site of a chalybeate spring that could supposedly cure all ailments and was a popular attraction in the eighteenth century.
Church of the Holy Redeemer, south side
The church was designed in 1888 in the Italian-basilica style of Brunelleschi's Church of Santo Spirito in Florence by John Dando Sedding, who wanted a building 'stately and impressive, uplifting the minds and hearts of those who dwelt beneath its shadow'. It stands on a site previously occupied by the Ducking House tavern and the Pantheon, an entertainments centre which

failed to attract sufficient custom and was converted into a Methodist Chapel. William Gladstone, the Liberal prime minister, laid the church's foundation stone in 1887. The bell-tower, parish hall and institute were later additions.

Pine Street
Finsbury Health Centre
A building of graceful white curves, Finsbury Health Centre was designed by the Georgian-born architect Berthold Lubetkin in 1935–6, some ten years before the creation of the National Health Service, for Finsbury Borough Council, then London's most radical borough, in an overcrowded working-class community of cramped terraced housing plagued by bad nutrition and poor health. The centre originally contained a TB clinic, chiropodist and delousing station. Rooms were given partition walls to allow flexibility and set at angles to allow the maximum daylight to enter, and by the entrance was a communal waiting area, where a map showed Finsbury at the heart of London and a mural urged locals 'to live out of doors as much as you can'. Remarkably, the centre has survived more or less intact, despite little spending on maintenance.

▶ Lubetkin's Highpoint, p. 333.

Rosebery Avenue
Built between 1889 and 1892 and cut diagonally through the area, Rosebery Avenue was named after Archibald Primrose Rosebery, the first chairman of the London County Council and prime minister at the end of the nineteenth century, and is the main route between Holborn and the Angel.

north side: Farrington Road to St John Street
New River Head / Former Thames Water headquarters, east of Hardwick Street
The New River, a canal bringing fresh water to London, was built between 1606 and 1613 by Hugh Myddelton, who obtained a loan from James I to begin work. It soon began providing Londoners with 38,000 gallons a day of water, which was brought 38 miles from springs at St Chad's Well in Ware, Hertfordshire, to a duck pond that stood near the modern day Sadler's Wells. To maintain the purity of the water, bathing was forbidden and watchmen were employed to ensure no one entered the water. Nevertheless the poet Samuel Taylor Coleridge swam across the river fully clothed when he was seventeen and after remaining in his wet clothes for the rest of the day spent the following six months in Christ's Hospital with rheumatic fever. The New River Company built its headquarters at this site in 1920, its Oak Room containing woodwork carved by Grinling Gibbons. The building was used by the Thames Water Authority until 1987 and has since been converted into luxurious apartments.
Sadler's Wells, east of Arlington Way
Britain's premier dance venue since the 1930s, Sadler's Wells is named after Thomas Sadler, who discovered a well with supposed medicinal qualities at the London end of the New River in 1683 and created a garden and wooden concert hall briefly known as Miles's Musick-house. It was here in 1798 that the poet William Wordsworth saw 'Singers, Rope-dancers, Giants and Dwarfs, Clowns, Conjurors, Posture-masters, Harlequins', as he recorded in *The Prelude*. At the beginning of the nineteenth century the venue was managed by the clown Joseph Grimaldi, who had made his first public appearance here as an infant dancer aged fourteen months in 1781, and hosted Charles Dibdin's aquatic plays in a water tank under the stage. It was later used for actor-manager Samuel Phelps's bowdlerized versions of Shakespeare's plays, and after Phelps retired in 1862 it became a skating rink, boxing venue, music hall and cinema, until it closed in 1906. Lilian Baylis rescued Sadler's Wells in the 1930s and it reopened in 1931 with a performance of Shakespeare's *Twelfth Night*, starring John Gielgud and Ralph Richardson. Damaged in the Second World War, the venue reopened in 1945 with the première of Benjamin Britten's *Peter Grimes*, which heralded a successful

run of operas, and was completely rebuilt in the 1990s with a stage door that also serves as the public entrance and a borehole on the site from which water is bottled and sold.
▶ Covent Garden Opera House, p. 109.

St John Street
Spa Green Estate
One of the most thoughtfully designed postwar estates in Britain, and one of four local developments designed by Berthold Lubetkin's Tecton team, Spa Green was planned in the 1930s when Lubetkin, the Georgian-born architect, convinced Finsbury council of his grand vision of an estate incorporating new housing, schools and a health centre. Construction was held over until after the Second World War, however, when Lubetkin was joined by the Danish engineer Ove Arup and, using box-frame concrete imported from Denmark, created an estate of eight-storey and four-storey blocks. Living areas were arranged so that they received at least some sunlight during the day and bedrooms were placed in the shadier areas, as in Lubetkin's luxury High-point in Highgate. The lavish budget also allowed for woodblock floors and kitchen waste-disposal units using the latest technology, which still work.

(v) St Luke's

A large triangle of land between City Road and Goswell Road, populated by an almost entirely working-class community, St Luke's is buffered by sought-after Clerkenwell to the west and the newly fashionable Hoxton to the east and is named after the now disused Hawksmoor church of St Luke on Old Street.

Bunhill Row
The poet John Milton finished his epic work *Paradise Lost* (1667) and wrote its follow-up, *Paradise Regained* (1671), and *Samson Agonistes* (also 1671) in a house at **No. 125**, where he lived between 1663 and 1674 and which has long been demolished. The east side of the street is dominated by Bunhill

Fields, the largest green space in the vicinity.
east side: Old Street to Chiswell Street
Braithwaite House
The Kray twins, Reggie and Ronnie, were arrested for the last time in the early hours of the morning of 8 May 1968 at their mother's flat in the Braithwaite House tower block after a painstaking two-year investigation into their activities. When police smashed down the front door they found Reg asleep with a girl from Walthamstow and Ronnie in bed with his latest boyfriend, his jacket, lying beside the bed, containing a list of those he wished to see murdered. The twins received life imprisonment for the murders of Jack 'The Hat' McVitie and George Cornell, Ronnie never seeing freedom again and Reggie released only when the authorities knew he was dying.
▶ The Krays' gangland activities, pp. 306, 310; the Krays at the Old Bailey, p. 59.
Bunhill Fields
Known as Bone Hill Fields after the authorities moved a quantity of bones from St Paul's Churchyard to the site in 1549, it was used as a cemetery for Nonconformists from 1657 to 1854 and was where, according to Daniel Defoe in *A Journal of the Plague Year* (1722): 'many [plague victims] who were infected and near their end, and delirious also, ran wrapped in blankets or rags and threw themselves in and expired there'. Defoe himself was buried here, but as he had been hiding from creditors and other enemies when he died in 1731, his tombstone was marked 'Mr Dubow'. Nearly 150 years later, an obelisk was erected for the author by his grave after an appeal in *The Christian World* newspaper, but it later disappeared and was discovered in the 1930s in Southampton, after which it was moved to Stoke Newington Library. When Susanna Wesley, the mother of the founder of Methodism, John Wesley, was buried here in 1742, Wesley himself conducted the service in front of a large crowd. Others buried in what the early-nineteenth-century poet Robert Southey described as the

Campo Santo of Nonconformity include the writers John Bunyan and William Blake, whose stone receives regular bunches of fresh flowers. The southern section of the fields are used as playing fields by the Honourable Artillery Company, the oldest military body in the City, and it was here that some of London's first cricket matches were played in the eighteenth century.

City Road

The main road leading into the City from the Angel.

Independent (1986–c. 98), No. 40, west side
The youngest national newspaper in Britain by almost a hundred years, the *Independent* was set up in 1986 by three *Daily Telegraph* journalists – Matthew Symonds, Stephen Glover and city editor Andreas Whittam Smith – who wanted to take advantage of the latest developments in newspaper technology that had already seen an explosion of free mass-market titles to launch a quality daily and chose a City Road site for their offices, as it was neither in Fleet Street nor Docklands. Around one-third of the new posts were filled by journalists from *The Times* and *Sunday Times*, who were unhappy about the editorial direction of the papers under Rupert Murdoch and the titles' recent move to Wapping. The launch in October 1986 was an editorial, if not a financial, success, the public quickly warming to the paper's elegant typography, grand front-page photographs, quality writing, particularly in the foreign pages, and the idea of a newspaper that was independent of a figurehead proprietor and of party political bias.

Inevitably, costs were higher than budgeted, and circulation barely reached 250,000; however, by the end of 1988 the paper was making a profit and sales were being achieved at the expense of the *Guardian*. In April 1987 Whittam Smith published extracts from the banned book *Spycatcher*, the memoirs of Peter Wright, a former British spy, which alleged that MI5 had tried to destabilize the Labour govern-ment of Harold Wilson in the 1960s. Whittam Smith risked going to jail under the Official Secrets Act, but when the government backed down the editor became a hero. A Sunday edition was soon begun, with mixed results, failing to find its own identity in the market place, and in 1994, when circulation fell below 300,000 for the first time in six years, Whittam Smith announced that a consortium of investors led by Mirror Group Newspapers was to take over the paper, a move that ended the *Independent*'s autonomy and removed its unique status. The paper is now based at Canary Wharf.

► Fleet Street, p. 41.

Wesley's Chapel and House, No. 49, east side
In 1739 the Methodists opened their main chapel (converted from a foundry), which John Wesley, the founder of Methodism, who often preached in the fields outside before crowds of 10,000, described as 'perfectly neat, but not fine'. Wesley lived in a house to the west, on the modern-day City Road, which is now a museum of Methodism.

John Wesley's general rules of employing time
In creating a 'method' for living his life Wesley drew up a list of nine guiding points:
1. Begin and end every day with God; and sleep not immoderately.
2. Be diligent in your calling.
3. Employ all spare hours in religion; as able.
4. Keep all holidays as holy-days.
5. Avoid drunkards and busybodies.
6. Avoid curiosity, and useless employments and knowledge.
7. Examine yourself every night.
8. Never on any account pass a day without setting aside at least an hour for devotion.
9. Avoid all manner of passion.

BLOOMSBURY, WC1

With its university buildings, Georgian squares, and the British Museum, Bloomsbury has been a centre of intellectual and creative activity since the nineteenth century and was where the Bloomsbury Group, whose members included Virginia Woolf and Lytton Strachey, hosted their salons early in the twentieth century.

In 1201 William de Blemund bought land locally and set his manor house to the south of what is now Bloomsbury Square. Although de Blemund's descendants were forced to relinquish the land after the baronial revolt against Henry III in the 1260s, they are remembered in the name of the area. In 1375 the land was acquired by Charterhouse, the Carthusian monastery near Smithfield, and after Henry VIII dissolved the monasteries in the 1530s he apportioned Bloomsbury to his Lord Chancellor, Thomas Wriothesley, later Earl of Southampton (hence Southampton Row, the name of the main road that bisects Bloomsbury).

Bloomsbury grew substantially after the Building Act of 1774, which forced developers to adopt more professional practices, and it became the first part of London to be built with straight new streets (Southampton Row, Gower Street) and squares (Bloomsbury Square, Russell Square, Bedford Square).

Bloomsbury's two major institutions, University College and the British Museum, were created in the nineteenth century, and over the next hundred years the area was at its creative peak, home to progressive movements such as Christian Socialism, the Pre-Raphaelite Brotherhood and the Bloomsbury Group of writers. The relative absence of wartime bombing, compared with other parts of London, and the University of London's willingness to preserve the building fabric, has helped create the modern-day Bloomsbury, whose Georgian elegance and ordered streets make it an ideal antidote to the excesses of the neighbouring West End.

(i) around the colleges

The straight roads between Euston Road and Russell Square are dominated by academic institutions connected with the University of London, which, during its vast twentieth-century expansion, took over many of Thomas Cubitt's early-nineteenth-century buildings, preserving the façades but renovating within.

Byng Place
University Church of Christ the King, west side

Built between 1851 and 1854 in the Early English style for the Catholic Apostolic sect, its first preacher was Edward Irving, who had been expelled from the Presbyterian church in Regent Square, St Pancras, for encouraging the congregation to 'speak in tongues' (talk spontaneously in ancient biblical languages). The Apostolic movement died out in the twentieth century, and in 1963 the trustees leased the building to the Church of England for London University's chaplaincy, an arrangement that recently ended. Although the spire, which the architect wanted as the tallest in London, was never built, the poet John Betjeman praised the church as having 'the something extra which raises it out of mere copying into great architecture'. In the church basement is a room filled with ceremonial cloaks, including one reserved for the return of Jesus Christ.

Gordon Square

Begun by Thomas Cubitt in the 1820s, and completed after his death by his son, Lewis, designer of King's Cross station, Gordon Square was later home to members of the Bloomsbury Group of writers and intellectuals, including Virginia Stephen (Virginia Woolf), who lived at No. 46 from 1904 to 1907, and the economist John Maynard Keynes, who lived at the same address from

The Bloomsbury Group

The Bloomsbury Group of writers, artists and critics had its origins in the Apostles society at Cambridge University, which reassembled at 46 Gordon Square in the early twentieth century. Members included Virginia Stephen (later Woolf); Clive Bell; Vanessa Stephen, who staged Britain's first exhibition of Post-Impressionist paintings; the biographer Lytton Strachey; the critic Roger Fry; Gwen Darwin, granddaughter of the famous anthropologist Charles Darwin; the economist John Maynard Keynes; and the novelist E. M. Forster. The name 'Bloomsbury Group', along with the nickname 'Bloomsberries' for its members, first appeared around 1910. Unlike other contemporary bodies, such as the Vorticists, the Bloomsbury Group had no formal membership and published no manifesto, but followed the teachings of the philosopher G. E. Moore, whose *Principia Ethica* (1903) alleged that 'by far the most valuable things are . . . the pleasures of human intercourse and the enjoyment of beautiful objects'.

The Group's self-righteousness and risqué lifestyles – Virginia Woolf had a relationship with Vita Sackville-West; Lytton Strachey with Dora Carrington and Ralph Partridge – repelled many. The poet Rupert Brooke spoke of the 'rotten atmosphere in the Stracheys' treacherous and wicked circle',

D. H. Lawrence denounced 'this horror of little swarming selves'; Wyndham Lewis called them 'elitist, corrupt and talentless', satirizing them mercilessly in his 1930 novel *The Apes of God*; while the poet and critic Osbert Sitwell mocked their mannerisms with phrases such as 'how simply too extraordinary' and 'exquisitely civilised'. Although the Group's influence was minimal, its place in history was secured on account of what the *Encyclopaedia Britannica* described as the 'extraordinary number of talented persons associated with it'.

Bloomsbury Group sites

38 Brunswick Square Five members of the Bloomsbury Group, including Virginia Woolf and John Maynard Keynes, lived in 1911 and 1912 in **No. 38**, a house that was destroyed in the Second World War.

37 Gordon Square The painters and Bloomsbury Group acolytes Vanessa Bell and Duncan Grant had rooms at No. 37 in 1925.

46 Gordon Square When Virginia Stephen moved into No. 46 in 1904 Bloomsbury was down-at-heel and unfashionable, but the address soon became the main meeting place for the Bloomsbury Group. A later resident was the economist John Maynard Keynes. In 1974 No. 46 was leased to Birkbeck College.

50 Gordon Square Home from 1922 to

1916 to 1946. Many of the properties are now owned by the University of London.

Gower Street

One of Bloomsbury's most prominent streets – past residents include Charles Dickens and Charles Darwin, though the houses of both have since been demolished – Gower Street was named after Lady Gertrude Leveson-Gower, wife of the 4th Duke of Bedford, who in 1790 was in charge of building its first houses. It was described by the mid-nineteenth-century arch critic John Ruskin as the '*ne plus ultra* of ugliness in

street architecture', a description that now seems unfair. The first ever exhibition of a railway engine took place on a patch of waste ground at the northern end of Gower Street in 1802, when a steam-powered locomotive pulled a carriage on a small circular track enclosed by a high fence. The exhibition was organized by the mining engineer Richard Trevithick, who developed his high-pressure steam engine ten years before George Stephenson, but who after leaving for South America lost out to the latter in the race to develop a workable railway

1939 to Clive Bell, the art critic and promoter of the Post-Impressionists, and a regular meeting place for the Bloomsbury Group.

51 Gordon Square Lytton Strachey, the biographer and essayist, moved into No. 51 in 1919 shortly after writing *Eminent Victorians*, his controversial critique of Victorian values, which revolutionized biography writing.

34 Mecklenburgh Square Virginia Woolf addressed envelopes for the People's Suffrage Federation here before the First World War and later cast the property as the workplace of Mary Datchet in her novel *Night and Day*. **No. 34** was also home of the Women's Trade Union League and the National Anti-Sweating League.

37 Mecklenburgh Square The Woolfs, Virginia and Leonard, moved to Mecklenburgh Square in August 1939, and there Virginia wrote the last chapters of her biography of Roger Fry, despite her claims that the impending war with Germany made it hard to concentrate.

52 Tavistock Square Virginia Woolf wrote *Mrs Dalloway* (1925), *To the Lighthouse* (1927), *Orlando* (1928), *A Room of One's Own* (1929) and *The Waves* (1931) while living here from 1924 to 1939. The property was bombed in October 1940 and has since been replaced by the Tavistock Hotel.

system, and returned to Britain penniless in 1827. London's first underground railway would have been built under Gower Street had plans announced in the 1830s to extend the Euston–Birmingham railway to a new central London terminus by the Thames been approved. Gower Street is now dominated by university buildings and small hotels.

west side: Bedford Square to Euston Road
Birthplace of the Pre-Raphaelite Brotherhood, No. 7
The Pre-Raphaelite Brotherhood, Britain's best-known art movement, was founded here in 1848 by the painters Dante Gabriel Rossetti, William Holman Hunt and John Everett Millais who wanted to create a body of work similar in brightness of colour, attention to detail and honest simplicity to the period of Italian painting prior to Raphael Sanzio (1483–1520). Rossetti wanted the group's name to include the then fashionable term 'Early Christian', and when Hunt objected and proposed 'Pre-Raphaelite' Rossetti added the word 'Brotherhood', as he wanted the body to be secret, in line with the Italian political group the Carbonaris. In the summer of 1849 they staged their first exhibition, in which Dante Gabriel Rossetti's *The Girlhood of Mary Virgin* was signed 'PRB' to maintain the society's air of mystery, but the Brotherhood fell apart when Millais, whom Ruskin had taken under his wing, was elected to be an Associate of the previously despised Royal Academy and Holman Hunt left for Palestine.
► Dante Gabriel Rossetti in Chelsea, p. 419.

Frank Dutton Jackson's 'Temple of the Occult', No. 99
Frank Dutton Jackson, a fake cleric, and his wife, Editha, set up a Temple of the Occult at No. 99 in the early years of the twentieth century, where Jackson, or Theo Horos as he preferred to be called, debauched hundreds of young girls in mock religious ceremonies amid incense smoke and under subdued lights. Dutton told one girl, Daisy Adams, that he was Jesus Christ and that she would give birth to a divine child. But he and Editha (who claimed to be the illegitimate daughter of Ludwig I of Bavaria) were eventually prosecuted and tried at the Old Bailey where, despite Jackson's plea, 'Did Solomon not have 300 legal wives and 600 others?', he was convicted of raping and procuring girls for immoral purposes. The

Spectator magazine occupied the building from the 1920s to 1975 and No. 99 now belongs to the Catholic chaplaincy.

east side: Euston Road to Montague Place

𝔐𝔍5 𝔥𝔢𝔞𝔡𝔮𝔲𝔞𝔯𝔱𝔢𝔯𝔰 (1970–94), No. 140 MI5, the semi-secret government department responsible for combating terrorism and subversion, was based in a drab 1950s block at the corner of Gower Street and Euston Road, known to those who worked in it as 'Russia House', until 1994. Three years previously Stella Rimington had been appointed as MI5's first woman Director General following an unprecedented public announcement, part of prime minister John Major's policy of limited openness regarding the security services, something which had been unthinkable during the Cold War. The block was demolished at the end of the decade and rebuilt by Michael Hopkins as the Wellcome Trust's new headquarters.

▶ MI5 in Millbank, p. 247.

University College, south of Gower Place University College, founded in 1826 and based on William Wilkins's classical revival building of 1829, came into existence after a group of radical early-nineteenth-century freethinkers that included James Mill (father of the better-known philosopher John Stuart Mill), the poet Thomas Campbell and the law reformer Lord Brougham decided that Regency London would benefit from a university that was non-residential and included students and lecturers regardless of their religious beliefs, unlike Oxford and Cambridge, which had an Anglicans-only policy. The new institution opened as University College in 1826 and was derided as 'the Godless College on Gower Street' by critics who established an Anglican rival, King's College, on the Strand two years later. Parliament, asked to choose between the two in 1836, decided to favour neither college but to create an umbrella body, the University of London, to administer exams for both sets of students. University College was the first British university to grant degrees to women.

Jeremy Bentham

Jeremy Bentham, the eighteenth-century philosopher, bequeathed a large sum of money to University College on condition that his own skeleton be preserved and displayed every year at the annual general meeting. Every year the mummified Bentham is taken along to the AGM enclosed in a mahogany case with folding glass doors, seated in an armchair and holding his favourite walking stick. Over the years there have been some cosmetic changes to the skeleton: the head is a wax model, the original being stored in the college safe, and the underclothes were changed as recently as 1935, a visiting academic insisting on it before giving a lecture. The late philosopher, who resides in a prominent public position in the South Cloister, is also taken to the board of governors' meeting once a week where he is registered as present but not voting.

Malet Street

The street, which lies to the east of Gower Street, is home to a number of academic buildings including the London School of Hygiene and Tropical Medicine, the Vanbrugh Theatre, where plays are staged by students from the nearby Royal Academy of Dramatic Arts, Birkbeck College and Senate House, the administrative headquarters of the University of London.

Senate House, east side opposite Keppel Street

Headquarters of the University of London and model for George Orwell's Ministry of Truth in *1984*, Senate House was one of London's first skyscrapers, built by Charles Holden between 1927 and 1936, and three years later, at the start of the Second World War, was commandeered by the government to house the Ministry of Information, which was satirized by Evelyn Waugh as 'that great mass of masonry . . . the vast bulk of London University insulting the autumnal sky' in his 1942 novel about the Phoney War, *Put Out More Flags*. According to the poet Dylan Thomas, the ministry attracted 'all the shysters in London . . . all the half-poets, the boiled newspaper men, submen from the island of crabs . . . trying to find a safe niche'. Among those who worked here alongside Thomas were the poet John Betjeman and the novelist Graham Greene, who claimed staff often had to wait up to twenty-four hours to receive replies to memos, and that the building was like a beacon 'guiding German planes towards King's Cross and St Pancras stations', although some believe the Luftwaffe spared the block as Hitler wanted it for his post-conquest London headquarters. After the war Senate House reverted to its original role, as headquarters of the University of London.

● Other Charles Holden buildings in London include Birkbeck College, also on Malet Street, and the highly praised suburban stations on the Piccadilly Line, with Park Royal and Arnos Grove of particular note.

Russell Square

London's second-largest square stands on land used during the English Civil War by the Parliamentarians, who constructed bulwarks later moulded into a terraced walk for the gardens of the 1657-built Southampton House. The square features in William Thackeray's *Vanity Fair* (1848) and Virginia Woolf's *Night and Day* (1919).

Russell Hotel, Nos. 1–9, east side
Victorian architecture at its most flamboyant, Charles Fitzroy Doll's 1898 hotel, built in the French Gothic style, features colonnaded balconies, cherubs and four female figures in period costume above the main entrance representing the four Protestant pre-twentieth-century English queens – Elizabeth, Mary II, Anne and Victoria. While dining at the hotel on 3 September 1939, the day the Second World War broke out, the Sunderland football team, hearing the sound of air raid sirens, rushed into the street to see what was happening but were chased back into the hotel by the police who made the team take refuge on the *third* floor, believing it to be the safest place in case of flying glass.

Tavistock Square

Built in 1820 by Thomas Cubitt, the first London builder to use a permanent workforce, who was responsible for constructing parts of Barnsbury, Belgravia and Stoke Newington, and once a quiet residential enclave, Tavistock Square is now part of the main route between Holborn and Euston, dominated by the grotesque brickwork of the British Medical Association's headquarters.

It stands on the site of the house where Charles Dickens lived from 1851 to 1860 and wrote *Bleak House* (1853), *Hard Times* (1854), *Little Dorrit* (1857) and parts of *A Tale of Two Cities* (1859). The gardens opposite contain a memorial stone dedicated to conscientious objectors, unveiled by the composer Michael Tippett in 1994, and a statue of the Indian leader Mahatma Gandhi designed by the Polish born artist Fredda Brilliant.

(ii) around the British Museum

Bedford Square

Bloomsbury's oldest complete Georgian square, spoilt by over-zealous pedestrianization, Bedford Square was financed by the money that flowed into London after the 1763 Peace of Paris, a treaty which recognized the independence of the American colonies and, according to the 4th Duke of Bedford, 'excited a rage for building'. The square was home to a number of publishers during the twentieth century, providing offices at various times for Jonathan Cape, Frederick Warne, Michael Joseph, Hodder and Stoughton and the Publishers' Association.

No. 6, east side
During the nineteenth century the property was the official home of the Lord Chancellor, its best-known incumbent of the period being Lord Eldon, who held the

office from 1804 to 1815 and was characterized acerbically by the poet Shelley in the
lines 'next came Fraud, and he had on / Like
Eldon, an ermined gown' in his vitriolic 1819
work, 'The Mask of Anarchy'.

Eldon, as Attorney-General, had antagonized opponents by suspending Habeas
Corpus between 1794 and 1801, prosecuting
members of the radical London Corresponding Society, and helping pass the
Corn Laws, which protected landowners
from cheap imports of grain and ensured an
artificially high price for bread. In 1815 he
bore the brunt of the anti-Corn Law
protests when a mob besieged his house for
three weeks. When at one point a rioter
broke into the property and came face to
face with Eldon the latter thundered: 'If you
don't mind what you are about you will be
hanged,' which led the man to reply:
'Perhaps so, but I think it looks now as if
you will be hanged first.'

Bloomsbury Square
Bloomsbury Square, the first junction of
roads in London to be called a square, was
created as Southampton Square in 1657 by
the Earl of Southampton with the unusual
layout of housing for wealthy families on
three sides and servants' houses on the
fourth. Its status declined when the south
side became a major traffic route in the
late nineteenth century, and around a
hundred years later the north side became
blighted while the authorities debated the
merits of a scheme to build a new British
Library in the neighbourhood, an idea
abandoned in 1981. None of the original
houses survives.

east side
The east side of Bloomsbury Square is occupied by Victoria House, a huge Beaux Arts
block built between 1925 and 1932 for the
Liverpool Victoria Friendly Society, which
was abandoned at the end of the twentieth
century and briefly considered for the headquarters of the London mayor and the
newly formed Greater London Authority
until a site by Tower Bridge was preferred.

In the late eighteenth century **No. 29** was
home to the Lord Chief Justice, Lord Mansfield, and was attacked and razed to the
ground in June 1780 by the anti-Catholic
Gordon Rioters who suspected Mansfield of
having sympathy for Catholicism. Mansfield
fled the property by the back door as the
rioters, fuelled by a rumour that the king
had been buried in the ruins of Buckingham
Palace and Lord North, the prime minister,
hanged in Downing Street, gathered outside,
eventually breaking in and destroying his
law library. Mansfield himself later presided
over Lord George Gordon's trial for inciting
the riots, and won much acclaim among
anti-slavery campaigners for refusing a
request to repatriate a black slave, James
Somersett. Dickens incorporated the riots
into his 1841 novel *Barnaby Rudge* in which
the half-witted eponymous hero is due to be
hanged in the square for his part in the
events but wins a last-minute reprieve.
▶ The Gordon Riots, p. 125.

Bloomsbury Way
St George, north side between Museum
Street and Bury Place
St George, the most complex architecturally
of Nicholas Hawksmoor's eight churches,
took fifteen years to complete (1716–31), due
to the inaccessibility of a site hemmed in by
houses. On completion it was criticized by
James Ralph, the architecture writer, who
complained: ' 'Tis built all of stone, adorned
with a pompous portico, and yet is ridiculous and absurd even to a proverb.'
'Pompous portico' refers to the steeple, in
the form of a stepped pyramid and
modelled on Pliny's description of the
Mausoleum at Halicarnassus, at the top of
which stands a statue of George I – the only
statue of the non-English-speaking king in
Britain. The church's burial ground was
unpopular until Robert Nelson, the religious
pamphleteer, was interred there, leading the
historian Timbs to remark: 'people like to
be buried in company, and in good
company'. The funeral of the suffragette
Emily Davison, who threw herself under the

king's horse at the 1913 Derby, was held at St George's.

► Christ Church Spitalfields, p. 285.

Great Russell Street

Renowned for its peaches and snipes at the end of the seventeenth century, according to the historian Lord Macaulay, the street's rural nature began to disappear when a seven-acre plot of land to the west of Bloomsbury's manor house was granted in 1675 to Ralph Montagu. He in turn then built Montagu House, which later became the first home of the British Museum.

north side: Tottenham Court Road to Bloomsbury Street

No. 106

When the Second World War Home Guard refused to allow women to join their ranks, even though they were teaching male recruits to fire guns, fifty women, including Marjorie Foster, a winner of the King's Prize for shooting, met here and formed the Amazon Defence Corps. Before long similar units had been set up across Britain.

No. 62

The Bloomsbury Dispensary opened at this address in 1801 and employed as Superintendent of Inoculation Edward Jenner, who conducted pioneering work into vaccination, carrying out more than 800 inoculations over a ten-year period and treating all the children at the nearby Foundlings Hospital.

No. 59

The travel pioneer Thomas Cook opened his first London office at this address in 1862. As the lease forbade him to advertise the business, he named the premises Cook's British Museum Boarding House.

British Museum, between Bloomsbury Street and Montague Street

Britain's foremost museum, home to one of the world's greatest collections of antiquities and manuscripts, was established from the 1753 bequest of the physician Sir Hans Sloane, who left a wealth of plants, fossils, minerals, pathological specimens, coins, books, prints and drawings. It opened on 15 January 1759 in Montagu House, the property that then stood on the site, for three hours a day to those who had made a written application for tickets.

The collection soon grew beyond all expectations. An Act of Parliament passed the year Sloane died allowed the founders to buy Robert Harley's manuscript archive; public lottery raised £300,000; George II donated his 12,000-volume library, which comprised volumes collected by every monarch since Henry VIII, in 1757; and when British troops defeated Napoleon in Egypt in 1801 more treasures, including the Rosetta Stone, key to Egyptian hieroglyphics, and the Elgin Marbles, were accumulated.

During a visit to the museum in 1818 the poet Shelley, inspired by the many Egyptian artefacts, including the granite statues of Rameses II, which had recently been added to the collection, was inspired to write the sonnet 'Ozymandias'. John Keats, Shelley's contemporary, wrote 'Ode on a Grecian Urn' (1820) after seeing on a visit to the museum, what he mistakenly took for a Greek antiquity. It was, in fact, a Wedgwood copy of a Roman copy of a Greek urn, made not in Etruria, Italy, but near Etruria, Stoke-on-Trent.

Sir Robert Smirke was hired to expand Montagu House for the growing collection in the 1820s and thirty years later Smirke's younger brother, Sidney, designed the Reading Room with the second-largest dome in the world after the Pantheon in Rome, later immortalized by Virginia Woolf in her 1929 essay 'A Room of One's Own' ('the vast dome . . . the huge, bald forehead which is so splendidly encircled by a band of famous names'). The Reading Room closed in 1997 when the museum's book collection, known since 1973 as the British Library, moved to new headquarters in St Pancras.

British Museum glossary

British Library (1759–1997) After the eighteenth-century novelist Tobias Smollett complained that the museum lacked a good book collection, the trustees began accumulating a copy of every book, newspaper and magazine published in Britain. The library soon became the main literary research centre in the country and after nearly 250 years moved to St Pancras in October 1997. The space has since been reworked into the Great Court.

Elgin Marbles Sculptures dating back to the fifth century BC, they were removed from the Parthenon in Athens by Lord Elgin in the early years of the nineteenth century, sold to the museum for £35,000 in 1816, and have been the subject of much wrangling between the British and Greek governments since.

Flood Tablet A seventh-century clay tablet written in cuneiform script that was once in the Assyrian royal library, it relates the story of the Epic of Gilgamesh, a flood similar to that ascribed to Noah in the Bible.

Lindisfarne Gospels The first written translation of any part of the Bible into English, the gospels were produced by a monk, Eadfrith, on the island of Lindisfarne (Holy Island), off the Northumbrian coast, *c.* 698.

Lindow Man The preserved remains of an Ancient Briton who was garrotted and thrown into a peat bog in Lindow, Cheshire, *c.* 300 BC, it was discovered in 1984 and sent to the museum.

Manuscripts The museum contains two of the four surviving copies of the Magna Carta, King John's treaty with the barons in 1215; a manuscript of *The Canterbury Tales*; the first folio editions of Shakespeare's plays; the manuscript of James Joyce's *Finnegans Wake*; and Lewis Carroll's handwritten *Alice in Wonderland*.

Nereid Monument The monument of a reconstruction of a Greek tomb from Asia Minor, originated *c.* 400 BC, which was discovered during an archaeological dig in 1838 and put back together over the next 100 years.

Rosetta Stone A slab of black basalt, 4 ft by 2½ ft, discovered near the Egyptian town of Rashid (Rosetta), it took fifteen years to be deciphered and was found to be the key to the Egyptian hieroglyphs. Its worth was established when researchers discovered that the frequently occurring elongated ovals always contain a royal name.

Tutankhamun In 1972 the museum exhibited 'Treasures of Tutankhamun', loaned from Egypt, and received 1,694,117 visitors.

south side: Bloomsbury Street to Tottenham Court Road

New Oxford Street

A relatively new major street for central London, built in the 1840s as part of the slum clearance scheme that wiped out the St Giles Rookery, it soon became a busy shopping street. An early shopkeeper was the pharmacist Thomas Holloway, one of the first businessmen to use newspaper advertising to promote his wares, who amassed a fortune, which he mostly gave to charity, and founded the Royal Holloway College in Egham, Surrey. Nineteenth-century New Oxford Street also sported a huge lending library (Mudie's), cheap restaurants, and oddities such as James Smith and Sons' umbrella store at No. 53, founded in 1830, which survives today with an unspoilt Victorian frontage. In the 1940s a number of bleak, utilitarian, steel-framed buildings with deep shafts and linked by tunnels were constructed on New Oxford Street so that they could be used by civil servants for governing London if the war intensified. They are now office blocks but the tunnels remain in place.

(iii) east Bloomsbury

Doughty Street

One of Bloomsbury's most sought-after streets, on account of its luxurious Georgian terraced houses and the presence of Charles Dickens's one-time address at No. 48 (now the Dickens Museum), it was built by Henry Doughty as Upper John Street between 1792 and 1822 with security gates at each end. This led the journalist Edmund Yates, who lived at No. 43, to declare: '[Doughty] is none of your common thoroughfares to be rattled through by vulgar cabs and earth-shaking Pickford vans'. Harriet Vane, the fiancée of Lord Peter Wimsey in Dorothy L. Sayers's stories, lives at No. 100, a fictitious address, and in George Orwell's *Keep the Aspidistra Flying* (1936) Gordon Comstock, the anti-hero and would-be poet, takes a furnished room in the street as 'it felt vaguely literary living in Bloomsbury'.

Guilford Street

𝔉𝔬𝔲𝔫𝔡𝔩𝔦𝔫𝔤 𝔥𝔬𝔰𝔭𝔦𝔱𝔞𝔩 / **Coram's Fields**, north side
Coram's Fields, a large, oddly shaped expanse of greenery in the centre of Bloomsbury, stands on the site of the Foundling (orphan) Hospital which Thomas Coram, a shipwright whose mother had died when he was seven, established in 1741 in Hatton Garden and moved to this 56-acre site, then known as Conditeschotte Field, four years later. Within a few years of moving to Bloomsbury the hospital was taking more than 1,000 children a year, and it ran what was for the time a humane regime: each child was given a name (usually of a hospital governor or his wife, or a biblical character); boys left at fourteen with an apprenticeship or a place in the army arranged; and the girls went into service. The hospital moved to Berkhamstead in 1926 after the governors decided that living in central London was no longer conducive to the good health of its charges (it has since closed), and the Bloomsbury site was demolished. The new owner of the field, James White, proposed a plan to move Covent Garden market here, which he dropped after a public outcry, and instead a campaign was launched to buy the land and build children's playing fields on the site, a scheme that was achieved with help from Harold Harmsworth (Lord Rothermere), owner of the *Daily Mail*. The playing fields are still in use, entry available to adults only when accompanied by a child, and some of the hospital architecture survives, including the eastern colonnade, the gateway and the lodges, in whose niches mothers used to leave their babies in a basket before ringing the bell and running away.

Lamb's Conduit Street

William Lambe, a member of the Clothworkers' Company City trade guild, constructed a conduit to take water from local springs to Snow Hill in the City in 1577 (a plaque in nearby Long Yard states that 'Lamb's conduit is the property of the City of London. This pump is erected for the benefit of the publick'). It fell into disuse after the New River opened in 1613, but it was not until 1851 that the reservoir which fed the conduit was rediscovered in the cellar of the now demolished 𝔑𝔬. **88**. The Lamb at No. 94, Bloomsbury's best-known pub, still contains original Victorian 'snob screens' made of cut glass which pivot at head height and which were installed to allow gentlemen in the lounge to avoid being looked at by working-class drinkers in the public bar. For much of the twentieth century the street was home to a variety of small shops and offices, including a phonograph maker's run by the French Pathé brothers, founders of the eponymous news company, at the now demolished 𝔑𝔬. **15**. Its elegance was recently ruined by partial pedestrianization.

Marchmont Street

A well-preserved street of mostly Victorian shops, it includes two popular bookshops, Judd Two (No. 82) and Gay's The Word (No. 66), named after an Ivor Novello musical, which was founded in 1979 and

Lenin's Bloomsbury haunts

While in London in the early years of the twentieth century the Russian revolutionary V. I. Lenin spent much of his time in a variety of local 'safe' houses inhabited by fellow revolutionaries, as well as researching at the British Library on Great Russell Street and working on the revolutionary *Iskra* newspaper in Clerkenwell Green.

22 Ampton Street *Iskra* editors met in the property, home of Nikolai Alexeyev, a doctor who went on to take part in the 1917 October Revolution, in October 1902, and it was here the following July that Lenin and associates welcomed delegates to London for the 2nd Congress of the Russian Social-Democratic Labour Party.

British Library Reading Room, Great Russell Street. Lenin signed himself into the British Library in 1902 as Jacob Richter, researching at seat L13 some fifty years after Marx had written *Das Kapital* in the same room.

14 Frederick Street This four-storey house with its pretty ironwork veranda was Lenin's London mailing address and home in early 1902 of Nikolai Alexeyev (see above).

26 Granville Square The editorial board of *Iskra*, the revolutionary newspaper, used this three-storey house, home of contributor Leo Deutsch, in 1902–3.

30 Holford Square Lenin's first London address in April 1902 was the now demolished 30 Holford Square where he and his wife, Krupskaya, posed as the German Mr and Mrs Jacob Richter. The landlady, who was concerned that Krupskaya had no wedding ring, provided them with food they could not eat – 'ox-tails, skates fried in fat and indigestible cakes not made for Russian stomachs'.

Pindar of Wakefield, 328 Gray's Inn Road Lenin brought Bolshevik delegates to this pub during the 1903 Russian Social-Democratic Labour Party Congress and they took up a corner of the room singing Russian songs.

16 Percy Circus Lenin lived here when he came to London for the second time in April 1905 to attend the 3rd Congress of the Russian Social-Democratic Labour Party, an event shrouded in such secrecy that no one knows where in London it was held. A number of delegates stayed at other Percy Circus addresses, including Nos. 9 and 23.

20 Regent Square It was the home of the Bolshevik K. M. Takhtarev and used by particularly Lenin, who later became the Soviet Union's first leader.

raided five years later by Customs and Excise, who seized works by Tennessee Williams, Gore Vidal, Christopher Isherwood and Jean Genet and charged the shop's owners with conspiracy to import indecent books. After a vigorous protest campaign the charges were dropped.

Percy Circus

A once genteel but now down-at-heel junction of radiating roads east of King's Cross Road named after Robert Percy Smith, nineteenth-century director of the New River Company, it was colonized in the early twentieth century by a number of Russian revolutionaries on the run from the Tsarist police,

Queen Square

An immaculate and secluded enclave to the east of Southampton Row, dominated by hospitals, which the novelist Henry James described as 'smelling strongly of the last [eighteenth] century with a hoary effigy of Queen Anne in the middle'. The square was built between 1716 and 1720 and originally named Devonshire Square before being rededicated in honour of Queen Anne. In the north-east section of the gardens a plaque marks the spot where a Zeppelin dropped a bomb in 1915, without anyone

Iskra as a mailing address. Letters sent here from Russia were intercepted by Russian police and sent to the Metropolitan Police with the warning: 'correspondence between members of the criminal *Iskra* society goes via this address'.

Sidmouth Street In 1902 the Russian Social-Democrats had a commune in an unknown house on this street where they secreted *Iskra*'s paperwork and welcomed colleagues who had escaped to Britain. When Lenin visited he found specks of tobacco in the sugar tin and thereafter refused to take sugar in his tea.

36 Tavistock Place Lenin lived here in 1908 after returning to London from Geneva to research philosophy at the British Library. In his letters he railed against associates such as the writer Maxim Gorky, who he claimed were 'prone to moods of depression evoked by episodes of the struggle abroad and splits, dissension and quarrelling'.

Twentieth Century Press, 37a Clerkenwell Green. Lenin and associates worked on the revolutionary paper *Iskra* at the printing house on Clerkenwell Green set up by William Morris (now the Marx Memorial Library) until April 1903, when *Iskra* moved to Geneva.

being killed, and lines of poetry by Philip Larkin and Ted Hughes have been set in the paving stones. Two benches commemorate the lives of sixteen doctors from the nearby homeopathic hospital who died in the 1972 Trident air disaster.

north side
Until 1960 the north-western corner of the square was occupied by **No. 20**, whose garden contained a trapdoor and steps leading to the stone tunnels of a stream known as the Devil's Conduit. Occupants of No. 20 over the years included a Dr John Campbell, who was regularly visited by Dr Johnson on Sunday evenings; Edmond

Hoyle, the eighteenth-century playing cards expert; and Louisa Twining, the eighteenth-century social worker and reformer who housed homeless women inside the house, to the astonishment of her neighbours. William Morris lived at **No. 26** from 1865 to 1871. His design shop, Morris, Marshall, Faulkner & Co., was located on the ground floor, and workshops were built into a converted ballroom at the back.

Working Women's College (1864–1901), No. 29
Elizabeth Malleson, who famously omitted to include the word 'obey' when she married, and Barbara Bodichon, a landscape painter once described by Dante Gabriel Rossetti as being 'blessed with large rations of tin [money], fat, enthusiasm and golden hair, who thinks nothing of climbing up a mountain in breeches, or wading through a stream in none, in the sacred name of pigment', founded the **Working Women's College** here in October 1864. As an alternative to the Revd F. D. Maurice's Working Men's College on Great Ormond Street which refused to accept women, it offered cheap evening classes in a wide range of subjects. Those who taught here, persuaded by Malleson to volunteer their services free, included the housing reformer Octavia Hill and the doctor Elizabeth Garrett Anderson. The college closed in 1901.

south side
Italian Children's Hospital, south-east corner
Giovanni Ortelli opened the Ospedale Italiano in his own house (No. 41) in 1884 and after the last patients left in 1989 the building reopened as the Italian wing of the Great Ormond Street children's hospital, which stands to the north-east.

Mary Ward Centre, No. 42
An adult education and community centre named after the late-nineteenth-century novelist, Chartist and death-penalty reformer, which from 1861 to 1908 was used as the Female School of Design.

west side
St George the Martyr, west side
The church predates the square and was
built as a chapel-of-ease to St Andrew,
Holborn, in the early eighteenth century,
with alterations to the building carried out
by Nicholas Hawksmoor from 1717 to 1720.
St George was promoted to the status of
parish church in 1723 and from 1747 to 1765
the rector was William Stukeley, who first
promoted the idea that Stonehenge may
have been a druid temple. S. S. Teulon
inserted the zinc steeple in 1868 and until
1875 the church was the setting for an
annual Christmas dinner for 100 chimney-
sweep apprentices (it is still occasionally
referred to as the Chimney Sweeps' church).
The poets Ted Hughes and Sylvia Plath
married here on 16 June (Bloomsday, from
James Joyce's *Ulysses*) 1956 before going off
to their honeymoon in Benidorm, then a
quiet fishing village.
Queen Charlotte's
The pub is named after Charlotte, wife of
George III, who prepared his favourite
dishes in the cellars while the king was being
treated for his madness in the hospitals of
Queen Square.

Southampton Row
The main road connecting Russell Square
with Theobald's Road, named after the
former landowner, the Earl of Southampton.
east side: Guilford Street to Theobald's Road
Imperial Hotel, east side south of Guilford
Street
When Learie Constantine, the mid-
twentieth-century West Indies test cricketer
who became Trinidad and Tobago's
Minister of Transport in the 1960s, tried to
book a room in the hotel in 1943, his party
was told: 'We are not going to have all these
Niggers in our hotel. He may stop tonight
but if he doesn't go tomorrow his bags will
be put outside and his door locked.' As
there were no laws against racial harassment
at that time Constantine sued on grounds of
'personal distress and injury', and the courts
found that although he was a 'man of

colour, no ground existed on which the
defendants were entitled to refuse to receive
and lodge him'. In his 1954 book *The Colour
Bar* Constantine explained that 'most British
people would be quite unwilling for a black
man to enter their homes, nor would they
wish to work with one, nor stand shoulder
to shoulder with one at a factory bench'.
The hotel, built from 1905–11, was designed
with many ornate flourishes by Charles
Fitzroy Doll and included a Winter Garden
and Turkish Baths.
► The West Indies at Lord's, p. 369.
International Times **(1966–8)**, No. 102
International Times (*IT*), the main journal
of London's 1960s counter-culture, began
publishing its uncompromising mix of
offbeat articles, drug information, icono-
clasms of sexual taboos and paeans to avant-
garde literature, art and music in 1966 in
what had previously been the Indica bookstore. Early issues included pieces on the
surrealist André Breton, the Vietnam War,
Yoko Ono's exhibitions and Ezra Pound's
pro-fascist views. On 9 March 1967, after a
reader complained about a supposedly
obscene article, twelve plain-clothes detectives raided the premises and seized every
back issue, all the scrap paper, the phone
books and, most importantly of all, the
contents of every ashtray. The haul, except
for the ashtray contents, was returned after
two months, but though the police declined
to press charges against the magazine, John
Hopkins, one of the editors and the driving
force behind the publication, was arrested
for possessing pot and sentenced to six
months in Wormwood Scrubs, where he
was joined for a few days by Rolling Stones
Mick Jagger and Keith Richards, who were
also being arraigned on drugs-related
charges. *IT* moved to Covent Garden in
1968.
► *Oz* magazine, p. 456.

Theobald's Road
Occasionally pronounced by locals as
'Tibbalds' Road, it follows the route the
Stuart kings took from the royal hunting

fields in Soho towards Theobald's Park in Hertfordshire and was where, according to Pepys, the royal coach containing Charles II overturned one day in 1669 as it came out of the King's Gate (junction of Theobald's Road and Drake Street), throwing the king and his courtiers into the gutter, unharmed. Theobald's Road was widened in 1878 when it was linked with adjacent streets and laid with tramlines. Samuel Coleridge-Taylor, Britain's first notable black musician, was born at **№. 15** on 15 August 1875. According to legend he was spotted playing marbles in the street while holding a violin by a violin teacher who asked him if he would like lessons. Coleridge-Taylor later studied at the Royal College of Music and at twenty-four was conducting at the Royal Albert Hall. He is best known for a musical version of Long-fellow's *Hiawatha*.

(iv) High Holborn / Gray's Inn

The streets between Bloomsbury Way/ Theobald's Road and High Holborn, first developed in the late seventeenth century, became a trading area for craftsmen in the eighteenth and nineteenth centuries, their workshops being mostly replaced in the mid twentieth century by large office blocks.

Bury Place
British Museum station (south of Barter Street)
British Museum station opened on the Central Line in July 1900 but being particu-larly close to the Piccadilly Line station of Holborn was chosen for closure when London Transport decided to extend Holborn to take Central Line trains. The station shut down on 24 September 1933 and two years later was used in shooting the film *Bulldog Jack*, which made use of rumours that it was haunted by the real-life incar-nation of one of the British Museum's Egyp-tian artefacts. The film also features a sarcophagus that opens to reveal a secret passage leading from the museum to the station, named Bloomsbury in the film.

British Museum station also features in the 1974 horror film *Death Line*, which is based around the fantastic story of a gang of navvies, entombed by a landslip during the station's construction, having mutated into a race of man-eating ghouls. The station was commandeered by the Ministry of Defence during the Second World War and has since been occupied by offices for the Brigade of Guards and the civil defence body, the London District Military Command, which would take over London in the event of flooding.
➤ Disused Aldwych station, p. 128.

Gray's Inn Road
The section of Gray's Inn Road south of Theobald's Road is dominated by the Gray's Inn legal institution, entrance to which can be obtained through a gate on Gray's Inn Road, beside which Richard Nelthorp, a member of the Inn, was executed in 1685 for taking part in the Duke of Monmouth's rebellion against James II. Samuel Romilly, the law reformer, and a band of men defended the Inn from the Gordon Rioters in June 1780.
Gray's Inn, north of Chancery Lane station, west side

> Gray's Inn, gentlemen. Curious little nooks in a great place, like London, these old Inns are – *The Pickwick Papers*, Charles Dickens (1837)

One of the four remaining Inns of Court, along with Lincoln's Inn, the Middle Temple and the Inner Temple, where lawyers have traditionally lived and studied, Gray's Inn was founded as a *hospitium* for lawyers *c.* 1370 and named after Sir Reginald de Grey, chief justice of Chester, who lived in a manor house on the site. The Inn declined in status and its finances dwindled during the eighteenth century, and when the new Courts of Justice on the Strand opened in 1882 Gray's Inn became the most distant of the four Inns from the building, although the closure of the many Inns of Chancery soon after helped bring about a revival in its fortunes. The Inn's most illustrious past member is Francis Bacon, the essayist, historian and statesman, who occupied chambers in the Inn from 1576 until his death in 1626, and as Lord Chancellor had considerable influence on the English legal system, particularly the concepts of fairness and impartiality. Other past members include the historian Lord Macaulay, the poet Robert Browning and the essayist Hilaire Belloc.

▶ Lincoln's Inn, p. 123; the Temple, p. 46.

Geographers' A–Z shop, No. 28, east side
Phyllis Pearsall supposedly walked every road in London, rising at 5 a.m. in her Holloway Road bedsit and walking until midnight every day, covering 3,000 miles in all, to compile the first A–Z of London, published in 1936. A–Z now produces guides to nearly 300 cities from offices here.

Gray's Inn Square

Nos. 4–5

The premises were chambers at the end of the twentieth century for George Carman, the leading libel lawyer of the period, who made his name in 1979 successfully defending the Liberal Party leader, Jeremy Thorpe, from a charge of conspiracy to murder his former lover Norman Scott. In his closing speech he told the jury: 'In his time Mr Thorpe has won millions of votes from people in this country, but now come the 12 most precious votes of all', and pointing at each juror in turn, repeated: 'Yours, yours, yours . . .' Carman success-fully defended the comic Ken Dodd from accusations of tax evasion in the 1980s, with the quip 'some accountants are comedians, but comedians are never accountants', and later represented the *News of the World*, which was being sued for libel by Sonia Sutcliffe, the wife of the Yorkshire Ripper, whom he accused of 'dancing on the graves of her husband's victims'. In the mid 1990s Carman defended the *Guardian* from a libel suit brought by former Tory minister Jona-than Aitken, having been hired when the paper's editor, Alan Rusbridger, announced, on receiving a letter from Aitken: 'We'd

better get Carman, before Aitken gets him.' Aitken dropped his action on the eve of the trial and was later convicted of perjury. After Carman died in 2001 his son, Dominic, published a book which claimed his father was plagued by a 'dark side' that involved drink, gambling and beating up his wife.

High Holborn

Originally a Roman road, but not a straight route on account of the swampy nature of the land, High Holborn became a centre for popular entertainment and leisure in the nineteenth century, with the **Royal Amphi-theatre**, where the Marquess of Queensberry's boxing rules were first enforced to help regulate the sport, at Nos. 81–87; the **Holborn Empire** at No. 242; and the grand **Holborn Restaurant** at No. 218, none of which survives on what is now a purely commercial street.

north side: Shaftesbury Avenue to Gray's Inn Road

Old Red Lion, No. 72

After being exhumed from their graves, the bodies of those responsible for the death of Charles I – Oliver Cromwell; his son-in-law, Henry Ireton; and John Bradshaw, the officer who had given the order for the King's execution – were displayed overnight in 1660 in the previous Red Lion that stood on this site, before being taken to the Tyburn gallows to be hanged and decapi-tated. Bradshaw's body had not been satisfac-torily embalmed, and as it had badly decayed, the tavern was filled with a considerable stench during the overnight exhibition. Following the display at Tyburn the heads were then skewered on to poles outside Westminster Hall.

▶ Tyburn gallows, p. 433.

Cold War bunker, No. 32

The government's Cold War-era bunker, built as part of the capital's defence against envisaged nuclear attack in the 1950s, can be reached through two doors, one of glass, one of steel, at 32 High Holborn. It was originally constructed in the 1940s as a telecommunications centre for the Kingsway telephone exchange, and by the 1950s had been converted to a bunker equipped with an artesian well and enough fuel, tinned and dried food to last six weeks. It was also later linked with other government tunnels under Whitehall, Bloomsbury's Judd Street and the Post Office Tower in Maple Street, Fitzrovia. Although defence staff in the 1950s calculated that a bomb falling on London similar in impact to the A bombs which the Americans had dropped on Nagasaki and Hiroshima would not be able to penetrate the bunkers, subsequent improvements in nuclear weaponry soon made such thinking, and the bunkers, redundant. Since the ending of the Cold War the site has been abandoned and in 1996 it was put up for sale.

► The Whitehall bunker, p. 233.

Cittie of Yorke, Nos. 22–23
The impressive interior of this 1430 pub, rebuilt in 1923 and known as Henekey's Wine Lodge from 1695–1982, includes fine panelling, one of the longest bars in the country and enormous vats in which Henekey's used to store their wine. There are also wooden cubicles constructed so that patrons, who would most likely come from Gray's Inn, could enjoy privacy with their clients, and an old Gothic stove in the centre, originally installed in Gray's Inn Hall, which allows smoke to escape, surprisingly, through a chimney running *under* the floor.

south side: Staple Inn Buildings to Shaftesbury Avenue

The George and Blue Boar, Nos. 268–280
The George and Blue Boar was a medieval inn where those being taken from Newgate Prison to be hanged at Tyburn could stop for a glass of beer, as noted by Jonathan Swift in his 1727 poem 'Tom Clinch' in the lines: 'As clever Tom Clinch, while the rabble was bawling / Rode stately through Holborn to die in his calling / He stopt at The George for a bottle of sack / And promised to pay for it when he came back.' The inn lost much trade when the railways

were built and it was replaced by a hotel, the Inns of Court, which catered for railway travellers until it too was sold in 1923. The Kingsway telephone exchange (see No. 32) was built on the site in 1929.

Holborn Empire, No. 242
Built in 1858 as Weston's Music Hall, and hosting music hall acts such as Marie Lloyd and George Robey, it became the **Holborn Empire** in 1900, and was where fourteen years later, on 9 April 1914, the 100-minute melodrama *The World, the Flesh and the Devil* was shown as the first full-length feature film in Kinemacolor. Louis Armstrong, the pioneer jazz trumpeter, appeared at the venue on 31 July 1933, despite a recent article in the *Daily Express* which claimed he had died, backed by a hastily assembled group of musicians and spending much of the show clowning and joking. The chaotic performance divided the crowd, with older members of the audience leaving in disgust and younger elements cheering wildly. By the end of the week Armstrong, realizing that he was losing friends, played down the showmanship, to the delight of the audience and press. The Empire was bombed in the Second World War and stood derelict until demolition in 1954 when the site was subsumed into the adjacent Pearl Assurance Building.

Princess Louise, No. 208
An ornate Victorian public house named after Queen Victoria's fourth daughter, the Princess Louise was built in 1872 and refurbished in 1891 by Arthur Chitty with fine craftsmanship, particularly the tiles, glasswork and joinery, much of which has been preserved.

In the 1950s the pub was home to the Ballads and Blues club, organized by James Miller, a Salford-born songwriter who had changed his name to Ewan MacColl and composed the song 'Dirty Old Town', where songs by American country blues artists were sung alongside English murder ballads, sea shanties and work songs. MacColl's club was replaced in the early 1960s by gigs featuring the virtuoso guitarists Davey Graham and Bert Jansch and the pub also became a popular haunt for musicians using the nearby De Lane Lea studios, such as the Who's Pete Townshend who devised the humorous fake adverts which segue tracks on the group's 1968 album, *The Who Sell Out*, while relaxing in the pub in between recording sessions.

Dennis Nilsen, the homosexual serial killer who murdered at least fifteen men in the late 1970s and early 1980s, met Kenneth James Ockenden, a 23-year-old Canadian, in the Princess Louise on 3 December 1979 and at the end of the evening took him back to his Cricklewood flat and killed him. In recent decades the Princess Louise has become one of London's leading real ale pubs, winning a number of awards from the Campaign for Real Ale.

Red Lion Square

Originally Red Lion Fields, setting for executions and punishments, the square was developed in 1684 by Dr Nicholas Barbon, a surgeon and speculative builder, whose plans were vociferously opposed by Gray's Inn lawyers. Annoyed about losing their green views, the lawyers attacked Barbon's builders with bricks. (Of Barbon's 1680s development only Nos. 14–15 remain.) In the 1850s the painter-poet Dante Gabriel Rossetti, the designer and poet William Morris, and the artist Edward Burne-Jones, lived at No. 17, where the landlord warned Rossetti to keep his models 'under some gentlemanly restraint, as some artists sacrifice the dignity of art to the baseness of passion'. A demonstration organized by the National Front in Red Lion Square on 15 June 1974 ended in violence when Front members clashed with members of the International Marxist Group (IMG) and Warwick University students, one of whom, Kevin Gately, was killed in the fighting.

COVENT GARDEN, WC2

The heart of London, a buffer between the great buildings of state of Westminster and the nightlife centre of Soho, and an area of considerable importance for shopping and tourism, Covent Garden is built on what was the Saxons' Thames port of Lundenwic and is probably the same as Bede's 'Metropolis . . . a mart of many peoples coming by land and sea', which was abandoned *c.* 900. After Westminster Abbey bought the lands at the beginning of the thirteenth century it established a *convent* garden, later Covent Garden, which grew into London's major flower and vegetable market, giving its name to the area in a corrupted form, and now located in Nine Elms, Battersea.

(i) *around Leicester Square*

Charing Cross Road

Now one of the most heavily used roads in the capital, the boundary between the western and eastern sides of the metropolis, and home to London's greatest conglomeration of bookshops, Charing Cross Road was previously Hog Lane, upgraded after Charing Cross station opened in 1864, to become one of the liveliest in London, with nightclubs, theatres, cheap restaurants and bookshops, but also a centre for crime. Frank Norman, the Barnardo's boy who became a celebrity in the 1960s after writing his prison memoirs, once explained how he first came to be involved in the central London underworld: 'You are 14 years old. You walk down the Charing Cross Road. You are accosted by a man wearing a flashy tie. The rest follows on from there.'

west side: St Martin's Place to St Giles Circus

Cambridge Circus

Previously known as Five Dials, on account of the number of intersecting roads, it briefly became Shaftesbury Circus after the opening of Shaftesbury Avenue in 1886, and later Cambridge Circus. The office block on the south-west corner, above the bank, was depicted as the Circus, the headquarters of a spy ring which organizes espionage across Britain, in John Le Carré's George Smiley books.

Palace Theatre, Charing Cross Road at Shaftesbury Avenue
The theatre, renowned for its extravagant brick façade, and now owned by the musical impresario Andrew Lloyd Webber, was built as the Royal English Opera House in 1891. Money was supplied by the Gilbert and Sullivan impresario, Richard D'Oyly Carte, who wanted it to be a home for English opera but had to settle for a music hall, the Palace Theatre of Varieties, when he realized his original ideas were too ambitious. Anna Pavlova made her West End debut here in 1910, and a year later the theatre was the setting for the first Royal Command Performance, with the music hall star Marie Lloyd excluded from the bill for being too vulgar. Since the 1960s it has been the setting for long-running musicals: *The Sound of Music* (1961–7), *Jesus Christ Superstar* (1972–80) and *Les Miserables* (1985–).

St Martin's Art College, No. 107
The college, founded in 1854, was where in the late 1960s Gilbert Proesch, born in a small Italian village in the Dolomites, met Flete George Charles Ernestine Passmore and formed the infamous duo Gilbert and George, communicating at first by sign language, for Gilbert could speak no English. Their first collaboration was a human face in which, as Gilbert explained, 'we had a mould and poured in liquid colour. We arranged for photos to be taken of us with the sculptures, and that's when we realised we were the sculptures.' The first Sex Pistols gig took place at the college on 6 November 1975 in front of fewer than twenty people, with Johnny Rotten, wearing baggy pin-stripes held up with braces and a ripped Pink Floyd T-shirt with the words 'I hate' scrawled over it, menacingly prowling the stage impersonating Ian Dury. The students' union organizers failed to

appreciate the Pistols' performance as a defining point in rock history and pulled the plug after five numbers.
► Gilbert and George in Spitalfields, p. 288.

Foyle's, Nos. 113–117
London's best-known yet most eccentrically run bookshop was opened by William and Gilbert Foyle in 1904 in Islington and moved in 1929 to Charing Cross Road. One of the first customers was the novelist Arnold Bennett, who used to walk from floor to floor holding a £5 note which he said he would offer to anyone he found reading one of his books, but which he never parted with. The following year Christina, William's nineteen-year-old daughter, launched Foyle's famous literary lunches, and when in the mid-1930s she heard that Hitler's brownshirts were burning books she cabled him with the message: 'Don't burn books, we'll give you a very good price.' Christina Foyle took over as owner of the shop in 1963, after her father died, and over the next thirty years Foyle's became a byword for cultivated chaos, the art of finding volumes made more enticing by the vast size of the shop, but also more exasperating by the arranging of novels by publisher, rather than author. Staff were hired and fired on an erratic basis, successful applicants rarely stayed, or were allowed to stay, longer than six weeks, trade unions were outlawed, women were confined to cashier jobs, and there was a glut of people with unusual classical names. (When one customer asked where he could find *Ulysses* he was told he had just gone out to lunch.) Foyle also steadfastly refused to modernize the shop's bureaucracy and customers were obliged to take part in a Kafkaesque queuing system if they wished to leave the store with a book by legal means. Since Foyle's death in 1999 the shop has been brought into the modern world.
► Foyle's literary luncheons at the Dorchester, p. 160.

east side: St Giles's Circus to Cambridge Circus

Centre Point, Charing Cross Road at Andrew Borde Street

Central London's best-known skyscraper, designed by Richard Seifert and built between 1956 and 1967, was intended to be one of a number of government-operated air-conditioned tower blocks standing above a network of bunkers which, in the event of chemical or biological warfare, could be used to accommodate civil servants and ministers who could quickly make their way below to man the bunkers if danger increased. Other blocks included in the scheme were Euston Tower, New Scotland Yard, the Post Office Tower (now Telecom Tower), Telstar House in Paddington, Bowater House (Knightsbridge) and the Meteorological Office at 281–288 High Holborn. By the time most of these blocks had been constructed advances in weaponry had rendered their defence capabilities obsolete. Centre Point stood empty, amid much controversy, throughout the sixties and seventies, the public being spun a spurious tale about office rents rising so sharply that it was better to leave the tower empty than rent it out and tie its value down to a particular rent review period. Little use has been made of the tower since, although it now contains offices for the Confederation of British Industry.

No. 84

The bookshop immortalized in Helen Hanff's *84 Charing Cross Road* was based on Marks & Co., a shop housed here for much of the twentieth century and visited by Charles Chaplin, George Bernard Shaw and the elderly Sigmund Freud. Too weak to climb the stairs to the third floor where the rare books on religion and the occult were stored, Freud would wait at the bottom while an assistant carried them to him. The shop had a policy of awarding expensive books a secret code, so that staff would know how much discount to give to awkward customers, and when the owner's eight-year-old son, Leo, saw a copy of Edgar Allan Poe's *The Gold Bug* valued at £850 he decided he had to read the story. It set off an interest in codes that eventually led to his becoming one of the government's leading wartime codebreakers. Helen Hanff began a twenty-year correspondence with the shop owner in 1949, compiling the letters into book form in 1971.

▸ Leo Marks's codebreaking exploits, p. 149.

Cranbourn Street

William Hogarth was apprenticed here, under the sign of the Golden Angel, in 1713. In the eighteenth century Cranbourn Street, which connects Leicester Square and Long Acre, was a bonnet market where girls were positioned outside shops to entice customers inside, and it is now one of the busiest side streets in London, even though its name is barely known to most of its users.

Hippodrome

The Hippodrome, one of London's best-known and largest night spots, was designed by Frank Matcham with 1,340 seats and opened on 15 January 1900 to stage music hall, circus and variety acts. The country's first performance of *Swan Lake* was staged at the Hippodrome in 1910 and it was here on 7 April 1919 that live jazz was heard in Britain for the first time, thanks to the Original Dixieland Jazz Band, mostly white musicians from New Orleans playing piano, cornet, clarinet and trombone. The magazine *Performer* was not impressed and wrote how 'the best qualification for a jazzist is to have no knowledge of music and no musical ability beyond that of making noises', but when Irving Berlin's 'Alexander's Ragtime Band' was performed here in 1926 the *Daily Express* excitedly proclaimed: 'Go where you will you cannot escape from the mazes of music he has spun. In all London restaurants, parks and theatres you hear his strains. Ragtime has swept like a whirlwind over the earth and set civilisation humming.' In 1947 the twelve-year-old Julie Andrews was an instant hit when she sang an aria during the show *Starlight Roof*. The theatre was converted to the Talk of the Town nightclub in 1957 and later reverted to its original name.

Leicester Square

It will never be known, I suppose, why this square itself should look so alien and in some ways so continental. It will never be known whether it was the foreign look that attracted the foreigners or the foreigners who gave it the foreign look –
The Man Who Was Thursday, G. K. Chesterton (1908)

Leicester Square, London's busiest quarter and a major gathering place for tourists and visitors, was laid out in the 1630s by Robert Sidney, the 2nd Earl of Leicester, who built a mansion, **Leicester House**, on what is now the north side of the square and enclosed the central grassy area, Leicester Fields, paying £3 annually to the parish to compensate for the loss of grazing land. By the end of the seventeenth century the square was attracting wealthy merchants from the City who wanted to live closer to the royal court and the seat of government, but it was also full of 'ruffians around the livery stables and horse-dealers, and there were rows of hotels with foreign names where moustachioed loungers breathed garlic and tobacco', according to Jenny Uglow, the modern-day biographer of the artist William Hogarth, who played chuck in the square as a boy in the early eighteenth century and later moved his studio here.

In 1717 the royal court attached to Prince George (later George II) came to Leicester House, but after the property was demolished in the 1790s the square declined in importance. Various schemes were enacted to revive its fortunes, including the opening of the Panopticon display of scientific exhibits in 1854, but it was not until the late nineteenth century, when theatres, including the Empire (later replaced by a cinema of the same name), and music halls were built, attracting hordes of visitors, both Londoners and foreigners in equal measures, that Leicester Square's popularity grew, and the square now features London's highest concentration of cinemas and largest crowds, despite the inferiority of its cafés, eateries and architecture compared with similar continental squares.

● Maurice Micklewhite, an up-coming actor, making a phone call from a booth on Leicester Square in the early 1960s, noticed a poster for *The Caine Mutiny* and decided to change his name to Michael Caine.

north side

Though one of the largest properties in seventeenth-century London, **Leicester House** was marred by the presence of four lock-up shops at the front. It nevertheless attracted royalty, including Elizabeth, Queen of Bohemia, who came to England penniless in 1661 and died in the property a week later, and from 1717 George, Prince of Wales (later George II), who left St James's Palace after a row with his father, the king, and brought to Leicester House a large retinue of attendants and servants, who moved into the adjacent **Ailesbury House**. When George I died in June 1727 Prince George was crowned king in the gateway of Leicester House and moved back to St James's Palace. In 1774 the Manchester bird-fancier Sir Ashton Lever moved into Leicester House, where he opened his Holophusicon, a natural history collection of some 26,000 items, but the public were unmoved by his birds, fossils and Sandwich Islands Room, and Lever was forced to close the venture after a year. Leicester House was demolished soon after and the site is now occupied by a cinema.

east side

Edward Clarke opened the Royal Panopticon of Science and Art, an institution for 'Scientific Exhibitions, and for Promoting Discoveries in Arts and Manufacturers', in a vast exotic Moorish building on the east side of the square in 1854. After a local cholera outbreak it closed and was sold to the theatre impresario E. T. Smith, who installed a circus ring and in 1856 reopened the premises as the **Alhambra Theatre**. The London debut of the Parisienne Quadrille, better known as the Can-Can, took place here fourteen years later, causing such public outcry that the theatre's licence was removed for three years. A fire destroyed the building, costumes and stage sets in 1882, and it was rebuilt as a music hall, Gracie Fields winning rave reviews for her performance in *Mr Tower of London* in 1923. The 𝔄𝔩𝔥𝔞𝔪𝔟𝔯𝔞 was demolished in 1936 and rebuilt as the Odeon Cinema.

𝔚𝔦𝔩𝔩𝔦𝔞𝔪 𝔥𝔬𝔤𝔞𝔯𝔱𝔥'𝔰 𝔰𝔱𝔲𝔡𝔦𝔬 (1733–64), No. 30

William Hogarth, England's greatest satirical painter, moved into a shop at the sign of the Golden Head, in what was then Leicester Fields, in 1733. He soon made himself a new shop sign, a bust of Van Dyck, the Dutch artist who had settled in England, out of 'several thicknesses of cork compacted together' and built a studio where he began to work on his many 'modern moral subjects' – witty and caustic paintings and engravings conveying a message. The first of these was *The Rake's Progress*, which in eight parts details the tragic life of the irresponsible Tom Rakewell from birth to fortune to penury. Hogarth held back from releasing it until the passing of the 1735 copyright act that he himself helped draw up to prevent pirating of artists' work. In June 1748 Hogarth, the arch Anglophile, visited France to do some drawings and to his horror was expelled at Calais for supposedly being a spy. Incensed, he returned to Leicester Fields and painted the mocking *The Roast Beef of Old England (The Gate of Calais)*, which savaged French claims of superiority and promoted supposedly English virtues, such as reliability. The following year Hogarth bought a country retreat in Chiswick, but continued to work occasionally in Leicester Fields, and died here of an aneurism on 25 October 1764. The house later became the area's first restaurant, the Hôtel de la Sablionère, and was eventually demolished. Capital Radio is now based in an office on the site.

west side

The artist Joshua Reynolds, who became the

Demonstrations and rallies in Trafalgar Square

Trafalgar Square has long been the setting for major political meetings, demonstrations and events, despite regular bans from the authorities.

Demonstration against the raising of income tax, 6 March 1848 Ten thousand people assemble to protest against the raising of income tax from 3 per cent to 5 per cent and when the authorities order Cochrane, the campaigner for low tax, not to speak G. W. M. Reynolds, the Chartist leader, takes the stage, brandishing a placard proclaiming: 'A Republic for France – The Charter for England'. Asked by a member of the crowd if he would kill Louis Philippe (the French king) if he met him, Reynolds replies: 'No, I would put him in Woombles Menagerie instead', at which point he is seized by two police officers. The crowd then attacks the police with stones and as the cry 'To the Palace! Bread and Revolution' goes up, the mob advances towards St James's Park, but is halted by sealed-off entrances.

'Black Monday', 8 February 1886 Those made redundant by the closure of the sugar refineries gather to protest in a demonstration organized by the Fair Trade Association and backed by the Conservative Party but taken over by the left-wing Social-Democratic Federation. A crowd of around 10,000 then leaves the square and makes its way along Pall Mall throwing missiles at the Reform Club after members, intrigued to see what is happening, make the mistake of appearing at the windows. Leaders of the Social-Democratic Federation are

first president of the Royal Academy in 1768, lived at **No. 47** on the west side of the square, building himself a 'detached gallery and painting rooms' where he entertained the writers James Boswell, Oliver Goldsmith and Fanny Burney. When Reynolds introduced Dr Johnson to Laurence Sterne, the latter read him a few lines from the dedication of his recently completed comic prosecuted for sedition, but found not guilty. Nevertheless for the next few weeks London goes into a state of siege.

'Bloody Sunday', 13 November 1887 Organized to protest against the jailing of the radical Irish MP William O'Brien, the demo is taken over by radicals wanting to test their right to free speech and results in considerable violence when a Socialist League contingent that includes William Morris, Annie Besant (leader of the match girls' strike) and George Bernard Shaw reaches the square and is rushed by the police. Eventually the crowd disperses, but 200 people are injured and two are killed. The following Sunday a smaller version of the rally takes place, with the police again attacking marchers at points leading into the square.

Coronation of Edward VII, 9 August 1902 The radical American writer Jack London watches the coronation of Edward VII from a vantage spot in the square, writing in his London travelogue *The People of the Abyss* (1903): 'Vivat Rex Eduardus! They crowned a king this day, and I am perplexed and saddened . . . nor did I ever see anything so hopeless and so tragic.' While waiting for the procession, London reflects on how 'the people of Israel first took unto themselves a king', and how 'five hundred hereditary peers own one-fifth of England'. When the royal party arrives London notes: 'Everybody has gone mad. The contagion is sweeping me off my feet – I, too, want to shout, "The King! God save the King!" and I check myself with a rush, striving to convince myself that it is all real and rational.'

novel *Tristram Shandy*, but Johnson was unimpressed, later intimating to an associate that he had told Sterne 'it is not English, Sir'.

St Martin's Place
A short stretch of the main road north of Trafalgar Square.

VE Day, 8 May 1945 Hundreds of thousands of people gather in the square to celebrate the ending of the Second World War in Europe and sing songs, the most popular of which is Charles Coborn's 'Two Lovely Black Eyes'.

Aldermaston anti-nuclear march, 4 April 1958 Four thousand marchers set out on the first anti-nuclear march, which leaves Trafalgar Square en route for Aldermaston, Berkshire, headquarters of the Atomic Energy Research Establishment, on a cold and wet Good Friday, sleeping overnight in church halls and schools. The last mile of the 50-mile route is marched in complete silence. Many further anti-nuclear demonstrations take place in the square over the following decades.

Anti-Vietnam War demonstration, 22 October 1967 The first of three mid-1960s anti-Vietnam War demonstrations hears speakers call not for peace in Vietnam, but for victory to the communist forces, before marching to the United States Embassy in Grosvenor Square (p. 164). At the second rally on 17 March 1968 a crowd of around 25,000 hears speeches from Tariq Ali and Vanessa Redgrave.

Anti-poll tax demonstration, 31 March 1990 A rally attended by some 200,000 people ends in violence when police clash with anarchists, resulting in considerable looting and destruction in the Whitehall area. Commentators cite the demonstration as a significant factor in the demise of Margaret Thatcher as prime minister later that year.

National Portrait Gallery, west side
The gallery was established in Westminster in 1856 according to the wishes of the historian the Earl of Stanhope, moving to the present site in 1895, and until 1969 featured only those who had been dead for at least ten years. It now contains more than 9,000 portraits arranged chronologically,

with Hans Holbein's cartoon of Henry VIII among the oldest works.

St Martin-in-the-Fields, east side
A church has stood on the site since the thirteenth century, when it was reachable only by walking across fields. The current church, described by the poet Francis Thompson as 'Jacob's ladder / Pitched between Heaven and Charing Cross', designed by James Gibbs between 1722 and 1726, was adopted by American pioneers as the model for church building, resulting in replicas throughout New England. St Martin's also contains a café, a bookshop, a homeless shelter, a craft market and the London Brass Rubbing Centre, and promotes lunchtime and evening classical music concerts. The steeple can be seen in the William Hogarth painting *Beer Street*, and the church served as the model for the Museum of Propaganda in George Orwell's *1984*.

Trafalgar Square

Trafalgar Square, London's main meeting point, along with Piccadilly Circus, was built from 1827 to 1835 according to the designs of John Nash and replaced the 𝕶ing's 𝕸ews, a prison where the Parliamentarians imprisoned Royalist captives during the Civil War, and the 𝕲olden 𝕮ross 𝕳otel, depicted by Charles Dickens in *The Pickwick Papers* as the place where Mr Pickwick meets Tupman, Snodgrass and Winkle. As Nash died before work was complete the square was finished by Charles Barry, who levelled the sloping land and paved the central area, surrounding it with a low wall on the northern side in which the Imperial measures of inch, foot and yard are etched in metal. In 1848 the square was the setting for the capital's first-ever display of electric lighting, when arc lamps lit up the area, and every 30 January, the anniversary of Charles I's execution, it is the setting for a memorial service to the executed king. The square is ringed with grandiose buildings of questionable architectural merit, such as William Wilkins's National Gallery and Herbert Baker's 1935 South Africa House, and the centre is dominated by Nelson's Column, other statues including those of Charles I, George IV, Admirals Beatty, Cunningham and Jellico, and Generals Napier and Havelock. There is also a plinth that was meant for a statue of William IV which never transpired and was filled in 2001 by Rachel Whiteread's amusing *Monument*, a cast of the very same plinth in crystal-clear resin placed upside-down on the stone original.

centre of square
Nelson's Column
E. H Baily's statue of Lord Nelson, victor of the 1805 Battle of Trafalgar, carved between 1840 and 1843, looks towards Plymouth, from where Nelson left England for the last time, and is surrounded by lions designed between 1859 and 1867 by Edwin Landseer, who used as his model a dead animal brought to his St John's Wood studio by cab from Regent's Park Zoo. On 30 May 1884 the Dynamiters, a socialist terrorist group, left sixteen cakes of explosives at the base of the column. They were defused, but that evening at 9.20 p.m. a bomb exploded at Scotland Yard police headquarters, injuring many people, while a bomb went off at the Junior Carlton Club at the same time causing much damage. To Adolf Hitler, Nelson's Column represented 'a symbol of British naval might and world domination' which he wanted to remove, boasting 'it would be an impressive way of underlining the German victory if it were to be transferred to Berlin', which may explain why the Germans failed to bomb the column during the Second World War. In the government bunker underneath Nelson's Column lies the Whitehall Telephone Exchange, installed in the 1950s as part of London's preparations for dealing with nuclear war.

north side
National Gallery
The National Gallery, London's oldest major art gallery, highlights of which include Leonardo da Vinci's *Cartoon* (1504), John Constable's *The Haywain* (1821) and Van Gogh's *Sunflowers* (1888), was established at 99 Pall Mall in 1824. George IV

persuaded the government to buy thirty-eight paintings belonging to the banker John Julius Angerstein, whose collection included works by Raphael and Rembrandt and a large altarpiece by Sebastiano del Piombo, *The Raising of Lazarus*. But following public criticism of the venue there were calls for a permanent gallery to be built to house the growing collection, and once the site of the former King's Mews at Charing Cross had been chosen, John Nash, who was in charge of creating Trafalgar Square out of the jumble of medieval buildings that stood here, hired as architect William Wilkins, who used the portico from 𝕮𝖆𝖗𝖑𝖙𝖔𝖓 𝕳𝖔𝖚𝖘𝖊 (George IV's recently demolished palace to the south, which stood where Carlton House Terrace can now be found) to front his 1832–8 building.

The new gallery opened in 1838 and originally had no formal collection policy, new pictures being acquired according to the personal tastes of the Trustees, but by the 1850s the Trustees were being criticized for neglecting to buy works of the earlier Italian Schools, and so Sir Charles Eastlake, the first director, journeyed to Italy to buy around 140 paintings of the Italian Renaissance, including Botticelli's *Adoration of the Kings* and Uccello's *The Battle of San Romano*. In 1856 J. M. W. Turner bequeathed over 1,000 paintings, drawings and watercolours and in 1871 the gallery's collection grew further when seventy-seven works, including Dutch and Flemish paintings, were bought from the collection of the late Tory politician Sir Robert Peel.

In 1876 the gallery was enlarged again, but by this time British works were being exhibited in other buildings, leading to the creation of what became the Tate Gallery on Millbank, which opened in 1897. In 1914 the suffragette Mary Richardson damaged Velázquez's *The Rokeby Venus*, telling reporters: 'I have tried to destroy the picture of the most beautiful woman in mythological history as a protest against the government destroying Mrs Pankhurst [who was then on hunger strike in support of votes for women]'.

Richardson received a six-month sentence, and later explained that she had chosen the Velázquez because she did not like the way 'men gaped at it all day'. In 1985 Lord Sainsbury financed the construction of a new wing to the west of the gallery which opened in 1991 and was filled with the entire early Renaissance collection.

➤ Tate Britain, p. 246; Tate Modern, p. 376.

(ii) St Giles

St Giles, the area between New Oxford Street and Shaftesbury Avenue, was developed in the twelfth century on the marshy ground around a leper hospital situated where the Church of St Giles now stands. After suffering considerable loss of life during the 1665 Plague St Giles became a slum, one of London's most unruly, with thieving and prostitution rife, and a population of poor Irish immigrants and black beggars, mostly escaped slaves who became known as St Giles blackbirds, crammed into crumbling houses in the narrow courts and alleys. The desperate conditions attracted considerable attention from the country's foremost writers. When Henry Fielding, the novelist and barrister, conducted a survey into London crime in the middle of the eighteenth century, he noted how 'in the parish of St Giles's there are great numbers of houses set apart for the reception of idle persons and vagabonds'. Lord Byron told the House of Lords in 1812: 'I have been in some of the most oppressed provinces of Turkey, but never under the most despotic of infidel governments did I behold such squalid wretchedness as I have seen since my return in the very heart of a Christian country', and it was probably St Giles that Oscar Wilde had in mind when describing the slum inhabited by 'women with hoarse voices and harsh laughter' in *Lord Arthur Savile's Crime*. The derided buildings were demolished when New Oxford Street was built in the 1840s and the area then gradually became commercialized, with Crosse and Blackwell's pickle factory one of the main local employers. Since the construction of Centre Point and the introduction of a one-way system in the 1960s the area has become something of a backwater at the edge of the West End and Covent Garden.

Gin Lane

William Hogarth set one of his best-known works, *Gin Lane* (1750–51), in St Giles, one of the areas of London most affected by the abundance of gin imported from Holland following the accession of William of Orange to the British throne in 1688. Within a few years every fourth house was a gin-shop, a state of affairs that led the prime minister, Robert Walpole, to bring in an Act in 1736 restricting its sale, resulting in riots and cries of: 'No Gin, No King'. In Hogarth's picture the Madonna and Child are personified in the gin-sodden mother dropping her baby underneath a pawn-broker's sign bearing the legend: 'Drunk for a penny / Dead drunk for two pence / Clean straw for nothing', while in the background is the steeple of Hawksmoor's church of St George, Bloomsbury Way, and a tumble-down building typical of the jerry-building of the day.

Denmark Street

The centre of Britain's music industry for much of the twentieth century, Denmark Street was named after Prince George of Denmark, Queen Anne's consort. Music publishers moved here in the nineteenth century to be close to the theatres and concert halls where new songs could be aired. The street later came to be filled with recording studios and offices for promoters, showbiz journalists and songwriters, its heyday being in the early 1960s, before the Beatles revolutionized the industry. Denmark Street is nowadays dominated by musical instrument shops.

north side: Charing Cross Road to St Giles High Street
No. 19
Melody Maker, until recently one of Britain's major music magazines, was launched at 19 Denmark Street in 1926 by Lawrence Wright, a music publisher and songwriter who doubled as Horatio Nicholls, composer of romantic songs with a desert theme, as popularized by Rudolph Valentino in *The Sheikh*. Early issues did little more than promote Wright's own songs, but things changed when the media group Odham's bought the title in 1929, the first post-Wright edition containing a thinly disguised swipe at the previous owner which read: 'The passing of central control will not affect the *Melody Maker* in any way except that it will ensure complete editorial independence from vested interests.' *Melody Maker* later became the leading magazine for jazz in Britain but lost ground to *New Musical Express* in the rock era and ceased publishing in 2000.
Mills Music Ltd, No. 20
Elton John worked as office boy earning £5 a week for publishers Mills Music in 1965, when he was still known by his original name, Reg Dwight. When he told his former history teacher, Bill Johnson, that he had secured the job the latter replied: 'When you're forty you'll still be some sort of glorified office-boy or you'll be a millionaire.' Paul Simon tried to sell his song catalogue, which included 'Homeward Bound' and 'The Sound of Silence', without success to Mills Music in 1965.
Peter Maurice Music (1960s), No. 21
In the early 1960s chart-topping British singers such as Adam Faith and Marty Wilde used to drop into the office to pick up songs from in-house songwriters who included Lionel Bart. In the 1990s No. 21 was home of Acid Jazz Records, which issued early records by the Brand New Heavies and Jamiroquai.
Rhodes Music, No. 22
One of Britain's best-known musical instruments shops, its customers have included

Pete Townshend, Jeff Beck and Eric Clapton. In the 1960s Manfred Mann and the Small Faces recorded in the Tin Pan Alley Studios in the basement.

Denmark Productions (1960s), No. 25
Denmark Productions handled the Kinks and the Troggs in the 1960s, while Gordon Mills, who also worked here, ran the affairs of Engelbert Humperdinck and Tom Jones.

south side: St Giles High Street to Charing Cross Road

Job Centre, No. 1
Dennis Nilsen, the serial killer who murdered at least fifteen men at his home in north-west London in the late 1970s and early 1980s, worked at the Job Centre at 1 Denmark Street while engaged in his killing spree. To help with the catering for the 1980 staff Christmas party Nilsen brought in a huge cooking pot in which he had previously boiled the heads of some of his victims.

Regent Sound Studios (1960s) / Helter Skelter, No. 4
The Rolling Stones cut most of their debut album here in January 1964, and over the next few years Elton John recorded cover versions of well-known songs for the budget label Embassy at Regent. Cat Stevens, whose real name was Steven Georgiou and who was born only a few hundred yards away on New Oxford Street, made his first demonstration record at the studio in 1965. The bookshop Helter Skelter, London's only store devoted to rock books and magazines, has been based on the ground floor since 1995.

No. 5
New Musical Express's first address in 1952 was at No. 5, while on the top floor was Lorna Music where in 1964 Paul Simon tried to sell his songs, only to be told they were too intellectual and uncommercial.

No. 6
The then unnamed Sex Pistols rehearsed and slept in the flat above the ground-floor shop in late 1975.

No. 7
No. 7 was home in the early years of the twentieth century to music publishers Box & Cox, founded by H. Elton Box and Adrian Cox, whose biggest hit was 'I've Got a Lovely Bunch of Coconuts'.

Southern Music, No. 8
A number of well-known chart hits of the 1960s were recorded in the ground-floor studio, including Donovan's 'Catch the Wind', the Ivy League's 'Funny How Love Can Be' and the Flowerpot Men's Summer of Love cash-in 'Let's Go to San Francisco'.

Barino Coffee Bar, No. 9a
As La Gioconda Restaurant it was a hang-out for mods in the sixties and was where David Bowie (then David Jones) met his first backing band, the Lower Third, and where the Small Faces decided to turn professional. By the late 1970s No. 9a had become a popular meeting place for punk bands, including the Clash and Slits.

St Giles High Street

Despite its curved shape, St Giles High Street was built as a Roman road, linking the western route out of London with the City, the bend being necessary to ford the marshy land. Criminals being taken from Newgate Gaol to the gallows at Tyburn at the western end of Oxford Street before 1783 would be taken to one of the many inns on St Giles High Street for a last drink from what became known as 'the St Giles bowl'. The road's status declined following the construction of New Oxford Street in the 1840s.

St Giles-in-the-Fields
The 1733 church, which is the oldest building in the area and was designed by Henry Flitcroft in a style similar to that of St Martin-in-the-Fields, half a mile south, stands on the site of a leper hospital built by Queen Matilda, wife of Henry I, in 1117. The spire can be seen in the Hogarth painting *The Times of Day: Noon* (1736) in which Cupid, Venus and Apollo lounge among the Huguenot crowd outside the building.

(iii) Covent Garden

One of London's main tourist spots, along with Leicester Square and Westminster, Covent Garden stands on the site of Westminster Abbey's thirteenth-century convent, which later reverted to the Crown and was granted to the Duke of Somerset following the dissolution of the monasteries in the mid fifteenth century. When the duke fell out of favour in 1552 the land was handed to John Russell, the 1st Earl of Bedford, whose descendants still own large tracts of land locally, who built himself a mansion, 𝔅𝔢𝔡𝔣𝔬𝔯𝔡 𝔥𝔬𝔲𝔰𝔢, near the modern-day junction of Southampton Street and Strand. In 1613 the 3rd Earl walled the former convent garden and his successor, Francis Russell, chose to develop the suburb, paying £2,000 for a licence to build houses 'fitt for Gentlemen and men of ability'. He also hired Inigo Jones to design a grand Palladian piazza which has remained the centrepiece of the area since the 1630s.

After a market developed in the 1650s the area declined as a prestigious residential location, but it became a centre for theatre and opera following Charles II's decision to license two Theatre Royals in 1660. It also attracted coffee houses, gambling dens, brothels and criminals, particularly the Mohock gang of aristocratic hooligans, feared throughout London for their speciality of assaulting elderly women, throwing them into empty barrels, and rolling them along the road. The Bedford Estate, which ran the market, lost interest in administering it at the beginning of the twentieth century, and in 1918 sold the lease to a new company, the Covent Garden Estate Co. Ltd.

By the mid twentieth century it was apparent that the narrow streets of central London could no longer take the market-bound traffic, but it was not until 1961 that the authorities took action, recommending that the market be moved to Beckton, east London, and when that choice was vehemently opposed, Nine Elms.

Locals formed an association at a meeting in 1971 to oppose plans to allow Covent Garden to be redeveloped for hotels, conference centres and corporate tower blocks. A worldwide recession in the 1970s meant many of the proposed schemes were abandoned and the environment secretary, Geoffrey Rippon, then listed some 245 local buildings and surrounding properties, so that when the market left for Nine Elms the buildings, instead of being demolished and replaced with skyscrapers, were converted to an indoor flea market. Covent Garden has since re-emerged as a popular shopping area.

Bedford Street

The street dates back to 1633 and became a publishing centre in the late nineteenth century with offices for Macmillan, Edward Arnold, Joseph Dent and Heinemann, who first published Robert Louis Stevenson, H. G. Wells, Somerset Maugham and Joseph Conrad. The Dutch artist Vincent Van Gogh worked at Goupil's, the art dealer's at No. 25, in 1875 but his moody behaviour annoyed his bosses so much he was transferred to Paris. In 1860 the Jewish tailor Moses Moses moved his East End clothes shop to Bedford Street and changed his name to the anglicized Alfred Moss, hiring out suits from 1897 when a customer, Charles Pond, unable to afford a new one, persuaded the manager to lend him a suit he could return and borrow a number of times. By 1920 Moss Bros owned the entire west side between No. 25 and King Street. *The Lady*, Britain's oldest women's magazine, is based at Nos. 39–40.

Bow Street

Built between 1633 and 1677 in the shape of a bow, the street attracted a number of well-known figures as residents, including the Dutch wood carver Grinling Gibbons and the novelist-barrister Henry Fielding. The Covent Garden Theatre (now the Covent Garden Opera House) opened on Bow Street in 1732 and eight years later the magistrates court that has since become one of London's most famous first sat.

west side: Russell Street to Long Acre

𝕭𝖔𝖜 𝕾𝖙𝖗𝖊𝖊𝖙 𝕸𝖆𝖌𝖎𝖘𝖙𝖗𝖆𝖙𝖊𝖘 𝕮𝖔𝖚𝖗𝖙 (1740–1880), No. 4

Thomas de Veil, a 'trading justice' who aimed to make a profit and kept accounts, opened London's first magistrates court here in 1740, a time when there was little official protection for members of the public. After he died in 1747 de Veil was replaced by Henry Fielding, barrister, circuit judge and novelist, who set up a small force of 'thief-takers', known as 'Mr Fielding's Men', who were unpaid but received a share of the reward money. The public, understandably, assumed Mr Fielding's Men were involved in trading stolen goods, so when the team broke up a gang of thieves, in the first major haul of criminals for thirty years, the Recorder of London would not give them the rewards to which they were entitled.

After Fielding died in 1754 he was replaced by his blind half-brother, John, who had written a crime report entitled 'Thieving Detected: Being a True and Particular Description of the Various Methods and Artifices Used by Thieves and Sharpers to Take in and Deceive the Public; with Proper Cautions to Guard against Such Destructive Measures'. John reformed Henry's thief-taking unit, allowing them to claim expenses but be paid a retainer for their work in combating crime.

Fielding's troupe, known from 1785 as the 'Bow Street Runners', did not wear uniforms but carried short tip staves with gilt crowns so that they could be identified, and they continued as an independent force until 1839 when they were disbanded following the founding of the Metropolitan Police.

When blue lamps were introduced outside police stations in 1861, Queen Victoria objected to being reminded every time she visited Covent Garden Opera House of the blue room in which Prince Albert had died, and so Bow Street station had a unique white lamp. The court moved across the road in 1880 and the site is now occupied by the Floral Hall.

Covent Garden (Royal Opera House), Bow Street at Floral Street

London's grandest opera venue opened on 7 December 1732 with a performance of the William Congreve play *The Way of the World* under the management of John Rich, who had made his name with his superlative dance routines, founded the Sublime Society of Beefsteaks (motto: 'beef and liberty'), and had once killed a fellow actor in a fight over a wig. Until the Theatres Act of 1843, Covent Garden was one of only two London venues allowed to present drama, as well as musical works, but it was best known for the latter and was where the premières of several works by the German-born George Frederick Handel, including *Alexander's Feast*, *Judas Maccabaeus* and *The Messiah*, were held in the 1730s.

In 1807 Joseph Grimaldi, known as the 'Garrick of Clowns' and the 'Jupiter of the practical joke', began his seventeen-year association with the theatre. The following year Covent Garden burned down in a fire that killed more than twenty firemen and resulted in the destruction of Handel's original manuscripts. It was rebuilt soon after, in the style of the Temple of Minerva at the Acropolis, but the opening night was marred by noise from protestors complaining about the increased admission prices who released pigs and pigeons into the auditorium, or as the publisher Leigh Hunt put it: 'the actors became the audience, and the audience the actors'. The demonstrations, known as the Old Prices Riots, lasted for two months before the managers, John Kemble and Thomas Harris, conceded defeat. Charles Macready took over as manager in 1837 and introduced a new calcium light known as limelight, which revolutionized stage lighting. After Covent Garden lost the drama part of its duopoly in 1843 there was a lull in its fortunes until Michael Costa and Giuseppe Persiani took over the theatre and redesigned it as an

Italian opera house, hiring the leading singers of the day.

The theatre burned down again on 3 March 1856 and was rebuilt in a Romanesque style by E. M. Barry, son of the House of Commons architect Charles, reopening as the Royal Opera House Covent Garden on 15 May 1858 with a production of Meyerbeer's *Les Huguenots* that was ruined when the last act had to be cancelled because the audience had taken so long to return to their seats after the intermission. Yet despite its superficial grandeur Barry's design was second-rate, the public spaces cramped and poorly designed, and many seats suffered from appalling sightlines. But with few rivals the theatre achieved its aim of becoming a prestigious opera venue. Augustus Harris promoted German as well as Italian opera, with Gustav Mahler conducting Wagner's *Tristan* and *The Ring Cycle* in 1892. When Hans Richter became conductor early in the twentieth century he demanded that all performers, even the principal singers, rehearsed. Richter's standards were maintained by his successor, Thomas Beecham, who promoted relatively new composers such as Richard Strauss and Frederick Delius. When the venue reverted to opera in 1953 after being used as a Mecca dance hall during the Second World War there were performances by Maria Callas and Joan Sutherland and visiting conductors such as Otto Klemperer and John Barbirolli.

At the end of the twentieth century £200 million-worth of refurbishment overseen by Jeremy Dixon so pleased the dancers of the Royal Ballet they broke into spontaneous applause after their first rehearsal. Nevertheless, at the same time, technical problems meant that a performance of Ligeti's *Le Grand Macabre* had to be cancelled at a cost of several hundred thousand pounds, forcing managers to admit that the reopening had been rushed.
► Royal Albert Hall, p. 422.

east side: Long Acre to Russell Street
Bow Street Magistrates Court (1880–)
London's main magistrates court was where Oscar Wilde was charged with gross indecency in April 1895 and thrown into a cell, waking after a fretful night to order a breakfast of tea, toast and eggs from the nearby Tavistock Hotel, which was brought across on a tray. It was also where the trial of Radclyffe Hall's lesbian novel *The Well of Loneliness*, indicted on the grounds of obscenity, took place in November 1928. The novel had achieved notoriety after the *Sunday Express*'s James Douglas wrote in his review: 'I would rather give a healthy boy or girl a phial of prussic acid than this book', and during the trial it was found to contain 'acts of the most horrible, unnatural and disgusting obscenity' and banned. After prominent members of the Campaign for Nuclear Disarmament demonstrated outside the Russian Embassy in 1961, thirty-six of the organization's members were taken to Bow Street, where they were bound over for a year. When all thirty-six defied the order the authorities sent them to prison for two months, although one of the group, the 89-year-old Lord (Bertrand) Russell, was released after a week in Brixton Prison.
► Brixton Prison, p. 406; CND in Trafalgar Square, p. 103.

Covent Garden (Piazza)

The paved piazza at the centre of congested Covent Garden was designed by Inigo Jones in the 1630s to attract wealthy Londoners wishing to move out of the City into hitherto semi-rural areas. It was based on the piazza of Livorno, northern Italy, with luxurious stuccoed houses (none of which survives, the current piazza buildings being mostly Victorian) around a colonnaded square and church. Early inhabitants included Sir Thomas Trenchard, a member of Oliver Cromwell's Long Parliament, who lived at **No. 1**, and Thomas Killigrew, who built the first Theatre Royal Drury Lane, at **No. 8**. The Civil War of the 1640s saw many aristocrats flee; the best houses were vacated and shops opened.

Within ten years a market had developed that grew into one of London's greatest, selling fruit, flowers, roots, herbs and animals. By the eighteenth century London's most expensive prostitutes had begun renting the upper rooms of the piazza buildings for £250 a night, punters buying Harris's *New Atlantic: The Whoremonger's Guide to London* to help them make the right choice. But by the following century the market had grown so large it had pushed almost all other activities out.

After the market left for Nine Elms in 1973 there was an opportunity to convert the piazza into a central square for London, in the manner of Madrid's Plaza Mayor, or Rome's St Peter's Square, but instead the authorities opted to convert the main market building into an indoor flea market that has become one of the most popular locations in London.

north side
Rock Garden, Nos. 6–7
A former banana warehouse, converted into a rock-themed restaurant in the style of the Hard Rock Café in 1976, it has since become an important venue for bands at early stages of their careers, including the Stranglers, who were showered with spaghetti thrown by unimpressed diners, Talking Heads, Dire Straits, the Police and U2. The Smiths made their London debut at the Rock Garden on 23 March 1983 billed as the 'Mancunian 5-piece whose sound though difficult to pigeon-hole leans towards pop and the dance floor'.

east side
The artist William Hogarth had his studio at the north-eastern corner of the piazza from 1729 to 1733, by which time Covent Garden had lost its allure, thanks to the ramshackle market in the piazza, the local brothels and bawdy taverns. The playwright Richard Brinsley Sheridan watched the Theatre Royal, which he owned, burn down while sitting in the 𝕲𝖗𝖊𝖆𝖙 𝕻𝖎𝖆𝖟𝖟𝖆 𝖈𝖔𝖋𝖋𝖊𝖊 𝖍𝖔𝖚𝖘𝖊 on 24 February 1809 and when asked by a

fellow customer how he could remain so composed replied: 'Can't a fellow enjoy a drink by his own fireside?'

Floral Hall / London Transport Museum
The hall, designed by E. M. Barry and built in 1859 by the owners of the Covent Garden Opera House, made use of the possibilities afforded by cast iron and glass that had inspired Joseph Paxton's Crystal Palace, but was not a success and a rival flower market opened in Bedford Street soon after. It was converted to a fruit market in 1887 and just 100 years later, in 1980, the western section became the home of the Transport Museum, based around a collection of vehicles first assembled in Chiswick in the 1920s by the London General Omnibus Company. The museum features the work of Harry Beck, designer of the first structured underground map in 1931, while the shop, one of the best of the many London museum shops, contains a large collection of E. McKnight Kauffer's art deco Underground posters.

south side
The south side of the piazza was occupied by the wall of the 𝕭𝖊𝖉𝖋𝖔𝖗𝖉 𝕳𝖔𝖚𝖘𝖊 mansion until the latter was demolished in 1706 and is now home to the 1985 Jubilee Market, during the construction of which archaeologists uncovered evidence of the Saxon settlement of Lundenwic, including traces of timber buildings and burial sites. The adjacent Jubilee Market Hall, built in 1903 for vegetable traders and florists, now contains a smaller version of the main flea market.

west side
St Paul
Where Covent Garden's famous temple stands / That boasts the work of Jones's immortal hands – *Trivia*, John Gay (1716)
Known as the actors' church – the late-Victorian actress Ellen Terry is buried here and the church contains memorials to the actress Vivien Leigh and the music hall star Marie Lloyd – St Paul was the work of the 4th Earl of Bedford who on informing the architect Inigo Jones that he wanted a

chapel, but nothing too expensive, 'nothing much better than a barn', was told: 'you shall have the handsomest barn in England'. Between 1631 and 1633 Jones erected what was central London's first classical building and the capital's first new Anglican church for nearly 100 years, placing the altar at the western end so that the Tuscan portico façade could face the piazza, but annoying the clergy, who ensured that the altar was moved to the east and the main entrance to Bedford Street. In his 1662 diary Samuel Pepys recorded seeing the English version of the Italian Punchinello (Punch and Judy), which had been introduced to England by the Italian puppeteer Pierro Gimonde, under the church's portico, which is also the setting for the opening of George Bernard Shaw's play *Pygmalion* and its musical version, *My Fair Lady*. A fire in 1795 destroyed much of Jones's original work, although the church was rebuilt to his designs.

Earlham Street

At the junction of Earlham Street, Mercer Street, Monmouth Street and Shorts Gardens stands Seven Dials, a Doric pillar with, strangely, only six dials, copied from the 1693 original which was torn down in 1773 by a mob who, believing a horde of treasure was buried at its base, had dug away, but found nothing. The surrounding area of small compact streets was laid out by Thomas Neale, Charles II's Master of the Mint, at the end of the seventeenth century, and soon became a slum noted for, according to Dickens, its 'wild visions of prodigies of wickedness, want and beggary'. It was also a poor Jewish area, as Flora Tristan noted in her *London Journal* of 1840, in which she described how 'the cellars are nothing but kennels where the hapless people of Israel are crowded pell-mell'. The slums were wiped out at the end of the nineteenth century and subsequent commercialization led to the almost complete removal of the residential population and the creation of streets that soon filled with small workshops making furniture, watches, clocks, musical instruments, fittings for the nearby Covent Garden market and at one firm, Comyn Ching, at 15–21 Shelton Street, furnishings for the *Titanic*. When the market moved away in the 1970s the buildings were left untouched and were subsequently gentrified into designer shops, particularly around Neal Street and Neal's Yard, a courtyard off Monmouth Street filled with shops selling vegetarian food and New Age wares.

Donmar Warehouse, No. 41, north side
A nineteenth-century banana warehouse, it became a rehearsing centre in 1961 and was used by the Royal Shakespeare Company as a studio theatre from 1976 until 1981 when it was taken over by Ian Albery, who renamed it the Donmar Warehouse after his father Donald (Don) and the dancer Margot Fonteyn (Mar) and reopened it as a fringe theatre venue. Sam Mendes was appointed artistic director in the late 1980s, and staged successful productions of *Cabaret* and *The Glass Menagerie*, before achieving greater fame with the film *American Beauty*. He left the theatre in 2002 and was replaced by Michael Grandage.
▶ Almeida Theatre, Islington, p. 325.

Garrick Street

More than 5,500 people were displaced to build Garrick Street, named after the actor David Garrick. In the 1860s the street replaced an area described by Maud Stanley, the campaigning social worker, as having the 'poorest, the dirtiest, and the lowest houses that this part of London can boast of'. Below street level is the oldest section of London's tiled 9-mile 1850s utility subway which carries cables and pipes in purpose-built tunnels.

Garrick Club, No. 15, west side
The club, named after the famous eighteenth-century actor David Garrick and established in nearby King Street in 1831 to cater for actors who could not gain admittance to the Pall Mall gentlemen's clubs, moved to the newly constructed Garrick

Street in 1864 and was where in the early 1960s society osteopath Stephen Ward met Captain Yevgeny Ivanov, the Soviet naval attaché with whom he became embroiled in the Profumo Scandal (p. 157). In 1998 the Disney Corporation paid the Garrick £50 million for the rights to Winnie the Pooh, which the author A. A. Milne, a Garrick member, had bequested to the club.

Henrietta Street
north side
No. 33
The Boy Scouts, founded by Robert Baden-Powell, had their first office at the address of Baden-Powell's publisher, Pearson's, and grew from the success of the latter's *Scouting for Boys*, first published in 1908.

south side: Southampton Street to Bedford Street
No. 4
The early-twentieth-century military hero, Arabist and writer T. E. Lawrence (Lawrence of Arabia), disillusioned with Britain's role in dividing up the Middle East at the end of the First World War, tried to enlist in the Royal Air Force under the pseudonym John Hume Ross at the Air Recruitment Office based here in August 1922. Racked with nerves, Lawrence paced up and down Henrietta Street for two hours, relieved himself by St Paul's church, and then entered the building, only to fail the medical because 'You aren't as good as we want'. One of the officers in charge was Captain W. E. Johns (author of the Biggles books), who was suspicious of 'Ross' and checked his appearance with photographs of wanted criminals. When Johns could find no entry for a John Hume Ross in the public records at Somerset House, he scolded Lawrence and sent him away. A few hours later Lawrence, to Johns's astonishment, returned with an Air Ministry messenger who had an order for the recruit to be enlisted immediately. When Johns expressed his surprise, the messenger warned him, 'For heaven's sake watch your step. This

man is Lawrence of Arabia. Get him into the Force or you'll get your bowler hat.'

Jane Austen's address (1813–14), No. 10
The early-nineteenth-century novelist stayed with her brother in the flat above the bank he owned at No. 10 in the summer of 1813, and again in March 1814, describing the property as 'all dirt and confusion, but in a very promising way'. While in Covent Garden Austen saw *Don Juan* at the Lyceum Theatre and *The Merchant of Venice* at Drury Lane's Theatre Royal. The property was later used as a hospital and is now offices.

Gollancz (1928–1994), No. 14
Victor Gollancz opened a publishing firm on Henrietta Street in 1928, where one of his first projects was *A Scullion's Diary* by Eric Blair, a retired Burmese military policeman, which arrived at the firm courtesy of a friend of the author who ignored instructions to destroy the script but save the paper clips. Gollancz contacted Blair and told him he would publish the book pseudonymously, to which the author replied: 'I have no reputation that is lost by doing this and if the book has any kind of success I can always use this pseudonym again.' The pseudonym Blair adopted was George Orwell – George because it was archetypically English and Orwell after the Suffolk river near where he was raised – and the book was given the title *Down and Out in Paris and London*.

In 1936 Gollancz, John Strachey and Harold Laski founded the Left Book Club, a socialist reading circle modelled on commercial book club lines to propagate Soviet communism. It was an instant success, attracting some 50,000 members, who received a new title in a garish orange cover every month and frequent newsletters, whose frantic production schedule led to complaints about clattering typewriters from the nearby Covent Garden Opera House. Having spent the 1930s promulgating communism and denouncing fascism, the Left Book Club was caught unawares by the Hitler–Stalin pact of 1940.

However, the vanquishing of fascism at the end of the war led to an upturn in its fortunes, and during the campaigning for the 1945 general election, which returned a huge Labour majority, the LBC's yellow-backed anti-Tory pamphlets each sold around a quarter of a million copies. Once Labour was elected the Left Book Club's popularity declined and it was dissolved in 1948.

King Street
Named after Charles I, who was on the throne when the street was laid out to the west of the newly built Covent Garden Piazza in the 1630s, King Street, until twentieth-century commercialization, was one of the most popular residential streets in Covent Garden, home at various times to the actor David Garrick, the poet Samuel Taylor Coleridge and Thomas Arne, composer of 'Rule Britannia', who was born at **№. 31** in 1710.

No. 43 / Middle Earth (1960s), north side
One of the few surviving early-eighteenth-century properties in the area, No. 43 was built in 1716 by Thomas Archer, also responsible for the church of St John the Evangelist in Smith Square, Westminster, and was immediately castigated by the architectural critic Batty Langley, as 'certainly one of the most expensive and worst buildings about London'. In 1772 it became a hotel and in 1856 a theatre where, eighty years later, Leonard Sachs and Peter Ridgeway formed the Players Theatre Club so that Londoners could still hear music hall, by then disappearing from the London stage. Many of the Players' sets were designed by Rex Whistler, and a large rooftop view of Covent Garden from 43 King Street, painted by Whistler for an early production, hung in the foyer of the Players Theatre in Charing Cross. In 1967 43 King Street became home to the psychedelic rock club the Electric Garden, a rival to the UFO club on Tottenham Court Road, where Tyrannosaurus Rex played their first gig. The premises are now occupied by a PR firm.
► **UFO club**, p. 148.

Communist Party of Great Britain headquarters (1920–1980), No. 16, south side
Soon after the British Communist Party opened its first London office at 16 King Street with money donated by Lenin, it was raided by the police, acting under 'emergency regulations', who used information gleaned from tapping the Party's telephones and arrested Party Secretary Albert Inkpin for publishing Soviet literature deemed to be seditious, resulting in the latter serving six months' hard labour. In October 1925 police raided King Street again, this time carrying away 250,000 letters, a statue of the Soviet leader Lenin, and an interesting lump of metal which turned out to be the toilet ballcock. Inkpin was again jailed for seditious libel, as well as incitement to mutiny. On a later occasion Special Branch officers rented rooms in nearby Bedford Street, burrowed into the building, and by means of an open trapdoor sat taking notes directly under the stage where the Party was holding a meeting. Eventually the officers were spotted and CP officials called the police, who found themselves arresting their plain-clothed superiors.

With the intensification of the Cold War in the 1950s, MI5 stepped up its surveillance of King Street and in 1955 the security service obtained a complete membership list after raiding a wealthy member's Mayfair flat while he was away for the weekend, microfilming it and replacing it before he returned. To no one's surprise the names included those of thirty-one Labour MPs. Later that decade, MI5 agent Peter Wright (who would go on to attain public notoriety with his book *Spycatcher*) devised an ingenious means of bugging No. 16. He constructed a false door wired up with a microphone which could be fixed over the coal chute, but wary of installing it by day, when the street would be full of office workers, in the evening, when it would be thronged with theatre-goers and other revellers, or late at night, when any such activity would immediately look suspicious, he sent a group of MI5 officers and their wives to the street one Saturday afternoon. They staggered along, pretending to be drunk, until they reached No. 16. There, one of their number dropped to his knees and, as the party laughed and joked, took out a drill, quickly bored a few holes in the coal chute door, removing the brick dust in his handkerchief, and placed the new, bugged door over the old one.

► Lenin's Bloomsbury haunts, p. 92.

Long Acre

The main east–west route through the area, Long Acre was laid out in 1615 on gardens owned by the monks of Westminster Abbey and was where in June 1780 the painter-poet William Blake, on his way to the Great Queen Street shop where he was being taught engraving, was caught up with the anti-Catholic Gordon Rioters, following the mob to Newgate Prison, where he watched them burn it down. Long Acre has long enjoyed important commercial associations. In the seventeenth century it was renowned for its coach repairers, who worked from premises later adapted to showrooms for motor cars; in the eighteenth century it was dominated by cabinet makers; and in the twentieth century its major firm was the publisher Odham's, owners of the *Daily Herald* and *Sunday People*, which was based in a huge complex half-way along the northern side of the road. Although the street is now central to local shopping, an unofficial Covent Garden High Street, it is filled mostly with chainstore outlets, a rare exception being Stanford's at Nos. 12–14, London's best-known shop for maps and travel books, founded in 1852, and believed to be the largest of its kind in the world.

north side: Upper St Martin's Lane to Drury Lane

John Logie Baird's studio (1927–31), No. 133

Baird, the pioneer of television, moved from Frith Street, Soho, to Long Acre in 1927 to work in a small studio the size of a living room, and there constructed what he called a 'televisor' out of an old tea chest with a circular rotating cardboard disc, a knitting needle as spindle, a projection lamp set in an empty biscuit box and lenses bought from a bicycle shop at fourpence each, the apparatus assembled with glue, sealing wax and string. Nevertheless it was good enough to allow Baird to make his first outdoor television transmission on the roof of No. 133 on 12 June 1928 and to make a film, *The Bride*, a monologue with the comedian George Robey, transmitted from the studio on 19 August 1929, although he struggled to show sound and vision at the same time. Baird began transmitting a daily experimental picture on 30 September 1929, but it was the BBC rather than Baird who synchronized sound and vision, making it possible for 'televisors' to be sold, one of the first people to buy a set being the prime minister, James Ramsay MacDonald.

► Baird's pioneering television work in Soho, p. 197.

St Martin's Hall / Odham's, No. 94

St Martin's Hall was the setting for the first meeting of the International Working Men's Association (the First International) on 28 September 1864, the delegates including Karl Marx, and was converted into the Queen's Theatre in 1867 and a gymnasium in 1878. The building was later taken over by the publisher Odham's to produce magazines such as *Racing Pigeon*, *Vanity Fair* and *John Bull*, a red light flashing whenever the presses were not working, and from 1925 the ailing *Sunday People*, which Odham's owner, Julius Elias, revived by introducing sensationalist articles and offering free insurance to new readers.

Even by 'Fleet Street' standards Elias was seriously eccentric. He refused to keep pennies in his pocket, had an irrational loathing of green (he refused to allow his wife to wear a green dress), and hated any design that featured peacocks, so much so that arriving home one day and finding a new carpet bearing an heraldic pattern he announced: 'looks like peacock to me' and had it removed. Elias died in 1946, but even that was not enough to curtail his involvement with his papers according to his successor, A. C. Duncan, a keen spiritualist, who claimed he held regular 'consultations' with his deceased predecessor.

In the 1950s the *People*'s chief crime reporter, Duncan Webb, pioneered the modern style of crime reporting, each Sunday producing a detailed investigative report, usually on a disturbing moral matter such as West End vice or south London protection rackets. In these articles he would breathlessly 'lift the lid' on the 'dangers threatening London', explain how he had sent the article, in the form of a 'dossier', to the Home Office (who, needless to say, were not in the least bit interested), and at the end reveal how he had extricated himself from danger using a phrase he coined that is now one of the archetypal newspaper clichés – 'I made my excuses and left'.

The *Mirror* Group took over Odham's in the early sixties, leaving the *People* intact but giving the *Herald* a new image and a new name – the *Sun* – whose first issue was described by the left winger Tony Benn as 'appalling . . . basically the same minus the *Herald*'s political content'. When the paper flopped it was sold, in 1969, to Rupert Murdoch for £1 million, moving to Bouverie Street, off Fleet Street. The building was demolished after Covent Garden market closed in the 1970s.

▶ *Sun*, Bouverie Street, p. 50.

St Martin's Lane

In medieval times the route was West Church Lane, an open drain, 'full of great muckhills', but it soon began to attract the wealthy looking for places to live west of the City following the Fire of London, and one of the first residents was James I's physician, Sir Theodore Mayerne. The road later attracted Thomas Chippendale, the furniture maker, and Sir Joshua Reynolds, the artist. The St Martin's Lane Academy, London's first art school, was founded in 1720, with the satirist William Hogarth and the architect William Kent early students.

west side: St Martin's Place to Cranbourn Street

Duke of York's Theatre, north of Great Newport Street

Opening as the Trafalgar Theatre in 1892, it became the Duke of York's three years later and was where in 1900 the Italian opera composer Giacomo Puccini was inspired to write *Madame Butterfly* after watching a performance of David Belasco's play of the same name. Four years later, on 27 December 1904, the première of J. M. Barrie's *Peter Pan* took place here. The theatre is supposedly haunted by the ghost of Violet Melnotte, a former owner.

Salisbury tavern, No. 90

A pub long popular with theatre-goers, actors and journalists, it was originally the Coach and Horses, later became Ben Caunt's, named after the prize-fighter known as 'the Nottinghamshire Giant', and was renamed the Salisbury Stores in 1866, 'Stores' denoting that take-home sales of alcohol were available. The pub was rebuilt as the Salisbury in 1892, furnished with etched glass, bronze nymphs and mahogany, and features in the 1961 Dirk Bogarde movie *Victim*, one of the first British films to deal sympathetically with homosexuality.

Albery Theatre

Built as the 877-seater New Theatre by W. G. R. Sprague for Charles Wyndham in 1903, it was where John Gielgud scored a number of triumphs in the 1930s, particularly with *Hamlet*, which ran for 155 nights in 1934. During the 1940s it was home to the Old Vic and Sadler's Wells companies, which had been bombed out of their homes, and featured memorable performances from Ralph Richardson in *Peer Gynt* (1944) and *Uncle Vanya* (1946). The theatre turned down John Osborne's *Look Back in Anger* in the 1950s because of the play's risqué language but achieved success with Lionel Bart's musical *Oliver!* which ran for over 2,000 performances from 1960 to 1967. It was renamed the Albery after the impresario Sir Bronson Albery in 1973.

east side: Long Acre to St Martin's Place
London Coliseum

The Coliseum, London's largest theatre with 2,354 seats, designed by Frank Matcham and built in 1904 with a roof topped with a globe resting on carved figures of Art, Music, Science and Literature, was the first in the capital to have a revolving stage and lifts. It opened with a four-shows-a-day variety programme that was replaced two years later by *The Revue*, an ambitious cabaret with a 300-strong cast which nearly bankrupted the impresario Oswald Stoll and forced him to close the building temporarily. When Stoll invited Sergei Diaghilev's Russian ballet company to perform here the latter thundered 'and have the Russian ballet between a fat lady playing a silver trombone and performing dogs? Never!', but changed his mind in 1917. Musicals dominated the Coliseum in the 1950s, but the theatre failed to compete with Drury Lane, where *My Fair Lady* was running, or Her Majesty's, which was showing *West Side Story*, resulting in MGM's buying the venue for use as a cinema in 1961. Seven years later MGM pulled out and was replaced by Sadler's Wells Opera, which in leaving its Islington home for St Martin's Lane renamed itself English National Opera. Despite the excellent acoustics, described by the conductor Mark Elder, a former music director, as the best for Wagner in Britain, the building is unsuitable for large-scale opera as its fly tower cannot be raised to allow large scenery to be moved, there are inadequate side stages, and a lack of storage room.

Marquis of Granby, No. 20

The pub is named after the peer who ordered 300,000 pints of porter to be drunk after winning a battle in the Seven Years War (1756–63), resulting in grateful members of his regiment naming public houses they opened on their retirement from the army after him.

Wellington Street

Originally Charles Street and named after Charles I when built in 1631, it was renamed Wellington Street after the Duke of Wellington, the victor at Waterloo, in 1844, by which time it had filled with brothels. Charles Dickens moved the office of his popular magazine *All the Year Round*, whose contributors included Elizabeth Gaskell and Wilkie Collins, to No. 26 in 1859 and when Collins's novel *The Moonstone* was serialized in the magazine nine years later, it proved so popular crowds gathered in the street outside waiting for the latest instalment. Dickens himself lodged above the shop in the late 1860s, shortly before he died, while visiting London to do public readings.

Lyceum, west side

Built in 1772 at the eastern end of the Strand, the Lyceum theatre moved here in 1834 and was where the Victorian actor Henry Irving made his name in the 1870s with his performance of Hamlet. Much of the theatre was demolished for road widening schemes in 1902 and was rebuilt as a music hall by Bertie Crewe, who hoped it would rival the Coliseum on St Martin's Lane. Instead it was a spectacular flop and opened only sporadically, mostly for melodramas. Demolition was planned, but the Second World War intervened, and the Lyceum was revived as a discotheque which became popular with mods. By the end of the 1960s it was staging rock concerts; Led Zeppelin played here in October 1969 on the fifty-fourth anniversary of the dropping of a Zeppelin bomb on the theatre. The most celebrated Lyceum gig was the Bob Marley and the Wailers concert of 18 July 1975 recorded for the live album that included 'No Woman No Cry'. The venue closed down in 1991 and has since been refurbished for staging musicals.

(iv) Holborn

A mostly commercial area between Covent Garden and the Strand, Holborn takes its name from the now culverted Holebourne stream and was one of the first suburbs outside the Romans' walled town (now the City of London) to be built. In the nineteenth century Holborn became overcrowded and over-commercialized, as the Scottish historian Thomas Carlyle noted in writing to his brother about 'the black vapour brooding over [Holborn], absolutely like fluid ink; and coaches and wains and sheep oxen and wild people rushing on with bellowings and shrieks and thundering din'. It was cleaned up at the end of the nineteenth century when a major new road, Kingsway, was driven through the old slums.

Aldwych

The street, which takes the form of a crescent at the southern end of Kingsway, dates back only as far as 1905, but the name is considerably older, Via de Aldewych being the name by which Drury Lane was known in 1398 when the surrounding area was called Aldwic, 'the old settlement'. When Aldwych was built a number of small streets in what was the densely packed Clare Market area, as well as a number of theatres, including the Gaiety and the Opéra Comique, the first home of the Gilbert and Sullivan operas, were demolished.

south side: St Clement Dane's end to Wellington Street end

Aldwych's south side is dominated by three monumental blocks: the Beaux Arts Australia House, home of the Australian High Commission from 1907; Bush House, associated mostly with the BBC; and India House, offices for the Indian High Commission.

Bush House, Strand at Montreal Place

Built as a trade centre in the 1920s by Irving T. Bush, it was where a decade later the advertising agency J. Walter Thompson took offices, converting the basement swimming pool into a studio where sponsored programmes for Radio Luxembourg could be recorded. One of the less conspicuous tenants around that time was Colonel C. E. M. Dansey, who ran his 'Z' network of spies, consisting mostly of journalists and businessmen, from a set of rooms on the eighth floor which masqueraded as the export office of a diamond company. Another intelligence department partly based at Bush House was the Political Warfare Executive which during the Second World War made radio programmes in German to be broadcast to the Reich. Every night at 6 p.m. programmes would begin on the Radio Deutschland frequency with a burst of military music, followed by an announcer proclaiming in German: 'Here is the soldiers' Radio Calais. We bring music and news for comrades in the command areas west.' So effective was the programme it received praise from the Nazis' own chief propagandist, Joseph Goebbels.

Since the war the building has been used by a number of radio stations, including the BBC World Service. It is likely that most celebrity interviewees have met with better treatment at the reception desk than the Norwegian king, Haakon VI, who announced his arrival and was asked by the receptionist: 'Sorry, dear, where did you say you were king of?'

Drury Lane

Best known as a night-time haunt of theatre-goers, Drury Lane was called Via de Aldewych ('route of the old town') in the Middle Ages when a stone monument, the Aldewych Cross, stood at the northern end, and became Drury Lane after Sir William Drury built a property, 𝔇𝔯𝔲𝔯𝔶 𝔥𝔬𝔲𝔰𝔢, at the southern end in 1590. In 1665 London's worst outbreak of the Plague, inadvertently caused by Flemish weavers who opened a parcel of contaminated goods imported from Holland, occurred on Drury Lane. The diarist Samuel Pepys noted a number of houses marked with a red cross, which meant that the occupants had fallen victim to the disease, and the words 'Lord have mercy upon us' written on the door in regulation one-foot high letters. Shortly afterwards armed guards were installed to prevent people leaving the area, and that summer 100,000 Londoners died of the plague.

By the eighteenth century Drury Lane had become a popular haunt of con-men, thieves and prostitutes, as captured by William Hogarth in *The Harlot's Progress* – in 1725 a visitor counted 107 brothels in and around the street – and things had barely improved by the nineteenth century. Charles Dickens described how 'the filthy and miserable appearance of this part of London can hardly be imagined by those who have not witnessed it' in 'A Gin Shop' from *Sketches by Boz* (1837). The area was cleaned up towards the end of the century, its impoverished residential character giving way to small shops including the first Sainsbury's, which opened at No. 173 in 1869.

Theatre Royal Drury Lane, west side
One of London's most famous theatres, the Theatre Royal dates back to 1660 when Thomas Killigrew, a former page to Charles I, obtained one of two licences granted by Charles II to stage drama and took a lease on the land, owned by the Duke of Bedford, to build a playhouse, which was burned down in 1672 by footmen, annoyed at being refused free entry. The theatre was rebuilt in a grander style by Christopher Wren and was where on 28 September 1745 'God Save the King' was sung publicly for the first time, just as the Young Pretender's Jacobite forces were landing in Scotland preparing for their ultimately unsuccessful march south to overthrow George II.

David Garrick, the revered actor who became manager-owner in 1747, spent the next thirty years improving the quality of the productions and the facilities, but the playwright Richard Brinsley Sheridan, who took over from Garrick as manager in 1777, did not get off to a good start when his play *The Rivals* was panned on the opening night following a poor performance by John Lee, who was accidentally hit on the head with an apple. Then in 1795 he staged a disastrous performance of *Vortigern*, a play which the forger William Ireland claimed had been written by Shakespeare and had been locked away for 200 years. Many were suspicious about Ireland's claims, but Sheridan went ahead with the production, despite the publication of a damning inquiry into the play's authenticity the night before the première. If the doubters had not managed to convince Sheridan to pull the play, the audience did, finding the language increasingly unconvincing and laughing uproariously at the line 'And when this solemn mockery is o'er'.

In 1811–12 the current building was designed by Benjamin Wyatt with the Grand Theatre of Bordeaux in mind and two royal boxes: one for the reigning monarch and one for the royal heir, George III having publicly rowed with the Prince of Wales in the theatre foyer. By the late nineteenth century the Theatre Royal was putting on spectacular pantomimes, Dan Leno setting the standard for the male pantomime dame in a series of renowned performances, the last being in 1903 a year before his surprise death at forty-three. In 1961 Rudolf Nureyev made his London debut at the theatre, having defected from the Soviet Union earlier that year.

Great Queen Street
Work began on the street, which is named after James I's queen, Anne of Denmark, in 1623, and early residents, such as Thomas Fairfax, the Parliamentary Civil War general, and the artist Joshua Reynolds, enjoyed northern views of the Highgate and Hampstead hills. In the eighteenth century Great Queen Street began attracting traders connected with coach building and repairing, and since the nineteenth century it has been the centre of Masonic activity in London. The north side contains offices, shops and charities associated with the movement, such as the Masonic outfitters Central Regalia Ltd at No. 23, and the south side is dominated by the huge bulk of Ashley and Newman's formidable neo-classical Freemasons Hall of 1933, the headquarters of English Freemasonry and a meeting place for London Lodges and Chapters, and the New Connaught banqueting

rooms, formerly the Freemasons Tavern and a major nineteenth-century meeting place. **New Connaught Rooms (former Freemasons Tavern)**, Nos. 61–65, south side Banqueting rooms with a long and varied history, the New Connaught Rooms stand on the site of the seventeenth-century 𝕮𝖔𝖓𝖜𝖆𝖞 𝕳𝖔𝖚𝖘𝖊, the residency of the Lord Chancellor, whose best-known incumbent of the period, Heneage Finch, hid the Great Seal of England under his pillow to prevent its theft. In 1774 Conway House was replaced by the Freemasons Tavern which soon became a popular venue for public meetings. Thomas Taylor, a vehement opponent of Isaac Newton's scientific theories, gave a lecture here on the subject of perpetual light, using supposedly 'everlasting' lamps filled with phosphorus, but succeeding in little more than setting light to the room. On 28 October 1863 the Football Association was founded here by eleven clubs – Barnes, Blackheath, Blackheath Proprietary School, Crystal Palace, Crusaders, Forest (Leytonstone), Kensington School, No Names Kilburn, Perceval House (Blackheath), Surbiton and War Office.

The clubs met here a number of times over the next few months to debate ways of uniting the various rules being played around the country, with the most contentious issues being the use of hands and the physical charging of players. Representatives of Blackheath were keen on approving a rule that allowed a player 'to run with the ball towards his adversaries' goal if he makes a fair catch', and another which noted that if 'any player shall run with the ball towards his adversaries' goal, any player on the opposite side should be at liberty to charge, hold, trip or hack him, or wrest the ball from him'. After losing the vote that December the club withdrew its membership and Association Football developed without players being able to use their hands or make full-bodied assaults on opponents.

On 12 November 1867, following the passing of the Reform Act, which gave the vote to a million more people, the National Union of Conservative and Constitutional Associations met here to organize working-class support for the Conservatives at what is now considered to be the first party political conference. In 1888 the venue staged the first meeting of the Lawn Tennis Association, and in 1910 it was rebuilt as the luxurious new Connaught Rooms, named after the first Duke of Connaught, Grand Master of the Freemasons. The Social Democratic Party was launched here on 26 March 1981.

Kingsway

Built in 1905 as the centrepiece of the improvements to the slum area of Clare Market, and lined with large ostentatious office blocks such as Craven House, Beacon House and Africa House, Kingsway was hailed fulsomely by the historian Harold Clunn as a road of 'unsurpassed beauty . . . nothing of the kind is to be seen in Paris, Berlin or New York'. By the end of the twentieth century Kingsway had lost much of its commercial importance with the departure of many firms to greenfield sites. Estate agents then optimistically tried to revive the area by labelling it Midtown, in the American manner, and by the end of the century a number of bars and coffee shops had opened in the abandoned buildings, although the new name had failed to capture the public imagination.

⁕ Visible at the junction of Southampton Row and Theobald's Road is a former tram tunnel, the only one connecting the north and south sides of the river, which ran under Kingsway and after closing in 1952 was mostly used as a control centre for London's flood defences. The southern section is now a traffic underpass linking Kingsway and Waterloo Bridge.

west side: Aldwych to High Holborn
Kingsway Hall (twentieth century), No. 75 An important meeting place during the twentieth century, Kingsway Hall was run by Donald Soper, the Methodist minister,

who during the Second World War opened a canteen where he cooked breakfasts of porridge, fried potatoes and spam for those sleeping in the air raid shelter in Holborn tube station. Muhammad Ali Jinnah and Jawaharlal Nehru shared a platform on 3 December 1946 during the campaign for the independence of the Indian subcontinent from British rule, and it was Jinnah's call for Britain to 'give Muslims their homeland and Hindus Hindustan' that led to the subsequent partition of Pakistan and India. One of Britain's first blues concerts took place in Kingsway Hall in September 1951, with Big Bill Broonzy playing to what *Melody Maker* described as a 'small but discerning audience' who gave Broonzy a particularly warm welcome as at that time a Musicians' Union ruling meant that blues performers had to be promoted in Britain as 'variety acts' and therefore rarely played. In 1971 the hall roof collapsed only minutes after a service had finished on a Sunday evening and the building was subsequently closed.

№. 129

A supermarket stands on the site of the nineteenth-century Holborn Restaurant which in 1955 was replaced with the De Lane Lea recording studio where Jimi Hendrix recorded his first single, 'Hey Joe', on Sunday 23 October 1966. The record failed to captivate executives from Decca Records – the label which had previously turned down the Beatles – who rejected the single, telling his manager, Chas Chandler, 'He hasn't got anything.'

Tavistock Street

Tavistock Row, the predecessor to Tavistock Street, attracted artists such as Willem Vandevelde, the Dutch court painter, and Samuel Scott at the end of the seventeenth century, and was where at No. 36 in the 1820s Thomas de Quincey wrote *Confessions of an English Opium Eater*, the first and still the best-known drugs book in English literature. *Confessions* first appeared in September 1821 in the *London Magazine*, which ran a

banner proclaiming: 'we cannot neglect the opportunity of calling the attention of our readers to the deep, eloquent and masterly paper which stands first in our present Number. Such Confessions so powerfully uttered cannot fail to do more than interest the reader.'

(v) Lincoln's Inn

Lincoln's Inn, one of the four remaining Inns of Court in London, and Lincoln's Inn Fields, the large leafy square to the west of the Inn, dominate the area to the immediate east of Kingsway. East of the Inn is Chancery Lane, the spiritual heart of legal London.

Chancery Lane

The first street of consequence west of the City of London, Chancery Lane has been associated with the legal profession since Edward III took possession of the 𝔥ouse for 𝔠onverted 𝔍ews at the south-east end of what was then New Street in 1377 and handed it to the Keeper of the Rolls of Chancery, the court of public records and archives. New Street later became known as Chaunceleres Lane and then as Chancery Lane, being close to the courts of Chancery, the body that settled trusts, legacies and wills. The arrival of the Royal Courts of Justice at the south-west end of the street from Westminster in the 1870s put the street at the centre of the legal profession in London.

west side

A wine bar at No. 115 occupies what was Hodgson's book auction rooms, an eccentrically decorated property festooned with carvings of turbaned and bearded heads and winged dogs, while nearby are several buildings connected with the legal profession, including the former Law Fire Insurance Office, designed in the Renaissance style, with carved firemen's helmets on both sides of the doorway, and offices for the Law Society, a voluntary organization of solicitors, at Nos. 100–113. The tailors Ede and

Ravenscroft at No. 93 have supplied ermine, used for ceremonial robes in medieval times as a symbol of moral purity, to members of the House of Lords since 1689. An ermine suit now costs around £7,000.

east side: High Holborn to Fleet Street
London Silver Vaults, Nos. 53–64
The vaults were set up in 1882 under the name Chancery Lane Safe Deposit to house local jewellery dealers' valuables and have also held the personal papers of the Liberal politician David Lloyd George and the Spanish republican government's secret documents.

Public Record Office (1860–1996), Chancery Lane, south of Bream's Buildings
Now being renovated for King's College, the building stands on the site of a medieval 𝕳𝖔𝖚𝖘𝖊 𝖋𝖔𝖗 𝕮𝖔𝖓𝖛𝖊𝖗𝖙𝖊𝖉 𝕵𝖊𝖜𝖘, or *Domus Conversorum*, which Edward III appropriated in the mid fourteenth century to store the rolls of Chancery (public records). As the records grew so did the number of sites in which they were stored, and by the beginning of the nineteenth century some fifty buildings, including the Tower and Chapter House of Westminster Abbey, were being used. In the 1830s the authorities decided to create one vast public record office, which was designed in the mock-Tudor style by James Pennethorne. In the late twentieth century, by which time the quantity of records was growing at around a mile a year, there were proposals for a new, larger public record office, which was duly built at Kew.

Houghton Street
London School of Economics
Henry Hunt Hutchinson, a Fabian socialist who committed suicide in 1894, left instructions in his will for Sidney Webb and other trustees of his estate to establish an institution 'to promote the study and advancement of Economics or Political Economy, Political Science or Political Philosophy, Statistics, Sociology, History, Geography, and any subject cognate to any of these'. The college was founded the following year at 9 John Street, south of the Strand, moving here in 1902, and later took over a number of neighbouring buildings, resulting in a sprawling site that lacks an obvious main entrance. In the 1960s the LSE was a focal point for student unrest and on 23 May 1968 students showing solidarity with their French counterparts' anti-establishment activities in Paris – *les événements* – held a number of protests, including an all-night vigil. They were visited a month later by two of the leading figures of the Paris student demonstrations, Danny Cohn-Bendit and Alain Geismar, who were attending a conference entitled 'Students of the World Ignite'. That October, students occupied the main building to campaign against American involvement in Vietnam and the following year, when it emerged that the college had investments in Rhodesia and South Africa, students broke down new gates the authorities had installed and a number of students were arrested, resulting in the shutting down of the college. The lockout lasted four weeks and the LSE took out injunctions against thirteen people including the sociology don Robin Blackburn.

Lincoln's Inn Fields
Lincoln's Inn Fields, London's largest square, was used in medieval times for sports and jousting and was where in September 1586 the fourteen Babington Plotters who had planned to murder Elizabeth I and install Mary Queen of Scots on the throne were hanged, drawn and quartered. The architect Inigo Jones introduced plans for the fields in 1618, but nothing ensued until 1638 when thirty-two houses were built (of which only Nos. 59–60, Lindsey House, remain), the green space in the centre remaining unspoilt as promised to members of the legal body, Lincoln's Inn.

Development did not immediately improve the area and it remained a shabby, ill-kempt spot where rubbish accumulated and executions took place, the most famous being that of Lord William Russell, convicted of participating in the Rye House Plot to assassinate the Duke of York (later James II) and Charles II on their return from the Newmarket races. In 1734 the residents applied for an Act of Parliament which would allow them to raise funds and enclose the fields, keep the area clean and appoint watchmen to police it. The residents' trustees ran their affairs in this way for more than 100 years before municipal legislation reduced their powers. The square's best-known past resident is John Soane, architect of the Bank of England, whose late-eighteenth-century home, which he designed, has been splendidly preserved as a museum. Other major architects responsible for Lincoln's Inn Fields properties include Charles Barry (the Royal College of Surgeons, on the south side, in the 1830s), Philip Webb (No. 19, 1868–70), Alfred Waterhouse (Nos. 17–18, 1871–2) and Edwin Lutyens (No. 66, 1930).

north side

No. 3

The first headquarters of the Labour Party, formed in 1900, were at No. 3, then home of James Ramsay MacDonald, the party's first secretary and in the 1920s its first prime minister.

Sir John Soane's Museum, Nos. 12–14

A remarkable museum created from the cultured eccentricity of the architect Sir John Soane, designer of the Bank of England and an obsessive collector of arcana, who lived here from 1792 to 1837, it is filled with classical curios, fragments of Gothic architecture, paintings squeezed into every imaginable corner, and architectural surprises and illusions created from unexpected sources of light and a multitude of mirrors that alter and obscure shape and size. In the crypt is the sarcophagus of Pharaoh Seti I, who died in 1279 BC, carved out of a single piece of Egyptian alabaster that has turned yellow in the London air, which was discovered in the Valley of the Kings in 1817. Soane arranged for it to be shipped to London but needed to construct a hole in the back of the house to bring it through. Its arrival in 1825 was marked with a three-day party attended by

around 1,000 people including the painter J. M. W. Turner and the poet Samuel Taylor Coleridge.

The Picture Room contains more than 100 works, mostly fixed to hinged screens which fold away to reveal further walls of paintings, and is crowned with William Hogarth's *The Election* (1754), which satirizes the corrupt hustings in Oxford, and *The Rake's Progress*, an eight-part morality tale detailing the rise and fall of the dilettante Tom Rakewell. Before he died Soane, concerned about the fate of his collection should it come into the hands of his prodigal son, bequeathed the house to the nation, ensuring through a private Act of Parliament in 1833 that the building and its contents would be kept unaltered in perpetuity.

east side

Lincoln's Inn

One of four surviving Inns of Court, the others being Gray's Inn and the Inner and Middle Temple, Lincoln's Inn's origins are uncertain but it was founded either by Henry de Lacy, Earl of Lincoln (1272–1307), or by Thomas de Lincoln, a law officer who trained legal apprentices, in the mid fourteenth century, and was originally located near modern-day Holborn Circus, moving to Furnival's Inn on the Strand, and finally to the present site *c.* 1412. In 1659 eighty members of the Long Parliament met in the chapel's open undercroft to campaign for the restoration of Charles II to the throne. During the eighteenth century unmarried mothers would leave their babies in the undercroft and the Inn would offer five shillings to anybody wishing to take one, until 1750 when it decided to keep the children, give them the surname Lincoln, and take care of their welfare until they reached apprenticeship age. Alumni of Lincoln's Inn include the Catholic martyr Thomas More, Oliver Cromwell, the poet John Donne, and the politicians Benjamin Disraeli, William Gladstone, Muhammad Ali Jinnah (founder of Pakistan), Margaret Thatcher and Tony Blair.

south side

The south side of Lincoln's Inn Fields, formerly known as Portugal Row, is dominated by huge corporate blocks of antiquated design, including the Royal College of Surgeons and the neo-Jacobean Land Registry Office.

west side

Lindsey House, Nos. 59–60

The square's only surviving original property, Lindsey House was described by Sir John Summerson, the leading twentieth-century expert on Georgian London, as 'perhaps, historically, the most important single house in London'. It was designed from 1638 to 1641 by David Cunningham (not as commonly believed for many years Inigo Jones) for Robert Bertie, the 1st Earl of Lindsey, Charles I's commander-in-chief, who was killed at the battle of Edgehill in 1642. The block was divided into two addresses in the late eighteenth century, No. 59 being the home of Spencer Perceval, the only British prime minister to be assassinated, but has since been reconverted into one address.

Portsmouth Street

The Old Curiosity Shop, No. 13

Though billed as the Old Curiosity Shop of Charles Dickens's novel and believed to be the oldest surviving shop in England (it dates back to 1657), the building, formerly a dairy and antiques shop, took the name in 1868 nearly thirty years after the book was published and is the only survival from Clare Market, swept away at the end of the nineteenth century when Kingsway and Aldwych were created.

Sardinia Street

The street is named after the Sardinian Embassy and chapel that stood here in the seventeenth and eighteenth centuries, when it was one of the few places in London where mass could legally be heard at a time when Catholicism was forbidden. The chapel was attacked in 1688 when news reached London that the Protestant William

of Orange had landed in England to take the throne and again nearly 100 years later in June 1780 at the outset of what became the anti-Catholic Gordon Riots. In 1861 the chapel became the church of St Anselm and St Cecilia and moved to a nearby site on the newly built Kingsway in 1910.

Took's Court

A small dog-leg-shaped street to the east of Chancery Lane built in 1650 by Thomas Tooke, a City merchant, it features in Charles Dickens's 1853 novel, *Bleak House*, as Cook's Court, where law stationer Mr Snagsby 'pursues his lawful calling, [dealing] in all sorts of blank forms of legal process, in skins and rolls of parchment, in paper – foolscap, brief, draft, brown, white, whitey-brown, and blotting'. No. 15 has been renamed Dickens House in honour of the author.

No. 14, north side

The premises are chambers for Michael Mansfield QC, the leading left-wing barrister of the late twentieth and early twenty-first centuries, who first came to public notice in 1972, defending Angela Weir, one of those accused of being a member of the Angry Brigade, an English anarchist group which had planted scores of bombs throughout London. Mansfield discredited key scientific evidence and Weir walked free. The following year Mansfield defended two sisters accused of taking part in an IRA bombing of the Old Bailey, which had destroyed his own car, and he secured his reputation with a number of high-profile cases of miscarriages of justice, such as those involving the Birmingham Six and the alleged IRA bomber Judith Ward. He has also represented the family of Stephen Lawrence, the black youth murdered by racist assailants in Eltham in 1993.

south side

London Centre of Regional Government

The ungainly brick and concrete structure by the bend in the road was built in the late 1940s at the outset of the Cold War to house

The Gordon Riots

The week-long Gordon Riots, the most violent protests in London history, took place in June 1780 after Parliament voted to grant more rights to Catholics, who were then not allowed to belong to the House of Commons or Lords, buy land, keep arms, hold military office, practise medicine or teach. The mob was spurred on by Lord George Gordon, a peer in his late twenties who made rousing speeches in Parliament against 'Popery', and by rumours that 20,000 Jesuits were hidden in a network of secret tunnels under the Thames, ready on the order of Rome to overrun the capital. They took to the London streets after Gordon delivered an anti-Catholic petition to Parliament on Friday 2 June 1780 and attacked the Sardinian Chapel by Lincoln's Inn Fields and the Bavarian Chapel on Warwick Street, Soho, two of the few places in London where Catholics could worship openly.

Outbreaks of violence increased throughout the weekend, and on the Monday a procession marched to Lord George's house in Welbeck Street, Marylebone, bringing him relics ransacked from the looted chapels. The following day hundreds of protestors attacked Newgate Prison, battering down cell doors with sledgehammers and pickaxes, releasing prisoners, and setting fire to the building. On the Wednesday the rioters stormed Langdale's Distillery in Holborn, rolling out the casks and smashing them open, which resulted in the raw spirit catching fire, a pillar of flame reaching up to the sky, and hot gin running down the road, rendering those who gorged themselves on the liquid dead drunk, or just dead.

As the violence increased thousands of householders chalked up the warning 'No Popery' on their doors – the Italian (Catholic) parents of the clown Joseph Grimaldi daubed on their door 'No religion' – while in the Jewish ghetto around Houndsditch houses were chalked with the words: 'This is the home of a true protestant.' The authorities regained the upper hand on the Thursday, when troops poured into London, and the destruction was counted as 285 people dead, 200 wounded, £200,000-worth of damage caused and 450 rioters in prison. Although Lord George was charged with high treason and sent to the Tower, where he languished for eight months, he was cleared of blame but later forsook the Anglican church for Judaism, changing his name to Israel Abraham George Gordon. He died at the age of forty-two in Newgate Prison where he had been incarcerated for libelling Marie Antoinette.

senior government figures who would run London in the event of a nuclear attack. It contains a supposedly bombproof bunker and tunnels connected with government departments under Whitehall and strategic properties such as Centre Point, the former London Weather Centre on High Holborn, and Telecom Tower (former Post Office Tower). Once the advances in nuclear weaponry had rendered the system redundant the buildings were abandoned.
► High Holborn bunker, p. 96.

(vi) Strand

Strand

Until the construction of Victoria Embankment in the 1860s the Strand, named after the shore of the Thames, was the closest road to the river linking Westminster and the City of London and was lined with aristocratic mansions, all of which have been demolished, apart from Somerset House. In the nineteenth century Strand became home to Charing Cross station, the monumental Cecil Hotel, the Savoy, King's College, Somerset House and the Royal

Courts of Justice, leading the Conservative politician Benjamin Disraeli to describe it as 'perhaps the finest street in Europe'. It was also the home of many music halls, its place in popular music immortalized in William Hargreaves's song about Burlington Bertie who 'rises at 10.30 and saunters along like a toff / walks down the Strand with [his] gloves on each hand / and walks back again with them off'. During the twentieth century the street gradually lost its exclusivity, its theatres, stamp shops and restaurants standing alongside discount clothes shops, amusement arcades and run-down office blocks, but the late twentieth-century rejuvenation of Somerset House has brought about improvements.

north side: Trafalgar Square to Temple Bar
Coutts, No. 440

> The aristocrat who hunts and shoots /
> The aristocrat who banks with Coutts –
> *The Gondoliers*, W. S. Gilbert (1889)

The bank, probably London's most prestigious, with many royal clients, was founded by Scottish goldsmith John Campbell at the sign of the Three Crowns in 1692 and a few years later was sold to an Edinburgh banker, James Coutts, who moved it to 440 Strand in 1904. It was rebuilt in 1973 with a tree-filled atrium, then an unknown feature in London, and is now independently operated within the National Westminster Bank.

Zimbabwe House, No. 429
Designed in 1907 for the British Medical Association by Charles Holden, best known for his impressive modernist stations on the Piccadilly Line, the building's façade features sculptures by Jacob Epstein that were immediately denounced as obscene by religious figures. Dr Cosmo Lang, who later became Archbishop of Canterbury, climbed the scaffolding to examine them and declared them acceptable. They were partly destroyed by the Southern Rhodesia government after it took over the building in 1937, leaving the incongruous spectacle of several headless figures adorning the building's outer wall.

Adelphi Theatre, No. 414
Built as the Sans Pareil in 1806 by John Scott, a tradesman who wanted to launch his daughter, Jane, as an actress, it became the Adelphi in 1819 and was rebuilt in 1858 by T. H. Wyatt to resemble the Opéra Comique in Paris. Oscar Wilde pulled the production of his first play, *Vera*, due to be premièred here in 1881, when the Russian Tsar Alexander II, married to the Prince of Wales's sister-in-law, was assassinated. On 16 December 1897 the actor William Terris was stabbed to death by a jealous colleague outside the theatre. During the twentieth century the Adelphi staged a number of long-running musical comedies including *Charlie Girl* with Anna Neagle (1965–71) and more recently *Me and My Girl* (1985–92) and *Chicago* (1998–).

Observer (1791–1911), No. 396
Now the oldest Sunday newspaper in the world, the *Observer* was founded at 396 Strand on 4 December 1791 by A. S. Bourne, who promised a paper 'unbiased by prejudice and uninfluenced by party, whose principle is independence'. Despite believing the paper would enable him to make a rapid fortune, Bourne was £1,600 in debt within three years. Bourne tried to cut his losses by selling the title to the government, and though ministers were unwilling to buy the paper, they agreed to subsidize it (from Home Office funds) in return for influencing its content. The *Observer* gradually began to move away from its role as a propaganda sheet in the nineteenth century, taking on the call for reform, and eventually universal suffrage, while Rachel Beer, editor at the end of the century, was responsible for one of its greatest exclusives, the admission by Count Esterhazy that he had forged the letters that condemned the innocent Jewish officer Captain Dreyfus to Devil's Island. The *Observer* moved nearer Fleet Street early in the twentieth century.

▶ Fleet Street, p. 41.

St Mary-le-Strand
The church, which stands on an island in the middle of the Strand, was first built in

1147 as the Church of the Nativity of Our Lady and the Innocents and after it was demolished some 400 years later the site lay vacant until a new church was planned as part of the 1711 New Churches Act. Thomas Archer was chosen to be architect of the new church, with James Gibbs selected to build a column and statue to Queen Anne outside, but when Anne died in 1714 work stopped and Archer's ideas were stolen by Gibbs who resubmitted a design that omitted the column to the late monarch. Charles Edward Stuart, the Young Pretender (known as 'Bonnie Prince Charlie'), tried to boost his claims to the British throne by entering into the Anglican faith at the church during a secret visit to England in 1750. thereby incurring the displeasure of Pope Clement XIII, who refused to support the prince's campaign, but reverted to Catholicism before his death. The church was saved from destruction in the mid 1980s following protests led by the poet John Betjeman, who wrote a poem in its honour which ran: 'There's nothing quite so grand / as the Baroque of your Chapel / of St Mary in the Strand'. St Mary-le-Strand is now the official church of the Women's Royal Naval Service, the Women's Royal Naval Reserve and the Association of Wrens.

𝖣𝖆𝗂𝗅𝗒 𝖳𝖾𝗅𝖾𝗀𝗋𝖺𝗉𝗁 (1855–82), No. 253

Lt-Col Arthur Sleigh launched the *Daily Telegraph and Courier* from No. 253 on Friday 29 June 1855, taking advantage of the abolition of stamp duty on newspapers and undercutting his rivals by selling the paper for a penny. After running into financial difficulties Sleigh sold the paper to his printer and chief editor, Joseph Levy, who changed its name to the *Daily Telegraph* with the slogan 'the largest, best, and cheapest newspaper in the world'. Within six years the paper was selling nearly 150,000 copies a day, and had overtaken *The Times*. When Levy retired he was succeeded by his son, Edward, who changed his name to Edward Lawson-Levy, converted from Judaism to Christianity, and moved the paper away from the Liberals towards the Conservative Party. Lawson-Levy adapted the format of James Gordon Bennett's *New York Herald* in incorporating sensationalist stories with incredible headlines such as 'A Child Devoured by Pigs', 'Extraordinary Discovery of Man-Woman in Birmingham' and 'Shocking Occurrence: Five Men Smothered in a Gin Vat'. His star writer was the flamboyant G. A. Sala, who once filed an expenses chit: 'To expenses in Persia – £3,000', and when asked for more detail seized a scrap of paper and scrawled: 'To arsing and buggering about in Persia – £3,000'. The *Telegraph*'s sales continued to rise, nearing 250,000 in 1877, by which time it was the biggest-selling paper in the world, and it moved to 135 Fleet Street in 1882. The site is now partly covered by the Royal Courts of Justice.

▶ *Daily Telegraph* on Fleet Street, p. 43.

St Clement Danes, Strand at Aldwych, east end

No accurate records exist to explain the church's Danish connection, but it is believed that when Alfred the Great banished the Danes from England those who had married English women were allowed to live locally and they built the Ecclesia Clemtis Danorum, from which the present names derives. The first church, which was wooden, was replaced with a stone building in the eleventh century and came into the possession of the Knights Templar, the warrior monks after whom the Temple is named, in 1189. Christopher Wren rebuilt the church from 1679 to 1682, even though it had escaped damage in the Fire of London, and James Gibbs added the tower in 1719. St Clement Danes, which is the RAF's main church, has several literary connections. In Shakespeare's *Henry IV, Part II* (1600) Falstaff's line, 'We have heard the chimes at midnight, Master Shallow', refers to the chimes of the church and inspired Orson Welles to call his film based on Falstaff *Chimes at Midnight*; Dr Johnson attended services in the 1770s, sitting at seat No. 18 in the north gallery, and is remembered with a statue behind the

building; and in George Orwell's *1984*
St Clement Danes serves as the model for
the 'oval building with rectangular windows
near the Palace of Justice' [the Law Courts
on the Strand], which Winston remembers
when shown the picture by the secret police
agent Charrington.

Royal Courts of Justice

Britain's major civil courts, where libel
suits, divorces and appeals are heard, were
designed by George Edmund Street and
built from 1874 to 1882 to contain the Court
of Appeal, the Crown Court and the High
Court of Justice (which itself comprises the
Queen's Bench, Chancery and the Family
Divisions). Many famous personalities have
fought libel battles here, including the infamous occultist Aleister Crowley, who in
April 1934 sued the painter Nina Hamnett
for libel after she accused him of practising
black magic. The jury found for Miss
Hamnett and the judge, Mr Justice Swift,
who had researched Crowley's writings,
complained that he had never heard 'such
dreadful, horrible, blasphemous stuff'. In
1987 the Tory politician and blockbuster
novelist Jeffrey Archer won £500,000
damages from the *Daily Star* over allegations that he had paid for sex with a prostitute, Monica Coghlan, but fourteen years
later Archer himself was jailed for perjury
and perverting the course of justice over the
case and was forced to pay the *Star* £2.7
million compensation. The libel case that
received the most attention at the end of the
twentieth century was the so-called 'McLibel
trial', the longest in English legal history, in
which the hamburger company McDonald's
sued two protestors, David Morris and
Helen Steel, who had distributed leaflets
entitled: 'What's Wrong with McDonald's?'
Although McDonald's won, the judge was
critical of some of the company's practices,
and Morris emerged from court brandishing
a clenched fist and a briefcase emblazoned
with the scrawled message: 'Judge for yourself. Read the leaflet.'

► Old Bailey, p. 58.

south side: Temple Bar to Trafalgar Square

Wig and Pen Club, Nos. 229–230

One of only a few buildings remaining in
the Strand from before the 1666 Fire of
London, the property is the home of the
Wig and Pen Club, patronized by those
connected with the law, and was a regular
haunt of journalists trying to catch interesting gossip relating to cases at the Royal
Courts of Justice, opposite, in the days when
the newspaper industry was based around
Fleet Street.

Aldwych station (1907–94), Strand at
Surrey Street

The station opened as Strand, a one-stop
branch of the Piccadilly Line, in 1907, with
trains run as a shuttle service to and from
Holborn, and was renamed Aldwych in 1915.
In the 1930s London Transport announced
plans to close the station, rather than extend
the line south, and it shut at the outset of
the Second World War to be used for
storing treasures from the British Museum,
including the Elgin Marbles. Aldwych
reopened in the late 1940s, and plans were
announced to extend the line to Waterloo,
but nothing happened until 1978 when the
Greater London Council announced that
exploratory work was to start on the Jubilee
Line extension, which would include
Aldwych station. Tunnels were constructed
under the Strand, but when the newspaper
industry left Fleet Street for east London the
authorities wavered and work ceased with
the tunnel half-built, and in 1994 Aldwych
closed again. Over the years the station has
featured in a number of novels and films
including Geoffrey Household's 1939
thriller, *Rogue Male*, in which the hero,
having unsuccessfully attempted to assassinate Hitler, being cornered by his pursuers
in the station, and the John Landis 1981
horror comedy *An American Werewolf in
London*, in which David Kessler (David
Naughton) kills a man on the escalator
while gripped by lupine disease.

► Former British Museum station, p. 95.

King's College, Strand, opposite
St Mary-le-Strand
Established in 1828 by the Duke of Wellington and the bishops of the Church of England as an Anglican alternative to the non-denominational University College, it came under the jurisdiction of the newly formed University of London in 1836. Extensions to the building were constructed in the 1960s, the stark brutalism of the new block resting uneasily alongside Robert Smirke's classical revivalist architecture.

Somerset House, north-east of Waterloo Bridge
A monumental eighteenth-century riverside complex, home of the General Register of Births, Deaths and Marriages until 1973, and now mostly a tourist attraction, Somerset House is named after Edward Seymour, Duke of Somerset, uncle of Edward VI, who built a palace here by the Thames from 1547 to 1554 using stone taken from the church of St John in Clerkenwell, which was extracted with the aid of gunpowder. However, he was beheaded on Tower Hill in 1552 before he was able to see the fruits of his work.

Six years later Princess Elizabeth (later Elizabeth I) moved here, but she preferred Whitehall Palace when she became queen in 1558, and Somerset House later became the official residence of Anne of Denmark, consort of James I. During the residency of Henrietta Maria, wife of Charles I, the building became a centre of opposition to the government, and when the English Civil War broke out in 1642 it was one of the first London buildings to be attacked by Parliamentary forces. Somerset House was used as an auction hall for the royal treasures during Oliver Cromwell's 1649–60 Commonwealth, and the building was itself put on sale, but when there were no takers it was converted into the headquarters of Cromwell's New Model Army. Cromwell himself lay in state here for eleven weeks before his funeral in 1658, members of the public, no longer enamoured with his regime, throwing dirt on his shield which had been placed over the gate.

In 1771 the Royal Academy, founded by leading artists of the time, took rooms in Somerset House, and five years later the 21-year-old William Blake passed his interview for the Academy here after finishing his apprenticeship as an engraver. Around the same time William Chambers began rebuilding Somerset House in a Palladian style for civil service offices, creating four grand blocks around a courtyard. The navy took the plum riverside view, while the less desirable blocks were occupied by the Sick and Hurt Offices, the Office of the Clerk of the Estreats, the Comptroller of the Pipe and the Registry of Births, Deaths and Marriages, for the latter of which Somerset House was best known for the next two centuries.

By the 1970s decline had set in – the courtyard had become little more than a glorified car park – encouraging the journalist Simon Jenkins to launch a campaign in the *Evening Standard* to revitalize the building and restore its grandeur, a project that won support from the poet laureate, John Betjeman, and the leading art historian, Kenneth Clark. In 2000 the refurbished Somerset House opened as a tourist attraction and as a repository for the Courtauld Institute Galleries and the Gilbert Collection of mosaics and jewellery.

Simpson's-in-the-Strand, No. 100
Opening as a 'home of chess' in 1818, it later became the Grand Cigar Divan, where chess players relaxed on divans and sofas, refreshments being provided when John Simpson reopened the premises as Simpson's Divan and Tavern in 1848. The building was demolished when the area was redeveloped at the end of the century and rebuilt by T. E. Collcutt, who incorporated art nouveau elements, and it reopened in 1904 as an exclusive restaurant which, according to the comic writer P. G. Wodehouse, offered 'two great advantages, namely that you need not dress, and, secondly, that you paid your half-crown, and were then at liberty to eat till you were helpless, if you felt so disposed, without extra charge'. Simpson's was

refurbished again at the end of the twentieth century and now, as part of the Savoy Group, is an exclusive, if old-fashioned, eaterie offering traditional British food.

Shell-Mex House, No. 80

A monumental office block, previously home of the Shell company, 80 Strand stands on the site of the Cecil Hotel, which was built by a group of building societies headed by Jabez Balfour, who at the time had just begun a fourteen-year jail sentence for fraud. The Cecil opened as the largest hotel in Europe in 1896, with 1,000 rooms decorated with coloured marble and tapestries, each with a canopied bed and Doulton chamber pot. The hotel was portrayed by H. G. Wells as the magnificent Hardingham in his 1908 novel *Tono-Bungay*, while a famous *Punch* cartoon of the time depicted a lady asking a bus conductor: 'Do you stop at the Cecil?', to which the conductor replies: 'What, on 28 bob a week?'

It was a particular favourite of American businessmen such as William Barry Owen, the recording pioneer, who booked into the Cecil in 1897 and began trading under the name of The Gramophone Company, the forerunner of EMI. Owen's compatriot Irving Guy Ries, a corn merchant who stayed here in 1915 during the First World War, was however unmasked by the British authorities as a German spy, taken to the Tower, and shot. Most of the building was demolished in 1930, when the site was bought by the Shell Oil Company, but the architect Milton Cashmore retained the Cecil's façade when he designed a new office block for the site, adding the huge distinguished clock, London's biggest, and incorporating into the decor globe-shaped gaslights taken from the stations and tunnels of the first underground line, the Paddington–Farringdon Metropolitan Railway.

During the Second World War the government requisitioned the building for the Ministry of Supply, which was responsible for two-thirds of Britain's war production, and after the war, when Shell returned to its headquarters, the government continued to use parts of the building; it was here in 1945 that the Labour prime minister Clement Attlee gathered his most trusted Cabinet ministers and outlined plans for Britain's new atomic weapons. In January 1999 environmental demonstrators occupied the building as a protest against the company's oil policies. Filing cabinets, desks, computers and chairs were piled high in front of doors and inner walls and during their four hours in the building the protestors set up and maintained a website, giving the world's media a live commentary from the occupation, until Shell employees and the police smashed through the walls. Soon after, the building was sold to US private investor Steven Winkoff for £100 million and leased to various companies, including Pearson, owners of the publishers Penguin.

Charing Cross station

Charing Cross station, the railway terminus closest to the West End, was designed by E. M. Barry in the 1860s and built on the site of Hungerford Market, a location chosen by Samuel Smiles, author of the libertarian classic *Self-Help* (1859), who was also secretary of the South Eastern Railway. At the front is the Charing Cross Hotel, built to entice travellers taking the boat train to stay in the station the night before. Facing the hotel is A. S. Barry's Eleanor's Cross, often mistakenly described as Charing Cross, a replacement of the cross that Edward I erected nearby in 1293 to mark the funeral route of his queen, Eleanor of Castile, which was pulled down in 1647 by the Long Parliament. The station was rebuilt by Terry Farrell in 1991 in an exotic Egyptian-influenced style best seen from the south side of the river.

No. 1

The property that stood at the western end of the street is believed to have been the first house in London to be numbered and during the seventeenth century was the official residence of the Secretary of State, the most powerful politician in the country given that there was no prime minister.

(vii) Adelphi

An area to the south of Charing Cross station dominated by handsome streets and alleyways, some of which run into the bowels of imposing office blocks, it is named after the Adam Brothers' 1770s river-side terrace, which was built around the many wharves, hovels, factories and dark corners that abutted the river and was demolished in the 1930s. The area buzzes with life around Charing Cross station but is silent and eerie further east.

Adelphi Terrace
The Adelphi
The Adam Brothers' grand colonnaded classical development of twenty-four terraced houses, built between 1778 and 1785 and designed in the style of the ruined palace of Diocletian at Spalato (Split), was named Adelphi from *adelphoi*, Greek for brothers, and had as its centrepiece a forty-one-bay row of eleven four-storey terraced houses which stood by the river's edge, the Thames then running further to the north than it does now. The houses were luxuriously fitted with the finest interior decorations, courtesy of Angelica Kauffman, among others, while below were servants' cottages, each of which had street access. There were problems with the foundations, which kept sinking into the mud, and a perennial threat of flooding at high tide. Nevertheless the area attracted a number of well-known figures, including the Gilbert and Sullivan impresario Richard D'Oyly Carte, who lived at **No. 4** from 1888 to 1901 and hired James Whistler to decorate the library walls with a tint of yellow so that they appeared warm with sunshine even during winter; and the playwright George Bernard Shaw who lived at **No. 10** from 1896 to 1927, mostly with Charlotte Payne-Townshend, with whom he shared an unconsummated marriage.

At **No. 6** in the late nineteenth century was the Savage Club, whose members included the future Edward VII. In 1899 the American author Mark Twain gave a literary lecture at the club and told the audience: 'Chaucer is dead, Spenser is dead, so is Milton, so is Shakespeare, and I'm not feeling very well myself.' After Victoria Embankment was constructed between 1864 and 1870 the threat of flooding receded and the arches were used to store coal and wine, as well as becoming a convenient bolt-hole for criminals. Most of the Adelphi was demolished in 1936, despite much opposition, and replaced by Collcutt and Hamp's intimidating Adelphi office block, London's most authentic example of totalitarian 1930s architecture, the façade of which is decorated with N. A. Trent's 'heroic' relief of workers.

Buckingham Street
The Dukes of Buckingham occupied **York House**, a mansion that stood south of the Strand, and whose grounds ran down to the Thames, in the sixteenth century. In 1679 the diarist Samuel Pepys moved into No. 12, the house of his friend Will Hewer, after being released from the Tower, where he had been imprisoned for baseless allegations of betraying naval secrets to the French. By then Pepys had lost his powerful job as Secretary to the Lord High Admiral of England, but the charges against him were dropped and in 1684 Charles II made Pepys Secretary for Admiralty Affairs. The latter stayed in Buckingham Street and moved the Admiralty into No. 12. Pepys was obliged to move out in 1688 when a nearby wooden water tower caught fire but he later moved into the rebuilt **No. 14**. In 1698 the Russian Tsar, Peter the Great, stayed at **No. 15**, a property occupied by the novelist Henry Fielding in 1735 and by Charles Dickens around a hundred years later.

Craven Street
Craven Street, described by the novelist Henry James as being 'packed to blackness

with accumulations of suffered experience', was named after William, Earl Craven, who won acclaim for his selfless deeds in helping victims of the 1665 Great Plague and who, according to legend, was secretly married to Elizabeth, Queen of Bohemia, daughter of James I. The American scientist and politician Benjamin Franklin briefly lived at No. 36 in the eighteenth century, and the American author Herman Melville stayed at No. 25 in 1849 before leaving for New York to start work on 'The Whale', the story that became *Moby Dick*. The street is now dominated by hotels and smart offices.

Hungerford Lane
A small dark alleyway almost entirely covered by buildings, Hungerford Lane leads off Craven Street, plunges unexpectedly under the Charing Cross Hotel, and then runs along the back of the houses on the east side of Craven Street in place of the expected gardens.

John Adam Street
Originally John Street, it was later renamed after one of the developers of the nearby Adelphi.
The Royal Society for the Encouragement of Arts, Manufactures and Commerce, No. 8, north side
Founded in 1754 by William Shipley, Viscount Folkestone and Lord Romney to 'embolden enterprise, enlarge science, refine art, improve manufacture and to extend our commerce', its first offices were in Covent Garden and meetings were held above a library in Crane Court, off Fleet Street. In 1760 the society organized Britain's first contemporary art exhibition, showcasing works by sixty-nine artists including Joshua Reynolds, and fourteen years later moved to John Adam Street. It was a society member, William Ewart, who in 1866 proposed erecting blue plaques commemorating the residences of famous people, beginning with one for Lord Byron at 24 Holles Street, Marylebone. The society also helped organize the Festival of Britain in 1951 and now has some 30,000 members or fellows.

Lower Robert Street
A concealed street with a blind turn which runs through the buildings south of John Adam Street.

Northumberland Avenue
The south-western boundary of wc2, connecting Trafalgar Square and Victoria Embankment, it was built in 1876 on the site of 𝔑𝔬𝔯𝔱𝔥𝔲𝔪𝔟𝔢𝔯𝔩𝔞𝔫𝔡 𝔥𝔬𝔲𝔰𝔢, seventeenth-century home of the Earl of Northumberland, and was later lined with luxurious hotels built in a grand baroque style, including the Metropole.
south side: Victoria Embankment to Charing Cross
Former Metropole Hotel, between Whitehall Place and Great Scotland Yard
The grand nineteenth-century hotel was commandeered at the start of the Second World War by British Intelligence's wartime escape and evasion section, MI9, whose director, Christopher Clayton-Hutton, set up office in Room 424 and immediately sent agents to scour second-hand bookshops to find books on how prisoners-of-war escaped during the First World War. MI9 also contacted Bartholomew's, the Edinburgh-based map makers, to order maps of Germany, about 18 inches square and made of silk, which could be stored in flying kits. Meanwhile agents set to work constructing a multitude of ingenious gadgets, including hacksaws that could fit into trouser legs, fountain pens containing poison, RAF uniforms which could easily be converted into Luftwaffe uniforms, and blankets that could quickly be turned into civilian overcoats. Clayton-Hutton's best creation was the Escape Box, a pair of flat plastic boxes, one fitting inside the other, which were handed to airmen before a flight and contained everything they could need – malted milk tablets, boiled sweets, a bar or two of chocolate, benzedrine tablets for energy, halazone tablets for purifying water, rubber water bottle, soap, needle and thread, matches, chewing gum, fishing line (not for fishing, but as a substitute for

braces, or to be used as a sling in case of a broken arm) and a razor with a magnetized blade so that anyone taken prisoner and allowed to keep his shaving gear always had one compass. MI9 moved out when a German bomb skimmed a corner of the building in September 1940.

▶ MI5 on St James's Street, p. 217.

Former Victoria Hotel, between Great Scotland Yard and Charing Cross

During the Second World War the government's Special Operations Executive, which was in charge of sabotage and subversion, recruited agents for its F (French) section in the hotel's Room 238, which was furnished with nothing other than two chairs, a table, a bare light bulb and blacked-out windows. The interviewing officer, Major Selwyn Jepson, never gave his name and after a sentence or two in English would suddenly switch to fluent French to test whether the interviewees could cope. Applicants would also be tested on the nature of their opposition to Hitler and National Socialism, with those deemed too fanatical or too casually opposed weeded out. After the war it was calculated that out of some 470 agents sent into France 118 failed to return.

▶ SOE in Baker Street, p. 149.

Northumberland Street

Sherlock Holmes, Northumberland Street at Craven Passage

A pub and restaurant crammed with mementoes and ephemera relating to the Sherlock Holmes stories, it was previously the Northumberland Arms, possibly the model for Arthur Conan Doyle's Northumberland Hotel where Sir Henry Baskerville stays in *The Hound of the Baskervilles*. In 1957 the pub was renamed the Sherlock Holmes and filled with curios taken from an exhibition about Holmes held at 221B Baker Street – Holmes's address in the detective stories – held during the 1951 Festival of Britain. The collection includes briar pipes, bent poker sticks, posters, placards and newspaper cuttings relating to the stories, while upstairs, next to the restaurant, is a life-size reconstruction of the 221B Baker Street sitting room complete with Holmes mannequin (as used in 'The Empty House'), violin, books, period furniture and shelves laden with foul-looking bottled chemicals.

Villiers Street

The street covers the grounds of **York House**, which once belonged to George Villiers, 2nd Duke of Buckingham, powerbroker for Charles I, and is dominated by the east side of Charing Cross station. Rudyard Kipling, the late Victorian/early twentieth-century poet and novelist, lived in rooms at No. 43 from 1889 to 1891 above Harris, 'the Sausage King', who would give him as much sausage and mash for tuppence as he could carry upstairs.

York Place *(formerly Of Alley)*

This tiny alley to the east of Charing Cross station was formerly known as Of Alley, thanks to the literal application of the will of George Villiers, the seventeenth-century Duke of Buckingham, who lived here in his mansion, **York House**. The will stipulated that neighbouring streets be renamed after him using all parts of his name, thereby leading to the creation of <u>George</u> Court, <u>Villiers</u> Street, <u>Duke</u> Street, <u>Of</u> Alley and <u>Buckingham</u> Street.

(viii) Savoy

The tiny lanes and blind alleyways to the west of Waterloo Bridge are dominated by the name Savoy – Savoy Buildings, Savoy Court, Savoy Hill, Savoy Place, Savoy Row, Savoy Steps, Savoy Street and Savoy Way, as well as the Savoy Hotel, the Savoy Theatre and Savoy Chapel – the name being in honour of the medieval **Savoy Palace**, sacked during the Peasants' Revolt of 1381, when thirty-two men inside the wine cellar found themselves trapped and drank themselves to death. The palace was rebuilt by Henry VII as a hospital in 1505 and closed in the 1820s to make way for the building of Waterloo Bridge, only Savoy Chapel remaining.

Savoy Court

The road where the Savoy Theatre and the Savoy Hotel are located is the only one in Britain where traffic drives on the right.

Savoy Theatre

Built by Richard D'Oyly Carte in 1881 to stage his productions of Gilbert and Sullivan's operettas, it opened with a performance of the latter's *Patience*, starring George Grossmith, later the co-author of *The Diary of a Nobody*. The theatre was the first building in the country to be lit entirely by electricity, D'Oyly Carte reassuring the public that there was no danger from the hundreds of electric lamps bathing the auditorium in a rich yellow light by holding a bulb covered with muslin in his hand, smashing it with a hammer, and brandishing the cloth to show there were no scorch marks. W. S. Gilbert, the operetta's librettist, who refused to sit through early performances of his works, would prowl the streets outside the theatre or go for long walks until the show had finished. One night, dressed in all his finery, he slunk out of the theatre only to be mistaken at the door for a commissionaire. 'You sir,' shouted the theatre-goer, 'call me a cab.' 'All right,' replied Gilbert. 'You're a growler.' When the man made a puzzled face, he explained: 'Well, I can hardly call you hansom.' The theatre was redesigned in 1929 so that the exterior would match that of the Savoy Hotel and reopened with a revival of Gilbert and Sullivan's *The Gondoliers*, which began a trend for regular revivals of the repertoire.

Savoy Hotel

The Savoy, one of London's most famous hotels along with the Ritz, was financed by the profits the Gilbert and Sullivan impresario Richard D'Oyly Carte made from the light operas performed at the nearby Savoy Theatre and opened on 6 August 1889. It had its own power generator, an independent water supply courtesy of an artesian well, and seventy bathrooms, at a time when even the largest hotels had only four or five. The Savoy's first manager was Cesar Ritz,

who went on to found the Ritz Hotel, and the main chef was Auguste Escoffier, and the two men helped revolutionize the concept of eating out, at a time when such an activity was not considered very British, by concocting a number of famous dishes including Peach Melba in honour of a visit from the opera singer Dame Nellie Melba.

In 1898 Ritz was accused of conducting his own commercial affairs on hotel property – he and Escoffier admitted taking £8,000 in commissions – and to avoid a scandal they resigned in exchange for the hotel refraining from commenting, moving to the Carlton in Haymarket and then to Piccadilly where Ritz opened the hotel named after him. Nevertheless the Savoy continued to be a haunt of royalty, society figures, artists and writers including Oscar Wilde, who conducted his affair with Lord Alfred Douglas in the hotel's Room 346 in the early 1890s, and after being arrested for gross indecency appeared in court, where the presiding magistrate remarked: 'I know nothing about the Savoy, but I must say that in my view chicken and salad for two at sixteen shillings is very high. I am afraid I shall never supper there myself.'

The French artist Claude Monet, who used to take lunch and dinner at the hotel, painted *Waterloo Bridge, Grey Day* in 1903 from a hotel balcony, describing the view of the river as 'the finest riparian coup-d'oeil in Europe'. Fred Astaire and his sister, Adele, danced on the roof when they stayed at the hotel in 1923, and the novelist Arnold Bennett based his last and longest novel, *Imperial Palace* (1930), on life in the hotel, protecting himself from accusations of libel by claiming the hotel was located in St James's rather than the Strand.

During the 1980s the hotel was a regular haunt of Britain's two most powerful newspaper magnates, Robert Maxwell and Rupert Murdoch, and one day the two men were lunching separately when Murdoch approached Maxwell and casually mentioned that he was about to take

Concorde to New York for a business dinner in Manhattan's Four Seasons Grill Room. On his way back to his Holborn office Maxwell decided he would beat Murdoch there. He called for a helicopter, which picked him up from the helipad atop the *Mirror* offices, and whisked him to an airfield on the outskirts of London, and there he transferred to his recently acquired private Gulfstream G-4 jet. As Maxwell flew over the Atlantic, *en route* for New York and the Four Seasons, he contemplated the look of amazement that would appear on Murdoch's face when the Australian spotted him and realized that as Maxwell had not been on Concorde he must have travelled by private jet. Everything went to plan, and Maxwell duly arrived at the Four Seasons before Murdoch and waited there for his rival for several hours, until he realized that Murdoch had changed his mind at the last minute and was not going to turn up.

Savoy Hill
Savoy Chapel
The oldest building in the area and now a private chapel for the queen, Savoy Chapel dates from 1510, when it was built as part of the hospital that replaced the medieval Savoy Palace, and in 1890 became the first London church to be lit by electricity. The chapel features stained glass memorials of the *Canterbury Tales* author Geoffrey Chaucer and John Wycliffe, the religious reformer who was one of the first translators of the Bible into English.

Savoy Place
BBC offices (1923–32), No. 2
The BBC, founded in 1922, moved in April 1923 to 2 Savoy Place, described in an early anonymous broadcasting review as 'quite the most pleasant club in London', where there was always the chance of running into a famous figure such as H. G. Wells, George Bernard Shaw or G. K. Chesterton. Here broadcast journalism was a relaxed affair, a newscaster one night announcing, so legend has it, 'This is the BBC. There is no news tonight.' In March 1929 John Logie Baird gave his first demonstration of television to the BBC at Savoy Place. Three years later the Corporation moved to Broadcasting House. The Savoy Place premises are now occupied by the Institute of Electrical Engineers.
► BBC Broadcasting House, p. 155.

The West End

The West End, the commercial and social centre of London, is based around the four areas – Fitzrovia, Marylebone, Mayfair and Soho – that emanate from Oxford Circus, with Oxford Street running east–west through its centre.

Oxford Street

In Oxford Street there are too many bargains, too many sales, too many goods marked down . . . the buying and selling is too blatant and raucous – 'The London Scene', Virginia Woolf (1932)

London's main shopping street, home of the department stores Selfridges, John Lewis and Debenhams, was a Roman route, the Via Trinovantica, which by the Middle Ages had become the Waye from Uxbridge, or the Tyburn Way, as the Tyburn stream flowed underneath. It was renamed Oxford Street in 1739, in honour of the landowner Edward Harley, the 2nd Earl of Oxford, and after the Tyburn gallows moved to Newgate Prison it became a shopping centre, 'a street taking half an hour to cover from end to end with double rows of brightly shining lamps', according to the German novelist Sophie von la Roche, who visited London in 1786. Most of the main stores date from the nineteenth and early twentieth centuries, Peter Robinson opening a linen draper's shop at No. 103 in 1833, John Lewis setting up a shop at No. 132 in 1864, Marshall & Snelgrove (now Debenhams) taking the corner of Oxford Street and Vere Street in 1870 and Gordon Selfridge launching his store in 1909. Today, Oxford Street is responsible for around 10 per cent of retail spending in the capital.

north side: Edgware Road to Tottenham Court Road
Cumberland Hotel, between Great Cumberland Place and Old Quebec Street
Jack Spot, one of the major West End underworld figures of the 1950s, had a daily routine which began with a shave and brush-up in a barber's on Edgware Road, a saunter along the road waving and wishing passers-by good morning, and a few hours spent holding court in the Cumberland Hotel's Bear Garden where people would drop in and seek his advice on a wide range of topics. Jimi Hendrix occupied a suite, Room 507, during the last week of his life in September 1970, broadcasting his last radio

performance for Radio One's *Scene and Heard* from the room.

Selfridges, No. 400, between Orchard Street and Duke Street

One of London's best-known department stores, together with Harrods and Harvey Nichols, was opened on 15 March 1909 by Gordon H. Selfridge, a self-made Chicago millionaire, who had arrived in London determined to build the capital's first American-style superstore. It featured 130 departments, including a post office, roof garden and soda fountain – shopping on a scale never previously witnessed in London. Believing that the British knew how to make goods but not how to sell them, Selfridge concentrated on developing a new retailing philosophy that involved a credit scheme, bargain basement, sales, innovative window displays, themed departments, publicity and advertising, his opening slogan being: 'Why not spend the day at Selfridges?', thereby introducing the idea of shopping as leisure pursuit in its own right. He was rewarded by the arrival of a million people at the store in its first week.

John Logie Baird gave one of the first demonstrations of television in Selfridges in April 1925 and three years later the store made the world's first sale of a television set. The store fared badly during the economic crises of the 1930s, and after the company's board forced the founder to resign in October 1939 Selfridge sold his fifteen provincial department stores to the John Lewis Partnership.

In 1968 the Situationist group King Mob (named after a nickname the 1780 Gordon Rioters gave themselves), one of whose number was Malcolm McLaren, who later created the Sex Pistols, visited Selfridges with their own Santa Claus and began handing out the store's toys as 'alternative' presents to queuing children, along with a leaflet which proclaimed 'Christmas: it was meant to be great but it's horrible'.

Debenhams, Nos. 334–348, between Marylebone Lane and Vere Street

The department store Marshall & Snelgrove opened here in 1870 and in 1919 merged with Debenham's, which had been set up as a drapery shop in nearby Wigmore Street in 1778. The company was sold to the Burton Group in September 1985 for £550 million but broke away in January 1998.

House of Fraser (D. H. Evans), No. 318

Dan Harries Evans, a Welsh lace-maker, bought a property on this site in 1879 and opened a draper's store, staying with the firm until 1915 when he lost his money in an unsuccessful property deal that resulted in his dying penniless in 1928. In 2000 the store was renamed after its new owners, the House of Fraser.

John Lewis, Nos. 278–306, corner Oxford Street and Holles Street

John Lewis, a silk buyer, opened a shop here in 1864, and in 1906 bought Peter Jones's store in Sloane Square, making it over to his eldest son, John Spedan Lewis, on the condition that the latter worked a full day at the Oxford Street store before attending to the new shop. The two men later clashed over the development of the company, but it was Spedan's policy of equitable sharing that was implemented, and in 1929 Spedan transferred his shares to a trust 'for the happiness of all its members' which is set to expire twenty-one years after the death of the last descendant of King Edward VII alive at the time of its creation. At the beginning of the twenty-first century only two descendants remained alive: Queen Elizabeth II and Lord Harewood.

Oxford Circus

Sir Henry Tanner designed the four identical corners of the quadrant, which were built between 1913 and 1928.

100 Club, No. 100

London's oldest jazz club was opened in October 1942 by Robert Feldman, a jazz clarinettist, and taken over in 1954 by trumpeter Humphrey Lyttelton, who renamed it Humph's. It began to attract a fashionable crowd that included 1960s fashion pioneer

Mary Quant, wearing clothes – black tights – that caused an outrage, until the crowd spotted her companion, Alexander Plunkett-Green, wearing his mother's cast-offs. By 1964 it had become the 100 Club (unkindly claimed to derive from the number of people it could hold in comfort), putting on beat groups. But it was not until the early days of punk that it became an important rock venue, being where the Sex Pistols played in front of an audience of fifty in March 1976 and where Britain's first major punk festival – an event that saw the debut of Suzie [sic] & the Banshees, with the distinctly unmusical Sid Vicious on drums – was held in September 1976. Since 1978 the 100 Club has returned to being mainly a jazz venue.

► Ronnie Scott's, p. 196.

Kinetoscope Parlour (nineteenth century), No. 70

Moving pictures were shown in London for the first time on 17 October 1894 at 70 Oxford Street, where Franck Z. Maguire and Joseph D. Baucus, using the Edison Kinetoscope, which showed films on a loop to a single viewer at a time, presented a dance by Carmencita, a cock fight, bar scenes and pictures from a blacksmith's and a barber's.

Virgin (1970s), No. 24

Richard Branson set up the first Virgin record shop at 24 Oxford Street in 1970, having been forced to turn to retailing records when a postal strike threatened the existence of his fledgeling mail order company. As a record shop Virgin broke the mould, providing bohemian decor, floor cushions and headphones to listen to the latest hip releases, with no pressure placed on customers to buy.

south side: Charing Cross Road to Park Lane

Marquee I (1958–64), No. 165

The Marquee, which became London's most revered rock venue in the 1960s, opened as a coffee bar-cum-jazz club on 4 January 1958, in rooms below the Academy Cinema, then one of the few places in London to see art-house films. It was here that the Rolling Stones played their first gig on 12 July 1962, billed as 'Brian Jones, Mick Jagger and the Rollin' Stones', the night ending in violence when the audience was attacked by a group of Mods. When the Marquee's owner decided to install a new cinema screen in the basement in 1964 the club moved to 90 Wardour Street, taking most of the fixtures and fittings with it. No. 165 is now a bank.

► Marquee II, 90 Wardour Street, p. 201.

Pantheon, No. 173

Faith may grow bold / And take to herself all the wonders of old / Near the stately Pantheon you'll meet with the same / In the street that from Oxford hath borrowed its name – 'The Power of Music', William Wordsworth (1806)

James Wyatt built a grand entertainment palace, the **Pantheon**, here between 1770 and 1772, incorporating galleries framed by Corinthian columns and niches modelled on those of St Sophia, Istanbul. More than 1,500 people attended the opening ceremony, the aesthete Horace Walpole, unsure whether to marvel or mock, exclaiming: 'imagine Balbec in all its glory! The ceilings, even of the passages, are of the most beautiful stuccos in the best taste of grotesque', and later deciding that the building was 'the most beautiful edifice in England'. Although the **Pantheon** became the most talked about venue in London, it was not as commercially successful as expected and was converted into a theatre in 1791. Destroyed by fire the following year, possibly in an arson attack caused by those involved with the rival King's Theatre, Haymarket, it was rebuilt and continued as a theatre until 1813, when Nicholas Wilcox Cundy defied the Lord Chamberlain by staging opera without a licence, the latter exacting revenge by ruling that the **Pantheon** must close. The building was later converted into a department store and was demolished in 1937 by Marks and Spencer when they bought the site for a new store, also known as the Pantheon.

► Marks & Spencer, p. 150.

HMV, No. 363

The composer Edward Elgar officially opened what was the first HMV store here on 21 July 1921, and it was at No. 363 just over forty years later that the Beatles cut their first demonstration disc. The premises are now a shoe shop.

► Abbey Road studios, p. 367.

William Morris's showroom (1877–83), No. 449

William Morris's design company, The Firm, opened a showroom here in 1877 specializing in painted glass, embroidery, tapestry, carpets and wall-hangings, decorations that were unknown in London at the time. The shop attracted householders from the new Bedford Park estate, London's first garden village, and aesthetes such as Oscar Wilde, whose Morris wallpaper in his Tite Street home in Chelsea popped and split when poked. Although Morris's conscience was troubled by dealing with well-heeled clients ('ministering to the swinish luxury of the rich'), he noted that the poor did not have the money or time to take an interest in his medieval-style decorations and compromised by moving The Firm to Manchester in 1883.

► William Morris in Hammersmith, p. 250.

Marble Arch

John Nash's monument, constructed of white Carrara marble, is based on Rome's Arch of Constantine and commemorates Nelson's and Wellington's early-nineteenth-century victories over France. The arch stood outside Buckingham Palace from 1827 to 1851, when it became too small to accommodate the new enlarged coaches and was moved here.

CENTRAL LINE

The Central Line opened in July 1900 to link Shepherd's Bush and the Bank of England below what was then the most congested route of horse-drawn traffic in the capital. It attracted workers and shoppers by day and theatre-goers by night, its popularity assured as there were no railways in the areas linked by the new line. The line was extended west of Shepherd's Bush to Ealing Broadway in 1920 and east beyond Liverpool Street after the Second World War, using redundant Great Eastern Railway track, which resulted in the incongruous sight of tube trains moving through open Essex countryside alongside grazing cows. The 34-mile journey from the western terminus, West Ruislip, to the eastern terminus, Epping, is the longest on the system.

West Ruislip Opened as West Ruislip (For Ickenham) in 1948.

Ruislip Gardens Featured by John Betjeman in his 1954 poem 'Middlesex', in which the 'red electric train' [runs] gaily' into the station.

South Ruislip Designed with a drum tower and translucent laminated glass curtain walling.

Northolt The footpaths climb 'twisty . . . out of Northolt on and upward to the heights of Harrow Hill', according to John Betjeman's poem 'Middlesex'.

Greenford When the station opened it had the surprising feature of an escalator that carried passengers *up* to the platforms.

Perivale Early plans to adorn the station with the motif of a pear were abandoned when funds ran out during the Second World War.

Hanger Lane The station sits in the middle of a major traffic roundabout and can only be reached by subways.

Ealing Broadway Opened in July 1879 as the District Line's western terminus.

West Acton The only station on the 1940s Central Line western extension entirely built according to the wishes of the architect, Brian B. Lewis, following the scaling down of plans for the other stations when the Second World War broke out.

North Acton A Great Western Railway station that has been subsumed into the underground system.

East Acton Has a wooden platform shelter like a Victorian country station.

White City Opened in 1947 a few yards from Wood Lane, a station built for the 1908 Franco-British Exhibition at White City stadium that closed in the late 1940s but whose disused platforms and antiquated posters can still be glimpsed while travelling east from White City station to Shepherd's Bush.

Shepherd's Bush The original western terminus, which opened in July 1900, it has no connection with the other Shepherd's Bush station on the Hammersmith and City line.

Holland Park Named after the grounds of nearby Holland House, one of London's few surviving Jacobean mansions.

Notting Hill Gate There was no connection with the adjacent District/Circle Line station until 1959.

Queensway Originally Queen's Road and renamed Queensway in 1946.

Lancaster Gate Named after an awkwardly shaped nearby street of sumptuous stucco villas.

Marble Arch Named after the nearby arch that originally stood outside Buckingham Palace.

Bond Street In 1909 Gordon Selfridge, the owner of the nearby store, was refused permission to build a tunnel connecting Selfridges with the station, which he wanted to rename after his store.

Oxford Circus The underground network's second busiest station, with the equivalent of 53 million users a year.

Tottenham Court Road The station is decorated with millions of tiny tiles that make up a mosaic designed by Eduardo Paolozzi.

Holborn Before 1933 Holborn served only the Piccadilly Line, the nearest Central Line station being British Museum. But when the lines were upgraded Holborn began taking Central Line trains and British Museum closed.

Chancery Lane Britain's central telephone exchange was moved into a tunnel below the station during the Second World War for safety purposes.

St Paul's Plans to build a wartime bomb shelter in the tube station, originally known as Post Office, were abandoned for fear of damaging the cathedral's foundations.

Bank The original booking hall occupies the crypt of the church of St Mary Woolnoth.

Liverpool Street To promote one of their first events, a 1968 show in the staff canteen of a meat-packing factory on Bethnal Green Road, the performance artists Gilbert and George stood outside Liverpool Street station handing passers-by invitations. Few people took up the offer, but the couple did arouse the interest of Robert Fraser, one of the leading gallery owners of the time, who gave the young artists their first major break.

Bethnal Green One hundred and seventy-three people taking refuge in the station's air raid shelter on 3 March 1943 died when a crowd of around 1,500 rushed for the south-east entrance as rockets began dropping on nearby Victoria Park. As the victims fell people at the top kept pushing, thinking that they had been locked out, and more were killed. It was later determined that all 173 died within ninety seconds. Two days after the disaster the Ministry of Home Security released a statement saying there had been an accident at a 'London tube shelter', revealed only two years later as Bethnal Green station.

Mile End So named as it is a mile from Whitechapel, rather than a mile from the City of London.

Stratford Part of what is now the largest transport interchange in suburban London.

Leyton The station was originally built for the Great Eastern Railway.

Leytonstone The then unfinished tunnel between Leytonstone and Newbury Park was used as an aircraft components factory during the Second World War when work on the new line stopped.

Wanstead Designed in the style of the Gemeente Museum in The Hague.

Redbridge Originally planned as West Ilford, and then as Red House, after a nearby pub, it was eventually called Redbridge, after the nearby red bridge over the River Roding, the name now being used for the surrounding area and borough.

Gants Hill The station's design, with its huge central hall between platforms and generous use of space, is reminiscent of the grand stations on the Moscow metro system.

Newbury Park The station's huge curved bus shelter won the Festival of Britain award for architectural merit in 1951.

Barkingside It was built in a grand style at the end of the nineteenth century to please dignitaries visiting the nearby Barnardo's children's home.

Fairlop Home of an ancient fair that was held every July under the branches of a huge oak tree until it blew down in 1820.

Hainault The name comes from Henehout, 'the community's wood', rather than from Edward III's queen, Philippa of Hainault.

Grange Hill The station has no connections with the TV programme of the same name.

Chigwell The arrival of the tube helped create Chigwell's modern-day prosperity, but nowadays the station is, ironically, underused and often shut.

Roding Valley Named after the River Roding which rises in Dunmow, Essex, and flows into the Thames in Barking.

Snaresbrook Trains used to run non-stop from here to Liverpool Street.

South Woodford Originally George Lane on the Great Eastern Railway.

Woodford The ford is over the River Roding.

Buckhurst Hill The station nearest to Epping Forest.

Loughton Built in the early 1940s with innovative sound-proofing inspired by the 1939 New York World's Fair.

Debden Originally Chigwell Lane.

Theydon Bois One of three ancient adjacent Epping parishes, the others being Theydon Gernon and Theydon Mount.

Epping The shuttle section east of Epping to Ongar, the most remote part of the underground network, closed in 1994 after years of underuse, with passenger numbers at one of the stations, Blake Hall, barely reaching double figures.

FITZROVIA, W1

The area to the north-east of Oxford Circus was known until the mid twentieth century as Marylebone at its western end, Bloomsbury at its eastern end and North Soho, near Oxford Street, but later became Fitzrovia, a neologism coined in the 1930s by an unknown party, possibly the painter Augustus John, in homage to the Fitzroy Tavern, the nerve centre of the louche local bohemian scene.

Once the manor of Tottenhall, which stretched north to Highgate, it belonged to the canons of St Paul's at the time of the Domesday Book (1086), the manor house, 𝕿𝖔𝖙𝖙𝖊𝖓𝖍𝖆𝖒 𝕮𝖔𝖚𝖗𝖙, being situated to the north of where Warren Street station now stands. The estate was seized by Parliament in 1640 and later came into the possession of Henry Fitzroy, an illegitimate son of Charles II, who became Earl of Euston, and the names of Euston and Fitzroy have since been used for local streets and buildings. During the eighteenth century the area became fashionable, but when the wealthy began moving west the following century the houses were turned into workshops, mostly making furniture, or divided into cheap flats. These were often taken by artists, particularly on and around Charlotte Street, where John Constable lived in the 1820s and 1830s, and Italian and German immigrants. The latter included a number of political agitators, who took over the cafés, restaurants and clubs of Tottenham Street, Goodge Place and Charlotte Street.

The mid twentieth century was Fitzrovia's heyday, when pubs such as the Fitzroy

Tavern on Charlotte Street and the Wheatsheaf on Rathbone Place played host to the artists Roger Fry, Duncan Grant, Rex Whistler and Augustus John and writers such as Dylan Thomas and Julian Maclaren-Ross, whose unfinished *Memoirs of the Forties* is the definitive work on the area. After the Second World War the local bohemian scene slowly died out and the area became little more than a shabby land of small offices and workshops for the rag trade until the arrival of media organizations such as Independent Television News at 48 Wells Street and Channel 4 at 60 Charlotte Street in the late 1970s, which led to the area's rebirth as a favoured media stamping ground, with advertising agencies, recording studios and magazine offices filling the pleasant Victorian streets.

Charlotte Street

Named in 1787 after Charlotte of Mecklenburg-Strelitz, wife of George III, it was colonized by artists who in turn attracted frame-makers, art supplies shops and craftsmen, its bohemian character continuing into the twentieth century when poets and artists such as Dylan Thomas and Augustus John congregated at the Fitzroy Tavern at No. 16. (It was said of John that during the 1930s he would pat the head of every child walking along Charlotte Street in case it was one of his.) Anthony Powell described Charlotte Street as retaining 'a certain unprincipled integrity of character' in *A Buyer's Market*, the 1952 instalment of his novel sequence, *A Dance to the Music of Time*. In recent decades the street has become more glamorous with advertising agencies, media companies and fashionable restaurants moving in.

west side: Percy Street to Howland Street
Bertorelli's, Nos. 19–21
A restaurant opened in 1913 by the Italian Bertorelli brothers, one of whom died in 1995 aged 101, it was home in the 1950s to the Wednesday Club, a literary group founded by the reviewer Philip Toynbee, named in honour of Richard Hannay's

Thursday Club from John Buchan's *The Three Hostages*. Its members included Rex Warner, John Berger, Christopher Isherwood and T. S. Eliot. The restaurant was featured in the 1997 film *Sliding Doors*.
Anti-Apartheid offices (1960s), No. 89
Charlie Richardson, the south London gangland leader, burgled Anti-Apartheid's Charlotte Street offices on 3 March 1966 at the request of the South African security service, BOSS, which had agreed to protect Richardson's mining interests in South Africa in exchange for political help in London. The job was not one of Richardson's most taxing. He went to the offices late in the afternoon, hid in the toilet, and when the staff left, removed the membership lists which he then air-mailed to his contact in Johannesburg.
▶ The Richardsons in South London, p. 378.
Communist Working Men's Club (1902–18), No. 107
The 1903 congress of the devoutly communist Russian Social-Democratic Labour Party was transferred to the club following police harassment in Brussels and was where the 23-year-old Leon Trotsky helped Lenin secure a majority for his policies, following which the latter organized his group as the 'majoritarians' (*bol'sheviki* in Russian), with his defeated opponent, Martov, coining a similar name, 'minoritarians' (*men'sheviki*), for his group. The congress later moved to the Brotherhood Church on Southgate Road, near Dalston. When it was over the delegates went on an outing to Karl Marx's grave in Highgate Cemetery, where Lenin warned them that British and Russian police officers who knew that the delegates were in the country could be staking out the cemetery waiting to photograph them. The Charlotte Street club was closed by the police in 1918.
east side: Howland Street to Percy Street
Épicerie Française, No. 78
In the 1870s the restaurant at this address was the headquarters of an anarchist cell that supported terrorism and assassination and drew up, as Hugh David outlined in

The Fitzrovians, a list of handy phrases French members needed to use to ingratiate themselves with locals, including 'if you deun't g'hive mi a sixepen'ce, aille breke your nose'. One of the restaurant regulars, Enrico Malatesta, was later involved in the planning of the Houndsditch murders of 1910 (p. 32).

Fitzroy Tavern, No. 16
Fitzrovia's most famous pub was built in 1897 with typically ornate *fin de siècle* touches and became the major gathering place for the area's bohemian set in the mid twentieth century when regulars included the poet Dylan Thomas, the artist Nina Hamnett, who would approach men she did not know and cajole them into buying her a drink by rattling a money box in their face, the hangman Albert Pierrepoint and the satanist Aleister Crowley, the so-called 'Great Beast', who invented a cocktail for the pub, Kubla Khan No. 2, made of gin, vermouth and laudanum. By the time the Second World War broke out the pub's in crowd, moaning that the Fitzroy had become too popular, had moved to the nearby Wheatsheaf (see p. 146). In the 1950s the Fitzroy became popular with homosexuals at a time when male homosexuality was illegal. After a police raid the landlord was taken to court, which heard that 'there can be very little doubt that this house was conducted in a most disorderly and disgusting fashion', but he won the case.
► Coach and Horses, Soho, p. 198.

Cleveland Street
The street, which runs north–south through the centre of Fitzrovia, was named after the Duchess of Cleveland, mistress of Charles II, and was where, according to the historian Stephen Knight, Prince Eddy, the eldest son of the future Edward VII, was secretly apprenticed to the painter Walter Sickert, masquerading as the latter's brother, learning about everyday life so diligently that he fathered an illegitimate child with Annie Cook, a shop girl who worked at **No. 20**. The prince then secretly married

Cook, who was later sent to a mental institution, while the baby went to her friend Mary Kelly, murdered in 1888 by Jack the Ripper, who some believe was the prince himself. Prince Eddy was also involved in the so-called Cleveland Street scandal (see below).
► The Jack the Ripper murders, p. 276.

No. 18, east side
A Victorian brothel at 19 Cleveland Street (since renumbered No. 18 and rebuilt) was the setting for one of the major homosexual scandals of the late nineteenth century, which came to light when a boy who worked at the General Post Office in St Martin's-le-Grand and had been accused of stealing explained that he had earned the money 'by going to bed with gentlemen' at 18 Cleveland Street. Scotland Yard launched an investigation and found that boys supplied by a George Veck, who worked at the Post Office, were paid 4 shillings for sexual favours by 'a number of men of superior bearing and apparently good position', including the Earl of Euston, Lord Arthur Somerset (an equerry to the Prince of Wales) and Queen Victoria's grandson Prince Eddy. Arrests followed, and a number of clients were convicted of gross indecency and conspiracy, with Veck, who tried to leave the property disguised as a vicar, receiving a light sentence and Charles Hammond, who ran the brothel, tipped off in time to flee the country. The 24-year-old prince left on a tour of India just before the scandal broke.

Eastcastle Street
If they get us, I'll tell 'em she planned the job. I'll tell 'em she planned the big one, the Eastcastle Street job – *The Ladykillers* (1955)
London's first major postwar armed robbery took place on Eastcastle Street, a small quiet road to the north-east of Oxford Circus, on 21 May 1952, when a gang led by West End crime boss Billy Hill, posing as a film crew making a gangster movie, stole £287,000 from a mail van at quarter past four in the

morning. Hill's team had planned the raid with military precision. The van had been followed for months, so that the robbers would be acquainted with all its movements, the nine-strong team was taken to a secret location where they were locked in and briefed only on the night before the raid, and a few hours before the robbery one of the gang broke into the van while the drivers were on their tea-break and disconnected the alarm. Because the booty was the largest single sum that had ever been stolen, the prime minister, Winston Churchill, ordered daily updates on the police's progress, but Scotland Yard's investigating team of more than 1,000 officers never apprehended anyone and none of the money was ever recovered. In his memoirs Hill boasted about being the main perpetrator and handing Jack Spot, his main rival for the West End underworld crown, £14,000 from the proceeds.

Fitzroy Square

One of London's great showpiece squares, rich in architectural detail and history, although spoiled in recent years by excessive and ugly pedestrianization, Fitzroy Square was created in 1790 by Charles Fitzroy, 2nd Duke of Grafton, and designed by Robert and James Adam. The chapel and houses on the south side, which many claimed was the finest of the Adams' four sides, were destroyed in the 1940 Blitz but later rebuilt to resemble the original. The east side, dominated by a giant order of columns, escaped destruction.

Roger Fry's Omega Studios (1913–19), No. 33, south side
Fry, a member of the Bloomsbury Group, opened Omega Studios to make 'well-designed articles of daily use' in 1913, three years after organizing London's first exhibition of Manet and Post-Impressionist paintings (held at the Grafton Galleries, Mayfair). Fry had the walls padded with seaweed to keep out the noise and paid artists a wage to produce Post-Impressionist-style pottery, paintings and furniture. Those who worked here included the painter Wyndham Lewis, who left after a row in 1914 to set up the Vorticists and in his ire described Omega as 'Mr Fry's curtain and pin-cushion factory'.

George Bernard Shaw's address (1887–98) / Virginia Stephen's address (1907–11), No. 29, west side
Shaw moved to Fitzroy Square when he was largely unknown, having written several unsuccessful novels, and here wrote his first play, *Widowers' Houses* (1892), an attack on slum landlords, which received poor reviews, and his second, *Mrs Warren's Profession* (1893), which was banned by the Lord Chamberlain for containing suggestions of incest. Shaw moved out in 1898, and nearly ten years later Virginia Stephen (later Woolf) and her brother, Adrian, moved into the same five-storey house, much to the consternation of their friends, who thought the area to be socially beneath the Stephens.
► Virginia Woolf in Bloomsbury, p. 84.

Fitzroy Street

Like much of the area, Fitzroy Street was a haunt of writers and painters in the nineteenth century and was where George Bernard Shaw lived with his mother (at No. 37) from 1881 to 1886, writing a novel, *Cashel Byron's Profession*, that sold badly, and contracting smallpox. The artist Walter Sickert lived at **No. 8** in the early twentieth century, hosting tea parties in what many critics have since derided as a very 'English' set-up, and in 1907 hired a studio at **No. 19**, where he, Harold Gilman, Walter Sickert, Spencer Gore and others set up the Fitzroy Street Group of artists, 'celebrating the minutiae of everyday domestic life', as Hugh David noted in *The Fitzrovians*. The studio was open to anyone who wanted to peruse the artists' creations and art collectors were quick to take advantage. The protagonists later moved a mile north and established what came to be known as the Camden Town Group.

Maple Street
Telecom Tower
Built as the Post Office Tower from 1963 to
1966 – then the tallest building in London –
on the site of the former Museum Telephone Exchange and the BBC's 1930s
national distribution centre, as part of a civil
defence programme linking a network of
similar buildings deflecting high-frequency
microwave beams across the country, the
next one in the chain being in Stanmore,
12 miles north-west. It was also one of a
number of London tower blocks (others
include Centre Point) that in times of military tension could house civil servants who
could quickly descend into the bunker
underneath to run London under emergency regulations. (Below the tower the
Victoria tube line links important central
London buildings.) Despite the building's
importance the Post Office allowed the
public access to the observation tower and
around a million people took advantage
until an IRA bomb exploded in a toilet in
1971. The tower is still used for broadcasting
purposes, its slender circular frame and
massed aerials one of the most potent
symbols of postwar London.
► Secret history of the Victoria Line, p. 247;
Centre Point, p. 100.

Percy Street
A small street connecting Tottenham Court
Road and Charlotte Street whose restaurants
were heavily patronized by members of
Fitzrovia's literary set in the mid twentieth
century.
*south side: Tottenham Court Road to
Rathbone Place*
No. 18
George Orwell used the upstairs room at
No. 18, one-time home of his second wife,
Sonia Brownell, as the model for the room
in which Julia and Winston conduct their
ill-fated affair in *1984*.
No. 4
Alois Hitler, half-brother of Adolf Hitler,
lived at 4 Percy Street in the years leading
up to the First World War and was visited

here in 1912 by the future German dictator.
In 1914 the artist-novelist Wyndham Lewis
took rooms at No. 4 while working on his
avant-garde publication, *BLAST*, in which
he railed against various targets including
'BOURGEOIS VICTORIAN VISTAS'
and the 'purgatory' of Putney.
No. 1
The Restaurant de la Tour Eiffel at 1 Percy
Street was a major literary meeting place
during the middle of the twentieth century,
its first regulars being members of the Poets'
Club, led by Ezra Pound. In 1914 the icono-
clastic group the Vorticists, an avant-garde
art and literature movement led by
Wyndham Lewis, used the rooms to discuss
the contents of *BLAST*, their short-lived
publication, which was printed on yellow
paper with grotesque pink covers. Between
the wars the Eiffel Tower was run by an
Austrian, Rudolf Stulik, who had reputedly
been chef to Emperor Franz Joseph. It is
now the No. 1 Restaurant.

Rathbone Place
The first local street to be developed, and
named after a Captain Thomas Rathbone, it
was home in the early nineteenth century to
the Revd Henry Matthews, who lived at
No. 27, where he entertained, among others,
the painter-poet William Blake, who used to
sing his poems at parties. Some sixty years
later Karl Marx practised fencing at
Barthelemy's Salon, which was also on
Rathbone Place.
east side: Percy Street to Oxford Street
The Wheatsheaf, No. 25
One of a number of pubs popular with the
local mid-twentieth-century Fitzrovian
crowd, its best-known character was the
dilettantish writer Julian Maclaren-Ross,
who carried a silver-knobbed cane, was
court-martialled in 1943, and was memorably cast as the incorrigible X. Trapnell in
Anthony Powell's *A Dance to the Music of
Time*. After spending the early hours of the
afternoon in the Wheatsheaf, Maclaren-Ross
would take a late lunch at the Scala
restaurant in Charlotte Street, usually roast

beef with as much fat as possible and lashings of horseradish sauce, stroll down to the Charing Cross Road bookshops, and then return to the Wheatsheaf till closing time, after which it was back to the Scala for supper and coffee. Unsurprisingly, in view of this hectic schedule, Maclaren-Ross never finished writing his long-awaited memoirs.

Black Horse, No. 6

According to Julian Maclaren-Ross (see the Wheatsheaf, above) the Black Horse was where 'old dears in dusty black toasted departed husbands with port and lemon from black leather settees'. The folk singer Ewan MacColl ran his Ballads and Blues Club here in the early 1950s before moving it to the Princess Louise in High Holborn (p. 97).

Rathbone Street

Rathbone Street is Fitzrovia's main street for pubs, where mid-twentieth-century regulars included the writers Dylan Thomas, George Orwell and later Anthony Burgess. The newsagent on the corner of Rathbone Street and Percy Street was used in the 1959 Michael Powell thriller *Peeping Tom* as the establishment where respectable gentlemen buy 'glamour shots' of partly clothed women and where, in the flat above, the film's protagonist takes photographs of models in between committing murders.

west side: Percy Street to Charlotte Place

Duke of York, No. 47

During the middle years of the twentieth century the Duke of York was famed for its eccentric landlord, Alf Klein, who liked to cut off customers' ties and collected some 1,500 as trophies.

The Newman Arms, No. 23

Delightfully positioned over an alleyway, the Newman Arms, renowned for its pies, was a favourite of George Orwell who, being a beer snob, approved of its lack of a spirits licence and based scenes in the novels *Keep the Aspidistra Flying* and *1984* on the pub.

east side: Charlotte Place to Percy Street

Marquess of Granby, Rathbone Street at Percy Street

The poet Dylan Thomas enjoyed visiting the Marquess of Granby so that he could pick fights with guardsmen, who themselves had dropped by to pick on homosexuals. As the pub was in a different licensing area from most of its neighbours it stayed open half an hour later and attracted a large crowd once the Fitzroy Tavern and Wheatsheaf had closed.

Scala Street

The street took its name from the now demolished Scala Theatre on Charlotte Street.

Pollock's Toy Museum, No. 1

A lavishly stocked small museum, with puppets, theatrical material, Victorian dolls' houses and toys from around the world, it is named after Benjamin Pollock, a late-nineteenth-century toy maker, was founded in Hoxton in 1851, and became a favourite of the Scottish writer Robert Louis Stevenson, who once remarked: 'If you love art, folly or the bright eyes of children, speed to Pollock's.' It closed after being bombed in the Second World War and moved first to Seven Dials and then in 1969 to Fitzrovia.

Tottenham Court Road

A well-trodden medieval route from St Giles to the edge of the Hampstead hills, it was developed from 1760, when houses replaced the ash tip on the west side which people used to make rudimentary bricks, and soon began to attract furniture makers, there being more than 100 cabinet makers by 1850. Karl Marx, walking along Tottenham Court Road one day in the 1850s, attempted to solve a row between two people after hearing a woman crying out: 'Murder! Murder!'. He waded through the crowd to find a drunken woman arguing noisily with her husband, but the sound of his German accent caused the protagonists to turn on him as an interfering foreigner. Marx and a German companion later took a pub crawl along the road, visiting the Rising Sun at

No. 46, the Roebuck (No. 108), and the Northumberland Arms (No. 119), after which they ran down the street throwing stones and smashing a street lamp with several policemen giving chase. There are still furniture stores at the northern end of the road, while the southern end contains London's most intense concentration of hi-fi and computer shops.

west side: Oxford Street to Euston Road
𝔘𝔉𝔒 club (1960s), No. 31
The 1960s psychedelic club 𝔘𝔉𝔒 (Unlimited Freak Out), London's first all-nighter, which opened its doors in December 1966 and was run by the *International Times*'s John Hopkins and record producer Joe Boyd, featured underground films, poetry readings, plotless impromptu plays and the newly formed Pink Floyd, who played a set that consisted of seemingly interminable one-chord numbers. 𝔘𝔉𝔒 closed in the summer of 1967 when John Hopkins was convicted of possessing cannabis and jailed for nine months, but by then tourists had begun to edge out the regulars. The block was demolished in the seventies.
► Pink Floyd's first concerts, Notting Hill, p. 461.

Goodge Street station
In 1939 at the outset of the Second World War a planned new express tube system due to be run from Goodge Street station was abandoned (a notice warning of a deep shaft can still be seen at one end of the platforms). Three years later the space was allocated to the United States army for their signals centre, being where General Eisenhower, the US's wartime commander-in-chief, planned the D-Day landings in 1944. In 1951 the station was used as a hostel for visitors to the Festival of Britain, and five years later as a transit camp for troops on their way to Suez. Since 1956 the British Library has used the abandoned works for storage space.

east side: Euston Road to New Oxford Street
Heal's, Nos. 191–199
An innovative furniture store founded by John Harris Heal in 1810 at 33 Rathbone

Place, Heal's moved to Tottenham Court Road in 1840 and through the work of Ambrose Heal, one of John's sons, played a leading role in the development of the Arts and Crafts movement in England. The rebuilt store, the work of Smith and Brewer in 1916, alarmed the leading modernist architect Le Corbusier, who said: 'The existing plan of the dwelling . . . is conceived as a furniture store. This scheme of things, favourable enough to the trade of Tottenham Court Road, is of ill omen to society.' The store donated its archive to the Victoria and Albert Museum in 1978 and five years later was sold to Terence Conran's Habitat/Mothercare group.
► Liberty's store, p. 192.

Dominion, Tottenham Court Road at New Oxford Street
Now a venue for musicals, it was built as a concert hall in 1929 on the site of the Luna Park fairground, where a woman wrapped in cotton wool known as the Human Seal would set herself alight and dive into a water tank. It was converted into a cinema in 1932, being where in February 1957 Bill Haley and the Comets became the first American rock 'n' roll act to play Britain.

MARYLEBONE, W1

The least hectic of the four West End districts, Marylebone, owned in the twelfth century by the Knights Templar, a brotherhood of warrior monks established to protect pilgrims travelling to the Holy Land, was named after the church of St Mary-by-the-Tyburn or St Mary-a-le-Bourne, built *c.* 1400, by what is now the northern end of Marylebone High Street. The land eventually came into the possession of Thomas Hobson, one of Henry VII's exchequer officials, and was used as a hunting ground by Henry VIII. It was developed from 1719 by the architect James Gibbs (best known for the church of St Martin-in-the-Fields by Trafalgar Square) with a rigidity unusual for London but occasionally relieved by squares and mews. What has always been one of the wealthiest enclaves of inner London became fashionable at the end of the twentieth century when a number of chic boutiques and cafés opened on Marylebone High Street, which runs through the centre of the area.

● Marylebone is the quarter of w1 to the north-west of Oxford Circus. Entries for the Marylebone area around Marylebone station, in NW1, can be found on pp. 347–9.

(i) Baker Street and west

Baker Street *Also see p. 347*
The street, famous as the home of the fictional detective Sherlock Holmes (at No. 221B), was built by William Baker, who leased land from the Portman Estate in 1755, and originally ran from Portman Square to York Street, north of which it was known as Upper Baker Street. Many Baker Street properties were requisitioned during the Second World War by the Special Operations Executive, the government department responsible for sending undercover agents into enemy territory to engage in subversion and sabotage. The blocks reverted to offices for a number of major companies, including Marks and Spencer, in later decades.

west side: Orchard Street to Marylebone Road
No. 77
The Special Operations Executive used No. 77 during the Second World War as a homing station for its pigeons, which were trained to take coded messages from the American forces bases in Bedfordshire to strategic military and political locations in London.
Norgeby House, No. 83
The Special Operations Executive used Norgeby House as an overspill for officers working for F (French section), which was based at Orchard Court, Portman Square.

east side: Marylebone Road to Orchard Street
Apple boutique (1967–8), No. 94
The Beatles opened a boutique here in December 1967 with an announcement from Paul McCartney that it would be run according to 'Western communism principles'. The store was a financial disaster and closed on 30 July 1968 with all £15,000-worth of stock given away to members of the public.
No. 82
The Special Operations Executive interviewed potential codebreakers in a room above what was then Marks and Spencer's head office in 1940, inviting those who had sent in correct answers to the *Daily Telegraph* crossword. Among the first to be hired was Leo Marks, a member of the family that ran the bookshop at 84 Charing Cross Road (p. 100), later made famous by Helen Hanff's story of the same name, who on his first day was given a coded message to decipher but failed to solve it within the allotted half an hour. An unimpressed presiding officer revealed dismissively that most of his secretaries would have completed the task in that time; Marks took the rest of the day to solve the problem, and distraught handed in his work. The officer thanked Marks and asked him to hand back the codebreaker he had used to decipher the message. When Marks explained that he had not been given a codebreaker and had cracked the code with nothing more than the original cryptogram, the officer was so astonished he hired Marks straight away and immediately made him head of department. Marks's work was later instrumental in penetrating the Germans' coded messages.
► 84 Charing Cross Road, p. 100.
Special Operations Executive headquarters (1940–46), No. 64
Britain's wartime clandestine operations outfit, the Special Operations Executive (SOE), was set up in 1940 to 'organise movements in enemy-occupied territory comparable to the Sinn Fein movement in Ireland . . . using industrial and military sabotage,

terrorist acts and propaganda'. It was not immediately popular with war chiefs, for as espionage historian Roy Berkeley explained in *A Spy's London*, when the Chief of Air Staff was told about the newly formed group he commented that 'the dropping of men dressed in civilian clothes for the purpose of attempting to kill members of the opposing forces is not an operation with which the Royal Air Force should be associated'.

At the main headquarters in No. 64 the SOE's head, Major-General Sir Colin Gubbins, who had been Britain's first commando, also organized Britain's Auxiliary Units, teams based along the British coast primed to counter an expected German invasion, something that came close to fruition in August 1940 when eighty parachutes decorated with giant German eagles and loaded with maps, wirelesses and instructions were found in the Midlands. On 7 September there was another scare, when reconnaissance flights noticed an increase in enemy activity in the Channel, and at 8.07 p.m. that night the War Room in Whitehall flashed a message to all its posts across Britain. Church bells rang in seaside towns to herald the expected invasion and a couple of bridges were destroyed by enthusiastic members of the units, some of whom immediately went underground for five days. But again no invasion took place.

SOE's highpoint came after the 1944 D-Day Normandy landings when, thanks to the work carried out by the thousands of SOE agents stationed in occupied France, Belgium and Holland, the Nazis found it difficult to maintain their occupying forces and were obliged to surrender. In January 1946 following the end of the war Labour prime minister Clement Attlee closed down the entire SOE operation.
► SOE French section, p. 206.

Marks & Spencer, Nos. 47–67
The renowned retailing group, which has its headquarters here, was founded in a Leeds market in 1884 by Polish refugee Michael Marks, who went into partnership with Tom Spencer in 1894. It grew steadily during the early twentieth century, opening several stores in the north of England and London. In 1924 the then owner, Simon Marks, went to America to gain ideas on making and selling clothes using man-made fibres and on retailing in general, and when he returned Marks installed a 5s price ceiling on clothes and began refurbishing his stores using the latest American ideas. These developments helped the company dominate the British market after the Second World War, often being the first store to introduce innovative ideas such as self-service. Marks and Spencer remained Britain's most prestigious retailing chain until the end of the century, when a series of unsuccessful decisions particularly over clothing saw an alarming dip in its reputation.

Bryanston Mews West

Mandy Rice-Davies's address (1960s), No. 1
Mandy Rice-Davies, the 1960 Earls Court Motor Show's Miss Austin, best known for her later role in the Profumo Scandal, moved into this smart flat, owned by the west London slum landlord Peter Rachman, at the beginning of the decade, living on the £80 a week spending money that Rachman gave her along with expensive gifts such as a mink coat and a 3.2 litre Jaguar. She moved out in October 1962 to live with the society osteopath Stephen Ward at nearby 17 Wimpole Mews, the address that became central to the unfolding scandal.
► The Profumo Scandal, p. 157; Peter Rachman's property empire, p. 435.

Cato Street

Cato Street Conspiracy headquarters, No. 1a
A group of anarchists led by Arthur Thistlewood met in 1820 at this mews cottage, just off the Edgware Road, to plan the assassination of the entire British Cabinet, including the prime minister, the Duke of Wellington, while they dined at 44 Grosvenor Square, Mayfair. The plot was foiled when the police raided the cottage and found some twenty men armed with

guns, swords and other weapons standing next to the two sacks in which they intended to carry off the heads of senior ministers. When one constable, PC George Ruthven, shouted: 'We are officers! Seize their arms!', Thistlewood picked up his sword and thrust it into the body of another officer, Richard Smithers, who cried out: 'Oh my God, I am done!' and fell to the ground, dead. Thistlewood escaped, but was recaptured the following night near Moorgate, and after being imprisoned in the Tower, was hanged outside Newgate Prison on, ironically, 1 May. For being a traitor as well as a murderer Thistlewood was decapitated as well as hanged.

➤ 44 Grosvenor Square, Mayfair, p. 163; Newgate Prison, p. 10.

Portman Square

The centrepiece of Henry William Portman's estate, Portman Square was begun in the 1760s and became the most fashionable square in London outside Mayfair in the early nineteenth century. Its social nuances captivated the novelists William Thackeray, who set many scenes from his novels locally, and Anthony Trollope, who featured the square in *Phineas Finn* and *The Small House at Allington*. The two main Portman Square properties were **Home House**, designed by Robert Adam in 1772 to 1776 for Lady Home, heir to a fortune made in Jamaica and known for her foul language, and **Montagu House**, designed by James 'Athenian' Stuart for Elizabeth Montagu, whom the novelist Fanny Burney described as 'brilliant in diamonds, solid in judgment'. Elizabeth Montagu ran a literary salon that became known as the Blue Stocking Society after she told one of the guests, Benjamin Stillingfleet, who complained of having no formal wear, to come in his 'bluestockings' – ordinary clothes.

Montagu held a dinner for London's chimneysweeps every May Day, serving roast beef and pudding on the lawn, and when one sweep, David Porter, became a

builder he created a square, Montagu Square, in her honour a few hundred yards to the north-west. **Montagu House** was destroyed in the Blitz and parts of the gate are now in the grounds of Kenwood House, Highgate. When in the 1860s Lord Lyttleton, brother-in-law of the liberal politician William Gladstone, announced that he was leaving Portman Square for Grosvenor Place, Belgravia, his entire staff gave notice to quit. Portman Square was commercialized towards the end of the nineteenth century.

(ii) Marylebone village

Manchester Square
Hertford House (The Wallace Collection), north side

The Wallace Collection of porcelain, furniture and paintings is based in Hertford House, built in 1777 for the 4th Duke of Manchester, and was begun in the mid eighteenth century by the 1st Marquess of Hertford, Francis Seymour-Conway, who bought six Canalettos on his Grand Tour. The collection was enlarged by the 3rd Marquess, Francis Charles Seymour-Conway, Envoy Extraordinary to the Court of Russia, on whom Thackeray based the Marquis de Steyne in *Vanity Fair*. It was considerably improved by the 4th Marquess, who lived as a recluse in Paris but was a tireless accumulator of Old Masters and beat Baron de Rothschild into buying Frans Hals's *The Laughing Cavalier* in 1865, bidding six times the asking price. The 4th Marquess left the collection to his illegitimate son, Richard Wallace, whom he never publicly acknowledged, and Wallace's widow bequeathed it to the public, the gallery being opened by Edward, Prince of Wales, on 22 June 1900. The 775-strong painting collection also includes works by Rembrandt, Rubens, Van Dyck, Velázquez and Poussin, whose *A Dance to the Music of Time* gave Anthony Powell the title of his twelve-part series of novels.

➤ Sir John Soane Museum, Lincoln's Inn Fields, p. 123.

EMI (1960–95), No. 20, west side
Electrical and Mechanical Industries (EMI),
Britain's most successful record company,
had its origins in the National Gramophone
Company of New York, whose director,
William Barry Owen, arrived in Britain in
1897 and two years later bought Francis
Barraud's painting *His Master's Voice* as a
logo for his new company. EMI's early
recordings included speeches by the politicians Winston Churchill and David Lloyd
George, and in 1955 it bought America's
Capitol Records, an astute move that netted
millions of dollars in sales courtesy of Nat
King Cole, Dean Martin and Peggy Lee.
Three years later EMI signed Cliff Richard,
who went on to make more hit singles than
any other British act, and in 1962 it made its
most successful ever signing, the Beatles.
Success continued with Pink Floyd, signed
in 1967, Berry Gordy's Tamla group of
labels, distributed in Britain by EMI under
the logo Tamla Motown, and Queen. But
when in 1976 a new signing, the Sex Pistols,
enlivened a TV programme with a cascade
of Rabelaisian invective workers at the
company's Hayes plant refused to handle
the group's 'Anarchy in the UK' single and
EMI terminated the Pistols' contract, losing
much credibility. EMI continued to maintain its commercial status in the 1980s and
after acquiring other labels, such as United
Artists and Virgin, moved to Hammersmith
in 1995.
► Abbey Road studios, p. 367.

Manchester Street

Joanna Southcott, a Devonian upholsterer
who led a breakaway movement from the
Methodists in 1777, moved to **No. 38**
Manchester Street in 1801, announcing
herself as a millennial prophet – the 'woman
clothed with the sun' of Revelations 12 and
the 'bride of the lamb' of Revelations 19.
Her followers believed her to be a visionary
and claimed she had accurately predicted
the war with France and the failed harvests
of 1794, 1795 and 1797. In 1814, at the age of
sixty-four, Southcott announced she was

pregnant with what would be the virgin
birth of either 'Shiloh', as prophesied by
Jacob in Genesis 49:10 ('The sceptre shall
not depart from Judah, nor a law-giver from
between his feet, until Shiloh come'), or the
man-child of Revelations 12: 5 ('who is to
rule all the nations with a rod of iron').

After nearly twenty doctors asserted that
Southcott was pregnant gifts were sent and a
cradle was decorated with a gold crown and
the name Shiloh embroidered in Hebrew
letters at the head. Supporters thought it
best that Southcott acquire a husband
prior to the birth, so that the child would
not be declared illegitimate, and so on
12 November 1814 she married John Smith, a
steward to the Earl of Darnley. The newspapers of the day were not enthusiastic,
many alleging that the birth would be of the
'baby-smuggled-in-warming-pan' variety,
and by November, when the signs of pregnancy had disappeared, Southcott herself
declared it to have been an 'illusion'. The
pregnancy over, she grew increasingly weak
and when she died on 27 December 1814 her
followers placed hot-water bottles around
her body to keep it warm in expectation of
either a resurrection or the appearance of
Shiloh. When neither happened after four
days her remains were taken to St John's
Wood Cemetery where she was buried, with
supporters hopeful of her resurrection
vowing to refrain from shaving off their
beards until the great day.

Southcott left a box which she insisted
should only be opened in the presence of
twenty-four bishops, but it proved difficult
to find the required number willing to take
part in the ceremony, and it was not until
the 1920s, when a group of supporters
paraded through the streets of London
bearing sandwich-boards proclaiming 'The
Bishops must open Joanna's Box to save
England from ruin', that the box was
opened in the presence of one bishop at
Church House, Westminster. It was found
to contain some coins, a pistol, a nightcap,
a lottery ticket and a cheap novel.
► Richard Brothers, millennial prophet, see

below; controversial birth of James II's son, St James's Palace, p. 209.

Marylebone High Street

The main road through the centre of Marylebone was the location of the local manor house and the parish church of St Mary which stood by the Tybourne stream; the church was known as St Mary-by-the-Tybourne and gave its name to the area, since corrupted into Marylebone. The High Street is now lined with appealing shops, including a number of designer clothes outlets, smart restaurants and the renowned travel bookshop Daunt at No. 83.

St Marylebone, west side

Originally St Mary-by-the-Tybourne, or St Mary-a-le-Bourne, the church that gave its name to the area was built close to the present site, by the Tybourne stream, in 1400 and was where the 45-year-old Francis Bacon, Lord Chancellor and philosopher, married the fourteen-year-old daughter of an alderman in 1606, 'clad from head to toe in purple', according to contemporary reports. The church was pulled down in 1740, rebuilt in 1774, and demoted to a parish chapel when Thomas Hardwick built the current church, a short distance to the south, in 1817. The poets Elizabeth Barrett and Robert Browning were married in the new church on 12 September 1846 in secret, as her father disapproved of their relationship, and after the wedding the couple temporarily parted, Barrett returning home as if nothing had happened. A week later they eloped to Italy with her maid and dog, Flush. The older church was destroyed by Second World War bomb damage and demolished in 1949, the site now being marked by a garden.

Paddington Street

While living at №. **57** from 1792 to 1795 the preacher Richard Brothers proclaimed himself to be the Prince of the Hebrews and published *A Revealed Knowledge of the Prophecies and Times*, a mixture of extracts from the Bible interspersed with his own commen-

tary, adopting some of the popular Protestant teachings of the day (Rome as the great whore of Revelations 17, the Pope as the scarlet-coloured beast, the cardinals as the ten horns, and so on), fixing the day of the Millennium as 19 November 1795. *The Times* nicknamed him 'The Great Prophet of Paddington Street', his book became a bestseller, and he was visited by large numbers of people. But in March 1795 the authorities, worried about the scope of Brothers's influence, arrested him, and after an interview with the Privy Council Brothers was declared insane and sent to an asylum in Islington where he stayed for eleven years. Brothers's incarceration only served to reinforce the views of his supporters, who saw his plight as proof of his status as a true prophet persecuted by his own people, and his influence continued into the new century, with much publicity given to his unsuccessful plan to return the Jews to the Holy Land.

► Joanna Southcott, millennial prophet, p. 152.

(iii) around Harley Street

Many of Britain's most prestigious and most expensive private medical consultancies have their offices on and around Harley Street.

Cavendish Square

Edward Harley, 2nd Earl of Oxford, laid out what was originally Oxford Square, renamed Cavendish Square after his wife, Lady Henrietta Cavendish Holles, in 1717, and its excellent location soon came to the attention of the Duke of Chandos, who owned much land between here and **Canons**, his mansion in Edgware, which Daniel Defoe described as 'the finest in England'. The duke announced that he would build himself a mansion to take up the north side of the square, and line the 12-mile route to it with luxurious properties that would form a grand processional way, but his plans were spoiled by the South Sea Bubble financial crash of 1720, in which he lost a fortune, and he settled for just two mansions at the northern corners of the square. Cavendish Square was also meant to include a market, but the scheme was obstructed by Lord Craven, owner of Carnaby Market, south of Oxford Street. The square's gardens, which used to contain a statue of the Duke of Cumberland ('Butcher Cumberland', victor of Culloden), were uprooted during the building of the Victoria Line in the 1960s and replanted when the work was completed.

► Bloomsbury Square, p. 88.

west side

Harcourt House / Portland House

A grand property designed by Thomas Archer, architect of the former church of St John in Westminster's Smith Square, for Lord Bingley, Chancellor of the Exchequer, it became Portland House when the Duke of Portland moved here in 1825. The house was later at the centre of one of the strangest legal tussles London has ever witnessed when a Mrs Druce, the daughter-in-law of a local shopkeeper, the late Thomas Druce, petitioned the home secretary for permission to open Druce's coffin on the grounds that the duke and Druce had been one and the same. The duke had created the shopkeeper persona as an elaborate hoax, she claimed, the coffin would be empty, and she would be entitled to a share of the millions that the childless Duke of Portland had left in his will. A legal battle of Jarndycean proportions ensued, but Mrs Druce remained unsuccessful in her attempts to prove that her father-in-law's coffin was empty, the coffin remained unopened, and after seven years Mrs Druce was consigned to a mental hospital, the case unsolved. Meanwhile, the Druce family formed a public company to continue the case and speculators, sensing a killing, took up their cause. At last, in 1907, the coffin was opened. Inside, to no one's surprise, was the body of Druce and the case collapsed. The house was demolished in 1904 and replaced by a block of flats.

Harley Street

Suspecting myself of a cardiac disease, I went one morning to Harley Street – *An Error of Judgement*, Pamela Hansford Johnson (1965)

The London street most associated with private medical consultants was built in 1729 and named after Edward Harley, 2nd Earl of Oxford, becoming connected with medicine in 1828 when John St John Long opened a practice for wealthy women clients at No. 84. The street's first private consultants, whom Joseph Lister struggled to convince of the need for sterilizing their instruments, would use their ground-floor dining rooms and libraries as waiting and consulting rooms and live in the quarters above. There are now estimated to be more than 1,400 doctors and dentists in the Harley Street area and eight private hospitals, the most famous of which is the London Clinic, which has treated King Hussein of Jordan, the tycoon Paul Getty, Elizabeth Taylor and Charlie Chaplin.

west side: Cavendish Square to Marylebone Road

No. 19

Morell Mackenzie, the late-nineteenth-century throat specialist who was the first doctor to suggest a link between smoking and lung cancer, had his consulting rooms at 19 Harley Street where he treated Frederick, Emperor of Germany, Queen Victoria's son-in-law, but was unable to save him from dying from cancer of the larynx. Mackenzie earned the royal family's displeasure for writing a book about the affair and suggesting that Frederick might have contracted syphilis.

east side: Marylebone Road to Cavendish Square

No. 90

Florence Nightingale became Superintendent of the Establishment for Gentlewomen During Illness at what was then 1 Upper Harley Street in 1863, her improvements to nursing including piping hot water to every floor and arranging for the installation of a lift to bring patients their meals. A year later

Nightingale left to serve in the Crimean War, where her nursing work reduced the death rate among soldiers from 42 to 2 per cent.

No. 84

John St John Long, the first well-known Harley Street physician, nicknamed 'the King of the Quacks', began practising at No. 84 in 1828, attracting wealthy women, whom he would ask to inhale from a long length of pink tubing filled with a potent gas and whose resistance to undergoing massage would then usually decrease. Long's star waned after the death of two of his patients and he was convicted of manslaughter, for which he was fined £250. He died of tuberculosis at the age of thirty-six.

No. 64

At the end of the 1950s the aspiring actors Terence Stamp and Michael Caine shared a flat in the house where the painter J. M. W. Turner had lived in the early nineteenth century. One day Caine, who had married young and divorced soon after, was visited by bailiffs acting for his former wife who wanted alimony and he was obliged to attend debtors' court, where the magistrate refused to believe that the actor had no money yet lived in Harley Street.

Langham Place

Langham Place, the short stretch of road between Portland Place and Regent Street, takes a sharp curve rather than a straight line due to the activities of Lord Foley, a wealthy eighteenth-century resident, who in 1767 won a guarantee from the landowner, the Duke of Portland, that no building would spoil his view of the Highgate and Hampstead hills. Daniel O'Connor, the champion of Catholic emancipation, lived on Langham Place in 1836 while representing Kilkenny in Parliament, southern Ireland then being controlled by Westminster. When he was denounced by the young Benjamin Disraeli, who wanted to impress Conservative Party leaders, he in turn criticized Disraeli as an 'abominable, foul and atrocious miscreant'. Disraeli

challenged him to a duel but O'Connor, who had previously killed a challenger and had promised not to duel again, ignored him. Disraeli was eventually arrested and bound over to keep the peace.

Langham Hotel, Langham Place at Portland Place, west side

Built on the site of the demolished mansions of 𝕱𝖔𝖑𝖊𝖞 𝕳𝖔𝖚𝖘𝖊 and 𝕷𝖆𝖓𝖌𝖍𝖆𝖒 𝕳𝖔𝖚𝖘𝖊, the Langham Hotel, designed in the style of a Florentine palace, with room for 600 guests, opened in 1865 with a celebratory dinner attended by over 2,000 people. It was soon attracting custom from Napoleon III and the writers Mark Twain and Ouida (Marie Louise de la Ramée), who kept a suite with black velvet curtains fully closed to keep out the sunlight and hosted a number of literary evenings at which the visitors included the poet Robert Browning. At a dinner held in the hotel in August 1889 and organized by the American magazine publishers Lippincott, Oscar Wilde was commissioned to write *The Picture of Dorian Gray* and Arthur Conan Doyle the Sherlock Holmes novella *The Sign of Four*. The hotel was bombed during the Second World War, when its 38,000-gallon water tank was destroyed, and was later taken over by the BBC. It reverted to its earlier status in 1991.

east side: Portland Place to Mortimer Street
BBC Broadcasting House

The BBC, which first began broadcasting from Savoy Hill, off the Strand, in 1922, chose this larger site for its rapidly expanding organization in 1928 and hired G. Val Myers to create a huge Portland stone block with art deco touches. Figures of Prospero and Ariel for the outside of the building were commissioned from Eric Gill, the sculptor notorious for having sex with his sisters, daughters and dog. When he worked outside the building on a scaffold he wore a smock but no underclothes, shouting down to those who looked up: 'It's all balls, you know.' The building opened in 1932, the year the corporation began regular television transmissions using John Logie Baird's 30-line system, but the BBC soon decided even Broadcasting House was insufficient for its needs and further nearby extensions were made, followed by the construction of Television Centre in White City in the early 1950s, which left Broadcasting House devoted to radio. In the 1990s the corporation moved many of its radio stations to White City in west London, leaving a shadow service in Broadcasting House.

► The BBC at Savoy Hill, p. 135.

All Souls, Langham Place at All Souls Place
The church, designed by John Nash as part of his grand 1820s development of the area around Regent Street, was not immediately popular with the public and an early cartoon showed the architect impaled on the spire. Nevertheless All Souls soon became fashionable with the London aristocracy and was described in an 1864 brochure, published to advertise the construction of the Langham Hotel, opposite, as that 'quaint church with its peculiar steeple'. Bombed in the Second World War, it was restored in the 1950s.

► John Nash's Regent's Park, p. 350.

Portland Place

Portland Place, the main route linking Oxford Circus with Regent's Park, was designed in 1778 by Robert Adam, who envisaged a street lined with palaces, but was obliged to scale down his plans after the decline in house building following the outbreak of the American War of Independence in 1776. It was later reconstituted by James Adam as a picturesque terrace of exquisitely decorated façades disguising the separate houses, and an early resident was James Holroyd, editor of the memoirs of the historian Edward Gibbon. When Lord George Gordon brought his anti-Catholic petition to the Houses of Parliament in June 1780, at the outset of what became the Gordon Riots, Holroyd seized his throat and threatened to run his sword through him should the mob gain access to the building. Until the middle years of the nineteenth century Portland Place's residents were

mostly aristocrats or diplomats, but it later became commercialized and now consists almost entirely of prestigious offices, including at No. 66 those of the Royal Institute of British Architects.

► The Gordon Riots, p. 125.

Special Operations Executive research section offices (1940s) / IBC studios (1960s), No. 35
The research section of the government's wartime subversion unit, the Special Operations Executive (SOE), was based in 1940 at 40 Portland Place where officers trained new recruits in a variety of unusual skills: how to wire up dead rats with explosives, how to destroy the same part of every machine – and its replacement – so that nothing would work, how to kill with one's bare hands, how to remove a pair of handcuffs with a piece of thin wire and a pencil, and how to derail trains, for which agents were sent to practise on a stretch of rail track in the Midlands. After an enemy bomb fell on the property in 1940 the SOE moved to Aylesbury.

The premises were later taken over by the IBC recording company. It was here that the Rolling Stones recorded their first demonstration discs in 1963, the Yardbirds cut 'For Your Love' in 1964, and the Who their early singles such as 'I Can't Explain' (December 1964) and 'Anyway Anyhow Anywhere' (April 1965). The building is now occupied by architects.

► SOE in Marylebone, p. 149 and p. 150.

Chinese Embassy, No. 49
Sun Yat-sen (1867–1925), the Chinese revolutionary leader who at nineteen had taken part in an unsuccessful rebellion against the Imperial government of the Manchu dynasty, was seized and kidnapped while in London in October 1896 and taken to the Chinese Embassy in Portland Place where he was held prisoner on the orders of the Emperor. After a week he smuggled out a note that explained his predicament and ended: 'I am certain to be beheaded. Oh woe is me.' The embassy officially denied all knowledge of the abduction, but eventually

released him. Sun Yat-sen later became President of China.

Wigmore Street

The major route east–west through the area, Wigmore Street was named after Baron Wigmore of Herefordshire, one of the subsidiary titles of Edward Harley, Earl of Oxford, and is best known for the Wigmore Hall concert venue.

Wigmore Hall, No. 36, north side
Friedrich Bechstein, who wanted to bring German music to London, built what is now London's major venue for chamber concerts as the Bechstein Hall in 1901, a time when London audiences were unfamiliar with much of what is today considered to be the standard concert repertoire. At the opening concert on 31 May 1901 the Italian composer Busoni performed piano music by Beethoven, Schubert, Bach, Schumann and Brahms. During the First World War, when German assets were confiscated, more than 100 instruments were auctioned off for just £56,000 and the venue was reopened as the Wigmore Hall, with the German repertoire scaled down. During the twentieth century the hall played host to the tenor Enrico Caruso, the cellist Pablo Casals and the pianist Artur Rubinstein, who made his farewell appearance here in 1976 at the age of eighty-nine.

Wimpole Mews

Stephen Ward's address (1960s), No. 17
The Wimpole Mews address of the society osteopath Stephen Ward was at the centre of the Profumo affair of the early 1960s, the major political scandal of the time, which led to the resignation of the war secretary John Profumo. Here Ward not only treated the aching bones of his wealthy clients, but provided many of them with call-girls, including the eighteen-year-old Christine Keeler, whom he moved into the property after meeting her at a Regent Street club. One of Keeler's clients was the Soviet naval attaché Yevgeny Ivanov, whom MI5 wanted to enlist as a double agent, and in June 1961 the security service approached Ward as a go-between, hoping that he could use his call-girls as bait so that they could take compromising photographs or arrange some other means of blackmail.

Ward's first opportunity to help MI5 came at a party on 10 July 1961 at Lord Astor's Cliveden mansion in Buckinghamshire, where the guests included Ivanov, John Profumo and Keeler, who soon began affairs with both men. When she moved out of Wimpole Mews in 1962 Ward moved another teenage girl, Mandy Rice-Davies, into her old room, and events might have tailed off without further interest but for an incident on 14 December 1962 when Johnny Edgecombe, a West Indian friend of Keeler, followed her to Ward's mews apartment, where she was visiting Rice-Davies, and fired a gun at the building.

Journalists picked up on developments and agreed to print Keeler's 'life story' in the papers. Prior to publication, however, Ward tipped off Ivanov, who immediately made arrangements to leave London, while Profumo, concerned that news of his dalliances was to be made public, sought help from MI5. When Keeler's story hit the news stands Profumo was adamant that he had had no physical connection with her and on Friday 22 March 1963 made what turned out to be an unfortunate statement to the House of Commons, when he announced: 'Miss Keeler and I were on friendly terms. There was no impropriety whatsoever in my acquaintanceship with Miss Keeler.' But three months later, on 4 June 1963, Profumo admitted that he had lied to the House – that there had been 'impropriety' between him and Christine Keeler – and resigned from the Cabinet.

Ward was charged with living off immoral earnings and after being sent for trial at the Old Bailey took an overdose while the trial was still taking place. The following day he was found guilty in his absence but he died before sentencing. Christine Keeler was found guilty of perjury that December.
► The Soviet Embassy in London during the Cold War, p. 439.

Wimpole Street

Dark house, by which once more I
stand, / Here in the long unlovely street, /
Doors, where my heart was used to beat –
'In Memoriam', Alfred Lord Tennyson
(1850)

Best known for the clandestine romance
between Elizabeth Barrett and Robert
Browning, which took place at 𝕹𝖔. 50 in the
1840s, Wimpole Street was developed by
John Prince in 1724 and named after the
Cambridgeshire estate of the landlord,
Edward Harley. The street is the setting for
Tennyson's 1850 poem 'In Memoriam', in
which he stands in the 'long unlovely street',
following the death of a friend, Arthur
Hallam, who lived here – a description that
irked Virginia Woolf who believed Wimpole
to be 'the most august of London streets'.
The author Wilkie Collins, a close associate
of Charles Dickens, died at No. 82 in 1889.
In the George Bernard Shaw play *Pygmalion*
Professor Higgins lives at No. 27a and there
teaches Eliza Doolittle to talk like a lady.

Elizabeth Barrett's address (1838–46),
No. 50

The love affair between Elizabeth Barrett
and Robert Browning, one of the best-
known romances in literary history, began
in this now rebuilt house in the 1840s, in
the face of considerable opposition from
Barrett's tyrannical father, after Browning
favourably reviewed a collection of her
poems and wrote her a note that read: 'I
love your verses with all my heart, Miss
Barrett.' He soon became more daring,
expressing his love for her, and by 1845 was
visiting her twice a week. The couple
married in secret at St Marylebone church
in September 1846 and she returned to
Wimpole Street as if nothing had happened, eloping with Browning a week later,
for which her father never forgave her.

No. 57

Paul McCartney lodged in the luxurious
five-bedroom house owned by the parents
of his girlfriend, Jane Asher, towards the
end of 1963, only a year after living in a
Liverpool council flat, and here wrote a
number of songs, including 'I Want to Hold
Your Hand' (together with John Lennon in
the basement) and 'Yesterday', which he
claimed came to him in a dream. Waking
up, he went over to the piano beside the bed
and played the complete melody. He called
the new piece 'Scrambled Eggs', in honour
of the Booker T & the MGs' instrumental
'Green Onions', and took it to Beatles
producer George Martin, expressing
concern that he might have subconsciously
lifted the tune from an existing song.
McCartney's fears turned out to be
unfounded and the song is now the most
commercially successful in the history of
recorded music. At the height of Beatle-
mania in the mid-sixties McCartney used to
escape from the house by clambering on to
the flat roof of the adjacent property,
No. 56, having made an arrangement with
the owner, and making his way out of the
latter's entrance. McCartney moved to
St John's Wood in 1965.

▶ Abbey Road studios, p. 367.

MAYFAIR, W1

London's aristocratic playground for much
of the last 300 years, Mayfair is named after
the annual spring festival, renowned for its
pedlars, jugglers and sideshows, held in
what is now Shepherd Market until the
1730s. The area expanded after wealthy
Londoners moved west following the Fire
of London and by the early eighteenth
century London's greatest concentration of
the rich and influential – peers, politicians,
merchants, bankers, playboys and princes –
was living on and around Grosvenor
Square, Brook Street and Duke Street. The
intricacies of the relationships between
members of the upper classes in Mayfair
were expertly encapsulated by novelists such
as William Thackeray in *Vanity Fair* (1847–
8), Michael Arlen in *The Green Hat* (1924)
and Evelyn Waugh in *A Handful of Dust*
(1934). But the regular social pattern of
lunch at the Ritz, sandwiches, iced cakes

and, according to Barbara Cartland, a pink fruit punch known as 'Turk's Blood' at 𝕲unter's on Berkeley Square, followed by formal dinner in white tie and tails or gowns at one of the area's many opulent mansions, died out after the First World War.

The financial crises of the 1920s and 1930s led to a decline in service and saw the moneyed families vacate the grand houses for the suburbs, or America. After the Second World War most of the grand properties that had survived bombing were converted into banks, hotels and headquarters for prestigious companies, and though Mayfair is still a centre of wealth, opulence and luxury living, it has none of the social whirl that once characterized the area and its small residential population is now almost entirely drawn from wealthy overseas visitors attracted by the idea of owning a London base.

● Mayfair is the quarter of w1 to the southwest of Oxford Circus.

(i) Park Lane

Park Lane

The West End's western boundary and one of London's showpiece roads, Park Lane was developed at the edge of Hyde Park in the mid eighteenth century and because of its outstanding position overlooking the park soon attracted the grandest private residences in London, the properties embellished with baroque flourishes and façades. By the end of the nineteenth century Park Lane was studded with the mansions of the aristocracy and the wealthy but in the twentieth century many of the buildings were demolished and replaced with smart office blocks, banks and luxurious hotels, most famously the Dorchester and Hilton. The oldest surviving properties, both dating back to the 1820s, are Nos. 93–99 and Dudley House at No. 100.

east side: Marble Arch to Hyde Park Corner
No. 140
During the Second World War 140 Park Lane was used as offices by the 'N' (Netherlands) section of Britain's secret guerrilla section, the Special Operations Executive, a branch so incompetent that almost every agent sent into Holland was captured and later murdered at Mauthausen concentration camp, according to the espionage historian Roy Berkeley. When one captured agent sent back coded warnings of the impending doom to 140 Park Lane he was ignored, which convinced him that HQ's lack of interest was part of a grand plan. It was only when twenty or so captured agents began communicating at Mauthausen via the camp's central heating system that they realized they were the victims of major incompetence rather than pawns in a clever game.
► SOE in Baker Street, p. 149.

No. 139
The property was the location of the Home Guard headquarters in the 1943 Powell–Pressburger film *The Life and Death of Colonel Blimp*.

𝕭rook 𝕳ouse, north of Upper Brook Street T. H. Wyatt's opulent 1869 house, which had a dining room that could hold 100 guests, was acquired by Edwina Ashley when she married Lord Mountbatten, a cousin of the royal family, in 1922. It was fitted out with London's first penthouse, which could be reached only by an express lift – then a rarity for London – in which Queen Mary became stuck when she visited. Mountbatten, who was a navy officer, soon had the property redesigned with a marine theme. One room was turned into a replica of the cabin on his navy ship, the walls and ceilings lined with cork, and a regulation officer-size bunk with a brass handrail installed (not that the weather in Park Lane was choppy enough to warrant it), while his personal bathroom was decorated with rocks, seaweed, shells and pictures of fish, to the bemusement of visitors such as George Gershwin and Noël Coward. The Mountbattens put the house on the market in 1931, claiming that heavy taxation under the new 'socialist' government meant they could no longer afford to live there. The property was demolished soon after and rebuilt by Edwin Lutyens.

▶ Mountbatten and the 1968 attempted coup, p. 402.

Grosvenor House Hotel, Nos. 87–89

The 1930s-built Grosvenor House stands on the site of the eighteenth-century 𝕲loucester 𝕳ouse which was used as a hospital for invalided soldiers during the First World War and was later bought by the soap magnate Lord Leverhulme, who, having no use for the building, demolished it. The new hotel, the first of Park Lane's many grand twentieth-century hotels, was designed by Edwin Lutyens and had 478 en-suite bedrooms (a radical concept at the time) with running iced water, and 160 private apartments. During the Second World War the hotel became a refuge for the wealthy and powerful, including the Dutch Cabinet, who fled after the Germans occupied the Netherlands, and the French resistance leader Charles de Gaulle, who rallied his followers with a speech here on Bastille Day 1941. At a party held in the hotel on 1 December 1944 to celebrate the twenty-fifth anniversary of the entry of women into Parliament, Lady Astor, who had been the first woman MP to take her seat, announced she was not seeking re-election to the House of Commons, telling the gathering: 'I believe I have something to give to the House of Lords, but I'm not sure they want what I've got.'

● Other Lutyens buildings in London include the Midland Bank on Poultry, in the City, and St Jude's church, Hampstead Garden Suburb.

Aldford House, between Aldford Street and South Street

When plans were announced for the building of the original Aldford House on the site in 1897 the local landowner, the Duke of Westminster, worried that the proposed house might not be of a sufficiently high standard, sent the businessman behind the venture, diamond merchant Alfred Beit, who co-founded the De Beers company, a note stipulating that he must spend at least £10,000 on the property. Beit explained in his reply that he intended to spend that much on the stables alone. Aldford House was pulled down in 1929 and rebuilt as a block of flats bearing the same name, with long concrete balconies designed by Val Myers and Watson Hart, Edwin Lutyens acting as consultant.

Dorchester Hotel, No. 53

A world-renowned hotel, it was built in 1931 on the site of 𝕯orchester 𝕳ouse, with 600 bedrooms and walls of reinforced concrete soundproofed with seaweed and cork. The Dorchester soon began hosting Foyle's literary luncheons, organized by the twenty-year-old Christina Foyle and attended in the early days by the novelist D. H. Lawrence, the actor Charlie Chaplin and the Ethiopian ruler Haile Selassie. When Sir John Gilbey of the gin distillers once spoke for one and a half hours, a guest fell asleep, whereupon William Foyle, the bookstore's owner, approached the sleeping gentleman and hit him on the head with his gavel, only to be told by the awakened guest: 'Hit me harder, I can still hear him.'

During the Second World War the hotel was considered to be one of the safest buildings in the capital against attack and became a refuge for the aristocracy, with a menu that despite rationing featured oysters, smoked salmon and lobster – although by 1944 the sandwiches were being made of soya paste. Those who made use of these wartime luxuries included society hostesses Diana Cooper and Lady Cunard (who died in her suite here in July 1948), members of Churchill's War Cabinet and the 66-year-old novelist Somerset Maugham who was wrongly thought to have gone missing when France fell to the Germans.

While staying at the hotel in 1958 John Steinbeck, author of *The Grapes of Wrath*, struck up conversation with the economist J. K. Galbraith, who was returning to Boston from Warsaw, and asked him to explain a particularly complicated piece of economic theory, only to be told: 'Under capitalism man exploits man, whereas under communism it is just the reverse.' Breakfasting with Adlai Stevenson, the American Democratic presidential candidate, during the same trip, both men agreed that the biggest threat to the American system was not Soviet Russia but Richard Nixon, who as US President was later impeached.

► Foyle's, p. 99.

London Hilton, No. 22
The thirty-storey hotel, with its famous rooftop restaurant, opened in 1963 and was where the following year the gangster Ronnie Kray met the leading New York mafioso, Angelo Bruno, to discuss ways of establishing a transatlantic crime syndicate. The Beatles first heard the Maharishi Mahesh Yogi lecture on transcendental meditation in the hotel in August 1967. Ten years later, in July 1977, Elvis Costello busked outside on the pavement during a conference held by the CBS record label, astounding company executives who had never heard of the singer, then with only two relatively obscure singles to his name. Costello was arrested, taken to Vine Street police station, and charged £5 for obstruction. The New York rap outfit the Beastie Boys drilled a hole through the floor so that they could reach the room below when they stayed in the late 1980s and were banned from the Hilton chain worldwide.

► The Krays in Bethnal Green, p. 310.

(ii) around Grosvenor Square

In 1720 the landowner Sir Richard Grosvenor (the name comes from the French *gros veneur* – fat hunter) designed a grid pattern of new streets with what would be one of London's largest squares as its centrepiece. The writer Daniel Defoe, who visited the development in September 1725, noted 'an amazing Scene of new Foundations, not of Houses only, but as I might say of new Cities, New Towns, New Squares and fine

Buildings, the like of which no City, no Town, nay no Place in the World can shew'. The square was completed in 1770 and by the end of the nineteenth century the Grosvenors, who were granted the Duchy of Westminster in 1874, were Europe's wealthiest family. Descendants are still the area's major landowners, the estate office being based on Grosvenor Street.

Brook Street
The brook is the Tybourne or Tyburn, which flows underneath the road by the junction with South Molton Lane and Avery Row.

south side: Hanover Square to Grosvenor Square
Jimi Hendrix's address (1969), No. 23
The flamboyant rock guitarist Jimi Hendrix moved into 23 Brook Street with girlfriend Kathy Etchingham in January 1969 and was soon visited by the *Daily Mirror*'s Don Short who reported that 'the attic, Hendrix's favourite room, contains an assortment of bric-a-brac and a bed with a Victorian shawl pinned to the ceiling as a canopy'. Short also noted how Hendrix had described Etchingham to him as 'my girlfriend, my past girlfriend, my next girlfriend. My mother and my sister and all that bit. My Yoko Ono from Chester.' When Jane de Mendelssohn from *International Times* interviewed Hendrix that March the guitarist opened the door naked and conducted the interview from his bed, the journalist sitting on the edge by a table stashed with 'grass, amyl nitrate, pills and three different types of hash'. Hendrix moved out of Brook Street later that month, but despite the brevity of his tenure the property was awarded English Heritage's first blue plaque in honour of a rock star in 1997.

Handel Museum / George Frederick Handel's address (1723–59), No. 25
Handel, the German-born composer, moved into No. 25 in 1723 after ten years as musical director of the Italian Opera Company at the Queen's Theatre, Haymarket, converting the front parlour

into an office where he sold tickets for his concerts and copies of his published music, the back parlour into a sitting room and the first floor into a room for entertaining. Handel composed a number of works in Brook Street, including the operas *Giulio Cesare* and *Tamerlano* (1723–4), but his *annus mirabilis* was 1741 during which he wrote *Samson* and *The Messiah*. After composing the Hallelujah chorus for the latter he proclaimed: 'I did think that I did see all Heaven before me, and the great God himself seated on His throne, with His company of angels.' Handel died in the house in 1759 and in 2001 it was opened as a museum to the composer after an exorcism had been held in one of the rooms to remove a troublesome ghost.

Claridge's, No. 57
One of London's most exclusive hotels, Claridge's was opened by William Claridge, a butler, in 1855 and bought forty years later by the owners of the Savoy. Winston Churchill, when prime minister during the Second World War, often used the hotel to hold all-night meetings with US army intelligence personnel that would end at 6 a.m. when the hotel barber would appear and whisk the prime minister off for a haircut and shave. Churchill moved into the hotel penthouse in 1945 after his shock defeat at the general election left him homeless. When Nikita Khrushchev, the Soviet politician, stayed at Claridge's during his April 1956 visit to Britain he was bugged by MI5, who used a radio beam to activate his phone, as was the Soviet premier, Alexei Kosygin, when he visited Britain five years later, MI5 agents feeding prime minister Harold Wilson details of his conversations.

When he took over Mirror Group Newspapers in 1984, Robert Maxwell invited editors of all the group's titles to Claridge's for an expensive lunch. But the publisher arrived late for the meeting, for *en route* his chauffeur was so annoyed at being bullied into jumping the lights, overtaking the car in front, and taking unnecessary short cuts that he got out of the car and shouted to

Maxwell: 'If you're so bloody good, you drive,' leaving him alone in the vehicle.
➤ Ritz Hotel, p. 183.

Carlos Place
The Connaught, No. 16
A prestigious hotel, as exclusive but not as famous as nearby Claridge's, where film stars visiting London are likely to stay, the Connaught was opened as the Coburg Hotel, in honour of Victoria's consort, Prince Albert of Saxe-Coburg, in 1897 and renamed after the Duke of Connaught in 1917. The thriller writer Raymond Chandler was thrown out in 1955 for the heinous crime of having a woman in his room, and thirteen years later when Richard Nixon, then president of the USA, was staying at the hotel the telephonist, asked by a caller if he could be put through to the president but bound by the strictest rules of protocol, replied: 'Nixon? And the initial, sir?'

Grosvenor Square
Fortunately in England at any rate, education produces no effect whatsoever. If it did, it would prove a serious danger to the upper classes, and probably lead to acts of violence in Grosvenor Square – *The Importance of Being Earnest*, Oscar Wilde (1895)

The Grosvenor Estate's showpiece, one of London's largest squares and the last part of the capital to be lit by gas rather than electricity, was built from 1725 to 1731. With its houses conveniently located within walking distance of Hyde Park, it soon attained popularity with the aristocracy and politicians; Lords Rockingham, Grafton and North, all British prime ministers at various times, took residence here in the late eighteenth century. When the Second World War broke out many of the square's wealthy residents fled to the country, or to the nearby Dorchester Hotel, which was believed to be impregnable, and were replaced by US army intelligence personnel, who set up office in the relinquished buildings. After the war, businesses took over the properties and the entire west side of the

square was later demolished to make way
for Eero Saarinen's stark American Embassy
building. Grosvenor Square is still one of
the most prestigious locations in the West
End, but almost entirely commercial.

north side
No. 20
Dwight Eisenhower, commander of the US
armed forces during the Second World War,
who wanted a base at least fifty miles outside London but was told such a development was impossible as he would not be
able to drive 'even 20 miles in the blackout',
moved his London headquarters into No. 20
in 1944.
No. 9
One of few surviving original houses on the
square, No. 9 was home to John Adams, the
US statesman who became the first
American ambassador at the Court of
St James's in 1785. Adams was one of the
signatories of the American Declaration of
Independence in 1776 and became the
USA's second president in 1796.

east side
The now demolished 𝔑𝔬. **7** on the east side
of the square was home from 1926 to 1940 to
Lady Cunard, who acquired the nickname
'Emerald' on account of her dazzling jewellery and threw Mayfair's most glamorous
parties between the wars, 'a rallying point
for most of London society', according to
the diarist Chips Channon. When the
author Somerset Maugham left one of her
soirées early with the excuse 'I have to keep
my youth,' she replied: 'Why don't you
bring him with you?' When Lady Cunard
returned to Grosvenor Square during the
Second World War she found her home
destroyed by bombs and, salvaging what she
could, she moved to Suite 707 of the Dorchester Hotel, where she hosted parties for
leading politicians and society figures.
▶ Dorchester Hotel, p. 160.
No. 4
Now the Italian ambassador's residence,
No. 4 is one of the square's oldest original
houses, sold by raffle in 1739.

No. 1
The building, used as the American
Embassy in the 1950s, was visited in 1954 by
the musicians Lonnie Donegan and Wally
Whyton who came to examine the
embassy's Information Service Library, a
treasure trove of US blues and folk records
by artists then barely known in England,
such as Big Bill Broonzy, Leadbelly and
Muddy Waters. Their music inspired
Donegan into trying to replicate such
sounds on *ad hoc* instruments – guitar,
stand-up bass and home-made drums – a
style that came to be known as skiffle, soon
copied by thousands of teenage aspiring
musicians across the country, including the
teenage Beatles. The building is now occupied by the Canadian High Commission.
▶ The 2I's club, p. 200.

south side
News of Wellington's victory over Napoleon
at the 1815 Battle of Waterloo officially
arrived in London on 21 June, three days
after the event, when a chaise and four
decorated with French flags pulled up
outside **44 𝔊𝔯𝔬𝔰𝔳𝔢𝔫𝔬𝔯 𝔖𝔮𝔲𝔞𝔯𝔢**, home of the
Earl of Harrowby, where the British Cabinet
were dining and out stepped the Honourable Henry Percy, Wellington's aide-de-
camp, bearing a dispatch for the Earl of
Bathurst, the war secretary, confirming the
victory. Five years later, on the night of
23 February 1820, the Cabinet, including the
prime minister, the Duke of Wellington,
were again meeting here at the same time
as anarchist conspirators in Cato Street,
Marylebone, were plotting to kill them and
install a revolutionary government. The
Cato street mob, led by Arthur Thistlewood,
planned to knock on the door, rush in,
overcome the servants, enter the dining
room and kill the ministers, Thistlewood
having boasted that he would 'cut off every
head in the room and bring away the heads
of Lord Castlereagh and Lord Sidmouth in a
bag'. The plan was foiled when the police
caught up with the plotters at their hide-
away; Thistlewood, who murdered a

Anti-Vietnam War demonstration in Grosvenor Square

> Where has Harold Wilson gone? Crawling to the Pentagon – Anti-Vietnam War banner (February 1965)

British protest against the American government's involvement in Vietnam and the Labour government's support for the US stance reached a peak in 1967 and 1968 at three well-attended demonstrations around the US Embassy on Grosvenor Square.

First Vietnam Solidarity Campaign demonstration, 22 October 1967 Nearly 10,000 people call for victory for communist Vietnam at the first Vietnam Solidarity Campaign demonstration in October 1967 at which 350 police officers forming a cordon around the square to protect the embassy are attacked with missiles. Some demonstrators force their way into the embassy garden but are dissuaded from entering the building by the thought of meeting sterner opposition inside. Not all the protestors have serious political intentions. As the main body chant: 'Ho, Ho, Ho Chi Minh' (the name of the anti-colonialist leader), the Situationist King Mob group, equally sceptical of the establishment and left-wing opponents, chant 'Hot chocolate, drinking chocolate', as in the popular advertising jingle of the day.

Second Vietnam Solidarity Campaign demonstration, 17 March 1968 Around 20,000 meet for the second demonstration which starts at Trafalgar Square and makes its way to Mayfair amid the usual chanting of 'Ho, Ho, Ho Chi Minh'. Posters advertising the event have urged the crowd to 'come armed', an order which the Vietnam Solidarity Campaign denies is its work. Once in the square the crowd storms towards the embassy, hurling smoke bombs and throwing marbles under the hooves of the police horses. One girl who tries to offer a mounted policeman a flower is truncheoned to the ground. The fighting lasts two hours and 117 officers and forty-five demonstrators are injured. The events inspire Mick Jagger, an onlooker, to write 'Street Fighting Man', a sardonic swipe at his own inability to do anything more worthwhile than play for a rock and roll band, the song summing up better than any other the political mood in London at the time.

Third Vietnam Solidarity Campaign demonstration, 27 October 1968 In the run up to the third, the biggest and the policeman during the raid, was later hanged.

west side

American Embassy, Nos. 24–31

The American government bought land on the west side of the square, site of much wartime bomb damage, in 1950 on a 999-year lease – a deal that resulted in the landowner, the Duke of Westminster, making around £1 million – and hired Eero Saarinen to construct a new embassy. After the building was completed one of the first visitors was President John F. Kennedy who, remarking how the United States owned the land on which all their embassies were built, apart from the one in London, asked the Duke of Westminster if he could buy the freehold, to which the latter replied that Kennedy could have the land in exchange for the American territory the US government had seized from his ancestors in the 1770s, which included the Cape Canaveral rocket launch site. The embassy has been the target for a number of demonstrations against American government policies, particularly during the Vietnam War, but on 11 September 2001 was visited by thousands demonstrating *in support* of America following the attack on the World Trade Center.

Grosvenor Street

Grosvenor Street, which leads from Grosvenor Square to New Bond Street, was built from 1720 to 1734. Past residents include the chemistry pioneer Humphry last anti-Vietnam War demo, the authorities, with the May student riots and strikes in Paris fresh in mind, have tapped phones, opened the mail of leading campaigners, and infiltrated socialist groups, often as *agents provocateurs*. On the day of the demonstration, the Vietnam Solidarity Campaign at the last minute redirects the march from Grosvenor Square to Hyde Park, but a splinter group from the Britain–Vietnam Solidarity Front ignores the call and clashes with police outside the US Embassy, leading to forty-two arrests and injuries to four policemen and fifty demonstrators. The bulk of the 100,000 marchers congregates on Hyde Park, where at the end of the demonstration the marchers and police together sing 'Auld Lang Syne'. The newspapers later congratulate themselves at the failure of the campaigners to bring down the government, the royal family and world capitalism. The year of 1968 is later seen as a watershed for direct-action socialism following the failure of the Paris student *événements*, the assassinations of Robert Kennedy and Martin Luther King, and Soviet Russia's brutal repression of the Prague Spring in Czechoslovakia.

Davy, who made many breakthrough discoveries in chemistry at the Royal Institution on Albemarle Street (p. 166), and the nineteenth-century statesman and free-trade pioneer Richard Cobden. The properties are now mostly offices.

north side: Grosvenor Square to New Bond Street

OSS headquarters (1940s), No. 70
Members of the US army's intelligence outfit, the Office of Strategic Services (OSS), moved in October 1943 into the heavily guarded No. 70, one of a number of local properties taken up by the American army towards the end of the Second World War. The fresh-faced recruits, mostly hired from Wall Street banks and described by the journalist and historian Malcolm Muggeridge as being like '*jeunes filles en fleur* straight from a finishing school', included William Casey, later head of the CIA.

No. 16
In the early 1930s No. 16 was home to Laura Corrigan, the dazzling Wisconsin-born society hostess, who had worked as a waitress in Cleveland, Ohio, and had become fabulously wealthy after marrying the owner of the Corrigan–McKinney Steel Company, who died soon after, following a heart attack and left her $60 million in his will. Failing to win acceptance in American high society, Laura Corrigan moved to London and rented 16 Grosvenor Street from Alice Keppel (one-time mistress of King Edward VII and great-grandmother of Camilla Parker Bowles), where she became famed for her solecisms and malapropisms, complaining to Keppel that the Chippendale chairs were spoiled by their 'petit pois' covers and when listing the merits of Gothic architecture discoursing on a cathedral's 'flying buttocks'. Few could resist her social invitations, although one who did was the playwright George Bernard Shaw who, when sent a card that read: 'Mrs Corrigan At Home 6–8 p.m.', replied 'GBS Ditto'.

Charlie Richardson's office (1964–6), No. 65, south side
At the height of his power in the 1960s London underworld Charlie Richardson, the south London gangland leader, rented an office in Mayfair to impress his wealthy contacts in the South African diamond industry.
► The Richardsons in South London, p. 378.

Upper Grosvenor Street
Built in 1724 to 1741 to link Park Lane with Grosvenor Square, the street was dominated in the nineteenth century by 𝕲𝖗𝖔𝖘𝖛𝖊𝖓𝖔𝖗 𝕳𝖔𝖚𝖘𝖊, which stood on the south side until 1916. Adlai Stevenson, the American Democratic politician, collapsed in the street in July 1965 only yards from the US Embassy, dying in the ambulance taking him to hospital.

No. 48

No. 48 was home in the 1950s to the Duchess of Argyll, Debutante of the Year in 1930 and the subject of Cole Porter's song 'You're the Top'. The duchess was implicated in a famous 1950s divorce case enlivened by photographs found by the duke that showed the duchess fellating an anonymous man (the frame cut him off at the neck) in the bathroom, while wearing a three-stringed pearl necklace and a wide smile. The public was gripped by debate over the identity of the 'headless man' and expert opinion narrowed it down to two possibilities – the actor Douglas Fairbanks Jnr and the Tory Cabinet minister Lord Duncan Sandys. The latter, alarmed by the thought of a sex scandal, said he would resign if it were proved to be him, and so the prime minister, Harold Macmillan, enlisted the legal expert Lord Denning to solve the mystery. Denning came up with an ingenious solution. He invited Sandys, Fairbanks and an outsider, Sigismund von Braun, the brother of the Nazi rocket scientist Werner von Braun, to the Treasury to discuss the matter. As the words 'before', 'during' and 'finished' were written on the incriminating polaroids Denning ensured that each suspect signed the Treasury visitors' register. A graphologist matched the handwriting and identified Fairbanks as the culprit.

(iii) around Berkeley Square

The south-west corner of Mayfair, built around the 1730s Berkeley Square, contains a number of small residential eighteenth-century streets which still exude some of the atmosphere of the old rural village, although the square itself has been spoiled by insensitive twentieth-century development.

Albemarle Street

The 2nd Duke of Albemarle briefly became the major local landowner in the late seventeenth century and the street soon attracted wealthy figures, early residents including George, Prince of Wales (the future George II), and the architect Robert Adam. Albemarle Street is now home to expensive art galleries and prestigious offices.

east side: Grafton Street to Piccadilly
The Royal Institution, No. 21, east side
Humphry Davy discovered the elements sodium and potassium and Michael Faraday made a number of pioneering discoveries involving electricity and magnetism in the Albemarle Street premises of the Royal Institution, one of London's most prestigious scientific organizations, in the early nineteenth century.

Davy began lecturing here as a 23-year-old in 1801 and the following year was appointed professor, Britain's only professional scientist other than the Astronomer Royal. He gave lectures which drew huge crowds and made groundbreaking scientific discoveries including isolating two new elements, potassium and sodium, in 1807 after passing an electrical current through the alkalis potash and soda held in a platinum spoon over a flame. When Davy resigned from the Royal Institution in 1812 to go on a continental tour with passports granted to him, his new wife, her maid and valet by Napoleon Bonaparte, his place at the institution was taken by his assistant Michael Faraday, a member of the Sandemanian Christian sect that had broken away from the Church of Scotland. Faraday was guided in his work by Matthew's stricture: 'Lay not up for yourselves treasures upon earth', in contrast with his mentor's ostentatious materialism.

On 3 and 4 September 1821 in the Royal Institution's basement laboratory Faraday discovered electromagnetic rotation (the principle behind the electric motor), which led to the invention of the electric telegraph, first used in 1838 along the Paddington–West Drayton railway line. After he became director of the laboratory in 1825 Faraday hosted a series of Friday evening lectures here at one of which, in 1846, he suggested that matter was made not of billiard ball-like indestructible atoms but of wave-like particles.

On 29 August 1831, ten years after his discovery of electro-magnetic rotation, Faraday discovered electro-magnetic induction, the principle behind the electric transformer and generator, which enabled electricity to be adapted for everyday purposes. He spent the remainder of the decade engaged in further experiments in electricity, proposing the notion that electricity was a force that passed from particle to particle and coining a number of new scientific terms, which are now part of everyday speech, including electrode, anode and cathode. There is a reconstruction of his 1850 laboratory in the basement.
▶ John Logie Baird's pioneering television work, p. 197.

Albemarle Club, No. 13

Oscar Wilde's descent into public disgrace began at the Albemarle Club in February 1895, the day before the opening of his play *The Importance of Being Earnest*, when the Marquess of Queensberry, father of Lord Alfred Douglas, with whom Wilde was having an affair, left at the club a note which read: 'To Oscar Wilde Posing Somdomite [*sic*]'. Wilde issued libel proceedings, and the peer was arrested for 'unlawfully and maliciously publishing a certain defamatory libel'. But when Wilde failed to win the case he was prosecuted for gross indecency – in effect sodomy, as opposed to somdomy – and sent to jail. The club moved to 37 Dover Street in 1909 and the basement of No. 13 then became one of London's first nightclubs, Uncle's, designed as an American speakeasy with 'hard liquor' served in paper cups.
▶ Oscar Wilde in Chelsea, p. 415.

Berkeley Square

The square made famous by Eric Maschwitz's 1940 song 'A Nightingale Sang in Berkeley Square' was named after the 1st Lord Berkeley of Stratton, Royalist commander during the Civil War, but without being planned architecturally came

together haphazardly around the peer's 1660s mansion, **Berkeley House**. Well-known residents of the square have included Colly Cibber, poet laureate in the 1730s and lampooned by Alexander Pope in 'The Dunciad' (1728), who died in a house which stood at No. 19 in 1757; and Horace Walpole, son of the first Prime Minister, Robert Walpole and the main instigator behind the Gothic revival of the nineteenth century, who lived at No. 11 after curtailing his Grand Tour before reaching Italy. When the square's railings were torn down at the start of the Second World War one MP complained that it was a 'barbaric piece of socialism'. Since the war Berkeley Square has consisted mostly of offices. The plane trees, which are its most famous landmark, date from 1789.

east side

Horace Walpole, the novelist and Gothic revivalist, moved into **No. 11** in 1747 and was so taken with the view that he compared the statue of George III to the work of the Athenian Phidias, something of which he would have been barely aware, having failed to reach Greece on his Grand Tour. A later tenant, the Earl of Orford, staked the house on a game of cards at Almack's club in 1770 and lost. At **Nos. 7–8** in the eighteenth and nineteenth centuries stood Negri's tea rooms, founded by an Italian pastry-cook, Domenico Negri, 'making and selling all sorts of English, French, and Italian wet and dry sweetmeats'. In 1799 it became Gunter's, popular for its ice creams and sorbets, which gentlemen would eat while leaning against the railings watching the ladies sitting in carriages eating theirs. The original houses were demolished in 1937 to build the Berkeley Square House office block.

south side

The south side of the square was the location of the 1665-built mansion **Berkeley House**, sold at the end of the seventeenth century to the Duke of Devonshire, who renamed it Devonshire House. It was a Whig stronghold in the late eighteenth century under the tenure of the 5th Duke and his colourful wife, Georgiana. The property was demolished in 1924 and the Mayfair Inter-Continental Hotel built on the site.

west side

Annabel's / The Clermont club, No. 44

The architectural historian Nikolaus Pevsner described No. 44, one of the square's original houses, which was built by William Kent from 1742 to 1747 for Lady Isabella Finch, a member of George II's court, as 'the finest terrace house in London', on account of its ornate staircase and wrought iron-balustrade. In 1959 the property was bought by John Aspinall, the zoo owner, who converted it into the exclusive Clermont club, and it was here that Lord Lucan planned to meet friends the night he disappeared in 1974, never to be seen again. In the 1960s Mark Birley opened the basement as a nightclub, Annabel's, named after his wife, who later married the tycoon James Goldsmith. It soon became the most fashionable in London among the super rich and once refused entry to George Harrison for not wearing a tie. When in 1986 a policewoman and traffic warden turned up at the door a journalist put his finger through the lens of the traffic warden's spectacles to prove they contained no glass and then realized that the 'traffic warden' was the Duchess of York and the 'policewoman' Princess Diana. The Maître D turned them away on the grounds that no uniforms are allowed inside.

➤ Lord Lucan's disappearance, p. 403.

No. 42

No. 42, headquarters of the Polly Peck company, was raided by the Serious Fraud Squad in 1990 during investigations into the running of the company. Accused of insider trading, its founder, Asil Nadir, fled to Cyprus. In the 1990s the premises were converted into Pasley-Tyler and Co., an exclusive gentlemen's club aimed at American businessmen.

No. 40

The US government's Second World War intelligence agency, the Office of Strategic Services (OSS), moved here in the early 1940s to train hundreds of agents, mostly from Ivy League universities. Before long the OSS had taken over a number of Mayfair addresses, including 68 Brook Street (for its clothing department), 70 Grosvenor Street (for the planned invasion of Europe) and Hay's Mews (for the agents' residential quarters). After the war the premises were leased by the J. Walter Thompson advertising agency.

Grafton Street

Grafton Galleries (early twentieth century), No. 7, north side

Roger Fry held the first British exhibition of Post-Impressionist paintings, showing the works of Gauguin, Van Gogh and Cézanne for the first time to an incredulous British public, at the Grafton in November 1910. The exhibition attracted a barrage of opposition epitomized by the critic Robert Ross, who denounced the show as part of a 'widespread plot to destroy the whole fabric of European painting'. A second Post-Impressionist exhibition of British, French and Russian artists was held here in the autumn of 1912. By the 1920s the Gallery also incorporated a popular nightspot that featured a black jazz band, rare for Britain at the time, playing popular new numbers such as 'I'm Just Wild About Harry' before a crowd that included the young Barbara Cartland.

➤ Mayor Gallery, Cork Street, p. 173.

(iv) around Shepherd Market

A secluded enclave of passageways, antique shops, expensive restaurants, delicatessens and wine bars off the north-west end of Piccadilly, Shepherd Market is named after Edward Shepherd, the architect who laid out the street pattern in 1735 on the site where the annual May Fair had taken place. It has long been one of London's best-known haunts of prostitutes, one of whom in the 1980s was Monica Coghlan, the call-girl who received £2,000 in £50 notes at

Victoria Station in 1987 from a friend of the Tory Party deputy chairman, Jeffrey Archer.

Audley Square

Reduced by demolition and redevelopment to a fraction of its former size, Audley Square is now little more than a kink in South Audley Street, but in the 1950s and 1960s Soviet spies regularly used the lamp-post outside No. 2 as a message post, chalking a mark below the number '8' to show that a new operation was about to start and later looking for a chalk mark on a bench in nearby St George's Gardens to check whether or not it had been seen.

In the early 1960s No. 3 was home to Eon Productions, the film company that produces the James Bond films, and it was here that the series' first producers, Harry Saltzman and Cubby Broccoli, looking for an actor to play the secret agent in the first Bond film, *Dr No*, considered Roger Moore, Rex Harrison, Trevor Howard, Patrick McGoohan, Cary Grant and Noël Coward who, in his inimitable style, responded to their interest with a telegram that read simply, 'Dr No? No! No! No!' Eventually, Eon chose Sean Connery, a former milkman and labourer, because they 'liked the way he moved', claiming that 'for a big man to be light on his feet is most unusual'.

Chesterfield Street

One of Mayfair's most desirable streets, named after Philip, the eighteenth-century 4th Earl of Chesterfield, it was home at the end of the century to the society dandy Beau Brummell (No. 4) and in the early years of the twentieth century to the writer Somerset Maugham (No. 6).

east side: Charles Street to Curzon Street
Somerset Maugham's address (1911–19),
No. 6

Somerset Maugham, one of the most finan-cially successful writers of the early twen-tieth century thanks to the money generated by his West End plays, bought this tall red-brick house in 1911 and here set to work on his epic semi-autobiographical novel, *Of Human Bondage* (1915), in which he purged

himself of his childhood demons – his nervousness, sexual confusion and sense of inferiority – and showed critics that he could deal with weightier formats than drawing-room dramas. In 1917, during the First World War, Maugham was hired by British intelligence and sent to Moscow, where he gained sensitive political infor-mation for the prime minister, David Lloyd George. After hostilities ended Maugham returned to Mayfair to write another well-received novel, *The Moon and Sixpence* (1919), which relates the story of a banker who flees his humdrum life and responsibili-ties to paint in Tahiti and is partly based on the life of Paul Gauguin.

No. 4

George Bryan ('Beau') Brummell, the iras-cible Regency dandy, narcissist and confi-dant of the Prince Regent (later George IV), lived at 4 Chesterfield Street at the end of the eighteenth century, shocking friends by taking a daily bath at a time when personal cleanliness was low down the list of social requirements. Brummell was so fastidious about his attire that if his cravat was not tied properly at the first try it was discarded. Brummell was also fussy about his surround-ings. When his regiment was sent north he beseeched the prince to be excused: 'I really could not go. Think your Royal highness – Manchester!'

In Derek Marlowe's 1966 novel, *A Dandy in Aspic*, No. 4 is the location of the espionage headquarters.

Curzon Place

Mama Cass, the Mamas and Papas singer, and the Who's drummer, Keith Moon, both died in the 1970s, in Flat 12, 9 Curzon Place, a property owned by the singer Harry Nilsson. Although press reports said that the cause of death for Cass in July 1974 at the age of thirty-two was inhalation of vomit after choking on a sandwich, the pathologist found no traces of food blocking her trachea and concluded that she had died of natural causes. Four years later, on 7 September 1978, Moon overdosed on chlormethiazole pills prescribed to fight his alcoholism. Thirty-two Heminevrin tablets were found in Moon's stomach, twenty-six of them undissolved.

Curzon Street

A winding street that is one of the busiest in Mayfair, built in the 1720s and named after Nathaniel Curzon, an early eighteenth-century Derbyshire aristocrat, it has contained several important buildings connected with the British security services over the years and is now best known for the luxurious Curzon cinema.

north side: Park Lane to Lansdowne Row
Crewe House
Mayfair's most impressive surviving mansion with its exquisite stone façade and sumptuous grounds, Crewe House was built as Wharncliffe House in 1730 by Edward Shepherd, the architect after whom nearby Shepherd Market is named, and was bought in 1899 by the Marquess of Crewe. The property was requisitioned by the government during the First World War for the Ministry of Propaganda, run with much success by the newspaper proprietor Lord Northcliffe. The latter appointed the novelist H. G. Wells as director (he resigned when Northcliffe refused to employ anyone with German parents) and placed Wickham Steed, the *Times*'s foreign editor, in charge of campaigning in the Balkans, where many people had been forced into fighting for the Austro-Hungarian Empire. Steed and Northcliffe installed printing presses at Crewe House and turned out thousands of leaflets decorated with nostalgic Balkan imagery which were then dropped by aeroplane over divisions of wavering enemy troops. But Northcliffe's *coup de grâce* was to send Allied soldiers near to enemy lines armed with gramophones that played stirring nationalist songs. Hundreds of Polish, Romanian and Czech troops fighting unenthusiastically for Austria-Hungary downed arms and later admitted that the turning point for them had been when they heard a few stirring bars of their native songs. The building was

bought by the Saudi Arabian government in the 1970s to house its embassy.
▸ Death of Lord Northcliffe, p. 206.
MI5 headquarters (1945–70), Leconfield House, west junction with Chesterfield Gardens
The security service MI5 set up base after the Second World War in a building that had been the army's London District Command headquarters and was fortified with gun ports in its south-west corner, installed in case German paratroopers landed in the nearby parks and began street battles in Mayfair. Even after the war MI5 continued to man the ports, especially on Sundays, just in case mobs from Speaker's Corner stormed the streets. MI5 moved to Gower Street near Euston in 1970 and returned to Curzon Street (see below) in 1976.
▸ MI5 on Gower Street, p. 86; MI5 at Thames House, Millbank, p. 247.
Heywood Hill, No. 10
The novelist Evelyn Waugh claimed this long-running bookshop was 'a centre for all that was left of fashionable and intellectual London' during the Second World War, when the author Nancy Mitford worked as an assistant and customers included the society diarist Chips Channon and the designer Cecil Beaton. Heywood Hill still retains its period charm, using handwritten bills and selling books wrapped as parcels.
MI5 (1976–1990s), Curzon Street House, Nos. 1–4, east of Clarges Street
Curzon Street House, built in 1939 on land that had been occupied by some thirty houses, has a fortified bunker, constructed as part of Lord Beaverbrook's mass tunnel-building programme at the start of the Second World War, which is connected, it is believed, to the tunnels under Buckingham Palace where members of the royal family sheltered during air raids. After hostilities ceased the authorities set up the War Department Prisoners of War Information Bureau here and in 1976 MI5 moved its Administrative and Technical Department headquarters into the building, mostly to house

its 2 million personal files on suspected subversives. MI5 left for Thames House on Millbank in the 1990s and the premises have since been renovated into offices.

► MI5 at Thames House, Millbank, p. 247.

Old Park Lane
The main route of Park Lane until nineteenth-century road widening turned it into a side street.

Hard Rock Café, No. 150, west side
Two expatriate Americans, Isaac Tigrett and Pete Morton, opened a restaurant at this address in June 1971, claiming that it was the only way they could get a good burger in Britain. The company now has branches throughout the world and the Old Park Lane original displays more than 300 items of rock memorabilia.

Metropolitan Hotel, No. 19, east side
The hotel, formerly the Londonderry, was built on the site of 𝕷𝔬𝔫𝔡𝔬𝔫𝔡𝔢𝔯𝔯𝔶 𝕳𝔬𝔲𝔰𝔢, a 1760 mansion where in the 1930s Joachim von Ribbentrop, the Nazi German ambassador to Britain, was a regular guest of the Marquess (nicknamed 'the Londonderry Heir' by the diarist Chips Channon). The Londonderry was closed down at the outset of the Second World War after it was bombed. General Raymond E. Lee, the US military attaché in London, noting the owners' pre-war courting of the Nazi ambassador, later recalled remarking as he passed the bomb site, 'I could only wonder what that chump Londonderry thinks now of his friends Hitler, Ribbentrop and Goering.'

(v) Bond Street

Home to scores of smart shops and world-renowned names such as Vidal Sassoon, Asprey's and Sotheby's, Bond Street exudes an air of luxury and timeless style. The only street running the full length of Mayfair from Oxford Street to Piccadilly, it is known as New Bond Street north of Burlington Gardens and Old Bond Street to the south.

New Bond Street
Mayfair's high street, built *c.* 1720, some thirty-five years after Old Bond Street, lived in the shadow of its older relation for many decades, for whereas the aristocracy met on Old Bond Street to trade in fine art New Bond Street was dominated by tradespeople selling household goods, albeit luxury household goods. In the nineteenth century the street attracted sporting organizations such as the Pugilist Club, run by Gentleman Jackson, the bare-fist champion of England, but it gradually became a sought-after shopping street in its own right, with auctioneers (Sotheby's, Nos. 34–35), the jewellers Cartier (Nos. 175–176), stamp-sellers (Harmer's, No. 41), tobacconists (the original Benson and Hedges at No. 13) and department stores (Fenwick's, No. 63).

west side: Old Bond Street to Oxford Street 180–87

No. 171
The first Vidal Sassoon salon, where the geometric cut was pioneered in 1963, was at this address.

Asprey's, Nos. 165–169
Famous jewellers founded as a silk-printing shop by William Asprey in 1781, it moved to 49 New Bond Street in the 1830s, and in 1848 to the current site, where there is a fine unspoilt Victorian shop-front.

No. 147
The naval hero Lord Nelson stayed here in 1797–8, heavily sedated with laudanum to take away the pain from losing his right arm during a failed raid on Tenerife in the Canary Islands.

No. 143
Until the 1970s the premises were occupied by the chemist's Savory and Moore, famous for their Seidlitz powders, a laxative named after the German springs of the same name. In 1853 they won the contract to make medical supplies for troops fighting in the Crimean War.

Grosvenor Gallery (1877–1903), Nos. 135–137

A greenery-yallery / Grosvenor Gallery / Foot-in-the-grave young man – *Patience*, Gilbert and Sullivan (1881)

London's first independent art gallery opened in 1877 and soon came to be associated with the Aesthetic Movement, the body dedicated to the notion of 'art for art's sake' epitomized by the illustrator Aubrey Beardsley, the painter James McNeill Whistler and, most notably, Oscar Wilde. The gallery was painted in green and yellow, colours the Victorians thought not only unmanly but a sure sign of sexual depravity, especially once Aesthetic Movement members began appearing in public carrying colour-coordinated flowers. The opening ceremony was attended by Wilde, who wore a frock coat designed at the back in the shape of a cello, a display which got him into the papers and saw him become a celebrity; and John Ruskin, the critic and mentor of British art, who, after seeing Whistler's *Nocturne in Black and Gold: The Falling Rocket* here, declared that he had 'seen and heard much of Cockney impudence before now but never expected to hear a coxcomb ask two hundred guineas for flinging a pot of paint in the public's face'. Whistler sued for libel and won damages – of a farthing – but was ruined financially by the trial. The gallery's proprietor, Sir Coutts Lindsay, installed an electricity generating station, now the world's oldest surviving example, in the basement in 1883, and in 1903 the venue reopened as the Aeolian Hall to stage concerts. It was taken over by the BBC in 1941 and is now used by Sotheby's.
► Whistler in Chelsea, p. 416.

east side: Oxford Street to Old Bond Street
Sotheby's Auctioneers, Nos. 34–35
Now the largest fine art auctioneers in the world, the company was founded in 1744 by a bookseller, Samuel Baker. The first sale was that of Sir John Stanley's library containing 'several Hundred scarce and valuable books in all branches of Polite Litera-

ture', and the auction house was later involved in selling books Napoleon had taken with him into exile on St Helena and libraries owned by the French politician Prince Talleyrand and the radical agitator John Wilkes. It was Baker's nephew, John Sotheby, who joined the firm in 1776, who gave his name to the company, which moved from Wellington Street, off the Strand, to New Bond Street in 1917.

Sotheby's grew under the management of Peter Wilson in the 1940s and 1950s, capitalizing on the increased popularity of Impressionist and Modern paintings. At the Goldschmidt sale of 1958, attended by hundreds of art dealers, the novelist Somerset Maugham and the actor Kirk Douglas, seven pictures, including Cézanne's *Garçon au Gilet Rouge*, were sold in twenty minutes for nearly £800,000, then the highest total ever witnessed at a fine art sale. In the 1960s branches were opened in Paris, Los Angeles, Melbourne and Florence, and in 1977 the company went public. By the end of the twentieth century Sotheby's had more than 100 branches around the world and was selling nearly £2 billion-worth of art in New York and London.

Guy Burgess's address (1940s–50s), No. 10 Clifford Chambers
Clifford Chambers on New Bond Street was the last London address of Guy Burgess, the Foreign Office diplomat who defected to the Soviets in 1951, a year after he had been sent to the USA where he gained notoriety for his unusual behaviour which included emptying a plate of prawns into his pocket and leaving them there for a week. Burgess left New Bond Street on 25 May 1951 to help fellow spy Donald Maclean to defect and, expecting to return swiftly to Britain, left his Austin A70 at Southampton Dock. But neither Burgess nor Maclean returned, and once MI5 realized they had defected deputy director general Guy Liddell and an associate, Anthony Blunt, director of the Courtauld Institute, searched Burgess's flat for incriminating evidence. Liddell could not have made a worse choice of who to

help him, for Blunt, art adviser to George VI and later Queen Elizabeth, was himself a Soviet agent, and during the search, according to the espionage historian Roy Berkeley, made sure that he removed anything suspicious from the flat, particularly documents relating to himself.

Old Bond Street

The older of the two Bond Streets dates back to 1686 when Thomas Bond began development on what was a swamp, part of the Corporation of London's Conduit Meade Estate. By the early eighteenth century it had become a place where rich young men, 'Bond Street loungers', paraded in the fashionable clothes of the day. Old Bond Street was home to the writers Jonathan Swift (in 1727), Edward Gibbon (1758), Laurence Sterne (1768) and James Boswell (1769), the politician William Pitt the Elder (1766) and the naval hero Lord Nelson (1797–8), but is nowadays mostly commercial, dominated by art galleries.

(vi) around Savile Row

East of New Bond Street, village Mayfair gives way to commercial Mayfair, where the streets are lined with grand nineteenth-century office blocks and, around Savile Row, some of London's leading gentlemen's outfitters.

Burlington Arcade

One of three local arcaded walkways lined with exclusive shops selling expensive goods, Burlington Arcade was built from 1815 to 1819 by Samuel Ware for Lord Cavendish, who lived here in a large property and wanted to stop passers-by throwing rubbish on his land. The arcade is patrolled by top-hatted beadles who ensure that visitors are not carrying unfurled umbrellas or bulky parcels.

Burlington Gardens

A short street at the north-east end of Old Bond Street which contains on its south side an impressive thirteen-bay Italianate

mansion designed by James Pennethorne in 1866–7, built in the garden of the even more monumental Burlington House (now home of the Royal Academy), which was used as the main building of the University of London until 1900, was later taken over by the Civil Service Commission, and then became home of the Museum of Mankind. The block was bought by the Royal Academy and is currently being renovated.

New Burlington Galleries, No. 5, north side
In 1936 the galleries staged Britain's first exhibition of surrealist art, organized by the British surrealist Roland Penrose and the poet David Gascoyne, with exhibits selected by the art historian Herbert Read and the sculptor Henry Moore. The exhibition was heralded by a number of unusual events including the artist Sheila Legge's being photographed in Trafalgar Square as Salvador Dalí's 'la Femme au Tête des Roses', her head obscured by roses, and Dalí himself appearing for a lecture accompanied by two borzoi hounds and dressed in a diving suit, the helmet of which made his words inaudible and nearly suffocated him. Picasso's *Guernica* was first shown in Britain at the gallery in 1938.

Cork Street

The centre of fine art in London, Cork Street was named after the Irish seat of the landowners, the Earls of Burlington.

Mayor Gallery, No. 22a, west side
Fred Mayor opened Cork Street's first gallery at No. 22a in 1925 and it soon became the headquarters of the modernist Unit One group of artists which included Paul Nash, Henry Moore and Wells Coates (architect of Isokon in Belsize Park, p. 359). Unit One announced its formation through a letter in *The Times* on 2 June 1933 but split up after two years as it could not agree on its aims. Artists whose work was first exhibited commercially at the Mayor Gallery include Francis Bacon, Max Ernst, Paul Klee, Joán Miró and Eduardo Paolozzi.

Hanover Square

A busy traffic route just south-west of Oxford Circus lined by impressive office blocks, Hanover Square was laid out on the Kirkham Close Estate by the Earl of Scarborough in 1714 and named in honour of the accession to the British throne of George, Elector of Hanover. The development was an immediate success, attracting a number of titled people, and during the nineteenth-century growth of commercial London prestigious offices, fashion houses and clubs moved to Hanover Square as the residents moved away. At the south end of the square is Chantrey's statue of William Pitt the Younger, which supporters of the Reform Bill unsuccessfully tried to pull down on the day it was unveiled.

No. 17, north side

Lucy Christiana Sutherland, who as 'Lucille' was the leading British dressmaker of the *fin de siècle*, moved her clothes store to Hanover Square in 1897, and it soon became one of London's great couture houses, 'Maison Lucille', her clothes – 'a cascade of chiffons, of draperies as lovely as those of ancient Greece' – challenging the prevalent look of flannel underwear, woollen stockings and voluminous petticoats. Lucille was the first dressmaker to use live mannequins, pioneered the brassière and created skirts that revealed, rather than concealed, the leg. She opened a branch in New York and in 1912 booked herself on White Star Liners' new flagship, the *Titanic*, for the transatlantic voyage.

Disconcerted by the size of the vessel, Lucille went to bed each night fully dressed. When an iceberg fatally struck the ship at around midnight on 16 April 1912 she and her husband, Sir Cosmo Duff Gordon, fortuitously secured safety on the almost deserted Number 1 boat. When one of the crew remarked that as the ship had sunk their pay would stop and they would not be able to afford new uniforms, Duff Gordon promised to meet the men's costs. Once safely aboard the vessel *Carpathia* which had rescued them, Duff Gordon presented the

men with a cheque in a ceremony photographed by the ship's doctor. When the party reached New York, however, one of the men went to the press claiming that the money was a bribe Duff Gordon had paid him to row away from the *Titanic* to prevent the lifeboat from being swamped by drowning passengers. Although Duff Gordon was exonerated at the inquiry his reputation and Lucille's were damaged and she never regained her standing.

● Danny La Rue's 1960s club, where La Rue, Britain's first drag artist, appeared with the considerably shorter Ronnie Corbett as straight man, was situated in the basement at No. 17.

Hanover Square Rooms, No. 4, east side

The Hanover Square Rooms opened on the east side of the square on 1 February 1775 – Johann Christian Bach gave the first of many concerts here the following year – and annual performances of Handel's *Messiah* were staged in the rooms from 1785 to 1845. In 1791 the composer Joseph Haydn made the first of several visits, and he later wrote symphonies Nos. 93–104, popularly known as the London Symphonies, many of which were introduced here, in commemoration of his visits. The American novelist Mark Twain spoke at the rooms to an enthusiastic crowd on the subject of 'Our Fellow Savages of the Sandwich Islands' on 13 October 1873, and the following year the rooms were converted to the Hanover Square Club. The premises were demolished in 1900.

St George Street

St George, St George Street at Maddox Street

The parish church of Mayfair and one of London's most fashionable places of worship, St George was designed by John James, who had been apprenticed to Christopher Wren, and built in 1721 to 1724 with money raised by a tax on coal. As well as being a favourite with West End society, it specialized in cheap marriages at a guinea a time, without the requirements of banns or licences. One of those who took advantage was James Blake, father of the poet-painter William, who married Catherine Hermitage here in autumn 1752. A better-known marriage that took place here, fictionally, is that of Alfred Doolittle in George Bernard Shaw's *Pygmalion*, an incident depicted in the song 'Get Me to the Church on Time' in the play's musical incarnation, *My Fair Lady*.

Savile Row

Home of bespoke British tailoring since the early nineteenth century, Savile Row was built over the kitchen garden of Burlington House (now home of the Royal Academy) in 1695 and acquired its name in the 1730s from Lady Dorothy Savile, wife of the 3rd Earl of Burlington. Its first residents were mostly military officers and politicians and the first tailors set up here in 1806, establishing their reputations after gaining the custom of the society dandy Beau Brummell and the Prince Regent (later George IV), the supreme hedonists of the age.

It acquired a different kind of prestige during the 1930s when the firm of Kilgour, French and Stanbury at No. 8 made Fred Astaire's morning coat for the film *Top Hat*, and this set the pattern for the biggest Hollywood names – Cary Grant, Bing Crosby and Frank Sinatra – to come to Savile Row for their suits.

In 1948 Savile Row tailors successfully promoted an Edwardian revival style of velvet collars, long-lapelled waistcoats and narrow trousers that became known as the 'Teddy Boy' look. When, within a few years, the look was taken up by delinquent working-class teenagers one Savile Row customer was heard to complain that 'the whole of one's wardrobe immediately became unwearable'. In 1968 the Beatles, who bought their suits at Tommy Nutter's House of Nutter at No. 35, set up their Apple Corps company at No. 3, playing their last gig on the roof of the building on 3 January 1969. Savile Row continues to flourish, supplying suits to the world's wealthiest customers regardless of shifts in fashion.

west side: Vigo Street to Conduit Street
No. 35
Tommy Nutter shocked the traditional tailors of Savile Row in 1968 when, on setting up his House of Nutter outlet here with a cash injection from the singer Cilla Black, he laid a chocolate-coloured carpet in the store and installed a nameplate that read simply: 'Nutters'.

Anderson and Sheppard, No. 30
The tailors where Charles, Prince of Wales, has his suits made.

Savile Row police station, No. 27
During the Second World War the British secret service's subterfuge and subversion unit of the Special Operations Executive used the newly built police station basement for storing weapons and explosives. By the 1950s the station was in the pay of West End vice merchants who rewarded officers who turned a blind eye to clubs which sold alcohol outside licensing hours.
▶ SOE in Baker Street, p. 149.

east side: Conduit Street to Vigo Street
Henry Poole, No. 15
One of the leading Savile Row firms, it began by dressing local huntsmen and bankers such as the Rothschilds in the nineteenth century and won royal patronage from Queen Victoria. Its owner, Henry Poole, inadvertently created the tuxedo in 1860 when a new type of short smoking jacket designed for Edward, Prince of Wales, to wear at informal dinner parties at Sandringham caught the eye of a visitor from America, James Potter of Tuxedo Park, who asked Poole if he could design a similar garment for him to wear back home. After Poole died in 1876, his cousin, Samuel Cundey, took over the store, enlarging the premises and concentrating on civil, rather than military, tailoring, and by the twentieth century it had become the largest tailors in the world, employing some 300 staff. Poole's has since absorbed several other firms and, when the original Savile Row premises were demolished in 1961, it moved to No. 15, a

property built for the Countess of Suffolk in 1733.

Hardy Amies, No. 14

The most famous name on Savile Row, Hardy Amies opened a shop at No. 14 in 1946 and gained national fame in 1955 when he was appointed dressmaker to Queen Elizabeth II. Previously the property had been home to the playwright Richard Brinsley Sheridan, who lived here in poverty from 1813 to 1816 and who even after dying was not entirely free of creditors. A visitor who came to view the corpse claiming he was a long-lost relation wanting to look at his dear relative one last time revealed himself to be a bailiff when the coffin was opened and arrested the dead playwright for non-payment of bills. Jules Verne gave Phileas Fogg Sheridan's former address in his celebrated 1872 work *Around the World in Eighty Days*.

Apple Corps (1968–72), No. 3

Apple, the Beatles' chaotically run record label, moved into this tall eighteenth-century property, now home of the Building Societies Association, in July 1968. The following January the Beatles played their last gig on the roof of the building, which shows them at the point of breaking up, generating little warmth and perfunctorily running through the songs that formed the bulk of their last album. They were stopped after forty minutes by the police following complaints about the noise from nearby office workers. In September 1969 the four Beatles met for the last time at a business meeting held here and three years later Apple moved out. The graffiti'd front door was later shipped out to Lennon and Yoko Ono's New York apartment.

▶ Abbey Road studios, p. 367.

Gieves and Hawkes, No. 1

Founded as two separate firms by a Mr Gieves (in 1785) and a Mr Hawkes (in 1771), the former gave P. G. Wodehouse the idea for the name of his butler in the Bertie Wooster stories (spelled as Jeeves), while the latter, who secured a Royal Warrant from George III early in the nineteenth century,

replied to a note from George's successor, the Prince Regent, demanding his immediate attendance on a Sunday, by informing the Prince that 'for six days I serve my King, on the seventh day I serve my God'. The Prince Regent was not offended and continued his patronage. The two firms later merged and in the nineteenth century the company developed the Kitchener and Wolseley sun helmets that became essential items for those who travelled in hot climates, equipping David Livingstone and Henry Morton Stanley for their expeditions to central Africa. In 1912 the firm moved to No. 1 Savile Row, the 1732 town house that had previously been home to the Royal Geographical Society, where, ironically, Livingstone's corpse had lain in state in 1874. In the early 1930s it supplied Charles Laughton with corpulent costumes for his role as Captain Bligh in the film *Mutiny on the Bounty*, working with the same designs they had used for the real-life Bligh in the late eighteenth century.

(vii) Piccadilly

One of London's most famous roads, its name copied by a number of other British cities, Piccadilly is one of two traditional routes leading west from central London (the other being Oxford Street) and probably took its name from the 'picadil', a stiff collar made by a local seventeenth-century tailor, Robert Baker. The route was originally known as Hyde Park Road west of Berkeley Street, where a stone bridge took it over the now culverted Tybourne stream, and Portugal Street, in honour of Catherine of Braganza, the Portuguese wife of Charles II, further east, but became Piccadilly in the eighteenth century. On the north side were a number of aristocrats' mansions, of which only Burlington House and the Albany remain, while on the south side there was a succession of small, intimate shops such as the surviving Hatchards bookshop. Early in the twentieth century the street's wealthy residents, finding the noise of vehicles and the bustle of the capital not to their liking, moved away, but the modern-day Piccadilly retains its grandeur, thanks to the presence of the Ritz Hotel, the Royal Academy in Burlington House and the quality grocers, Fortnum & Mason, at No. 181.

• In Bram Stoker's vampire novel, *Dracula* (1897), the bloodsucking count buys the fictitious No. 347, a property 'grim and silent in its deserted condition among its more lively and spruce-looking neighbours'.

PICCADILLY LINE

The Piccadilly Line opened as the Great Northern, Piccadilly and Brompton Railway in 1906 to link Finsbury Park and Hammersmith, the soil excavated from the digging of the tunnels being used to shore up the terraces at Chelsea Football Club's Stamford Bridge ground. The line was extended west in 1911 along existing District Line tracks to Acton Town. Further extensions took place in the 1930s when new stations, mostly designed by Charles Holden, that were among the most exciting inter-war new buildings in London, were constructed.

Heathrow Terminal 4 In 1986 the line was extended to Terminal 4, ending in a loop which connects it with Terminals 1, 2, 3.

Heathrow Terminals 1, 2, 3 Opened in 1977 as Heathrow Central, the first ever underground station serving an international airport, it was renamed in 1986.

Hatton Cross A new station was built in 1977 when the line was extended to Heathrow.

Hounslow West This was the western terminus until the airport extension was opened in 1977.

Hounslow Central Opened in 1903 as Heston-Hounslow.

Hounslow East Opened in 1903 as Hounslow Town.

Osterley The station's architect, Charles Holden, took his inspiration for the design

from the tower and finial of Amsterdam's *Telegraaf* newspaper building.

Boston Manor Named after the nearby Jacobean house, which may have been designed by Inigo Jones and whose grounds are now bisected by the M4.

Northfields The station once used kestrels and hawks to kill pigeons which were setting up home within.

South Ealing Built with an innovative apsidal waiting room, a style much copied since.

Uxbridge Rebuilt in the 1930s with many distinctive period features, including brick massing and stripped-down classical motifs.

Hillingdon A grand rebuilding programme had to be curtailed because of the Second World War.

Ickenham The original station was so short that there was no room for more than three carriages at a time; trains had to stop twice.

Ruislip The station regularly used in the 1950s by a stream of Soviet spies visiting the notorious agents Helen and Peter Kroger at their nearby bolt-hole.

Ruislip Manor The 1912 halt was replaced with Charles Holden's expertly proportioned asymmetrical late 1930s brick building.

Eastcote Named after a local mansion, Eastcott House.

Rayners Lane The Piccadilly and Metropolitan lines meet just east of the station.

South Harrow There is a ghost station (the original South Harrow) to the south of the present-day stop.

Sudbury Hill A 1930 London Transport poster asked: 'Why not live at Sudbury Hill? Small, modern, labour-saving houses with garages and gardens. Live in the country where you have room to breathe.'

Sudbury Town The first of Charles Holden's modernist stations, built in 1930 to 1931 and designed in free-form brick with horizontal windows and no supporting frame, it was the first on the network not to be built on the side of the road, like a shop, but in its own cul-de-sac.

Alperton The only other station on the underground system apart from Greenford where passengers take escalators (originally used in the Dome of Discovery in the 1951 Festival of Britain) *up* to the platforms.

Park Royal John Betjeman recalled Park Royal as a 'little wooden platform, high above the football ground of Queen's Park Rangers' in a *Times* article in May 1963.

North Ealing Opened in 1903 on the Ealing and South Harrow Railway.

Ealing Common The 1931 ticket hall was designed by Basil Ionides, who also worked on the Savoy Theatre.

Acton Town Opened as Mill Hill Park in July 1879 and changed to Acton Town in 1910.

Hammersmith One of the few stations on the network where passengers can change from one line to another on the same platform, in this case from the Piccadilly Line to the District Line, and vice versa.

Barons Court A rare listed station building, the original 1905 fittings carefully preserved.

Earl's Court Location of the Underground's first escalator, which opened in October 1911. Bumper Harris, a man with a wooden leg, was hired to ride up and down all day to reassure passengers of its safety.

Gloucester Road The original station building contains a board that boasts, in mosaic lettering, 'Metropolitan Railway Station / Trains To All Parts Of London'.

South Kensington Captain Franz Rintelen von Kleist, a lieutenant-commander in the German navy who had been imprisoned on the Isle of Man during the First World War for spying for the Germans, was found dead in a tube train at South Kensington station in May 1949.

Knightsbridge Rebuilt for the benefit of Harrod's in 1934.

Hyde Park Corner A rare West End tube station serving only one line.

Green Park Extended in the 1960s to take the new Victoria Line and again in the 1970s to take the new Jubilee Line.

Piccadilly Circus Opened in 1906, the station was deemed too small by the 1920s and was rebuilt entirely underground, as there was no room for a surface level station. The new station, with its art deco booking hall, shops, world clock, maze of tunnels, walkways and painting showing Piccadilly Circus as the centre of the world, opened in 1928 as the biggest station the tube system had then witnessed.

Leicester Square When the station was rebuilt in the 1930s the nearby Hippodrome and Crown Hotel had to be underpinned.

Covent Garden Legend has it that the station is haunted by the ghost of Victorian actor William Terris, who was stabbed to death by a jealous colleague outside the nearby Adelphi Theatre in 1897.

Holborn Members of the Cabinet and the royal family, including King George V, took shelter in the deep tunnel of the Piccadilly Line spur from Holborn to Aldwych during First World War Zeppelin raids on London.

Russell Square At the start of Gary Sherman's 1974 horror film, *Deathline*, a bowler-hatted City gent is abducted from the station platform by a member of a mutant tribe of cannibalistic troglodytes who live in a nearby abandoned tunnel and prey on unsuspecting lone tube travellers at night.

King's Cross St Pancras The network's worst non-rail disaster took place on 18 November 1987 when a fire in the concourse at the top of the Piccadilly Line escalators led to the deaths of thirty-one people.

Caledonian Road A station was sited in this obscure back street location when the line was first built simply to provide stops at regular intervals.

Holloway Road The station faces major rebuilding work to deal with the planned new Arsenal stadium nearby.

Arsenal When opened in December 1906 the station was Gillespie Road and Arsenal

Football Club were based in south London, but after Arsenal moved to Highbury the club pressurized the transport authorities to change the name to Arsenal, and it is now the only station on the network named after its local team.

Finsbury Park British R&B pioneer Graham Bond died in mysterious circumstances beneath the wheels of a train at Finsbury Park station in May 1974, supposedly the victim of a demon who had entered his soul during an exorcism, dragged him to the station, and forced him in front of the train.

Manor House One of a number of stations (others include Swiss Cottage) named after a pub, rather than an area.

Turnpike Lane Rebuilt in the 1930s with a tube, tram and bus interchange and shopping precinct.

Wood Green Built in the 1930s, with ventilation grilles depicting idyllic rural scenes, in sympathy more with the station's name than with the nature of the surrounding area.

Bounds Green A remarkable piece of architecture, with a louvred ventilation shaft and a unique octagonal tower.

Arnos Grove Charles Holden's masterpiece, its cylindrical ticket hall modelled on Erik Asplund's public library in Stockholm, was described by the *Observer* on its opening in 1932 as 'an architectural gem of unusual purity'.

Southgate Another outstanding Holden station, it is designed in the shape of a drum with an upper storey of windows and has an accompanying shopping parade of similarly high quality.

Oakwood When the station was being built in the 1930s London Underground erected a board outside asking locals to suggest names to complement their own suggestions of East Barnet, Merryhills (a nearby pub) and Oakwood. Enfield West was chosen but Southgate council claimed the name was misleading, as the station was not in Enfield, and a compromise was reached with the station renamed Enfield West (Oakwood), which was shortened to Oakwood in 1946.

Cockfosters The line was taken this far north so that trains could reach their new depot, rather than to serve a transport-hungry community.

Piccadilly
north side: Hyde Park Corner to Piccadilly Circus

Hyde Park Corner

The traditional gateway to London from the west and now a fearsome traffic roundabout, Hyde Park Corner stands at the north-west corner of Green Park. Entrance to the park is through Constitution Arch – also known as Wellington Arch and designed by Decimus Burton between 1825 and 1828 as a monument to the Duke of Wellington's victory at Waterloo – which originally stood a little further to the north but was moved here after causing a traffic bottleneck. The statue of Wellington was removed in 1883 and in 1912 Adrian Jones's statue of the Goddess of Peace was installed on the roof. The arch used to contain a tiny police station, the second smallest in the capital.

Apsley House, No. 149

A Robert Adam mansion built between 1771 and 1778 for Henry Bathurst, the Lord Chancellor, one of whose family names was Apsley, it was later acquired by the Marquess of Wellesley who sold it to his brother, the Duke of Wellington, in 1817, and it was here that the duke exhibited trophies from the 1815 Battle of Waterloo, including Napoleon's coach. The duke preferred Apsley House to 10 Downing Street when he was prime minister in the 1820s and liked to sit on the roof watching troops march by without being observed. He was obliged to turn the house into a fortress in 1830 after the mob singled him out for abuse when he refused to accept political reform. After the 6th Duke was killed in action during the Second World War the property was granted to the nation and it is now a museum devoted to the victor of Waterloo and filled with paintings from the Spanish Royal Collection, including Velázquez's *Waterseller of Seville* and works by Goya, Rubens and Brueghel. The property's postal address is the quaint No. 1 London, awarded to it for being the first house east of the former Hyde Park toll gate.

No. 145

Princess Elizabeth (later Queen Elizabeth II) and Princess Margaret were brought up at 145 Piccadilly, which was the family home of their parents, the Duke and Duchess of York (later George VI and the Queen Mother), before the Second World War. When the duke assumed the throne in 1936 following the shock abdication of his brother, Edward VIII, he came home in a daze and asked his curtseying daughters: 'If anyone comes through on the telephone, who should I say I am?' In preparation for his coronation in May 1937 the new king paced his study for hours rehearsing his speech and wearing heavy weights on his head to ready himself to carry the 7 lb St Edward's Crown, which would be used during the ceremony.

The property was destroyed by a Second World War bomb and was later replaced by the Hotel Inter-Continental.

▸ Buckingham Palace, p. 212.

Park Lane Hotel, No. 112

The hotel, planned before the First World War for a site which had contained several Piccadilly mansions, was abandoned when hostilities broke out and the frame of the building stood forlornly until 1924 when work resumed. The author Evelyn Waugh, chronicler of upper-class Mayfair life, stayed here during the Second World War, after serving with the British Military Mission in Yugoslavia. Some forty years later the TV company making an adaptation of Waugh's *Brideshead Revisited* shot in the hotel scenes meant to be taking place on an Atlantic liner and the makers of the 1980s British movies *Dance with a Stranger* and *Mona Lisa* filmed in the ballroom.

In December 1991 George Graham, the manager of Arsenal Football Club, met his nemesis, the Norwegian agent Rune Hauge, in the hotel bar and accepted from him a hold-all 'as an appreciation of all you [Graham] have done to help me open doors here in England'. When Graham arrived home and opened the bag he found £140,500 in £50 notes. He later received a banker's draft for a further £285,000 and banked the money in Jersey without declaring it, on the grounds that it was an unsolicited gift, but when the news leaked out he was sacked by Arsenal and banned from football for a year, despite handing the money back.

▸ Arsenal Football Club, p. 331.

No. 94

An imposing Palladian building, set back from the road and built by Matthew Brettingham between 1756 and 1760 for the Earl of Egremont, it was the mid-nineteenth-century home of Lord Palmerston, one of the era's most formidable politicians and prime minister in the 1850s and 1860s. After Palmerston's death it was taken over by the Naval and Military Club, later being known as the In and Out club, on account of the signs painted by the gates. Early in the twenty-first century the club moved to 2 St James's Square and the building was sold to a mystery buyer from Kuwait.

Burlington House, east of Old Bond Street

A rare surviving Piccadilly mansion, now home to the Royal Academy of Arts, Burlington House was begun in 1665 by Sir John Denham, poet, architect and Surveyor-General to Charles II, and redesigned after Richard Boyle, the 3rd Earl of Burlington, returned from his Grand Tour of Italy in 1716 enthusing over the Palladian style. He upgraded the house from a plain brick structure to a grand Palladian mansion, its glory best seen in the lower storeys of the entrance arch on Piccadilly, which had considerable influence on the next generation of architects.

The government bought Burlington House in 1854, without having a plan for its use, and later leased it to a number of organizations including the Royal Academy, which now occupies much of the building and uses it to display its permanent collection of works by Constable, Gainsborough, Turner and others and to host its annual summer exhibition. In 1851 the Millais painting *Christ in the House of His Parents* met with a hostile reception when exhibited here on account of its extreme realism, which was unusual for the time, and the inclusion of the mysterious initials 'PRB' on the canvas, initials that were found to stand for 'Pre-Raphaelite Brotherhood'; the painting was one of the first created by the group of artists that also included Dante Gabriel Rossetti and William Holman Hunt. In 1997 Marcus Harvey's portrait of Moors murderer Myra Hindley made out of children's handprints was vandalized when it first went on show and its inclusion led to the resignation of a number of Academy members.

▶ Tate Britain, p. 246; the Pre-Raphaelites, p. 85.

Albany, Piccadilly at Albany Court Yard
The most exclusive bachelor apartments in London, Albany was built as Melbourne House between 1770 and 1774 for the 1st Viscount Melbourne by Sir William Chambers, who also redesigned Somerset House, and was soon taken over by Frederick, Duke of York, son of George III. When the duke ran into debt the complex was converted into luxury apartments, where only gentlemen, bachelors and those with no connections with trade were allowed to live. Since Lord Byron moved into No. 2 in 1814 – Lady Caroline Lamb disguised herself as a page-boy to get into the building – scores of writers have adopted an Albany suite as their *pied-à-terre* – Lord Macaulay, Arnold Bennett, Aldous Huxley and Graham Greene – while other wealthy socialites who have lived here include the actor Terence Stamp, Anthony Armstrong-Jones (Lord Snowdon), the former prime minister Edward Heath and the politician and diarist Alan Clark.

Piccadilly Circus

One of the world's great landmarks, dazzling in the flashing neon lights of its advertising hoardings, Piccadilly Circus is also the unofficial centre of the capital, a title for which it competes with Trafalgar Square and Leicester Square. It was created in 1819 as part of John Nash's work on the newly built Regent Street, originally taking the form of a French *place* with the curved corners of the buildings fronting a crossroads. The layout changed in the 1880s when the Metropolitan Board of Works, in creating Shaftesbury Avenue, demolished the north-east section. The tenants of the new buildings realized they could raise considerable revenue by fronting their façades with illuminated advertising, while the buildings on the other corners were prevented from following suit by the terms of the original leases. Although many London historians have decried the resulting awkward shape, Piccadilly Circus gains its character from the unusual angles and directions of the roads that meet here. The famous Eros statue was erected in 1892 as a memorial to the philanthropist the Earl of Shaftesbury.

south side: Piccadilly Circus to Hyde Park Corner

The Criterion, No. 224
Lavishly decorated inside in a neo-Byzantine style, the Criterion, a restaurant and basement theatre situated on the south side of Piccadilly Circus, was built by Thomas Verity in 1873, and soon attracted a raffish male crowd. It was here that Dr Watson bumps into an associate who later introduces him to Sherlock Holmes in the first Holmes book, *A Study in Scarlet*. It was also the haunt of villains such as the gangster Eddie Guerin who, while on the run from the police and private detectives in Chicago, came to London and in the Criterion told gullible associates how he had escaped by boat from Devil's Island, off the coast of French Guiana, and eaten his companions to stay alive. His story would have been immediately ruined had any of them

realized that Devil's Island was by then no longer in use as a prison. The Criterion's basement theatre was taken over by the BBC during the Second World War for the production of light entertainment shows such as the radio success *ITMA (It's That Man Again)*, and after the war staged an early run of Samuel Beckett's *Waiting for Godot*. In the early 1980s Ray Cooney's *Run for Your Wife!* played for over 1,500 performances, while more recently the theatre has been showing the *Complete Works of William Shakespeare (Abridged)*.

No. 213
Joe Lyons opened his first tea-shop here in 1894.

Waterstone's (former Simpson's), No. 203
Britain's largest bookshop was built into the former Simpson's store, the model for Grace Brothers in the TV sitcom *Are You Being Served?*, which was built of welded steel to the designs of Joseph Emberton in 1936. A customer during the Second World War was the French Resistance leader Charles de Gaulle, whose discussion with a colleague about plans involving the movement of Resistance fighters in France was accidentally overheard by an enemy agent trying on clothes in one of the changing rooms.

St James
A rare non-City Christopher Wren church, the only one he built on a site not previously occupied by another building and said to be the architect's favourite, it was consecrated in 1684 and has been one of London's best maintained and most fashionable churches since, now home to a radical ecumenical organization and the William Blake Society, the painter-poet having been baptized in the Grinling Gibbons-designed marble font. The church was bombed in 1940 and restored with a new spire, a replica of the original. The Piccadilly entrance is home to a small market.

No. 195
Built as the Royal Institute of Painters in Water Colours in 1881, it now houses Bafta, the British Association of Film and Television.

Hatchards, No. 187
John Hatchard opened a bookshop at 173 Piccadilly in 1797, moving to this site in 1801 and inscribing on a plate on the shop wall 'God blessed my industry and good men encouraged it.' Hatchards soon established itself as the leading bookshop in London, the destination for the wealthy installing libraries in their newly built mansions, and an early customer was the Duke of Wellington, who would ride here on horseback from his Apsley House residence further west on Piccadilly. Around 100 years later the eighteen-year-old Noël Coward was caught shoplifting by an assistant who saw him putting books into a suitcase, itself stolen. When challenged he quickly retorted: 'Really, look how badly this shop is run! I could have made off with a dozen books and no one would have noticed,' leaving with no further bother.

Fortnum and Mason, No. 181
London's most prestigious food store was founded in 1707 by William Fortnum, a footman to Queen Anne, who later formed a partnership with his landlord, Hugh Mason. By the end of the century it was supplying delicacies such as game in aspic jelly embellished with prawns and lobster to the wealthy of Mayfair and St James's. The store sent foodstuffs to British soldiers fighting in the Peninsular War (1808–14) and the Crimean War (1854–6), and officers wrote back asking Fortnum and Mason to leave the store's name off the products they were shipping out as it was a temptation to thieves. The firm has remained a major supplier to the royal family.
▶ Harrods, p. 397.

Egyptian Hall, No. 170
Egyptian House stands on the site of the 1812 **Egyptian Hall**, a museum that was the first building in London designed with Egyptian motifs, where curiosities brought back from the South Seas by Captain Cook, and Napoleon's carriage seized at Waterloo were exhibited. In 1844 the 25-inch-tall American, Charles Sherwood Stratton, known popularly as General Tom Thumb, took part in a

show organized by the flamboyant Phineas T. Barnum. Two years later the hall displayed Benjamin Haydon's enormous canvas, *Christ's Entry Into Jerusalem*, which had led the artist to exclaim: 'What fire, what magic!' on completion of the work. The building was demolished in 1905.

The Ritz

The famous luxurious Beaux-Arts hotel, built in 1904–5 with a steel frame, London's first, was financed by Cesar Ritz, who had revolutionized London dining in the 1890s at the Savoy – he resigned in 1898 after being accused of conducting his own business affairs on hotel property – but was not immediately popular with locals who claimed its vast bulk would stem the flow of fresh air from Green Park.

However, the hotel soon attracted the wealthiest and most celebrated guests, including the opera singer Enrico Caruso, the ballerina Pavlova and the Russian choreographer Diaghilev. Even during the First World War entertaining continued on a lavish scale, Francis Meynell writing scornfully in the left-wing *Daily Herald* of meals of 'hors d'oeuvres, rich soups, sole and lobster with cream everywhere – on the soup, in the fish sauce, on the fruit salad'. While lunching at the Ritz on 11 May 1920 the Conservative politician Oswald Mosley, who later founded the British Union of Fascists, was approached by the hostess Lady Cunard who asked him: 'Were you not being married five minutes ago?' Mosley realized that he should have been, rushed out, and ran along St James's Street to the Chapel Royal, St James's Palace, where he was just in time for his wedding to Lady Cynthia Curzon, daughter of the foreign secretary, Lord Curzon.

When Douglas Fairbanks and Mary Pickford stayed at the Ritz that June the crowds outside the hotel were so overwhelming that buses were stopped in the traffic for twenty minutes. A year later forty police were needed to ensure Charlie Chaplin could enter the hotel in safety when he stayed here. By the 1980s the hotel had descended into tastelessness, furnished with pink curtains that the journalist Victoria Mather described as 'looking like cami-knickers'. Since being bought by the Barclay brothers in the 1990s it has regained some of its former reputation.

► The Savoy, p. 134.

SOHO, W1

> 'Yes,' returned Mr. Hyde. 'It is as well we have met; and *a propos*, you should have my address.' And he gave a number of a street in Soho – *The Strange Case of Dr Jekyll and Mr Hyde*, Robert Louis Stevenson (1886)

If the City of London is the capital's historic and financial square mile, then Soho is its nightlife, social and glamour centre, a dynamic area of chic bars, packed pubs, smart restaurants and crowded clubs, its streets awash with tourists, day-trippers, celebrities and those looking for excitement.

The area was entirely covered in fields in 1582 when Elizabeth I passed a law forbidding the building of houses within three miles of the City, citing 'the improbability of supplying [the residents] with food, fuel and other necessaries of life at a reasonable rate and the danger of spreading plague and infection throughout the realm'. Nevertheless by the seventeenth century a number of houses had been constructed illegally, and in 1633 the name So-hoe, of uncertain etymology, first appeared in the parish rate book. Some thirty years later Charles II bestowed the land around what is now Soho Square to his bastard son, James Scott, Duke of Monmouth, who built a mansion, 𝔐𝔬𝔫𝔪𝔬𝔲𝔱𝔥 𝔥𝔬𝔲𝔰𝔢, there. He used the phrase 'So Ho!' as his battle cry in 1685 at the Battle of Sedgemoor, where his peasant forces were routed in his unsuccessful bid to usurp the throne of England from James II.

By the end of the seventeenth century those fleeing the devastation caused by the Fire of London, a few miles to the east, had

Soho's pubs and restaurants

Soho is London's most popular drinking and eating-out area with scores of well-known establishments.

Admiral Duncan, 54 Old Compton Street. Soho's leading gay pub, the target of a bomb attack in 1999.

Argyll Arms, 18 Argyll Street. A pub with well-preserved Victorian fittings where the novelist George Orwell chastised BBC colleagues for failing to show sufficiently proletarian credentials.

Bar Italia, 22 Frith Street. An authentic Italian café with giant TV screen, open until the early hours.

Coach and Horses, 29 Greek Street. The venue for *Private Eye*'s fortnightly lunches, presided over by Norman Balon, London's self-styled 'rudest landlord'.

Colony Club, 41 Dean Street. Soho's best-known private drinking club, run for many years by the foul-mouthed Muriel Belcher, and haunt of the artists Francis Bacon and Lucian Freud.

Crown and Two Chairmen, 32 Dean Street. Named after the two sedan chair-bearers who dropped by when taking Queen Anne to have her portrait painted opposite.

De Hems, 10 Macclesfield Street. Dutch pub where Resistance fighters met in the Second World War and which in the 1960s was popular with music business people, who claimed that the bottom three places in the pop chart could allegedly be bought in the pub's Oyster Bar.

L'Escargot, 48 Greek Street. One of Soho's most exclusive restaurants, where the civil servant Clive Ponting held a party after being cleared of leaking official secrets in the 1980s.

French House, 49 Dean Street. A favourite of Soho's literary crowd throughout the twentieth century and used by Charles de Gaulle during the Second World War.

Gay Hussar, 2 Greek Street. Favourite London restaurant of wealthy socialists.

Groucho Club, 45 Dean Street. Soho's most celebrated media club, patronized by Julie Burchill, Ben Elton, Damien Hirst and Salman Rushdie.

Intrepid Fox, 99 Wardour Street. A haunt of bikers and heavy metal fans and named after the great eighteenth-century Whig politician Charles James Fox.

The John Snow, 39 Broadwick Street. A pub built on the site of the surgery where John Snow discovered the source of Soho's 1854 cholera epidemic.

Kettner's, 29 Romilly Street. A former

---

begun to settle in the area alongside an influx of Greek refugees, the first of scores of foreigners settling in Soho after fleeing political or social persecution. Although Soho was popular with the aristocracy in the early eighteenth century, those with money soon moved further west to the pleasant lanes of Mayfair or the courts of St James's and many of their properties were taken over by foreign envoys who enjoyed the cosmopolitan atmosphere.

At the end of the century the area was colonized by Huguenots and other French citizens fleeing the Revolution. It also became popular with artists including Canaletto (who settled at 41 Beak Street),

Joseph Nollekens (29 Dean Street) and the sculptor John Flaxman (27 Poland Street), while a number of houses were converted into workshops by picture-framers, watchmakers, silversmiths and furniture makers.

During the nineteenth century Soho became one of the most densely populated parts of London, a shabby district teeming with life and energy, but also one of great poverty, the dingy streets as described by Robert Louis Stevenson in *The Strange Case of Dr Jekyll and Mr Hyde* typically containing a 'gin palace, a low French eating house, a shop for the retail of penny numbers and twopenny salads, many ragged children huddled in the doorways, and

French restaurant frequented by Oscar Wilde and Edward VII, now owned by Pizza Express.

King of Corsica, 90 Berwick Street. A pub named in honour of the Frenchman Theodore Neuhoff, who was invited to become King of the island of Corsica and died in Soho in 1756.

Leoni's Quo Vadis, 26–29 Dean Street. Exclusive Italian eaterie situated below Karl Marx's old rooms.

Patisserie Valerie, 44 Old Compton Street. A 1920s café renowned for its cakes and pastries.

Pillars of Hercules, 7 Greek Street. A favourite of the Victorian cricketing poet Francis Thompson.

Pollo, 20 Old Compton Street. London's best-known cheap Italian restaurant.

Soho House, 40 Greek Street. A 1990s rival to the Groucho (see above), popular with a more pop-oriented celebrity crowd.

Sun and 13 Cantons, 21 Great Pulteney Street. A charming pub named after the Swiss woollen merchants who were based locally.

Wong Kei, 41–43 Wardour Street. A cheap Chinese restaurant which caters for parties of pre-clubbers who come to be abused by the legendarily rude waiters.

women of many different nationalities passing out, key in hand'.

By the beginning of the twentieth century different ethnic groups occupied their own sections of Soho: Jews around Berwick Street market, where many of the stallholders spoke only in Yiddish; the Swiss in the Golden Square area; and Italians in the streets off Soho Square. In the 1930s Soho's Italian cafés were targeted by Benito Mussolini's ruling Italian fascists, and hundreds of local youngsters of Italian extraction were sent to summer camps that were little more than fascist recruitment centres. When the Second World War broke out in 1939 Soho's large Italian community feared for its existence. Violence erupted, crowds smashed windows, and in June 1940 Winston Churchill ordered that all London's Italians be rounded up and interned, thereby avoiding the need to differentiate between those who felt allegiances to their ancestors' birthplace and those who wanted to fight for their new homeland, a stance that infuriated loyal subjects such as the restaurateur Peppino Leoni, founder of the long-running Leoni's Quo Vadis restaurant.

Soho escaped the kind of war damage that ruined other parts of London and after the war a new feeling of egalitarianism, coupled with the area's tradition for tolerance, gave rise to a bohemian scene that thrived around the area's espresso bars, drinking dens and jazz clubs. In the 1960s the clothes shops on Carnaby Street briefly became the most fashionable in the western world, the centre of the Swinging London scene famously celebrated by *Time* magazine, while in the many after-hours drinking clubs, particularly the Colony and Caves de France on Dean Street, disreputable and dilettante writers and artists such as Jeffrey Bernard, Francis Bacon and Colin MacInnes held court. By the seventies sex shops had gradually become the area's dominant image. But as Soho's reputation sank, property prices became more attractive, resulting in the area's rebirth as publishers, advertising agencies and restaurateurs moved into the area.

● Soho is the quarter of W1 to the south-east of Oxford Circus.

(i) around Carnaby Street

Argyll Street
Pedestrianized and crowded with theatregoers and tourists walking between Oxford Circus station and the rest of Soho, Argyll Street is named after John Campbell, the 2nd Duke of Argyll, who owned the land in the 1730s when the street was created. His brother, who became the 3rd Duke, built the street's grandest property, 𝔄𝔯𝔤𝔶𝔩𝔩 𝔋𝔬𝔲𝔰𝔢,

Soho's clubs

Soho's growth as London's major nightlife centre dates back to the 1920s when nightclubs first opened to cater for soldiers who were banned from local restaurants.

Beat Route, 17 Greek Street. An early 1980s new romantic club, directions to which were provided by Spandau Ballet in 'Chant No. 1'.

Café de Paris, 3 Coventry Street. Soho's most exclusive nightspot, bombed in the Second World War, and later host to the singer Marlene Dietrich.

La Chase / Mezzo, 100 Wardour Street. A chic restaurant where the prog rock band Yes were conceived in May 1968 after Jon Anderson, working there as a cleaner, met Chris Squire and found they had a mutual interest in Simon and Garfunkel, the Beatles, Jimmy Webb and the 5th Dimension.

Les Cousins, 49 Greek Street. Soho's major 1960s folk club, where performers included Bert Jansch, John Martyn, Donovan and Al Stewart, and where Nick Drake played a rare gig. After busking around North Africa, Europe and London in 1964 Roy Harper secured himself a residency here, before being thrown out 'for not being Nana Mouskouri'. Not so confident was the young Cat Stevens, raised only a few hundred yards away on New Oxford Street, who told the music magazine *Mojo* that he was 'too shy to play more than one or two songs'. The club closed in the 1970s.

Dive Bar, 48 Gerrard Street. A gay venue below the King's Head pub mentioned by the Pet Shop Boys in 'West End Girls'.

Flamingo, 33–37 Wardour Street. A 1960s mod venue, favoured by black American GIs, where the house band was Georgie Fame and the Blue Flames, starring the

virtuoso guitarist John McLaughlin, who later played with Miles Davis.

Goings-On Club, 3–4 Archer Street. A regular venue for the 1960s beat poets Pete Brown, Johnny Byrne and Spike Hawkins and the location of early, experimental Pink Floyd gigs where members of the group would discuss their work with the audience at the end of the show.

Madame Jo-Jo's, 8–10 Brewer Street. In April 1964 the then unknown David Bowie received his first big break at what was then the Jack of Clubs, playing with his group at the wedding reception of the washing-machine tycoon John Bloom who, unimpressed, shouted: 'They're driving me mad, get them off!' Now Madame Jo-Jo's, it is one of Soho's most famous nightspots, particularly popular with transvestites, and the London club most associated with the 1990s 'cheesy listening' phase.

Marquee, 165 Oxford Street, 90 Wardour Street. The most famous of Soho's many rock clubs was where Mick Jagger made his stage debut and where, after the Marquee moved to Wardour Street in 1964, countless new acts, including the Yardbirds, Who, David Bowie, Pink Floyd, Led Zeppelin and Sex Pistols, played early gigs.

Miranda Club, 9 Kingly Street. More exclusive than most Soho nightspots, it was where members of the 1960s rock aristocracy would come to get away from the crowds and where Paul McCartney first met Linda Eastman, whom he later married.

La Poubelle, Great Marlborough Street. London's first discotheque opened in a Great Marlborough Street basement in 1959, a time when music in nightclubs was provided by live bands.

later replaced by the Palladium Theatre, the street's best-known building.

Palladium, No. 7, east side One of London's best-known concert halls, the Palladium was built in 1910, opening that Boxing Day with a variety bill, and was

where in July 1932 the pioneering jazz trumpeter Louis Armstrong, brought over at great expense from Los Angeles, appeared on a bill of variety acts backed by a scratch band. The London audience did not know how to react to a jazz instrumentalist and

Roaring Twenties, 50 Carnaby Street. It opened in 1961 when Carnaby Street was just beginning to establish its reputation for fashionable clothes and was initially aimed at Jewish teenagers, but when they failed to flock to the club, it was taken over by the Jamaican Count Suckle.

Ronnie Scott's, 39 Gerrard Street and 46 Frith Street. Britain's best-known jazz club opened in Gerrard Street in 1959 and moved to Frith Street in 1965.

Roundhouse, 83 Wardour Street. Alexis Korner and Cyril Davies pioneered their British version of the Chicago R&B sound above the Roundhouse pub in the late fifties, playing alongside US blues performers such as Muddy Waters and Big Bill Broonzy.

The Scene, Ham Yard, Great Windmill Street. Soho's leading early sixties mod club, celebrated by the High Numbers (who became the Who) on 'I'm the Face' and owned by Ronan O'Rahilly, who later founded Radio Caroline.

Top Ten Club, 10 D'Arblay Street. Run in the late fifties by Vince Taylor, Britain's first credible rock star and the model for David Bowie's Ziggy Stardust.

2I's (1950s), 59 Old Compton Street. Birthplace of British rock 'n' roll, where merchant seaman Tommy Hicks metamorphosed into Tommy Steele, Terry Nelhams into Adam Faith and Harry Webb into Cliff Richard.

Vortex, 203 Wardour Street. Punk venue mentioned by the Jam in ' "A" Bomb in Wardour Street', where the journalist Danny Baker, announcing the death of Elvis Presley in 1977 at the height of punk, was cheered – to his disgust and the delight of the crowd.

one punter remarked to the *Daily Herald*'s Hannen Swaffer: 'That man, why he did everything with the trumpet but play it,' while a theatre manager at the back of the auditorium explained that although he almost left immediately when Armstrong started to play, he stayed because he wanted to know what Armstrong was going to do next. 'I have never seen such a thing. I thought he might even play the trumpet before he was through.' *Melody Maker* was more supportive, claiming that Armstrong's 'technique, tone and mastery of his instrument is uncanny . . . The amazing thing is his personality. He positively sparkles with showmanship and good humour. When he is singing he carries a handkerchief and mops his face.'

On 12 June 1933 another jazz pioneer, Duke Ellington, made his British debut here, sharing a bill with the comedian Max Miller, the so-called 'Cheeky Chappie' of the music hall, watched by the ten-year-old Ahmet Ertegun, who later founded Atlantic Records. But further visits of leading jazz musicians to the UK were prevented by a deal struck between the US Ministry of Labour and the British Musicians' Union, who refused work permits to visiting jazz musicians until satisfactory reciprocal arrangements were set up with the American Federation of Musicians. As there were no British jazz outfits that Americans wanted to hear, Britain became a live jazz wilderness for the next two decades. When the performing ban was lifted in 1956, the first US act to take advantage were the banal rock 'n' roll copyists Bill Haley and the Comets.

During the 1960s the venue was host to the popular television show *Sunday Night at the London Palladium* and more recently has staged lavish musicals such as *Barnum* (the lead, Michael Crawford, had to be treated by his osteopath after every performance, such were his sprains), *Singing in the Rain*, and *Joseph and the Amazing Technicolor Dreamcoat*.

▶ Theatre Royal, Drury Lane, p. 119.

Beak Street

Full of appealing small shops, ranging from select clothes stores to places selling boxing ephemera and an ironmonger's, Beak Street was Silver Street when the Italian artist

Soho Sex

> In Soho, all the things they say happen,
> do: I mean, the vice of every kink – *Abso-*
> *lute Beginners*, Colin MacInnes (1958)

Giovanni Giacomo Casanova, the Venetian-born Lothario known simply by his surname, briefly lived on Greek Street in 1764, but sex in Soho has mostly been closer in spirit to the seedy back-street shop where Joseph Conrad's Adolf Verloc sells smutty magazines and naughty photos in *The Secret Agent*. In Graham Greene's novels Soho prostitutes were usually cast as Belgian or French – sex in the mid twentieth century was seen by the British largely as a conti-nental affair. Gangsters set up stables of prostitutes, often French and known in vice circles as 'Fifis', on streets such as Brewer Street or Rupert Street, whose liai-sons with clients would often be interrupted by men with cameras bursting in and taking shots that could be used for blackmail.

The 1959 Street Offences Act mostly cleared the streets of prostitutes, but the shabby properties around Brewer Street and Walker's Court were soon leased by 'models', while there was also a growth in the number of sex shops, outside which 'hostesses' would try to lure gullible men inside so that they could be relieved of large sums of money for the chance of talking to a member of the opposite sex.

The number of local sex shops grew to such levels that by the 1970s there were some 200 such premises, their prevalence dissu-ading many people from visiting the area. This led the Soho Society, formed in the 1960s to campaign for the preservation of Soho's character, to press the council to act, not out of concerns for morality but to combat local shabbiness and sordidness, and the MP Tim Sainsbury pushed a private member's bill through Parliament to ban overtly sexual window displays. In 1982 a law was passed forcing sex establishments to be licensed, which effectively led to scores of properties closing and saw Soho down to thirty-five sex shops by the end of the decade.

Canaletto took a lease on a studio at No. 41 in 1746 and was later renamed after Thomas Beake, one of Queen Anne's messengers. Charles Dickens alluded to Beak Street as 'a tumbledown street with two irregular rows of tall meagre houses' in *Nicholas Nickleby*, but the 𝕮rown inn on the corner of Beak Street and James Street, as recommended by Newman Noggs in the novel, and which was probably the pub used by Philip Carey and friends in Somerset Maugham's *Of Human Bondage*, no longer stands.

Berwick Street

> The League of Nations met in Berwick
> Market, to discuss on which side kippers
> ought to swim – 'The League of Nations',
> Billy Bennett (1934)

Soho's market street, which was developed in 1688 and named after the Duke of Berwick, bastard son of James II, has been one of the best places in London to buy fruit, vegetables, cheese, fish and olives since the 1840s – it was a Berwick Street market trader, Jack Smith, who introduced the grapefruit to London in 1890 – and was one of Soho's main mid-twentieth-century parading grounds for what local historian Mark Edmonds described as 'gentlemen with brilliantined hair who sold hot cases of whisky or organised impromptu card games'. Berwick Street is still a vibrant and noisy place, flanked by London's greatest conglomeration of record outlets, a state of affairs that led Oasis to use a shot of the street on the front cover of their 1995 album (*What's the Story) Morning Glory?* At the southern end of the street stands Kemp House, a rare Soho tower block, the sole example of the Pilkington Glass company's 1954 proposal to glass over much of Soho at roof level and build six twenty-four-storey towers, each equipped with heligarages for helicopter parking and canals to transport people around the area on hi-tech boats.

Although the scheme's seventeen-storey Kemp House was built, the heligarage or mooring facilities never materialized.

Broadwick Street

Broad Street until 1936, when it was merged with Edward Street to form Broadwick Street, it was where the painter-poet William Blake was born in 1758 (in a house where the tower block Blake House now stands), his parents running a hosiery shop where he later claimed he saw God's face pressed against the window. When Winston Churchill at the outset of the Second World War ordered that Soho's Italians be rounded up for internment or deportation, a group of local women marched along Broadwick Street heading for the Italian shops of Old Compton Street, ready to carry out the prime minister's injunction themselves, but were thwarted by a Rose Blau, who pleaded with them to reconsider, explaining that Soho's Italians were mostly English-born and did not support Mussolini. The march broke up.

The John Snow, No. 39, south side
The 1870s pub, originally the Newcastle-upon-Tyne, was built on the site of the surgery run by John Snow, one of the first surgeons to use anaesthetics, who gave Queen Victoria chloroform for the birth of Prince Leopold in 1853 and made startling discoveries concerning the 1850s cholera epidemic.

Carnaby Street

The centre of British fashion in the 1960s but now selling mainly tourist tat, Carnaby Street was built in the 1680s and named after the local seventeenth-century mansion, 𝕶𝖆𝖗𝖓𝖆𝖇𝖞 𝕳𝖔𝖚𝖘𝖊. In the late eighteenth century Carnaby Street was home to an abbatoir run by female butchers, as the artist William Blake depicted in the plates he produced for *Jerusalem*, which shows three women removing the entrails of a fallen man. In the early nineteenth century it was home to the 𝕹𝖆𝖌'𝖘 𝕳𝖊𝖆𝖉 public house, a hotbed of revolutionary political activity where the toast was 'May

---

Soho crime

Though no more violent than other parts of London – indeed many reports show that it is one of the safest places of its kind in the Western world – Soho has always attracted publicity on account of its glamorous reputation and the way local crime usually fits into a clichéd pattern involving nightclubs, casinos and clip-joints.

In the early years of the twentieth century the Soho underworld was run by the Italian Sabini brothers of Saffron Hill, Farringdon (p. 73). But when they were interned as undesirable aliens during the Second World War their place was taken by Billy Hill, a master of safe-breaking, smash-and-grab raids and illegal gambling, who in 1955 published his autobiography, *Boss of Britain's Underworld*, in which he claimed he was 'the undisputed king of Soho'. To celebrate the launch Hill threw a party (at Gennaro's, now the Groucho), the invitations for which read: 'The above-named person is hereby appointed as a free and virtuous citizen of the iniquitous and uninhibited province of Soho . . . known for its burglars, bandits, gangsters and con men.'

Hill's main rival was Jack Comer, a Jewish gangster known as Jack Spot (it was said that where there was trouble he was always on the spot), who looked the part in his perfectly tailored suits, fedora and crombie and ran illegal gambling dens and protection rackets. But Spot's standing was never as high as Hill's, especially after a bullion raid at London Airport he organized went awry, and in 1956 he was badly beaten up outside his flat by Hill's gang, which included a young Frankie Fraser, who was sentenced to seven years for the offence. In the 1960s the Kray twins ran a number of local clubs and in recent decades Soho's main criminal gangs have been the Chinese Triads.

the last of the kings be strangled with the guts of the last of the priests.' Tailors set up workshops here in the nineteenth century but there was no identifiable local clothing industry until photographer Bill Green opened a select shop, Vince, at nearby 15 Newburgh Street in the mid-1950s, selling dandified clothes to homosexuals and showbusiness celebrities.

John Snow and the 1854 cholera epidemic

When cholera, which had killed some 10,000 people in various parts of London in 1853, hit Soho the following year John Snow, a local surgeon, announced that the disease was spread through dirty water but had his findings rubbished, particularly by local water companies who claimed it was caused by a 'miasma in the atmosphere'. When 127 local people died of cholera early in September 1854 Snow began more research and after interviewing the families of those who had died found out that all the victims had drunk from a well on Broad Street (Broadwick Street). He took samples of the water, discovered that it contained infectious particles, and went to the guardians of the local parish, urging them to remove the pump handle. After they did so spread of the disease stopped, but still the authorities were not convinced, and cited the death of a Hampstead woman and her niece in Islington, neither of whom had been in Soho, to boost their argument. Snow visited their relatives and discovered that the woman had previously lived in Broad Street and liked the taste of the water so much she had engaged her servant to journey to Soho to raise water from the well and take it back to her house in Hampstead.

Soon after, a former Vince assistant, John Stephen, opened a menswear shop, His Clothes, on Beak Street, specializing in scarves loosely knotted around the neck, velvet suits and cheap throwaway clothes. When the shop burned down in 1960 Stephen opened a new branch at 41 Carnaby Street and before long Stephen owned more shops such as Male West One and His Clothes. By the mid-sixties Carnaby Street had become the shop window for men's fashion in England, with crowds flocking to the street at weekends. The Kinks simultaneously lionized and sent up the scene with their February 1966 single 'Dedicated Follower of Fashion' about a dandyish fop who does the rounds of the street's boutiques. The rest of the world caught up with the idea of London, rather than Paris, as a fashion centre on 15 April 1966 when *Time* published its infamous article on 'Swinging London', in which it described how 'On any twilight evening when the day's work is done, Carnaby Street pulses with slender young men in tight, black pants that fit on the hips like ski-pants, their tulip-like girlfriends on their arms, peering into the garishly-lit windows at the burgundy coloured suede jackets with the slanted, pleated pockets.'

The publicity killed Carnaby Street, which was soon filled with cash-in shops stuffed with inferior hipster jeans and second-rate Cuban-heeled boots, but even though it enjoyed a brief revival at the end of the 1970s, when its stores latched on to punk, stocking tartan bum-flaps, knee-length lace-up boots and zip-festooned leather jackets, it is now purely of nostalgic interest, its days as a cutting edge fashion centre long gone.

west side: Beak Street to Foubert's Place
His Clothes, No. 41

John Stephen opened his pioneering men's boutique, His Clothes, at 41 Carnaby Street in 1960, selling sharp Italian clothes to a young narcissistic crowd and introducing new concepts into marketing clothes, such as experimental window displays and goods on racks outside on the pavements. His customers included members of the new clothes-conscious groups such as the Small Faces, the Yardbirds and the Who. It was here that the latter's drummer, Keith Moon, would come with the eccentric performer Viv Stanshall to try out their trouser-testing gag, which involved Moon and Stanshall demanding the 'strongest pair of trousers in the shop', tearing them apart, to the horror of the store manager, and then being joined by a one-legged man who had been waiting outside, who would grab the trousers, announce that they were 'just the thing he was looking for' and order the confounded manager to 'Wrap them separately!'

Great Windmill Street
A windmill, built *c.* 1560, stood on what is now Ham Yard, opposite Archer Street, and was demolished at the end of the seventeenth century.

The Scene, No. 41, west side
The Scene, London's leading 1960s mod club, was previously Club 11, a jazz venue, where in the 1950s Ronnie Scott and Johnny Dankworth showcased Dixieland jazz of the 1920s, thereby launching the trad jazz scene of the period. It became the Scene in 1963 when it was taken over by Ronan O'Rahilly, who employed a dancer called Johnny Moke to showcase new moves – the Swim, Jerk, Mashed Potato, Pony, Watusi, Fly et al. – and hired as house DJ Guy Stevens who later produced the Clash's *London Calling*. The Scene's clientele dropped inordinate amounts of pills and after closing time would head to a café in Fleet Street and maybe to the south coast on their scooters, or catch the milk train from Waterloo. Many groups and budding musicians visited the club, including the Who in their High Numbers days, who immortalized the venue and its modish members, or 'tickets', in their first single 'I'm the Face', the Small Faces, Rod Stewart, and the Animals' Chas Chandler (later manager of Jimi Hendrix and Slade), who turned up during a visit to London from Newcastle and later recalled how 'there were no lights and no alcohol. When we saw it we couldn't believe it. On Tyneside people went to clubs to fight.' The building was demolished at the end of the sixties and a car park now occupies the site.
► The Marquee, Wardour Street, p. 201.

Red Lion, No. 20, east side
Karl Marx attended the communist debating club that met above the Red Lion pub in 1850, as did the Prussian government agent Wilhelm Stieber, who watched Marx under instructions from the Prussian Minister of the Interior, Ferdinand von Westphalen, Marx's brother-in-law. Stieber reported back to von Westphalen that the communists were plotting in code to kill Queen Victoria, and though von Westphalen in turn reported this to Lord Palmerston, the foreign secretary, the latter sat on the information. When the Prussians complained that the British authorities were not showing sufficient concern the home secretary explained that 'under our laws, mere discussion of regicide . . . does not constitute sufficient grounds for the arrest of the conspirators'. After the cell was wound up it moved to Cologne where it was rounded up by the Prussian police.
► Karl Marx's Soho addresses, p. 193 and p. 194; Anarchists in Fitzrovia, p. 143.

Newburgh Street
Vince (1950s), No. 5
Bill Green, a photographer who specialized in shots of muscle men, opened London's first men's *boutique* (as opposed to mere clothes shop) here in 1954, selling dandified clothes to homosexuals (according to the jazz performer and scene chronicler George Melly, it was the only shop where 'they measured your inside leg each time you bought a tie'), its celebrity clientele including the songwriter Lionel Bart, the actor John Gielgud and even the Spanish artist Pablo Picasso, who bought a pair of suede trousers. The store featured in the 1960 Wolf Mankowitz story *Expresso Bongo*, in which 'sweating teenagers [wear] Vince Man's Shop jeans with heavy rollnecks, close-fitting Charing Cross Road teddy trousers and velvet-collared coats bought on hire purchase', and its success paved the way for nearby Carnaby Street's growth

as a centre of British men's fashion in the 1960s.

▶ Carnaby Street, p. 189.

Regent Street

One of the most attractive streets in London, it was built by John Nash early in the nineteenth century for the Prince Regent (later George IV), who wanted to link his **Carlton House** mansion in St James's with Regent's Park and provide a boundary between the areas occupied by the 'Nobility and Gentry' (Mayfair) and the streets occupied by 'mechanics and the trading part of the community' (Soho). Regent Street's arrival caused much disruption to West End life and led to a considerable number of complaints from shopkeepers, residents and visitors. Nevertheless Nash's broad boulevard soon attracted the wealthy residents and the best shops, and the curving stretch between Oxford Circus and Piccadilly Circus, known as the Quadrant, was lavishly decorated with colonnaded terraces and buildings designed by many of the leading architects of the day, including Sir John Soane and Robert Smirke. (It was partly demolished in the 1840s as the colonnades had become overrun with prostitutes.) Today, Regent Street is still a major shopping area, one of the most popular in the capital, home to a number of the most famous names in retailing – Burberry, Aquascutum, Jaeger, Hamleys – its ornate architecture obscured by shop signs.

east side: Beak Street to Piccadilly Circus
Liberty's, at Great Marlborough Street
Arthur Lasenby Liberty opened a store here in 1875, selling silks and other goods from the Orient, and hired the painter James McNeill Whistler, to help him create what became known as *le style Liberty* – a blend of art nouveau, Arts and Crafts and art deco created by English craftsmen, which included printed cotton clothes and much of the Tudor-style furniture bought for the new villas springing up in London suburbs. Liberty also engaged William Morris to design prints and was himself hired by W. S.

Gilbert to create the Japanese-style sets for the first run of *The Mikado*. But the store was constantly prone to ridicule from detractors. Oscar Wilde described a dress designed by E. W. Godwin as 'looking like a badly made salad', while others poked fun at the shop being staffed not by assistants but by 'cicerones' who only spoke when approached and were expected to know the names of all the shop's customers, particularly that of Nicholas II, the last Tsar of Russia, who ordered new furnishings for the imperial palace from Liberty's in 1914 three years before his assassination.

Liberty's has remained a major store since, renowned for its fabrics, carpets and furniture, even if not for the innovation of its early days.

▶ Heal's, p. 148.

Café Royal, No. 68
London's best-known Parisian-style *fin de siècle* café was established by Daniel Thévenon, a French wine-merchant, as the Café-Restaurant Daniel Nichols at nearby 15 Glasshouse Street in 1865 and was extended on to the present site in 1870. Its lavish ornate decor, velvet seats and elaborate mirrors attracting the most flamboyant members of the Aesthetic Movement, such as Oscar Wilde, who lunched here at exactly one o'clock most days. In the middle decades of the twentieth century patrons included Edward, Prince of Wales (later Edward VIII), the Duke of York (later George VI), for whom waiters were instructed 'always plain food, no fuss', the poet John Betjeman and the painter Augustus John, on whose entrance younger artists would rise. An impoverished George Orwell's insistence on paying for a meal for himself and his friend, the much wealthier Richard Rees, editor of the literary magazine *Adelphi*, inspired the scene in the former's novel *Keep the Aspidistra Flying* in which Gordon Comstock embarrasses himself in the Café Imperial, a fictitious establishment based on the Café Royal. Charles Forte bought the Café Royal in 1954, and it continued to attract the crowds until the

seventies, by which time it had become unfashionable. Its reputation improved in the 1990s when Marco Pierre White took charge of the Grill Room. In the basement is the exclusive China White club, magnet for stars and celebrities.

▶ Gay Hussar restaurant, p. 198.

(ii) around Soho Square

Dean Street
One of three bustling streets running north–south through Soho around Soho Square, Dean Street was developed in 1680 and probably named after Henry Compton, Bishop of London and Dean of the Chapels Royal. Many of the early residents were French immigrants and by the eighteenth century the street was attracting craftsmen and artists. It is now best known for its restaurants, such as the Red Fort at No. 77 and Quo Vadis (No. 28).

west side: Shaftesbury Avenue to Oxford Street

Karl Marx's address (1850), No. 64
Karl Marx and family came to Soho in May 1850 to live at the now demolished No. 64 and were so badly in debt his wife, Jenny, went to Holland to beg money from her uncle, Lion Philips, one of the founders of the Philips electric company that now dominates the city of Eindhoven. Philips, worried about the effect socialist activity, of the kind that Marx advocated, was having on his business, refused her and when Jenny threatened that she and Karl would therefore have to emigrate to America he explained that such a move would be an excellent idea. Eventually Marx's financial problems were eased by his long-term collaborator, Friedrich Engels, who took a lucrative job in his father's Manchester textile firm and sent Marx money from the petty cash, cutting bank notes in two and sending them separately so that no would-be thief would prosper from opening an envelope. In June 1850 the *Spectator* printed a letter from a Charles Marx and Fredc. Engels of 64 Dean Street complaining about police spies, whom they had spotted watching their every move around Soho, but ruined their case by admitting they were revolutionaries on the run from Germany, their country of birth. Indeed the Prussian authorities had dispatched police spies throughout Europe's main capitals since the attempted assassination of the Prussian King, and the London agents were reporting back to Ferdinand von Westphalen, the Minister of the Interior . . . and half-brother of Marx's wife.

The Gargoyle / Gossip's, No. 69
The Gargoyle was a drinking club opened by the Hon. David Tennant and his fiancée, the actress Hermione Baddeley, in 1925. Edwin Lutyens had been hired as architect and no expense had been spared on the decor, with Henri Matisse as designer. Its membership register included the actors Noël Coward, Fred Astaire and Tallulah Bankhead, but the Second World War briefly put an end to the club's glamour days and some of the luxurious furnishings were sold – Matisse's Red Studio went to America when the Tate Gallery decided to turn it down. After the war the Gargoyle briefly reverted to being Soho's most prestigious nightspot, where swing bands played and men in white tuxedos, including the spies Guy Burgess and Donald Maclean, strutted on the dance floor. In 1978 Steve Strange and Rusty Egan ran a successful night playing records by David Bowie, Roxy Music and Kraftwerk, out of which grew the New Romantic movement of groups such as Culture Club, Depeche Mode and Spandau Ballet. The following year Don Ward opened the Comedy Store here, giving aspiring comics (one of whom was Alexei Sayle) the chance to prove they had the talent to perform live in front of a probably hostile crowd. In 1982 No. 69 began hosting the Batcave, a goth night, identified by its clientele of black-clad Dracula stylists, where according to the Cure's Robert Smith 'the people were really nice, but the music was awful'. It is now Gossip's nightclub.

east side: Oxford Street to Shaftesbury Avenue

No. 21

The Venetian ambassador's chapel, erected in 1746 as the first building on the site, later became Caldwell's Assembly Rooms, where in 1763 the seven-year-old Mozart played the harpsichord, accompanied by his four-year-old sister. It was rebuilt in the 1860s as St Anne's National School, converted into the West End Synagogue in 1944, and after that closed in the late 1990s became the Soho Theatre.

Leoni's Quo Vadis, Nos. 26–29

Peppino Leoni opened what is now one of Soho's best-known restaurants in 1926. Fourteen years later, when Italy joined the Second World War, he was interned as an enemy alien, later recalling how while walking to his cell he felt a 'sudden hatred for the police, for the British government which had issued the instructions for my internment, and for all forms of authority. I had starved for 33 years to establish my restaurant. I deeply resented the fact that after 33 years in England with no political or police blemish on my record I had been scooped up without proper consideration.' Leoni returned after the war, and built up the restaurant into one of the finest in the capital, but was later outraged again when a blue plaque was placed on the building commemorating the 1850s residency of Karl Marx (see below): 'My clientele is the very best . . . rich people . . . nobility and royalty, and Marx was the person who wanted to get rid of them all.' In the 1990s, after the founder had passed away, the restaurant was bought by superchef Marco Pierre White and the artist Damien Hirst.

▶ Gay Hussar restaurant, p. 198.

Karl Marx's address (1850–56), No. 28

Marx lived in extreme poverty with wife Jenny, maid Lenchen and a number of children, in what he called 'an old hovel', with no toilet or running water, on the top floor of No. 28 in the 1850s. Describing himself for the 1851 census as Charles Mark, Doctor (Philosophical Author), he signed letters 'A. Williams' in case the authorities opened his mail. Three of the Marxes' children died while they resided here, but one who survived was Eleanor, their last child, who was born here in 1855, and is known in her own right as a socialist campaigner and writer. Marx spent his time researching *Das Kapital* in the British Museum, and when in 1856 Jenny received an inheritance they moved to Kentish Town.

▶ Karl Marx's burial place, Highgate Cemetery, p. 334.

Caves de France, No. 39

A fiercely cliquey drinking club, 'the closest thing to Bohemia in Soho', according to mid-twentieth-century Soho chronicler Daniel Farson, the Caves de France attracted eccentrics such as the artist Francis Bacon, who used to drink here with the Scottish painters Robert MacBryde and Robert Colquhoun, the latter using their strong Scottish accents to full effect in intimidating tourists into buying them drinks.

Colony Club, No. 41

Soho's best-known drinking club was opened in 1948 by the incorrigible Muriel Belcher, a foul-mouthed harridan who attacked customers with her lashing tongue, gave all men feminine names, such as 'Miss Hitler', and who on meeting the novelist John Braine, author of *Room at the Top*, remarked out loud: 'There's plenty of room at her top.' Brian Howard, the social gadfly on whom Evelyn Waugh modelled Anthony Blanche in *Brideshead Revisited*, brought the artist Francis Bacon to the Colony in the 1950s, shortly after Bacon's father had thrown him out of the family home for wearing his mother's underwear, and Belcher was so impressed with Bacon she paid him £10 a week to bring in rich customers.

Others who patronized the club included the painters Lucian Freud and Frank Auerbach; the writer Daniel Farson, whose *Soho in the Fifties* is the definitive account of postwar life; the *Absolute Beginners* author Colin MacInnes, who liked sitting here on sunny days with the curtains drawn 'gossiping one's life away'; and the irascible homosexual Labour politician Tom Driberg, who would usually be accompanied by a leather-jacketed youth described as a 'constituent'.

When Belcher died in 1979 she was replaced by the even more bad-tempered Ian Board, who had been head barman, and when Board himself passed away in 1994 the more reasonable Michael Wojas took over. Nowadays the artist patrons include Damien Hirst, some of whose work is on permanent display around the room, the decor of which has barely changed since it first opened.

Groucho Club, No. 45

Soho's most celebrated media club, which takes its name from Groucho Marx's adage about not wanting to join anything that would have him as a member, was the brain-child of the publishers Carmen Callil and Liz Calder who wanted an alternative to the stuffy, male-only Pall Mall clubs. Soon after opening in May 1985 it became the favourite hangout of literary agents, authors (Salman Rushdie), artists (Damien Hirst) and the better-paid journalists (Julie Burchill) who, following the newspaper industry's move from Fleet Street to the Isle of Dogs, were unwilling to spend their evenings on a wind-swept Docklands quay. By the end of the 1990s the Groucho had a rival in Soho House and in 2001 there were ructions among members when it was revealed that Benjamin Fry, a member of the Sloane Square set and therefore *infra dig* in Soho circles, had launched a take-over bid, aiming to establish the Groucho as a worldwide brand with a branch in Los Angeles.

► El Vino's, p. 45.

The French House, No. 49

A popular haunt for writers and artists during the early decades of the twentieth century, this compact pub opened as the Wine House in 1910 and was run by a German, Schmidt, who was deported when the First World War broke out. He was replaced by the Frenchman Victor Berle-

mont, at the time the only foreign landlord in Britain, who would eject troublesome customers by announcing: 'I'm afraid one of us will have to leave, and it's not going to be me.' Berlemont changed the pub's name to the York Minster, and during the Second World War it became a meeting place for the French Resistance, Charles de Gaulle allegedly drawing up his Free French call-to-arms after lunch upstairs. After the war painters such as Lucian Freud and Francis Bacon became regulars, and in 1951 Berle-mont was succeeded by his son, Gaston, who, despite being born in Soho and serving in the RAF during the war, played up his Gallic background to the full by sporting a flamboyant moustache and engaging in much hand-kissing. Officially renamed the French House, it has maintained its popularity.

Golden Lion, No. 51

A gay pub since the 1920s, it was frequented in the 1970s by Dennis Nilsen, the mass murderer who killed at least seventeen men in the London suburbs around that time, and was where in November 1981 Nilsen picked up Paul Nobbs, one of the few intended victims he failed to murder.

Frith Street

With its well-known restaurants such as Jimmy's (No. 35), dell'Ugo (No. 56) and Alastair Little (No. 49), the continental-style café Bar Italia (No. 22) and Ronnie Scott's jazz club, Frith Street is central to Soho nightlife. Originally parkland, it was bought by Richard Frith in 1677 and later became home to the young Mozart (No. 20, 1764–5), the poet Samuel Taylor Coleridge (No. 55, 1810), the painter John Constable (No. 49, 1810–11) and the essayist William Hazlitt (No. 6, 1830). The television pioneer John Logie Baird transmitted the first recognizable TV pictures from his attic workshop at No. 22 in October 1925.

west side

Ronnie Scott's, No. 46

Britain's best-known jazz club, which was founded in 1959 by the saxophonist Ronnie

Scott, moved here from 39 Gerrard Street in December 1965 and introduced the then radical policy for Britain of providing jazz six nights a week. Despite the predictable decor of whitewashed walls and tables covered in gingham cloths, uninteresting food, slow bar service and off-hand attitude (those who called requesting a table were sometimes asked: 'Certainly, Sir, would you like it here or taken away?'), the club thrived, booking many of the biggest names in jazz, including Count Basie, Sarah Vaughan, Ella Fitzgerald, more left-field performers such as Rahsaan Roland Kirk and Ornette Coleman, and even novelty acts such as Cheech and Chong and Scaffold. The club also put on rock and was where the Who premièred *Tommy* to journalists in 1969 and Jimi Hendrix made his last public appearance, jamming with the jazz-rock band War a few days before he died in September 1970. The ensuing decade was mostly a successful time for the club, its pivotal role in the jazz fusion boom resulting from a Weather Report show in 1972, but things later declined and it looked as if the club would close, until Chris Blackwell, owner of Island Records, made a £25,000 donation, with the stipulation that Scott continued to run the club in exactly the same way. In the eighties a jazz revival saw the venue regain its fashionability. Since the death in 1996 of Scott, himself a fine sax player, who played the break on the Beatles' 'Lady Madonna', the club has been run by his partner, Pete King.

► Ronnie Scott's in Gerrard Street, p. 204; Louis Armstrong at the Palladium, p. 186.

east side: Soho Square to Shaftesbury Avenue

Hazlitt's / William Hazlitt's address (1830), No. 6
A charming anachronism of a hotel, one of few in the area, Hazlitt's dates from 1718 and takes its name from the brief residency of the waspish, left-wing, early-nineteenth-century essayist William Hazlitt, a supporter of the French Revolution (unlike many of his contemporaries who withdrew their allegiance once details of the Terror emerged). Hazlitt wrote his four-volume *Life of Napoleon* here in the 1820s and died in the small back room on the third floor on 18 September 1830, at the age of fifty-two, dictating on his deathbed a note to the magazine editor Francis Jeffrey which read: 'Dear Sir, I am dying. Can you send me £10 and so consummate your many kindnesses to me.' The essayist faded from fashion during the twentieth century, and when the writer Tom Paulin opened Hazlitt's *Life of Napoleon* in Oxford's Bodleian Library he discovered that the pages needed cutting, no one having opened the book in the sixty years it had been in stock.

As a hotel Hazlitt's offers a gentility that contrasts sharply with Soho's cosmopolitan vigour – its walls covered in old prints and cartoons and its rooms, with their antique furniture, named rather than numbered. Although it provides none of the usual hotel 'facilities', hundreds of restaurants and bars are within easy walking distance, or as Nigella Lawson once pointed out: 'It's quicker to get from your room in Hazlitt's to Ronnie Scott's or L'Escargot than to get from a Penthouse suite in the Hilton to its coffee shop.' Bill Bryson began the jaunt around England recounted in his bestselling travelogue *Notes from a Small Island* from Hazlitt's, which he chose 'because it's intentionally obscure'.

Mozart's address (1764–5), No. 20
The eight-year-old Mozart came to London with his father, Leopold, and sister in September 1764, played before George III at **Buckingham House** and began giving recitals at No. 20 after Leopold, acting as the young prodigy's manager, placed a notice in the *Public Advertiser* which read: 'Tickets may be had at 5s. each, of Mr Mozart, in Thrift [sic] Street, Soho; where such Ladies and Gentlemen . . . will find the Family at home every Day in the week from twelve to Two O'clock, and have an opportunity of putting his [the younger Mozart's] Talents to a more particular proof by giving him anything to play at sight, or any Music

without a Bass, which he will write upon the spot, without recurring to his harpsichord.' While he was living here Mozart composed 'God is Our Refuge', a sonata for piano, violin and flute dedicated to Queen Charlotte, and began work on music for the opera *Idomeneo*. The family left the property in July 1765.

John Logie Baird's address (1924–7), No. 22

Baird, the inventor of television, transmitted the world's first recognizable television pictures from his attic workshop at No. 22, above what is now Bar Italia, in October 1925, at a time when science accepted that the technology might be possible but had not yet seen the results. Self-taught, Baird had borrowed £200 to indulge in his experiments and once installed in Frith Street began improving upon his early, crude machines, developing a sophisticated model using a large rotating disc studded with a spiral of holes to achieve a scanning effect and selenium cells to convert light and shade to electrical impulses. Once Baird had succeeded in displaying stationary objects on screen, he began work on more ambitious plans, which would involve televising people, and on 30 October 1925, needing a model for his experiment, went downstairs to the Cross Pictures company and borrowed the office boy, William Taynton. Baird tried to screen Taynton, but the experiment was unsuccessful as the boy, scared by the intense light, had moved too far away from the equipment. To win Taynton's co-operation Baird handed him half a crown, and this time Taynton stayed in the right position. Baird, watching in the next room, saw the boy's head on screen in what was the first recognizable television picture of an individual – Taynton not only becoming the first person ever to appear on TV but also, after a fashion, the first paid performer.

Baird was not so successful with his next subject, the Australian baritone Peter Dawson, who had to stop singing as only the middle of his body was showing on screen. Nevertheless, forty members of the Royal Institution of Great Britain, clothed in full evening dress, were impressed when they visited the workshop on 26 January 1926 to see what Baird called 'noctovision'. Baird then moved operations, first to Motograph House, Upper St Martin's Lane, Covent Garden, and then to nearby Long Acre. Ten years later, when the BBC launched television, pictures were transmitted over alternate weeks for six months using two methods, Baird's (with 240 lines) and those of Russian émigré Isaac Shoenberg (with 405 lines), and it was Shoenberg's system that was adopted. Baird's models can now be seen in the Science Museum.
▶ Baird's television work in Long Acre, p. 115.

Bar Italia, No. 22

Opened in 1950 by the Polledri family, Bar Italia, its walls festooned with mirrors and pictures of boxers, has become the best known of Soho's many coffee bars, thanks to mentions in books (Will Self's *Grey Area*), films (*Absolute Beginners*) and rock records (Pulp's 'Bar Italia'). Much of the back wall is taken up with a huge TV screen which proves popular when football matches (especially those involving Italian players) are shown. When Italy lost the final of Euro 2000 the distraught owners closed early – the only time in the bar's history.

Moka (1950s), No. 29

Moka was the first fifties Soho café to feature its own gleaming espresso machine, taking advantage of the Italian Achille Gaggia's 1948 invention of a machine that pumped a jet of hot water through the coffee, supposedly producing a more satisfying drink. After the first Gaggia machine was installed at Moka's Frith Street briefly became popularly known as Froth Street. The premises are now occupied by a building society.

Greek Street

Named after the Greeks who settled here in the 1760s after escaping Turkish persecution, the street became a centre for craftsmanship in the eighteenth century when its most famous resident was briefly the Italian Lothario Casanova (a different kind of craftsman). Later residents included the hallucinatory writer Thomas de Quincey, best known for his autobiographical *Confessions of an English Opium-Eater* (1822), the first literary work of fiction to discuss drugs at some length, and the pottery manufacturer Josiah Wedgwood. Today, Greek Street is famous for the Coach and Horses pub at No. 29 and smart restaurants (the Gay Hussar, No. 2; L'Escargot, No. 48), as well as the Soho House media club (No. 40).

east side: Soho Square to Shaftesbury Avenue

House of St Barnabas-in-Soho, No. 1
One of the oldest surviving properties in Soho and retaining many original fittings, No. 1 was built in the 1740s for Richard Beckford, a West Indian planter who became MP for Bristol in 1754, and bought in 1862 by the House of Charity, founded sixteen years previously for 'deserving persons in distress', which received a £50 donation from Queen Victoria. Some of its first residents were women waiting to emigrate to Australia, while others were prostitutes 'rescued' from the West End streets by the Liberal politician William Gladstone. Now a women's hostel, it took its present name in 1945.

Gay Hussar, No. 2
A Hungarian restaurant named after the Magyar cavalrymen who would gallop up to restaurants demanding buckets of wine for their horses, the Gay Hussar was opened in 1953 by Victor Sassie, a Barrow-in-Furness native of Italian stock who had studied catering in Budapest and was therefore the closest thing London then had to a continental restaurateur. It soon began attracting the Bevanite left wing of the Labour Party – Tony Benn, Barbara Castle and Michael Foot – along with a number of Soviet diplomats whom Sassie was obliged to discourage for fear of the restaurant becoming known as a centre for intelligence gathering. Its

popularity in exalted left-wing circles survived throughout the 1960s, and it was here towards the end of the decade that Mick Jagger, Marianne Faithfull, journalist Paul Foot and Labour MP Tom Driberg met to discuss forming a new socialist party, Logos (Greek for word), a venture that never came to fruition. In 1987 Sassie sold the establishment to the Wheeler's fish restaurant company, and it is still popular with the country's best-known journalists, media figures and champagne socialists.

The Pillars of Hercules, No. 7
The pub that has stood here since 1733 was a favourite of Francis Thompson, the cricketer-poet, who in 1888 was supposedly rescued from the doorway, where he was lying in a drunken stupor, by Wilfred Meynell, editor of *Merry England*, who subsequently gave Thompson his first chance of being published. In the 1970s the pub was frequented by up-coming authors Martin Amis, Julian Barnes and Ian McEwan, and used as a home-from-home by those who worked for the literary magazine the *New Review*, then based at No. 11.

Establishment Club (1961–4), No. 18
In October 1961 Peter Cook opened the Establishment Club to showcase comedy and satire in what had been the Club Tropicana ('All-Girl Strip Revue – Dancing to 3-D Sound'), putting on performers such as himself, Dudley Moore and the American iconoclast Lenny Bruce, which led one tabloid newspaper to howl: 'Get this vile creature out of Britain!' When the club tried to book Bruce again in April 1963 Henry Brooke, the home secretary, banned him from entering the country.

Coach and Horses, No. 29
Soho's most famous pub, presided over by Norman Balon, the self-styled 'rudest landlord in London', it gained its reputation towards the end of the twentieth century as the home-from-home of the *Spectator* columnist and professional alcoholic Jeffrey Bernard, the archetypal pub bore, who could regularly be found perched on a favourite stool and who, according to

Daniel Farson, 'paid for his formidable intake of drinks by writing very funnily about the disastrous effect the drinks have on him'. Keith Waterhouse turned Bernard's life into a West End show, *Jeffrey Bernard Is Unwell*, the excuse often found on the page where his *Spectator* column should have been. The pub is also the setting for the fortnightly lunches hosted by the satirical magazine *Private Eye*, which is based in nearby Carlisle Street.

Old Compton Street

Soho's high street and the centre of London's gay scene, Old Compton Street was built in the 1670s as Compton Street, being named after Henry Compton, Bishop of London, who raised the money for the nearby church of St Anne on Wardour Street. In the 1950s it attracted coffee bars and clubs such as Act One Scene One ('Real French coffee where the film and theatrical celebrities gather'); Heaven and Hell (No. 55), where the basement was in total darkness (hell) and the ground floor bathed in light (heaven); and most famously of all the 2I's, birthplace of British rock 'n' roll (No. 59). Since the 1970s the street has been dominated by gay culture – there is a branch of the Manchester gay bar Manto's at No. 30, and other popular establishments include Compton's (No. 53) and the Admiral Duncan (No. 54) – and such is its popularity that it is packed with revellers until the early hours. As with other main Soho streets its restaurants are particularly well known and include Amalfi at Nos. 29–31, the Soho Brasserie (Nos. 23–25) and the much-loved Hungarian pastry emporium Patisserie Valerie at No. 44. Two well-known food outlets can be found here as well: the Algerian Coffee Stores, which opened in 1887 at No. 52; and Camisa's delicatessen at No. 61. At the end of the twentieth century Westminster councillors introduced pedestrianization and bollards that might have killed off the street's vibrancy, but the scheme was soon abandoned.

north side
Admiral Duncan, No. 54

Soho's leading gay pub, the scene of a horrendous nail bombing incident in 1999, was where in October 1953 the poet Dylan Thomas left the only copy of the original handwritten manuscript of *Under Milk Wood*, a few weeks before leaving Britain for good, launching a treasure hunt that was eventually won by a BBC producer, Douglas Cleverdon, who was spurred on by Thomas's promise that if he found the original he could keep it. Cleverdon later sold the manuscript for the then princely sum of £2,000. On 30 April 1999 David Copeland, a loner and Nazi sympathizer, hid a bomb packed with 500 nails in the bar as part of a one-man war against minority groups, nervously asked the barman directions to the nearest bank, and left the building. Fifteen minutes later the bomb exploded, killing three people and injuring scores of bystanders. Copeland also planted bombs in Brixton and Brick Lane that spring. The pub has since been refurbished but the presence of bouncers has spoiled the atmosphere.

► Copeland's Brick Lane bomb, p. 284; Copeland's Brixton bomb, p. 405.

south side: Charing Cross Road to Wardour Street
No. 19

Now the Boheme restaurant, the property was until recently Wheeler's fish restaurant where during 1950s' rationing sole and lobster were cooked in thirty-two different ways, but with no vegetables. An account in 'Bon Viveur in London' at the time described Wheeler's as a 'temple devoted to shell-fish . . . oysters in season are whipped open by Jack, once a wrestler, now a renowned oyster opener'. Its best-known patron then was the artist Francis Bacon, who would arrive around noon most days after completing his morning work in the studio, accompanied either by fellow artists or his latest favourite East End bruiser.

2I's (1950s), No. 59

Soho's best-known 1950s club, quoted by many as the birthplace of British rock 'n' roll, took its name from the first letter of the surname of its founders, the Irani brothers, and was run by two Australian wrestlers, Ray Hunter and Paul Lincoln (Doctor Death). At first there were few customers and the 2I's could barely compete with the more enterprising Heaven and Hell club next door at No. 57, but its fortunes improved in the summer of 1956 when Wally Whyton and his group began playing skiffle, a British revivalist take on American street folk and Southern blues played on crude home-made instruments.

Before long other skiffle groups, encouraged by the chart success of Lonnie Donegan's skiffle version of Huddie Leadbetter's 'Rock Island Line', began to play the 2I's, the most exciting of whom were the Vipers, whose Tommy Hicks, a merchant seaman, so impressed a watching A&R man from Decca Records that he signed him, rather than the band, and convinced him to change his name to Tommy Steele.

Hicks's success made the 2I's the most talked about music venue in Britain and it began to attract agents, managers and impresarios looking for the next star, as captured in the 1959 film *Expresso Bongo*, a superb exposé of the ruthless superficial world of the local showbiz scene. Thousands of young hopefuls came to the 2I's searching for success, among them the Worried Men, featuring Terry Nelhams (later Adam Faith); the Newcastle guitarist Brian Rankin (later Hank Marvin); and the Drifters, fronted by Harry Webb, an extraordinarily confident and charismatic singer who changed his name to the sleeker Cliff Richard and secured a recording contract with EMI, which led to an unmatched run of hit singles. The club failed to keep up with the changes in popular music and closed in 1970, after which it was converted into a restaurant.

Camisa, No. 61
Soho's best-known delicatessen opened in 1929 at No. 66 and shut ten years later at the outbreak of the Second World War, when the authorities rounded up Soho's Italians,

including the owners, Ennio and Isidor Camisa, taking them to Lingfield racecourse in Surrey, and then to Warth Mills in Bury, while the Foreign Office decided on their future. When a list of those to be deported to Canada on the luxury liner *Arandora Star* was read out, the Camisas' names were omitted and they discovered, to their disappointment, that they were to be imprisoned on the Isle of Man instead. A few days later the *Arandora Star* was sunk in the Atlantic by a German torpedo with the loss of 730 lives. After their internment, the Camisas returned to Soho to reopen their deli.

Soho Square
Laid out in 1681 on land that had been a military yard, Soho Square was originally King's Square (it was designed by a Gregory King) and became one of London's most desirable addresses after Charles II's bastard son, James Scott, the Duke of Monmouth, built a house here. Ironically, one of its first residents was Oliver Cromwell's daughter, Mary.

The square was popular with foreign ambassadors in the eighteenth century and is now home to various prestigious companies and organizations, including Paul McCartney's MPL Communications (at No. 1), the British Board of Film Classification (No. 3), 20th Century Fox (No. 31) and the publishers Bloomsbury (No. 38). The well-tended gardens contain Caius Gabriel Cibber's statue of Charles II and a rickety mock Tudor hut that originally housed a transformer for the Charing Cross Electric Light Company. Underneath are bomb shelters constructed to protect Soho people during the Second World War.
east side
Carlisle House / St Patrick, No. 21a
Soho's Roman Catholic church, the oldest place of worship in London dedicated to the patron saint of Ireland, stands on the site of **Carlisle House**. In 1760 the Viennese opera singer Theresa Cornelys began staging the Temple of Festivities here, masked balls that

soon became the leading events in the social calendar and were attended by, among others, the rake Casanova and Joseph Merlin, the French inventor who pioneered a form of roller-skates and was so drunk one night he crashed into mirrors at the end of the room. The house was demolished in 1791 and soon after a Catholic chapel opened in the extension, which had escaped demolition. The chapel was rebuilt in 1893 and is now St Patrick's church.

Wardour Street

Soho's spine, a narrow street running through the heart of the area from Oxford Street to Shaftesbury Avenue, was originally Colman Hedge Lane and took its current name from Sir Edward Wardour, a Treasury official who in 1633 obtained a licence from Charles I to draw water from a local spring for the benefit of householders. It was developed in the late seventeenth century and soon became a centre for furniture makers, antique dealers and music publishers. In the nineteenth century the publisher Leigh Hunt advised anyone wanting the 'richest books for ninepence' to come here. Later the term 'Wardour-street English' came to be used to describe pseudo-archaic fanciful words such as 'erstwhile', 'hither', 'howbeit', 'peradventure' and 'quoth', as used by writers of historical romances. After the Second World War the street began to attract the nightclubs, music venues, advertising agencies and film companies for which it is still best known.

Flamingo (1950s, 1960s), Nos. 33–37, west side

A 1960s mod venue which sold no alcohol (although a lot of the coke was laced with scotch), it gained public notoriety in 1963 when a club member collapsed outside and was later found to have seventy-six purple hearts (Drinamyl) in his stomach. Henry Brooke, the Conservative home secretary, made an incognito visit to Soho's nightclubs and later announced that anyone found with Purple Hearts would be fined £200 or face six months in jail. His warning had

little effect on those US soldiers who, as pop manager Simon Napier-Bell explained in his autobiography, came to the Flamingo 'every weekend and paid for their night out by selling Benzedrine tablets taken from their cockpit emergency kits'. In 1968, in a desperate bid to cash in on the new psychedelic scene, the club became the Pink Flamingo, a scuzzy dive decorated with stuffed pigeons (no stuffed flamingos could be found), which failed to draw in the punters and later became the Temple, catering for the new underground rock scene. In recent years it has been home to the popular WAG club.

east side: Oxford Street to Shaftesbury Avenue

Marquee II (1964–88), No. 90

For nearly thirty years the Marquee was London's major rock venue for breaking new bands, the Yardbirds, the Who, David Bowie, Pink Floyd, Led Zeppelin, Yes, Jethro Tull, the Police and the Sex Pistols all playing early gigs here, but there were also more unusual events. In 1966 New Yorker Steve Stollman began organizing the outré Spontaneous Underground on Sunday afternoons, featuring beat poets Johnny Byrne, Spike Hawkins and Pete Brown, film makers, magic artists and the then unknown Pink Floyd. Billed as the Pink Floyd Sound, as house band, they played versions of 'Louie Louie' and 'Roadrunner', with what Julian Palacios described as 'freak out explorations in the middle'. On Sunday afternoons around that time David Bowie would perform his three-hour 'Sunday Showboat', watched by around twenty people, in which he engaged in mime and first wore make-up.

When Jimi Hendrix played a gig, his only ever appearance at the Marquee, in 1967, just after he had starred at the Monterey festival, the queue stretched down Wardour Street and along Shaftesbury Avenue as far as Cambridge Circus. After the Sex Pistols supported Eddie and the Hot Rods on 12 February 1976 they trashed the main act's equipment and terrorized members of the audience, or as guitarist Steve Jones explained in an interview with the *New Musical Express*: 'We're not into music. We're into chaos.' The club declined in the 1980s although visiting American bands such as ZZ Top and Metallica were keen to pay homage. In 1988 the Marquee moved to Charing Cross Road and 90 Wardour Street was later redeveloped as loft apartments with the Mezzo restaurant downstairs.

▶ Marquee I, p. 139.

St Anne, Wardour Street at Old Compton Street

Only the tower remains of the seventeenth-century church built by William Talman – not Christopher Wren, as some claim – with money donated by an unknown benefactor. It was consecrated in 1686 when still unfinished and without a spire and bombed in the Second World War, after which a campaign led by the poet John Betjeman resulted in its restoration as a community centre. Those buried in the churchyard include the essayist William Hazlitt and the mystery novelist Dorothy L. Sayers.

(iii) Chinatown

Europe's biggest Chinatown, *Tong Yan Kai* – Chinese Street – a dynamic, bustling, endlessly fascinating enclave, was first settled by Chinese in the 1920s. But it was not until the Chinese residents of Lime-house and Poplar, whose streets were heavily bombed in the Second World War, moved to Soho that the area acquired a significant Chinese presence. In the 1960s they were joined by farm workers from Hong Kong, forced out by economic changes in the Eastern rice markets, and as the local Chinese community's first generation of children born in England grew up and moved to the suburbs Chinatown became a commercial, rather than a residential area. The most exciting time to visit Chinatown is during Chinese New Year, in February, when huge *papier mâché* lions dance in the streets to a cacophony of fire-crackers and devour cabbages hung from the upper floors on strings pinned with bank notes.

Coventry Street

Henry Coventry, Charles II's Secretary of State, gave his name to the street which, being near the major meeting places of Charing Cross, Leicester Square and Picca-dilly Circus, has long attracted some of London's most popular restaurants and places of entertainment.

north side: Piccadilly Circus to Wardour Street

Trocadero, west junction with Rupert Street
Opened in 1882 as a music hall, it was where some of the era's best-known songs, such as Charles Coborn's 'Two Lovely Black Eyes' and Albert Chevalier's 'Wot Cher! (Knocked 'em in the Old Kent Road)', attained popularity. In 1895 the premises became a restaurant, renowned for its magnificent frieze and marble decor, and was later taken over by Lyons, becoming a shopping centre in 1980. It was renovated in 1996 as an indoor entertainments complex.

Café De Paris, No. 3

> As to class, at the top there's the Café de Paris, booked solid with Dietrich, Coward, Bankhead and Steele – *Expresso Bongo*, Wolf Mankowitz (1958)

One of London's first nightclubs, the Café De Paris, opened in 1924, decked out with the most ostentatious decor – twin staircases curving down from the balcony based on the Palm Court of the *Lusitania* ocean liner, and a dance-floor modelled on the ballroom of the *Titanic* – and was where some of the greatest entertainers of the time, including Marlene Dietrich and Josephine Baker, performed. At the outset of the Second World War the singer Inge Anders premièred here a new novelty song that went: 'We're going to hang out our washing on the Siegfried Line', jokingly referring to the Germans' First World War western defensive line, which quickly became one of the most popular in the country. Harry Roy's Band, the club's regular act, contributed to the war effort with the song

'God Bless You, Mr Chamberlain [the prime minister], We're all mighty proud of you / You look swell holding your umbrella, All the world loves a wonderful feller . . .'

Another Café De Paris regular was the bandleader Ken 'Snakehips' Johnson, a native of British Guiana, who announced: 'I'm determined to make them like swing at the Café or die in the attempt.' He did both, for on 8 March 1941 as Johnson's band played to a packed crowd, a bomb fell on the club killing the band leader and thirty-three others, the explosion so intense that the musicians and dancers were instantaneously killed. Survivors included a Dutch officer, who had his injured leg washed with champagne, the only liquid at hand, and Betty Baldwin, daughter of the erstwhile Prime Minister, Stanley, who complained about looters arriving on the scene and making off with handbags and rings torn off the fingers of the dead. The venue soon reopened to entertain troops, with Tommy Trinder as main performer, and was where Princess Elizabeth (Elizabeth II) celebrated her twenty-third birthday in 1949. The Café De Paris was relaunched as a plush nightclub in the 1990s.

Gerrard Street

Chinatown's main street, home of restaurants, bun shops, tea houses, herbalists and acupuncturists, is named after Baron Gerard of Brandon, Suffolk, who commissioned Nicholas Barbon, the property developer responsible for large parts of central London, to develop the land in 1680. The street was soon known for its taverns and coffee houses, and colonized by the wealthy, being home to the Restoration poet John Dryden at the end of the seventeenth century and also to Samuel Johnson's Literary Club. By the twentieth century Gerrard Street had a down-at-heel look, full of prostitutes and seedy clubs, but it also had a smattering of foreign restaurants, and it was this as well as the peppercorn rents that attracted Chinese restaurant owners

bombed out of Limehouse in the 1940s. Pedestrianized in 1971, the street has since become one of the busiest in London and features a variety of Chinese furnishings, including Oriental gates, Chinese street signs, stone lions and red telephone boxes in the form of mini-pagodas.

south side: Newport Place to Wardour Street
Happening 44 (1950s), No. 44
London's first all-night 'raves' were held in the early 1950s in what was then the West End Jazz Club, George Melly describing the scene as being where 'an extreme sloppiness was *de rigueur*, both on stage and off. The duffel coat was a cult object, sandals with socks a popular if repulsive fad, beards common, and bits of battle dress, often dyed navy-blue, almost a uniform.' Following the success of the 2I's rock 'n' roll club on Old Compton Street, No. 44 was renamed the New 2I's and by the mid-1960s had become Happening 44, where the pioneering folk rock outfit Fairport Convention played some of their first gigs after placing adverts in *Melody Maker* which read: 'Friday: Fairport Convention stays home tonight'; Saturday: 'Fairport Convention stays home again, patiently awaiting bookings.' The building is now a Chinese restaurant.
➤ 2I's, p. 200.

No. 43
Home of John Dryden (poet laureate 1687–1700), it was the 43 Club in the 1920s, patronized by artists, writers, aristocrats and gangsters, such as the burglar Ruby Sparks and the Sabini brothers, who would make regular raids on the wealthier members' furs and wallets. It was also the centre of drug dealing in Soho, and the owner, Kate Meyrick, was convicted a number of times of running a disorderly house and allowing after-hours drinking. At one court hearing the actress Tallulah Bankhead, asked why she went to the club, explained: 'It's useful for early breakfasts', and when asked 'What time is breakfast, then?' replied '10 p.m.' When Meyrick died London's nightlife

crowd was shocked, not at her demise, but at the size of her estate – just £58.

Ronnie Scott's (1959–65), No. 39
Ronnie Scott's jazz club opened at No. 39 beneath a Chinese fan-tan gambling den on Friday 30 October 1959 and was at the time the only place in London to listen to modern jazz – Charlie Parker, Miles Davis, Thelonious Monk – as opposed to trad (traditional) jazz in the style of Louis Armstrong and Bix Beiderbecke. The club's fortunes rose in 1963 when the Musicians Union dropped its ban on American musicians, who had been allowed to play in Britain only if British players went out to the States in exchange. It moved to superior Soho premises at 47 Frith Street in Christmas 1965.

▶ Ronnie Scott's, Frith Street, p. 196.

Westminster | Whitehall

Westminster and Whitehall are home to the nation's great buildings of state – the Houses of Parliament, Westminster Abbey, Buckingham Palace, 10 Downing Street, the Treasury, Home Office and Foreign Office.

(i) St James's

Long associated with the aristocracy and the wealthy who wanted to be close to the royal palaces and now containing some of the most expensive real estate in the world, St James's was first laid out by Henry Jermyn, Earl of St Albans, in the 1660s. It was soon home to a number of coffee houses – opened to take advantage of the arrival of chocolate in England in 1652 – many of which were later transformed into the gentlemen's clubs such as the Athenaeum, Reform and Travellers that still provide St James's with its air of exclusivity. • St James's is the area south of Piccadilly, around Pall Mall and St James's Palace.

Carlton Gardens

An oddly numbered street of sumptuous stucco-clad villas designed by John Nash and built between 1830 and 1833.

west side

Privy Council office, No. 2

Lord Kitchener devised his First World War poster recruitment campaign with its famous slogan, 'Your Country Needs You', at 2 Carlton Gardens, where he would turn up for work every day at 9 a.m. in full field marshal's uniform. In March 1915 Kitchener moved to York House in St James's Palace and four years later the property was bought by the Duke of Devonshire who soon after let the house to Lord Northcliffe, owner of the *Daily Mail*, *Daily Mirror* and *The Times*. Northcliffe was by then suffering from a mixture of stomach pains and acute paranoia and he would phone *The Times*'s office to make bizarre pronouncements, such as telling the night editor, C. Robert Mackenzie, that he would henceforth be known as Crobert Mackenzie, to distinguish

him from other office Mackenzies, and to randomly sack members of staff ('to whom am I speaking?', 'this is the news editor, sir', 'correction, the ex-news editor'), unaware that his orders were being disregarded. Northcliffe slept alongside a loaded revolver, which he once cocked at his own dressing gown believing it to contain a body, and told aides that his stomach problems stemmed from having had his ice cream poisoned during the First World War by a German gang during a visit to the Dutch border. This was not as far-fetched as it seems, for Northcliffe, Director of Allied Propaganda during the First World War, may have been recognized by enemies during a visit to Holland and targeted. Northcliffe spent his last days in a hut on the roof, incarcerated there for his own safety, and died of general paralysis of the insane in August 1922. No. 2 is now used by the Privy Council, a body of ministers past and present of mostly symbolic importance. ► Fleet Street, p. 41.

No. 1

The official residence of the foreign secretary.

east side

No. 4

Home in the eighteenth century to various statesmen, including the foreign secretary Lord Palmerston (from 1847 to 1855); A. J. Balfour, who became prime minister early in the twentieth century (1874–97); and Lord Curzon, early-twentieth-century foreign secretary (1898). Charles de Gaulle set up an office for his Free French resistance movement here in the early 1940s, after the Nazis had overrun France and installed a puppet government in Vichy. When the British press announced that the French government had condemned de Gaulle to death and confiscated his property sympathizers left jewellery including wedding rings on the steps of 4 Carlton Gardens as gestures of support.

No. 3

MI6's ultra-secret Section Y, unknown even to most of the administration, was based here after the Second World War, one of its staff being George Blake who, while working at No. 3, provided the Soviets with details of the West's covert operations. After confessing to espionage activities in 1961 he was brought back here to be interrogated. Blake was eventually sentenced to forty-two years' imprisonment but escaped from Wormwood Scrubs in 1966 and fled to Moscow. No. 3 is still used for recruiting MI6 agents.

▶ MI6, p. 235.

Carlton House Terrace

A long terrace coated in dazzling stucco, designed by John Nash in the 1820s, it was named after **Carlton House**, the mansion that stood here and which George III gave to his son, the Prince Regent, on his twenty-first birthday in 1783 but which the latter vacated on taking the throne in 1820 as he felt it was not of sufficient grandeur for a king. Carlton House was demolished in 1829 – Nash used its columns for the National Gallery and the Ionic screen for the Buckingham Palace conservatories – and the lavish houses of Carlton House Terrace, built in its place, were immediately taken up by the wealthy. Some of the properties were later taken over by institutions such as the German Embassy (now in Belgrave Square), the Royal Society (at No. 6) and the Mall Galleries, home of the Federation of British Artists and the Royal Society of Portrait Painters (at No. 17).

south side: Trafalgar Square end to Buckingham Palace end

Nos. 12–14

Home during the Cold War of the Information Research Department, a secret branch of the Foreign Office set up to combat nationalism in the British Empire and monitor the Left in Britain. The department's agents gleaned their information from radio broadcasts, smuggled newspapers, refugees and asylum seekers, and assisted in overseas missions, such as the 1965 overthrow of the Indonesian leader President Sukarno. It was closed down in 1977 by Labour foreign secretary David Owen who claimed it had too many links with Labour's opponents.

No. 11

Home from 1855 to 1875 of the Liberal politician William Gladstone, who continued to live here when he became prime minister in 1868 and occasionally hosted Cabinet meetings within. It is now offices for the Foreign Press Association.

German Embassy (1849–1936), No. 9

When the German ambassador, Leopold von Hoesch, died of heart failure after collapsing in the bathroom here in April 1936 rumours spread that he had been assassinated by the Nazis, with whom he had not shared political sympathies. His replacement was a Hitler favourite, Joachim von Ribbentrop, and around the same time the building was redesigned by Albert Speer, Hitler's architect. After the Second World War the contents of the building were auctioned off, the theatre producer Jay Pomeroy paying £590 for von Ribbentrop's mahogany desk.

No. 6

Headquarters since 1967 of the Royal Society, the world's oldest scientific society in continuous existence (founded in 1660 in the City), whose original members included the architect Christopher Wren.

Turf Club, No. 5

The Turf Club was founded in 1868 at 85 Piccadilly as the Arlington. Its members are mostly drawn from the racehorse-owning class.

No. 2

The Tories founded the Carlton Club here to revive the party's fortunes following their disastrous performance at the 1832 general election. The club is now at 69 St James's Street and No. 2 is occupied by the Royal College of Pathologists.

No. 1

From 1905 to 1925 No. 1 Carlton House Terrace was home to Lord Curzon, Viceroy of India (1899–1905) and foreign secretary (1919–22), a stiff and pompous figure derided by opponents as 'God's butler', who once famously defended his image by explaining: 'If you are leader of the House of Lords, it is your *métier* to be a snob.' Curzon hosted many society dinners at No. 1 in the early years of the twentieth century and put much effort into the arrangements, including instructions in his invitations to Labour MPs, whom he felt obliged to invite, on how the member should address any aristocrat or royal likely to be present. When the Labour member's secretary, unversed in aristocratic protocol, responded, predictably, in everyday language, Curzon would send back a stiff warning about the correct etiquette beginning: 'In the first place your secretary should address me (if he must address me at all) as My Lord . . .'

Curzon's daughter, Cynthia, married Oswald Mosley, then a Tory MP, in 1920, and soon after gave birth, to the consternation of Margot Asquith, wife of the former Liberal prime minister Herbert, who told her: 'You look very pale. You must not have another child for a long time. Herbert always withdrew in time. Such a noble man.' At a dinner party here on 7 June 1921 the king, George V, and various royals and politicians were entertained by the music-hall singer George Robey, the so-called 'prime minister of mirth', who gave a splendid performance until he stopped suddenly during one number and ran from the stage in fright at having to sing the next line in his song, 'I feel just as good as a jolly old queen'.

Constitution Hill
Charles II took walks – constitutionals – along this tree-lined route, which now separates Green Park and the gardens of Buckingham Palace. Queen Victoria survived three assassination attempts here in the 1840s.

Green Park
Fifty acres of land to the north-west of St James's Palace, used in the Middle Ages as a burial ground for lepers (which may account for its surprisingly bleak appearance), were enclosed by Henry VIII and converted into a royal park, Upper St James's Park, by Charles II in 1688, being renamed Green Park in 1746. An explosion during a royal fireworks display in 1749 destroyed a number of buildings, while in 1814 festivities marking the Prince Regent's gala were abandoned when the Temple of Concord exploded. The park no longer contains any buildings.

Cleveland Row
Cleveland Row, which occupies a secluded position by Green Park, is one of the most exclusive streets in central London as, unlike every other street bar The Mall, it contains a working palace – St James's.
Green Park end to Pall Mall end
Bridgewater House
When the Earl of Ellesmere discovered in the 1830s that 𝔠𝔩𝔢𝔳𝔢𝔩𝔞𝔫𝔡 𝔥𝔬𝔲𝔰𝔢, the property that stood on the site, was to be demolished he hired Charles Barry to build the grandiose Bridgewater House (1846–54), which was home to the Greek shipping magnate John Latsis until his death in 2003.
Stornoway House, No. 13
A fourteen-bedroom mansion built for Tory prime minister Lord Granville in the 1790s, it was bought in 1924 by the *Daily Express* owner Lord Beaverbrook and was where in 1933 he entertained the jazz bandleader Duke Ellington at a post-concert party attended by the Prince of Wales (later Edward VIII) who, to Ellington's surprise, was sipping gin, a drink the latter had always regarded as 'rather low', but which from that time on he decided was 'rather grand'. The two men soon established a rapport and jammed together, Edward on drums calling the bandleader 'Sonny' and Ellington calling the Prince 'The Whale'. When Beaverbrook, who had been in Lloyd George's Cabinet during the First World War, was appointed to Winston Churchill's Second World War Cabinet in 1940 as Minister for Aircraft Production, he turned Stornoway House into his ministry office and here organized the national campaign to get the public to send in pots and pans so that the metal could be reconstituted to

make aeroplanes. When Stornoway House was deemed too small, the ministry moved to the ICI building on Millbank. The Granada group bought the property in 1996 and put it up for sale in 2001.

▶ *Daily Express*, p. 44.

St James's Palace

London's major royal residence before Buckingham Palace, and still home to a number of royals, including the Prince of Wales when he is in the capital, St James's Palace was built by Henry VIII between 1532 and 1536 on the site of a leper hospital and was where Mary Tudor signed the treaty surrendering Calais, the last portion of France administered by England, to the French. Elizabeth I resided here during the campaign against the Spanish Armada, receiving news of the battle through a chain of beacons lit from the Cornish coast.

Charles I spent the last night before his execution, 29 January 1649, at St James's Palace, so that he would not be able to hear the hammering of the carpenters building the scaffold for him on Whitehall, and on the following morning awoke at six, calling to his servant: 'I will get up. I have a great work to do this day. This is my second marriage day; I would be as trim today as may be for before tonight I hope to be espoused to my beloved Jesus.' After receiving the sacrament of Holy Communion, Charles, wearing extra shirts so that the crowd would not see him shivering from the cold and think it cowardice, made his way across the park to Banqueting House, Whitehall, where he was beheaded.

Charles's two sons who became kings, Charles II and James II, were both born here, as was James's son, the Catholic James Francis Edward Stuart, whose birth in 1688 alarmed Protestants. They spread a rumour that the queen would give birth to two sons, one of whom would be king of England, the other Pope of Rome. But was James Francis Edward Stuart royal at all? Some historians believe that James's 'son' was a foundling, smuggled into the royal chamber to replace the girl that had been born, in order to provide James with a male heir, for even though a crowd of around thirty people were amassed by the queen's bedside the midwives took the newly born child into an adjoining room before it could be shown to onlookers.

When George, Elector of Hanover, took the throne in 1714 as George I he brought with him to St James's a court of some 700 Germans, most of whom spoke no English. George's successor, George II, also lived here but found it hard to get to grips with English ways, remarking to the writer Horace Walpole: 'This is a strange country, Sir. The first morning after my arrival I looked out of my window and saw a park with walks and a canal, which I was told was mine. The next day, Lord Chetwynd, the park ranger, sent me a fine brace of carp out of my canal; and I was told I must give five guineas to Lord Chetwynd's servant for bringing me my own carp, out of my own canal, in my own park.' George III, George II's grandson, moved the court to Buckingham Palace in 1762, but St James's has remained the monarch's official residence, which is why foreign ambassadors and high commissioners are nominally sent to the Court of St James.

▶ Buckingham Palace, p. 212.

Chapel Royal

One of only two surviving parts of the original 1530s palace, the other being the gatehouse, the Chapel Royal was where Elizabeth I prayed while the Spanish Armada remained a threat and Charles I received Holy Communion before his execution in 1649. In 1997 the coffin of Diana, Princess of Wales, lay before the altar so that family and friends could pay their respects prior to the Princess's funeral in Westminster Abbey. Every 6 January the Royal Epiphany Gifts service, a 700-year-old ceremony, takes place here during which officials of the royal household offer up gold, frankincense and myrrh, the gold later being returned to the Bank of England and its value donated to charity.

Occupants of Buckingham Palace

George III (1760–1820) After buying the property in 1762 George made many alterations, adding four new libraries and renaming the building the Queen's House in honour of his consort, Charlotte of Mecklenburg-Strelitz. In his declining years George, obsessed with protocol, forbade members of the royal household to pass a room occupied by a member of the royal family if the door was open and refused to allow anyone to sit in the presence of the king or queen. Frequent visitors to Buckingham House included the composers Johann Christian Bach, who gave Queen Charlotte music lessons, and Dr Johnson, who came to use the libraries.

George IV (1820–30) When George sought permission to convert the Queen's House into a palace suitable for his outré tastes and gargantuan ego Parliament, aware of George's profligacy and ability to amass debts in inverse proportion to the suitability of their worth, turned him down. But George concocted a devious plan to proceed regardless, and Parliament fell for the duplicity, voting through an initial £252,690 for the work and later forwarding more money for a triumphal arch – Marble Arch – which was found to be too small to allow coaches to pass through and was later removed to the north-east corner of Hyde Park.

William IV (1830–37) When the Duke of Clarence took the throne in 1830 as William IV, work on what was then known as Pimlico Palace was still unfinished and the new King had to live nearby in Clarence House.

Victoria (1837–1901) Victoria was the first monarch to use Buckingham Palace as an official residence. She gave receptions and musical evenings that were attended by composers such as Felix Mendelssohn, who sat at the piano and played 'Rule Britannia' with his left hand and the Austrian national anthem simultaneously with his right hand. After Prince Albert, her consort, died in December 1861 the queen went into prolonged mourning and the palace became a mausoleum, the rooms and Albert's possessions left untouched, with a manservant filling a basin with water for the deceased prince every night.

Edward VII (1901–10) Loathing the palace as a child, Edward, on becoming king, went through the rooms smashing objects that he remembered from his youth, in particular busts of Victoria's one-time close confidant, John Brown, but he later brightened it up, rearranging all the clocks to run half an hour fast to satisfy his mania for punctuality, and installing modern plumbing, which was just as well given his penchant for breakfasts of eggs, bacon, haddock and chicken and dinners of pheasant stuffed with snipe and woodcock. On 21 June 1902 leading European royals arrived in London for the Coronation and travelled to Buckingham Palace for a feast to end all feasts. For Edward it nearly was an end feast, for he collapsed with acute appendicitis and was taken for surgery in an emergency theatre set up in one of the palace rooms. The coronation was cancelled and rearranged for 9 August, the uneaten food, including 2,500 quails, given to charities in Whitechapel.

George V (1910–36) After the lechery and debauchery of the Edwardian palace a sense of calmness and order was restored with the accession of George V, described by Antonia Fraser as the first great constitutional monarch. On hearing the band of Grenadiers play Richard Strauss's *Elektra* one day, George sent them a note stating that 'His Majesty does not know what the band has just played but it is never to be played again.' In 1931 the king met 'the little man with no proper clothes on' – India's spiritual leader Mahatma Gandhi – at the palace, warning him not to encourage terrorism 'in my empire' and being told in response that Gandhi would 'not be drawn into a political argument in Your Majesty's Palace, after receiving Your Majesty's hospitality'.

Edward VIII (1936) Edward assumed the throne on the death of his father, George V, in January 1936 and was soon embroiled in scandal for having a married mistress – Wallis Simpson. Even though she later divorced her husband, Edward abdicated the following December, without being crowned, and countless conspiracy theories have since emerged to boost claims that Edward did not simply step down to 'marry the woman he loved', but was forced to quit by government figures who felt he was incapable of ruling competently, might become a focus for Tory dissidents such as Winston Churchill, and was too sympathetic to the Nazis. Some people believe that Wallis Simpson was a Nazi honeytrap (it later became known that Hitler wanted to reinstate Edward to the throne if Germany won the war) or, more bizarrely, that Edward was a homosexual and Wallis Simpson a man in drag.

George VI (1936–52) Unprepared for the throne and, many felt, psychologically unsuitable on account of his shyness and stammer, Prince Albert assumed the throne as George VI on 11 December 1936, following the abdication of his brother, Edward VIII, overcoming his initial problems through devotion to duty, selflessness and capacity for hard work. When the palace was bombed for the first of nine occasions during the Second World War in 1940, wrecking the chapel where Princess Elizabeth had been christened and smashing a hundred windows, a policeman turned to Queen Elizabeth (the future Queen Mother) and remarked: 'A magnificent piece of bombing, Ma'am, if you'll pardon my saying so.'

Elizabeth II (1952–) Elizabeth II originally intended to live in nearby Clarence House and use the palace only for state business and ceremonial occasions, but the prime minister, Winston Churchill, insisted that the people would expect the Queen to work and live in Buckingham Palace. In the summer of 1982 labourer Michael Fagan made two uninvited entries into the grounds and buildings, scaling a drainpipe and wandering at will around the palace corridors during his first visit, on 7 June 1982, and entering Room 108, where he helped himself from a bottle of Californian Riesling and waited for the Duke of Edinburgh. When nobody came Fagan made his way out, just before a helicopter containing the US president Ronald Reagan landed on the palace lawn.

A month later, on 8 July, Fagan broke into the palace grounds at four in the morning, scaled a wall and entered the building through the Stamp Room. In the Throne Room he tried different seats for size, urinated in the corgis' food bowl, and accidentally made his way into a bedroom where his movements woke the Queen who shouted: 'What are you doing here? Get out! Get out!' The Queen pressed the alarm bell and phoned for the police, but having recovered from the shock, calmly chatted to Fagan, despite the fact that he was holding a broken glass ashtray with which he intended to slash his wrists. Five minutes later, when help had still not arrived, the Queen summoned a maid who, when she saw Fagan sitting on the edge of the bed, exclaimed: 'Bloody hell, Ma'am. What's he doing in here?' Eventually the police rescued the Queen and arrested Fagan, who told them he was Michael Hess, son of the Nazi war criminal, Rudolf.

In 1993 the Queen opened parts of the palace to the public to help pay for the restoration of Windsor Castle after the fire.

Jermyn Street

Along with Savile Row, Jermyn Street is a leading street in London for bespoke men's tailoring, with Turnbull and Asser at Nos. 70–72, Russell and Bromley shoes at No. 95, and Harvie and Hudson shirtmakers at No. 97. Named after Henry Jermyn, the seventeenth-century Earl of St Albans – the poet Andrew Marvell claimed he looked like a butcher with 'drayman's shoulders' – who was granted a sixty-year Crown lease on 45 acres of land in St James's Fields in 1660, the street was laid out in the 1680s, a relief at No. 73 showing Charles II, who was then on the throne, handing the deeds to Jermyn. Past residents of what is now an almost entirely commercial street include the scientist Isaac Newton, who lived at No. 87 from 1696 to 1710, and the poet Thomas Gray. At No.40 is the exclusive nightclub Tramps.

The Mall

A grand boulevard central to state ceremonies and usually filled with tourists on their way to Buckingham Palace, it was cut through St James's Park in 1660 by Charles II as a pitch for the game of paille-maille, with two long avenues of trees in the French style. By the eighteenth century it had become a haunt of prostitutes and robbers, but was cleaned up between 1904 and 1907. Underneath is a network of tunnels connecting Buckingham Palace with major government departments and buildings, including 10 Downing Street, which allows the prime minister to visit the monarch without venturing into the open air, but is never obviously used. Street level indication of the tunnel can be seen through an extractor fan outside the gentlemen's toilets in the Institute of Contemporary Arts.

north side: Buckingham Palace to Admiralty Arch

Buckingham Palace

Home of the British monarchy since 1762, the site was covered with fields by the Tyburn and Westbourne streams before the seventeenth century. James I planted a grove of black mulberry trees here sometime around 1605, hoping to produce silk, but although the trees blossomed in the marshy ground no silk was forthcoming and the grove became a place of outdoor entertainment and courting, which the diarist Samuel Pepys found to be 'a very silly place [full of] rascally, whoring, rouging sort of people'. In 1633 George Goring, Earl of Norwich, built himself a property, **Goring House**, by the garden, which later burned down and was rebuilt as Buckingham House for John Sheffield, who became the Duke of Buckingham in 1703, and in 1762 George III bought Buckingham House for £28,000, making it his London home. After considerable reconstruction it became Buckingham Palace, which all British monarchs since William IV have used as their London seat.

ICA (Institute of Contemporary Arts), opposite Horse Guards Road

The Institute of Contemporary Arts, which opened in Mayfair in 1947, moved in 1968 to larger premises on The Mall where there was room for galleries, a cinema, a lecture hall and a theatre. In the 1970s, under the directorship of Mike Laye, the ICA became the champion of the avant-garde and controversial. The Socialist Theatre season included a lunchtime production by the Gay Sweatshop, a play about the 1972 miners' strike, the Women Theatre Group's feminist *Work to Role* and Monstrous Regiment's *SCUM – Death, Destruction and Dirty Washing* about the women of the 1871 Paris Commune, and when in 1976 the governing council announced they were closing the theatre, citing financial problems, many saw the decision as politically loaded. The theatre reopened in January 1977 with a different programme. However, by that time the ICA's galleries were causing more consternation. In 1976 Mary Kelly's exhibition, 'Post Partum Document', featured dirty nappy liners as a statement against the stereotyping of the mother and child, causing predictable outrage in the press. That October COUM Transmissions' multimedia exhibition, 'Prostitution', organized by Genesis P-Orridge, featured bondage photos of his girlfriend, Cosey Fanni Tutti, taken from the porn magazine *Whitehouse* and framed like museum artefacts alongside four boxes on a wall called 'Tampax Romana', one of which featured an art deco clock whose workings had been replaced by used tampons. The *Sun* claimed that P-Orridge was 'prostituting Britain – and sending us the bill', while the Arts Council, outraged, scrapped the ICA's grant. In 1984 P-Orridge, returning in musical guise with his band Throbbing Gristle, destroyed part of the stage using electric saws, generators and torches, and some time later the German noise band, Einsturzende Neubaten, drilled through the stage and broke through into a section of the Underground. In recent years the ICA has failed to make the headlines with quite the same impact, although in 1992 it staged the first solo Damien Hirst exhibition.

Admiralty Arch

A triumphal arch incorporating offices and apartments for the Sea Lords, it was designed in 1911 by Aston Webb as part of a memorial to Queen Victoria and as a means of reaching Buckingham Palace from Trafalgar Square.

south side

St James's Park

London's first royal park was created in 1532 by Henry VIII and, though initially covering an area larger than the West End, was later reduced to 90 acres between Buckingham Palace and Whitehall. In 1660 Charles II opened the park to the public and, wishing to convert its lake into a 'Little Venice', imported specially built gondolas. Unfortunately the ships bringing the vessels to Britain ran into storms off the toe of Italy and the gondolas were so badly damaged that the scheme was abandoned. As late as the eighteenth century there were no powers of arrest within St James's Park, which had become a haven for robbers and a gang known as the Mohocks, who roamed the park brandishing swords. On 1 August 1814 a re-enactment of the 1798 Battle of the Nile

took place in St James's Park to celebrate the 100th anniversary of Hanoverian rule, but disaster occurred when the gas-lit pagoda caught fire, killing two men and injuring several others as well as the royal swans. The watching crowd, assuming that this was part of the organized spectacle, applauded wildly. After Victoria moved into Buckingham Palace in 1837 the lake was dredged and the park cleaned up to create what now ranks as the most attractive green setting in central London, all the more astonishing for its proximity to the West End and Whitehall.

► Regent's Park, p. 350.

Marlborough Road
Queen's Chapel, east side

When the future Charles I announced his intended marriage to the Spanish infanta in the 1620s Inigo Jones built a Catholic chapel at St James's, basing the structure on the Temple of Venus in Rome. The marriage never took place and work on the building ceased, recommencing in 1626 for the king's marriage to Henrietta Maria.

Pall Mall

A once elegant and prestigious street which takes its unusual name from the croquet-like game paille-maille (related to the Italian *pallo a maglio* – 'ball to mallet') that the aristocracy used to play in nearby St James's Park in the seventeenth century, it is home to several of St James's best-known gentlemen's clubs, including the Athenaeum, the Reform Club and the Travellers'. The street no longer enjoys its once enviable status, having been spoiled in recent decades by a one-way system.

● Pall Mall became the first London street to be lit by gas on 4 June 1807 after Friedrich Albrecht Winzer laid a pipe under the road outside **Carlton House**.

north side: St James's Street to Haymarket
Horatio Bottomley's address (1879–1912), No. 56a

One of the great swindlers of the early twentieth century, Horatio Bottomley, nicknamed Hot-air-io Bottomley, made his fortune publishing newspapers in Hackney, where he became MP, was worth £3 million by his late thirties, and during the First World War styled himself Britain's leading patriot, encouraging people to persecute anyone with a German-sounding name. He also promoted a Victory Bond Club whose brochure contained a biography of its publisher and the caption: 'Who is Mr Bottomley? He is the finest orator in the kingdom. He is the first lay lawyer in the land; He is our best recruiter; He is a fine sportsman; He is a great financier; He is a fearless politician. There are many people who think Mr Bottomley is the greatest man in Britain today', which raised some £900,000. When demobbed servicemen who had invested in the scheme tried to cash their bonds after the war they found that he had absconded with their money. Bottomley was arrested and sentenced to seven years' imprisonment. In prison, according to a popular story, spotted by an inmate one day working on mailbags and asked whether he was sewing, he replied: 'No, reaping.'

south side: Cockspur Street to St James's Street

All the properties except for No. 79 belong to the Crown.

The Athenaeum, No. 107

The leading intellectual club of St James's, the Athenaeum was founded in 1824 as The Society by John Croker, who first coined the term 'Conservative', and moved to Decimus Burton's Pall Mall building in 1830, when it took its present name. The novelist and Conservative politician Benjamin Disraeli wrote many of his novels at the Athenaeum, despite having once been blackballed, while the novelist Anthony Trollope promised to kill off Mrs Proudie after hearing two members at the club complain about the character during the serialization of *The Last Chronicle of Barset* in 1867.

Travellers' Club, No. 106

Founded in 1819 at 12 Waterloo Place through the wishes of the despised foreign secretary Lord Castlereagh as a reunion point for English gentlemen who had trav-

elled abroad, the club later moved here, to Charles Barry's *palazzo* building of 1829 to 1832, the first in that style in London. The initial requirement that members must have travelled at least 1,000 miles from London no longer applies.

Reform Club, Nos. 104–105

A radical club founded in 1836 by supporters of the 1832 Reform Bill, it is where Phileas Fogg takes on the bet that results in his travelling around the world in eighty days in the Jules Verne novel of the same name.

Carlton Club (1835–1940), No. 94

The Conservatives' main social and political club, which was formed at 2 Carlton House Terrace after the party's poor showing at the 1832 general election, moved here three years later. Despite the energy members expended in creating a strong party organization based around the three tenets of the long-serving Tory prime minister Lord Liverpool – defence of the Crown, Church and Constitution – the party was torn apart in 1846 when Tory PM Robert Peel repealed the Corn Laws, a move opposed by the majority of members. In the 1870s the Carlton was replaced as the most powerful bastion of Conservatism by the party's Central Office, and in 1886 the windows of the Pall Mall building were smashed by demonstrators following a march by the London United Workmen's Committee in demand of jobs. At a meeting in the Carlton in October 1922 the Tories withdrew their support for the Coalition government of the Liberal David Lloyd George, which led a group of Tory MPs to form the 1922 Committee, the major powerbase for backbench MPs since. The building was destroyed in the Second World War and the Carlton moved to St James's Street in the 1950s.

Royal Automobile Club, No. 89

The club, founded 'for the protection, encouragement and development of Automobilism' in 1897 at Whitehall Court, moved here, the site of the eighteenth-century **York House**, in 1911 and was where the spies Guy Burgess and Donald Maclean had lunch before defecting to the Soviet Union in June 1951. When it was revealed in the early 1990s that the roof of the new Jubilee Line tunnel lay only 16 ft below the bottom of the club's swimming pool, a member of the committee told the *Sunday Times* that 'the prospect of members diving into the pool and ending up in Neasden is not one I relish'. In 1999 RAC members received a windfall of £34,000 each after the club's motoring services section was sold for £437 million.

Schomberg House, Nos. 80–82

Built in 1698 for the 3rd Duke of Schomberg, the property was home to James Graham's late-eighteenth-century Temple of Health and Hymen, where women having trouble conceiving could engage with their partners in the 'Grand celestial bed', supported by forty pillars of glass, and under a mirror-lined dome 'obtain the desire of their lives'. The venture ended in farce and Graham was committed to a lunatic asylum in 1787. From 1859 to 1956 various departments of the War Office were based at Schomberg House and after the civil servants moved out the building was restored to resemble its original appearance.

Marlborough House

Now used by the Commonwealth Secretariat, Marlborough House was built between 1709 and 1711 for the Duchess of Marlborough. She completed the design herself after sacking the architect, Christopher Wren the Younger, son of the more famous architect of the same name, for allegedly cheating his contractors, and the building was extended by Sir William Chambers, architect of Somerset House, in the 1770s. The house remained in the Marlborough family until 1817, when the Crown bought it for Princess Charlotte, heir to the throne, and her husband, Prince Leopold of Saxe-Coburg-Saalfeld. From 1863 to 1903 it was home to Edward, Prince of Wales (later Edward VII), and was where the prince conducted his extensive socializing. It was at Marlborough House in December 1936 that

Prince Albert, hearing that his brother, Edward VIII, had abdicated the throne and that he, Albert, would now become king (George VI), cried on the shoulder of his mother, Queen Mary, for an hour. The house was badly damaged in the Second World War and was donated to the government in 1959.

St James's Place

Spencer House, No. 27

A Palladian mansion built by John Vardy between 1756 and 1766 for the 1st Earl Spencer, who assumed ownership after the intended owner, Henry Bromley (Lord Montfort), shot himself shortly after making his will on New Year's Day 1755. It was home to the Spencer family until 1895 when the building was let to various tenants, including Barney Barnato, the diamond merchant who had been brought up in poverty in the East End. When Barnato was obliged to appear in court one day and gave his address as 'Spencer House, St James's' the judge inquired: 'Are you the owner's major-domo?', to which Barnato replied, 'No, I'm my own bleedin' major-domo.' From 1926 to 1943 the house was used as the Ladies' Army and Navy Club, was later requisitioned by the government as administrative offices for nurses, and after the Second World War was taken over in turn by the auctioneers Christie's, the British Oxygen Company and the Economist Intelligence Unit think-tank. In 1980 Lord Rothschild redeveloped the property at a cost of £17 million and filled it with works of art, opening it to the public on Sundays.

St James's Square

The grand centrepiece of St James's was built from 1667 to 1677 as the 'Place Royale' by Henry Jermyn, Earl of St Albans, 'for the conveniency of the Nobility and Gentry who were to attend upon his Majestie's Person, and in Parliament', and it was later lined with some of the finest Georgian town houses in London, attracting leading politicians such as William Pitt the Elder and

William Gladstone. The square is no longer residential and is dominated by institutions and businesses.

north side

No. 12

Built by Thomas Cubitt in the 1830s and later home to Lord Byron's daughter, Ada, Countess of Lovelace, who worked with Charles Babbage on his nineteenth-century forerunner of the computer.

Chatham House, Nos. 9–10

A 1736 building which has been home to three prime ministers – William Pitt the Elder (Lord Chatham), the Earl of Derby and William Gladstone – and is now the headquarters of the Royal Institute of International Affairs, a think-tank founded in 1920 funded by the Rothschild family and various South African mining houses, which in the first few decades after the Second World War was a major influence on British foreign policy.

No. 8

It was used by the French ambassador in the eighteenth century and as a showroom by the Wedgwood firm from 1796 to 1830.

No. 7

Built by Edwin Lutyens in 1911 for the banker Gaspard Farrer, No. 7 was requisitioned by the government in 1943 for espionage activities and is now home of the Royal Fine Art Commission.

Former Libyan People's Bureau (1980s), No. 5

On 17 April 1984 a policewoman, Yvonne Fletcher, standing by the square's railings, was killed by shots fired from a sub-machine gun during a raid on the building, then the Libyan People's Bureau, carried out by dissidents opposed to the regime of Colonel Muammar Al-Gaddafi. British police and troops besieged the embassy for eleven days, the longest siege ever witnessed in London, but could not enter due to diplomatic immunity and the culprits were allowed to leave Britain on the day Fletcher was buried. Later, some sixty embassy officials were deported for refusing to co-operate with the police.

east side

No. 4

Nancy Astor was living in this 1728 property in 1919 when she became the first woman to take her seat in the House of Commons. From 1943 to 1945 No. 4 was used as a refectory for the Free French resistance movement, who were plotting to overthrow the Nazis from occupied France. The Naval and Military Club recently moved here after leaving its Piccadilly premises.

Norfolk House, No. 31

The original Norfolk House, the birthplace of the future George III, was rebuilt in 1938, and used during the Second World War as the headquarters of Anglo-American intelligence, being where General Eisenhower directed the Allied Expeditionary Forces for the D-Day landings in 1944.

west side

Winchester House, No. 21

Two of James II's mistresses – Arabella Churchill and Catherine Sedley – lived at No. 21 in the late seventeenth century and in 1829 the property was taken over by the Bishops of Winchester, being renamed Winchester House. In 1901 one of British intelligence's earliest organizations, the Mobilization and Military Intelligence Department, moved into the block, which was demolished after the Distillers Company bought it in 1934 and then rebuilt to resemble the adjacent Adam-designed house.

Adair House, No. 20

Designed from 1775 to 1789 by Robert Adam for Sir Watkin William Wynn, it was bought by the Distillers Company in 1935 when it was combined with No. 21.

No. 18

From 1815 to 1822 No. 18 was home to Lord Castlereagh, the late-eighteenth-century Tory politician involved in the subjugation of the 1798 Irish rebellion, which brought Ireland under British rule. In 1819 he was vilified by the poet Shelley in the lines: 'I met Murder on the way / He had a mask like Castlereagh / Very smooth he looked, yet grim / Seven bloodhounds followed him', in his poem 'The Mask of Anarchy', a diatribe against the Manchester Peterloo Massacre which was brought about, it was said, by Castlereagh's repressive policies. By 1822 Castlereagh was deemed insane and after telling colleagues 'I'm mad. I know I'm mad', he asked his doctor for the precise location of his jugular vein and deliberately cut an artery with a small knife, bleeding to death at his Kent country seat. When his coffin was borne on a gun carriage to Westminster Abbey it was booed in the street.

No. 16

Now occupied by the East India, Devonshire, Sports and Public Schools Club, No. 16 was where a bloodstained Major Henry Percy arrived from Europe on 21 June 1815, interrupting a ball to announce news of the British army's victory over the French at Waterloo three days previously. He later travelled on to Grosvenor Square, Mayfair, to inform the Cabinet who were dining at No. 44.

Lichfield House, No. 15

Built by Richard Frith in 1678–9, it was later occupied by the Duchess of Richmond, who sat for the model of Britannia used on coins.

London Library, No. 14

A private library with a vast stock, it was founded in 1841 by the writer Thomas Carlyle who, fed up with the protracted methods for borrowing books at the British Library and 'the man with the bassoon nose' who sat next to him, organized a group that included the philosopher John Stuart Mill to establish a library that would 'supply good books in all departments of knowledge'. Five hundred subscribers donated £6, setting annual fees at £2, and the library opened at 49 Pall Mall that year with 3,000 volumes, moving to St James's Square in 1845. The premises have been extended considerably since and the number of books has now surpassed one million.

St James's Street

The street, which is the main route between Piccadilly and Pall Mall, grew as St James's Palace expanded, early notable residents

including the architect Sir Christopher Wren, who is believed to have died here in 1723, and the poet Alexander Pope. In the eighteenth century St James's Street became home to many of London's most celebrated coffee houses – White's, the **Cocoa Tree** and the **St James's** – which later developed into the gentlemen's clubs for which the area is still renowned. Exclusive shops soon opened alongside the coffee houses, the most famous modern-day names including Lock, the hatters (at No. 6), and John Lobb, bootmakers to the Crown since 1911 (No. 9). In Plate 4 of William Hogarth's *The Rake's Progress* (1732–4) Tom Rakewell is thrown out of his sedan chair and arrested at the northern end of St James's Street, the gatehouse of St James's Palace clearly visible in the background.

west side: Pall Mall to Piccadilly

Carlton Club, No. 69

Britain's major Conservative club moved here after its Pall Mall headquarters was bombed in the Second World War. When Margaret Thatcher was elected leader of the Conservative Party in 1975 she was declared an 'honorary man' to keep up the tradition that every Tory leader automatically becomes a life member of the club.

Brooks's Club, No. 61

A gentlemen's club founded by William Almack on Pall Mall in 1764, it moved here in 1778 and was run by the wine merchant William Brooks, whom members buried under the club floor after he died so that creditors could be kept at bay. The original twenty-seven members were known as 'macaronis', dandies who specialized in wearing flamboyant clothes and enormous wigs. Brooks's later became a major gambling venue and a meeting place for Whigs.

MI5 headquarters (1940–45), Cassini House, Nos. 57–58

The security service MI5 moved into St James's Street during the Second World War and appointed Victor Rothschild, the millionaire scientist, peer, banker, jazz pianist and county cricketer, who had been involved in developing atomic weapons ahead of the Nazis, to head the unit organizing the dismantling of bombs entering Britain. Rothschild knew that the Nazis had inserted bombs into thermos flasks, or even lumps of coal, which would explode if slivers were removed, and at St James's Street he once made safe a device placed inside a crate of onions while giving staff a running commentary: '. . . I have taken the primer out . . . I can now see the detonator buried in the middle of the plastic [long silence] . . . I have taken the primer off. The other detonator is off. All over, all safe now.' For this deed Rothschild was awarded the George Cross and immediately entrusted with the task of ensuring that presents given to Churchill were safe for consumption, which meant that the prime minister's cigars were X-rayed for explosives and foods such as hams or bottles of brandy were tested for poison without it looking obvious that they had been examined. After the war the building was used as offices by the entertainments company MGM.

➤ MI5, p. 247.

east side: Piccadilly to Pall Mall

White's, Nos. 37–38
St James's oldest and most illustrious club was founded in 1693 by Francis White (an Italian whose real name was Francesco Bianco) as White's Chocolate House at No. 28 (now the location of Boodle's, see below), moving to various other nearby addresses before relocating here in 1755. Membership was hard to come by, and when the Tory prime minister William Pitt who was passing White's one day was asked by a colleague if he could propose him he replied: 'At the end of the year we shall be making some new viscounts and some new barons. Can you accept a viscountcy instead?' In 1811 the famous bow window was inserted into the façade, and it was by the window that the society dandy Beau Brummell held court with the Duke of Argyll and Sir Lumley Skeffington, in the nineteenth century.

Boodle's, No. 28
Now Boodle's, a favourite of MI6 officers, and the model for Blade's in the James Bond books, it was White's Chocolate House from 1693 to 1783, a club notorious for gambling, where members would wager sums on the most trifling of matters, such as which of two raindrops would reach the bottom of a window pane first, an event on which Lord Arlington gambled £3,000. The novelist Horace Walpole recalled in 1755 how a man who collapsed at the door was carried into the club while members bet on whether or not he was dead, complaining that efforts to revive him would affect the fairness of the wager. In 1783 the premises were taken over by Boodle's, becoming popular with country gentlemen betting on hazard, a game of chance, in which the players threw dice against a number between five and nine, and faro, a form of roulette.

MI9 headquarters (1940s), No. 5
MI9, the government's Second World War escape and evasion unit, was based in a room at this address, and here agents preparing to be sent into enemy territory were provided with a host of ingenious devices, such as compasses hidden in toothbrushes or combs and blades secreted in cricket bats, to be passed to prisoners of war through fake charities, Red Cross parcels being considered too risky. In charge of MI9 was Colonel Claude Dansey, whom the historian Hugh Trevor-Roper once described as an 'utter shit; corrupt, incompetent, but with a certain low cunning', who had run spy networks in Somaliland during the First World War, established the Americans' first secret service unit, and been in charge of MI6's activities in the 1930s, hiring businessmen expert in areas such as avionics or steel-manufacturing. During the Second World War Dansey was also in charge of passing German secrets to Soviet allies without letting the latter know that the British had cracked the Germans' Enigma code. He was depicted by Graham Greene, who had lived in the flat below in the late

1940s, as the spymaster, Colonel Daintry, in the 1978 novel *The Human Factor*.

Berry Brothers and Rudd, No. 3
Established in 1690 as a grocer's, Berry's has been one of London's best-known wine merchants for more than a hundred years and below the shop are extensive cellars which stretch for hundreds of yards under St James's Street and can house 18,000 bottles of wine. The shop also contains human weighing scales which have been used by Lord Byron, Napoleon III and the actress Vivien Leigh.

Stable Yard

Access to this road and Stable Yard Road is restricted for security reasons.

Warwick House
The only large private building in an area of court property and company headquarters, Warwick House was built in 1770 by Sir William Chambers, architect of Somerset House. In 1924 Warwick House passed to Esmond Harmsworth, the 2nd Lord Rothermere, proprietor of the *Daily Mail*, who closed it down during the Second World War at a time when many similar London mansions were being vacated by their wealthy owners. Ann, Esmond's wife, reopened Warwick House in 1946 and, hoping to become one of London's leading society hostesses, threw a number of lavish parties and invited a panel of guests to discuss the important issues of the day, a move that Evelyn Waugh described as an 'utter failure'.

Stable Yard Road

Lancaster House, west side
Built to the designs of Benjamin Wyatt in 1825 and used for government hospitality, meetings and conferences, Lancaster House was where Giuseppe Garibaldi, the Italian nationalist, was greeted by some 50,000 supporters when he came to London in 1864. The building was later sold to the soap magnate Sir William Lever (Lord Leverhulme) who gave it to the nation so that it could be used for government entertaining and as a home for the London

Museum. Queen Elizabeth II's coronation banquet was held here in 1953 and in the 1970s Lancaster House hosted the 1979 Rhodesian independence talks that resulted in the creation of Zimbabwe. Film crews regularly used Lancaster House until government ministers clashed with cameramen shooting Warren Beatty's *Reds* and banned filming.

Clarence House, east side
Home of the Queen Mother from 1953 to 2002, Clarence House was designed by John Nash in 1825 to 1828 for William, Duke of Clarence, younger brother of George IV, who on hearing here in 1830 that George had died and that he would now take the throne told a servant: 'I will now return to bed, as I have always wanted to sleep with a queen.' After his accession, William continued to live at Clarence House, as work on Buckingham Palace was still proceeding, and after his death the house passed to various members of the royal family, including his sister, Princess Augusta, and the Duchess of Kent (mother of Queen Victoria). The Red Cross was based here during the Second World War and the property later became home to Princess Elizabeth who on succeeding to the throne in 1952 moved to Buckingham Palace.
► St James's Palace, p. 209.

(ii) Buckingham Gate

An estate of well-constructed, handsome houses built to the south of St James's Park in the eighteenth century on land known as the Almonry – the land of the alms giver – where the most prestigious address was, and still is, Queen Anne's Gate. Though now mostly commercial, the area that remains exudes an effortless charm helped by the consistency and elegance of the architecture and the presence of the park.

Birdcage Walk

James I's aviary was situated at this end of St James's Park and, though the roadway was created as early as the 1660s, until 1928 only the Hereditary Grand Falconer was allowed to drive along it.

Broadway

No trace remains of pre-twentieth-century Broadway, an awkwardly shaped street in two parts, once home of the 𝕭𝖑𝖆𝖈𝖐 𝕳𝖔𝖗𝖘𝖊, the pub where Dick Turpin planned his highway raids. Since the mid twentieth century Broadway has been dominated by offices for major organizations such as MI6 (from 1924 to 1966), London Transport (since 1929), and Scotland Yard (since 1967). In the late 1930s a German spy positioned outside St James's Park station, disguised as a match-seller, spent a number of days surreptitiously photographing those who went in and out of MI6's headquarters opposite, sending the results on to the Gestapo, as various British officers discovered when they were interrogated during the Second World War. Absent from the agent's pictures, however, were shots of MI6's senior personnel, who entered and left the building via the director's residence at 21 Queen Anne's Gate, which was connected to the MI6 building by a passageway.

MI6 headquarters (1924–66), No. 54, north side

MI6, Britain's secret intelligence service, moved into what the biographer Tom Bower described as a building full of 'dust, decay and dark corridors' in 1924, at a time when the organization did not 'officially' exist (the sign on the door of No. 54 claimed the premises were the headquarters of the previous occupants, the Minimax Fire Extinguisher Company) and few of the staff even knew the identity of their director general, who was always known as 'C'. During the Second World War 'C' was Sir Stewart Menzies, rumoured to be one of Edward VII's illegitimate children and the model for 'M' in the James Bond books, who sat behind an antique desk that had allegedly belonged to Lord Nelson and kept a pigeon loft on the roof as he did not trust the radio. Once, when asked by George V to identify 'our man in Berlin', Menzies told the king: 'Sire, if my service has a man in Berlin, I may not divulge his identity', and when the king then asked him: 'What would you say if I said, "Give me the name of our man in Berlin or off with your head!"', Menzies retorted: 'Sire, were you to give such an order, and were that order carried out, my head would roll with my lips still sealed.'

► MI6, Westminster Bridge Road, Lambeth, p. 386.

Caxton Street

Named after Britain's first printer, William Caxton, who lived and worked close to here in the fifteenth century, the street is best known for Caxton Hall and also features a luxurious hotel, St Ermin's, which was requisitioned by the government at the outset of the Second World War to train agents in guerrilla warfare.

► William Caxton's printing shop, p. 222.

Caxton Hall, north side

And afterward she saw a very much larger and more enthusiastic gathering, a meeting of the advanced section of the women's movement in Caxton Hall, where the same note of vast changes in progress sounded – *Ann Veronica*, H. G. Wells (1909)

A public meeting place and registry office which opened as the Westminster City Hall in 1878, Caxton Hall was where in February 1907 the first Women's Parliament met during the early days of suffragette activity. Here in 1937 Sir Michael O'Dwyer, former lieutenant governor of the Punjab, was assassinated by Udham Singh, who had been his chauffeur and held him responsible for the 1919 Amritsar massacre, during which British officers ordered soldiers to open fire on the unarmed crowd, killing hundreds of people. Singh was hanged at Pentonville on 31 July 1940. Celebrities married at Caxton Hall include the nineteen-year-old Elizabeth Taylor (to Michael Wilding, twenty years her senior) on 19 February 1952, Peter

Sellers (to Britt Ekland), Diana Dors (twice), George Harrison and Ringo Starr.

Queen Anne's Gate

One of the best-preserved Georgian streets in London, Queen Anne's Gate was originally two streets – Queen Square (the eastern end, built 1704) and Park Street (to the west, built 1774) – divided by a wall, the old names still being visible on wall plates half-way along. Popular with the upper echelons of government as a residential area until around the time of the First World War, the street is now mostly offices, with the Home Office based in a postwar tower block at No. 50 and the National Trust at No. 36.

north side: Petty France to Old Queen Street
Home Office, No. 50
An unpopular block of consummate ugliness designed by Basil Spence and completed in 1976.

No. 42

No. 42 was home in the 1770s to Lord Simon Harcourt who acted as proxy groom in the marriage of the future George III and Princess Charlotte Mecklenburg-Strelitz and died in 1777 when he fell into a well trying to retrieve his dog. A later resident, in 1839–40, was Sir James Pennethorne, assistant to the architect John Nash, who worked on designing Battersea Park and Victoria Park.

National Trust headquarters, No. 36
Built for the Anglo-American Oil Company in 1909, No. 36 is now home to the National Trust, founded in 1895 as the National Trust for Places of Historic Interest or Natural Beauty by the housing reformer Octavia Hill, among others, to preserve traditional aspects of Britain.

No. 26

Outside the property, which the MP Shaun Woodward, who defected from the Tories to Labour in 1999, put up for sale in 2002 for £6.75 million, is a cone-shaped link snuffer, which was used for extinguishing visitors' torches in the days before electric lighting, and a fire insurance plaque indicating that the householder could be certain of receiving help in the event of fire in the days before free municipal cover.

No. 20

Henry John Temple, the future Lord Palmerston, nineteenth-century statesman and prime minister, was born here in 1784.

No. 16

The 1780s home of William Smith, known as the pioneer of English liberty, whose family fortune was made from slavery but who fought to abolish the system, it was used as the headquarters of British Army Intelligence from 1884 to 1901. Posing as a lepidopterist, Robert Baden-Powell, founder of the boy scouts, was sent from here as a spy to Dalmatia, where he was dismissed by locals as a harmless eccentric but sketched the fortresses of Cattara, disguising the guns and forts in pictures of butterfly wings. Admiral of the Fleet Lord John Fisher, who modernized the navy, lived here from 1904 to 1910.

south side: Old Queen Street to Broadway
Queen Anne statue
In the nineteenth century the statue had no title and when a group of local children, believing that it represented the sixteenth-century Catholic queen Mary Tudor, called upon the monarch to descend from her pedestal and found her unable or unwilling to do so, they threw stones at the figure and damaged it. The statue was repaired and the words 'Anna Regina' carved on the plinth, and legend has it that the queen descends from the pedestal every 1 August, the anniversary of her death, to walk up and down the street three times. Behind the queen's head are the faded street signs for Park Street and Queen Square, the names of the two former streets that now constitute Queen Anne's Gate. Below is a plaque bearing the initials C.H., standing for Christ's Hospital, the original landowners.

Tothill Street

A 'tot' is a sacred mound, and druids used the land as a meeting place in the sixth century. In 1482 William Caxton, who had set himself up as Britain's first printer in a shop by Westminster Abbey, rented a house at the south-eastern end of Tothill Street, printing books under the sign of the 'reed pale', a shield with a vertical red band, and there over the next fifteen years printed 18,000 pages, translated more than twenty works from Latin and French into English, and produced the first edition of *The Canterbury Tales*, a copy of which was sold at Christie's in 1998 for a world record £4.6 million. After Caxton died, his press was maintained by his assistant, Wynkyn de Worde, who moved to Fleet Street in 1500. Caxton's house was demolished in the nineteenth century.

(iii) Whitehall

The name Whitehall is synonymous with government – the Houses of Parliament, the Treasury, the Foreign Office, 10 Downing Street and a host of government departments and ministries are based on or near the road. Whitehall dates back to medieval times, when it linked the Palace of Westminster and the village of Charinge (now Charing Cross) and was known as King Street, its name coming from the colour of the sixteenth-century palace where Henry VIII lived, outside which Charles I was executed in 1649.

Axe Yard

Samuel Pepys, clerk to Sir George Downing, the secretary to the Treasury after whom Downing Street is named, moved to Axe Yard, which stood just to the south of Downing Street, in 1658 and on 1 January 1660 bought an octavo notebook, lined the margins in red ink, and made a New Year resolution to begin a diary. That day he wrote the first entry: 'Blessed be God, at the end of the last year, I was in very good health, without any sense of my old pain, but upon taking of cold. I lived in Axe Yard, having my wife and servant Jane, and no other in family than us three.' For the next ten years Pepys continued to write his diary, a frank and detailed description of his

personal life and the political world of the Restoration period, as he rose through the bureau-
cratic ranks to become Secretary to the Admiralty, and historians owe much of their knowledge of the period to it. Pepys, who never intended the diary to be published in his lifetime, compiled it in shorthand, obscuring the more controversial passages by using foreign languages and coded names. It was sent with his personal papers to Cambridge University after his death, and was not deciphered until 1822.

Bridge Street
north side: Parliament Street to Victoria Embankment
Westminster station
The station opened on the Metropolitan District Railway (now the District Line) in 1868 and was redesigned by Michael Hopkins at the end of the twentieth century to accommodate the Jubilee Line.

DISTRICT LINE

Following the success of the Metropolitan Line, London's first underground railway, which opened in 1863, some fifty-three proposals for new lines were sent to the authorities, including a plan to drain Regent's Canal and lay tracks on the bed and one for a 10-mile circular railway covered in glass around central London. But the proposal which gained most support was for an underground railway by the Thames – what became the District Line and was originally called the Metropolitan District Line. Building began in June 1865 and the first section, from South Kensington to Westminster, opened in Christmas 1868, soon being extended eastward under Victoria Embankment to Blackfriars. Later extensions to the District were built to Hammersmith (in 1874), Richmond (1877), Ealing Broadway (1879), Putney Bridge (1880) and Wimbledon (1889).

Richmond Queen Victoria and a royal party that included Nicholas, the heir to the

Russian throne, who was eventually murdered by the Bolsheviks during the Russian revolution, arrived at Richmond station en route to the White Lodge to see the newly born Prince (the future Edward VIII) in 1894.

Kew Gardens The British nuclear scientist Klaus Fuchs, who was later jailed for handing British atomic secrets to the Soviets, met his KGB contact at this station in the late 1940s. In 1993, fourteen years after he died, Fuchs was honoured by Russian nuclear scientists who admitted that they had built their first bomb based on material he provided.

Gunnersbury In 1954 a tornado hit west London, destroying the station.

Ealing Broadway The 1911 station building survives, but not for railway use.

Ealing Common The original station had an attached stationmaster's house.

Acton Town Misnamed, as it is about three quarters of a mile from Acton town centre.

Chiswick Park A superbly designed station, courtesy of Charles Holden, featuring a striking semicircular ticket hall, a rare cantilevered platform canopy, and an elegant side tower in brick containing the underground roundel.

Turnham Green Stands on the site of a failed assassination attempt on William III in 1696.

Stamford Brook Named after the now-culverted stream that rises on Wormwood Scrubs and pours into the Thames between Upper Mall and Lower Mall in Hammersmith.

Ravenscourt Park Originally Shaftesbury Road.

Hammersmith When the District Line first reached Hammersmith in 1874 it was competing directly with the Metropolitan Line whose station stood opposite.

Barons Court The station contains church-styled pews for waiting passengers.

West Kensington North End (Fulham) when opened in 1874.

Olympia Until 1986 the station opened only when exhibitions were being staged at the adjacent Olympia centre.

Wimbledon There are connections here to the new south London tram system that links Wimbledon and Croydon.

Wimbledon Park The station nearest the All-England Lawn Tennis Club, home of the annual Wimbledon tennis tournament.

Southfields Celebrated in a classic tube poster of 1933 promoting the tennis championships at Wimbledon.

East Putney Built on the site of a plague pit.

Putney Bridge The station, being in Fulham, should properly be named Fulham Bridge.

Parsons Green The parsonage after which the station was named in 1880 was demolished two years later.

Fulham Broadway Where Ian Dury could have been a ticket man instead of a writer with a growing reputation, according to the 1978 song 'What a Waste'.

West Brompton The station was upgraded as an interchange with the adjacent West London Railway at the end of the twentieth century.

Earl's Court The original 1871 station was a small wooden affair, the huge present-day structure dating from the early twentieth century.

High Street Kensington Opened in 1868 as Kensington (High Street).

Notting Hill Gate Named after the now-demolished nearby tollgate.

Bayswater Originally Queen's Road, the latter itself since changed to Queensway.

Paddington On 30 October 1883 a bomb planted by the Dynamiters, a revolutionary organization, in a third-class carriage of a train exploded as it passed through the station, injuring sixty-two people.

Edgware Road The northern terminus of a District Line spur that runs to Wimbledon.

Earl's Court Part of the station was used for manufacturing torpedoes during the Second World War.

Gloucester Road In the Arthur Conan

Doyle short story 'The Bruce-Partington Plans' Sherlock Holmes wanders along the tracks leading to the station while investigating a murder.

South Kensington The original western terminus of the District Line in 1868.

Sloane Square Two bombs fell on the station in 1940 while two trains were there and an unknown number of people were killed. The station remained closed for eleven years, reopening in time for the Festival of Britain in 1951 as the nearest station to Battersea Fun Fair.

Victoria The busiest station on the London underground.

St James's Park Rebuilt by the underground's greatest architect, Charles Holden, in the late 1920s, with a façade decorated with statues by Jacob Epstein and Henry Moore and an office block above, at 55 Broadway, that was then the tallest building in London.

Westminster When work on the station began in the 1860s engineers had to ensure that Westminster Abbey did not fall into the gully.

Embankment Plans for a surface building modelled on Wren's extensions to Hampton Court Palace were rejected by Parliament.

Temple The roof promenade was once a haunt of prostitutes.

Blackfriars Originally part of an important railway terminus known as St Paul's.

Mansion House Originally intended as a vast junction of all planned London underground lines, it was later downgraded and given an erroneous name, the building known as Mansion House being situated some distance to the east by Bank station.

Cannon Street Built in 1884 to complete the Circle Line.

Monument Built in 1884 as one of the last two stations on the Circle Line and the only station on the network connected to another (Bank) by escalator.

Tower Hill Named not after the Tower, London's oldest building, but the hill on which prisoners used to be executed.

Aldgate East The station has the longest platforms on the network.

Whitechapel One of the network's few interchanges with the East London Line.

Stepney Green Named after what is now the last remaining exclusive address in the area.

Mile End Crowds stampeded the station during an air raid in January 1918, leading to several deaths.

Bow Road The model for *EastEnders*' fictitious Walford East station.

Bromley-by-Bow A rare station located on a motorway (the A102M).

West Ham A station in an almost deserted locale, surrounded by branches of the River Lea and factories.

Plaistow Opened in 1902 on what was then the Whitechapel and Bow Railway.

Upton Park The stop for West Ham football club, as opposed to the more likely West Ham, a mile west.

East Ham An IRA bomb accidentally exploded on a tube train at East Ham station in 1976.

Barking The station is also the eastern terminus of the Hammersmith and City Line.

Upney The line's least used station.

Becontree Built in 1932 for the Becontree housing estate, then the largest in the world.

Dagenham Heathway The nearest tube station to the Dagenham Ford Motor Works.

Dagenham East Scene of a train collision in 1958.

Elm Park Opened 1935.

Hornchurch The surrounding area is named after the horns on the gable of St Andrew's church.

Upminster Bridge The bridge is over the Ingrebourne River.

Upminster The most easterly station on the network.

Portcullis House

An office block for MPs, it was designed by Michael Hopkins, who was responsible for the Mound Stand at Lord's, and built between 1992 and 2000 with a no-expense-spared £250 million budget (£1.2 million for each MP), £30 million of which was spent on bronze cladding, £500,000 on restaurant furniture, £200,000 on plants for the restaurant, £150,000 a year on renting fig trees from Florida and £75,000 for the reception desk. Yet no sooner had it been built than the glass panels slipped from their frames in the atrium, crashing to the ground, and MPs began complaining about the lack of storage space, water leaking from the fountains, and sprinklers and fire alarms going off without warning. Despite the phenomenal cost Hopkins's building, with its forest of tubular steel chimneys and dormer windows topped with stainless steel flaps, is also a visual disappointment for a site as important as Westminster Bridge.

Downing Street

One of the most famous streets in the world, Downing Street was built in 1682 by Sir George Downing, secretary to the Treasury and the second person to graduate from Harvard University. Of the original buildings only No. 10, the official home of the prime minister since 1732, and No. 11, used by the Chancellor of the Exchequer since 1828, survive. Until 1989 it was possible for members of the public to enter the road and directly deliver petitions to the prime minister, but this privilege was removed in the 1980s by Tory prime minister Margaret Thatcher, who had gates installed at the ends of the road. Underneath the street is a tunnel that connects No. 10 with Buckingham Palace and the huge underground citadel, Q-Whitehall, built at the height of the Cold War in the 1950s as a bunker where politicians, business leaders and royalty could take shelter in the event of a nuclear war.

No. 10, north side

The most famous house in Britain was built without foundations in 1581 and was first occupied by Sir Thomas Knyvet, the Justice of the Peace who arrested Guy Fawkes for trying to blow up the Houses of Parliament in 1605. It later passed to a Mr Chicken, who was evicted by George II so that the property could be used as an office and home for Robert Walpole, Chancellor of the Exchequer and First Lord of the Treasury, the first politician to be described as 'prime minister'. Until the twentieth century prime ministers preferred to live in their own (superior) properties, mostly around Whitehall, and even as recently as the 1970s Harold Wilson lived in Lord North Street, half a mile south, when PM. No. 10 appears to be a typical Georgian town house from the outside but is of an unexpected size inside, having been extended north and east to incorporate some 160 rooms.

Great George Street

A short street connecting Birdcage Walk with Parliament Square, Great George Street is dominated on the north side by the Treasury and on the south side by the buildings of the Royal Institution of Chartered Surveyors, which partly occupy No. 11, built in 1756, and the only original property. Demolished houses include **No. 13**, where in 1762 John Wilkes, London's most prominent eighteenth-century radical, set up a printing press to publish the satirical journal *The North Briton*, which led to his being charged with seditious libel and being sent to the Tower; **No. 24**, where in 1845 Joseph Bazalgette, the engineer who built London's sewer systems in the late nineteenth century, had his first practice; and **No. 29**, first home of the National Portrait Gallery in 1857.
➤ John Wilkes, p. 76; Joseph Bazalgette's clean-up of London, p. 255.

Occupants of No. 10

● When **Robert Walpole** became Chancellor of the Exchequer and First Lord of the Treasury in 1721 he was obliged to converse with the king, George I, who spoke no English, in schoolbook Latin and so effectively became first, or prime, minister. After George II assumed the throne in 1727 he offered Walpole the house as a gift, and when Walpole rejected the offer, George persuaded him to accept the property as his official residence as First Lord of the Treasury. On the morning Walpole moved in, 23 September 1735, the *London Daily Post* announced: 'Yesterday the Right Hon. Sir Robert Walpole, with his Lady and Family, removed from their House in St James's Square, to his new house, adjoining to the Treasury in St James's Park.'

● **Francis Dashwood**, Chancellor of the Exchequer and rogue, who once took a whip to penitents in Rome's Sistine Chapel, moved into No. 10 in 1762, but spent more time with his Dilettanti friends than on Exchequer business. Despite, or perhaps because of, his enthusiasm for drink he imposed a tax on cider and perry, which led to riots among fruit growers. He moved out of No. 10 when the 100-year-old house began to crumble.

● **Lord North**, the second Tory PM (1770–82), refused to consider himself prime minister, claiming the title was not in the British Constitution, and presided over a regime that lost control of the American colonies. Because of the length of time it then took to send information from America to Britain North and his ministers were unaware of how Britain's hold on the New World was slipping. For instance, although a group of Bostonians threw the East India Company's tea chests into Boston Harbour (the so-called 'Boston Tea Party') on 18 December 1773, the government did not find out until the following February, when it resolved that the Port of Boston be closed 'immediately', a directive which Boston learned about at the end of March.

● **William Pitt**, the youngest ever prime minister, who took office in 1783 when he was twenty-four, presided over imperial advances in India and Canada which went some way towards compensating for the earlier loss of the American colonies. In 1799 Pitt introduced the most unpopular policy in British history – income tax – set at 10 per cent, to pay for the war against Napoleon. Supposedly a temporary measure, it has never been rescinded.

● The **Duke of Wellington**, who presided over Britain's victory at the Battle of Waterloo in 1815, is the only military figure to have become prime minister, arriving at No. 10 in 1828 on his horse, Copenhagen. He organized races along No. 10's corridors in which women would sit on rugs and be pulled by male guests, but he spent little time here, preferring his own property, Apsley House, by Hyde Park Corner, lending No. 10 to Earl Bathurst, Lord President of the Council.

● **Earl Grey**, the first Whig to take the premiership for twenty-five years, led the campaign in the 1830s for political reform but failed to placate the mob, who surged round No. 10 chanting 'Liberty or death', to which one soldier replied: 'Liberty I don't know much about, but if you come any further I'll show you what death is.'

● When **Robert Peel** became PM in 1834 he chose to live in his house in Whitehall Gardens, something unbeknown to Daniel Macnaghten, a Glasgow woodcutter, who, having a grievance with Peel, waited for him outside No. 10 one night in 1843, and shot Edward Drummond, the prime minister's secretary when he emerged, mistakenly assuming Drummond was Peel. Drummond died five days later.

● **Benjamin Disraeli**, who lived at 2 Whitehall Gardens, had a brief spell at No. 10 in 1868 and moved back reluctantly in 1877 when he was seventy-two and suffering from ill health. As the rooms had been empty for decades the prime minister sought funds for expensive redecoration, which resulted in a barrage of correspondence being banded forth between the tenant and the Treasury. A year later the state began paying for the upkeep of No. 10, a cost previously borne by the occupant.

● **William Gladstone**, four times prime minister between 1868 and 1894, was never a favourite of Queen Victoria, who described the Liberal statesman as a 'half-mad firebrand who would soon ruin everything'. He lived at 11 Carlton House Terrace, using No. 10 as an office and home for his grand piano.

● **A. J. Balfour**, who moved into 10 Downing Street when appointed First Lord of the Treasury and Leader of the Commons in 1891, was the nephew of the prime minister, Lord Salisbury (Robert Gascoyne-Cecil), a state of affairs which led to the coining of the saying 'Bob's Your Uncle'. Balfour returned to No. 10 as prime minister in 1902 and was the first PM to use a car, a De Dion Voiturette, which he parked outside.

● During the premiership of **H. H. Asquith** (1908–16) suffragette activity increased, with women chaining themselves to the railings and Annie Kenney and Adelaide Knight being arrested for trying to enter No. 10.

● **David Lloyd George** became prime minister of a Coalition government in December 1916 during the First World War and moved into No. 10 his large household that included five children, his wife, Dame Margaret, and his mistress, Frances Stevenson. Barricades were erected at the Whitehall end of the street in December 1920, as Lloyd George, who had antagonized the Irish by sending the Black and Tans [special members of the Royal Irish Constabulary] on to the streets of Dublin, feared reprisals, as have recent prime ministers who have intervened in Irish affairs. Lloyd George's tenure came to an end when the Tories pulled out of the coalition on 19 October 1922.

● When **James Ramsay MacDonald** became the first Labour prime minister in 1924 London society was awash with concern over whether a socialist premier could be trusted to run 10 Downing Street with sufficient decorum and good taste. But doubts were swiftly dispelled when vans from the Co-op pulled up outside No. 10 bringing deliveries of food and MacDonald's daughter, Ishbel, furnished the property after a trawl through the winter sales. On 31 March 1930 John Logie Baird installed a television receiver at No. 10 and the following week Ramsay MacDonald told Baird in a letter: 'When I look at the transmissions I feel that the most wonderful miracle is being done under my eye . . . You have put something in my room which will never let me forget how strange is this world – and how unknown.'

● Huge crowds gathered in Downing Street for **Neville Chamberlain**'s return to No. 10 after his meeting in Germany with Adolf Hitler in September 1938. With his assistant, Lord Dunglass (later to become prime minister himself as Alec Douglas-Home), Chamberlain appeared on the balcony and announced: 'My good friends, this is the second time in our history that there has come back from Germany to Downing Street peace with honour.' A year later Britain was at war with Germany and after another six months Chamberlain was replaced by Winston Churchill.

● In running the Allies' war effort **Winston Churchill** made little use of No. 10 which was, after all, a prime bombing target, moving operations to the nearby underground Cabinet War Rooms (p. 230). When No. 10 was indeed bombed, pictures of the attack were withheld from the public lest they sapped morale and aided German propaganda.

● A visit from Charles de Gaulle, the French president, during the late 1950s premiership of the Conservative **Harold Macmillan** caused the staff of No. 10 much consternation. De Gaulle travelled everywhere with a quantity of blood, in case he needed a transfusion in the event of an assassination attempt, and when his entourage declared their intention to store the supply in the No. 10 fridge the cook, Mrs Bell, remonstrated vigorously that it was too full of haddock to accommodate the president's wishes.

● During the premiership of **Harold Wilson** the south London gangleader Charlie Richardson bugged No. 10 on orders of the South African intelligence agency, BOSS, for whom he was then working. Friends of Richardson who worked in the GPO went to Downing Street in overalls, opened the manhole that carried the cables from No. 10's telephones and doctored the wires. Wilson later claimed that he suspected that the phones were tapped around that time but was not sure whether the perpetrators were MI5 or MI6.

● **Edward Heath**, the first Tory prime minister to be educated at a state school, and the first to be elected by fellow MPs, moved his Steinway grand piano and harpsichord into No. 10 on taking office in 1970. When Parliament voted for Britain to join the European Community in 1971 Heath celebrated by playing Bach's *First Prelude* to friends.

● To **Margaret Thatcher**, the longest-serving prime minister for more than 150 years, some parts of No. 10 were like a 'down-at-heel Pall Mall club' and others like a 'furnished house to let'. Worried about terrorist attack and unwilling to accept protest, she installed security gates at the end of Downing Street, which helped protect her from the mob that gathered near Downing Street on several occasions.

● No. 10 was the target for a mortar attack by the IRA during a Cabinet meeting held by **John Major** (prime minister 1990–97) on 7 February 1991. It was launched from a white van parked in Whitehall, and when one mortar exploded in No. 10's garden Major's private secretary, Charles Powell, pulled the PM to the ground to take cover. Two more bombs landed on the grass near the Foreign Office, but when no further bombs fell over the next few minutes Major calmly announced: 'I think we'd better start again somewhere else.' The Cabinet then reconvened in an underground room in the block.

● **Tony Blair** and family occupy a flat in No. 11 more capacious than the official prime ministerial quarters at No. 10 but enter at night through the door of No. 10, making their way along the connecting corridor.

British Union of Fascists headquarters
(1932–3), No. 1, south side, corner with
Storey's Gate

Oswald Mosley, a former Labour Cabinet
minister as well as an ex-Conservative MP,
founded the British Union of Fascists (BUF)
here on 1 October 1932 with a manifesto,
The Greater Britain, that gave a detailed
critique of Marxist economics and advocated an Italian-style corporatist state with
industry run by representatives of both
owners and workers. Initially, the party
was 'neither pro- nor anti-Jewish', as the
historian Geoffrey Alderman explained in
Modern British Jewry, and it was only later
through the attitude of members such as
William Joyce, the party's Propaganda
Director (later to become the notorious
wartime traitor Lord Haw-Haw), that the
party began to move towards full-blown
anti-Semitism. The BUF moved to Chelsea
in 1933.
▶ The British Union of Fascists in Chelsea,
p. 411.

Great Scotland Yard

Scottish kings visiting London in the
sixteenth century stayed in an outpost of
Whitehall Palace that came to be known as
Great Scotland Yard and was used in the
seventeenth century as the official residence
of the Royal Architect, an incumbent of the
time being Inigo Jones who planned Covent
Garden. In the nineteenth century the name
Scotland Yard came to be used as a popular
term for the Metropolitan Police as their
first headquarters had an entrance for the
public on Great Scotland Yard. The force
now has its department of technology and
police stables on the north side of the street.
▶ Metropolitan Police first headquarters, Whitehall Place, p. 235.

Horse Guards Road
east side: The Mall to Great George Street
The Citadel, Horse Guards Road at The
Mall (south-east junction)

A vine-covered windowless concrete extension to the Admiralty, still used by the
Ministry of Defence, and secure enough to

withstand a 1,000 lb bomb, it was built in
1940 to house a wartime communications
system. Dubbed Lenin's tomb by critics, it
remains a grim reminder of the Second
World War, despite the extensive land-
scaping.

Horse Guards Parade, north of Downing
Street

London's largest meeting place, the name
commemorating the military practice of
parading flags and banners to familiarize
troops with the battle colours, it was where
Henry VIII held jousting tournaments and
where the Changing of the Guard and the
Trooping of the Colour take place.

King Charles Street

Running parallel to Downing Street to the
south, King Charles Street is lined with the
vast blocks of the Foreign Office on one side
and those of the Treasury on the other.
north side
Foreign and Commonwealth Office

The first foreign secretary, the eighteenth-
century Whig Charles James Fox, was
assisted by the playwright Richard Brinsley
Sheridan, MP for Stafford, with the work
administered from two houses on Cleveland
Row by St James's Park. The fledgling
Foreign Office moved in 1793 to Lord
Sheffield's house in Downing Street, a property that was not popular with politicians,
Sir Horace Rumbold describing it as 'dingy
and shabby to a degree, made up of dark
offices and labyrinthine passages'. Although
proposals to rebuild were shelved after a fire
destroyed the Houses of Parliament in 1834,
politicians reconsidered after a ceiling fell
down and narrowly missed Lord Malmes-
bury, the foreign secretary, in 1852. Four
years later the government held a competition to find an architect for a new Foreign
Office. The eventual choice was George
Gilbert Scott who, when told that his Gothic
design was inappropriate and that he should
build in an Italianate style, bought some
'costly books on Italian architecture and set
vigorously to work to rub up what though I
had once understood pretty intimately, I

had allowed to grow rusty by 20 years neglect', and created what he considered to be a 'national palace or drawing room for the nation' between 1861 and 1868.

south side: Whitehall to Horse Guards Road
The Treasury
The Treasury has been based in John Brydon and Henry Tanner's huge Portland Stone block, built between King Charles Street and Parliament Square between 1898 and 1917, since 1940. It was previously shunted around various Whitehall sites, including 𝕎hitehall ℙalace, Henry VIII's ℭockpit, near Horse Guards Parade, and William Kent's 1734 building between Horse Guards and Whitehall, which still stands and is now used as the Cabinet Office. Two tributaries of the Tyburn River run under the western end of the building.

Cabinet War Rooms, corner with Horse Guards Road
Winston Churchill based his Second World War operations room in an underground complex deep below the current Treasury building, made safe from enemy attack by a 3-foot layer of concrete, and consisting of twenty-one windowless rooms large enough to accommodate more than 500 people, a canteen, a hospital and a shooting range. In December 1940 Churchill moved in to command the British war campaign, vowing to 'sit here until either the Germans are driven back or they carry me out dead', and in April 1941 he set up the highly secret London Controlling Section. Based here, it co-ordinated an operation which involved laying false trails to trick the enemy, and was staffed by a dozen men including Sir Roger Wingate, who spoke various Arab and Indian dialects, the horror writer Dennis Wheatley, and John Harvey-Jones, who became chairman of ICI in the 1980s. In 1948, after the war, the rooms were converted into a museum, open at first only by special arrangement and from 1981 to the public. On view are Churchill's desk, the phone on which he and American president F. D. Roosevelt spoke, and the Map Room,

which has been restored to its wartime appearance with the appropriate coloured marker pins in place.
► Churchill on Hampstead Heath, p. 361.

Parliament Street
Created in 1750 when some of the slums around the Houses of Parliament were demolished, Parliament Street serves as the southern continuation of Whitehall, connecting Richmond Terrace Mews with Parliament Square.
No. 1, east side
Offices in the early years of the twentieth century for the honours broker Maundy Gregory, who charged £10,000 for those wishing to become a knight bachelor, £40,000 for a baronetcy, and £100,000 for a peerage. His main customer was the Liberal David Lloyd George (prime minister 1916–22), who told Lord Davidson: 'You and I know that the sale of honours is the cleanest way of raising money for a political party. The worst of it is that you cannot defend it in public.' In this way a host of pushy businessmen and newspaper magnates received titles from Lloyd George, who created forty-three baronetcies a year compared with his predecessor, Asquith's, twenty, and 354 knighthoods annually, compared with Asquith's 154.

Storey's Gate
A short street to the west of Parliament Square covering a branch of the River Tyburn, Storey's Gate is named after Edward Storey, keeper of Charles II's aviary in nearby St James's Park.
Central Hall
A huge Beaux Arts hall designed by Lanchester and Rikards and built in 1912 on the site of the Royal Aquarium for the Methodist Church after a campaign of 'one million guineas from one million Methodists'. It played host to the first general assembly of the United Nations from 10 January to 14 February 1946 and the first meeting of the Campaign for Nuclear Disarmament (on 17 February 1958), which

was attended by some 5,000 people, many more than expected, speakers including the mathematician and pacifist Bertrand Russell, the writer J. B. Priestley and the historian A. J. P. Taylor.

Whitehall

Synonymous with government, Whitehall takes its name from the sixteenth-century 𝔚𝔥𝔦𝔱𝔢𝔥𝔞𝔩𝔩 𝔓𝔞𝔩𝔞𝔠𝔢 and began as a lane linking Westminster Abbey and the Palace of Westminster with the village of Charing. It was popular with the aristocracy, who could live near the court in houses whose long gardens (if they were on the east side) led down to the river. Around the year 1240 some of the properties came into the possession of the Archbishop of York, after which the street became known as York Place, serving as home to several archbishops until the reign of Henry VIII. When the archbishops' residence was renamed Whitehall Palace, York Place became Whitehall, as Shakespeare noted in his play *Henry VIII* ('Sir, You must no more call it York-Place, that's past; / For, since the Cardinal fell, that title's lost: 'Tis now the King's and call'd Whitehall'). After fire destroyed 𝔚𝔥𝔦𝔱𝔢𝔥𝔞𝔩𝔩 𝔓𝔞𝔩𝔞𝔠𝔢 in 1698 the court moved away and government buildings gradually filled the area.

west side: Parliament Square to Charing Cross

Cenotaph, centre of road opposite Richmond Terrace Mews

Edwin Lutyens's 1920 war memorial takes its name from the Greek *kenos* (empty) and *taphos* (tomb) and was designed using the Greek device of *entasis*, whereby lines that look straight are imperceptibly curved. At 11 a.m. on the Sunday nearest 11 November every year (Remembrance Sunday) royalty, politicians and war veterans attend a ceremony at which the monarch places a wreath of red poppies by the cenotaph to remember the war dead.

Foreign and Commonwealth Office, south of Downing Street

See King Charles Street (p. 229).

Cabinet Office, Nos. 68–70, north of Downing Street

Built on the site of the royal cockpit by William Kent in 1733 to 1736 as offices for the Board of Trade, the building later became the Treasury and was enlarged by John Soane in 1827 and Charles Barry in 1844, both of whom, like Kent, incorporated remains of the Tudor and Jacobean buildings into their façades. The complex was severely damaged by bombs during the Second World War and restored for the use of the Privy Council (now at 2 Carlton Gardens) and the Cabinet Office.

Dover House / The Scotland Office

Dover House was built by James Paine for Sir Matthew Featherstonehaugh in 1758 on the site of the Whitehall Palace Tilt Yard ground, was later used as the French ambassador's home, and offered to the Liberal prime minister William Gladstone as an official residence in 1884. When he turned it down, fearing that he would be obliged to host more social events there, the building was handed to the Scottish Office, recently renamed the Scotland Office.

Horse Guards

William Kent designed the Palladian-style guard house between 1750 and 1758 on land where jousting had taken place in the sixteenth century, basing the windows on the St James's Park side on a Palladio drawing owned by Lord Burlington. Only members of the royal family are allowed to ride through the arch; in Plate 2 of the William Hogarth painting *The Election* the royal coach is being driven through by a headless driver. The Changing of the Guard takes place here twice a day.

Parliamentary Counsel / Paymaster-General's Office (1836–1986), No. 36

Built in the seventeenth century as an office for the Paymaster of the Forces, No. 36 was rebuilt from 1732 to 1733 by John Lane, Surveyor of the Horse Guards and Clerk of the Works at Chelsea Hospital, and became the Paymaster-General's office in 1836. It was bombed in the Second World War and restored over twenty years with some of the original panelling, doors and plasterwork, as well as a carved wooden chimneypiece salvaged and incorporated into a reconstruction of the Paymaster-General's original room on the ground floor. Since 1986 it has been used by the Parliamentary Counsel, a specialized team of lawyers who draft government bills for introduction into Parliament.

Admiralty House

Home of the First Lord of the Admiralty until 1960, and now general government offices, the property was built in 1786 to 1788 by Samuel Pepys Cockerell and occupants over the years have included Winston Churchill (from 1911 to 1915 and from 1939 to 1940) and Austen Chamberlain – the only twentieth-century Tory leader apart from William Hague not to become prime minister – in 1931. The Cabinet used Admiralty House, rather than 10 Downing Street, during a wave of terrorist attacks in the 1990s, a move that caused enormous problems on Black Wednesday, 16 September 1992, when ministers were forced to deal with the ERM financial crisis without their usual means of communication, resulting in the Chief Whip's being sent out to find a radio so they could keep up with events. By the beginning of the twenty-first century Admiralty House was being used as their residence by various MPs, including John Prescott, deputy prime minister, whose tenure was marred by blown fuses, exploding lights and faulty microwave ovens courtesy of the property's antiquated electrics.

Old Admiralty

Long-time home to the Navy, the building was designed by Thomas Ripley in the 1720s to replace a Christopher Wren block that had been constructed only twenty-five years previously and is shielded from Whitehall by Robert Adam's Admiralty Screen of 1759–61. Before the invention of the telegraph the Admiralty was equipped with rooftop semaphore, and when the British general Charles Cornwallis surrendered at Yorktown in 1781, a defeat which hastened the end of the American War of Independence, news was sent across the Atlantic, received in Britain at Falmouth, and dispatched to the Admiralty, from where it was sent by semaphore to Lord Germain's house on Pall Mall, Germain then speeding off to 10 Downing Street to inform the prime minister, Lord North. News of the Battle of Trafalgar was brought to the Admiralty on 6 November 1805, sixteen days after it ended, by a panting officer who burst in on William Marsden, first secretary to the Admiralty, and told him: 'Sir, we have gained a great victory but lost Lord Nelson.' The Admiralty Board continues to hold meetings in the boardroom within.

Charing Cross

Charing Cross, the point from which distances to London are measured, refers to the northern tip of the street that leads into Whitehall and takes its name from the Caen stone cross (the last of twelve) that Edward I erected in 1290 at the medieval hamlet of Charinge where the cortège carrying the corpse of his wife, Eleanor, stopped on its way to Westminster Abbey. The cross was pulled down during the Commonwealth, so that it could be used to make knife handles, and a replacement has stood in front of Charing Cross station since 1863. In the late seventeenth century Charing Cross was used as a place of capital punishment for those who had taken part in the execution of Charles I, Samuel Pepys writing in his diary: 'I went out to Charing Cross to see Major-General Harrison hanged, drawn and quartered . . . he looking as cheerfully as any man could do in that condition.' Dr Johnson, in answer to the point made by his biographer, James Boswell, that Fleet Street had 'a very animated appearance', famously responded that 'the full tide of human existence is at Charing Cross'.

east side: Charing Cross to Parliament Square

Silver Cross, No. 33

The pub stands on the site of the thirteenth-century 𝔥𝔢𝔯𝔪𝔦𝔱𝔞𝔤𝔢 𝔬𝔣 𝔖𝔱 𝔎𝔞𝔱𝔥𝔞𝔯𝔦𝔫𝔢 and was first licensed in 1674. The landlord is obliged to renew his licence annually with the Board of Green Cloth at Buckingham Palace.

Old War Office, between Whitehall Place and Horseguards Avenue

Built from 1899 to 1906 on the site of the 𝖂𝖍𝖎𝖙𝖊𝖍𝖆𝖑𝖑 𝕻𝖆𝖑𝖆𝖈𝖊 kitchen quarters, and now home to the Defence Intelligence Staff, a department of the Ministry of Defence, it was where MI5 was set up as MO5 (Military Operations Five) on 23 August 1909 to ease government concerns about German spies in England. Its one member of staff was Captain Vernon Kell, a Sandhurst graduate, who had fought in China during the Boxer Revolution and became its first director-general, secretary and sole spy-catcher – Agent 001. Underneath the Old War Office is the £42 million Pindar bunker, used by Margaret Thatcher as a military command centre during the Falklands War of 1982. It was modernized in 1993 at a cost of some £125 million and was where in 1998 the Queen and leading government figures, including the prime minister, Tony Blair, took part in a full-scale practice 'Doomsday' exercise to test the government's ability to defend itself from chemical and biological warfare. In 1999 foreign secretary Robin Cook, Foreign Office ministers and chiefs of defence staff met in Pindar to discuss military strategy during the Kosovo conflict.

➤ MI5, p. 247; the High Holborn bunker, p. 96.

𝖂𝖍𝖎𝖙𝖊𝖍𝖆𝖑𝖑 𝕻𝖆𝖑𝖆𝖈𝖊, between Horseguards Avenue and Derby Gate

England's major late medieval royal residence grew out of York Place, the Archbishop of York's London base, which after being seized by Henry VIII in 1529 was extended into a complex containing more than 2,000 rooms. The palace sprawled over a 23-acre site from the Thames to St James's Park, and included a cockpit, bowling green and four tennis courts, the site described by the historian Lord Macaulay as the 'most celebrated palace in which the sovereigns of England have ever dwelt'. After Henry died here on 28 January 1547 the building

became the royal seat of his devoutly Catholic daughter, Mary Tudor, and one day Protestants broke into her chamber and left the body of a dead dog, its head shaved like a priest's and a rope tied around its neck, as a protest against her decision to restore the Catholic Mass and make the (Protestant) Book of Common Prayer illegal.

Elizabeth I, Mary's successor, preferred Richmond Palace to Whitehall, and though Charles I drew up plans for further enlargement with a series of grand quadrangles to replace the muddle of alleyways and courtyards, few of his plans were carried out and in 1644 the Puritan-led Parliament carried out a purge of the palace, removing 'all Papists . . . all other ill-affected persons, and persons of scandalous conversation'. Five years later the king was beheaded outside Banqueting House, now the only surviving part of the palace.

Charles II moved into the palace following the restoration of the throne in 1660 and it soon became the setting for 'luxury, profaneness, gaming and dissolution', according to the diarist John Evelyn, who was even more shocked when James II opened a Catholic chapel in the palace in 1685, commenting: 'I could not believe I should ever have seen such things in the King of England's palace.' The entire palace, save for Banqueting House (see below), was destroyed in a 1698 fire caused by a Dutch washerwoman who lit a charcoal blaze to dry her clothes, and although Christopher Wren drew up plans for a replacement that would have rivalled Versailles in size and status the king, William III, decided that the smoke of central London and damp of the nearby Thames would have a debilitating effect on his chronic asthma and chose to live in Nottingham House, now Kensington Palace, resulting in 𝖂𝖍𝖎𝖙𝖊𝖍𝖆𝖑𝖑 𝕻𝖆𝖑𝖆𝖈𝖊 never being rebuilt.

➤ St James's Palace, p. 209; Buckingham Palace, p. 210.

Banqueting House, south junction of White-hall and Horseguards Avenue

The only surviving building from 𝔚𝔥𝔦𝔱𝔢𝔥𝔞𝔩𝔩 𝔓𝔞𝔩𝔞𝔠𝔢 and the setting for Charles I's execution, Banqueting House was originally part of three banqueting halls constructed in the sixteenth century of wooden poles and canvas, decorated with ivy, fruit and flowers. It was rebuilt in 1619 by Inigo Jones who used mathematical proportions – Banqueting House is a double cube and there are no superfluous sections – in constructing the first building in London erected in the Italian Renaissance Palladian style, the ceiling painted by Peter Paul Rubens. Because the building glorified the institution of monarchy, Oliver Cromwell chose it as the execution site for Charles I, who went to the scaffold outside the hall on 30 January 1649, his last words (to Dr Juxon, the Bishop of London) being: 'I go from a corruptible to an incorruptible Crown, where no disturbance can be. Remember,' after which his head was lifted up to the crowd (which included the sixteen-year-old Samuel Pepys) by the executioner with the cry: 'Behold, the head of a traitor.'

To avenge the death of his father, Charles II chose Banqueting House as the venue for celebrating the restoration of the monarchy in 1660. But following the 1698 fire that destroyed the rest of 𝔚𝔥𝔦𝔱𝔢𝔥𝔞𝔩𝔩 𝔓𝔞𝔩𝔞𝔠𝔢 Banqueting House's status declined and it came to be used for minor ceremonial events, as the Museum of the Royal United Services Institution from 1892 to 1964, and now contains an art exhibition hall. In the entrance is a seating plan for the coronation of Edward VIII, which was meant to take place here in 1937 but never occurred. Every 30 January, the anniversary of Charles's execution, a wreath is laid outside.

Ministry of Defence

The Ministry of Defence, an amalgamation of the Admiralty, War Office, Air Ministry and Ministry of Aviation, occupies E. Vincent Harris's bleak white 1957-built fortress, beneath which are extensive medieval cellars that were once part of 𝔚𝔥𝔦𝔱𝔢𝔥𝔞𝔩𝔩 𝔓𝔞𝔩𝔞𝔠𝔢. It has been the setting for a number of demonstrations against government military policy over the years. On 18 February 1961, the day on which the first US submarines arrived at Holy Loch, Scotland, 6,000 people, led by the 89-year-old mathematician and pacifist Bertrand Russell, marched on the ministry to stage a sit-down protest outside the building. As Russell gingerly approached the MoD's main entrance, ready to bang on the door and hand over a petition, an official voluntarily opened the door and came out carrying a roll of Sellotape to help him secure the document to the entrance.

Gwydyr House / Wales Office

Built as a private house in 1772 and leased to the Reform Club in 1838, it was home to the Charity Commissioners for England and Wales from 1842 to 1972, after which it became the Welsh Office, unnecessarily renamed the Wales Office at the end of the twentieth century.

Whitehall Court

An immense luxury apartment block (now the Royal Horseguards Thistle Hotel), designed by Archer and Green in the French Renaissance style, lines the south side of Whitehall Court, its skyline, seen from St James's Park, the most striking in London. It was built in 1884 as Whitehall Court, a speculative development by Jonathan Carr, who was also involved with the building of Bedford Park in Chiswick but later went broke, taking down with him many small investors. He fled his Whitehall Court apartment for Argentina, from where he was extradited in 1895. Early residents included the novelist H. G. Wells and the playwright George Bernard Shaw, who never realized that the building's commissionaires were Special Branch officers recruited to guard MI6, which occupied part of the building from 1911 to 1923.

MI6 headquarters (1911–23), No. 2, east side

MI6 left cramped offices in unfashionable Vauxhall Bridge Road near Victoria station in 1911 and moved into the top floor of 2 Whitehall Court, a maze of oddly shaped rooms, narrow staircases, small alcoves and false corridors which the organization's director-general, Mansfield Smith-Cumming, using a complicated system of pulleys and levers, would rearrange for his own amusement and to perplex new recruits. A memorable figure who wore a monocle and indulged in chemical experiments in his office, Smith-Cumming was obliged to use an alias and he was not at liberty to tell anyone where he was, what he was doing, or receive mail, visitors or telephone calls, which probably explains why a typical diary entry for the time reads: 'Went to the office and remained all day, but saw no one, nor was there anything to do.' Smith-Cumming left for France when the First World War broke out in 1914 and driving through the countryside with his son crashed his Rolls-Royce. Unable to reach the boy, as his shattered leg was trapped in the wreckage, he shook himself free by amputating his own leg with a penknife, but by the time he reached his son the boy was dead. After the war Smith-Cumming would strike matches on his new wooden leg to light his pipe, or stab it with a penknife to test the nerve of potential recruits. MI6 moved to Broadway, St James's Park, in the 1920s.
► MI6, St James's Park, p. 220.

Whitehall Place
Scotland Yard's first headquarters, Nos. 3–8, north side
The Metropolitan Police was formed in September 1829 – a time when London was at the mercy of criminal gangs, particularly in Alsatia (between Fleet Street and the river), Covent Garden, Saffron Hill (where Dickens set Fagin's Den in *Oliver Twist*), St Katharine's Dock and Limehouse – and

moved into government offices at 4 Whitehall Place, at the back of which was a police station that was entered from Great Scotland Yard, the name soon being used for the force itself. In the 1890s the Metropolitan Police moved to New Scotland Yard, a grand Norman Shaw-designed block at the junction of Victoria Embankment and Bridge Street, and is now based on Broadway near St James's Park tube station. At the outset of the Second World War the government's Auxiliary Units, which secretly trained groups of civilians to defend Britain against a possible German invasion, were based there. The buildings are now offices.

(iv) around the Houses of Parliament

The Houses of Parliament and Westminster Abbey are built on the ancient Thorney Island, a small marshy patch of land surrounded by the Thames and two branches of the River Tyburn, where, according to legend, St Peter rewarded the ferryman who rowed him across the water to consecrate a chapel by promising him a bountiful catch of fishes. After Edward the Confessor moved his palace to the same site in the 1040s and built an abbey dedicated to St Peter (what is now Westminster Abbey), the locality began to attract a sizeable population, its number later including Geoffrey Chaucer, author of *The Canterbury Tales*, who was Clerk of the King's Works at the Palace of Westminster from 1389 to 1391, and the printer William Caxton, who moved into a house by the abbey in 1476 and there the following November produced the first book to be printed in Britain, *The Dictes or Sayengis of the Philosophers*. The area's residential nature petered out in the nineteenth century, when the houses were cleared away to create the Westminster of today, where the great buildings of state stand in an uncluttered setting.

Dean's Yard

A quiet square with the character of a genteel village green, despite its proximity to Westminster Abbey and the Houses of Parliament, it was known as The Elms in the Middle Ages, when it was dominated by monastic buildings attached to the abbey. It is now enclosed by educational and religious buildings such as Westminster School and Church House, the headquarters of the Church of England, where Parliament assembled during the Second World War and the War Crimes Commission and fledgeling United Nations met in 1945. On the east side is an archway leading to Little Dean's Yard, a square within a square and an even more secluded world than that of Dean's Yard, where various Westminster Abbey outbuildings can be found, and where the sound of the choir rehearsing in the abbey can often be heard.

Great College Street

The 'Great College' is Westminster School, which backs on to the early-eighteenth-century street that marks the southern boundary of the ancient Thorney Isle, the marshland between the river Thames and Tyburn on which Westminster Abbey was built. The street is now home to various political lobbyists.

Great Smith Street

A branch of the River Tyburn runs under the street on which London's first public library was built in 1857, a site now occupied by Church House, headquarters of the Church of England.

Little Dean's Yard

A well-secreted courtyard within the shadow of Westminster Abbey, entrance to which can only be gained from Dean's Yard (see above).

Westminster School, south side
One of London's most prestigious schools, founded *c.* 1340 according to the decree of Pope Alexander III, who urged all monasteries (in this case Westminster Abbey) to support a school. It was originally a

charitable organization, providing free education for sons of local tradesmen and became independent of the abbey in 1868. Its buildings, severely damaged by a 1941 bomb, have since been restored. Ancient school customs include tossing the pancake on Shrove Tuesday, during which the boys fight for possession and the winner is awarded a guinea, and the right of the pupils to be the first to proclaim the sovereign on entry into the abbey. Famous alumni include the Elizabethan playwright Ben Jonson, the architect Christopher Wren, the Labour politician Tony Benn and the musical impresario Andrew Lloyd Webber.

► Charterhouse, p. 77.

Old Palace Yard

The roadway south of Westminster Hall takes its name from a yard in Canute's eleventh-century Palace of Westminster and was where the *Canterbury Tales* author, Geoffrey Chaucer, lived when he was Clerk of the King's Works in the fourteenth century. Much of the Gunpowder Plot to blow up Parliament was hatched at the Old Palace Yard house of Thomas Percy, cousin of the Earl of Northumberland, which stood where the southern section of the Parliament buildings can now be found. In January 1606, after the plot was uncovered, Guy Fawkes and his fellow conspirators were hanged in Old Palace Yard, the executioner cutting out the heart of each of the seven men, lifting it up before the crowd, and exclaiming: 'Here is the heart of a traitor.' Sir Walter Ralegh was executed on the same site in October 1618, and as his head was placed on the executioner's block he remarked: 'What matter how the head lie, so long the heart be right.' The Yard and its houses burned down during the 1834 fire that destroyed the medieval Houses of Parliament.

Jewel Tower, west side
The Jewel Tower, the only substantial survival of the medieval Palace of Westminster apart from Westminster Hall, and

now a museum on the history of Parliament, was built in 1365–6 as a store for Edward III's royal valuables by Henry de Yevele, 'deviser of the king's works of masonry', who used ninety-eight boatloads of Kentish ragstone transported along the rivers Medway and Thames from Maidstone. From 1621 to 1864 the Jewel Tower housed the records for the House of Lords and from 1869 to 1938 it was home to the Weights and Measures office. The Tyburn River runs through the moat that surrounds the building during heavy rain.

Parliament Square

The centre of Westminster, framed by the Treasury, the Houses of Parliament, St Margaret's church and Middlesex Guildhall, Parliament Square is a relatively new creation, constructed by Charles Barry in 1868 to replace much slum property, which became London's first modern traffic roundabout in 1926. The lawn was enclosed in the 1960s when the authorities realized that the impact of a driver crashing on to the grass might open up the cavity leading to the tube line below, and at the end of the twentieth century millennium celebrations were banned from the square because of similar structural concerns.

Middlesex Guildhall, west side
The former Middlesex County Council headquarters, now used by the Crown Court service, it was built from 1906 to 1913 in a Gothic revival style with art nouveau touches by J. S. Gibson and Partners. It stands on a site previously occupied by a medieval sanctuary and Tothill Fields Prison, whose seventeenth-century doorway is set into the west wall. During the First World War courts martial of those accused of passing information to the enemy were held here.

The Treasury, north side
See p. 230.

New Palace Yard, east side
The open space between Westminster tube station and the Palace of Westminster was named New Palace Yard when it was created

in 1099 as part of the newly built Westminster Hall, in contrast with Old Palace Yard (see above), which dates back to the early eleventh century, and was where crowds would gather on coronation day, when the fountains would flow with wine. But it was also a place of punishment, where Perkin Warbeck, the Flemish pretender to the English throne who led a putsch against Henry VII, was placed in the stocks in 1498. Lord North, the late-eighteenth-century prime minister, was nearly killed when the mob attacked his coach in New Palace Yard to show its support for the radical John Wilkes.

► John Wilkes, p. 76.

St Margaret, south side
Dwarfed by the adjacent Westminster Abbey, St Margaret, where the pioneering printer William Caxton (died *c.* 1491) and the explorer-statesman Walter Ralegh (1618) are buried, was built between 1485 and 1523 'for the great honour and peace of the monks as of the parishioners', according to the fifteenth-century *Liber Niger Quaternus*. For several centuries it hosted a festival on the third week after Easter during which young men would bring girls they had taken captive, who would be released only if they made donations to the church; the girls swapping places with the men the following day.

On Easter Day 1555 William Flower, a Protestant fundamentalist, attacked the priest as he was administering the sacrament and was arrested and imprisoned in the Gatehouse before having his hand cut off and being burned alive in the churchyard, following which the church's clergy celebrated by holding a feast at which a sirloin of beef, half a veal, four green geese, three capons, a dozen pigeons and a dozen rabbits were consumed. Since 1614 St Margaret has been the official church of the House of Commons and during the 1649–60 Commonwealth was raided by Puritans, who removed all the statues and 'scandalous' pictures in the windows (i.e. the stained glass) and denounced the

Houses of Parliament / Palace of Westminster glossary

Big Ben One of the best-known sights in the world, Big Ben is the 14-ton bell in the clock tower on Bridge Street, rather than the clock itself, which was cast in Stockton-on-Tees in 1856 and installed by the rotund Sir Benjamin Hall, Commissioner of Works. The bell was originally to be called St Stephen's, but the newspapers renamed it Big Ben, in honour of Hall and the 18-stone boxer Benjamin Caunt, landlord of the Coach and Horses pub in Covent Garden. The original bell cracked in October 1857 and a new one cast in Whitechapel was found to have cracks too. In August 1976 metal fatigue caused another disaster when the bell came loose and crashed against the clock room wall, breaking the main frame. When Parliament is sitting after dark a light shines at the top of the Big Ben clock tower.

House of Commons chamber There was no clear separation between Commoners and Lords until around 1377 and in its early days the House of Commons had no permanent base, meeting in a variety of rooms, including the Abbey's Chapter House and the Abbey Refectory. Its first settled home, from 1547 to 1834, was St Stephen's Chapel, in the Palace of Westminster, where members would bow to the altar as they arrived; hence the tradition of members' bowing to the Speaker's chair. A new Commons chamber built after the 1834 fire was destroyed during the Second World War and rebuilt.

House of Lords chamber Ever since a chamber for the Lords was built into Charles Barry's mid-nineteenth-century Houses of Parliament the Upper House has faced regular reform. Life peers were admitted for the first time in 1876, and during the passage of the 1884 Reform Bill the very existence of the House was questioned by the Liberal John Bright, who asked the Commons: 'Shall the policy of a great and free country be thwarted by men, sitting in the hereditary chamber, who are not there by right of votes given them, and through whom the voice of the millions of the United Kingdom is not heard?' The powers of hereditary peers were cut in 1911, and although there were plans for their imminent abolition Tory members ensured that the measure was dropped. In 1948 an all-party conference voted for their abolition, but it was not until 1999 that a bill was passed removing the right of hereditary peers to sit in the House of Lords (they keep their titles and land).

House of Lords crypt At midnight on Wednesday 5 November 1605 Guy Fawkes was discovered in the crypt under the House of Lords guarding twenty barrels of gunpowder, his pockets loaded with touchwood, preparing to blow up Parliament and the king, James I, who it was feared would increase the persecution of Catholics. Fawkes stayed behind to set the fuses and was discovered only because the gang had argued among themselves and one of them had sent a letter to the Catholic Lord Monteagle warning him not to attend Parliament. He was arrested and tortured for three days. Eventually, eight men were caught and stood trial, being sentenced to death in January 1606. To this day members of the Yeoman of the Guard search the Lords cellars before the State Opening of Parliament.

Lobby The only assassination of a British prime minister took place in the House of Commons lobby on 11 May 1812 when Spencer Perceval was shot dead by Henry Bellingham, a businessman who felt aggrieved at the collapse of a Russian business deal and was probably intending to shoot the former ambassador to Russia, who was in the prime minister's party. On being shot Perceval cried out: 'Oh, I am murdered!' and died a few minutes later. When Bellingham was seized he nonchalantly exclaimed: 'My name is Bellingham. It is a private injury – I know what I have done – it was a denial of justice on the part of the Government.'

St Mary Undercroft The crypt below St Stephen's Chapel is a rare survival from the 1834 fire which destroyed the Palace of Westminster and is now used for christenings and the marriages of MPs. On Saturday 24 January 1885 a policeman discovered a bomb in the undercroft and carried it almost as far as St Stephen's Hall before having to put it down due to the excessive heat. The bomb then exploded, injuring the PC and blowing out the south window.

St Stephen's Hall The Hall stands on the site of the medieval 𝔖𝔱 𝔖𝔱𝔢𝔭𝔥𝔢𝔫'𝔰 ℭ𝔥𝔞𝔭𝔢𝔩 where the monarch worshipped and which was used for meetings of the House of Commons from 1550 to 1834. It was here in January 1642 that Charles I burst in on MPs and demanded to know the whereabouts of five members whom he wished to arrest; seeing that they were absent he remarked: 'The birds have flown.' Although Charles ordered the Speaker, William Lenthall, to tell him where the five were, Lenthall replied: 'I have neither eyes to see, nor tongue to speak in this place, but as this House is pleased to direct me'. No monarch has since been allowed into the House of Commons. The chapel was destroyed in the 1834 fire.

Speaker's House The Speaker, the supposedly non-partisan MP who presides over the House of Commons, lives in the Speaker's House within the Palace of Westminster and when Parliament is in session walks to the chamber in a slow-moving procession led by the Commons Bar doorkeeper, dressed in a black cloth court suit with linen bands, knee-breeches, buckled shoes and wig – what passed for typical parliamentary attire in the eighteenth century – followed by the Serjeant at Arms, who carries the Mace, and a police officer who shouts: 'Speaker . . . Hats off, strangers.'

Victoria Hall and Tower The royal entrance to the Palace of Westminster, known as the King's Tower when rebuilt in the 1850s and then the biggest tower in the world, now contains the 3 million parchment records of every law passed in England since the eleventh century.

Westminster Hall The main survival of the medieval Palace of Westminster, escaping the 1834 fire that burned down practically every other building in the vicinity, it is now the vestibule of the House of Commons. Built by William Rufus in 1097 to house the royal treasure, it hosted the first meeting of Parliament, Simon de Montfort's Great Parliament of 1265, which consisted of leading members of the clergy, five earls, eighteen barons, two knights from each shire, two citizens from each city and two burgesses from each borough (it is uncertain who attended). From 1100 to 1834 Westminster Hall was used as the law courts. Edward II was deposed here in his absence before a crowd of citizens, earls, barons and leading members of the clergy. Sir Thomas More was tried for treason in the hall in 1535 and accused of acting 'traitorously and maliciously . . . to deprive our Sovereign lord the king of his dignity, title and name of Supreme Head on Earth of the Church of England'. He was condemned to be hanged, drawn and quartered but was spared the ordeal by the king, who took pity on him and reduced the sentence to a simple beheading. Charles I was tried here in January 1649, accused of abusing his authority by 'introducing arbitrary and tyrannical government' and beheaded three days later outside Banqueting House (p. 234). Since the removal of the law courts to the Strand Westminster Hall has been used mostly for ceremonial events. In 1911 the suffragette Emily Davidson hid for forty-eight hours in the Crypt Chapel under the Hall so that she could put 'House of Commons' as her address in the 1911 census.

uncrowned king, Charles II, as 'the great Barabbas, murderer, tyrant and traitor'.

After the throne was restored in 1660 Christopher Wren commissioned renovations, but as central Westminster's residential population declined, particularly after nineteenth-century slum clearance, the parish withered away, being abolished in 1972. The church has long been a popular venue for society weddings, hosting those of the diarist Samuel Pepys (1655), the poet John Milton (1656), Winston Churchill (1908) and the Hon. Frank Pakenham (the future Lord Longford) in November 1931, which was attended by the writers John Betjeman, Nancy Mitford and Evelyn Waugh, with the flamboyant Tory politician Lord Birkenhead (Fred Smith) as best man.

St Margaret Street
Houses of Parliament / Palace of Westminster
The Houses of Parliament occupy the medieval Palace of Westminster, begun by Canute *c.* 1020, used by William the Conqueror some fifty years later as his London base, and transformed into a dignified palace by William's successor, William Rufus, at the end of the eleventh century, a time when the seat of government was wherever the king placed his Seal. Successive monarchs made the palace their London base until a fire in 1512 resulted in Henry VIII's moving the court to what became Whitehall Palace, the Palace of Westminster then becoming solely a seat of government.

Almost the entire palace perished in a fire on 16 October 1834, caused when two cartloads of tallies, ancient accounting sticks made of elmwood, being burned in the stoves beneath the Lords' chamber, set the flues alight. A large crowd, including the artist J. M. W. Turner, who later painted a number of watercolours of the fire, gathered to watch and one man was arrested for 'excessively huzzaing'. Immediately after the fire Parliament announced the launch of a competition to choose an architect to rebuild the palace and the winner was

Charles Barry, who argued that Gothic was the only style suitable for a Christian country, but died before the work was complete.

The fittings and furnishings were the work of A. W. Pugin, the leading Gothic revivalist, who employed intense Gothic detail even in the nails used on the chairs and 'down to the very inkstands and coat hangers', according to the essayist V. S. Pritchett – and died in a madhouse in 1852 from a condition brought on by overdecorating. The complex was damaged during the Second World War, when the House of Commons chamber was destroyed, and it was rebuilt by the Ministry of Works and Giles Gilbert Scott in the 1940s.

The Sanctuary
The small triangle of land to the immediate west of Westminster Abbey is named after the medieval place of refuge for those fleeing authority, which was abolished in the seventeenth century when the Gatehouse Prison was built. The Elizabethan explorer and statesman Sir Walter Ralegh was imprisoned in the Gatehouse in 1618 shortly before his execution, and the Cavalier poet Richard Lovelace was jailed for seven weeks there in 1642 for petitioning the House of Commons in support of King Charles. Inside he wrote the poem 'To Althea, from Prison', which contains the famous lines 'Stone Walls do not a Prison make / Nor Iron bars a Cage'. The Gatehouse was torn down in 1776, fifteen years after Dr Johnson claimed that the building brought shame to London.

Westminster Abbey
Westminster Abbey, officially the Collegiate Church of St Peter in Westminster, is England's main religious building. Originally built by Sebert, King of the East Saxons, in 616, being first recorded as West Minster *c.* 730, it was rebuilt as an abbey with seventy monks in 1065, when Edward the Confessor set his throne in the adjacent Palace of Westminster (now the Houses of Parliament). Its subsequent

Westminster Abbey glossary

Chapter House Used for storing state papers from 1540. George Gilbert Scott uncovered the wall paintings when he restored the building in the nineteenth century.

Choir The choir, which sings a daily service, is made up of boys from the nearby Westminster Choir School, and was where the monks worshipped before the Benedictine abbey was dissolved.

Henry VII Chapel Cited by many as the finest example of late Perpendicular Gothic architecture in England, it was begun in 1503 as a burial place for the saintly Henry VI, but later became a burial place for monarchs, including Henry VII, Elizabeth I, Mary Tudor and George II. Since 1725 the chapel has been used for swearing in the Knights of the Bath.

Nave Abbot Litlington, a master mason, began work on rebuilding the nave of Edward the Confessor's original abbey in 1376 and by 1502 what is the tallest Gothic nave in England was complete. Here can be found the tomb of the Unknown Warrior, an unidentified soldier buried in the abbey on 11 November 1920 to represent the unknown British dead of the Great War, and the graves of a number of famous Britons, including the explorer David Livingstone (1873) and the 1940s Labour prime minister Clement Attlee (1967).

North Transept Rebuilt by Christopher Wren in the early eighteenth century, the North Transept became the Statesmen's Aisle after the burial of the former prime minister William Pitt the Elder (Lord Chatham) here in 1778.

St Edward's Chapel The chapel houses the coronation chair, Edward the Confessor's shrine and the tombs of medieval kings.

Sanctuary The spiritual heart of the abbey, containing the High Altar and reredos designed by George Gilbert Scott.

South Transept (Poets' Corner) Almost every major English poet is either buried or remembered in the south transept's Poets' Corner, described by Oliver Goldsmith as 'the place of sepulchre for the philosophers, heroes and kings of England'. It owes its existence to the fifteenth-century printer William Caxton, who mentioned in the inscription he placed on the grave of Geoffrey Chaucer in the abbey garden that the latter had been a poet, beginning a fashion for burying poets and writers alongside.

Stone of Scone From 1296 to 1996 the Stone of Scone, a relic which looms large in Scottish history, was on display in the Abbey, to the chagrin of nationalists. A block of sandstone believed in Scots legend to be the pillow on which the Hebrew Patriarch Jacob rested, it was taken from the Holy Land c. 700 BC. After a journey through Egypt, Sicily, Spain and Ireland, where it was used to crown the kings at Tara, it made its way to Scotland where it was captured by the English in 1296. On Christmas Day 1950 four Scottish nationalists stole back the Stone from the Abbey, resulting in police closing the border between England and Scotland for the first time in 400 years. Three months later, on 11 April, the Stone was discovered on the altar of Arbroath Abbey, with a letter addressed to George VI lying nearby, and returned to Westminster. In November 1996 it was removed to Edinburgh Castle.

development into one of the world's great religious buildings stems from Edward's successors' desire to honour his name, ascertain their legitimacy to the throne through connection with him, and be buried near his ashes. By the mid sixteenth century the abbey had become the setting for coronations, royal marriages and funerals, which continued despite the dissolution of the Benedictine abbey in 1540. At the end of the seventeenth century it was discovered that four pillars at the central crossing had swayed inward and Christopher Wren supervised major repairs, continued after his death by Nicholas Hawksmoor, whose western towers are one of the abbey's

best-known images. Since the early eighteenth century little major work has been
needed on the structure.

(v) Houses of Parliament to Horseferry Road

The land was once Bulinga Fen, marshland
reclaimed by Westminster Abbey in medieval times, and features an enclave of small
Georgian streets whose properties are
mostly taken up by MPs keen to live within
range of the Commons' division bell.

Lord North Street

One of the best preserved Georgian streets
in the capital, central to English political life
for over a century, Lord North Street was
built in the late eighteenth century as North
Street, being the northern entrance to Smith
Square, and its first residents were professionals, an early inhabitant (at No. 15)
being Thomas Gayfere, the mason who
restored the Henry VII Chapel in Westminster Abbey. In the nineteenth century
the houses were broken up into flats to cram
in tenants, including a number of MPs'
mistresses, but the growth in public transport saw the poorer inhabitants move to
the new suburbs, such as Battersea and
Clapham, and North Street gradually began
to attract wealthier residents and MPs who
wanted to live in quiet surroundings but be
able to reach the nearby Houses of Parliament quickly enough to answer division
bells.

In 1936 the street's name was augmented
to Lord North Street – a perverse joke on
behalf of the council, given that Lord
North was the British prime minister when
America won the War of Independence –
and around that time it first began to
feature in political intrigue, being the home
of Brendan Bracken, the Tory MP who gave
shelter to Winston Churchill when the latter
was in the political wilderness in the 1930s.
More recently its best-known inhabitant has
been Jonathan Aitken, the disgraced Tory
Cabinet minister who was jailed for perjury

in 1999. A few houses on the street still
quaintly bear original painted signs pointing
to subterranean wartime air-raid shelters.

west side: Smith Square to Great Peter Street
No. 14
Hugh 'Binkie' Beaumont, a formidable
theatre impresario who was a master at
using the casting couch (for male hopefuls),
lived at No. 14 from 1943 to 1973, a period
during which his visitors included many of
the biggest names in theatre and cinema
such as Laurence Olivier, Ingrid Bergman,
Noël Coward, Richard Burton and Marilyn
Monroe, who once stayed overnight with
Arthur Miller. No. 14 has been home since
1978 to the maverick Tory MP Teresa
Gorman.

Lady Sybil Colefax's address (1939–50),
No. 19
A leading society figure of the 1930s and
1940s, Lady Sybil was notorious for inviting
guests to dinner, switching the venue to the
Dorchester at the last minute, and then
sending guests the bill. Among her visitors
were the authors Cyril Connolly, Evelyn
Waugh and Somerset Maugham, and
society figures such as the Duke and
Duchess of Windsor (the former Edward
VIII and Mrs Wallis Simpson), who came
for lunch on 27 September 1939, a few days
after the start of the Second World War,
travelling to London from the continent
incognito. Edward Du Cann, chairman of
the Tories' 1922 Committee of backbench
MPs during Edward Heath's premiership,
lived here in the 1970s, and the property is
now home to the former Tory MP Alistair
Goodlad, Chief Whip in John Major's last
government, who lent Major the property
as a campaign headquarters during the 1995
Tory Party leadership election.

east side: Great Peter Street to Smith Square
The Institute of Economic Affairs, No. 2
Home in the early 1920s to Sir Stuart
Samuel, Liberal MP for Whitechapel, Presi-
dent of the Board of Jewish Deputies, and
an avowed *anti*-Zionist, it was used as an
officers' club for the Free French navy in the
Second World War and since 1969 has been

home of the Conservative think-tank the Institute of Economic Affairs, which reached its peak of influence during Margaret Thatcher's government.

Harold Wilson's address (1970s), No. 5

A 1720s property, home in its time to a carpenter and later a police sergeant, it was where Harold Wilson lived during his last term as prime minister (1974–6), despite being paranoid that the house was being bugged by MI5 (which it probably was). On one occasion Wilson invited the journalists Barrie Penrose and Roger Courtiour to a private meeting here to inform them that there had been a series of burglaries on the property, probably by 'forces threatening democratic countries like Britain' and agents hired to find incriminating evidence again him, and told them that he saw himself as a 'big, fat spider in the corner of the room'. 'Sometimes, I speak when I'm asleep,' Wilson continued. 'You should both listen. Occasionally, when we meet, I might tell you to go to Charing Cross Road and kick a blind man standing on the corner. That blind man may tell you something, lead you somewhere.' A little while later Wilson resigned as prime minister through ill health.

► Harold Wilson in 10 Downing Street, p. 225.

No. 7

Home in the 1920s to Gavin Henderson, a Labour MP and one of the original Bright Young Things, who on his stag night set the Thames alight with eight 2-gallon cans of petrol. A longer staying resident, from 1951 to 1991, was the Conservative thinker Diana Spearman, a research worker at nearby Central Office and a leading exponent of economic liberalism within the Tory Party before Margaret Thatcher made such views popular.

Brendan Bracken's address (1933–58) / Jonathan Aitken's address (1981–2001), No. 8

The largest property on the street, featuring ten bedrooms and its own ballroom, No. 8 was home at the end of the twentieth century to the disgraced former Tory MP

Jonathan Aitken, jailed in June 1999 for perjury and perverting the course of justice. But the house witnessed political intrigue as far back as the 1930s when another notorious (but non-criminal) Tory politician, Brendan Bracken, moved in, filling No. 8 with antique furniture, though a bed he imported from Venice turned out to be too large to fit in the house. Bracken was a ruthless schemer and social climber, who used to get his servants to interrupt dinner parties with pronouncements such as 'the prime minister would like to speak to you on the telephone, sir'. He would dash away even though there was, of course, no such call. Bracken revelled in the nickname 'B.B.', which George Orwell purloined as the epithet for Big Brother in *1984* (the less notorious Rex Mottram in Evelyn Waugh's *Brideshead Revisited* was also based on him), and was rumoured to be Winston Churchill's illegitimate son, something neither party refuted convincingly, Randolph Churchill, Winston's legitimate son, calling him 'my brother the bastard'. Indeed Winston Churchill stayed here in the 1930s, when he was in the political wilderness, using No. 8 to hold meetings with other leading Tories opposed to the appeasement policies of prime minister Neville Chamberlain, and when Churchill took over from Chamberlain as PM in 1940 he appointed Bracken Minister of Information.

Jonathan Aitken, a backbench Tory MP and a millionaire financial adviser, moved into No. 8 in 1981, hosting meetings of the Conservative Philosophy Group attended at various times by Tory MPs Keith Joseph and Enoch Powell, the arch-monetarist Milton Friedman, Henry Kissinger and even Richard Nixon, who came here to help Aitken with his hagiography, *Nixon: a Life* (1990). Though overlooked for promotion by Margaret Thatcher, probably for slighting her daughter, Carol, Aitken was later invited to join the government by John Major, who made him Minister of State for Defence Procurement in 1992, promoting him to the Cabinet in 1994 as

Chief Secretary to the Treasury. A year later Aitken resigned from the Cabinet following allegations in the *Guardian* that while he was Minister for Defence Procurement he had concealed his links with a Lebanese arms dealer and that a hotel bill for his stay at the Paris Ritz in 1993 had been paid by a Saudi businessman, in breach of parliamentary guidelines.

Distraught, Aitken vowed to sue the *Guardian* (and Granada TV) using 'the simple sword of truth and the trusty shield of fair play to cut out the cancer of bent and twisted journalism', and for a while it looked as if he would be exonerated. But the *Guardian* staged a clever coup to ensnare him. The paper's editor, Peter Preston, sent the Ritz Hotel a fax on House of Commons notepaper, purportedly from Aitken, requesting information about the bill, and received the required information in response. Aitken's case collapsed, he was subsequently tried for perjury, and in June 1999 convicted and jailed.

There are painted letters on the house wall pointing down to the wartime air-raid shelter and the mail box has a video camera trained on it, part of the surveillance installed in the late nineties to ensure that Aitken did not break the terms of his release by leaving the house between 7 p.m. and 7 a.m.

No. 11

In the 1990s No. 11 was home to Greville Howard, former political secretary to Enoch Powell and friend of Lord Lucan, and was where Michael Portillo installed forty telephone lines while preparing to enter the 1995 Tory Party leadership election contest. In 2001 Iain Duncan Smith ran his successful campaign for the Tory Party leadership from here.

Smith Square

Central Westminster's major square, created in 1725 in honour of the landowner, Henry Smith, and dominated by the former church of St John the Evangelist (now a concert hall), it was home at various times during the twentieth century to the Trades Union Congress, the Labour Party and the Conservative Party, of which only the last remains, at No. 32.

Former St John the Evangelist

> A very hideous church with four towers at four corners, generally resembling some petrified monster, frightful and gigantic, on its back with its legs in the air
> – *Our Mutual Friend*, Charles Dickens (1865)

A major example of the English Baroque, St John was designed by Thomas Archer between 1715 and 1728 as the most expensive of the fifty new churches planned in the 1711 Act, the foundations having to be sunk securely into swampy land. Queen Anne, irritated by architects asking for her approval of the design, kicked over her footstool and told Archer 'build it like that', resulting in the church becoming known as Queen Anne's footstool. The church was not immediately popular, Robert Walpole, the prime minister, dismissing the architect as 'a Mr Archer, the groom porter'. It burned down in 1742, was struck by lightning in 1773 and was bombed during the Second World War, after which it was rebuilt for use as a concert hall.

Transport House (1920–99), east junction with Dean Bradley

Built in the 1920s as the headquarters of the Transport and General Workers' Union (TGWU), much to the delight of the dockers' leader Ernest Bevin, who took pride in a working-men's association being able to move into a costly eight-storey building within the precincts of the Palace of Westminster, at a time when no union had so salubrious a headquarters. It soon became home to the Trades Union Congress and the Labour Party, who shared the property until 1957 when the former moved to Great Russell Street, Bloomsbury. The Labour Party left for Walworth Road, south of Elephant and Castle, in 1981, the TGWU moved out in 1999, and the building is now the home of the Local Government Association.

► Birth of the Labour Party, p. 56.

(vi) Pimlico

A mostly down-at-heel triangle of land south of Victoria, dominated by crumbling stucco terraces, Pimlico's unusual name relates either to the Pamlico tribe of Red Indians, who exported timber to London in the seventeenth century, or to a Ben Pimlico, a Hoxton brewer, who developed a popular 'nut browne' ale around the same time. In the tenth century the land was a swamp, Bulinga Fen, into which the Tyburn stream drained, and in the nineteenth century attained its modern-day look when Thomas Cubitt began development on earth brought by river from the excavations of St Katherine Dock, near the Tower, and created street upon street of stucco houses with little interruption and no greenery. The new Pimlico's first residents contained a large proportion of artists, musicians and writers, including the composer Arthur Sullivan, the authors Joseph Conrad and George Eliot and the aesthete and designer Aubrey Beardsley, but bohemian Pimlico gradually disappeared during the twentieth century.

Cathedral Piazza
Westminster Cathedral
The Catholic cathedral for the north side of the Thames was designed by John Bentley in a Byzantine style with a striking striped campanile and built in 1895 to 1903 after several delays, Bentley being the third architect to be involved with the project. The first, Henry Clutton, who controversially was a relative of the powerful Catholic Cardinal Manning, the owner of the land, was removed following delays in raising the money to fund the building, resulting in Sir Tatton Sykes, a Yorkshire businessman, being brought in as benefactor and choosing a different architect, Baron von Herstel, who died soon after. When the project was

revived by Cardinal Vaughan he appointed Bentley, but as there were still insufficient funds to realize the latter's ambitious plans, the cathedral opened with the upper areas unfinished, and they remain unfinished over 100 years later.

Passport to Pimlico
A much-loved Ealing comedy, directed by Henry Cornelius in 1949, *Passport to Pimlico* is set during a summer heatwave, shortly after the Second World War, that is shattered by an explosion in a Pimlico bombsite which opens up an Aladdin's cave of treasure and unearths a parchment proving that the district of Pimlico belongs to the Duchy of Burgundy. Locals, realizing they are no longer answerable to Whitehall, tear up their ration books, ignore the licensing laws, ban the police from entering 'foreign' territory, and stop tube trains at the frontier (Victoria) for passport checks. But Whitehall fights back, imposing frontier and currency controls, putting Pimlico-en-Burgundy under siege and leaving residents torn over their identity. (When one character is accused of being a foreigner she memorably retorts: 'We always were English, and we always will be English, and it's just because we're English we're sticking out for our right to be Burgundians!') Eventually, the old order is restored and Pimlico is readmitted to the United Kingdom. Ironically, the film was shot not in Pimlico but in Lambeth, across the river.

► King's Cross on film, p. 356.

Chichester Street
Dolphin Square, west side
A stark, totalitarian-looking block of luxury flats, the largest of its kind in Europe with some 1,250 apartments, it was designed in 1937 by Cecil Eve and Gordon Jeeves in the shape of a doughnut around a central garden. Socially, if not architecturally, Dolphin Square comes close to Le Corbusier's vision of an all-inclusive estate,

enjoying its own shops, leisure facilities, bars and restaurants. It has been home at different times to Princess Anne, Labour prime minister Harold Wilson, the singer Shirley Bassey and currently some fifty MPs. It has also long been popular with spies and spymasters: in the 1930s MI5's Maxwell Knight ran a small, select band of recruits, who dubbed themselves Knight's Black Agents (the name adapted from Macbeth's 'night's black agents'), from 10 Collingwood House; MI5 used 308 Hood House as a safe house during the Second World War; while 807 Hood House, the postwar home of the spy William Vassall, was raided in 1962 by police who found 140 photographs of top-secret Admiralty documents hidden in the bookcase.

Churchill Gardens Road
Churchill Gardens Estate
Regarded by many architecture experts as the finest postwar estate in London and selected by the Civic Trust in 2000 as the outstanding British building of the previous forty years, Churchill Gardens was designed by Philip Powell and Hidalgo Moya while they were still at architecture school and erected between 1946 and 1962. A deliberate contrast to traditional stucco Pimlico, the estate consists of a series of seven- to nine-storey concrete blocks coated in yellow brick, set at right angles to the river and positioned to allow maximum sunlight to flood the rooms – in the manner devised by Walter Gropius, founder of the Bauhaus – and is expertly landscaped with lawns and children's play areas.

Millbank
Millbank began as a riverside walk from Westminster Abbey towards Chelsea, named after the fourteenth-century abbey mill that stood at the modern-day junction of Millbank and Great College Street, and by the nineteenth century had become a slum. Its cramped houses were demolished in the early twentieth century, after which the street was redeveloped with grandiose blocks including Thames House (home of

MI5), Millbank Tower (late-twentieth-century Labour Party headquarters) and the Tate Britain art gallery.
north side: Bessborough Gardens to Horseferry Road
Morpeth Arms, No. 58
A well-preserved Victorian pub, featuring cut glass and wood panelling, that was built for the warders of 𝔐𝔦𝔩𝔩𝔟𝔞𝔫𝔨 𝔓𝔢𝔫𝔦𝔱𝔢𝔫𝔱𝔦𝔞𝔯𝔶.
𝔐𝔦𝔩𝔩𝔟𝔞𝔫𝔨 𝔓𝔢𝔫𝔦𝔱𝔢𝔫𝔱𝔦𝔞𝔯𝔶, Millbank at Bulinga Street
Built in 1816 under the guidance of the social reformer Jeremy Bentham as the largest prison in the world, it was used mostly for convicts awaiting transportation to Australia, who were kept separate and silent for the first half of their sentence, a system that was scrapped after a cholera outbreak in 1823 when the women were released and the men transferred to prison boats on the Thames. Twenty years later the penitentiary was converted into a general prison, and after it closed in 1890 the site was taken up by the Tate Gallery. Parts of the penitentiary tunnel, along which convicts were taken *en route* to Thames barges, remain.
Tate Britain, Millbank at Bulinga Street
Henry Tate, the nineteenth-century sugar magnate, wanted to present the state with fifty-seven paintings from his collection, but as he stipulated that they could not become part of the National Gallery, a new gallery was built on land donated by the government. The new gallery, with an £80,000 grant from Tate, opened in 1897 as the National Gallery of British Art, with the works of the recently deceased Pre-Raphaelite John Millais as the main feature. At first only paintings by those born after 1790 were exhibited, but it was considered inferior to the National Gallery until a Turner wing opened in July 1910 to take the 180 oils and 19,000 drawings and water colours the painter J. M. W. Turner had donated in his will. Over the following decades the Tate gathered much of the best of British art from 1500 to the present day – works by William Hogarth, John Constable, Thomas Gainsborough, George Stubbs,

William Blake (which can be found in a room devoted to the artist), Dante Gabriel Rossetti and David Hockney – but the opening of the Tate Modern in 2000 for the gallery's huge twentieth-century collection saw the Millbank building become increasingly forlorn and visitor numbers dropped from 160,000 in April 2000 to 62,000 the following August, tempered by a subsequent revival in its fortunes.

Millbank Tower

A lofty late-1950s tower, until recently the tallest office block in London, it was built for the Vickers group and contained the headquarters of the Labour Party from 1955 to 2002.

MI5 headquarters (1937–9, 1994–), Thames House, No. 11

MI5, the government department involved with internal security, first moved into Thames House in 1937, when it was unknown to members of the public, and its twenty-odd staff were mostly engaged with monitoring the activities of Germans in England and investigating the possibilities of a British fifth column of Nazi sympathizers. When war broke out with Germany in 1939 agents photographed all their important files, only to discover after the war that the negatives had been overexposed and ruined. MI5 moved to Wormwood Scrubs and later occupied various London addresses until it returned to a refurbished Thames House in 1994, by which time staff numbers had grown to some 2,000 and it was no longer secret.

Terminus Place

Victoria station

LADY BRACKNELL: In what locality did this Mr James, or Thomas, Cardew come across this ordinary hand-bag?

JACK: In the cloak room at Victoria Station. It was given to him in mistake for his own.

LADY BRACKNELL: The cloak-room at Victoria Station?

JACK: Yes. The Brighton line.

LADY BRACKNELL: The line is imma-
terial, Mr Worthing – *The Importance of Being Earnest*, Oscar Wilde (1895)

Built in 1860 for the London, Brighton and South Coast Railway, it was extended two years later for the London, Chatham and Dover Railway, resulting in the older tenants erecting a wall between the two sections of the station to prevent its passengers having to gaze upon those using its arriviste rival, whom it slighted as the 'London, Smash 'Em and Turnover Railway'. Nevertheless, the two companies formed a partnership in 1899, but it was not until the arrival of Southern Railway in the 1920s that the wall between the two stations was removed.

VICTORIA LINE

The Victoria Line, which opened in 1968 as London's first new tube line since 1907, owes its existence more to civil defence needs than transport requirements, dating back to government concerns in 1944 about German A-bomb-tipped V2 rockets dropping on London. This led the authorities to construct a number of bomb-proof tunnels that could take cables between strategically important buildings: Buckingham Palace; the Curzon Street bunker in Mayfair where the royal family took shelter during the war, later used by MI5; BBC Broadcasting House; the Museum Telephone Exchange, which was also home of the BBC's national distribution centre, on Maple Street, Fitzrovia (where Telecom Tower now stands); and the railway termini of Euston, St Pancras and King's Cross.

When the war finished the authorities decided to build tunnels large enough for trains alongside the cable lines and in 1946 unveiled the route. Because of the existence of the cable network a number of major organizations later moved into properties located above the Victoria Line, including MI5, who were based in offices near Warren Street station in the 1960s; MI6, whose 1990s headquarters were built near Vauxhall station, as was Scotland

Yard's computer department, Tintagel House; and the British Library, the Victoria Line running between two of the latter's underground floors. The line also runs close to Buckingham Palace (between Victoria and Green Park stations).

Inter-government department bickering resulted in lengthy delays to the building of the tube line, with work not starting until September 1962, and the southern route needed to be redirected to Stockwell and Brixton after springs of water were discovered by the Oval. The line opened in September 1968, with the link to Brixton reached in 1971, but the original plan, to take the line further south to Streatham, Norbury, Mayday [Thornton Heath] and Coulsdon North, has not materialized.

Walthamstow Central The Victoria Line's eastern terminus was built into the existing British Rail station, part of the Liverpool Street–Chingford route.

Blackhorse Road Another existing British Rail station, serving the Gospel Oak–Barking line.

Tottenham Hale The ticket hall contains barriers that can be quickly installed to prevent flood water running down the escalators if the nearby River Lea overflows.

Seven Sisters The section of tunnel from here to Finsbury Park is the longest between any two stations in London.

Finsbury Park The busiest station on the network still not to have electronic barriers by 2003.

Highbury & Islington The first station was built here in 1849 for the overground line to Fenchurch Street and twenty-five years later a much enlarged Highbury, with a station building resembling St Pancras, was constructed, being demolished after Second World War bombing.

King's Cross St Pancras In rebuilding the station in the 1960s to accommodate the Victoria Line, the subterranean River Fleet had to be encased in a new concrete pipe.

Euston The inclusion of a Doric arch motif in the station design enraged the many protestors who had unsuccessfully campaigned to stop the railway authorities demolishing the grand Doric arch that used to front the entrance to Euston.

Warren Street The walls and corridors by the Victoria Line platforms are decorated with the predictable pattern of a warren.

Oxford Circus A huge steel umbrella was inserted under the station to protect the buildings and roadway during construction of the Victoria Line in the late 1950s.

Green Park A plague pit was discovered when work began on the tunnels under the station in the 1960s.

Victoria Six 50 million-year-old fossil nautiloids were discovered when the line was dug under Victoria.

Pimlico Decorated with artist Peter Sedgley's op art design of yellow spray bursts on a white ground, inspired by his 1968 painting *Go*.

Vauxhall Navvies excavating the new tunnel in 1968 claimed they saw a 7-ft ghost, 'the Quaire Fellow', which allegedly had been disturbed from one of the nearby plague pits.

Stockwell American troops used the station as a hostel during the Second World War.

Brixton The station motif features a laboured rebus based on a 'ton of bricks', even though bricks are not the produce most associated with the area.

River Thames

London's main artery and the second longest river in England, the Thames, which rises in Gloucestershire, meanders through Oxfordshire and Berkshire to London where it was easily forded in ancient times, a factor that led the Romans to set up camp in what is now the City of London in AD 50. The river became its main transport network, and by the nineteenth century was filled with ships unloading goods at one of the world's busiest ports. Since the closure of the docks and the building of motorways in the second half of the twentieth century the Thames has emptied of craft, but in recent years much of the land along its banks has been reborn for residential and commercial use.

● The Thames section covers sites and buildings of interest by the river in and near the centre of London, from Hammersmith to Bow Creek on the north bank, and from Barnes to the Millennium Dome on the south bank.

North bank: Hammersmith to Bow Creek

HAMMERSMITH, W6

One of London's most dynamic communities, thanks to its intensely commercialized centre, underground lines and motorway, with a riverside that contains some fine houses and a number of popular pubs.

Hammersmith Terrace The building of a row of Bloomsbury-style town houses in the eighteenth century in what was then open countryside by the river amazed locals. An early-twentieth-century resident (at No. 13) was A. P. Herbert, the Independent MP for Oxford University, who steered the divorce bill through Parliament and wrote musical comedies and books about the Thames.

Upper Mall An attractive stretch of town houses and boating clubhouses, popular with drinkers in summer, on account of its many welcoming pubs.

Latymer Preparatory School, 36 Upper Mall. Built on the site of 𝕽𝕚𝕧𝕖𝕣𝕤𝕔𝕠𝕦𝕣𝕥, home of Catherine of Braganza, consort of Charles II, it was occupied by the writer Naomi Mitchison in the early twentieth century.

Old Ship A pub furnished with nautical ephemera that was originally the garden lodge for the mansion of 𝕽𝕚𝕧𝕖𝕣𝕔𝕠𝕦𝕣𝕥.

William Morris's address (1878–96), Kelmscott House, 26 Upper Mall. Morris, the larger than life Victorian designer and writer, moved into the house where in 1816 Francis Ronalds had built the world's first electric telegraph and changed its name

from The Retreat to Kelmscott House, in honour of his Oxfordshire mansion, Kelmscott Manor, often journeying between the two properties by boat. A more recent occupant has been the playwright Christopher Hampton, best known for the screenplay of *Dangerous Liaisons*.

The Dove, 18 Upper Mall. A cosy 1790s-built pub where the Scottish poet James Thomson wrote 'Rule Britannia' and which has the smallest snug in Britain.

Furnival Gardens The gardens that separate Upper Mall and Lower Mall were named after Dr Frederick Furnival, one of the first people to promote rowing as a sport, and were laid out in the 1950s over the mouth of Hammersmith Creek.

Lower Mall A short stretch of roadway to the immediate west of Hammersmith Bridge lined with rowing clubs.

Blue Anchor, 12 Lower Mall. The pub where the composer Gustav Holst wrote some of his *Hammersmith Suite*.

Hammersmith Bridge Built in 1824 to 1827 by William Tierney Clarke as London's first suspension bridge, it has since earned the dubious honour of being the most bombed of London's bridges. The IRA left a device under the bridge in March 1939, which was spotted by a passer-by, who threw it into the river, where it exploded, causing minimal damage, and in 1996 an IRA bomb resulted in the closure of the bridge for four years. Soon after Hammersmith Bridge reopened in 2000 it was the target for another bomb, detonated at 4.30 in the morning and causing no injuries. Although the media blamed Irish terrorists, no one was ever apprehended for the crime, and rumours circulated that the device might have been placed by militant Barnes residents to prevent the bridge reopening and maintain the peacefulness of their community when free of Hammersmith traffic.

Riverside Studios, Crisp Road. Built as a water-pump factory in the late nineteenth century, it was used as a munitions factory in the First World War and was converted in 1934 into a film studio, becoming

Europe's biggest TV studios by the 1950s – the first to broadcast colour television – where BBC programmes such as *Hancock's Half Hour*, *Blue Peter* and *Doctor Who* were recorded. The building was converted into the Riverside arts centre in 1974 and, though occasionally used for television, it is best known for its repertory cinema.

Thames Wharf, Rainville Road. Offices for Lord (Richard) Rogers's architectural practice and also home of the River Café, the renowned restaurant run by his wife, Ruth, and Rose Grey.

FULHAM, SW6

One of London's most popular inner suburbs since 1960s gentrification, it is separated from Hammersmith by Parrs Ditch, a tributary of Stamford Brook.

Fulham Football Club Perennial under-achievers, now owned by Harrods' proprietor Mohamed Al Fayed, Fulham used to play in the most pleasant location of any of London's football clubs, Craven Cottage, built on the site of a property of that name which burned down in 1888, but moved out in 2002.

Bishop's Park A half-mile-long narrow park that belonged to the Bishop of London and was featured in the 1976 horror film *The Omen* in the scene in which a priest vainly tries to flee the wrath of Satan.

Fulham Palace Summer residence of the bishops of London from 704 to 1973 and home in the sixteenth century to London's major botanical gardens.

Putney Bridge In 1729 a wooden bridge that was the only means of crossing the river on foot upstream of Westminster opened here and was where Mary Wollstonecraft, the eighteenth-century feminist and mother of Mary Shelley, tried to commit suicide in 1795 after her partner – she daringly defied convention by refusing to marry – eloped with an actress. The bridge was replaced in 1882 by a granite structure designed by Sir Joseph Bazalgette and is where the annual

Oxford–Cambridge Boat Race, first staged in 1845, begins.

Hurlingham Park Large, mostly inaccessible, grounds, partly designed by Humphrey Repton, where polo was first played in England, it contains the 1760-built Hurlingham House, home to the exclusive Hurlingham Club, and the athletics stadium used in the film *Chariots of Fire*.

Wandsworth Bridge The ugliest of London's many Thames bridges, designed by T. Pierson Frank in 1936 to 1940 to replace J. H. Tolmé's private toll bridge of 1873.

Sands End A mile-long stretch of land consisting mostly of mud banks.

CHELSEA, SW3, SW10

The most exclusive riverside community in London, Chelsea, originally a fishing village, attained popularity with royalty in the late Middle Ages and later with artists on account of its excellent light.

Chelsea Harbour, off Lots Road. An exclusive, well-concealed luxury estate beloved of pop stars and footballers, memorably described by the novelist Iain Sinclair in *Radon Daughters* as being 'neither in Chelsea, nor a harbour', it contains apartments, a hotel and a yachting marina.

Chelsea Creek The waterway, which rises near Kensal Green Cemetery, where it is known variously as Billingswell Ditch, Pools Creek and Counters Creek, was converted to an industrial canal by Lord Kensington in 1820. After enjoying a brief period of usefulness it was taken over in 1839 by the Birmingham, Bristol and Thames Railway, which filled it in north of King's Road to build what is now the West London Railway, resulting in considerable wasteland abutting the railway line by Scrubs Lane and Wood Lane in Shepherd's Bush. The land around the mouth of the creek in Chelsea is still industrialized, being the location of the Sands End gas works and the Lots Road power station.

Lots Road power station, Lots Road. Built in 1902 to 1905 for powering the London Underground, it soon became the biggest power station in the world, using 6,000 tons of coal brought in each week by barge. It was converted to apartments at the beginning of the twenty-first century.

Cremorne Gardens, Cremorne Road Pleasure gardens which stood to the east of Chelsea Creek in the early nineteenth century, it was where Madame Genevieve performed a tightrope walk across the Thames and Charles Green ascended in a balloon accompanied by a lady friend and a leopard. The gardens closed in 1877 after complaints about the patrons' rowdy behaviour.

World's End A huge housing estate of tower blocks, built in 1966 to 1978, and named after the World's End pub on King's Road. A late 1970s resident was the Clash's Joe Strummer, who was inspired to write the group's best-known single, 'London Calling', with its chorus 'London is drowning and I live by the river', while living in a World's End flat.

Cheyne Walk The most prestigious riverside street in London, whose residents have included the artist J. M. W. Turner; the James Bond author, Ian Fleming; the Victorian novelist George Eliot; and the Rolling Stones Mick Jagger and Keith Richards.

J. M. W. Turner's address (1846–52), 119 Cheyne Walk. Turner moved to what became his last address, then 6 Davis Place, in 1846 when he was in his seventies, living here incognito as 'Mr Booth', to avoid attention, and building a gallery on the roof so that he could watch sunsets. Here Turner painted his last four works and died on 19 December 1851. A later resident was the young Ian Fleming who went on to create James Bond.

Battersea Bridge A wooden bridge was built in 1771 at the point where Thomas More, Henry VIII's ill-fated Lord Chancellor, had his private landing stage, but was financially unsuccessful, the receipts from tolls failing to cover the cost of repairs, and was demolished in 1885 for being dangerous to vessels, which often crashed into the piers. It was mistily captured by the artist James Whistler in his 'Nocturnes'. The new bridge was designed by Joseph Bazalgette, who also constructed Chelsea Embankment.

Chelsea Old Church (All Saints) The oldest building in the area, bombed in the Second World War and carefully restored.

48 Cheyne Walk Home to the Rolling Stones Mick Jagger from 1967 to 1978.

Albert Bridge An exquisitely designed bridge, courtesy of R. M. Ordish, in 1873, who based the suspension on the Franz Josef Bridge in Prague, it was meant to take the heavy traffic that nearby Battersea Bridge could not cope with but by the 1950s was wobbling when pedestrians crossed. The authorities wanted it demolished, but the poet John Betjeman campaigned for its retention, describing how 'shining with electric lights to show the way to Festival Gardens or grey and airy against the London sky, it is one of the beauties of the London River'. Instead of being demolished the bridge was strengthened and saved. A sign warns that troops must break step while crossing it.

Cadogan Pier, south of Oakley Street. Every July a group of people re-enact the last journey of the ill-fated Thomas More, Henry VIII's Lord Chancellor, taking a boat from Cadogan Pier downriver to the Tower, where they visit the cell in which he was imprisoned and the place on Tower Hill where he was executed.

Henry VIII's manor house, 19–26 Cheyne Walk. Henry VIII built a manor house on this site in 1536 when he made himself Lord of the Manor of Chelsea, but was not able to fulfil his wish that it should become the residence of his queen, Jane Seymour, as she died the following year, nine days after bearing him a male heir (the future Edward VI). In 1543 Henry gave the building to Catherine Parr, his sixth wife, as a wedding present, and although it was demolished in the 1780s traces of the brickwork and gardens remain.

Dante Gabriel Rossetti's address (1862–82), 16 Cheyne Walk. Rossetti, the Pre-Raphaelite painter and poet, moved into the 1719-built property in 1862, while mourning the death of his wife Elizabeth Siddal, and converted it into a temple of Aestheticism that incorporated a menagerie of exotic animals including a zebra, kangaroo and racoon.

4 Cheyne Walk The novelist George Eliot died here in 1880 only a few weeks after moving in.

3 Cheyne Walk Home to the Rolling Stones guitarist Keith Richards from 1969 to 1978.

Chelsea Embankment Built by Joseph Bazalgette in 1871 to 1874 to conceal a newly constructed sewer, it swept away the old riverside village where the water lapped the properties, and contains several houses, including No. 17 (Old Swan House) and No. 18 (Cheyne House), built for the tea merchant E. J. Horniman, designed by Norman Shaw, England's leading domestic architect of the late nineteenth century.

Chelsea Physic Garden, Swan Walk. The second oldest garden in England, it was created in 1673 and ran down to the river before the Embankment was built. It is home to England's first cedar trees, the largest olive tree and the oldest rock garden in England.

Chelsea Royal Hospital, Royal Hospital Road at West Road. Built in the style of Paris's L'Hôtel Royal des Invalides by Christopher Wren in 1682 to 1694 to provide accommodation for discharged soldiers, the Chelsea Pensioners. It also houses the National Army Museum.

Ranelagh Pleasure Gardens A major eighteenth-century centre for entertainments, banquets, balls and fireworks, now used for the annual Chelsea Flower Show.

PIMLICO, SW1

A triangle of land south of Victoria dominated by crumbling stucco houses, Pimlico was named either after the Pamlico tribe of Red Indians, who exported timber to London in the seventeenth century, or a Ben Pimlico, a Hoxton brewer who developed a popular 'nut browne' ale in the seventeenth century.

Chelsea Bridge Thomas Page constructed a bridge connecting Sloane Square and Clapham in 1858 at a fording point where the Romans and Ancient Britons are believed to have clashed in battle, the Romans winning after producing their trump card – an elephant they had secreted in the woods. The current bridge was erected in 1936.

River Westbourne / Former Grosvenor Canal The Westbourne, which rises in Hampstead, flows in a pipe through Kilburn and Paddington into Hyde Park, where its waters feed the Long Water and Serpentine. It then runs under Knightsbridge (hence the name) and Sloane Square, where it is conveyed above the tube station platforms in a huge pipe, and splits in two south of the station, the western branch reaching the Thames near the Royal Hospital, the eastern reaching it here, by Chelsea Bridge. In 1725 the eastern section was converted into the Grosvenor Canal, which ran north to where Victoria station now stands, but was closed in 1899 when the station was expanded.

Churchill Gardens Estate A highly regarded postwar council estate, it was designed by Philip Powell and Hidalgo Moya in 1946 to 1962 on the site of war-damaged terraced housing, its blocks set at right angles to the river to allow maximum sunlight to flood the rooms.

St George's Square The only London square facing the river, it was created in 1839 with its own pier for steamers. Bram Stoker, author of *Dracula*, died of syphilis at No. 26 in 1912.

Dolphin Square A starkly totalitarian-looking block of luxury flats, the largest in Europe with some 1,250 apartments, designed by Cecil Eve and Gordon Jeeves in 1937 and now home to scores of MPs, it was originally heated with untreated Thames water heated at Battersea Power Station, which lies opposite on the south bank. A proposed landing stage for residents' craft was never built.

River Tyburn The mouth of one branch of the now culverted river which gave its name to the Tyburn tree gallows by Marble Arch and which rises in Hampstead, flowing south under Regent's Park, Marylebone Lane and Buckingham Palace, emptying into the Thames just west of Vauxhall Bridge.

Vauxhall Bridge Opened by the Prince Regent as Regent's Bridge in 1816, there was a 1d charge for pedestrians, 2s 6d for a coach of six, and sixpence for each score of cattle. The tolls were withdrawn in 1879 and the bridge was replaced in 1895 by Alexander Binnie's structure.

Millbank Named after the fourteenth-century Westminster Abbey mill that stood at the modern-day junction with Great College Street, it began as a riverside walk from the Abbey to Chelsea and, though a slum in the nineteenth century, is now dominated by large office blocks.

Morpeth Arms, 58 Millbank. A well-preserved Victorian pub with cut-glass partitions and wood panelling, which was built for the warders of Millbank Penitentiary.

Millbank Penitentiary, Millbank at Bulinga Street. A nineteenth-century prison where inmates, mostly convicts awaiting transportation to Australia, were originally kept in silence in a huge circular area. The prison closed in 1890 but parts of the penitentiary tunnel, along which convicts were taken to Thames barges, survive.

Tate Britain, Millbank at Bulinga Street. An art gallery mostly devoted to the Tate's huge pre-twentieth-century collection, housed in a baroque building designed in 1890 to 1897 by Sidney R. J. Smith.

Queen Alexandra Hospital Located to the immediate east of the Tate, it opened in 1905 as a military hospital and its buildings are now used by the gallery.

Millbank Tower, 30 Millbank. A soaring 1960s glass tower block built as the headquarters of the Vickers group – there was a Spitfire on the forecourt – and used by the Labour Party as its headquarters from 1995 to 2002.

MI5 headquarters (1937–9, 1994–), Thames House, 11 Millbank. MI5 first used Thames House in 1937, moving to Wormwood Scrubs two years later when war was declared, and returning here in 1994, by which time it had expanded out of all proportion to its 1930s size.

Horseferry Road The eastern end of Horseferry Road marks the point where an ancient horse ferry took passengers between Thorney Island (now subsumed into Westminster) and Lamb Hythe (Lambeth). Occasionally heavily laden carriages would sink, despite the relative tameness of the river at this point, and one of those who suffered this hardship in 1656 was Oliver Cromwell. When James II fled London on 10 December 1688 he threw the Great Seal of England into the Thames by the horse-ferry quay. It was later recovered by fishermen.

Lambeth Bridge Built on the site of the ancient horse ferry in 1862 and replaced in 1932.

WESTMINSTER, SW1

The political and royal centre of Britain, whose riverside is dominated by the Houses of Parliament.

Nobel House, 9 Millbank. A monumental block built in 1928 for ICI and taken over by the Department of Environment, Transport and the Regions in 2000.

1 Millbank Headquarters of the Church Commissioners.

Abingdon Street Its junction with Great College Street marks the ditch boundary of the ancient Thorney Island, the marshy land between the Thames and the branches of the Tyburne River on which Westminster is built. Before wartime bombing Abingdon Street was lined with houses inhabited by members of Parliament.

College Green A small green space opposite the sovereign's entrance to the House of Lords, where MPs are often interviewed for television.

Houses of Parliament / Palace of Westminster King Canute famously commanded the waves to obey him by the Thames outside the Palace of Westminster which he built here in the eleventh century and which was later vacated by royalty to become the Houses of Parliament. When the palace was rebuilt after the disastrous 1834 fire the Duke of Wellington insisted that the building should back on to the river so that it could not be surrounded by mobs.

The great clean-up of London

During the hot dry summer of 1858 the smell of sewage from the Thames was so foul – the politician Benjamin Disraeli described it as a 'Stygian pool reeking with ineffable and unbearable horrors' – MPs were obliged to cover the windows of the Houses of Parliament in sheets soaked in chloride of lime. A solution was found by Joseph Bazalgette, chief engineer to the Metropolitan Board of Works, who built an 82-mile network of sewers and drains lined with special bricks, Staffordshire Blues, baked to extremely high temperatures to make them more durable, to take waste and rainwater to treatment plants at Barking and Plumstead.

Westminster Bridge Resisted by river watermen, who ferried pedestrians across the river at this point, and by Southwark residents, who feared increased flooding, the bridge was none the less built (in the 1750s), with money raised by a state lottery, the work resulting in the demolition of the alleyways and courts by the Houses of Parliament. By 1759 it was unsafe and had to be rebuilt. William Wordsworth wrote 'Upon Westminster Bridge', with its famous opening line, 'Earth has not anything to show more fair', on the roof of a coach after crossing the bridge with his sister Dorothy on 3 September 1802.

Portcullis House There is a side view from the river of Michael Hopkins's late-twentieth-century building, the most expensive office block ever constructed in London.

Victoria Embankment Built in 1864 to 1870 as part of engineer Joseph Bazalgette's ambitious land reclamation and road-building project to cover his newly constructed sewer and the new District Line underground railway.

Westminster Pier Until the growth in air travel in the 1970s the pier was used as a landing area for foreign dignitaries arriving in Britain by boat, one of the last to do so being Marshal Tito, the Yugoslav leader, who in 1953 was met here from his vessel by Prince Philip and Winston Churchill.

Former New Scotland Yard Headquarters of the Metropolitan Police from 1890 to 1967 and now used by MPs, it was immediately derided by the home secretary, Sir William Harcourt, who claimed it was architecturally inferior to Crosse and Blackwell's pickle factory across the river.

Ministry of Defence A bleak white fortress of a building, designed in 1957 by E. Vincent Harris, it stands above the cellars of the medieval 𝔚𝔥𝔦𝔱𝔢𝔥𝔞𝔩𝔩 𝔓𝔞𝔩𝔞𝔠𝔢, the royal seat that occupied a huge site between the Thames and Whitehall.

Victoria Embankment Gardens The gardens, which stretch from Horseguards Avenue to the Temple in three separate sections, were built in the 1860s on land reclaimed from the river.

Whitehall Court A monumental late-nineteenth-century French Renaissance-style block, whose early residents included H. G. Wells, George Bernard Shaw and MI6.

STRAND, WC2

Wharves, jetties and narrow lanes filled the land between Strand and the river before the construction of Victoria Embankment in the 1860s, the area now being mostly one of imposing office blocks with no traces of the old riverside community.

New Hungerford Bridge (I) One of the newest Thames bridges, it was designed by Alex Lifschutz and opened in 2002 alongside the Hungerford rail bridge despite fears that laying the foundations would unsettle wartime bombs that had been buried in the river bed and trigger time-delay fuses that could flood the tube network.

Hungerford Railway Bridge Built to the design of Sir John Hawkshaw in 1864 to take trains and pedestrians across the river, it replaced Brunel's 1845 suspension bridge, the chains of which were taken to Bristol to be used for the Clifton Bridge. To the north is Terry Farrell's Egyptian-style shell containing Charing Cross station.

New Hungerford Bridge (II) The second of the new, 2002-opened, Hungerford bridges, built to connect Charing Cross and Waterloo.

Warren's Blacking Factory, Villiers Street at Embankment Place. Embankment station fills the site of the blacking factory at 30 Hungerford Stairs where the twelve-year-old Charles Dickens covered pots of paste with paper and string, alleviating the boredom by entertaining workmates with stories. He later recreated the factory as Fagin's den in *Oliver Twist* (1839) and as Murdstone and Grinby's, 'a crazy, tumble-down old house abutting the river and literally overrun with rats', in the semi-autobiographical *David Copperfield* (1850).

Water Gate, end of Buckingham Street. Built in 1626 as a triumphal arch leading from the river through the Duke of Buckingham's private gardens to his mansion, **York House**, previously the London home of the Archbishop of York.

The Adelphi, Adelphi Terrace. Collcutt and Hamp's intimidating Adelphi block, London's most authentic example of totalitarian 1930s architecture, stands on the site of the Adam Brothers' spectacular late-eighteenth-century Adelphi development, a terrace of twenty-four houses, designed in the style of the ruined palace of Diocletian at Spalato (Split), which was home for nearly 150 years to the rich and famous, including the actor-manager David Garrick and the Gilbert and Sullivan impresario Richard D'Oyly Carte. It was demolished in 1936.

Cleopatra's Needle, Victoria Embankment, south of Adam Street. A 60-ft high 186-ton obelisk, the oldest exposed artefact in London, Cleopatra's Needle was cut from granite quarries in Aswan, Egypt, around 1475 BC, carved with dedications to various gods and rulers, and erected in Alexandria, where it fell into the sand. It was presented to the British by Mohammed Ali, Viceroy of Egypt in 1819, and transported to London amid much difficulty in 1877.

Shell-Mex House, No. 80 Strand. A monumental 1930s office block built on the site of the grand Victorian Cecil Hotel, whose river façade contains the largest clock tower in London.

Savoy Hotel, Strand at Savoy Court. T. E. Collcutt's flamboyant 1889 hotel, the epitome of late-Victorian glitz, has been a haunt of royalty and society figures since.

Institute of Electrical Engineers, 2 Savoy Place. The first permanent home of the BBC, from 1923 to 1932.

Brettenham House, Lancaster Place. A 1930s Portland Stone office block at the north-west end of Waterloo Bridge.

Waterloo Bridge Built in 1811 to 1817 as Strand Bridge to the designs of John Rennie, and renamed following the Battle of Waterloo, its opening was captured by John Constable in his 1832 painting *The Opening of Waterloo Bridge*, in which the Prince Regent (later George IV) is shown about to take the short river journey from Whitehall Stairs to the bridge. The bridge was painted over forty times by Claude Monet between 1899 and 1905, before being demolished amid public outcry in 1936, and later rebuilt to the designs of Giles Gilbert Scott.

Georgi Markov, a 49-year-old Bulgarian exile who worked for the BBC's World Service, was waiting for a bus at the southbound stop on 7 September 1978 when he was stabbed in his right thigh with the sharpened end of an umbrella by a man who apologized to him and fled in a taxi. The Bulgarian later slipped into a coma and died, and in his thigh was found a 1.7 mm platinum-iridium pellet filled with ricin, a poison for which there is no known antidote. The murderer is believed to have been working for the Bulgarian secret service agency *Durzhavna Sigurnost*, which was planning to rid the country of troublesome opponents as a birthday present to President Todor Zhivkov.

Somerset House, Strand, east of Lancaster Place. The only surviving medieval riverside Strand palace, now a tourist attraction, with offices for civil servants alongside, it was built in the late eighteenth century with a river entrance that was rendered unusable by the construction of Victoria Embankment 100 years later. The grandeur of the north frontage is compromised by the shops of the Strand.

King's College, Strand, west of Surrey Street. Part of the University of London, King's College was founded in 1828 by the Duke of Wellington and the bishops of the Church of England as an Anglican alternative to the non-denominational University College. The various college buildings visible from the river include Robert Smirke's original Classical-style college of 1829 to 1831.

Temple station The tube station opened in 1870 as part of the eastern extension of the Metropolitan District Railway. Its colonnaded rooftop, built to complement the local surroundings, had to be closed after a few months as it had become a haunt of prostitutes.

Temple Place A street behind Victoria Embankment dominated by corporate blocks, including Arundel House, headquarters of the military think-tank the International Institute for Strategic Studies; Globe House at No. 4, offices for the British American Tobacco Company; and No. 2, the former Astor family estate office, designed in 1895 in an ostentatious Elizabethan style.

Electra House, Temple Place. One of a number of substantial interwar office blocks on and around the Strand, it was built as the headquarters of the Cable & Wireless Company and was home to a secret Foreign Office department, CS, involved in planning propaganda, during the Second World War. Beneath the building, the authorities laid a number of telephone lines linked to the Central Telegraph Exchange at Moorgate which monitored calls made to and from every foreign embassy in London.

HQS Wellington The Honourable Company of Master Mariners' floating livery hall was built at Devonport in 1934 and used in the South China Sea during the Second World War.

CITY OF LONDON, EC4, EC3

Two griffins saved in 1963 from the demolished Coal Exchange on Lower Thames Street mark the western riverside boundary of the City of London, the ancient heart of London.

Middle Temple Garden The gardens of the Middle Temple Inn of Court.

Middle Temple Lane The dividing line between the Middle Temple and Inner Temple, which originally ran down to the water's edge.

Inner Temple Garden Home of the Royal Horticultural Show, that became the Chelsea Flower Show, which was first held here in 1888.

Hamilton House, 1 Temple Avenue. Built by William Emerson in the Renaissance style in 1898 to 1901, it used to be the home of the Employers' Liability Corporation and is now offices for various legal and accountancy firms.

Telephone House, 2 Temple Avenue
A baroque building that is home to British Telecom's archives.

Audit House, 58 Victoria Embankment
A 1903 Wren-influenced building, home of the Employment Appeal Tribunal.

9 Carmelite Street An 1890s red-brick Gothic block with a 'sugar icing' interior, built as a library for the Carmelite monks and converted in 1909 into offices for the Thames Conservancy.

Sion Hall, 56 Victoria Embankment. Built in 1884 to 1887 in red-brick Tudor Gothic by Arthur Blomfield as a social centre for London's Anglican clergy, it contained Sion College's 100,000-volume library until 1996.

City of London Boys School (1883–1986), John Carpenter Street. A prestigious school founded by John Carpenter, town clerk of London in 1442, which moved into Davis and Emmanuel's French Renaissance-style building, now occupied by J. P. Morgan bank, in the 1880s and is now based east of Blackfriars Bridge.

Unilever House, Victoria Embankment
A vast baroque office block faced in Portland Stone, built by Burnet, Tait and Partners in 1930 to 1932 for the Unilever company.

Blackfriars Bridge Built in 1760 to 1769 as Pitt Bridge, at the place where felons had boarded ships to be transported to Virginia, it was paid for with money from fines paid by men who had refused to take up the post of sheriff, and replaced with a Joseph Cubitt-designed structure in the 1860s. The body of Roberto Calvi, a banker with the Italian Banco Ambrosiano and known popularly as God's banker, as his client list included the Pope, was found hanging from the underside of the bridge on 15 June 1982. Calvi was a member of the Italian P2 Masonic Lodge and murdered, probably by the Mafia. The Fleet River flows into the Thames under the bridge.

Blackfriars Railway Bridge There are remains of the western bridge, designed by Joseph Cubitt and F. T. Turner in 1862 to 1864 for the London, Chatham and Dover Railway, alongside the 1880s eastern bridge, designed by John Wolfe-Barry and H. M. Brunel, which now takes Thameslink trains.

Puddle Dock Geoffrey Chaucer is believed to have been born by Puddle Dock in 1343 or 1344.

City of London School The fifteenth-century school moved to this new block in 1986.

Millennium Bridge An unusual addition to the many Thames bridges, with horizontal, rather than vertical, suspension, it was built at a cost of £12.8 million in 1999, to link the newly created Tate Modern with the area south of St Paul's Cathedral, and was inspired according to its chief architect, Lord (Norman) Foster, by 'the most primeval of bridges, like ropes slung across peaks in the Himalayas, or a plank across a stream' and by the Flash Gordon comics' fantastical 'ray of light' bridges. The bridge became an embarrassment to the national millennial celebrations within days of opening in December 1999 when it was found to be wobbling, or as the official description put it, suffering from 'pedestrian induced vibration, synchronization resonance', and was closed. The architects blamed the engineers, Ove Arup, and the latter blamed the architects, while the dismayed public quickly renamed the structure the Wobbly Bridge. It reopened in 2002 after major repairs.

Queenhithe Dock All vessels entering the Port of London in medieval times were obliged to moor either at Queenhithe, to the immediate south of the modern-day Mansion House tube station, or Billingsgate, further east, so that the authorities could impose the appropriate charges.

Vintners' Hall, Thames at Vintner's Place
The hall of the City livery company in charge of wine importing, it is where members give five, rather than three, cheers in their toast in commemoration of a 1363 feast attended by five kings – those of

England, Scotland, France, Denmark and Cyprus.

Southwark Bridge A steel structure built in 1912 to 1921 replaced John Rennie's 1819 bridge, on which John Chivery proposes to Little Dorrit in the 1857 Dickens novel of the same name, while 'putting his penny on the toll plate of the iron bridge'.

Bracken House, 1 Southwark Bridge. Built for the *Financial Times* in 1959 to the design of Sir Albert Richardson and based on the 1679 Palazzo Carignano in Turin, it was unsympathetically refurbished in the 1990s.

Location of the *Marchioness* disaster A collision between the dredger *Bowbelle* and the passenger vessel *Marchioness*, at this part of the river on 20 August 1989 resulted in the deaths of fifty-one people, mostly in their twenties, in what was the worst Thames disaster of the twentieth century. Stringent new safety laws have since been introduced for Thames travelling.

Cannon Street rail bridge Built to carry South-Eastern Railway trains using Cannon Street over the Thames by the site of the steelyard used by the Hanseatic merchants from the tenth to the sixteenth centuries.

Mondial House, 90–94 Upper Thames Street. Europe's largest international tele-communications complex, built on the site of Christopher Wren's 𝔄ll 𝔥allows t𝔥e 𝔊reat church, is designed in a style that so vexed Prince Charles he wrote in 'A Vision of Britain' (1988): 'As you continue down the river . . . you pass the dreadful Mondial House. To me this building is redolent of a word processor. I don't see that people particularly want a perpetual view of a word processor when they find themselves living with them all the time in the office or at home.'

Fishmongers' Hall, King William Street The 1834 hall for the Fishmongers' company, founded at the beginning of the fourteenth century, and one of the most important medieval City livery companies on account of the religious importance of fish. The hall suffered considerable damage during the Second World War and was restored from 1943 to 1953.

London Bridge London's main bridge, around which the Romans established a camp in the first century AD, and the only bridge over the Thames in central London until 1750. Here, according to Norse legend, Danes who had seized control of London in 1014 stood throwing stones and weapons on Ethelred the Unready, king of England, and Olaf, king of Norway, who were sailing in a boat on the Thames underneath. Eventually, Ethelred and Olaf recaptured the city by tying ropes to the wooden slats, rowing along the river and pulling down the bridge.

The first stone London Bridge, which opened in 1209, rested on nineteen arches – the number being that great to prevent unwelcome ships travelling further upriver – caused a change in the river flow and allowed the Thames to freeze easily in winter. On the bridge itself a chapel, houses, and eventually as many as 150 shops, were built and when the bridge burned down in 1212 many people jumped in the river to flee the flames and drowned. Once rebuilt, the bridge again became home to more than a hundred shops and houses, whose inhabitants would empty their chamber pots from the windows on to the heads of those journeying by river below, if they spotted the opportunity.

The accession to the throne of the boy-king Richard II in 1377 was toasted with a pageant and banquet on the bridge, after which 'one hundred and thirty Citizens with innumerable Trumpetts, Sackbuts, Cornetts and Wax Lights, rode from Newgate through Chepe over the bridge to Suth-warke to meet the yonge Prince'. Around the same time began the practice of placing the heads of executed wrongdoers on the end of poles on the bridge, the heads first parboiled in the gatehouse to dissuade scavenging birds from pecking at them. Among those exhibited were William Wallace, the Scottish nationalist; and Sir Thomas More, Henry VIII's Lord Chancellor, who was executed at the Tower for treason in 1535.

The houses were demolished in 1762, when the bridge was widened, and in 1831 a new bridge, designed by John Rennie, was constructed a little to the west of the existing structure. Rennie's bridge was itself dismantled and transported to Lake Havasu City, Arizona, in the early 1970s and replaced by Harold Knox-King's reinforced concrete structure.

Adelaide House, London Bridge. A 1924 office block by London Bridge designed by Sir John Burnet in the American skyscraper style, it was, at 148 ft, the tallest office block in London at the time and included what were then unusual features, such as air-conditioning, an internal mail system and a rooftop golf lawn.

Billingsgate market (1016–1982), Lower Thames Street. London's main fish market, built on the site of one of three Roman harbours in London, stood here for over 900 years until it was moved to the Isle of Dogs in 1982. The current building, designed by Sir Horace Jones in 1874 to 1877, is now used as offices.

Custom House, Lower Thames Street. A building where the authorities could collect duty payable on goods imported into London by river was first built on the site in 1275 and rebuilt by Christopher Wren after burning down in the Fire of London. It was severely damaged by a gunpowder explosion in 1714 and rebuilt by Thomas Ripley in 1717 to 1725. The present building dates from 1817 and is now used as offices.

Tower of London, Tower Hill. Built by William the Conqueror as a fortress against invasion from the river, and since used as an armoury, mint and prison, it has been a major London tourist attraction for the last hundred years. Visible from the river is Traitors' Gate, the medieval water-bound entrance for prisoners such as Princess Elizabeth (later Elizabeth I), who was brought to the Tower in 1554 when suspected of taking part in a plot to replace the Queen, Mary Tudor.

Tower Bridge One of London's best-known sights, thanks to Sir John Wolfe Barry and Horace Jones's Gothic towers, it opened in 1894 as the last of the Victorians' new London bridges and the only bascule bridge in the capital. In its first year the roadway opened to allow ships to travel further upstream over a thousand times, but nowadays it opens only on rare occasions.

WAPPING, E1

A maritime community of considerable mercantile activity until the closure of the docks in the 1960s, Wapping nestles by the section of the river known as the Pool of London, which became so congested with boats during the nineteenth and early twentieth centuries, when London was the busiest port in the world, that it was commonly believed it was possible to cross from one bank to the other along the decks of waiting vessels.

Irongate Stairs Tens of thousands of Jewish immigrants – 'flocks of aliens, mostly Russians in top-boots and leather leggings and little round fur hats; wild-looking people from the most outlandish parts of that great uncivilised land', according to the former head of the Flying Squad, Nutty Sharpe – first set foot in England at Irongate Stairs at the north-eastern end of Tower Bridge during the great waves of immigration from continental Europe at the end of the nineteenth century. On leaving their boats many of the new arrivals would bend down and kiss the ground in thanks for arriving in a country where they were free to practise their religion, and they were then greeted by Jewish welfare workers from the nearby Jewish Temporary Shelter at 84 Leman Street, set up by the Rothschild family to remove the uncouth manners and alien ways of the refugees. 'We have now a new Poland on our hands in East London. Our first business is to humanise our Jewish immigrants and then to Anglicise them,' Rothschild once explained. Mass immigration from Russia eased off after the passing of the 1905 Aliens Act, which allowed the authorities to turn back immigrants they thought to be 'undesirable'.

Entrance to former St Katharine's Dock
St Katharine's, the dock closest to the City of London, was built by Thomas Telford in the 1820s and replaced the warren of crowded alleyways with names such as Cat's Hole and Dark Entry that were home to some 11,000 people, few of whom received any compensation for being forced out. New warehouses were built to store tea, perfume, wine, wool, ivory, silver and live turtles (for turtle soup, a Victorian delicacy), but they were mostly bombed during the Second World War. Those that survived were demolished during 1970s redevelopment when the area was renovated as a leisure and commercial area with a hotel (the Thistle Tower), offices, wine bars, health clubs and a yachting marina.

Devon House A 1980s development built on the site of Devon Wharf, a tea and wool warehouse once managed by the father of the local author W. W. Jacobs, it contains the Dickens Inn, a former spice warehouse that has no links with the author.

Presidents' Quay Luxury apartments built around the ship HMS *President*, which occupies the lower three floors.

Wapping High Street An unusual high street, almost devoid of shops, it once boasted some thirty pubs, including the 𝔗𝔲𝔯𝔣'𝔰 𝔥𝔢𝔞𝔡 𝔍𝔫𝔫, which had a licence to serve the last quart of ale to condemned pirates on their final journey from Newgate Prison to Execution Dock. Since the 1970s closure of the docks its tall, brick, nineteenth-century warehouses have been renovated into luxury apartments, the smell of spices has been obliterated, and the street has emerged as an unlikely magnet for the rich, albeit one devoid of conspicuous life or community.

Hermitage Basin Once the western entrance to London Docks.

Wapping Pierhead houses Built from 1810 to 1813 for senior officials of the London Dock Company.

Wapping Entrance The former eastern entrance to London Docks, it was filled in during the 1970s and converted to a garden. The water course is marked by old cannon barrels.

Wapping Old Stairs Captain Blood was captured here in 1671 while attempting to leave London with the stolen Crown Jewels. The stairs were also where convicts being deported to Australia boarded their boats.

Town of Ramsgate, 62 Wapping High Street
A seventeenth-century pub named after the Ramsgate fishermen who left their catches here before they were taken to Billingsgate market, it was also where in 1688 Judge Jeffreys, James II's unpopular Lord Chancellor, was seized while attempting to flee to the continent to avoid the troops of William III, who had taken the throne from James. Jeffreys was arrested and taken to the Tower of London where he tried unsuccessfully to drink himself to death and was rendered unable to eat anything but poached eggs for months. The pub cellars used to hold convicts awaiting transport to Australia.

Oliver's Wharf, Wapping High Street
A former tea warehouse, built in 1870 for George Oliver, it was the first of the Wapping dock warehouses in the 1970s to be converted to luxury apartments, one of which was taken by the American singer Cher.

Wapping Pier (𝕰𝖝𝖊𝖈𝖚𝖙𝖎𝖔𝖓 𝕯𝖔𝖈𝖐) In medieval times pirates were hanged from the gibbets at 𝕰𝖝𝖊𝖈𝖚𝖙𝖎𝖔𝖓 𝕯𝖔𝖈𝖐 until three tides had washed over them. Alongside the dock was the Bell pub, a major centre for press-ganging locals into joining the navy. In September 1736 the *Daily Post* reported how one reluctant internee staying here overnight hanged himself using the catch of the door; when his friends came to wake him in the morning and found him on his knees they assumed he was praying and departed.

Captain Kidd, 108 Wapping High Street
A pub converted from a warehouse named after the seventeenth-century pirate William

Kidd, who was hanged in 1701 at nearby 𝕰𝔵𝔢𝔠𝔲𝔱𝔦𝔬𝔫 𝔇𝔬𝔠𝔨.

Wapping station Dating from 1884, it is the East London Line station at the northern end of Marc Isambard Brunel's 400-yard Thames tunnel, the first to be constructed under the river, which opened for pedestrians, not trains, in 1843.

Shipworming under the Thames
The first tunnel under the Thames, built amid considerable difficulty from 1825 to 1843 to connect Wapping and Rotherhithe, was designed by Marc Isambard Brunel, a royalist exile from revolutionary France, who came upon the idea in debtors' prison while watching a shipworm making its way through wood, passing the material through its body and excreting it as it moved on. To build the tunnel Brunel constructed a huge iron shipworm with corkscrew blades and a honeycomb of thirty-four cells in which miners dug four or five inches, shoring it up with planks, before moving on to another cell and repeating the process, masons and bricklayers lining the receding tunnel as the contraption moved forward. It took eighteen years to complete the job – the Thames broke through three times, workmen fell ill and ten men died – but once the tunnel opened new problems emerged. Public patronage was not as high as expected and the tunnel became the haunt of prostitutes and 'tunnel thieves', who lay in wait for pedestrians in the arches. The structure was taken over by the East London Railway in 1869 and it is now part of the Underground network.

Wapping police station When the world's first river police was established here in 1798 local thieves were so upset that their reign of lawlessness was over that they attacked the station. A museum inside is open by appointment only.

Metropolitan Wharf A converted tea warehouse, home to more than a hundred small firms.

Prospect of Whitby One of London's oldest pubs, it dates back to 1520 and is named after a coal boat, the *Prospect*, registered at Whitby, Yorkshire, which was positioned outside in 1777.

Entrance to Shadwell Basin A narrow inlet leads to the former London Docks basin, where in 1945 a German U-boat captured in the Atlantic in the Second World War was publicly displayed.

King Edward Memorial Park Laid out in 1921 on land previously occupied by a fish market, it was the only riverside land between the Tower of London and the Isle of Dogs open to the public when the docks were in use.

Rotherhithe Tunnel The tunnel, which runs from Shadwell to Rotherhithe under King Edward Memorial Park, was designed by Sir Maurice Fitzmaurice in 1904 to 1908 and contains a footpath which allows pedestrians an unusual, if noisy, means of crossing the river.

Free Trade Wharf, The Highway, south of Schoolhouse Lane. One of the busiest parts of the river during its trading heyday, filled with lighters and barges carrying coal from collier ships, it was rebuilt in the 1980s with a large block of ziggurat-shaped flats.

LIMEHOUSE, E14

Limehouse, named after the long-vanished local lime industry, was where Englishmen set off on ocean-going trips to open up new trade routes in the sixteenth century and was home of London's Chinatown between 1850 and 1950.

Ratcliffe Cross Stairs, south of Butcher Row. The point where the Thames met the red cliff ('ratcliffe') and the Pool of London became Limehouse Reach was used as a boarding point for those crossing the oceans in late medieval times. Their number included the explorer Sir Hugh Willoughby, whose party left in three ships to try to find the elusive North-East Passage, a sea route north of Scandinavia and Russia to China and America. Ratcliffe Cross faded into insignificance once the first docks were built locally in 1800.

Sun Wharf, 30 Narrow Street. The home in the 1980s of David Lean, the film director responsible for *David Copperfield*, *Brief Encounter* and the Oscar-winning *Bridge on the River Kwai*.

Entrance to Limehouse Basin An inlet leading to a 10-acre marina created in 1812 to 1820 as the southern terminus of the Regent's Canal.

The Grapes, 76 Narrow Street. The pub on which Charles Dickens supposedly based the Six Jolly Fellowship Porters in *Our Mutual Friend*, at the back of which a wooden ladder leading down to the shore acts as a reminder of the time when watermen would use it to leave the pub carrying drunks to the middle of the river, where they would drown them to sell the corpses to dissectors.

David Owen's address, 78 Narrow Street The original four members of the Social Democratic Party – the so-called Gang of Four former Labour ministers, David Owen, Roy Jenkins, Bill Rogers and Shirley Williams – issued the Limehouse Declaration, a statement in favour of social democracy, as opposed to traditional Labour Party-style socialism, here on Sunday 25 January 1981, forming the Social Democratic Party and creating a brief three-party race for power before merging with the Liberals.

Dunbar Wharf, 138 Narrow Street. The first travellers journeying from England to Australia left from Dunbar Wharf.

Limekiln Wharf, 148 Narrow Street England's first porcelain factory was built here in the 1740s.

ISLE OF DOGS, E14

A low-lying U-shaped peninsula bounded on three sides by the Thames, it was home to London's main docks and considerable heavy industry in the nineteenth and twentieth centuries, when every inch of riverside was filled with factories and works, and is now best known for Canary Wharf, Britain's most densely developed business park.

Canary Wharf Pier A jetty directly west of the imposing Canary Wharf towers.

Entrance to West India Dock An inlet leads to what was London's first enclosed dock, built in 1802 to protect merchandise from thieves and ensure that traders bringing produce from the Caribbean paid a tariff to the authorities. The area was restored after Second World War bombing and saw a short-lived boom in trade but closed in 1980 after which the site was spectacularly transformed into Canary Wharf.

Cascades, 2 Westferry Road. A cleverly designed housing development built in 1987–8 by CZWG Architects, the most striking feature of which is the 45 degree northern slope.

Launch site of the *Leviathan* / Burrell's Wharf, off Blasker Walk. Isambard Kingdom Brunel's 19,000-ton ship *Leviathan* – at least four times bigger than any other ship in the world and able to hold 4,000 passengers – was built here between 1853 and 1857 and unsuccessfully launched in November 1857, when the crush caused by the excessive number of people who gathered to watch resulted in one man being killed and the ship getting stuck on its rollers. Another three aborted launches took place and the vessel was not waterborne until the end of January 1858, by which time the owners had gone bankrupt. The ship, which was later renamed *The Great Eastern*, plied the trade routes between India and Australia and laid telegraphic cables in the Atlantic until 1886, when it came to be used as a showboat for the Lewis's store of Liverpool, being broken up two years later. Some remains of the timber slipway are still in place.

Island Gardens The gardens, laid out by the Commissioners of the Royal Naval Hospital in Greenwich in the nineteenth century, mark the south-east point of the Isle of Dogs, and it was here that pirates were hanged in chains, often watched by the pensioners of Greenwich Hospital through their spyglasses.

Foot Tunnel dome A red-brick rotunda marks the northern entrance of the 1217-ft Edwardian foot tunnel that connects the Isle to Greenwich and which until the recent opening of the Docklands Light Railway extension was the only non-marine means of negotiating the Thames between Rother-hithe and Woolwich.

Blue Bridge, south of Coldharbour. Until modern-day transport improvements the bridge, built in 1969 over the inlet to Blackwall Basin, was one of two swing bridges that provided the only communication between the Isle and the rest of London.

The Gun, 27 Coldharbour. Named in honour of the ship *The Henry Addington*, which fired its guns from the river outside, according to legend it is connected by underground passage with No. 3, where Nelson is believed to have stayed in 1799 before leaving to fight in the Battle of Aboukir.

Blackwall Stairs, continuation of Blackwall Way. A major place for embarking on ships crossing the ocean in the seventeenth and eighteenth centuries, it was where in 1606 nearly 150 men, women and children departed in three ships to found the state of Virginia, the first American colony.

Blackwall Tunnel The first traffic tunnel connecting the north and south sides of the river, Blackwall Tunnel was built as one tunnel from 1889 to 1897 and complemented by a companion tunnel in the 1960s. The gangster James Moody, dressed as a policeman, once hijacked a security van in the tunnel, blocking the traffic and forcing motorists who had stopped nearest him to hand over their keys to prevent their raising the alarm. Moody later escaped from Brixton Prison but was shot dead in the Royal Hotel pub in Hackney in 1993.

Reuters A dramatic-looking glass-faced block designed for the news agency by the Richard Rogers partnership in 1987–8.

Brunswick Wharf, south of East India station. A late-twentieth-century office development stands on the site of 𝕭𝖗𝖚𝖓𝖘𝖜𝖎𝖈𝖐 𝕯𝖔𝖈𝖐, built in 1789 for fitting-out and masting vessels and later transformed into East India's Export Dock. The dock company also built a public house, the 𝕭𝖗𝖚𝖓𝖘𝖜𝖎𝖈𝖐 𝕿𝖆𝖛𝖊𝖗𝖓, here, on the Meridian line, which provided superb views over the Thames and surprisingly, given its isolated location, became a popular nineteenth-century haunt, renowned for its whitebait suppers, with day-trippers arriving by train to what was affectionately nicknamed 'East End-by-the-Sea'. The dock was heavily bombed in the Second World War and closed in 1967.

Entrance to East India Dock The East India Company built its own deep-water docks at the beginning of the nineteenth century to allow the vast quantity of goods from Java, Bali, China and India, particularly tea and spices, that had previously lain in boats for weeks waiting to be discharged, to be stored in secure conditions off the river before being taken under armed guard to the company's Cutler Street warehouses near Petticoat Lane. Occasionally, some of the chests would break open and the contents spill on the floor, where they were trodden on by men returning from the overflowing toilets before being repackaged. In the Second World War the import dock was drained and used for storing craft, prior to the Normandy beach landings. The Port of London Authority closed the docks in 1967 and filled in much of the site.

Trinity Lighthouse, Orchard Place London's only lighthouse, built in 1860, now used to train lighthouse keepers.

Bow Creek A short stretch of waterway which leads to the River Lea, the Thames's main London tributary and the traditional border between London (Middlesex) and Essex.

South bank: Barnes to the Millennium Dome

BARNES, SW13

The most attractive of London's many riverside villages, with street after street of handsome well-appointed Edwardian houses.

The Terrace A particularly glorious riverside stretch lined with houses in coloured pastel wash, closer in spirit to Lyme Regis than London, with their bow windows, maritime embellishments and graceful terraces overlooking the Thames. The composer Gustav Holst lived at No. 10 from 1907 to 1913 when head of music at St Paul's Girls School, the house featuring a large music room on the top floor perfectly positioned to capture the light from one of London's most expansive horizons and a terrace where he and fellow composer Ralph Vaughan Williams would watch the annual Oxford–Cambridge boat race.

Bull's Head An ornate Victorian pub which doubles as a major jazz venue.

St Paul's School Founded alongside St Paul's Cathedral in 1509, it moved to West Kensington in 1884 and to Barnes in 1968.

Hammersmith Bridge See p. 250.

Harrods Furniture Depository, off Riverview Gardens. An 1890 warehouse where Harrods used to store its furniture and which now contains luxury apartments, including one inhabited at the beginning of the twenty-first century by Harrods owner, Mohammed Al-Fayed.

West Middlesex reservoirs Built from 1886 to 1897 and decommissioned by Thames Water in 1990, the reservoirs are now home to the 105-acre Wildfowl and Wetlands Trust Centre, which features lagoons, reed beds and grazing marshes.

Barn Elms Open land named after the 𝔅𝔞𝔯𝔫 𝔈𝔩𝔪𝔰 manor house which in the sixteenth century was owned by Sir Francis Walsingham, Elizabeth I's Secretary of State, and was used by the exclusive Ranelagh Club from 1894 to 1939. Since the mansion burned down in 1954 the land has been used mostly as school playing fields.

PUTNEY, SW15

An attractive late nineteenth-century suburb with a glorious river setting.

Embankment Created 1888 and one of the most picturesque riverside stretches in London, it is lined with boating clubs and grand Victorian pubs, outside one of which (the Star and Garter) John Christie, the serial killer of 10 Rillington Place (p. 454), was arrested after a police manhunt in 1953.

Putney Bridge See p. 251.

St Mary the Virgin Oliver Cromwell's New Model army had its headquarters at the Putney church in the autumn of 1647, holding discussions about a new constitution – the Putney debates – around the communion table.

WANDSWORTH, SW18

A traffic-choked lower-middle-class suburb with an unattractive and mostly industrialized river frontage.

River Wandle The mouth of the river that rises in Croydon and flows through south London, giving its name to Wandsworth, is one of only three London waterways south of the Thames which remains above ground for much of their length, the others being the Ravensbourne and Beverley Brook. Visible a few hundred yards to the south of the river's mouth is London's main brewery, Young's.

Jews Row An unusual name for a riverside street in this part of London, the local Jewish community having long departed.

Wandsworth Bridge See p. 251.

BATTERSEA, SW11

A barely inhabited swamp when Chelsea was an eighteenth-century fishing village, it grew into a land of market gardens until the arrival of the railways in the mid nineteenth century created a working-class suburb that away from the river has recently been gentrified.

Battersea Heliport, Lombard Road. One of few heliports in London, it is owned by Harrods.

West London Railway An underused rail route, connecting Kensington Olympia and Clapham Junction.

St Mary The church, which has Norman origins and was granted to the monks of Westminster Abbey by William I, was rebuilt in 1379 and was where in 1782 the painter-poet William Blake married Catherine Boucher, who marked the register with an 'X'.

Battersea Bridge See p. 252.

Foster Associates Headquarters of the architectural firm led by Lord (Norman) Foster, which was responsible for the Millennium Bridge, the new Greater London Authority building for the London mayor and the redesign of Wembley stadium. All 300 or so staff work at long benches, there is no division between design and production, and the building is open twenty-four hours a day, seven days a week.

Albert Bridge See p. 252.

Battersea Park The park was created in 1853 by John Gibson, who raised the river embankment to add more drama to the surroundings, built hillocks out of earth excavated in the building of London Docks, and planted some 40,000 trees and 45,000 bushes. Here the first football match to be played under Football Association rules, between the Secretary's XI and the President's team, took place on 9 January 1863. The park hosted concerts and political meetings in the early years of the twentieth century and pleasure gardens were added for the 1951 Festival of Britain, but they were demolished after the collapse of the Big Dipper in 1974. The park contains the *Three Standing Figures* sculpture by Henry Moore, the bronze *Single Form* by Barbara Hepworth and a Buddhist Peace Pagoda presented in 1985.

NINE ELMS, SW8

Named in 1645 after the trees that lined the roadway, it was once home to breweries, lime kilns, potteries, timber yards and gas works but is now one of the most blighted districts in London.

Chelsea Bridge See p. 253.

Battersea Power Station, off Nine Elms Lane. Designed in the late 1920s in the shape of an upside-down billiard table by Giles Gilbert Scott, of red telephone booth fame, it was soon producing 400,000 kilowatts of electricity and was later enlarged to become the largest brick building in Europe, but has lain dormant since closure in 1983. In the summer of 1963 the Great Train Robbers staged a full-scale dress rehearsal of their crime at Stewarts Lane railway depot by the power station.

River Effra, western continuation of Parry Street. The source of the river which rises in Upper Norwood and flows underground through Norwood Cemetery, Dulwich (whre it forms an ornamental lake), Herne Hill, Brixton and the Oval.

LAMBETH, SE1

Loamhithe meant a 'muddy landing place' and the area, never a wealthy or confident locality, has a riverfront of considerably less interest than its northern counterpart.

Vauxhall Bridge See p. 254.

Albert Embankment Built by Joseph Bazalgette in 1866 to 1870, it swept away much of the riverside industry of boat yards and timber yards and is now dominated by corporate blocks of mostly dubious architectural quality, saved only by Terry Farrell's MI6 building.

MI6 headquarters (1994–) A flamboyant building with Egyptian and South American touches, nicknamed the Aztec Temple and Ceaucescu Towers after the late Romanian dictator, it was designed by postmodernist pioneer Terry Farrell and built at a cost of

£240 million for the secret service branch concerned with overseas intelligence work at a time when it did not officially exist. Parliamentary rules were broken to allow the spending to exceed the agreed budget on new building, and by the time MI6 moved in, in 1994, John Major's Tory government had admitted the existence of the organization. In the opening sequence of the 1999 James Bond film *The World is Not Enough*, the building is blown up by a bomb smuggled in by a terrorist. The following September life almost imitated art when the building was attacked by a missile launched, it was claimed, by the Real IRA, which caused little damage and which some espionage experts believe was the work of MI6 itself, carried out to induce public support for increased security measures.

Vauxhall Gardens, between Glasshouse Walk and Kennington Lane. Riverside pleasure gardens from 1661 to 1859, where the diarist Samuel Pepys ate lobster and syllabub and the poet William Wordsworth saw 'green groves, and wilderness of lamps / ... gorgeous Ladies, fairy cataracts'. The gardens were so popular that other cities used them as a model for their pleasure grounds – Copenhagen's Tivoli Gardens were based on Vauxhall – and the Russians adopted the word 'vokzal' as the name of the country's first railway station and now as their word for station itself.

Tintagel House Police offices housing Scotland Yard's computer room and disciplinary wing from where the late 1960s investigation that netted the Kray twins was run, as Scotland Yard was believed to contain corrupt officers who would tip off the gangsters. After Tintagel House was bombed by the Angry Brigade on 22 May 1971 the anarchist organization released Communiqué No. 9 which announced: 'The Angry Brigade is the man or woman sitting next to you. They have guns in their pockets and hatred in their mind. We are getting closer. Off the system and its property. Power to the People.'

Peninsula Heights A 1960s-built tower block overlooking the Thames, formerly Alembic House and once an MI6 safehouse, it is filled with luxurious apartments, occupied at various times by Tommy Steele, John Barry and Jeffrey Archer who has the penthouse suite when he is not in jail.

Lambeth Bridge See p. 254.

Lambeth Palace Home of the archbishops of Canterbury since 1197, it stretched down to the Thames until the embanking of the river in the late nineteenth century.

St Thomas's Hospital Previously based where London Bridge station now stands, it moved here in the 1860s.

St Thomas's Steps, by Westminster Bridge Lord Noel-Buxton walked into the Thames at this point at low tide in 1952, wearing ordinary clothes, to try to prove the river was still fordable here. When the water reached his neck and was still rising, he was forced to admit that the ford had disappeared.

Westminster Bridge See p. 255.

THE SOUTH BANK, SE1

An area rich in theatres, cinemas and attractions, mostly built on industrial land that had been used for the 1951 Festival of Britain.

County Hall, north of Westminster Bridge Ralph Knott's London County Council headquarters, later used by the Greater London Council, is built on the site of Eleanor Coade's Coade Stone manufacturing works, where the hard-wearing artificial stone popular in housing developments was made until 1840. After the Greater London Council was abolished in 1986 County Hall was partly converted into a hotel which also contains an aquarium and museum devoted to the surrealist painter Salvador Dalí.

Jubilee Gardens Created in 1977 to mark the Queen's Silver Jubilee on land that was used for the 1951 Festival of Britain Dome of Discovery.

London Eye One of the few successes of the various late-twentieth-century millennium projects, the London Eye, a giant wheel

designed by Julia Barfield and David Marks, revolves through a complete vertical circle every forty-five minutes and provides users with an unrivalled panorama of London.
Hungerford Railway Bridge See p. 256.
Royal Festival Hall Robert Matthew's concert hall is the only permanent legacy of the 1951 Festival of Britain and the western-most of the various South Bank venues.
Waterloo Bridge See p. 256.

'Waterloo Sunset'
A view of the sky, river and buildings at this part of the river which the Kinks Ray Davies saw when he was taken outside by a nurse while in hospital in the early 1960s inspired the 1967 song 'Waterloo Sunset', one of the best-loved singles of the period. Ironic-ally Davies originally chose to ignore the London inspiration and call the song 'Liverpool Sunset', the 'dirty old river' being the Mersey, but changed his point of reference when the Beatles released 'Penny Lane'.

National Film Theatre Britain's leading art house cinema opened in 1952 and is home of the annual London Film Festival.
National Theatre More than 100 years in the planning, Denys Lasdun's bleak, stark concrete building opened in 1976, some twenty-five years after Princess (now Queen) Elizabeth laid the foundation stone, and has since been the setting for many memorable productions courtesy of successive artistic directors Peter Hall, Richard Eyre and Trevor Nunn.
London Weekend Television, Upper Ground. Headquarters of the television company that was founded in 1968.
Oxo Tower The surviving section of an early-twentieth-century power station, it was bought in the 1920s by the Liebig Extract of Meat Company, makers of Oxo, who circumvented rules on advertising by picking out the letters of the brand name in the design of the windows. Derelict by the early 1970s, it was later restored to include

apartments and what has become a renowned restaurant.
Sea Containers' House, 20 Upper Ground A 1970s hotel redesigned in the 1980s as offices for Customs and Excise.

BANKSIDE, SE1

Home of the 1990s-built Shakespeare's Globe Theatre and the Tate Modern art gallery.
Blackfriars Bridge See p. 258.
Albion Mill, east of Blackfriars Bridge A 1786 mill which was the first to grind corn by steam power and was soon producing 6,000 bushels of flour a week, it burned down in 1791, and in the charred remains the graffiti 'Success to the mills of Albion but no Albion Mills' was found, leading many to assume that the fire was an arson attack carried out by disgruntled indepen-dent millers.
Founders Arms The bells used for Wren's St Paul's Cathedral were cast on this site, now occupied by a pub.
Bankside Gallery, 48 Hopton Street. Head-quarters of the Royal Watercolour Society.
Tate Modern An ambitious art gallery created in the shell of Giles Gilbert Scott's disused Bankside power station and the most spectacular London development of the new millennium.
Cardinal's Wharf A rare surviving south London seventeenth-century terrace which includes at No. 49 the house where Chris-topher Wren may have lived while working on the reconstruction of St Paul's Cathedral opposite.
Shakespeare's Globe A 1990s theatre built in an Elizabethan style near the site of the original Globe Theatre and which hosts mostly Shakespeare plays in the open-air every summer.
Southwark Bridge See p. 259.
Anchor, 34 Park Street. A pub owned in the eighteenth century by Henry and Hester Thrale, friends of Dr Johnson.
Pickford's warehouses, Clink Street. Built

in 1864 for storing flour, hops and seeds over five floors.

St Mary Overy's Wharf A replica of the *Golden Hind*, the ship in which Sir Francis Drake circumnavigated the globe, stands here in dry dock.

'Nancy's Steps', west of London Bridge Once a popular spot for boarding boats to travel along the river, it is where in Charles Dickens's *Oliver Twist* (1839) Nancy tells Rose Maylie Oliver's story.

London Bridge See p. 259.

BERMONDSEY, SE1

A run-down area, built on marshy land, it was an important religious centre in the Middle Ages, and after the opening of the Surrey Docks to the east in the early nineteenth century was developed with tall warehouses built for storing flour, fish, maize, grain, syrup and spices.

St Olaf House An art deco 1932 block built for the Hay's Wharf company on the façade of which the name of the company is picked out in gold lettering.

Hay's Galleria A smart shopping area built into a former enclosed wharf, it was designed by Thomas Cubitt in 1857 for the Hay's Wharf group of companies, founded by Alexander Hay in 1651, which by the 1930s owned almost all the warehouses on the south side of the river between London and Tower bridges. Here, large ships unloaded their dairy cargoes, resulting in the area being nicknamed 'London's larder', and smelling, according to the docks writer H. M. Tomlinson, 'distinctly curious. A funny blended odour of the wood and straw of boxes of eggs, and of tea, cheese, butter and bacon'. The warehouses closed in 1969, the dock was filled in and the site was given a glass roof to house the new shops.

HMS *Belfast* A former Royal Navy cruiser which in 1943 helped sink the German cruiser *Scharnhorst* and has been used as a floating museum since 1971.

GLA building Foster Associates' Greater London Authority building has a transparent façade to symbolize the openness of the democratic process, incorporates energy-saving features such as natural ventilation and uses water from its own well.

Tower Bridge See p. 260.

Butler's Wharf, Shad Thames. Built in 1873 as the largest collection of warehouses on the Thames, it was converted into luxury flats in the 1980s and has long been popular with television and film producers, featuring in the scene in the comedy *A Fish Called Wanda* in which Otto (Kevin Kline) holds the lawyer Archie Leach (John Cleese) upside down from an upper window.

Design Museum Opened in 1989 as the first museum in the world devoted to the design of everyday objects.

St Saviour's Dock Once the mouth of the lower course of the River Neckinger, used as a port by the monks of the medieval Bermondsey Abbey.

ROTHERHITHE, SE16

A marshy peninsula which became a maritime area, it was from here that the Pilgrim Fathers sailed for America in the *Mayflower* in 1620.

Bermondsey Wall The river was embanked here in the eleventh century by the monks of the nearby Bermondsey Abbey who found a Saxon cross, the Rood of Grace, in the Thames in 1117 and claimed that it had fallen from heaven and had miraculous powers. During the sixteenth century the Rood was placed on Horselydown Common (near the junction of Abbey Street and Bermondsey Street), but was pulled down by a Protestant mob in 1559. The surrounding land was until the late nineteenth century Jacob's Island, a disease-ridden slum in which Dickens set the home of the villain Bill Sikes in *Oliver Twist*.

New Concordia Wharf Warehouses built in 1885, now apartments, sold to the Butler's Wharf company in 1934 with the agreement that they could not use the buildings for flour milling. Scenes from the film version of *The French Lieutenant's Woman* were shot here.

Cherry Garden Pier, Bermondsey Wall East Site of an eighteenth-century pleasure garden where J. M. W. Turner painted the *Fighting Téméraire* ship on its return from the Battle of Trafalgar.

Edward III's Manor House, Bermondsey Wall East / Cathay Street. Remains of the moated 1361 manor house of King Edward III, excavated in the 1980s, can be found here.

The Angel A fifteenth-century pub, founded by the monks of Bermondsey Abbey, where Samuel Pepys drank, according to his 1660s diary.

St Mary, St Marychurch Street. A church has occupied the site since the tenth century, the present building being erected from 1715 to 1737, and is where Christopher Jones, captain of the *Mayflower*, on which the Pilgrim Fathers sailed to America, is buried.

Rotherhithe Street Built as an embankment against the Thames and a bustling thoroughfare during Rotherhithe's maritime heyday.

Mayflower, 117 Rotherhithe Street. A pub named after the boat that took the Pilgrim Fathers from Rotherhithe to the New World, it is the only one in the country licensed to sell UK and US stamps.

Entrance to Surrey Docks An inlet leading to a string of docks, now mostly filled in, the first of which – Howland Great Wet Dock – was built in 1699, and the last – Quebec Dock – in 1926.

Cuckold's Point The point directly opposite Canary Wharf takes its name, according to local tradition, from the story of how King John seduced the wife of a local miller and in compensation gave the wronged husband (the cuckold) a portion of land from Rotherhithe to Charlton. The annual Horn Fair (the horn being a symbol of cuckoldry) used to depart from here *en route* to Charlton.

DEPTFORD, SE8

A great maritime centre until the twentieth century, Deptford became prosperous from shipbuilding and the naval yard founded by Henry VIII by the River Ravensbourne in 1513 so that England could prepare against the threat of invasion from France and Spain. After attracting wealthy residents, particularly sea captains and merchants looking for a pleasant residential environment away from the smoke of London, it became industrialized, covered with repair yards, gasworks, factories and jerry-built housing. Second World War bombing, a decline in maritime activity in the late 1960s and the building of crude municipal housing stock saw the creation of the modern-day slum, the Thames-side area desolate and the main streets lined with poundsaver stores and takeaways.

Royal Naval Yard (1513–1871), east of Grove Street. Henry VIII founded a yard to service England's first navy, which included a wet dock for fitting out ships and a dry dock for building and repair, in 1513, and it was soon the best-equipped dockyard in Britain, being where the ships used in defeating the Spanish Armada in 1588 were constructed. The yard was also the departure point in 1575 for the explorer Martin Frobisher, who left to find the North-West Passage, a sea route north of America linking the Atlantic with the Pacific, and was where ten years later Francis Drake departed from to sail around the world.

After the naval yard closed in 1871 the site was used for the Foreign Cattle Market, a source of employment for many local women, known as the 'Gut Girls', who earned considerably higher wages than they would have done in service in the grand houses of Blackheath and Lee, but who were also obliged to clean out the innards of slaughtered animals in the offal sheds. Their working conditions – alongside coarse, foul-mouthed men – and their after-work behaviour in the local taverns (which, no doubt, they learned from the men) caused much consternation among members of the Humanitarian League, who urged them to join the local Albany Institute so that they could spend their after-work hours engaged in 'useful' or 'wholesome' Christian activities. The market closed during the First World War, when the land was used by the War Office for storing supplies, and is now derelict.

Deadman's Dock, east of Grove Street. So named because when excavated in the 1920s it was found to contain large numbers of corpses, probably plague victims from the seventeenth century. It was also where prisoners from France, Spain and Holland were executed during the Napoleonic Wars. The site is now covered by the Pepys council estate.

Deptford power station (1887–1960s), north of Stowage. Sebastian de Ferranti chose the site to build what became the world's largest power station to harness the river water for cooling and to allow easy access for coal ships.

Deptford Creek The river inlet for the Ravensbourne River, which rises in Bromley and flows through Lewisham and Deptford.

GREENWICH, SE10

Long the wealthiest riverside settlement east of the City, Greenwich is now a major tourist centre, thanks to its many popular attractions.

Gipsy Moth, north of Greenwich Church Street. The 54-ft ketch in which Francis Chichester in 1966, at the age of sixty-six, became the first man to sail around the world single-handed rests at the spot where he finished his 226-day journey. Here Chichester was knighted by the Queen with the same sword that Elizabeth I had used in knighting Francis Drake here some 400 years previously.

Greenwich Foot Tunnel dome The Edwardian dome covers the stairwell leading down to the tiled tunnel that was the easiest means of crossing the river until the Docklands Light Railway was extended in 1999.

Cutty Sark, King William Walk. The fastest of the late-nineteenth-century tea clippers, named after the shirt worn by Nan, the witch in Robert Burns's 'Tam o' Shanter', it was built in Dumbarton in 1869, used for plying the route between Britain and the Far East until 1922, and brought to this site, home of the nineteenth-century Ship's Tavern, destroyed in the Second World War, in 1954.

Royal Naval College Wren's riverside masterpiece began as a refurbishment of Greenwich Palace and, when money ran out in 1664, was converted to a seamen's hospital. After the hospital closed in 1869 it was converted into the Royal Naval College, which moved out in 1998. The building is now part of the University of Greenwich.

Greenwich Park The oldest royal park in London, first enclosed in 1433, it became home of the Royal Observatory (now a museum), which is located at the highest point of the park, in 1675, and following the observatory's pioneering work in timekeeping was made the setting for the 0° Meridian in 1875.

Trafalgar Tavern, Park Row. Built in the 1770s and featuring large bowed windows and balconies that provide splendid views of the river (and now the Millennium Dome), it was renowned for its whitebait dinners in the nineteenth century but was converted into a seamen's hostel in 1915. Refurbishment to something approaching its original splendour came in 1965 when whitebait returned to the menu.

Crane Street Home of the Curlew Rowing Club, believed to be the oldest in London.

Highbridge The road is named after a fifteenth-century bridge beyond which, according to a decree issued by the Venetian Senate in 1453, Venetian galleys were forbidden to proceed upstream.

Trinity Hospital, Riverside Walk. Almshouses founded in 1613 by Henry Howard, Earl of Northampton and now run by the

Mercers' City Livery Company. A tablet set in the river wall commemorates the abnormally high tides recorded here in 1874 and 1928.

Greenwich Power Station Built in 1906 to power London's tram network.

Granite Wharf, north of Cadet Place. Stone for many of London's best-known buildings, including Admiralty Arch, was stored here after being quarried.

Enderby's Wharf, west of Mauritius Road Enderby's rope and cable factory, which made the cable for the first transatlantic telephone lines, opened here at the south-western end of the Bugsby Marshes peninsula in 1834 and made cables until 1979.

Millennium Dome The single most spectacular government-sponsored financial disaster in British history, built at the end of the twentieth century to house exhibitions during the year 2000 at a cost of almost £1 billion of taxpayers' money.

Blackwall Point The northern tip of Bugsby Marshes, where pirates were hanged in chains.

East London

THE EAST END, E1

> The East End is a vast city . . . a shocking
> place . . . an evil plexus of slums that hide
> human creeping things; where filthy men
> and women live on . . . gin, where collars
> and clean shirts are decencies unknown,
> where every citizen wears a black eye, and
> none ever combs his hair – *Tales of Mean
> Streets*, Arthur Morrison (1894)

The dark corner of London, shaped by
poverty, deprivation and violence, the East
End was barely inhabited when the Romans
journeyed along the Thames in AD 43,
reaching a huge lake by what is now

Wapping and setting up a military camp
'lost in a wilderness, like a needle in a
bundle of hay – cold, fog, tempests, disease,
exile, and death', as Joseph Conrad mused
in *Heart of Darkness*. When William the
Conqueror's forces reached London in 1066
a fort was built on Bryn Gwyn, a sacred
pagan site, which gradually grew into the
Tower of London – in turn fortress, prison,
barracks, palace, royal mint and tourist
attraction. Churches and religious institutions were founded nearby and the Tower
spurred on the growth of the surrounding
villages – the Tower Hamlets of Mile End,
Stepney, Wapping, Whitechapel et al. –
which developed through maritime trades
such as shipbuilding, repairing, sail-making
and cargo unloading which relied on poorly
paid, semi-skilled, casual labour, the volume
of work depending on the unpredictable
arrival and departure of the vessels.

As trade increased so did immigration.
Huguenots fleeing religious persecution in
France arrived at the end of the seventeenth
century; the Irish came after the potato
famine of the 1840s; the Chinese and Lascars
arrived in the mid nineteenth century; Jews
fleeing the pogroms of northern Europe
settled locally between 1860 and 1905; and
since the Second World War Pakistanis and
Bangladeshis have moved into the area. As
the population grew so the East End became
an ever more hostile area, home to 'every
type of delinquent – thieves, brigands, cut-
throats, coiners, forgers, bigamists, profli-
gate priests and pederasts – in holy order',
according to the twentieth-century Jewish
historian Chaim Bermant; it was the setting
for some of London's most infamous
crimes, in particular the Ratcliff Highway
murders of 1811 and Jack the Ripper's
murders in the 1880s.

The horrors of these events plus the
poverty, disease and depravity of the surroundings spurred on local philanthropists
to redouble their efforts to improve conditions: George Peabody created the
Peabody homes in 1864; in 1867 Thomas
Barnardo set up the Barnardo's children's

homes; the Salvation Army was founded by William Booth in 1878; and the Toynbee Hall welfare centre was opened by Canon Samuel Barnett in 1884.

Nevertheless, the East End remained the most deprived and depressed part of London, where life was a daily struggle for work, food and safety from attack. The Second World War destroyed much of the area, tearing apart communities and wiping away streets, houses, schools, shops and factories, and though the decimated landscape gave the authorities the chance of creating an improved East End, the opportunity was wasted and the landscape was blighted with socially divisive housing and shambolic estates. The closure of the docks and the decline of its attendant industries in the 1970s led to further impoverishment and the dereliction of vast tracts of land – problems that have been only partly alleviated by the recent gentrification of Wapping and Spitalfields.

(i) Mile End

A humdrum district between Whitechapel and Bow, Mile End is named after the first milestone eastwards from the City, which stood near the corner of Mile End Road and Stepney Green, a mile from the old Roman gate to the City (Aldgate), where in 1381 marchers from Kent and Essex allied with Wat Tyler's rebellion against the poll tax met the sixteen-year-old king, Richard II, and where 200 years later Henry VIII's bowmen practised. The fields were built over from the eighteenth century to house those employed at the various local breweries, railways, workshops and docks. Much of the area was wiped out in the Second World War, after which it was rebuilt with an uneven mix of poorly designed municipal flats set behind the road line in their own shabby grounds.

Mile End Road
Rickety shops built into the frontages of Victorian terraced houses and the widest

pavements in England can be found along the main road that connects Whitechapel and Bow, home to the market known as the Mile End Waste, where in the nineteenth century, according to Charles Dickens, 'Old iron and fried fish, cough drops and artificial flowers, boiled pigs' feet and household furniture that looks as if it were polished up with lip-salve, umbrellas full of vocal literature and saucers full of shell-fish in a green juice, which I hope is natural to them when their health is good, garnish the paved sideways.' The Waste was also home to the Penny Gaffs, described by Daniel Farson in *Limehouse Days* as 'the lowest form of entertainment in which a girl turned the handle of an organ until a man without arms appeared who could shave himself, play a violin and perform numerous feats with his toes', as well as oddities such as John Lee, the amateur boxer known as the Southpaw Cannonball and grandfather of the Kray twins, who made money by licking a white-hot poker. In October 1936, a week after fascists and Jews clashed in the Battle of Cable Street, half a mile south, all the windows of the Jewish shops on Mile End Road were smashed by supporters of the British Union of Fascists who during the violence lifted up a Jewish hairdresser, threw him through his shop window, and then attacked a four-year-old girl. In recent decades the street has declined as a shopping centre.
▶ The Battle of Cable Street, p. 279.

north side: Cambridge Heath Road to the Grand Union Canal
Trinity Almshouses, west of Bardsey Place Stone ships mark the entrance of the Trinity Brethren's almshouses which may have been designed by Christopher Wren and were built in 1694 to 1697 for '28 decayed masters and commanders of ships or widows of such', with money donated by sea captains Richard Maples and Henry Mudd. When the authorities proposed demolishing the almshouses in 1895 there was considerable opposition, particularly from the designer C. R. Ashbee, who had recently set up a

The Jack the Ripper murders

London's most infamous murders have inspired countless books, films, studies, pamphlets and tourist walks, gripping the public imagination more than any other crime in the capital's history due to their gruesome details, lack of motive and identifiable culprit. They had all the most clichéd but mesmerizing ingredients of the Victorian Gothic nightmare – the dirty, shabby, badly lit, fog-enveloped East End streets out of which the murderer appeared a number of times without warning, killing violently and disappearing without trace before vanishing for ever.

The Ripper's first victim is believed to be Martha Tabram, or Turner, who was found lying in a pool of blood in Gunthorpe Street, near Aldgate East station, on 8 August 1888. At the end of the month a woman later identified as Mary Ann Nichols, a prostitute, was found disembowelled and with her throat cut from ear to ear, on Buck's Row (now Durward Street), Whitechapel, half a mile east. On 8 September, two days after Nichols was buried, the murderer struck again, this time in Hanbury Street, Spitalfields, killing, mutilating and disembowelling Mary Ann Chapman.

As the news leaked out a crowd of several hundred gathered outside Chapman's lodgings, remaining there for several days. But though locals feared that the murderer would strike again nothing happened until 28 September when a letter sent to the Central News Agency warned: 'Dear Boss, I keep on hearing the police have caught me but they won't fix me just yet . . . I am down on whores and I shan't quit ripping them till I do get buckled. Grand work the last job was. I gave the lady [Annie Chapman] no time to squeal. How can they catch me now? I love my work and want to start again. You will soon hear of me and my funny little games. The next job I do I shall clip the lady's ears off and send to the police officers just for jolly . . . Keep this letter back till I do a bit more work, then give it out straight. My knife is nice and sharp. I want to get to work right away if I get a chance. Good luck. Yours truly, Jack the Ripper.'

The appearance of the letter, which some experts believe to be a hoax, proved timely, for in the early hours of 30 September two more women were violently murdered: Elizabeth Stride was found with her throat cut on Berner Street, off the Commercial Road; and Catherine Eddowes was found in Mitre Square, Aldgate, with her throat cut and her intestines protruding. A few hours later police received a postcard which read: 'I was not codding [joking], dear old Boss, when I gave you the tip. You'll hear about Saucy Jack's work tomorrow. Double event this time. Number one squealed a bit. Couldn't finish straight off. Had not time to get ears for police. Thanks for keeping last letter back till I got to work again. Jack the Ripper.' A few days later a gruesome package, containing a kidney, which may have been the one missing from the body of Catherine Eddowes, was delivered to George Lusk, chairman of the Whitechapel Vigilance Committee, with a note that ran: 'Mr. Lusk. Sir I send you half the Kidney I took from one woman preserved it for you. The

committee to campaign for the preservation of buildings of historical and architectural interest. The saved almshouses became the first buildings on Ashbee's preservation register, which eventually led to the Grade I and Grade II list of protected buildings.

Vine Tavern, No. 31, in front of almshouses William Booth first began preaching, promising 'heaven in east London for everyone', on 2 July 1865 outside the **Vine**, being greeted with jeers, oaths and rotten eggs. Undeterred, Booth founded the East London Revival Society, which in 1878 became the Salvation Army, a Christian other piece I fried and ate it was very nice. I may send you the bloody knife that took it out if you only wait a while longer. Signed "Catche me when you can Mister Lusk".'

A month of fruitless police work followed before the worst of the Ripper murders took place on 9 November 1888 when Mary Kelly, also a prostitute, was found lying on her bed in Dorset Street, Spitalfields, her throat cut and her body mutilated. There were no further similar murders locally until the following July, when Alice M'Kenzie was found murdered and mutilated on Castle Alley (now Old Castle Street), Aldgate. The last murder attributed to the Ripper, that of Frances Coles, occurred eighteen months later.

Despite assembling a huge investigation team and making several arrests, the police failed to find the culprit. Hampered in their inquiries by the absence of policewomen to act as decoys, police chiefs ordered a few male officers to patrol the streets in women's clothes. One heavily moustachioed officer, who kept his whiskers hidden behind a veil, stopped a male journalist, also dressed as a woman, and asked him: 'You're a man, aren't you? Are you one of us?', to which the journalist replied: 'I don't know what you mean, but I'm not a copper.' Meanwhile, bloodhounds, brought in to track the killer by tracing the scent through the alleyways of Spitalfields and Whitechapel, were taken to Tooting Common to be trained but immediately ran off, leaving the police to dispatch telegrams throughout the force to track down the dogs. The Ripper was never found.

welfare movement modelled on quasi-militaristic lines that paid for itself through donations and sales of the organization's newspaper, *War Cry*. In 1890 Booth published his ground-breaking work on poverty, *In Darkest England and the Way Out*, the title a pun on Henry Stanley's lecture series *In Darkest Africa*, which, with its down-to-earth prose, unembellished by moralizing tone ('When it's wet we stand about all night under the Arches . . . there are women who sleep out here. They are decent people, mostly charwomen and such like who can't get work'), became a best-seller. The Salvation Army now has some 16,000 branches in more than 100 countries.
▶ Toynbee Hall, p. 301.

Genesis Cinema, Nos. 93–95

The East End's only cinema stands on the site of the Eagle pub and music hall which was destroyed by a fire in 1884 and replaced by the Paragon Theatre of Varieties (designed by Frank Matcham, the greatest theatre designer of the late nineteenth century), where Charlie Chaplin appeared in Fred Karno's *Mumming Birds*. The Paragon was replaced by a cinema in the 1930s and was where on 26 February 1963 the première took place of the locally filmed *Sparrers Can't Sing*, produced by Joan Littlewood and starring Barbara Windsor. It was attended by the actor Stanley Baker, the comedian Roy Kinnear, the gangsters the Kray twins and society figures such as the Earl of Snowdon, but not his wife, Princess Margaret, who staged a diplomatic withdrawal after being advised against appearing in public alongside the Krays. The building closed in the 1980s and was reopened by Barbara Windsor in 1999.
▶ The Krays in east London, p. 310.

Charrington brewery (1760s–1975)

One of three large former breweries in the East End, the others being Ben Truman on Brick Lane and Mann's on Whitechapel Road, it was opened by John Charrington in 1766 and handed down through the family without incident until Frederick Charrington gave up his inheritance in 1870, at the age of twenty, after experiencing an epiphany outside an East End pub. There he saw a woman and her three children beg her husband for money to buy bread, only for the man to knock her into the gutter and enter the pub. As the brewery heir watched the wretched scene, his eyes glanced up at the pub sign with his own

name, 'CHARRINGTON', written in large letters above the door. Shocked at what he believed to be the effect of the family business on the local population, he chose to give up brewing and campaign for temperance.
► Ben Truman brewery, p. 284.

People's Palace (1887–1945) / Queen Mary College Graduation Hall, east of Bancroft Road

The creation of the People's Palace, the East End's first cultural centre, was inspired by a passage in the Walter Besant novel *All Sorts and Conditions of Men*, in which the heroine, Angela Messenger, uses her brewing fortune to demolish a 'whole four-square block of small houses' and replace it with a 'Palace of Delight . . . to awaken in dull, lethargic brains . . . a craving for things of which as yet they knew nothing'. The People's Palace opened in 1887 as a 'centre of intellectual and material advancement, recreation and amusement', incorporating a technical school, library and concert hall, and it was there that the local results of the 1945 general election, which resulted in a Labour landslide, were declared and photos of the winning candidates taken. When the pictures were relayed around the world they showed the new prime minister, Clement Attlee, standing next to the Stepney victor, Phil Piratin, a communist, much to the horror of the Americans who, having helped Britain win the Second World War, were about to embark on the Cold War with the Soviets to vanquish communism. Queen Mary's College has since taken over the site.

(ii) St George's

Caught between the glamorous Docklands developments to the south and east and bohemian Spitalfields to the west, St George's, ungentrified and little known, is named after the Nicholas Hawksmoor-designed church of St George-in-the-East, built at the junction of Cable Street and Cannon Street Road in 1729, and was developed in the eighteenth century with streets of cheap housing for sailors and Irish immigrants whose presence led to considerable unrest, culminating in anti-Irish riots in 1736. There was more fighting in 1813, this time between locals and Chinese Lascars, and the feeling that violence was always imminent led one incoming nineteenth-century preacher to announce memorably in his first sermon, 'Woe is me that I sojourn in Mesach, but dwell in the tents of Kedar', and to choose to live in more comfortable surroundings in the Strand.

Opium smoking in the East End

Chinese immigrants who arrived in St George's in the nineteenth century soon opened opium dens where, according to the *Pall Mall Gazette*'s James Greenwood, the opium master would hold in a flame a piece 'as large as a common grey pea' till it was done to his liking and then 'clap the precious morsel into the pipe that one of the Chinamen was already greedily sucking, and, to all appearance, be at once translated from earth to heaven'. The local opium scene transfixed the country's best writers. Charles Dickens, researching what became his last novel, *The Mystery of Edwin Drood* (1870), visited such a den where, according to the American J. T. Fields, who accompanied him, 'in a miserable court we found a haggard old woman blowing at a kind of pipe made of an old penny ink-bottle. We heard her croon as we leaned over the tattered bed on which she was lying . . . "Ye'll pay up according, deary, won't ye?"' Oscar Wilde had the eponymous hero of his 1890 novel, *The Picture of Dorian Gray*, search for an opium den where he could 'cure the soul by means of the senses, and the senses by means of the soul', eventually arriving at a 'small shabby house and [entering] a long low room which looked as if it had once been a third-rate dancing-saloon [where] some Malays were crouching by a little charcoal stove, playing with bone counters and grotesque things lay in fantastic postures on the ragged mattresses'. The opium dens faded away in the twentieth century.

Nor did the ill-feeling go away when the next wave of immigrants, Jews from eastern Europe, arrived, antipathy to the Jewish community culminating in the 1936 Battle of Cable Street in which Jews and communists blockaded Cable Street to prevent a British Union of Fascists march. The area was devastated by Second World War bombing, and in the 1970s the decline of the local dock industry brought about severe economic depression tempered a decade later by Pakistani and Bangladeshi immigration which has helped revitalize the local clothing industry.

● St George's is the area to the south-east of Aldgate.

Cable Street

An eighteenth-century street named after the ship's cables made locally, and originally the length of a nautical cable – 608 ft – it was later colonized by Scandinavians and Irish at its eastern end and Jews at the western end, leading George R. Sims to note in 1911 in *Off the Track in London* that 'you will not see a single curling-pin [on Cable Street]. The young alien Jewess dresses her hair very much as the work-girl of Paris does. It is neatly and artistically arranged, and it frequently boasts an ornamental comb, which, though cheap, is effective and picturesque.' When the British Union of Fascists tried to stage a march along the

The Battle of Cable Street

The most famous of London's many anti-fascist skirmishes took place on Sunday 4 October 1936. After months of simmering tension between Oswald Mosley's British Union of Fascists (BUF) and opponents fierce fighting prevented Mosley's followers marching along Cable Street through the heart of the local Jewish community. The BUF planned the march as a celebration of the fourth anniversary of the founding of the party and in the weeks leading up to the march the fascists stirred up tension by defacing the walls in Jewish areas with insulting slogans and on one occasion riding through the streets shouting through loud-hailers: 'The Jews have got the money. And how do you think they got it? From you of course! Jewish sweat-shops! The Yids drive in big cars on the money they make out of you.'

By 1 p.m. on the day itself over 2,000 Blackshirts were congregated around Cable Street, while some 500 anti-fascists and Jews, who feared the march might presage a pogrom, assembled at Gardiner's Corner, the junction of Whitechapel High Street and Commercial Road, chanting: 'They shall not pass'. When the cry went up 'Everyone to Cable Street' the crowd surged along Leman Street, throwing marbles at the police horses' hooves, tearing down a barricade, arming themselves with the jagged wooden pieces, and on Cable Street itself overturning a lorry, which they used as a barrier to prevent the fascists marching through. At 3.30 p.m., while some of the worst street fighting London has ever witnessed continued, Oswald Mosley's Bentley turned into Dock Street and was pelted with bricks. The fascists began chanting 'M-O-S-L-E-Y', the communists retorted with the *Internationale*, and the fascists' leader, surrounded by his wrestler bodyguards, gave a Hitler-style salute as his car was attacked.

When the police told Mosley to retreat and head west through the City of London, which was empty on a Sunday, rather than through the Jewish areas, he made a short speech in which he claimed 'the Government has surrendered to red violence and Jewish corruption'. Fascists in the crowd then began to sing the *'Horst Wessel Lied'*, but at four o'clock they headed off. The anti-fascists claimed they had won the day, as they had prevented the BUF marching along the predominantly Jewish Cable Street.

► The British Union of Fascists in Chelsea, p. 411.

street on Sunday 4 October 1936 to provoke the local Jewish community they met with considerable resistance, the events later passing into popular mythology as the Battle of Cable Street. In the 1950s a number of Caribbean merchant seamen moved to the area, and the following decade, around the time that the singer Paul Simon was an unlikely resident, most of the houses were demolished and rebuilt with low-rise council flats.

Cannon Street Road
St George-in-the-East
One of a small number of churches designed by the enigmatic Nicholas Hawksmoor, eighteenth-century Britain's leading exponent of the European Baroque, St George was built between 1714 and 1729 in the shape of a basilica, featuring a tower with an octagonal lantern and four pepper-pot turrets at the corners. In 1859 it was the setting for 'No Popery' riots when parishioners, on discovering that the vicar, Bryan King, had co-founded a secret brotherhood for priests, the Society of the Holy Cross, threw rubbish at the altar and brought in barking dogs to disrupt the services. Following the riots the church was forced to close for six weeks. St George's interior was destroyed during the Second World War and restored in the 1950s.
▶ Christ Church Spitalfields, p. 285.

Commercial Road
Commercial Road, the longest road in east London, was built in 1803 to allow imported goods unloaded at Poplar's docks to be brought into central London by road, and in its early days aspired to a level of gentility rare for the East End, with houses built on 'Places' or 'Terraces'. Industrialization wiped out the smart properties, which were replaced with cheap lodging houses used by seafaring people and travelling labourers. In 1875 a tiger which had escaped from **Jamrach's**, the exotic animal shop on Ratcliff Highway, made its way along Commercial Road where it picked up a small boy by the collar and made off with him, doubtless

with lunch in mind. The sight of the tiger, with attendant unwilling child, walking along the road caused much alarm, and led one passer-by to fetch a crowbar, but in trying to prise the child from the beast's jaws the man struck the boy a fatal blow. The tiger was eventually captured. Much of Commercial Road was destroyed by Second World War bombs but the shops that survived at the Aldgate end are now Asian-run rag trade cash-and-carry outlets.

Grace's Alley
Wilton's Music Hall
The oldest surviving music hall building in England, Wilton's was originally a pub, the Prince of Denmark, incorporating a concert hall with ornate mahogany furnishings, and was taken over in 1858 by John and Ellen Wilton, who ran it as a music hall for thirty years. From 1888 to the 1950s the building was used as a Wesleyan Mission Hall and when it was outlined for demolition in 1964 the poet John Betjeman led a successful campaign to save it from destruction. Wilton's has since been used by film companies looking for an authentic slice of Victoriana, featuring in *The Krays*, *Chaplin* and *Interview with the Vampire*, and it is now run by the Broomhill Opera Company.
▶ **Britannia Music Hall**, Hoxton, p. 330.

Henriques Street
A gloomy and uninviting street to the south of Commercial Road, it was known as Berner Street in the nineteenth century and later renamed Henriques Street after the philanthropist Sir Basil Henriques, known locally as 'the Gaffer'.
west side: Boyd Street to Commercial Road
Location of the fourth Jack the Ripper murder, No. 40
On 30 September 1888 Elizabeth Stride, a 45-year-old Swedish woman, was found with her throat cut and the blood still pouring out in the entrance to Duffield's Yard by No. 40, a spot where prostitutes regularly took their clients. The Ripper, presumably, struck again later that night at Mitre Square, near Aldgate station, half a

mile west, committing another bloodthirsty murder, and the following day a mob gathered on Berner Street protesting against the continuing killings and the police's inability to catch the culprit.

▶ Location of the fifth Jack the Ripper murder, p. 34.

Hessel Street

The street, which runs parallel to Cannon Street Road, is named after Phoebe Hessel who served for seventeen years in the 5th Regiment of Foot in the British army dressed as a man and died in Brighton in 1821 aged 108. By the early twentieth century Hessel Street was a centre of Jewish life which, the playwright Steven Berkoff later explained, 'could have been torn out of a European ghetto', the people speaking 'a dense soup of languages with Yiddish being the unifying one . . . [and where] old bent backs sold bagels in the street out of giant sacks'. The street is now dominated by halal butchers and small shops selling cheap clothes.

Royal Mint Street

Location of the eighth Jack the Ripper murder, north side, under the railway arch Frances Coles, a prostitute, was found dying under the railway arch to the north of Royal Mint Street by a policeman on 13 February 1891, some eighteen months after the previous East End murder attributed to Jack the Ripper. Police soon arrested Thomas Sadler, a merchant seaman who had consorted with Coles, and believed, understandably, that they might have caught Jack. But witness statements claimed that Sadler was so drunk at the time of the crime he could not have been the murderer and the jury returned a verdict of 'Willful Murder against some person or persons unknown', to the delight of crowds who had gathered outside the magistrates' court to lend Sadler their support. There were no further murders in the style of Jack the Ripper.

▶ The Ratcliff Highway murders, p. 298.

Eastminster / Former Royal Mint, south side at Mansell Street
Edward III founded the abbey of St Mary

Graces, briefly known as Eastminster and a Cistercian rival to the Benedictine abbey at Westminster, here in 1349, having previously vowed to build a monastery after surviving a shipwreck. It was shut down in the mid sixteenth century during Henry VIII's dissolution of the monasteries. In 1811 the Royal Mint moved here from the Tower of London and in 1968 the last minting of coins took place, after which the Mint moved to Llantrisant in Wales. The building is now an office block.

Swedenborg Gardens

And lo! Swedenborg is the Angel sitting at the tomb; his writings are the linen clothes folded up. Now is the dominion of Edom, & the return of Adam into Paradise – *The Marriage of Heaven and Hell*, William Blake (1790–93)

Swedenborg Gardens, a run-down stretch of cheap municipal houses, is all that remains of Swedenborg Square, originally Prince's Square, which was built by a John Prince in the eighteenth century and became the centre of London's small Swedish community with a Swedish church, gardens and pond. It was later renamed after Emmanuel Swedenborg, the Swedish philosopher and theologian who claimed to be in contact with biblical characters, kings, popes and saints and was a major influence on William Blake, who was buried in the church in 1772. When the church was demolished in 1908 Swedenborg's body was exhumed so that it could be taken to Sweden, and the skull removed by a Swedish sailor, who hoped to sell it as a relic, but when it went on display in an exhibition it was mixed up with another skull and the wrong one was returned to the coffin.

Wellclose Square

Wellclose Square was a Sherlock Holmes sort of place; not exactly producing lepers, abominable lascars and wicked Chinamen, but giving that impression all the same. – *The Plant Hunters*, Tyler Whittle (1970)

Severely blighted and pockmarked with council-owned buildings of astonishing ugliness, Wellclose Square was until the early twentieth century the most desirable address in the East End, lined with solid brick houses built around Caius Gabriel Cibber's 1696 Danish church that became home to the Danish ambassador, merchants made wealthy by the local silk industry and naval officers. Its most unusual resident was Chaim Samuel Jacob Falk, one of the leading Cabbalistic exponents of eighteenth-century Jewry, who fled to England penniless after being sentenced to death for sorcery in Westphalia, Germany, but was soon living in extreme comfort in Wellclose Square where he had his own private synagogue. Falk made a number of trips from Wellclose Square to Epping Forest to hold ritualistic ceremonies and, according to local legend, to bury chests of gold that are still in the ground. By the late nineteenth century Wellclose Square had become predominantly Jewish, the home of Jewish almshouses and the Hand in Hand Asylum for 'aged and decayed tradesmen'. It was destroyed by enemy bombs during the Second World War.

➤ Joanna Southcott, millennial prophet, p. 152.

(iii) Spitalfields

> Spitalfields meant Architecture, the Prince, Development schemes . . . gay vicars swishing incense – *Downriver*, Iain Sinclair (1991)

A cosmopolitan community of lively street markets, thriving cottage industries, brash neon-lit curry houses and carefully restored Georgian houses, Spitalfields is one of the oldest suburbs of the City and grew in the Middle Ages around the late-twelfth-century priory and hospital of the 𝕭𝖑𝖊𝖘𝖘𝖊𝖉 𝕭𝖎𝖗𝖌𝖎𝖓 𝕸𝖆𝖗𝖞 𝖂𝖎𝖙𝖍𝖔𝖚𝖙 𝕭𝖎𝖘𝖍𝖔𝖕𝖌𝖆𝖙𝖊, which came to be known as 𝕾𝖙 𝕸𝖆𝖗𝖞 𝖔𝖋 𝖙𝖍𝖊 𝕾𝖕𝖎𝖙𝖆𝖑. After the priory was dissolved in 1538 the land around the former hospital buildings, the Hospital Fields (since corrupted into Spitalfields), was built over. In 1682 Charles II granted a charter to hold a market, which took place until the 1970s

and was later replaced by the flea market that now occupies the Spitalfields market building.

In 1685 Huguenot silk weavers (French Protestants) fleeing persecution began to arrive locally. Refusing to work in factories, they set up workshops in the attics of the closely packed houses, planted in the gardens the mulberry trees they had brought with them and established London's first textile industry. By the end of the seventeenth century there were hundreds of weavers' workshops in Spitalfields, and on streets such as Elder Street, Folgate Street, Fournier Street and Spital Square the silk merchants built grand houses with marble chimneypieces and rococo plasterwork, some of which survive thanks to the high-profile conservation campaigns of the 1970s.

The local silk-weaving industry died out after the government lifted duties on the importing of French silks in 1860, but the clothing industry has remained, operated at the end of the nineteenth century by Jews based in small workshops, who sold their wares at the nearby Petticoat Lane (p. 289), and since the departure of the Jewish community in the 1970s, by Bengalis.

◉ Spitalfields is the area around Spitalfields Market, Commercial Street and Brick Lane.

Artillery Lane

> Well, I say, thrive brave Artillery Yard / that has not spar'd / Powder or paper to bring up youth / Of London in the military truth – *Underwoods*, Ben Jonson (1640)

A winding medieval lane running east from Bishopsgate, previously known as Artillery Yard, it was where Henry VIII's Royal Artillery Company practised until 1640 and features at No. 56 a 1756-built property that contains what many experts believe to be the finest Georgian shop-front in London. At No. 41 is a wedge-shaped late-eighteenth-century building which the Spitalfields Trust bought in 1977 when the grocer's that had been run by the same family since 1912 closed. When Trust members entered the property for the first time they discovered hundreds of antiquated food boxes and sixty years' worth of shop displays that had been sent by food manufacturers and never thrown away. The property was saved, but to the horror of the Trust was converted into an estate agent's office, decorated with 1980s 'period-style' fittings.

Bell Lane

Bell Lane was the 'worst area in all London', according to the *East End News* of July 1888, a time when the surrounding streets were so densely populated there were around 800 people to the acre, compared with a capital-wide average of fifty per acre. Next to the chicken slaughterhouse on the west side of the street from 1821 to 1939 stood the Jewish Free School, at one time the largest school in the British Empire, with 4,300 pupils. Though denominational, the establishment aimed at anglicizing its pupils and ridding them of their guttural European accents, and its alumni included the diamond merchant Barney Barnato; the comic Bud Flanagan; the danceband leader Joe Loss; Morris 'Two-Gun' Cohen, the only non-Chinaman to become a member of the Kuomintang, China's nationalist party; and the novelist Israel Zangwill, the leading Jewish writer of the late nineteenth century. №. 12, on the east side, was home in the 1820s to Ikey Solomons, the Jewish 'fence' (receiver of stolen goods) on whom Charles Dickens based Fagin in *Oliver Twist*. Twentieth-century renovation eradicated the worst poverty and modern-day Bell Lane has little to differentiate it from its neighbours.

Brick Lane

Brick Lane was a hotbed of villainy. Women sold themselves for a few pence. Thieves hung about the corner of the street. In the back alleys there was garrotting – *East End Underworld: Chapters in the Life of Arthur Harding*, Samuel Raphael (1981)

Home to successive waves of immigrants – Huguenots, Jews, Bengalis – and famous for its Sunday flea market and for having London's highest concentration of curry houses, Brick Lane is lined with Indian music shops, cafés, art galleries and twenty-four hour bagel bakeries, and is where underage prostitutes from eastern Europe ply their trade and Slavonic-looking men hawk trinkets and contraband cigarettes.

Named after the local sixteenth-century brick works and mostly fields in 1685 when the poorer of the Huguenot immigrants who came to London moved here, it grew after Ben Truman established the Black Eagle Brewery at the junction of Brick Lane and Hanbury Street in 1724. In the nineteenth century it became home to thousands of immigrant Jews fleeing persecution in eastern Europe, who crowded into the tenements and cheap lodging houses to man the sweatshops of the local rag trade. The Jews' unusual garb, strange accents and alien customs caused much resentment from the local native Englishmen, the novelist and journalist Arthur Morrison complaining of 'German-Hebrew provision shops [displaying] food of horrible aspect; greasy yellow sausages, unclean lumps of batter fried in grease; and gruesome polonies and other nondescript preparations repellent to look upon'.

As the Jewish population began to move away after the Second World War, Bengalis, mostly Chittagong seamen, arrived in Brick Lane and soon settled into the ways of the dwindling number of Jews, living in poverty in the same streets, taking up similar trades, but setting up halal butchers where there had been kosher ones, and opening curry houses where there had been kosher restaurants. The author Salman Rushdie, who later set parts of *The Satanic Verses* in the area, which he renamed Brickhall, was fascinated by the demographic changes and wrote how: 'When people board an Air India jet and come halfway across the planet, they don't just bring their suitcases. They bring everything. And this can lead to such strange things . . . teen-age girls [with]

Levi 501s, Madonna T-shirts, spiky hair [who] never think at all of going back to India or Pakistan, even for a visit. And yet you find among them a willingness, an eagerness in some cases, to have an arranged marriage. An arranged marriage!'

Just as the Jewish immigrants had been subjected to racist attacks, so the Asian immigrants were singled out. In May 1978 Altab Ali was chased along Brick Lane and murdered near Aldgate East station, and on 11 June that year around 150 white youths, mostly skinheads, rampaged down the street attacking Bengalis and smashing shop windows. During the 1980s the violence gradually abated and Asians became grudgingly accepted, if not welcomed. Tower Hamlets council erected street signs in Urdu and in a much criticized move tried to rename the area 'Bangla Town'. Although by then the main criminal activity was not racist violence but, ironically, turf wars involving Asian heroin gangs, thoughts that Brick Lane was no longer a target for racist violence were proved wrong in April 1999 when a bomb left by a lone Nazi sympathizer exploded near the police station.

Despite its long history of violence Brick Lane continues to thrive: a bustling street by day, a restaurant centre at night, where waiters rush out to grab potential customers, and a magnet for bargain hunters at weekends.

west side: Wentworth Street to Bethnal Green Road
Ben Truman brewery (1724–1980s), north junction with Hanbury Street
  . . . the prevailing winds that gifted us all with the odours of Truman's Brewery: odours you can taste, Whitechapel Madeleine – *Downriver*, Iain Sinclair (1991)
Workshops, studios, media company offices, furniture showrooms and cafés fill the site of Ben Truman's Black Eagle Brewery which opened in 1724 and soon began producing some 200,000 barrels of porter a year. By 1873 the extended firm, Truman, Hanbury

and Buxton, was the biggest brewer in the world and the air was filled with the smell of hops and yeast. The brewery closed in the 1980s and the site was redeveloped as part of the rejuvenation of Spitalfields.
Beigel Bake, No. 159
One of few London eateries open twenty-four hours a day, seven days a week, it sells bagels filled in the traditional north European Jewish manner – egg, salt beef, smoked salmon and cream cheese being the most popular choices – at the cheapest possible prices, attracting queues of customers which stretch outside the door but are served with admirable speed and efficiency.
east side: Bethnal Green Road to Old Montague Street
No. 92
Until the 1990s, No. 92 was Katz's, the last Jewish shop on Brick Lane, which survived for decades despite selling little other than bales of string.
No. 58
Rebecca and Morris Bloom opened their first restaurant, Bloom's, at No. 58 in 1920, building a reputation through their unique recipe for pickling beef. They later moved to bigger premises at 2 Brick Lane, which became known as Bloom's Corner and was destroyed in 1943 by a German bomb. Bloom's then uprooted to 90 Whitechapel High Street and is now in Golders Green, with a rival branch, run by a scion of the family, in Farringdon.
▶ Bloom's on Whitechapel High Street, p. 304.
Location of 1999 Brick Lane bomb, Nos. 46–48
A bomb planted by David Copeland, a 22-year-old vigilante staging a one-man war against immigrants and homosexuals, exploded on 24 April 1999 in a car parked outside the Café Naz curry house at 46–48 Brick Lane, injuring six people and damaging buildings, but causing considerably less damage than envisaged as Copeland had wrongly believed that Saturday, rather than Sunday, was the main market day. He had placed the bomb in a black

Reebok sports bag on nearby Hanbury Street, but a passer-by picked it up and took it to Brick Lane police station. Finding it closed, the man put the bag in the boot of his car and began walking to Leman Street police station. En route he remembered the bomb that had recently exploded in Brixton and stopped to phone the police which was when the bomb exploded.

▸ Copeland's Soho bomb, p. 199; Copeland's Brixton bomb, p. 405.

Brushfield Street
Spitalfields market
Charles II drew up a charter in 1682 to allow for a market selling 'flesh, fowl and roots'. Spitalfields market thrived, being extended in 1928 to provide storage space for new heated cellars where bananas could be kept, and further extensions followed the lifting of food rationing in the 1950s, resulting in the destruction of much of neighbouring Spital Square. In the 1980s the market moved to Temple Mills, Leyton and when the 1928 market building was threatened with demolition in 1987 locals campaigned for its retention, bringing about its conversion into a lively flea market. Plans unveiled at the beginning of the twenty-first century to redevelop the site and demolish part of the property resulted in the loss of some of the market's vitality.

▸ Covent Garden market, p. 108.

Commercial Street *Also see p. 301*
The street was cut through the slums of Spitalfields in 1845 and is now the main traffic route through the area, busy at weekends with visitors moving between Spitalfields Market and Brick Lane.

west side
Peabody Buildings, Nos. 135–153
This was the first of the many austere blocks of flats built from funds provided by George Peabody, the mid-nineteenth-century American millionaire who came to England and, shocked by the poverty he saw in the East End, asked for a meeting with the philanthropist Lord Shaftesbury. In 1862 Peabody set up a trust fund to ease suffering in slum areas, which resulted two years later in the first Peabody estate of forty flats and shops with laundries and baths, opening on Commercial Street. There are now some 12,000 Peabody flats in London.

east side: Shoreditch High Street to Wentworth Street
The Ten Bells, No. 94
According to local legend, Jack the Ripper is believed to have chosen some of his victims at this pub where Annie Chapman, the third victim, was working as a prostitute the night she was murdered. The sixth victim, Mary Kelly, reputedly ordered her last drink here before returning home to nearby Dorset Street, where she was murdered. The pub was briefly renamed 'The Jack the Ripper' in 1988 to mark the 100th anniversary of the killings, selling a Ripper Tipple cocktail and Ripper T-shirts.

Christ Church Spitalfields, Commercial Street at Fournier Street
The most famous and striking of Nicholas Hawksmoor's six surviving London churches, its spire soaring high above Spitalfields, Christ Church was built following the Tories' Fifty New Churches Act of 1711, but was not immediately popular with all architecture experts. Writing in 1734, James Ralph claimed Christ Church was 'one of the most absurd piles in Europe' and Hawksmoor retorted in kind, deriding 'Mr Rafe the Critick' for using the term 'Gothick to signifye every thing that displeases him, as the Greeks and Romans call'd every Nation Barbarous that were not in their way of Police and Education'. Many of the furnishings were gutted in the nineteenth century: the original altarpiece and communion table were sold in 1851 when Ewan Christian, architect of the National Portrait Gallery, renovated the church following a fire on Ash Wednesday 1836; the side galleries and old box-pews were removed in the 1860s; and further destruction took place in the 1880s.

The American writer Jack London, passing by in 1903 while researching what became *The People of the Abyss*, described how 'in the shadow of Christ's Church I saw a sight I never wish to see again . . . a mass of miserable and distorted humanity, the sight of which would have impelled Doré to more diabolical flights of fancy than he ever succeeded in achieving'. By 1957 the church had become increasingly forlorn and it closed for worship because of structural problems. In the mid-sixties meths drinkers took over the building, and in 1978 a group of architectural enthusiasts started campaigning for funds to restore the church. In 1996 English Heritage and the Heritage Lottery Fund launched a scheme to renovate churches and granted Christ Church £2.9 million, which was spent on repairing the tower and spire and cleaning the south façade to uncover the whiteness of the stone. By 2000 the floor of the aisle galleries had been reinstated to Hawksmoor's original designs.

The church's imperious beauty has long captivated writers. In his 1975 collection, *Lud Heat*, Iain Sinclair claimed that the three East End Hawksmoor churches – Christ Church, St George-in-the-East and St Anne, Limehouse – 'were centres of power for those territories; sentinel, sphinx form, dynamos abandoned as the culture they supported went into retreat', while the novelist Peter Ackroyd drew inspiration for his 1985 mystery novel, *Hawksmoor*, from the church, setting much of the book here.

► Hawksmoor's St Anne, Limehouse, p. 316.

Dorset Street
Now an unnamed service road between Crispin Street and Commercial Street, Dorset Street in the nineteenth century was popularly known as Dosset Street, owing to the large number of lodging houses, and was where Jack the Ripper killed his sixth victim, Mary Kelly, in November 1888.
Location of the sixth Jack the Ripper murder, **No. 26**, north side 50 yards west of Commercial Street
On the night of 9 November 1888 Mary Jane Kelly was murdered and mutilated, presum-

ably by Jack the Ripper, in her lodgings at 26 Dorset Street (a site now occupied by a multi-storey car park), only a few hours after she was heard leaving the flats singing: 'Only a violet I plucked from my mother's grave'. The murderer spent considerable time mutilating Kelly's body, completely disembowelling her as the fire lay burning. By the time she was found the next day her body was empty, the entrails draped around the room as if they were Christmas decorations. The police failed to arrest anyone for the crime, much to the fury of Queen Victoria, who told the prime minister, the Marquess of Salisbury, 'this new most ghastly murder shows the absolute necessity for some very decided action. All these courts must be lit, and our detectives improved. They are not what they should be.' The Ripper next struck the following July.
► Location of the seventh Jack the Ripper murder, p. 303.

Elder Street
One of Spitalfields' best-preserved streets, its houses were central to the 1970s campaigns that led to the preservation of the area.
Nos. 30–36, west side
In 1977 Douglas Blain, one of the leaders behind the campaign to preserve Georgian Spitalfields, successfully fought to save this stretch of Georgian houses, which included a property that was being used as a brothel and No. 32, the home of Mark Gertler, the painter who in the 1930s threatened to kill himself if the Spanish Civil War ended in government defeat; he committed suicide when the fascist leader Franco won. Blain found himself negotiating with a Polish landlord who used two surnames, Field and Galinsky, depending on whether he was buying or selling, and bought the terrace of four houses for £3,000 each before establishing the Spitalfields Housing Development Trust to conduct further restoration.
No. 7, east side
The campaign to prevent the destruction of Georgian Spitalfields became national news

in 1977 when a group of architectural historians, including Dan Cruikshank, Colin Amery and Mark Girouard, squatted No. 7, one of the few remaining local purpose-built weaver's houses, and held an at-home to which they invited John Betjeman, the poet laureate. Betjeman offered his support for their campaign and after much publicity the owners agreed to sell to the conservationists.

Fashion Street
Unicorns can't grow in Fashion Street, but boys have to – *A Kid for Two Farthings*, Wolf Mankowitz (1955)

An untidy side street off Brick Lane which Israel Zangwill, the main chronicler of the Jewish East End, described in his best-known novel, *Children of the Ghetto* (1892), as a 'dull, squalid, narrow thoroughfare [which] a dead and gone wag called Fashion Street', whose name should have been swapped with Rotten Row, the smart horse-riding route in Hyde Park. In the early years of the twentieth century Abraham Davis opened the ill-fated Moorish Market, a covered arcade with 250 shops, reading room and bathrooms – at a time when few people had their own – on the north side of the street, hoping to pull trade from Petticoat Lane, but saw his scheme fail. The screenplay writer Wolf Mankowitz and the playwright Arnold Wesker were both born on Fashion Street, Mankowitz in 1924, Wesker in 1932, and set some of their work here.

Folgate Street
The south side of Folgate Street, north of Spitalfields market, contains the best-preserved stretch of Georgian houses in Spitalfields.

Dennis Severs's House, No. 18
An unusual museum, open on the first Sunday of every month as a performance art 'Huguenot experience', until 1999 it was presided over by Californian artist Dennis Severs, its founder, who would greet visitors dressed in top hat and tails and invite them to wander at will through the house, where they would hear in the distance noises of a family of Huguenot silk weavers going about their daily routine. To add to the period charm Severs kept a pot of his own urine under his bed. Despite Severs's death in 1999 the house is still open as before, with the format relatively unchanged, minus the founder's quirky presence.

Fournier Street
Spitalfields' best street, abutted at each end by religious buildings with interesting histories – Nicholas Hawksmoor's Christ Church Spitalfields at the western end; and the Jamme Masjid mosque, formerly a church and synagogue, at the eastern – was built in the late seventeenth century and colonized soon after by silk-making Huguenot refugees fleeing France (who erected a barrier across the road to ward off trespassers). It is lined on both sides with Georgian brick houses with wooden door-cases, segment-headed windows and keystones, the ones on the north side also featuring attics built to give more light to the weavers' looms. After the silk industry died out in the nineteenth century Fournier Street declined socially, along with the rest of Spitalfields, but the houses survived and the street became the centrepiece of the 1980s regeneration of the area.

north side: Commercial Street to Brick Lane
No. 3
The property was used as a hairdresser's in the 1992 Neil Jordan film *The Crying Game*.
Former Market Café, No. 5
The café where the performance artists Gilbert and George, who live close by, breakfasted for thirty years, even being known to remove their jackets when it became uncomfortably hot, closed amid much dismay in September 2000.
Jamme Masjid mosque, Fournier Street at Brick Lane
The only building outside the Holy Land to have housed the world's three major monotheistic faiths – Christianity, Judaism and Islam – it was built in 1742 as a Huguenot chapel, the Neuve Église, and was one of a

number of local places where John Wesley, founder of Methodism, hosted the earliest Methodist covenant services in 1755. In 1819 the property became a Methodist Chapel and headquarters of the Christian Evangelical Society for promoting Christianity among Jews, but in 1898 it reopened as the Spitalfields Great Synagogue, run by the Jewish sect Machzikei Hadas V'Shomrei Shabbas ('strengtheners of the law and guardians of the Sabbath'), who refused to do work of any kind on the Sabbath – even carry handkerchiefs (they tied them around their waists), employing for vital tasks a flunkey known by the semi-insulting Yiddish term, the 'Shobbos Goy', who could not be directly ordered but had to guess the nature of their tasks by convoluted osmosis. Ironically, the Machzikei found harassment not so much from gentiles but from non-religious Jews, and in 1904, on the Day of Atonement, a day of fasting and the most important date in the Jewish calendar, worshippers taking a break from the service were pelted with bacon sandwiches by members of a local Jewish anarchist group driving a food van along the street, who in turn were pelted with stones and broken bottles by the orthodox Jews. The synagogue closed in 1965 and at the beginning of the 1990s was converted into a mosque.
➤ Rodinsky's Room, p. 290.

south side: Brick Lane to Commercial Street
Howard House, No. 14
A 1726 weaver's house where the silk for Queen Victoria's Coronation gown was woven.

Gilbert and George's studio (1968–), No. 12
The well-known performance artists Gilbert Proesch and Flete George Charles Ernestine Passmore, better known as Gilbert and George, moved to Spitalfields in the late 1960s, when the area was at its lowest ebb and one of the least fashionable enclaves of the capital ('it was like walking into a book in the nineteenth century: amazing light, and few people in the street, more like literature than reality', according to Gilbert), but

decades later found that their locale had become one of the most fashionable places in central London, thanks to the surrounding gentrification and the influx of artists into Spitalfields and Shoreditch.
Nos. 4–6
Built as a silk merchant's house by Marmaduke Smith in 1726, Nos. 4–6 – used in the late-twentieth-century television version of Dava Sobel's *Longitude* – is grander than most of the other properties on the street and features a rusticated central doorway, carved surround, cantilevered canopy and full height Doric pilasters, as well as being decorated internally with much mahogany, used because the duty on the wood had been lifted only four years previously. By 1914 the property was part banana warehouse and part tenement residence, and in 1977 it was bought by the Spitalfields Trust, becoming the first local house to be saved from destruction at a time when Georgian properties were being bulldozed because they were unfashionable or uninhabitable. When the property went on the housing market in 2000 for £1 million estate agents pointed out that a similar property in Chelsea would fetch between £4 and £5 million pounds.
No. 2
Built between 1726 and 1728 as the house for the minister of the adjacent Christ Church, it was designed not by local jobbing builders, like most of Spitalfields' houses, but by Nicholas Hawksmoor, the major church builder of the period, and is the only Spitalfields house for which there are construction records, now kept in Lambeth Palace.

Hanbury Street

Once an important side street of small shops and houses, it was where in 1896 the comedian and Crazy Gang stalwart Bud Flanagan was born Reuben Weintrop at No. 12, some eight years after Jack the Ripper murdered his fourth victim at No. 29. Weintrop chose for his stage name that of a particularly nasty sergeant-major he had encountered during the First World War, vowing to exact revenge by turning the man's name into a laughing stock.

Location of the third Jack the Ripper murder, 𝔑o. 29, north side

Mary Ann Chapman, a 47-year-old prostitute known as 'Dark Annie', was found murdered and disembowelled, her head almost severed from her body, at the back of **29 𝔥anbury 𝔖treet** on 8 September 1888, a week after the similar murder of Mary Ann (Polly) Nichols on Buck's Row, Whitechapel. As the morning broke a huge crowd gathered outside **𝔑o. 29**, some of them paying to be taken to an upper window of a nearby block to gain a better view of the spot where the body had been found. The following day the public, looking for a scapegoat, turned their attention to the local Jewish community, singling out John Pizer, a bootmaker known as 'Leather Apron', who had a reputation for bullying prostitutes and had previously served six months hard labour for wounding. When Pizer heard that police had found a leather apron near Chapman's corpse he went into hiding. But though he was arrested he had alibis for the times at which Polly Nichols and Annie Chapman were murdered. No one was ever apprehended for Chapman's murder, which is believed to have been the work of Jack the Ripper.

▶ Location of the fourth Jack the Ripper murder, p. 280.

Lolesworth Close (formerly Flower and Dean Street)

> . . . the ragged wretch who has never been taught to work . . . lives in Flower and Dean Street, where the policemen walk two and two, and the worst cut-throats surround him – *Work*, Ford Madox Brown (1865)

In the nineteenth century Flower and Dean Street had a reputation for violence, poverty and overcrowding, and following a cholera outbreak in the 1870s the Rev. Samuel Barnett, the social reformer who later co-founded Toynbee Hall, suggested demolishing the street and its cramped tenement blocks, a proposal which was greeted with widespread opposition on the grounds that it would make 13,000 people homeless. Abe Sapperstein, the businessman who founded the Harlem Globetrotters basketball team, was born in Flower and Dean Street in 1900, and two years later Jack London, the American writer, researching East End poverty in the guise of an American sailor down on his luck, lodged here. London had originally looked for local accommodation at Thomas Cook's on Ludgate Hill but was told: 'You can't do it you know. It is so – ahem – so unusual. Consult the police. We are not accustomed to taking travellers to the East End; we receive no call to take them there, and we know nothing whatsoever about the place at all.' London later wrote up his exploits in *The People of the Abyss*.

Middlesex Street (Petticoat Lane)

> The Lane was the stronghold of hard-shell Judaism, the Alsatia of 'infidelity', into which no missionary dared set foot – *The Children of the Ghetto*, Israel Zangwill (1892)

London's most famous street market, now a shadow of its former self, was previously Hog Lane, lined in the seventeenth century, according to John Stow's *Survey of London*, with hedgerows and elm trees. Before long, local Huguenot silk weavers were selling their wares here and the street soon acquired the nickname 'Petticoat Lane' on account of the silk petticoats on sale. In 1830 complaints about the street being named after an item of underwear led to the authorities renaming it Middlesex Street (it formed the boundary between the City of London and the County of Middlesex), and by the end of the century the market was dominated by Jewish rag trade workers, its busiest day being Sunday, when 'every insalubrious street and alley abutting it [was] covered with the overflowings of its commerce and its mud', according to Israel Zangwill. Although the modern-day market is still crowded it sells little other than cheap clothes, fake jewellery and dismal toiletries, with discerning shoppers now heading for Camden Town, Portobello Road or Brick Lane.

▶ Portobello Road market, p. 459.

Norton Folgate

Norton Folgate, the short stretch of main road linking Shoreditch High Street and Bishopsgate, is an ancient liberty – an area by the City of London but outside its jurisdiction – which belonged to St Paul's Cathedral in medieval times and took its name from the Foliot family, one of whom, Gilbert, was Bishop of London from 1163 to 1186. At No. 5 until the mid twentieth century was the 𝕭𝖑𝖚𝖊 𝕮𝖔𝖆𝖙 𝕭𝖔𝖞 pub, the setting for a major East End gangland showdown on 23 December 1911 between the gang led by Arthur Harding, who had already taken part in a number of shootouts in the Brick Lane area, and the Jewish villain Ikey Bogard, a pimp who liked dressing as a cowboy, openly carried a gun at a time when it was still legal to do so and ran a number of stalls on Petticoat Lane market. When the two gang leaders met Bogard offered Harding a drink, but the latter threw it and the glass at Bogard, leaving his face 'looking like a map of England', according to one witness. After the fight the pub's manager fled to Southend, and when Harding's gang ambushed Bogard's men as they came out of Old Street Magistrates' Court a few weeks later they declared themselves victors.

Princelet Street

Now gentrified, Princelet Street was a slum at the centre of Jewish life in Spitalfields in the nineteenth century and home at No. 19 to a synagogue which later became the setting for the story of Rodinsky's Room, turned into a book in 2000 by the novelist Iain Sinclair and the artist Rachel Lichtenstein.

north side: Wilkes Street to Brick Lane
No. 17
The 1886 birthplace of Miriam Moses, who in 1935 became the first British woman to become mayor of a local authority (Stepney).

Rodinsky's Room / Former Princelet Street synagogue, No. 19

> Rodinsky's room was left as he had abandoned it: books on the table, grease-caked pyjamas, cheap calendar with the reproduction of Millet's *Angelus*, fixed for ever at January 1963 – *Downriver*, Iain Sinclair (1991)

Brought to public attention through the writings of Iain Sinclair and his collaborator, the artist Rachel Lichtenstein, No. 19, built in 1718 by Samuel Worrall, master carpenter for Nicholas Hawksmoor, was inhabited by Huguenot silk weavers in the eighteenth century – their spinning wheel remains in the attic – and in 1869 was bought by Russian and Polish Jews who built a synagogue in the garden using furnishings made in Poland and transported to London intact. The building ceased being a place of worship in 1963, but caretaker David Rodinsky, a reclusive polyglot scholar who had lived there since the 1940s without upgrading the furniture or decor, stayed on for six years before suddenly vanishing. When workmen renovated the derelict property in the late 1970s they discovered a locked room that had been Rodinsky's refuge, piled high with 78 rpm discs, a table laid for a meal, an opened copy of the newspaper *Israel Reborn* and a calendar for January 1963, amended to Julian time, marked in cuneiform and dotted with notes about the Hittite kings. In the early 1990s, around the time that Iain Sinclair was adapting fantastic tales around Rodinsky into his novel *Downriver*, the artist Rachel Lichtenstein began collecting information on the mysterious caretaker, discovering that he had died of bronchial pneumonia aged forty-four in a Surrey mental hospital the year he vanished. She then became No. 19's artist-in-residence, collaborating with Sinclair on a book about the building and its attendant East End myths, *Rodinsky's Room*. The property is now the Centre for Immigration Studies.

south side: Brick Lane to Wilkes Street
No. 18
Built like No. 19 by Samuel Worrall, master carpenter for Nicholas Hawksmoor (in 1723), it is enticingly set back from the building line behind gates leading to an alleyway and for much of the twentieth century was used as a beansprout farm.

Hebrew Dramatic Club (late nineteenth century), Nos. 6–10
The Hebrew Dramatic Club was the major local entertainments venue for Spitalfields' Jewish community in the late nineteenth century, featuring a grand orchestra pit, library and restaurant, but on 18 January 1887 seventeen people were crushed to death after a false cry of 'fire' was made during a performance of the Hurvitz operetta, *Gypsy Princess*. The *Jewish Chronicle*, far from being sympathetic, blamed the tragedy on Yiddish-speaking Jews keeping themselves in 'persistent isolation' and warned fellow Jews to 'avoid such performances of strolling minstrels acting in the jargon [and] hasten the process of "Anglicising"'. After the fire the actors left for America, where many became major players in the emerging film industry. There is a relief of a cello in the pavement outside the house to mark the site.

Shoreditch High Street
The start of the Romans' route out of the City of London towards Lincoln, it is dominated by wholesale shoe warehouses and packing factories but contains no trace of the recent arrival of artists into Shoreditch.
St Leonard
Although the church, which has stood by the junction of the Romans' Ermine Street and the route from Clerkenwell to Hackney since the twelfth century, features in the nursery rhyme 'Oranges and Lemons', the original words were 'When I grow rich, Say

the bells at Fleetditch', referring to a long-demolished City church. Soon after rebuilding work on St Leonard's began in 1711 to the designs of George Dance the Elder the builders were sacked and replaced by cheaper Irish labourers, which led to three successive nights of local rioting. By the 1960s the church had no parishioners, thanks to the depopulation of Shoreditch following wartime bombing, but it somehow continues to survive.
► Oranges and Lemons, p. 65.

Spital Square
Spital Square, once the area's Georgian residential showpiece and now a sad spectacle, its grand houses almost entirely destroyed and replaced by a hotchpotch of ugly buildings, was built on the site of the **priory and hospital of St Mary of the Spital** in the late seventeenth century and soon inhabited by silk merchants. In 1891 the City of London Girls School was built here, and in the 1920s the Corporation of London demolished the eastern side to extend Spitalfields market. The western and northern sides followed the east side into obliteration when the Co-operative Wholesale Society later built a fruit warehouse, and by the 1960s the remaining silk merchants' houses had been vacated or were being squatted by tramps. The properties were subsequently served with compulsory purchase orders and all save Nos. 20 and 37 were demolished, with No. 20 itself later destroyed by the GLC. Ironically, the market building, which had been the cause of some of the destruction, was demolished within twenty years. Over the centuries excavation work has uncovered various findings including a cache of Roman urns, coins and bones, and recently, on the south side of the square, evidence of a large reservoir which acted as the main water supply to the priory, rubbish pits, and the remains of small timber and stone buildings.

(iv) Stepney

The name given to much of the East End until 1900 when the borough of Stepney was created (it was abolished in 1965), Stepney is now a small East End enclave between Mile End Road and Commercial Road which, because of its lack of riverfront or proximity to the City, has missed out on the gentrification that has occurred elsewhere in the East End and now contains some of the most deprived communities in Britain, inhabited mostly by immigrants from the Indian subcontinent. The name Stepney is derived from the Saxon warlord Stibba and it was a land of market gardens until the late eighteenth century when houses were built and colonized by Jewish immigrants, leading the Bishop of Stepney to complain that its churches would be 'left like islands in the midst of an alien sea'. The bishop was supported by the local MP, Major Evans-Gordon, who moved an amendment to the Queen's Speech in which he argued that these 'strangers from abroad' were taking homes, jobs and school-places from the natives. Evans-Gordon helped form the British Brothers League to campaign against Jewish immigration, which in turn led to the passing of the Aliens Act of 1905 curtailing further immigration. The rise of the Nazi party in Germany in the 1930s brought more refugees, but during the Second World War one third of Stepney's properties were destroyed by bombs. Subsequent redevelopment has not been kind, resulting in a landscape of ugly, barely habitable council estates.

Stepney Causeway

Dr Thomas Barnardo, an Irish medical missionary, set up his first home for destitute boys in 1870 at № 18 under the patronage of Lord Shaftesbury and limited the number of inmates to twenty-five until a boy called John Somers, who had been told the home was full, was found dead from exposure a few days later by a porter at Billingsgate market. Barnardo then changed

his policy and erected a sign proclaiming: 'NO DESTITUTE CHILD EVER REFUSED ADMISSION'. In 1874 he opened a photographic department at the home, to take pictures of every child on arrival and then several months later, when they had recovered from life on the street. He sold the photos as 'before' and 'after' cards in packs of twenty to raise the homes' public profile and bring in money. By the time Barnardo died in 1905 he had rescued some 60,000 destitute children.

(v) Tower Hill

The Tower of London and the land immediately outside its walls, the Tower Liberty, came under the jurisdiction of the building in medieval times, which gave locals certain advantages, such as being excused jury service and most taxes. In 1900 the land became part of the Borough of Stepney (now Tower Hamlets).

Tower Hill

Tower Hill, where every spring Druids celebrate the Equinox, was used by locals in the Middle Ages as a dumping ground until the Tower authorities complained of contaminated possessions left there during the Black Death of the fourteenth century. In 1381 rebels taking part in the Peasants' Revolt broke into the Tower, dragged out Sir Robert Hales, the Chancellor, responsible for enforcing the poll tax, and took him to Tower Hill, where they killed him by hacking away until 'being mangled with eight several strokes in the neck and head, he fulfilled most worthy martyrdom'. Hales was the first public figure to be put to death here, and before long Tower Hill was being used for executions such as (in 1535) that of Thomas More, who refused to accept the Act of Supremacy which made Henry VIII head of the English church, and (in 1540) that of Thomas Cromwell, who organized the separation of the English church from Rome and dissolved the monasteries.

When the notoriously unreliable

executioner Jack Ketch tried to execute the Duke of Monmouth on Tower Hill in 1685 his first blow caused only a slight wound and even after his second the duke's head refused to budge. Eventually the executioner had to call for a knife to complete the decapitation, but when the headless duke was taken to the Tower the authorities, realizing that no official portrait of him existed, asked the royal surgeon to stitch the head back on and tie a white cravat around the neck to make him look more appealing so that his portrait could be painted. The portraitist, William Wissing, had twenty-four hours to complete his work before the body started decomposing. The picture now hangs in the National Portrait Gallery.

Tower of London

If the King finds out that you are not a lady, the police will take you to the Tower of London, where your head will be cut off as a warning to other presumptuous flower girls – *My Fair Lady*, Lerner and Loewe (1956)

London's oldest collection of buildings and its principal tourist attraction, which has been palace, prison, mint, armoury, observatory and menagerie, dates back to 1078 when William the Conqueror built a small timber castle (now the White Tower) on what was Bryn Gwyn, a sacred pagan site where Bran, the crow god, was allegedly buried, as a show of strength, a symbol of security for locals, and a warning to miscreants.

Richard I was responsible for constructing more towers and increasing the size of the enclosed estate and Henry III and Edward I further fortified the Tower in the thirteenth century, when many of its famous buildings, including the Beauchamp Tower, were erected. Edward IV made the Tower the centre of his court in the 1470s and Henry VIII added a range of timber-framed buildings which after the Reformation came in useful as prisons for dealing with non-compliant religious figures, such as Thomas More.

The last monarch to use the Tower as a palace was James I (1603–25), and after the execution of Charles I in 1649 the Tower was mostly abandoned. As the complex attained its present appearance so its role as a prison and state fortress diminished, revived only during times of political crisis such as the Chartist riots of the 1840s and the First and Second World Wars when it received its last inmate, the Nazi deputy leader Rudolph Hess.

(vi) Wapping

Come, then, let's go fight with them / but first, go and set London bridge on fire / and, if you can, burn down the Tower too. / Come, let's away. – *Henry VI Part II*, William Shakespeare

Occupying an isolated V-shaped peninsula at the southern tip of the East End, Wapping, named after a Saxon warlord, Weappa, developed from the fifteenth century through boat-building and riverside trade carried out at the local wharves, warehouses and docks. It was for centuries the place where sailors and immigrants bound for London landed and many of its houses were filled with maritime paraphernalia – model ships, quadrants, chronometers and huge compasses. Unlike other parts of the East End, Wapping never attracted a middle class, even during its seafaring heyday, because people were dissuaded from living locally by the sight of pirates being hanged in public by the river edge and left on the gallows until three tides had washed over them.

In the early nineteenth century thousands of houses were demolished for the building of London Docks (1805) and St Katharine's Dock (1828), which created a new industrialized Wapping that thrived until the Second World War, when they were bombed. Although the docks were patched up, they closed in the late sixties, leaving Wapping a forlorn and forgotten place until the 1980s redevelopment when the bonded warehouses by the river were converted to luxury flats taken up by City workers and

Tower of London glossary

Beauchamp Tower Named after Thomas Beauchamp, a fourteenth-century inmate, it was often used to hold prisoners of high rank. Those jailed here include Thomas More, Henry VIII's Lord Chancellor; the Elizabethan explorer Sir Walter Ralegh; and the diarist Samuel Pepys.

Beefeaters The Tower is patrolled by Yeoman warders known as Beefeaters (a name that may have been derived from the French *buffetier*, food taster), established in 1485 as Henry VIII's bodyguard, who are clad in scarlet and gold dress uniforms and armed with a halberd, or pike, known as a partisan. The chief Yeoman Warder carries a staff topped by a silver model of the White Tower.

Bell Tower Elizabeth Tudor (later Elizabeth I) was imprisoned here for three months in 1554 for allegedly taking part in a plan to depose her half-sister, the devoutly Catholic Queen Mary. Guy Fawkes and his fellow conspirators involved in the 1605 Gunpowder Plot were interrogated in the Bell Tower before their trial at Westminster Hall. The diarist Samuel Pepys staged an epic treasure hunt in the basement in 1662 and with permission from Charles II dug up the floor looking for £50,000 in gold supposedly buried in butter churns. After fifteen hours they gave up, none the richer.

Bloody Tower (Garden Tower) Built *c.* 1400 and named the Garden Tower after the Constable's private garden, it was where in 1483 the twelve-year-old Edward V and his brother Richard, Duke of York, the so-called Princes in the Tower, were last seen before being murdered, after which the Garden Tower became known as the 'Bloody Tower'. In 1674 two skeletons, believed to be those of the boys, were found in the White Tower, placed in an urn, and reburied in Westminster Abbey. They were forensically examined in 1933 but could not be definitely identified.

Bowyer Tower Edward IV's brother, the Duke of Clarence ('false, fleeting, perjured Clarence', according to Shakespeare), was incarcerated in the Bowyer Tower after being accused of high treason and drowned here in 1478 in a butt of malmsey wine.

Brick Tower The Elizabethan explorer and poet Sir Walter Ralegh was sent to the Brick Tower in 1592 for seducing one of the queen's maids of honour but lived a fairly comfortable life, lodging with his cousin, the Master of the Ordnance.

Byward Tower The main entrance through the outer walls, built at the end of the thirteenth century.

Ceremony of the Keys Every night the 700-year-old Ceremony of the Keys takes place in the Tower during which the chief Yeoman Warder locks the West Gate, Middle Tower and Byward Tower and is challenged at the Bloody Tower by a sentry whom he tells he is bringing 'Queen Elizabeth's Keys'. At the end of the ceremony at 10 p.m. the Yeoman Warder raises his Tudor bonnet and proclaims: 'God preserve Queen Elizabeth', to which the guard responds 'Amen' and a bugler sounds the Last Post.

Chapel Royal of St Peter ad Vincula (Peter in Chains) The oldest chapel royal in England, it burned down in 1512 and was rebuilt three years later. Most of those executed on Tower Hill and Tower Green, including Lady Jane Grey and the Scottish Lords who took part in the unsuccessful Jacobite Rebellion of 1745, are buried here.

Devereux Tower Named after Robert Devereux, Earl of Essex, who was imprisoned here by Elizabeth I in 1601 before being executed.

Lanthorn Tower Built in the 1220s, it gained its name from the night-time lantern placed in the small turret of the roof to guide ships on the river.

Lion Tower The Lion Tower, which stood from 1200 to 1834 on the site of the present-day ticket office and refreshment room, was the home of the Royal Menagerie, founded in 1235 when the Holy

Roman Emperor gave Henry III three leopards. At one time a polar bear donated by the king of Norway was kept on a chain so that it could fish in the Thames without being able to escape. The collection was moved to London Zoo in 1828.

Martin Tower The Martin Tower was where Colonel Blood and others tried to steal the Crown Jewels in 1671. Blood hid the crown under his cloak while an accomplice secreted the orb and another filed the sceptre in half, but they were eventually disturbed and captured. Nevertheless, Charles II pardoned them and even conferred a pension on Blood, leading some to suppose that the king had set up the robbery, or that Blood had incriminating information on Charles. Henry Percy, the 9th Earl of Northumberland, known as the 'Wizard Earl' because of his enthusiasm for scientific experiments, was imprisoned in the Martin Tower for being one of Guy Fawkes's Gunpowder Plotters and while incarcerated here carried out considerable renovations, having paths, a sundial and even a bowling alley built in the garden outside. Eleven German spies were shot outside the Martin Tower in the First World War.

Queen's House Built in 1530 as the Lieutenant's Lodgings and renamed the Queen's House in 1880, it was where Anne Boleyn was held for eighteen days in 1536 prior to her execution for adultery and where Guy Fawkes was interrogated following his arrest in 1605 for taking part in the Gunpowder Plot against Parliament.

Ravens Legend has it that should the Tower ravens fly away the kingdom will fall. Just to be on the safe side the authorities clip the birds' wings.

Rudolph Hess The last prisoner held in the Tower, Hess, deputy leader of the Nazis, was incarcerated here from 17 to 21 May 1941 after parachuting into Scotland without warning and being taken to the Foreign Office in London amid the tightest security, lest the public discover that he was in the country and assume the government was negotiating for peace. When the prime minister, Winston Churchill, heard the news of Hess's capture he remembered more pressing matters and announced: 'Hess, or no Hess, I am going to see the Marx Brothers.' The VIP prisoner was later sent to Aldershot and after the war was held in Spandau Prison, Berlin. Military experts have since argued at length over whether Hess was acting unilaterally, had arrived to make peace, had been set up by the Nazis, was acting under the orders of the KGB, or even whether he really was the former deputy Führer.

St John's Chapel The oldest intact church in England, St John's Chapel was built in 1078 by Gandulf, Bishop of Rochester, and renovated in 1241. On the eve of his coronation Henry IV chose forty-six followers to be spiritually cleansed in the baths adjoining the chapel and as the men washed, the king made the sign of the cross on their back and knighted them, thus initiating the Ceremony of the Bath. Mary Tudor was married to Philip of Spain by proxy in the chapel in March 1554, the real wedding being held four months later in Winchester Cathedral.

St Thomas's Tower Built in the thirteenth century, it contains a small chapel dedicated to Thomas à Beckett, murdered at prayer in Canterbury Cathedral, and was where Roger Casement, the Irish nationalist who spied for the Germans during the First World War, was imprisoned, before being hanged at Pentonville.

Salt Tower Previously known as Julius Caesar's Tower, it was built by Henry III *c.* 1235 and used as a prison for Jesuits. The walls contain a number of inscriptions including a diagram cut in stone for casting horoscopes and carved body parts symbolizing the wounds of Christ.

Tower Green The scaffold was erected on Tower Green for beheading public figures such as Anne Boleyn and Lady Jane Grey whose public execution might have incited a riot. The timber houses on the site were built *c.* 1520.

Traitors Gate Most prisoners held in the Tower arrived by boat, rather than on the muddy cart tracks to the north, and entered through Traitors Gate.

Wakefield Tower Named after William de Wakefield, the King's Clerk in the 1340s, the Wakefield Tower was where state records were kept from 1360 and where on 21 May 1461 Henry VI was murdered at prayer. On the anniversary of Henry's death, staff of the two institutions he founded – Eton College and King's College, Cambridge – place flowers in the Tower.

Waterloo Barracks The gangsters Ronnie and Reggie Kray enlisted for national service in March 1952 at the Tower's Waterloo army barracks, but walked out after listening to their corporal's welcoming speech, telling the amazed corporal: 'We don't care for it here. We're off home to see our mum.'

Wellington Barracks Home of the Crown Jewels, which mostly date back to the restoration of the throne in 1660, and which include the crown made in 1837 for the Coronation of the eighteen-year-old Victoria, since worn by the monarch at each state opening of Parliament.

White Tower The oldest part of the Tower, built from 1078 to 1097, and therefore London's oldest building, it was renamed the White Tower after being whitewashed in 1240. Some thirty years later London's Jewish community, which numbered fewer than a thousand, was imprisoned in the crypt on charges of coin-clipping, some 260 Jews later being executed here. Richard II, coerced into giving up the throne, signed his abdication statement in the White Tower in 1399. Henry VIII briefly lived in the White Tower in the early 1530s and Guy Fawkes was shackled by his ankles and wrists in the tower's dungeon, 'Little Ease', after the Gunpowder Plot of 1605.

even celebrities (most notably the American singer Cher) looking for an unusual metropolitan bolthole. Despite the influx of money the locale is still swamped by an all-pervading eeriness and solitude that is unusual for inner London and Wapping has failed to return to its dock-era dynamism.

EAST LONDON LINE

The East London tube line uses the oldest tunnel on the network, Marc Brunel's 1843 Thames Tunnel, originally a pedestrian walkway linking Wapping and Rotherhithe, which began taking trains between Whitechapel and Surrey Docks from 1869, being extended north to Spitalfields (Shoreditch station) in 1876. Four years later the line was extended south, taking trains to Croydon, and even Brighton, journeys which were curtailed when two new southern termini were created at New Cross and New Cross Gate stations. In the 1990s the line closed for repairs and for the building of the new Canada Water station, which was held up while English Heritage ensured that Brunel's original tunnel was not spoiled. In the early twenty-first century plans were announced to extend the line north-west of Shoreditch station and link up with the North London Railway.

Shoreditch London's least-used tube station, closed outside the rush hour but open on Sundays, and located not in Shoreditch, but in a hard-to-find spot off Brick Lane.

Whitechapel Until 2000 the line's only connection with the rest of the network.

Shadwell Named after the new town to the north of Wapping which was developed in the seventeenth century by Thomas Neale, a landowner remembered in the names of several streets in Covent Garden.

Wapping The station is located at the northern end of Marc Brunel's 1820 foot tunnel, the first to be built under the Thames.

Rotherhithe The station is located at the southern end of the first Thames tunnel.
Canada Water The newest station on the line and a link with the Jubilee Line.
Surrey Quays Previously Surrey Docks, named after the nine south London docks that opened here in 1807.
New Cross Gate One of two termini, half a mile west of New Cross.
New Cross The other local terminus on New Cross Road.

Asher Way

𝕷𝖔𝖓𝖉𝖔𝖓 𝕯𝖔𝖈𝖐𝖘, south of Pennington Street, between Thomas More Street and Wapping Lane

The docks nearest to central London, designed by John Rennie and opened on 31 January 1805 to accommodate the growing volume of trade in the Port of London and prevent traders from avoiding paying duty, enjoyed a twenty-one-year monopoly on tobacco, rice and wine imported on all routes except those covered by the East India Company. Henry Mayhew, founder of *Punch*, who visited 𝕷𝖔𝖓𝖉𝖔𝖓 𝕯𝖔𝖈𝖐𝖘 in 1850, wrote how the quay was filled with men whose faces were 'blue with indigo [alongside] gaugers, with their long brass-tipped rules dripping with spirit from the cask, a group of flaxen-haired sailors chattering in German, a black sailor with a cotton handkerchief twisted turban-like round his head, a blue-smocked butcher, with fresh meat and a bunch of cabbages in the tray on his shoulder; and a mate with green parakeets in a wooden cage'. 𝕷𝖔𝖓𝖉𝖔𝖓 𝕯𝖔𝖈𝖐𝖘 closed in 1969 and five years later the water was drained (scores of vehicles, mostly stolen, were lifted from the empty dock), the excavations were filled in, new flats were built alongside, and an ornamental canal was created to maintain the water theme.
► East India Docks, p. 264.

The 'Call On'

Dock work, the most arduous job in London (given the absence of coalmines), was reliant on casual labour hired by the dock foreman, who wielded tyrannical power and took his pick of labourers at the 'Call On' outside the main dock gates, where thousands would gather looking for work once a ship had arrived in the port and needed unloading. When the hiring began, the men would rush towards the foreman, shouting his name, or calling out their own names, and they would scuffle with each other to gain ground. Some would triumph by a look or a wink, others would scream for all their worth and still be ignored, and those who were turned away (the majority) had to return later in the hope of being picked, which prevented them searching for work elsewhere. It was also known that the foremen were open to bribes in the form of a few drinks the night before a ship was due in and that many of them were in the pay of gangs, such as the Watney Street mob from Shadwell.

A labour market dominated by casual, unskilled work did little for the community's sense of its own worth. Wages were low and irregular and women were forced into the worst-paid and most menial jobs to supplement the family income. In 1889, during the biggest of the various dock strikes, the dockers carried poles topped with rotting fish heads – what they claimed was their main diet – through the City demanding wages of 6d an hour ('the dockers' tanner') and a minimum working period of half a day. They received much public sympathy, people blaming the inept dock companies for the chaos, and received donations totalling £24,000. Ten years later the individual dock companies were abolished and the Port of London Authority was founded, leading to some improvement in working conditions.
► East and West India Docks, p. 263–4.

Garnet Street

Garnet Street, which connects the Highway and the Thames, was originally New Gravel Lane, where sand dug from pits in Dalston was deposited on its way to the riverside works. The pawnbrokers and pubs that lined the street in its seafaring heyday have long since vanished, replaced by small, burrow-like council houses.

Location of the second Ratcliff Highway murders, No. 81, west side

On 19 December 1811 the Williamsons, who ran the King's Arms pub at 81 New Gravel Lane (now Garnet Street), were killed by an unknown assailant in the second set of the so-called Ratcliff Highway murders twelve days after the Marr family of nearby 29 Ratcliff Highway had been murdered in the middle of the night, possibly by the same assailant. During the attack, one of the lodgers, John Turner, made his way out of an upper window, shouting as he descended: 'Murder! Murder! . . . they are murdering the people in the house!', and when a crowd forced their way in they found Williamson at the foot of the stairs with his throat cut and his wife and maid upstairs bleeding to death, their throats cut, too. The alarm went out through the district and police launched a huge manhunt, resulting in John Williams, who had been Marr's shipmate, being charged with the murders. Williams committed suicide in the House of Correction at Cold Bath Fields, Clerkenwell before he could be tried.
▶ Location of the first Ratcliff Highway murders, p. 299.

The Highway (former Ratcliff Highway)

As I was walking along Ratcliff Highway / a recruiting party came beating my way / They enlisted me and treated me 'til I did not know / And to the Queen's barracks they forced me to go' – 'The Deserter', Fairport Convention (1969)

Now little more than a speedway track for vehicles leaving the City and the setting for some of the worst violence perpetrated in the history of the capital, The Highway is one of London's oldest routes, dating back some 2,000 years, and was originally a Roman Pretorian Way connecting the lake fort, Llyndin, with the gravel spur by the river at Ratcliff ('red cliff'). In the mid sixteenth century it was lined with hedges and 'long rows of elme and other trees', but by the time John Stow came to write his *Survey of London* in 1598 it had degenerated into a 'filthy strait passage with alleys of small tenements'.

As maritime trade increased, Ratcliff Highway became the point where, according to *The Annual Register* of 1763, 'dissolute sailors, blackmailing watermen, rowdy fishermen, stock-fish hawkers, quarrelsome chairmen, audacious highwaymen, sneak thieves and professional cheats', disembarking from boats at Ratcliff Cross, could enjoy their first shore leave after weeks on the water, visiting the street's brothels, beer houses and gin palaces.

In 1811 the road's reputation as a centre of depravity was underlined by the savage and motiveless murder of the Marr family of **No. 29** in the first of the so-called Ratcliff Highway murders. The horrific nature of the crimes made Ratcliff Highway the most notorious street in the capital – a status it held until the even more gruesome Jack the Ripper murders took place in other parts of the East End at the end of the century – but little changed over the following decades. According to Charles Dickens in *Sketches by Boz* (1837), Ratcliff Highway was a 'reservoir of dirt, drunkenness and drabs', and nearly thirty years later in *Our Mutual Friend* the home of Gaffer Hexham was 'down by Ratcliff . . . where accumulated scum of humanity seemed to be washed from higher ground'. A few years later a police officer talking to James Greenwood, researching his book *The Wilds of London*, complained how 'at times it is unsafe for our men to perambulate it except in a gang of three. They'd have the hair off a man's head if they could get a penny a pound for it.'

To rid the street of its stigma its name was changed in the late nineteenth century to St George Street, and in 1937 to The Highway, while slum clearance and Second World War bombing removed many of its buildings, including 𝕹𝕠. **29**, which were replaced by shabby estates set back behind grass verges. In 1986 the road became the scene of violent clashes outside Rupert Murdoch's News International plant when printers who had lost their jobs following the removal of *The Times, Sunday Times, Sun* and *News of the World* to Wapping clashed with the police.

► Fleet Street, p. 41.

𝕵𝖆𝖒𝖗𝖆𝖈𝖍'𝖘, Nos. 179–180, north side, opposite Artichoke Hill

London's foremost nineteenth-century store for the purchase of exotic animals was founded by a German, Charles Jamrach, and was the only place in the capital where the casual buyer could obtain, for instance, a lion, no questions asked. The store's wild animals, which also included elephants and monkeys, were kept in the yard on Betts Street, while the main part of the shop held curios assembled from around the globe including a jewelled buddha, Javanese pottery, Burmese temple bells and Japanese medicine chests. The store is featured in the literature of the period, being the London home of an escaped wolf in Bram Stoker's *Dracula*.

► Exploits of a **𝕵𝖆𝖒𝖗𝖆𝖈𝖍'𝖘** tiger on Commercial Road, p. 280.

Location of the first Ratcliff Highway murders, 𝕹𝕠. 29, south side, opposite Betts Street

The so-called Ratcliff Highway murders, the most notorious London killings of the early nineteenth century, began on the night of 7 December 1811 when just before midnight the householder and shop-owner, Timothy Marr, sent his maid, Margaret Jewell, to buy oysters. Unable to find any, Jewell returned home, and found the house in darkness, to her surprise. Her knocks alerted the neighbours who came out to help, and when they gained entrance they found Marr, his wife, baby and assistant dead, their throats cut. Posters went up throughout the vicinity proclaiming: 'Fifty Pounds Reward. Horrid Murder!', and such was the outrage at the killings that 100 guineas, later increased by the government to 500 guineas, was offered for information.

Twelve days later another similar killing spree took place a little further east on New Gravel Lane (p. 298), and police eventually arrested a sailor, John Williams, who had been a shipmate of Marr, at the Pear Tree pub on nearby Cinnamon Street. Williams was charged with the murders, but committed suicide in the House of Correction at Cold Bath Fields, Clerkenwell (p. 71) before he could be tried. His corpse was then dragged through the streets of Wapping on a cart which stopped outside **29 𝕽𝖆𝖙𝖈𝖑𝖎𝖋𝖋 𝕳𝖎𝖌𝖍𝖜𝖆𝖞** for a quarter of an hour and came to a halt at the junction of Cable Street and Cannon Street Road, a crossroads being the traditional site for those whose destiny was uncertain. There, hundreds watched as the corpse, a stake driven through the heart to exorcize the devil, was thrown into a hole. Around 100 years later the body was exhumed and mutilated, after which the bones were shared out among criminologists searching for forensic clues, and the landlord of the Crown and Dolphin at the junction where Williams was cast to the ground kept the skull as a souvenir.

► Location of the second Ratcliff Highway murders, p. 298.

Pennington Street
News International

The headquarters of Rupert Murdoch's News International group of papers – *The Times, Sunday Times, Sun* and *News of the World* – was built in the early 1980s amid some of the most intense security ever seen at an industrial plant. Murdoch, aware of the controversial nature of introducing new technology at the expense of the traditional print unions and their Fleet Street base, took every precaution. The Wapping site was ringed with razor wire and a 12-ft high steel fence and monitored by searchlights and closed-circuit cameras. Computer equipment was smuggled in and installed in a room guarded by electronic security, all mail was considered to be a potential letter bomb and scrupulously checked, and all documents produced in the office, even shorthand notes, were immediately shredded after use. Staff were warned to beware of car bombs, to check their vehicles carefully as they left work and to continue being vigilant when they arrived home. 'To ward off undesirables,' they were told, 'remove or trim trees and shrubs near the house to minimize the possibility of concealment.'

On Friday 24 January 1986 the first journalists were bused into the plant past the pickets and through electronically controlled front gates beyond which they were photographed and issued with identity passes that gave them access only to their own news room – each clinically white, open plan, fluorescent-lit and devoid of the Fleet Street ephemera of leather armchairs, piles of newspapers, dog-eared dictionaries and tea cups. The pickets maintained their vigil throughout the winter, which had a demoralizing effect on Murdoch staff who had to go into work every day past jeering and cat-calling. Public opinion, which had grudgingly supported Murdoch at a time of disillusionment with trade unionism, began to turn against him. Murdoch cleverly outmanoeuvred his detractors, offering the sacked print workers and journalists who had refused to go to Wapping the old *Times* plant on Gray's Inn Road as an office for a new left-of-centre trade union-friendly newspaper, even though surprisingly he was turned down.

▸ Fleet Street, p. 41.

Wapping High Street
See River Thames.

(vii) Whitechapel

> . . . away went the coach up Whitechapel, to the admiration of the whole population of that pretty densely populated

quarter. 'Not a wery nice neighbourhood, this, Sir,' said Sam, with a touch of the hat, which always preceded his entering into conversation with his master. 'It is not indeed, Sam,' replied Mr. Pickwick, surveying the crowded and filthy street through which they were passing – *The Pickwick Papers*, Charles Dickens (1837)

A busy part of the East End, taking in the market streets to the east of Petticoat Lane, the Whitechapel Waste shopping stretch, the sweatshops of the local rag trade industry and the brightly lit curry cafés around New Road, Whitechapel takes its name from the white stones used to build the chapel of 𝔖𝔱 𝔐𝔞𝔯𝔶 𝔐𝔞𝔱𝔣𝔢𝔩𝔬𝔫, which stood near Aldgate East station and was demolished in 1952 after Second World War bombing.

Its history has been one of poverty, deprivation and violence, much of it directed at immigrants – Irish, German, Jewish and more recently Bengali. In 1736 there were anti-Irish riots, during which a circus strong man, Enoch Foster, ripped up floorboards and hurled them through the windows of homes owned by Catholics. In 1742 John Wesley, the founder of Methodism, was pelted with eggs while preaching locally and was struck between the eyes with a stone by opponents who tried to set a herd of cows on him, Wesley noting in his diary that the 'brutes . . . were wiser than their masters'. And in the late 1880s a number of prostitutes were brutally murdered by the unknown assailant Jack the Ripper – whose crimes are still the most notorious killings in London history.

Alongside the violence was poverty. John Hollingshead, in his 1861 survey of local conditions, felt that the district should go by 'its more appropriate name of Blackchapel . . . overflowing with dirt, and misery, and rags', where the children 'dart about the roads with naked, muddy feet; slink into corners to play with oyster-shells and pieces of broken china, or are found tossing half-pennies under the arches of a railway', while the Revd Samuel Barnett, when offered the local parish of St Jude's in 1873, was told by the Bishop of London that Whitechapel was the 'worst district in London, containing a large population of Jews and thieves'. During the twentieth century conditions continued to be among the most deprived in Britain and though Second World War bombing destroyed many of the worst houses they were replaced by similar deprivation.

Cavell Street
The side street, which runs south from the London Hospital, commemorates the early-twentieth-century nurse Edith Cavell, who trained locally and moved to Brussels to become head of nursing at the Rue de la Culture in 1906. When the First World War broke out in 1914 Cavell stayed in Belgium, treating wounded allied soldiers and helping smuggle allied prisoners to safety. Dis-covered by the Germans in August 1915, she was arrested and sentenced to death.
► London Hospital, p. 306.

Chicksand Street
One of a number of depressed streets between Brick Lane and Vallance Road, Chicksand Street was where Bram Stoker, author of *Dracula*, briefly stayed in the late nineteenth century at No. 197, using it as one of the London addresses where the vampire count sends his boxes in the novel. In the 1920s Chicksand Street was home to Isaac Glassman's coal depot and there he, his daughter, Minnie, and her husband, Edgar Lansbury, son of the Labour poli-tician George, secreted the Crown Jewels of Russia, which the communists had origin-ally hidden under the Kremlin before taking them to London. When the jewels were sold in the 1920s Glassman offered the proceeds to George Lansbury to help fund his *Daily Herald* newspaper, but the latter rejected the offer. The jewels are now on display in the USA.
► Dracula in Hampstead, pp. 360, 362 and 363.

Commercial Street *Also see p. 285*
Toynbee Hall, No. 28, east side
The social reformer Canon Samuel Barnett opened a mission hall named after Arnold Toynbee, the Oxford economist and social reformer who had worked in Whitechapel, in 1884, running it in the style of an Oxford College, with a range of educational and social activities as well as accommodation. Hall staff helped Charles Booth research what became *Life and Labour of the People of London* (1889), the work that inspired the authorities to combat the worst of the local poverty, and a number of influential groups – among them the Workers' Education Association (in 1903) and the Youth Hostel Association (1931) – were established here, staff at various times including William Beveridge, the welfare state pioneer, who was sub-warden from 1903 to 1905, and Clement Attlee, 1940s Labour prime minister, who was secretary from 1910 to 1911. Quentin Crisp, the flamboyant homo-sexual, posed naked for art students in the hall in the 1930s (hence the title of his well-known autobiography, *The Naked Civil Servant*). John Profumo, the 1960s Tory war secretary implicated in the Christine Keeler scandal, rebuilt his public profile by becoming involved with the hall's charity work.
► Profumo Scandal, p. 157.

Durward Street
Location of the second Jack the Ripper murder, south side of road, east of railway bridge
Mary Ann Nichols, a 44-year-old prostitute, was found murdered on Durward Street (then Buck's Row), to the north of White-chapel station, at around 3.45 a.m. on 31 August 1888. Being the second murder of a prostitute in the vicinity that year, it caused panic among the public, but there were no witnesses, no weapon, nor any clues. The murder was later attributed to Jack the Ripper.
► Location of the third Jack the Ripper murder, p. 289.

Fieldgate Street
Tower House (Former Rowton House)

> The best [lodging houses] are the Rowton
> Houses, where the charge is a shilling,
> for which you get a cubicle to yourself,
> and the use of excellent bathrooms. The
> Rowton Houses are splendid buildings,
> and the only objection to them is the strict
> discipline, with rules against cooking, card
> playing, etc. – *Down and Out in Paris and
> London*, George Orwell (1933)

One of six fearsome-looking lodging houses
built by the philanthropist Montague William Lowry-Corry (Lord Rowton), Benjamin
Disraeli's private secretary, to provide cheap
and clean accommodation for working
men new to London, Rowton House was
described by the American social commentator Jack London as 'the Monster Doss
House' in *The People of the Abyss*, his 1903
account of East End poverty. But for much of
the twentieth century it was considered to be
one of the best places of its kind in London,
as George Orwell noted in *Down and Out in
Paris and London*. The building's most
famous inmate was Joseph Stalin, the future
Soviet leader, who as a 28-year-old stayed
here in 1907 during the London-based fifth
congress of the Russian Social-Democratic
Labour Party, the organization that gave
rise to the revolutionary Bolsheviks, occupying a cubicle alongside Maxim Litvinov, who
became the Bolsheviks' representative in
London at the time of the Russian Revolution and later Soviet ambassador to Wash-
ington. Tower House closed in the 1990s and
the building is now awaiting redevelopment.
► Lenin's Bloomsbury haunts, p. 92.

Goulston Street

A vibrant market street to the north of
Aldgate East station and home to Tubby
Isaacs's seafood stall, it was a poverty black-
spot in the nineteenth century when a
Whitechapel sanitary inspector found
twenty people living in one house and
twelve fowls feeding under a bed in another.
According to the novelist Israel Zangwill,
though, the street came alive at Jewish

festival times with a 'pandemonium of
caged poultry, clucking and quacking, and
cackling and screaming. Fowls and geese
and ducks were bought alive, and taken to
have their throats cut for a fee by the official
slaughterers.' On the night that Jack the
Ripper claimed his fourth and fifth victims,
30 September 1888, a policeman discovered
graffiti on the wall of Wentworth Model
Buildings, on the east side, which read: 'The
Juwes [*sic*] are not the men That will be
Blamed for nothing', and on the ground
below the graffiti a fragment from the apron
of Catherine Eddowes, the fifth victim.

To prevent a pogrom the police wiped the
words from the wall of the block which, at
that time, was inhabited by many Jews, but
failed to photograph the wall for their
records. Twenty years later Sir Robert
Anderson, the Assistant Commissioner of
Police at the time of the Ripper murders,
explained how officers had been 'certain
that the murderer was a low-class foreign
Jew. It is a remarkable fact that people of
that class in the East End will not give up
one of their number to gentile justice.' Or
as the Jewish commentator Chaim Bermant
later explained: 'If Jack the Ripper was a
Jew then one can be fairly certain that his
fellows would have kept quiet about it, for
the simple reason that the whole
community could have been held culpable
for his deeds.'
► The Jack the Ripper murders, p. 276.

Gunthorpe Street
Location of the first Jack the Ripper murder, George Yard Buildings (Sunley House)

Martha Tabram, or Turner, a 36-year-old
prostitute, was found dead on the landing of
George Yard Buildings, a block of flats
(since demolished and replaced by Sunley
House) on Gunthorpe Street, near Aldgate
East station, on 8 August 1888 in what is
now believed to have been the first of the
Jack the Ripper murders.
► Location of the second Jack the Ripper
murder, p. 301.

Old Castle Street
Location of the seventh Jack the Ripper murder, west side

At 12.50 a.m. on 17 July 1889 Alice M'Kenzie, a prostitute, was found murdered and mutilated, her throat cut and abdomen sliced open, on what was then Castle Alley, a passageway between Middlesex Street and Commercial Street, described in *The Times* as 'one of the lowest quarters in the whole of east London'. At the inquest a verdict of murder 'by a person or persons unknown' was reached. A drunk named William Wallace Brodie confessed to murdering M'Kenzie and claimed responsibility for all the murders associated with Jack the Ripper. Scotland Yard dismissed Brodie as being of unsound mind and it was later discovered that he had been in South Africa when most of the murders had taken place. The street is now home to the Women's Library, which was opened in 2002.

▶ Location of the eighth Jack the Ripper murder, p. 281.

Sidney Street
Sidney Street Siege, 𝕹o. 100

Three Latvian anarchists on the run from the police following a botched raid on a jeweller's in Houndsditch were traced to 100 Sidney Street, south of Whitechapel station, home of one of the raiders, William Sokolow, on 3 January 1911. Finding their escape route obstructed by police they fired guns, one shot hitting a Sergeant Leeson who fell to the ground and spluttered to his superior, Detective Inspector Wensley, 'Mr Wensley, I am dying. They have shot me through the heart. Good-bye. Give my love to the children. Bury me at Putney.' The officers, in need of reinforcements, contacted the home secretary, Winston Churchill, who was enjoying his morning bath, but once roused Churchill sent in the Scots Guards, who took up positions in the street and on various nearby rooftops. When Churchill himself arrived at Sidney Street he was taunted with cries of 'Oo let 'em in?', a reference to the Liberal government's hospitable immigration policy towards east European refugees, but as shots rang from the house the heckling abated. After a couple of hours of stalemate the house caught fire and collapsed, just as the postman came by on his round. When the fire brigade arrived to quell the blaze the chief police officer told them they would be shot if they attempted to intervene, which led to a public row between officers from the two bodies. After the blaze died out a policeman entered the burnt-out property and found the bodies of two men, Fritz Svaars and William Sokolow, but no third party. At the inquest it was alleged that Churchill had muttered at the time of the fire 'Let the bastards burn'. 𝕹o. 100 has since been demolished.

▶ The Houndsditch murders, p. 32.

Wentworth Street

A major market street off Petticoat Lane where food rather than clothes was traditionally sold. By the beginning of the twentieth century the street was home to fifteen kosher butchers and, on Sunday mornings, women plucking chickens and stallholders selling bagels, cholla, smoked salmon and pickled cucumber. The Jewish presence began to die out in the 1960s and there are now no Jewish stalls, the food available consisting of little other than grease-soaked beefburgers and hot dogs.

▶ Petticoat Lane market, p. 289; Bloom's, p. 304.

Whitechapel High Street

One of the shortest high streets in London but a major traffic route through the East End, Whitechapel High Street was developed during the sixteenth century as part of the main route between London and the Essex countryside and was lined with coaching inns such as the Bull, which Dickens featured in *Pickwick Papers*, and the Blue Boar, mentioned by Dickens in *David Copperfield*, which closed when the railways were built in the mid nineteenth century. Its two best-known current buildings, Whitechapel Art Gallery and Whitechapel

Library, date from the end of the nineteenth century when great social improvements were made in the area.

north side: Aldgate High Street to Osborn Street

Bloom's (1952–96), No. 90

The East End's most famous Jewish restaurant moved to 90 Whitechapel High Street in 1952, its 2 Brick Lane address having been bombed during the Second World War, and thrived despite the gradual exodus of the Jewish community from the East End and the waiters' habit of rudely angling for tips. In January 1996 the branch had its kosher food licence removed by the Court of the Chief Rabbi following a breach of the Jewish dietary laws, and after it closed down Michael Bloom opened a new twenty-four-hour restaurant off Hatton Garden (p. 72).

Whitechapel Art Gallery, No. 82

East London's foremost art gallery, one of the capital's most important centres for exhibiting avant-garde works, was the brain-child of the Barnetts (Canon Samuel and his wife Dame Henrietta), local late Victorian philanthropists extraordinaires, financed by John Passmore Edwards. It was built in the early years of the twentieth century in the art nouveau style of Charles Harrison Townsend, who was also responsible for the Horniman Museum in Forest Hill. The gallery soon became renowned for experimentation. In 1914 avant-garde works by Wyndham Lewis and Mark Gertler were exhibited; twenty-five years later Picasso's *Guernica*, a condemnation of the fascist bombing of the defenceless Spanish town of the same name in 1937, was displayed; and in August 1956 the gallery held the *This Is Tomorrow* exhibition, its centrepiece being Richard Hamilton's *Just what is it that makes today's homes so different, so appealing?*, a collage mocking the American-ization of Britain, which kick-started the pop art movement. Two years later the first Jackson Pollock display in Britain took place here and in 1971 Gilbert and George held an exhibition that involved the pair asking each other questions. From 1976 to 1988 the gallery director was Nicholas Serota who improved the building, raised funds and later became the main force behind the Tate Modern. His success has been continued by Catherine Lampert and Iwona Blazwick.

Whitechapel Library, No. 80

In the early years of the twentieth century the library was known as the 'University of the Ghetto' as it was where hundreds of Jewish immigrant children, including Jacob Bronowski, who became an acclaimed scientist and author of *The Ascent of Man*, first learned to read and write English. In recent decades Tower Hamlets council has failed to maintain the quality of the building or book collection, and in 2000, despite a local unemployment rate of around 13 per cent and figures which show that around a quarter of the population can barely communicate in English, the council announced plans to close the service and convert the building into an 'Ideas Shop'. On the wall outside is a plaque to Isaac Rosenberg, the Jewish poet and artist who lived in Stepney and used the library, and who was killed in the First World War trenches.

south side

Nos. 19–20

In 1927 Levy's gramophone shop which stood on this site was responsible for the first jazz music ever released in Britain, with works by Jelly Roll Morton, Duke Ellington and Louis Armstrong recorded for the British labels Oriole and Levaphone.

Whitechapel Road

Whitechapel Road is the greatest public pleasure-ground of the East End, accessible to all. Large music halls with broad lobbies and high stories and galleries are located there, and small hidden penny gaffs, in which there is little to see on account of the tobacco smoke, and little to hear on account of the noise – *A Picture of Civilisation at the Close of the 19th Century*, John Henry Mackay (1891)

The road along which Boadicea travelled to burn the City in revenge for the rape of her daughters by Roman soldiers became the main route from London to Essex and was where in 1813 the coach taking Lord Castlereagh, the unpopular early nineteenth-century foreign secretary, to his boat for the first overseas meeting to be attended by a British foreign secretary became trapped in icy fog. Castlereagh's party, terrified at the prospect of being attacked (it was only two years since the Ratcliff Highway murders had taken place half a mile south), sat on the trunks until they were safely beyond the dangers of the East End. As the nineteenth century proceeded the road became lined with music halls, penny gaffs, raucous pubs and theatres, and on Saturday evenings it was a parading ground for young Jews dressed up in their finery at the end of the Sabbath. Although the entertainment venues and the Jewish population have long departed, the road is still lively around Whitechapel station, with a market selling food, flowers, boots, books and cheap clothes by day and crowds weaving from pub to pub by night.

north side: Osborn Street to Cambridge Heath Road

Jewish Socialist Club (early twentieth century), Whitechapel Road at Fulbourne Street

The fifth Congress of the Russian Social-Democratic Labour Party, the communist agitators behind the Russian Revolution, opened in the Jewish Socialist Club at this address in May 1907, the delegates including the author Maxim Gorky, the revolutionary leaders Rosa Luxemburg and Leon Trotsky, and Joseph Dzhugashvili (the future Joseph Stalin), who claimed to represent the Bolshevik workers from the Borchalo district even though no party branch existed there then. It was here that Stalin first met Trotsky, whose murder in Mexico he engineered when Soviet leader thirty-three years later. Twelve Tsarist spies infiltrated the meeting to check up on their exiled political adversaries and a number of Scotland Yard officers, disguised as Russians, also attended to check on the Tsarist spies. Experts now believe the congress contained more police and secret service infiltrators than socialists.

➤ Lenin's Bloomsbury haunts, p. 92.

No. 259

John Merrick, the so-called Elephant Man, who suffered from neurofibromatosis, a disorder of the lymphatic system that severely disfigured his face, was in 1884 kept in a cage in the window of the shop at No. 259 (now a homeopathy clinic) and made to act like a dog to entice people inside to see a freak show. Merrick was rescued from his plight by Dr Treves, a specialist in skin disorders, who took him to the London Hospital, where Merrick taught himself to read using the Bible. In 1889, shortly after the murders now associated with Jack the Ripper, the building housed an exhibition displaying waxwork models of the victims' bodies.

Grave Maurice, No. 269

A gloomy and uninviting pub, even by East End standards, the Grave Maurice is named after Graf Maurice, a German Royalist mercenary of the English Civil War, and was a regular haunt of the Kray twins and much of the East End underworld in the 1960s. In 1964 Scotland Yard asked Inspector Leonard 'Nipper' Read (the policeman who later brought the Krays to justice) to watch over the twins' activities and when Read learned that Ronnie Kray was to be interviewed in the Maurice by TV presenter Michael Barrett he visited the pub incognito to watch Kray in action. Looking out of the window, Read saw a flash American car draw up, the driver get out and feel in his pocket, presumably to check that his gun was still in place, and enter the pub, carefully looking around the room. The man then returned to the car and after checking that the way was clear opened the back door of the vehicle with a flourish to let out Ronnie Kray who was dressed like a 1930s gangster, his cashmere coat nattily tied at the waist and reaching down to his ankles.

Kray made a suitably grand entrance into the pub, ordered a minion to frisk Barrett, even though the latter was wearing a neck brace, and when the interview finished left as ostentatiously as he had arrived.

Blind Beggar, No. 337

> Amid the moving pageant, 'twas my chance / Abruptly to be smitten with the view / Of a blind beggar – *The Prelude*, William Wordsworth (1805)

The pub is named after Bethnal Green native Henry de Montford, who fell at the battle of Evesham in 1265 and was found, blind and dressed as a beggar, by a nobleman's daughter who nursed him back to health.

At the end of the nineteenth century William Booth, founder of the Salvation Army, began selling his *War Cry* newspaper outside the pub, around the same time that it became home to a gang of pickpockets, one of whose number, according to James Morton's *East End Gangland*, was accused of murdering a man here by pushing the ferrule of an umbrella through his eye and was cheered back to the pub from court by regulars after being acquitted.

But it is for another murder, that of George Cornell by Ronnie Kray on 9 March 1966, that the Blind Beggar is best known. Cornell, an associate of the rival, south London Richardson gang, was sitting on a stool by the small U-shaped bar drinking a light ale, when Ronnie Kray and an accomplice, Ian Barrie, entered. Cornell exclaimed what were to be his last words, 'Well, look who's here then,' and while Barrie fired a shot into the ceiling Kray aimed his gun between Cornell's eyes and shot him dead. The needle of the jukebox, which was playing the Walker Brothers song *The Sun Ain't Gonna Shine Anymore*, sticking on the word 'anymore' which it began to play repeatedly.

There was little immediate response to the killing. Albie Woods, who was drinking with Cornell, cleared the pub of any incriminating glasses that might yield fingerprints and the underworld code of 'not grassing'

meant that both the barmaid and Woods claimed not to know the identity of the murderer, although, as Woods later pointed out, Cornell would have probably not wanted it any other way. Kray himself felt invincible, returning to the pub some time after to order a pint of 'luger and lime', but he was jailed for life for the crime in 1969. Although the pub has been gentrified it continues to attract thrill seekers.

▶ The Krays' Vallance Road headquarters, p. 310.

south side: Sidney Street to Whitechapel High Street

London Hospital, opposite Whitechapel station

The 1752 hospital was where Thomas Barnardo, founder of the boys' homes of the same name, underwent his medical training and where John Merrick, the so-called Elephant Man, lived after being rescued from a freak show at 259 Whitechapel Road. His remains are kept in the hospital museum, which is not open to the public. Because of its East End location, the hospital's casualty wing has often tended injured villains, including Eric Mason, a member of the Kray twins' firm – believed to be the last man to have been flogged in prison – who was thrown out of a car wrapped in a blanket outside the hospital in 1965 and was subsequently sacked from the Kray gang with a £40 'redundancy' payment. The hospital is now a major emergency centre and incorporates a helipad.

Hospital Tavern, No. 176

A regular haunt of East End villains, the pub was the setting in 1960 for a showdown between the Watney Street gang from nearby Shadwell and the Kray twins' firm, who were looking to avenge a three-year sentence Ronnie Kray had received in 1956 after attacking one of the Watney Streeters. Both gangs arrived for the fight armed with knives, chains and knuckledusters, and the Krays won overwhelmingly, the local papers describing it as the worst East End gang fight seen since the Second World War.

East London Mosque, Nos. 84–92
It opened in 1985 to cater for East End immigrants from Sylhet, Bangladesh, following a £2 million donation from King Fahd of Saudi Arabia.

Whitechapel Bell Foundry, Nos. 32–34
Britain's oldest manufacturing company was established by Robert Mot in 1570 and was where 200 years later America's 2,000 lb Liberty Bell, with its inscription: 'proclaim liberty throughout all the land unto all the inhabitants thereof', was cast. The bell cracked on the first ring but the captain who had brought it from England refused to take it back, and even though cracked it was hung in the Philadelphia State House steeple. Big Ben was cast here in 1858 and after the Second World War the firm replaced many of the London church bells destroyed by German bombs.

Altab Ali Park, east of Whitechapel Lane
The park is named after a local Pakistani, Altab Ali, murdered in 1978 in nearby Adler Street by members of the National Front, who chased him along Brick Lane and across Whitechapel Road. The land marks the site of 𝔖𝔱 𝔐𝔞𝔯𝔶 𝔐𝔞𝔱𝔣𝔢𝔩𝔬𝔫 church, destroyed in the Second World War, whose white chapel gave the area its name and whose churchyard contains the Martyrs' Monument dedicated by the local Bengali community to those killed in Pakistan for refusing to give up their own language and speak Urdu.

BETHNAL GREEN, E2

I began visiting those of our society who lived in Bethnal Green. Many of them I found in such poverty as few can conceive without seeing it – John Wesley (1777)
Farmland in medieval times, Bethnal Green, which is believed to have taken its name from a Saxon warlord, Bledda, became a slum in the eighteenth century as the growth of the weaving industry to the south, in Spitalfields, brought the lowest-paid workers into the area. Before long it was covered with the crudest type of tenement blocks and cottages, populated, according to John Hollingshead writing in 1861, with 'poor dock labourers, poor costermongers, poorer silk-weavers, clinging hopelessly to a withering handicraft, the lowest kind of thieves, the most ill-disguised class of swell-mobsmen, with a sprinkling of box and toy makers, shoe-makers, and cheap cabinet-makers, its women mainly hawkers, sempstresses, the coarsest order of prostitutes, and aged stall-keepers'.

Although the authorities welcomed in the new century by making major social improvements and demolishing the worst slums, such as the Old Nichol, to the east of Shoreditch High Street, a 1932 survey found some 60 per cent of local children to be suffering from malnutrition and 85 per cent living in unsatisfactory housing.

By then Bethnal Green was as renowned for its crime as its poverty, and with each working-class district having its own speciality (thieves in King's Cross, cat burglars in Hackney), Bethnal Green became known for its villains – those who relied on intimidation and protection rackets, with every man for himself – a state of affairs that reached its apogee in the 1960s with the local Kray gang. Second World War bombing devastated much of the area, but the rebuilding staged by Bethnal Green council and later Tower Hamlets council was of the crudest to be found in London, being mostly in the form of stark, ungainly tower blocks and shabby deck-access low-rise estates.

Bethnal Green Road
Before Bethnal Green Road, now the main thoroughfare running east–west through the area, was developed in the nineteenth century the surrounding land was a haunt of cattle rustlers who would attack herds on market days, grab as many animals as they could capture and hide the beasts in the marshes. When in 1826 the rustlers began to turn their attentions to people, staging robberies that on occasions ended in

murder, the local police watch sent a group of forty mounted officers into the area and the trouble gradually abated. Even since development which followed the arrival of the railways in the 1840s, the vicinity has continued to be one of the most lawless in London, being a favourite for Oswald Mosley's fascists in the 1930s and the main stamping ground of the Kray twins in the 1950s and 1960s. At the western end of Bethnal Green Road a weekend street market attracts huge numbers of people to examine what Robert Sinclair once described as 'unsellable junk, rusty nails, mouldy books, broken records – that fill the pavements by the railway arches and act as a perverted museum of household rubbish'.

north side: Shoreditch High Street to Cambridge Heath Road
Pellicci's, No. 103
An old-fashioned working-class café with typical decor of chrome fittings, mirrors and family portraits, it was a regular mid-twentieth-century haunt of the Kray twins, who would scold customers who used bad language.

St James, east of Pollard Row
The wedding of Reggie Kray and Frances Shea, held at St James's church on 19 April 1965, was east London's wedding of the year, attended by 200 guests, including the boxers Ted 'Kid' Lewis and Terry Spinks; and the photographer David Bailey. Telegrams were read from the theatre impresario Joan Littlewood, the actress Barbara Windsor and the singer Judy Garland. Some Kray experts claim the marriage was never consummated; two years later Frances Kray killed herself with an overdose of drugs.

south side: Cambridge Heath Road to Shoreditch High Street
Salmon and Ball, No. 502
On 6 December 1769 two weavers who had taken part in the so-called 'Cutters Riots', a campaign against low wages in the local silk-weaving industry, during which the silk was cut from the looms, were hanged outside the pub. In the 1930s the Salmon and Ball was a favourite of local fascists who held

meetings here when planning their attacks against local Jews.

St Matthew
The funerals of the Kray twins, Ronnie (on 29 March 1995) and Reggie (11 October 2000), and their elder brother, Charlie (19 April 2000), were all held at this 1746 George Dance-designed church. The best attended was that of Ronnie, whose coffin was carried by four pallbearers – Johnny Nash, Freddie Foreman, Ginger Dennis and Charlie Kray – representing the four corners of the London gangworld. It was London's biggest funeral since the death of Winston Churchill thirty years previously. Reggie, Ronnie's twin brother, was allowed out of prison, where he was serving a thirty-year sentence for the murder of fellow villains George Cornell and Jack 'The Hat' McVitie, and attended handcuffed to a *woman* officer. Outside the church there were more unusual characters – young men who, as Duncan Campbell remarked in *The Underworld*, 'looked uncertain whether they were auditioning for *Pulp Fiction* or *The Lavender Hill Mob*'. After the service the coffin, resting on a carriage led by six black-plumed horses and decorated florally with the word 'Ron', along with twenty-five limousines toured the local streets of Ron's 'manor' and proceeded on to Chingford where Kray was buried. The later funerals of Charlie and Reggie were each in turn less ostentatious.

St Matthew's has long enjoyed associations with villains. In 1839 it was the setting for the funeral of Joseph Merceron, Bethnal Green's first gangster boss, who was born in poverty in Brick Lane but rose through the ranks, legitimately, to become treasurer of parish funds, commissioner of the local court of requests and a justice of the peace. Once ensconced in office Merceron became a law unto himself, appointing members of his family to parish office, and at one stage owned around twenty local pubs where the licensing laws were ignored and dog-fighting and duck-hunting proceeded without objection. In 1818 Merceron was tried for fraud and convicted, receiving a £200 fine and an eighteen-month prison sentence, but on his release regained most of his original positions.

Cheshire Street
north side: Brick Lane to Hereford Street
The Carpenter's Arms, No. 73
The last pub to be owned by the Kray twins, the Carpenter's was where their infamous, omnipotent mother, Violet, held court every weekend, surrounded by over-dressed, bejewelled women sporting huge peroxide-coloured beehive haircuts, until the imprisonment of the twins in 1969. In January 1965 Ginger Marks, a local villain, was shot dead outside the pub by Freddie Foreman, the south London gangster, who had driven around Bethnal Green looking for him and Jimmy Evans who, Foreman claimed, had shot his brother. When Foreman spotted Marks and Evans walking along Cheshire Street eating chips he drove up, leaned out of the window and aimed his .38 revolver at the pair, at which point Evans grabbed Marks and used him as a human shield to protect himself from Foreman's bullets. Marks died instantly and police later concluded he had probably been shot in the stomach as they found a chip embedded in the wall of the pub. Marks's body, however, was never found – there were rumours he had been put in a cement-mixer and used in the construction of Hammersmith flyover – but it is more likely that a compliant undertaker inserted his corpse into an already filled coffin, as in the Sherlock Holmes story 'The Disappearance of Lady Frances Carfax'. Foreman was later acquitted of the murder and has since told reporters that his only regret about the affair is that he 'didn't shoot the two of them that night'.
Repton Boys Club, Cheshire Street at Hereford Street
London's best-known boxing club, it was where the Kray twins, who lived close by, learned their moves in the 1940s and 1950s, becoming two of the most feared schoolboy boxers on the circuit, and where Audley

Harrison, who won a gold medal for Britain at the 2000 Olympics, trained. The card game featured in the Guy Ritchie film *Lock Stock and Two Smoking Barrels* was filmed at Repton.

Columbia Road
Now home to London's best flower market, Columbia Road was the location of the huge Gothic 𝕮𝖔𝖑𝖚𝖒𝖇𝖎𝖆 𝕸𝖆𝖗𝖐𝖊𝖙 financed by the Victorian banking heiress Angela Burdett-Coutts, which opened in 1869 at the north-western end of the road. The building, which featured soaring turrets, Tudor arches, a quadrangle, cloisters and crypt, looked more like a northern England town hall than a London market and was described in the 1950s by architectural historian Nikolaus Pevsner as 'one of the great follies of the Victorian age'. Once it was built costermongers no longer needed to work outdoors, but the scheme was a flop for the costermongers preferred the streets and were not thankful for rules preventing them opening on Sunday on religious grounds and for signs urging them to 'Be Sober, Be Vigilant, Be Pitiful, Be Courteous'.

𝕮𝖔𝖑𝖚𝖒𝖇𝖎𝖆 𝕸𝖆𝖗𝖐𝖊𝖙 was later relaunched as a fish market, but opposition from Billingsgate resulted in another failure and trading ceased in 1885. The buildings were then used as furniture workshops and after suffering bomb damage in the Second World War were left to rot until 1960 when in a display of municipal incompetence typical of the postwar history of the area they were demolished. Had they been retained they would now be the most sought-after artists' studios in London, given the popularity of inferior nineteenth-century warehouses among the growing art community that has moved east in recent decades.
▶ Petticoat Lane market, p. 289.

Old Nichol Street
The Old Nichol, one of London's worst Victorian slums, located to the east of Shoreditch High Street, was, according to John Hollingshead in 1861, 'rotten with mud and water; its houses black and repulsive

[where] at least fifty dark sinister faces look at you from behind blinds and dirty curtains as you pass up the rugged pavement'. Two years later the *Illustrated London News* called the locality as 'foul a neighbourhood as can be discovered in the civilised world', and in 1894 the local-born novelist Arthur Morrison renamed the district the Jago in his novel *A Child of the Jago*, the name created in honour of the Revd Osborn Jay, vicar of the local Church of the Holy Trinity and the model for the priest who in the story attempts to reform a criminal. The Old Nichol was demolished towards the end of the century and replaced with the London County Council's Boundary Estate, which comprised more than 1,000 flats in twenty five-storey walk-up tenement blocks, a school, workshops, a public garden and a bandstand. Ironically, the Boundary Street rents were too expensive for the poor people who had been moved out of the Old Nichol and they were then obliged to find accommodation in similarly impoverished conditions further east.

Vallance Road

A long road of run-down estates connecting Bethnal Green Road and Whitechapel Road, and cut in two by a railway viaduct whose arches are filled with scrap metal merchants and car dealers, it was known during the Second World War as 'Deserters' Corner', owing to the number of local able-bodied men who shirked war duty living in the houses nestling under the bridge. One of them was Charles Kray, father of the gangster twins, Ronnie and Reggie, who lived at No. 178 and who claimed that having never previously 'worked for a guv'nor', he was neither willing nor able to obey the instructions of an army officer. In 1943 the ten-year-old Ronnie Kray contemplated committing suicide by throwing himself off the bridge that takes Vallance Road over the East London tube line.

𝔎ray twins' headquarters, 𝔑o. 178

A two-up two-down terraced Victorian cottage at 𝔑o. 178, demolished in 1966, was where the Kray twins, Ronnie and Reggie, grew up in the 1940s and later ran their powerful crime network, assembling an arsenal of choppers, machetes, knives, revolvers, Luger automatics, Mausers and sawn-off shotguns which they stored beneath the floorboards. When Ronnie Kray was released from Long Grove mental asylum in 1959 he spent his first few months huddled around the fire at 𝔑o. 178. If he went out it was after dark, dressed in a double-breasted suit, tightly knotted tie and shoulder-padded overcoat, carrying a sword-stick and .32 Biretta. The Krays were visited every day by a barber who would massage their hair with olive oil and surgical spirit and divided their energies between their long firms, protection rackets, casinos and nightclubs, even becoming involved with the mafia, who once asked them to burn £250,000-worth of laundered bonds in the dustbin at the back of the house. A housing association property now stands on the site, bearing a plaque commemorating not the infamous former residents but Prince Charles, who opened the new estate in 1988.

BOW, E3

Bow takes its name from the shape of the original stone bridge across the River Lea, the area's eastern boundary, and developed around the 'stink' industries – tanning, which involved boiling blood for making dye, and fulling, in which woollen cloth was pounded with water and fuller's earth to clean and thicken it – that the authorities would not allow in central London. When industrialization became more sophisticated in the nineteenth century local factories began producing soap, rubber and matches, which increased pollution to unprecedented levels. Although parts of Bow later became a popular suburb for City workers commuting on the new railway lines, Second World War bombing spoilt the area's appearance.

(i) north of Bow Road

Coborn Road

Colin McCallum, an ambitious late-nineteenth-century music hall star, renamed himself Charles Coborn after talking to a friend about a change of name on Coborn Road, Bow, and went on to become one of the leading performers of the era, best known for the songs 'Two Lovely Black Eyes' (1886) and 'The Man Who Broke the Bank at Monte Carlo' (1891). After Coborn premièred 'Two Lovely Black Eyes' at the **Paragon Theatre**, Mile End Road, he found himself unable to walk the streets of Bow without groups of youths bellowing the chorus ('Two lovely black eyes, / Oh, what a surprise! / Only for telling a man he was wrong, / Two lovely black eyes') at him. Five years later the songwriter Fred Gilbert offered Coborn the song 'The Man Who Broke the Bank at Monte Carlo', and the latter turned him down. But Coborn soon had second thoughts, and after spending the day mulling over the chorus ('As I walk along the Bois Boulogne / With an independent air / You can hear the girls declare / He must be a millionaire! . . .') he realized the song's worth and desperately sought out Gilbert to retrieve the song, paying him £10 for the rights when he found him. Coborn eventually recorded it, changing the pronunciation with each verse and chorus as befitting somebody becoming increasingly drunk on the proceeds of his newly found wealth, but sold the copyright for £600, a fraction of what he and his estate, let alone Gilbert and his estate, could have earned.

▶ **Britannia Music Hall**, p. 330.

Fairfield Road

Bow Quarter (Former Bryant & May factory), east side, north of railway line
The match girls' strike of 1888, staged by some 1,500 Bryant & May workers over pay and conditions and now regarded as one of the most significant dates in English labour history, came about after Annie Besant, a member of the left-wing Social Democratic Federation, heard a Fabian Society talk about the conditions in which the matchmakers worked. The talk described how the yellow phosphorus, which was used to make the matches even though it was banned in many countries, caused a yellowing of the skin, loss of hair and the withering away of the jaw, resulting in what was known in the trade as 'phossy jaw', a form of bone cancer in which the face discharged a foul pus and which often ended in death. Besant visited the factory the next day and discovered that the women worked a fourteen-hour day for low wages, their pay often reduced to cover fines for talking or dropping matches. She also found out that when the factory owner, Theodore Bryant, had chosen to erect a statue to his political hero, William Gladstone, the former Liberal prime minister, he had forced his workers to contribute to the cost by taking a shilling from their wages and had deprived them of half a day's work by closing the factory to 'celebrate' the unveiling.

When Besant complained to Bryant & May about the way they were treating their workers the company tried to force the staff to sign a statement stating their enthusiasm for their working conditions. A group of women who refused to sign were sacked and on 5 July 1888 the women went on strike. Besant successfully lobbied her well-connected friends to boycott Bryant & May's matches and organized the workers into a union. After three weeks the company announced that it would rehire the sacked workers and end the fines system, an unexpected victory for the strikers.

Bryant & May stopped using yellow phosphorus in 1901 and a later proprietor, Sir George Paton, won praise for running the works as a model factory, which explains why the company avoided industrial disruption during the 1926 General Strike. The factory closed in 1980 and the attractive Italianate red-brick buildings have since been converted into luxury apartments that are surprisingly popular given the aural brutality of the nearby motorway.

Grove Road

The Germans' Second World War V1s, pilotless planes designed to explode on impact and nicknamed doodlebugs, first fell in London on Grove Road at around half past four in the morning of 13 June 1944. Herbert Morrison, Minister for Home Security, forbade any immediate mention of the bombs in the press, lest the Germans realized how much damage they had caused. Their arrival meant that Britain's existing air-raid warning system had been rendered useless. On the west side of Grove Road in August 1993 the sculptor Rachel Whiteread took possession of 𝔑o. 193, the last remaining property on a Victorian terrace, itself due for demolition, and with the permission of the local council began work on redecorating the house, lining the interior with a metal mesh sprayed with concrete before dismantling the house's walls, doors and windows to leave a mass of concrete she called *House*, which won the 1993 Turner Prize. Tower Hamlets, rather than expressing its support, were horrified and insisted on demolishing the building.

(ii) Bow Road

Bow Road

A wide straight road which developed in the nineteenth century as part of the main route between London and Essex.
north side: Mile End Road to the River Lea
𝔇ouble '𝔑' 𝔔lub, No. 145
The Kray twins' main east London nightclub, furnished with items stolen by members of the Kray firm, was officially opened by the boxer Henry Cooper in 1957 and was run by Reggie Kray, as Ronnie was in jail. The former found he had a talent for running a club and the 𝔇ouble '𝔑' began to attract a glamorous crowd of sharp-suited businessmen, West End socialites, villains, actors and sportsmen, the entertainment provided by Queenie Watts and her sentimental cockney songs. But after Ronnie escaped from Long Grove prison hospital he began turning up at the 𝔇ouble '𝔑' when he

knew the place was free of police officers, jeopardizing the smooth running of the club by meting out disproportionate violence to anyone who crossed him. After Reggie was jailed in 1960 the 𝔇ouble '𝔑' began losing money and it soon closed. There is now a car hire firm on the site.
► The Blind Beggar, p. 306.

St Mary

The church, which dates from 1311 and this building from 1719, stands in an island in the middle of the road, the carriageway having run on either side since the Middle Ages, and is often confused with St Mary-le-Bow in the City of London, the so-called 'Cockneys' church', within the sound of whose bells true Cockneys are born. The mistake is compounded by the nearby pub being called Bow Bells.
► St Mary-le-Bow, p. 62.

Bow Flyover, Bow Road at River Lea
Legend has it that parts of the body of Frank 'The Mad Axeman' Mitchell, a violent but genial giant whom the Kray twins sprang from Dartmoor Prison in 1966 and then killed when his presence became a threat to their safety, were buried in the concrete supports of the flyover when it was being built. During Ronnie Kray's funeral procession, some thirty years later, twenty-six hearses crossed the river on this stretch of highway heading for Chingford Cemetery where Kray was to be buried. Given that the procession had no need to take this route its inclusion perhaps indicated a nefarious association.

(iii) south of Bow Road (Bromley)

Powis Road
Kingsley Hall, No. 21
The Indian leader Mahatma Gandhi, invited to London in 1931 for talks on Indian independence, rejected the chance of staying in the kind of luxurious hotel usually chosen for visiting overseas dignitaries. Instead he chose to stay at Kingsley Hall, a hostel run by volunteers (now a community centre), 'set among the rotting row houses, smelly

gas works and soap factories' of Bow, according to his biographer, James D. Hunt. Gandhi rose early and with his hostess, Muriel Lester, would take lengthy strolls along Three Mill Lane, across the River Lea, and on to the Northern Outfall Sewer walk, before heading back and journeying across London for his meetings.

Three Mill Lane

The best view of the myriad of waterways that constitute the southern end of the River Lea can be seen from Three Mill Lane to the east of Blackwall Tunnel Northern Approach. Their existence dates back to the ninth century, when King Alfred diverted the waterway into a number of different channels so that the water level dropped and the Danes who had sailed north along the river were marooned. Re-cut and retrenched many times since to aid navigation and commerce and prevent flooding, the waterways now consist of a bewildering number of branches with exotic names such as the Channel Sea River, City Mill River, Pudding Mill River, Three Mills Wall River, Waterworks River, as well as the main River Lea (or Lee) itself.

The Clock Mill

A white clock tower denotes the mill, once a gin distillery, where the Russian-born scientist Chaim Weizmann, who became the first president of Israel in 1948, worked on producing acetone, a solvent used in making explosives, for the British government during the First World War. While in London Weizmann promoted Zionism, which eventually resulted in the Balfour Declaration of 1917 that paved the way for the founding of Israel after the Second World War. The mill buildings have since been converted into workshops and film studios used in the 1990s for films such as Guy Ritchie's *Lock, Stock and Two Smoking Barrels* and Mike Leigh's *Topsy Turvy*.

POPLAR / ISLE OF DOGS, E14

Now home to London's most intensely developed commercial estate, Canary Wharf, as well as some of its bleakest council estates, Poplar, named after the large amount of poplar trees that grew locally, developed through shipbuilding, maritime trade and the opening of large docks in 1800, which made it the most industrialized part of London. Slum clearance, Second World War bombing and the closure of the docks in the 1960s devastated the area, but the southern section, the Isle of Dogs, has been the setting for the most remarkable urban regeneration the capital has experienced and is now home to much of Britain's newspaper industry as well as its tallest buildings.

● For riverside sites and the former docks, see River Thames, pp. 262–4.

(i) *Isle of Dogs*

> So we were fain to stay there, in the unlucky Isle of Doggs, in a chill place, the night cold, to our great discomfort –
> *Diary*, Samuel Pepys (1665)

A low-lying, mile-and-a-half long, U-shaped peninsula, bounded on three sides by the Thames, the Isle of Dogs, until recently best known for its large docks, heavy industry and inhospitable residents, has now witnessed the most remarkable urban regeneration ever seen in Britain, particularly around the small riverside estate of Canary Wharf.

The Isle was deserted until a chapel was built in the late fourteenth century near the modern-day Chapel House Street, probably for pilgrims making their way between Canterbury and Waltham Abbey, and it was abandoned when the river overflowed in 1448. Originally known as Stebunhethe (Stepney) Marsh, it became the Isle of Dogs in the 1580s for reasons which remain unclear, perhaps as a corruption of 'Isle of Ducks', 'Isle of Dykes' (to keep out the Thames), because Henry VIII's royal hounds were kept on the land, or more fancifully from a local legend about a dog that swam around the body of his dead master, who had been thrown into the sea, and later growled at a waterman, who turned out to be the murderer.

The land was prone to constant flooding until the sixteenth century, when it was drained by a Dutchman, Vanderdelf, who built an embankment and made it suitable for cattle, but as late as 1800 the by now ruined chapel was the only building and there were only two inhabitants, the man who drove the cattle off the marshes and the man who operated the ferry. Development came swiftly following the construction of the West India and East India Docks at the beginning of the nineteenth century and before long the Isle had become one of the most industrialized parts of London, with not only docks, but warehouses, factories, ironworks, brass foundries, cement works, potteries, shipbuilding yards and engineering firms filling the land.

Alongside the factories and workshops locals lived in barely habitable houses with mud seeping through the floorboards, their children obliged to stand at the back in school photos to hide their bare feet. The Isle's isolated position and harsh way of life created a community that was distrustful of outsiders (anyone not living locally was known as a 'foreigner') and in 1920 a group of residents closed the two roads that connected the island with Poplar and briefly declared independence. Wartime bombing wiped away much of the worst housing, as well as many factories, docks and shipyards, and although the docks prospered in the 1960s they soon closed and the industry collapsed, leaving a devastated landscape and an even more impoverished population.

Various ideas, many outlandish, were proposed for dealing with the derelict area, including a park, zoo and prison, but the various local councils could not agree on a programme, and it was not until Margaret Thatcher's Conservative government formed a new quango, the London Docklands Development Corporation (LDDC), which was given authority over the local councils in 1981, that urban regeneration began. The LDDC's powers to attract investment capital and circumvent restrictive municipal planning regulations led companies looking for a change from the City and newspapers who wanted to break the power of the Fleet Street print unions to move here into new offices, particularly at Canary Wharf where Britain's tallest skyscrapers have been built.

Alongside the new office blocks well-appointed flats have been built or converted from redundant warehouses, fast roads have been cut through (major roads had deliberately not been built while the docks were active, to discourage thieves), the Docklands Light Railway has been constructed, and at the end of the century the Jubilee tube line extension was brought to the Isle.

Canada Square
Canary Wharf
A narrow strip of land between the West India Import and Export Docks, Canary Wharf, London's biggest commercial development, has a working population of some 50,000 based in Britain's three tallest towers: No. 1 Canada Square (the tallest), designed by Cesar Pelli, clad in stainless steel, topped with a distinctive louvred pyramid and popularly known as Canary Wharf; Norman Foster's HSBC building (Nos. 8–16); and the Citigroup building (No. 33), also designed by Pelli.

Following the opening of the docks in the early nineteenth century the land was known as Rum Quay, on account of the produce unloaded here, and it was renamed Canary Wharf after the Second World War, when the Fred Olsen Line unloaded bananas and tomatoes imported from the Canary Islands next to a two-storey warehouse, the only building on the site. After the docks closed in the late 1960s the warehouse became derelict but redevelopment began following a meeting between the restaurateurs, the Roux Brothers, and Michael von Clemm, the chairman of the Credit Suisse First Boston bank. At the meeting, held on a barge moored on the river nearby, Von Clemm remarked that the derelict warehouse reminded him of those in Boston harbour that had been converted into offices and small business premises.

By the summer of 1985 the Chicago architects Skidmore, Owings and Merrill, creators of parts of the Manhattan skyline, had been hired to devise a scheme and the Reichmann Brothers, Canadian owners of Olympia and York, who had built on Battery Park in New York, had been brought in as developers. When work began in 1987 locals dressed in black staged a mock funeral procession, objecting to what they called the despoiling of their area, and they greeted the collapse of Olympia and York in 1992 with barely restrained *schadenfreude*. However Canary Wharf was rescued by a new consortium of bankers, led by Lloyd's, which was then bought out by one of the previously humbled Reichmann brothers, Paul, for £800 million, and by the end of the decade the original vision of a new financial centre for London, allowing City companies to relocate three miles downriver rather than in Paris or Frankfurt, was taking shape.

The first companies moved into Canary Wharf in 1991 and the estate has since grown at a phenomenal rate, now being the London home of a number of international companies (Citigroup, Morgan Stanley Dean Witter, Credit Suisse First Boston, BZW and the Hong Kong and Shanghai Bank), media groups (the *Telegraph*, *Mirror* and *Independent* newspapers, the Reader's Digest Association), an up-market shopping centre, a Docklands Light Railway station and a state-of-the-art tube station.

(ii) Limehouse

There are in Limehouse many sounds;
A hundred different sounds by day and
night – *Dockside Noises*, Thomas Burke (1920)

Few areas of London can match the romantic history of Limehouse, thanks to its long maritime tradition, the presence of London's Chinatown between 1850 and 1950, and the vivid, descriptive name, a reference to the local lime industry which was conducted in what Oscar Wilde described as 'strange, bottle-shaped kilns with their orange, fan-like tongues of fire'.

Mostly fields until the mid nineteenth century, when Burdett Road was cut through grazing land, Limehouse gradually became industrialized following the 1770 opening of the mile-long Limehouse Cut, London's oldest industrial canal, which linked the Thames with the River Lea and allowed goods coming into London from Hertfordshire to avoid the long journey around the Isle of Dogs. Alongside the lime works locals made ropes, built barges, wove sails and fitted out rigging and masts.

The opening of the Strangers Home for Asiatics in West India Dock Road in 1856 gave rise to the growth of a local Chinese community, and after the government passed a law banning the sale of opium in 1908 the Limehouse opium dens that had gripped the imagination of Charles Dickens and Oscar Wilde began to be replaced by cafés, Fan Tan parlours and laundries. A new Limehouse emerged to entice the next generation of writers, such as Thomas Burke, who described how 'by daytime a cold, nauseous light hangs about it; at night a devilish darkness descends upon it' in *Limehouse Nights* (1916), and Arthur Sarsfield Ward (Sax Rohmer), who depicted 'the sordid drama of Limehouse, with its orchestral accompaniment of river noises, a monotonous symphony, its frequent fog effects and sinister sadistic crimes casting a queer spell' in the entertainingly mysterious Fu Manchu stories such as 'Dope: a Story of Chinatown' and 'The Drug Traffic' (1919).

Chinatown declined after the 1930s, when a new law made it illegal to sign on a Chinese crew in a British port, and in the

1950s the advent of the automatic washing machine and launderettes caused the Chinese to close their laundries and move to Soho – where the rents were then cheap – to concentrate on catering. Limehouse suffered further economic decline after the closure of the local docks in the 1980s and now remains a bedraggled community tempered by occasional snatches of gentrification by the river.

Three Colt Street

St Anne, west side
One of six surviving Nicholas Hawksmoor-designed churches in London, St Anne was built in 1714 to 1730 in open fields following the 1711 Fifty New Churches Act, which the government brought in as a means of taking Anglicanism to areas that were rife with dissent. For the following 200 years the steeple, its design evoking that of a ship's topmast and crow's nest, was the first London landmark glimpsed by those arriving in the capital by sea, captains setting their chronometers by its clock. The church was damaged by fire in 1850, and bombed during the Second World War, but has since been restored.
► Hawksmoor's St Alfege, Greenwich, p. 390.
The Five Bells and Bladebone, No. 27, east side
The pub's unusual name is a combination of the five bells that would ring in the local docks at 2.30 p.m. and the whalebone that used to be displayed outside.

(iii) Poplar

> . . . the inhabitants of that end of the town where life goes on unadorned by grace or splendour – *Chance*, Joseph Conrad (1913)

Poplar, the area between Bow Common and the Isle of Dogs, was developed around noxious industries such as paint-making, bone-boiling and glue-making and consisted in the 1860s of streets of dull terraced houses with Caledonian names – Blair, Culloden, Ettrick, Glencoe, Leven, Nairn, and so on – until practically every letter of the alphabet had been used up.

Conditions here were among the least healthy in London – during the cholera outbreak of the 1860s a Poplar man checking his water tank following the death of his two children found a decomposing 14-inch long eel blocking a pipe. Poplar began to attract Chinese immigrants, who set up laundries and introduced exotic foods

---

George Lansbury and 'Poplarism'

Poplar, with a long history of municipal initiative and radicalism, was among the first London authorities to build public baths, wash-houses and free public libraries, and in 1921 it made the national news when councillors voted to give more poor relief to the local unemployed rather than hand over their levy to the London County Council (LCC). The government took Poplar to court and on 29 July 1921 council leader George Lansbury, accompanied by a mace bearer, brass band and 2,000 supporters, marched from the town hall on Newby Place to the High Court to reiterate the authority's refusal to levy the precept. Twenty-five male councillors were arrested and sent to Brixton prison, where they continued to hold council meetings in George Lansbury's cell, while the five women councillors were sent to Holloway. When other councils expressed their support the jailed Poplar councillors were asked to negotiate but refused to do so from prison. They were released (after six weeks inside) and the government relented, agreeing to apportion the precept according to each borough's means. Lansbury later became leader of the parliamentary Labour Party and in 1939, when mayor of Poplar, journeyed to Berlin to meet Hitler and Mussolini in an ambitious, but fruitless, attempt to seek peace. He died on 7 May 1940, disillusioned by the outbreak of the Second World War. His home, at 39 Bow Road, was, ironically, one of the first East End houses to be destroyed by wartime bombing.

and opium, living on streets whose names alone – Pennyfields, Ming Street and Amoy Place – were enough to send a vicarious thrill through the mind of the imaginative Londoner. In the Second World War Poplar was carpet-bombed and was later redeveloped by planners who were given licence to experiment in the knowledge that there would be little opposition from the local inhabitants. The result was chaos. Undamaged buildings – town halls, public halls, theatres, cinemas, pubs, libraries – which had serviced the community for generations were demolished because they did not fit into the planners' vision, important roads were turned into culs-de-sac thus losing their vitality, while new fast roads were cut through communities to take traffic across the area. The early-twentieth-century vision of George Lansbury, Poplar's former council leader and mayor, of a strong, cohesive working-class community using popular, well-funded municipal services was replaced by a dystopia of violent run-down council estates reliant on some of the worst municipal services in London in an area of overwhelming impoverishment and deprivation.

East India Dock Road

East India Dock Road, the main thoroughfare running east–west through the area, was built in 1805 to provide access to the new docks and was then the only means of crossing the River Lea south of Stratford. Because the incline was so steep the brakes on early motorized vehicles could not cope, forcing drivers to negotiate the descent by twisting their front wheels along the kerb. On the north side of the road stood the 𝕴𝖗𝖔𝖓𝖇𝖗𝖎𝖉𝖌𝖊 𝕿𝖆𝖛𝖊𝖗𝖓, treated by locals as the 'last' building in London – children would stand with one foot on the Middlesex side and one foot on the Essex side – which had an early hours licence to cater for dockers and was run in the 1960s by the actress and singer Queenie Watts. There is little of interest to be found now.

Giraud Street
Lansbury Estate

Built as a showpiece 50-acre estate of maisonettes, shops, schools and churches, and incorporating Britain's first shopping precinct, the Lansbury Estate, designed by Frederick Gibberd (best known for Liverpool's Roman Catholic Cathedral), was created as a 'live' architectural exhibition for the 1951 Festival of Britain on a site devastated by wartime bombing and was named after the late Labour politician George Lansbury. It paved the way for thousands of similar municipal precinct centres built along culs-de-sac rather than traditional roads, with buildings separated by communal grass verges rather than private gardens and facilities dependent on the whim of the local authority rather than a private investor.

The estate was heralded by much triumphant publicity, and residents initially kept the communal spaces clean and tidy while a porter looked after the external areas. But the problems the council had created for itself by introducing modernist architecture and experimental ideas on a whim gradually appeared and it soon became clear that the blocks and their layout were not conducive to communal living – few inhabitants knew, trusted or could depend on their neighbours. As the council began to get bored with the estate, funding levels dropped, facilities closed, repair work was overlooked and problem families were moved in, resulting in the Lansbury becoming a 'no-go' estate riddled with drugs, street crime and racism, a blight from which it has yet to emerge.

Pennyfields

I was glad when I was through Pennyfields. It was the only street in the miles of East London that I traversed day and night that inspired me with any real fear – *East of Aldgate*, Horace Thorogood (1935)

Until the mid twentieth century Pennyfields was the centre of London's Chinatown for those from Shanghai and Ningpo, its menacing atmosphere and record of violence giving rise to the legend that any white girl naïve enough to visit the area alone would be grabbed by a sinister Oriental, injected with an opiate, and taken to a boat on the Thames bound for the South China Seas and the white slave trade. The street was lined with cafés and gambling dens, regularly raided by police, where Chinese men played Fan Tan, a game in which a cup of haricot beans is covered and bets are placed on how many beans will remain after the contents have been divided into four, and Puk-a-Pu, or Plucking Pigeons, a game played on a sheet marked with Chinese characters. In the 1930s many buildings were demolished as part of the council's slum-clearance project and further devastation followed in the Second World War. Pennyfields was redeveloped in the 1960s with low-rise flats and shops (now mostly boarded up) and has remained impoverished and crime-ridden.

Robin Hood Lane
Robin Hood Gardens
A frighteningly utilitarian concrete estate, the epitome of austere postwar council housing, it was built by the husband-and-wife team of Peter and Alison Smithson in 1968 to 1972 and consists of two long slabs of pre-cast concrete, separated by a no man's land of landscaped open space and surrounded by a concrete segmented wall. The Smithsons' reasoning behind its design was that they wanted to provide an alternative to tower blocks and hoped that a low-rise estate of long corridors would revive traditional east London street life but in a safer environment. Instead, the absence of traffic, both human and vehicular, the resemblance of the concrete exterior to a Stalinist concentration camp and the estate's location next to the thunderous Blackwall Tunnel approach road has resulted in one of the most dystopian estates in London.
► The Barbican, p. 14.

North London

THE ANGEL | ISLINGTON, N1

A coveted address for the stylish and moneyed and a place in tune with the most fashionable ideas and attitudes of the day, Islington began as Yseldon, a rural retreat near the City, where cattle were fattened before making the last leg of their journey to the slaughter-houses of Smithfield, and was pock-marked with a chain of ponds until nineteenth-century development saw elegant squares and terraces built in Barnsbury, Canonbury and De Beauvoir. Much of the ensuing development, however, was shabby, and a 1967 survey found that Islington had the highest proportion (60 per cent) of houses in London in multi-occupation, many with outside toilets and no baths. Gentrification came following the opening of the fast Victoria Line tube at Highbury in the early 1970s, which meant the West End was only a quarter of an hour's ride away and attracted those with money who wanted to live near central London. Islington's better houses were reconverted to family homes and its high street shops revitalized, and by the 1980s Barnsbury and Canonbury were desirable areas, with the main roads north of the Angel – Essex Road and Upper Street – home to scores of antique shops and restaurants.

(i) The Angel

The commercial centre of Islington takes its name from the former Angel Inn on Islington High Street. Outside stood the Islington turnpike through which hundreds of sheep and oxen would arrive in the capital each day and Oliver Twist and John Dawkins 'enter London at nearly eleven o'clock . . . as John Dawkins objected to their entering London before nightfall' in Charles Dickens's *Oliver Twist*.

Camden Passage
Camden Passage, a lane running to the east of Upper Street, near Angel station, contains the greatest concentration of antiques shops

in Britain, their number having grown apace since John Peyton, who ran a music shop at No. 112, led a campaign in the early 1960s to prevent Islington council replacing the street with council flats. In the early eighteenth century Camden Passage was home to Alexander Cruden, who completed a concordance to the Bible and strode through the streets of Islington removing all traces of the number 45 to show his contempt for the radical orator and pamphleteer John Wilkes, whose issue No. 45 of the *North Briton* had criticized George III.
► Portobello Road antiques' market, p. 459; John Wilkes, p. 76.

Chapel Market
Islington's main street market was originally Chapel Street, built in 1787 as a residential middle-class street, one of its earliest residents being the essayist Charles Lamb, who moved to 𝕹𝖔. 45 to be near the asylum where his sister, Mary, had been incarcerated for stabbing their mother to death. When Mary was released in 1799 she and Charles moved to 𝕹𝖔. 36, where Charles kept a strait-jacket to hand so that he could restrain Mary if she had a relapse. The market, for which the street is now best known, sells fruit, vegetables, shoes and cheap CDs, began in 1868; it gave its name to the street in 1936.
► Petticoat Lane market, p. 289.

Essex Road
The main road from the Angel to Newington Green was originally Lower Road, as opposed to nearby *Upper Street*, and between New North Road and the Angel it contains one of the best collections of small everyday shops – baker, greengrocer, butcher, fishmonger – in London. On the corner with Cross Street is Get Stuffed, a taxidermy house of horrors that includes cheetahs, tiger cubs and black panthers, whose owner was prosecuted for illegally buying and selling animals in 2000.

Alfredo's (1919–99), Nos. 4–8
One of the best loved of London's twentieth-century 'greasy spoon' cafés, decorated with much steel, Formica and Vitrolite, and renowned for its thickly cut chips and lavish helpings, was owned by the Deritis family for eighty years and closed to great dismay in 1999 after the owners retired. The fight scene from the 'mod' film *Quadrophenia* was shot here. The listed premises reopened in 2002.

Islington Green
A tiny triangle of land where Essex Road meets Upper Street, used as a plague pit in the seventeenth century.
Collins Music Hall (1862–1958), Nos. 10–11
Sam Vagg, a nineteenth-century chimney-sweep who toured public houses and music halls as 'Irish' singer Sam Collins, took over the Lansdowne Arms on Islington Green in 1862 and converted it into **Collins Music Hall**, a venue where most of the leading names in the genre, including George Robey, Marie Lloyd, Charlie Chaplin, Harry Lauder and Tommy Trinder, performed and where in 1896 the first public film show held in Britain took place. Laurence Olivier visited the venue in the mid-1950s while researching his role as Archie Rice in the Tony Richardson film *The Entertainer* shortly before the building was destroyed by fire. The premises are currently occupied by Waterstone's bookshop.
▶ **The Britannia**, Hoxton, p. 330.

Islington High Street
One of London's shortest but busiest high streets.
Angel Inn, No. 1
The former coaching inn at the junction of Pentonville Road and Islington High Street, which gave its name to the area and the nearby Northern Line tube station, was built c. 1225. Its signboard depicting the angel Gabriel and Virgin Mary was removed during the Reformation in the sixteenth century and the inn was rebuilt in 1638 with a galleried coach yard and theatre. In 1747 the artist William Hogarth painted *The*

Stage Coach here and some forty years later the radical philosopher Thomas Paine began writing *The Rights of Man*, a response to Edmund Burke's *Reflections on the Revolution in France*, at the inn. The Angel was rebuilt at the end of the nineteenth century and from 1921 to 1959 was used as a Lyons Corner House, after which the building remained derelict until 1981, when it became a branch of the Co-op Bank.

NORTHERN LINE

London's main north–south line began as two lines: the City and South London Railway, which opened as the first deep tube line on 4 November 1890 to link King William Street (near London Bridge) with Stockwell; and the Charing Cross, Euston and Hampstead Railway, the two merging in 1937.

HIGH BARNET BRANCH
The section from Camden Town to Highgate opened in 1907 and was extended north in 1941 using track that had belonged to the London North-Eastern Railway.
High Barnet An unlikely setting for the line's northern terminus, being some distance short of the ancient Barnet village and the New Barnet overground railway station.
Totteridge & Whetstone Built in the late 1930s by the Dollis Brook.
Woodside Park Redecorated in 1974 with a colour scheme chosen by Spike Milligan.
West Finchley Opened in 1933 in an obscure side-street location.
Mill Hill East Although the station, which opened in 1941 to serve a nearby barracks, was meant to be the first stop on a branch line to Edgware, work was abandoned because of the war, leaving Mill Hill East on a conspicuous stump jutting out from the main High Barnet branch.
Finchley Central The southbound platform has a reproduction of Harry Beck's original 1930s Underground map, as it was his local station.

East Finchley Located at the northern end of what until the end of the twentieth century was the world's longest tunnel, the southern section emerging at Morden.

Highgate Open-air platforms of the abandoned Highgate–Finsbury Park railway are visible from the Shepherd's Hill exit.

Archway Opened as Highgate station in 1907, it later became in turn Archway (Highgate), Highgate (Archway) and finally in 1939, to avoid confusion, Archway.

Tufnell Park One of the few London areas named after an individual, in this case, a William Tufnell Joliffe, who owned the manor in the 1750s.

Kentish Town Built alongside the now culverted River Fleet.

EDGWARE BRANCH

Early in the twentieth century the American entrepreneur Charles Tyson Yerkes, who had already financed the Bakerloo and District lines, took a carriage to Hampstead Heath and getting out near the Bull and Bush pub vowed to build a new tube line from there to central London. Work started on a station which was to be called North End, but was abandoned at an advanced stage in favour of a site to the west – now Golders Green station. The line opened as the Charing Cross, Euston and Hampstead Railway in 1907 and was later extended to Edgware, but plans to go further north to Elstree were dropped during the Second World War.

Edgware The station, built in 1924, resembles a Roman villa.

Burnt Oak The station opened in the 1920s in what was then open countryside to serve the London County Council's planned, but then unbuilt, Watling Estate.

Colindale Until the 1990s a set of semaphore signals outside the station was used for testing drivers' eyesight.

Hendon Central The original building was designed in 1922 by Stanley A. Heaps to look like a Roman basilica.

Brent Cross Originally planned as Wood-stock, it was known as Brent until the building of Brent Cross shopping centre in the 1970s.

Golders Green Like Burnt Oak, the station stood in undeveloped fields when first opened (in 1907), the American underground-railway entrepreneur Charles Tyson Yerkes remarking: 'It is a very pretty part of the country right away to the North, and a country which is eminently suited for building both the better class of houses and also houses for the labouring classes.'

Hampstead Before construction of what is London's deepest station – 192 ft below the surface of the road – took place in 1903 photographs were taken of the cracks in nearby buildings so that the builders could not be accused of causing structural damage through their excavations. In the 1950s Hampstead was chosen as London Transport's emergency headquarters in the event of nuclear attack.

Belsize Park David Martin, an armed robber, was cornered by police in the Northern Line tunnel near Belsize Park in January 1983. When he was searched, a tiny penknife was found gummed to the roof of his mouth.

Chalk Farm It is named after a nearby inn, 𝕮𝖍𝖆𝖑𝖐 𝕳𝖔𝖚𝖘𝖊 𝕱𝖆𝖗𝖒, itself a corruption of Chalcot's Farm.

CHARING CROSS BRANCH

Many of the stations have names other than their original 1907 ones, among them Warren Street which was originally Euston Road; Goodge Street (Tottenham Court Road); and Tottenham Court Road (Oxford Street).

Camden Town In the 1920s Welsh miners were hired to create a junction out of two existing lines here.

Mornington Crescent When the station was rebuilt in the 1990s members of the cast of the BBC radio comedy *I'm Sorry I Haven't a Clue*, which uses the station's name as one of its long-running gags, were invited to reopen it.

Euston The original station building on this

line lies derelict at the corner of Drummond Street and Eversholt Street.

Warren Street The station had the first lifts on the system, installed in 1928, although there are no lifts now.

Goodge Street General Eisenhower, the United States' Second World War commander-in-chief, briefly ran his London headquarters from the station.

Tottenham Court Road As part of his major redesign of the station in 1984 Eduardo Paolozzi depicted the demography of nearby Charing Cross Road in his mosaic, with saxophones for the Denmark Street music trade and cows and chickens to symbolize the growth of local restaurants and fast-food outlets.

Leicester Square Rebuilt in 1935, it reopened on Cup Final day to accommodate Sheffield Wednesday and West Bromwich Albion fans, who had been celebrating in the West End.

Charing Cross Formerly Strand.

Embankment Originally Charing Cross.

Waterloo The tunnel to the north was blocked up with concrete at the beginning of the Second World War as the authorities were worried about flooding.

CITY BRANCH

This section contains the oldest part of the line, the original City and South London Railway, which ran from King William Street (now replaced by Bank) to Stockwell from 1890 and featured none of the amenities enjoyed by passengers on the older Metropolitan Line, the coaches having basic wooden benches and no windows.

Camden Town In the 1970s the BBC shot episodes of *Dr Who* in the deep wartime shelters under the station.

Euston Rebuilt within the British Rail station in the 1960s.

King's Cross St Pancras The underground's biggest station's hybrid name comes from a long demolished statue of George IV and a third-century boy saint and martyr.

Angel The station has the longest escalators in Europe and is the largest on the network serving only one line.

Old Street Rebuilt in the 1960s as part of an unattractive shopping precinct.

Moorgate The London Underground system's worst train accident occurred at the Moorgate terminus of the Northern Line's Great Northern & City Railway branch (now part of WAGN) on 28 February 1975, when a driver failed to brake approaching Moorgate and slammed into the tunnel at the southern end of platform 9, killing himself and forty-two passengers. No reason for the crash was ever found, but new safety controls have since been installed in trains to prevent a recurrence.

Bank When the station was originally planned in the early twentieth century the authorities proposed demolishing the church of St Mary Woolnoth nearby, but so great was the public outcry they were forced to underpin the church's foundations instead.

London Bridge Built under London's first ever station, which had opened in 1836.

Borough Rebuilt by Charles Holden, the Underground's greatest architect, in the early 1920s.

Elephant and Castle The City and South London Railway (the predecessor of the Northern Line) was originally meant to be a cable railway powered by a stationary engine at Elephant and Castle station.

KENNINGTON TO MORDEN

Kennington The only station on this part of the line to retain its original dome, which shielded hydraulic lift machinery.

Oval The long submerged River Effra flows underneath and burst through during the Second World War when engineers tried to construct a bomb shelter.

Stockwell The 1890 southern terminus of the City and South London Railway.

Clapham North One of seven Northern Line stations planned for an express tube link that never materialized.

Clapham Common The stairwell entrance shelter is listed.

Clapham South The first West Indian immigrants to London were given temporary accommodation in the station's air-raid shelters on arriving in Britain in 1953.

Balham Sixty-four people died when the station was hit by a Second World War bomb on 15 October 1940.

Tooting Bec It is named after the medieval landowners, the Benedictine Abbey of St Mary of Bec in Normandy.

Tooting Broadway During construction in the 1920s the authorities discovered an underground lake on the site, so the work had to be carried out within air locks.

Colliers Wood Named after the local woodland used by charcoal burners.

South Wimbledon Originally Trinity Road.

Morden The authorities gambled on opening a station here in 1926 at a time when there were few buildings in the vicinity.

Penton Street

Much of Pentonville at the western end of Chapel Market was covered by fields before the growth of Islington, but near the modern-day junction of Penton Street and White Lion Street stood the 𝔚𝔥𝔦𝔱𝔢 ℭ𝔬𝔫𝔡𝔲𝔦𝔱 𝔗𝔞𝔳𝔢𝔯𝔫, which opened on 30 January 1649, the day Charles I was executed. It was converted into a fashionable tea house in the mid eighteenth century. There, according to Oliver Goldsmith in *The Citizen of the World*, 'the inhabitants of London often assembled to celebrate a feast of hot rolls and butter; seeing such numbers, each with their little table before them, employed on this occasion, must no doubt be a very amusing sight to the looker-on, but still more so to those who perform in the solemnity'. Cricket was played next to the tavern, and when the cricket club's wealthy members decided they could no longer play on a public field they asked an employee, Thomas Lord, to find a new ground. Lord chose a site in Dorset Square, Marylebone, and he and several White Conduit members left Islington to found the Marylebone Cricket Club (MCC), which played its first game the following year against the White Conduit at Dorset Square. A new tavern was built in 1828, and it was there that five of the Tolpuddle Martyrs were welcomed on their return from Australia in 1836. It is now the Penny Farthing.

► Lord's, p. 328.

Popham Street

Cathy Come Home, Ken Loach's harrowing TV drama of 1966, which followed the miserable social descent of a northern girl seduced by the prospects of living in London, was partly filmed on this side street off Essex Road.

Upper Street *Also see p. 328*

One of the liveliest roads in the capital, thanks to its abundance of cafés and restaurants, two famous pubs (the King's Head and the Hope and Anchor), the Screen on the Green cinema and the nearby Almeida Theatre, Upper Street is also part of the traditional main route north from London – the A1 – and was briefly known as King Street in the first decade of the seventeenth century after King James, riding southwards from Edinburgh, was met by the Lord Mayor of London at Stamford Hill and escorted along the road to the City. Upper Street's present-day look dates back to the nineteenth century when small shops and large pubs with mews replaced the Tudor houses.

west side: Liverpool Road to Almeida Street
Screen on the Green, No. 83

A popular cinema showing mostly art house new releases, it was here that the Clash first performed in public on Sunday 29 August 1976 on a bill also featuring the Buzzcocks, playing their first gig outside Manchester, and the Sex Pistols. Among the outrageously dressed audience was Suzi Ballion (later of Siouxsie and the Banshees), in black cupless bra, fishnet tights and swastika armband. The Clash's performance was derided by the *NME*'s Charles Shaar Murray who, to his later embarrassment, described them as 'the kind of garage band that should be speedily returned to the garage, preferably with the motor still running, which would undoubtedly be more of a loss to their friends and families than to either rock or roll'.

The King's Head, No. 115

London's best-known and first pub theatre, described by Steven Berkoff as 'a sanctuary for every maverick in the theatre world', was opened by Dan and Joan Crawford in 1970, its early successes including William Trevor's *Going Home* and Robert Patrick's *Kennedy's Children*, which transferred to the West End in 1974, the first time a fringe production had done so. Those that have appeared at the pub which, confusingly, sells drinks at today's prices but expressed in pre-decimal terms, include Joanna Lumley, Tom Conti, Ben Kingsley and Janet Suzman.

(ii) Barnsbury

A bland but elegant residential area lying between Caledonian Road and Upper Street, Barnsbury has come to be seen as the spiritual homeland of New Labour, as Tony Blair lived at 1 Richmond Crescent before he became prime minister and it was in a nearby restaurant, Granita (at 127 Upper Street), that he and Gordon Brown agreed the deal whereby Blair would become Labour Party leader and Brown shadow chancellor in 1994. In the thirteenth century the land came into the possession of Ralph de Berners, which led to the coining of the name 'Barnsbury', but it remained an inconsequential semi-rural outpost until the building of Charles Barry's Holy Trinity church in 1824, following which a host of squares – Barnsbury, Cloudesley, Gibson, Lonsdale, the singularly gloomy Milner and Thornhill – were built for City gentlemen who could live in a refined semi-rural setting but still be able to walk to work. In the early twentieth century, as suburbia moved further away from central London following the development of the Underground network, Barnsbury gradually lost its status as a haven for the wealthy middle class. However, the absence of damage to its housing stock in the Second World War laid it open to 'rediscovery' in the 1960s and gentrification has since increased, making it again one of the most desirable addresses in inner London.

Almeida Street

Almeida Theatre

What became London's leading small theatre at the end of the twentieth century was built in the 1830s for the Islington Literary and Scientific Society, on what was then Wellington Street, and converted to the Wellington Music Hall when the society moved to Camden Road in 1871. The street was renamed Almeida Street in 1890 in honour of one of the Duke of Wellington's military victories, and the hall was taken over by the Salvation Army then and by Beck's Carnival Novelties as a warehouse in 1952. Beck's put it up for sale in 1971 when proposals for its future included a light entertainment centre, courtesy of the former Goon Harry Secombe, and an alternative theatre, the idea of the landlord of the nearby King's Head. But when neither plan was approved it instead became the Almeida Theatre, which opened with Glenda Jackson appearing in Howard Barker's *Scenes from an Execution*. In the 1990s major figures such as Harold Pinter, Glenda Jackson and Kevin Spacey enhanced the Almeida's reputation by performing in this unlikely non-West End setting.

Barnsbury Street

Barnsbury Hall

Michael Collins, the leading early-twentieth-century Irish revolutionary, was sworn in as member of the Irish Republican Brotherhood at the hall in November 1909 by Sam Maguire – a fellow post office worker who is now remembered in the name of the All Ireland Gaelic Football trophy, the Sam Maguire Cup – and later enrolled in the Irish nationalist No. 1 Company of the London Volunteers, drilling each week with sawn-off shotguns in the German

Gymnasium (now the Railwaymen's Club) on Pancras Road, King's Cross.

Caledonian Road

The Battle Bridge and Holloway Road Company privately built what was then Chalk Road in 1826, the first houses being constructed in the 1840s, as was Pentonville Prison (see Holloway, p. 335). After King's Cross station opened in 1852 the road was renamed in honour of the Latin name of Scotland, the trains' northern destination. It gradually filled with small shops and houses but after Second World War bombing was rebuilt with shabby council estates.

No. 156, east side

Karl Gustav Ernst, a second-generation German, ran a spy ring from his barber-shop at this address in the early years of the twentieth century, receiving his instructions in the post together with packages of hair-cutting sundries. Ernst would hand agents their orders when they visited the shop, but his activities were exposed in 1910 following the funeral of Edward VII when two detectives, told to watch a German naval attaché, Baron Rostock, who was in London as part of the Kaiser's entourage paying respects to the late British monarch, followed the nobleman to the barber's. The detectives, suspicious of why the baron would go to so seedy a quarter for a haircut, and why so many smart-looking men continued to drop in over the next few weeks, decided to intercept Ernst's letters. In his mail they found a list of German agents, but took no action as they feared the Germans would simply establish a new network, which would itself have to be identified. Instead they watched and waited, rounding up the spies at the outset of the First World War in 1914. After a trial at the Old Bailey Ernst received a seven-year jail sentence.

► German Embassy in the early twentieth century, p. 207.

Stonefield Street

A small street off Cloudesley Square, it was where in 1973 residents won a campaign to prevent developers demolishing the Geor-

gian housing stock, an event crucial to the subsequent gentrification of the area. For years speculators had been buying up Stonefield Street properties and leaving the houses to deteriorate, so that there would be less controversy over their demolition. When householders who refused to sell formed an association to prevent the street being spoiled the developers responded by knocking down the front wall of No. 16 while the tenants, the Murphys, were at work. The protestors then successfully secured an injunction to halt demolition and Islington council bought the properties to prevent further disruption.

(iii) Canonbury

The best-preserved and most picturesque suburb in inner London, Canonbury is built on land which took the name of Canon's Burgh after coming into the possession of the Canons of St Bartholomew in the thirteenth century and became more popular when Hugh Myddelton's New River, bringing water from Hertfordshire to the City, was cut through local fields in the early seventeenth century. A residential estate for the wealthy middle class in the nineteenth century, it became shabby in the early twentieth century. But the destruction wrought to similar suburbs such as Kennington and North Kensington during the 'Second World War, and the subsequent decline of districts such as Bayswater and Lisson Green, gave Canonbury, with its homogenous early-nineteenth-century appearance, fresh appeal, and the opening of the Victoria Line in the early 1970s made it a sought-after address.

● Canonbury occupies the triangle bounded by Upper Street, St Paul's Road and Essex Road.

Canonbury Place

A narrow lane in two sections at the centre of Canonbury village, which is home to the ancient Canonbury Tower, it was developed in the 1770s when the Marquess of Northampton leased the land to a local stock-broker, John Dawes. Weedon Grossmith, co-author of *The Diary of a Nobody*, moved into No. 5, The Old House, in 1891. Basil Spence, architect of the postwar Coventry Cathedral, moved to No. 1 in 1956.

Canonbury Tower

The oldest building not only in Canonbury but also in Islington, Canonbury Tower has Roman origins but the structure in its present guise, with its unusual tower, is from the early sixteenth century when William Bolton, Prior of St Bartholomew (now St Bartholomew's Hospital), built a property two miles from the nearest settle-ment – with a tower as he was worried about astrological warnings of a flood – stocking it with food to last two months. The property passed to the Crown on the dissolution of the monasteries in 1539 and in 1616 it became home to Sir Francis Bacon, essayist, Lord Chancellor and Keeper of the Great Seal of England, who, according to a mid seventeenth century inscription on the wall in the top room, may have had a legiti-mate claim to the throne. (The Francis Bacon Society, which was formed to debate the theory that the essayist wrote the plays attributed to William Shakespeare, moved to the Tower in 1886.)

By the eighteenth century Canonbury Tower was a lodging house, its most illus-trious tenant of the period being the novelist and dramatist Oliver Goldsmith, who came here from 1762 to 1764 when hiding from his creditors. On 26 June 1763 Goldsmith was visited by the biographer James Boswell, who recorded how he 'walked out to Islington to Canonbury House, a curious old monastic building now let out in lodgings'. In 1770 John Dawes demolished the buildings to the south of the tower and built what is now Canonbury Place, and fifty years later Wash-ington Irving, the American author of *Rip Van Winkle*, moved into Goldsmith's former room in the tower, leaving after a few days 'stunned with shouts and noises from the cricket ground nearby'. Irving was also irked by the behaviour of his landlady who during

his short tenure brought several parties of guests to his door and allowed them to peer through the keyhole at him. From 1952 to 2003 the building was home to various theatre companies including the Tower Theatre.

Canonbury Square

The area's most prestigious address, lined with tall brick houses set around a pleasant ruled-off green space, was designed in 1807 by Henry Leroux, the Huguenot architect also responsible for the nearby Compton Terrace and Union Chapel, which towers over Highbury Corner. It was spoiled five years later when the authorities chose to build North Road (now Canonbury Road), an extension of Holloway Road leading to Shoreditch, through the middle. The pres-ence of a main road running through the square dissuaded the wealthy from moving in, Leroux was ruined and went bankrupt, and Canonbury Square began to attract mostly artisans and clerks.

By the time the author Evelyn Waugh moved to No. 17a in 1928 the square was down at heel, and Waugh left two years later, tired of having to explain to friends why he was living in so appalling a district. Ironically, some fifteen years later George Orwell, with typical contrariness, moved into No. 27B, where he wrote some of *1984* precisely because of its shabbiness. In the 1950s speculators and wealthy householders, including Vanessa Bell, sister of Virginia Woolf, began buying up the derelict proper-ties, refurbishing them into desirable homes, while Basil Spence, the modernist architect responsible for rebuilding Coventry Cathedral, moved his practice to North-ampton Lodge (No. 39), now home of the Estorick Gallery of Italian Art. Subsequent renovation and changes in the public's atti-tude towards Georgian squares and houses have made Canonbury Square a desirable location, despite the traffic.

George Orwell's address (1944–7), No. 27B

After writing *Animal Farm*, the allegorical fable and satire of communism that became his first commercial success – in local book-shops he would surreptitiously move it from the children's section to the adult fiction shelves – George Orwell and his wife, Eileen, moved to a Canonbury Square damaged by German bombs and there became renowned for their traditional English high teas, which included various jams and marmalades, gentlemen's relish, kippers, toast, scones and very strong tea which Orwell would pour from a two-handled gallon-sized pot. When Eileen died from complications after an operation in 1946 a distraught Orwell moved to the Hebridean island of Jura for the summer, returning to Canonbury for the winter. In fact, Orwell would probably have been better off in Jura, for 1946–7 was one of the worst winters in London's history and he was obliged to burn furniture and his son's wooden toys for firewood. It was at 27B and in Scotland that he began working on his dark satire of postwar bumptiousness, *1984*, basing Victory Mansions, dilapidated home of the novel's hero, Winston Smith, on his Canonbury address.

Upper Street *Also see p. 324*
west side: Almeida Street to Highbury Corner
No. 190
Sisterwrite, London's first feminist book-shop, opened here in 1978.
Hope and Anchor, No. 207
Dr Feelgood, the Stranglers, and Graham Parker and the Rumour sealed their repu-tations as some of the most exciting groups on the mid-1970s London circuit at gigs staged in the basement of what was London's leading pub rock venue. Barely large enough to contain a handful of musicians, let alone an audience, its size helped generate a livewire atmosphere that electrified even the most mundane gigs. The venue ignored punk, but swiftly moved on to new wave, allowing Joy Division to make their London debut on 27 December 1978, playing to only twenty people, mostly jour-nalists. The pub stopped booking bands in

1984, a time when the live music scene in London was in decline, and later resumed the gigs with little comparable success.
▶ Marquee I, p. 139.
No. 328
Tariq Ali, the Pakistan-born political acti-vist, opened The Other Bookshop at this address in 1968 to sell radical literature and political newspapers. It later became a general second-hand bookshop and has since closed.
Highbury Corner
The green area at the junction of the A1, St Paul's Road and Canonbury Road was the setting for regular political rallies and demonstrations before a Second World War bomb fell on Highbury station in 1944 and destroyed much of the surrounding prop-erty. Its best-known regular speaker was the Revd Donald Soper, the Methodist minister who railed against blood sports and child labour and once remarked that the House of Lords was proof that there was life after death.
east side: Highbury Corner to Cross Street
Union Chapel, Compton Terrace
Designed by James Cubitt and built in 1876–7, its attractive brick mass, based on the eleventh-century church of Santa Fosca in Torcello, Italy, is flanked by elegant Geor-gian terraces set back from Upper Street behind green space and railings. It is now also used as a meeting hall and concert venue.
Islington Town Hall
The ideological battles that beset the Labour Party following the election of Margaret Thatcher's Conservative government in 1979 were keenly felt in Islington where left-wing activists began to challenge traditionalists for control of the town hall, positions of influence within the party, and the chance to control the lavish budgets making grants to non-council organizations. The Left gained control of the party and Islington council after the borough's two Labour MPs and a number of councillors defected to the newly formed Social Democratic Party in 1981. On taking over the council hoisted the

red flag above the town hall, displayed a bust of Lenin in the lobby, and triumphantly announced an imminent campaign of rebellion against the Tories' plan to reduce the power of local government. But when the realities of being in charge saw pragmatism replace revolution Islington reverted to its earlier moderation; Lenin's bust is no longer in place.

Old Parr's Head, Upper Street at Cross Street

This boisterous pub is named after Thomas Parr ('Old Parr'), a Shropshire man born in 1483, who supposedly first married at eighty and was made to stand in his village church dressed in a white sheet twenty-five years later for making another woman pregnant. Parr was taken to London after his 152nd birthday to be presented to King Charles I. He died soon after and was buried in Westminster Abbey.

(iv) Hoxton

A run-down land of council estates and bomb sites, Hoxton, previously Hogsden, has been one of the poorest and most violent parts of London since it was colonized in the 1660s by those burned out of their homes in the Fire of London. In 1820 the Regent's Canal was cut through the fields, attracting light industry (timber, furniture, brewing) and closely packed streets of grim terraced housing, bringing about the exodus of the wealthy to Stoke Newington or Canonbury. In the 1890s Charles Booth, author of the seventeen-volume *Life and Labour of the People in London*, claimed that 'Hoxton is the leading criminal quarter of London, and indeed of all England'. In the early twentieth century Hoxton continued to be at the forefront of advances in villainy, being home to the notorious fifty-strong Titanic Mob – so named because members dressed in mockery of the liner's beautifully attired first-class passengers who took the best seats on the lifeboats – who were involved in racetrack robberies but were broken up by the Flying Squad in 1922 after a spate of pick-pocketing at an Arsenal–Tottenham football match. The area has never recovered from blanket bombing by the Germans in the Second World War, having been rebuilt in the 1960s with poor-quality blocks of flats. In the 1990s some of the redundant manufacturing warehouses around Old Street were taken over by artists and Hoxton briefly became chic.

Charlotte Road EC2

A short turning connecting Great Eastern Street and Old Street, lined with solid brick warehouses and showrooms, which is now at the centre of the new local art scene. At No. 63 is the Bricklayers' Arms, the area's most popular pub, which has its own gallery.

Factual Nonsense (1990s), No. 44a

The gallery was opened here in the early 1990s by the artist Joshua Compston with a street party at which the stalls were manned by up-and-coming artists such as Tracey Emin, who did palm reading, Gavin Turk, who offered punters the opportunity to hit a rat made of old socks stuck in a drainpipe, and Damien Hirst, dressed as a clown, who hired out his spin-painting equipment at 50p a go to anyone who wanted to attempt a work in his style. (For a further 50p Hirst would expose his genitalia, which had been decorated especially for the occasion by the artist Leigh Bowery.) Compston died in his bed here in March 1996 after taking a mixture of alcohol and ether.

Hoxton Square

Hoxton's 1683 centrepiece, now exhibiting 300-plus years of London architectural history in various stages of decay, was where the Ancient Deists of Hoxton, an academy for dissenters from the Church of England, was established in 1780, attracting 'Alchemists, Astrologers, Calculators, Mystics, Magnetisers, Prophets and Projectors of every kind', and where James Parkinson, the late-eighteenth-century physician who gave his name to Parkinson's disease, lived (at No. 1). In the 1990s Hoxton Square was 'rediscovered' by magazine writers and artists, leading to the opening of the Lux Cinema and the White Cube[2] art gallery at No. 48, designed in the shape of a double cube entirely top-lit with translucent ceiling panels.

Hoxton Street

𝕿𝖍𝖊 𝕭𝖗𝖎𝖙𝖆𝖓𝖓𝖎𝖆, No. 107, west side

𝕿𝖍𝖊 𝕭𝖗𝖎𝖙𝖆𝖓𝖓𝖎𝖆, which became London's most celebrated music hall, opened in 1841 as the **𝕭𝖗𝖎𝖙𝖆𝖓𝖓𝖎𝖆 𝕾𝖆𝖑𝖔𝖔𝖓**, where the management would send round trays of food piled high with ham sandwiches to satisfy the hungry patrons, and was rebuilt in 1858 as the Britannia Theatre to seat 3,200. In 1869 the nine-year-old Dan Leno performed a routine here with his uncle, Johnny Danvers, which ran: 'I once had an I.O.U.' / 'So had I, but now I've only got U.' / 'Yes, poor I. O. died.' / 'What did I. O. die of?' / 'Don't you know? Iodide of potassium.' Two later star attractions were Harry Weldon and Jack Melville whose repartee included the banter: 'Are you married?' / 'Yes, sixteen wives, no kids.' / 'Ridiculous. No man in England is allowed sixteen wives.' / 'Yes, he is. It says so in the Marriage Service, "Four richer, four poorer, four better, four worse".' The venue later became a cinema, was bombed in 1940, and was subsequently demolished.

Poole Street

Gainsborough Studios (1924–39)

North London's major early-twentieth-century film studio, where Alfred Hitchcock made some of his first films, began as a power station for the Metropolitan Railway and was bought in 1919 by the American company Famous Players-Lasky. Five years later, following a number of unmemorable films, it was taken over by Michael Balcon's Gainsborough Pictures, whose logo featured Thomas Gainsborough's picture of the actress Sarah Siddons, and who employed the young Alfred Hitchcock as a studio hand. An early success was *The Rat*, starring Ivor Novello, set in the Parisian underworld but filmed here, and it was followed by two of Will Hay's best comedies, *Oh, Mr Porter*

and *Good-Morning, Boys*, and Hitchcock's first masterpiece, *The Lady Vanishes* (1938), starring Michael Redgrave, Margaret Lockwood and the duo Basil Radford and Naunton Wayne as two cricket-mad eccentrics desperate to reach Old Trafford for a test match that is inevitably rained off.

Balcon left in 1936 to take over Ealing studios, which he converted into Britain's greatest film company, and Gainsborough closed in 1939 at the outset of the Second World War because it was feared that the chimney might collapse during an air raid. The Ministry of Defence used the studio to make training films and gradually regular filming was allowed, with Anthony Asquith's *Fanny by Gaslight* shot inside and by the adjacent canal. In 1945 J. Arthur Rank reopened Gainsborough, employing the Welsh poet Dylan Thomas as screenwriter for a number of unsuccessful, long lost films, but it closed in 1949 and later became a carpet warehouse, before being renovated in the 1990s as flats.

► King's Cross on film, p. 356.

Shepherdess Walk

The Eagle, No. 2

> Up and down the City Road, / In and out the Eagle / That's the way the money goes / Pop Goes the Weasel – traditional nursery rhyme

The tavern associated with the nursery rhyme 'Pop Goes the Weasel', which refers to local tailors pawning their flat-irons (weasels) so that they could buy drink, opened as the Shepherd and Shepherdess in what was then a rural area in the 1750s, changing its name to the Eagle when it was rebuilt to incorporate the Grecian music hall in 1825. The teenage Marie Lloyd, who became London's leading music-hall performer, made her first appearance (as Bella Delmere) here on 9 May 1885 when she was fifteen.

HIGHBURY, N5

By modern urban standards Highbury is a
barely spoilt village, free of system-built
postwar estates, blight and excessive
industry, which has escaped the intense
development of neighbouring districts such
as Holloway by the good fortune of occupying a hilly site between major roads. After
the Norman Conquest William I granted
the local manor, then known as Tolentone
and stretching from Crouch Hill to Hoxton,
to Ranulf and the land passed to the Order
of the Knights of St John Jerusalem in 1271.
The name Highbury was first recorded in
1370 and during the Peasants' Revolt, eleven
years later, rebels ransacked 𝕳𝖎𝖌𝖍𝖇𝖚𝖗𝖞
𝕸𝖆𝖓𝖔𝖗, which stood where Leigh Road
can now be found. By the mid eighteenth
century the only buildings in Highbury were
three terraces, the Highbury Barn pleasure
gardens, and some twenty villas, but expansion followed the opening of the railway at
Highbury Corner in 1849, with villas and
handsome red-brick terraced houses built
on Highbury Fields and the roads around
Highbury Park, and it soon became one of
the most attractive suburbs in north
London.

Avenell Road

Members of the Russian Social-Democratic
Foundation (forerunners of the Bolsheviks)
including Lenin used the now demolished
𝕹𝖔. 85, home of a sympathetic British
doctor, A. P. Hazell, as a mailing address in
1903 to foil officers from the Metropolitan
Police looking to intercept mail and inform
the Tsarist secret police in Russia. In 1913
Arsenal Football Club moved to a site
opposite.

Arsenal Football Club

London's most successful football club was
founded in 1886 by workers from the Royal
Arsenal, Woolwich, who as Dial Square, the
name of their workshop, played their first
game against Eastern Wanderers that
December on a patch of ground on the Isle

of Dogs, winning 6–0. Growing success in
the various south London cups saw Woolwich Arsenal join the Football League in
1893, but they achieved little until the
megalomaniac Henry Norris took over as
chairman in 1910. Norris wanted to merge
Woolwich with his other team, Fulham, and
move to the latter's stadium, Craven
Cottage, in south-west London, but when
the League turned down his proposals the
Arsenal chairman, realizing that the club
would never be able to make enough money
at their Plumstead ground, began looking
for a new location.

Sites in Battersea and Harringay were
considered, but in 1913 Norris found out
that St John's College of Divinity in Highbury wanted to sell its playing fields and
decided to move Woolwich Arsenal to north
London. The proposal enraged locals, who
objected to the 'undesirable elements of
professional football', and other nearby
clubs, such as Clapton Orient and
Tottenham Hotspur, but the deal went
ahead none the less. The deed of transfer for
the property was signed by the Archbishop
of Canterbury and the lease included a stipulation stating that Woolwich Arsenal could
not play at home on Christmas Day or
Good Friday. At the end of the First World
War the club, by then simply Arsenal, won a
place in an enlarged First Division despite
having finished only fifth in the Second
Division, after an intense lobbying
campaign by Norris and at the expense of
Tottenham Hotspur, who had finished
bottom of the First Division and expected to
be allowed to stay in the extended division.

Following the appointment of Herbert
Chapman as manager in 1925 Arsenal gradually began to achieve success, winning the
FA Cup in 1930 and becoming the first
London side to win the League Championship the following year. Not only did
Chapman transform a previously unremark-
able team into the finest in the land, he was
also behind some notable new initiatives
such as floodlighting, numbered players, the
white ball, rubber studs, training schemes

for schoolboys, and his greatest off-the-field achievement, the renaming of Gillespie Road tube station as Arsenal – a PR coup which cost the train companies a fortune in rewriting tickets, maps and signs. Chapman died suddenly of pneumonia on New Year's Day 1934 but so solid were the foundations he had laid that success continued seamlessly: a hat-trick of championships was completed in 1935, the FA Cup was won the following year and the Championship again in 1938, with only the Second World War interrupting the flow. The club continued to dominate until the 1950s, recently returning to success. In 1999 Arsenal announced plans to move from Highbury to a new state-of-the-art stadium on the other side of the nearby Great Northern Railway which would be able to accommodate more than 60,000 seated spectators, but plans stalled in 2003 due to lack of funds.

Highbury New Park
A long road containing many of the area's largest villas, it was built in the 1850s, following the shelving of plans to create a 500-acre park between Highbury Grove and Green Lanes, in a bizarre mixture of styles, including Venetian, Gothic and Greek (best seen at the hybrid No. 55) for City shopkeepers of comfortable, rather than wealthy means, who could easily reach their workplaces on the new North London Railway. At the southern end is Highbury Grove school, made famous in the 1970s by its Lancastrian-vowelled disciplinarian head teacher Rhodes Boyson, who went on to be a minister in Margaret Thatcher's government.
east side: Green Lanes to Highbury Grove
Matrix-Wessex Studios, No. 106
It was in this former Rank Charm School that the Sex Pistols recorded 'Anarchy in the UK', their provocative first single, in the autumn of 1976 and the Clash cut their lauded *London Calling* LP, chosen by critics on *Rolling Stone* magazine as the best album of the 1980s.

Highbury Film Studios, No. 96
Built in 1864 as a temporary church, which was later converted into the Athenaeum, a venue for debates and lectures, it became the **Highbury Film Studios** in 1936 and two years later was responsible for the locally set *Arsenal Stadium Mystery* (1939), the story of a footballer who dies of poisoning during a game at Highbury between Arsenal and the Trojans (played by Brentford). During the Second World War panic-stricken local residents, convinced that Nazi paratroopers had landed in Highbury, phoned the police but inquiries revealed that the 'German' invaders walking along the road were extras for the Boulting Brothers film *Pastor Hall*. ITV made some of their earliest television programmes here in the 1950s, including *Double Your Money*, *Take Your Pick* and *Noddy*. The building was demolished in the 1960s.

HIGHGATE, N6

North London's leafiest suburb, part picturesque village, part wild heathland, part brick villa suburbia, is named after the long vanished thirteenth-century gate to Hornsey Park and occupies a lofty position at the edge of Hampstead Heath. It grew slowly, owing to the difficulties vehicles and pedestrians endured to reach the top of the hill in the days before motorized transport, and has maintained its air of exclusivity and village atmosphere, despite industrialization and the twentieth century.

Fitzroy Park
An unadopted rural road by Hampstead Heath, Fitzroy Park covers the tree-lined drive designed by Capability Brown that led to Charles Fitzroy's 1775 mansion, **Fitzroy House** (demolished 1826). It features a number of desirable properties including The Elms – home in the early nineteenth century of George Basevi, the Jewish architect who converted to Christianity and was killed when he fell off the roof of Ely

Cathedral – which went on sale for £7 million in 1999, and No. 10, designed by the mid-twentieth-century civic architect E. Vincent Harris, which was later bequeathed to Camden Council. In 2002 council proposals to sell the house to developers resulted in a campaign of opposition led by locals whose number included Andrew Morton, the royal biographer.

The Grove
A well-preserved seventeenth-century terrace, secluded from Highgate village by an avenue of horse chestnut trees, The Grove is built on the site of 𝖣𝗈𝗋𝖼𝗁𝖾𝗌𝗍𝖾𝗋 𝖧𝗈𝗎𝗌𝖾, a sixteenth-century mansion so named when it was bought by the 1st Marquess of Dorchester, which was demolished in 1688. Past residents include the poet Samuel Taylor Coleridge, who lived at No. 3 from 1823 to 1834 and rarely left the house except to sit on Highgate Hill looking down on the smoke of London, and the violinist Yehudi Menuhin, who lived at No. 2.

Highgate High Street
Andrew Smith Hallidie, the Scottish engineer responsible for San Francisco's cable system, created a cable tramway linking Highgate High Street and Archway in 1884, but the scheme suffered a number of accidents and was scrapped early in the twentieth century. The High Street, which offers dramatic views of central London, is lined with seventeenth- and eighteenth-century buildings and quaint shops and was saved from ruin in the 1960s when locals successfully lobbied to prevent the authorities introducing a one-way system that would have brought heavy traffic through the village.

Highgate West Hill
Set amid beautiful woodland, Highgate West Hill winds down from Highgate village towards Parliament Hill and is mostly lined with luxurious properties set back behind huge gates. They included Witanhurst, the largest private house in London after Buckingham Palace, built in 1913 for the soap magnate Sir Arthur Crosfield whose wife,

Domini, demanded he provide her with the biggest domestic property in the capital, and The Eagles, at No. 33, home of the Russian trade delegation. The nursing pioneer Florence Nightingale recuperated at No. 37 after returning to Britain from the Crimean War; Dick White, head of MI5 and MI6 at various times, lived at No. 83 after the Second World War; and the poet John Betjeman was raised in the early years of the twentieth century at No. 31.

The Flask, No. 77, east side
Highgate's most delightful pub, parts of which date back to 1663, is the home of a bizarre local drinking ceremony known as 'Swearing on the Horns', which began as an initiation rite for travellers and involves the landlord brandishing a pair of stag's horns fixed to a pole in front of a visitor who must recite an oath before being granted the freedom of Highgate.

North Hill
Highpoint
> The building at Highgate is an achievement of the first rank, and a milestone that will be useful to everybody – *Architectural Review*, Le Corbusier (1936)

The supreme example of luxury modernist architecture in London, Highpoint was commissioned by Sigmund Gestetner, head of the office equipment firm of the same name, as housing for his workers, and was designed by Berthold Lubetkin, the Georgian-born founder of the pioneering design team Tecton, in the 1930s. The first block, Highpoint One, consists of fifty-six flats over seven storeys built in reinforced concrete, grouped in the shape of two linked crosses, designed so that the living rooms received sunlight during the day, and separated from the ground by slim columns (pilotis). When Gestetner saw the results he chose to sell the flats, rather than use them for his workforce. He also bought the adjacent plot of land to prevent unsympathetic new development, and it was there, in 1936, that Lubetkin created Highpoint Two, furnishing the grounds with models of the

Erechtheum's caryatids (draped female figures named after the priestesses of Artemis) and a penthouse in which Lubetkin himself lived until 1955. When the Swiss architect Le Corbusier, the master of modernism, visited Highpoint One in 1935 he remarked: 'This beautiful building sets a question of principle: to follow tradition or to break with it? I reply unhesitatingly by stating my personal point of view; a new tradition must be created . . . For a long time I have dreamed of executing dwellings in such conditions for the good of humanity.' Highpoint has since maintained its exclusivity.

► Trellick Tower, p. 446.

Pond Square

Full of unexpected twists and turns and attractive architecture, Pond Square is neither a uniform square nor home to a pond, the standing water having been removed in 1864. Francis Bacon, the early-seventeenth-century essayist and Lord Chancellor, died of pneumonia he caught while trying to refrigerate a chicken in the square in 1626.

South Grove

The social hub of Highgate village, forming a pleasant setting south of the High Street by Pond Square and West Hill, South Grove is home to St Michael's church, which contains the tomb of the poet Samuel Taylor Coleridge, and the Highgate Literary and Scientific Institution at No. 11, set up in 1839 'for the promotion of useful and scientific knowledge' – one of the few surviving clubs of its kind in the country.

Swain's Lane

Highgate Cemetery

Huge catacombs, Egyptian columns, stone angels and ivy-covered vaults create one of the wildest settings in London, a cemetery built in what was part of the Forest of Middlesex and opened by the London Cemetery Company in 1839 as one of seven new commercial London cemeteries. Those buried at Highgate include the scientist Michael Faraday, Charles Dickens's wife and daughter, the author George Eliot, William Foyle (of bookshop fame), Sir Leslie Stephen (father of Virginia Woolf and first editor of the *Dictionary of National Biography*) and the poet Christina Rossetti. The most famous of the 50,000 graves and one that attracts many visitors, however, is that of Karl Marx who, being Jewish, was buried in unconsecrated ground. The most elaborate architecture can be found in the mausoleum of Julius Beer, designed by J. Oldrid Scott and based on the tomb of the Greek king Mausolus at Halicarnassus.

Western Cemetery

The older section, which was designed by Stephen Geary and can be inspected courtesy of the Friends of Highgate Cemetery Society, has as its centrepiece the Circle of Lebanon, a ring of excavated vaults surrounding a huge cedar tree that is considerably older than the cemetery. The section contains the grave of Elizabeth Siddal, wife of the poet and artist Dante Gabriel Rossetti, who died of laudanum poisoning in 1862, leaving Rossetti so grief-stricken he buried a book of new poems in her grave. Seven years later, looking to raise money, Rossetti decided he needed to publish the poems and so, after obtaining permission from the authorities, he dug up the coffin and disentangled the book of poems from her hair. Each page had to be soaked with disinfectant before it could be published.

By the mid-1960s the western section had been abandoned and in its overgrown state was being used by Satanists, spurred on by the legend of the Highgate Vampire that had supposedly been seen by two teenage students walking past the North Gate late one night, who also claimed they saw graves opening and bodies rising. Local newspapers regularly featured stories about ghostly sightings, such as the report that a local vampire hunter accompanied a woman to the Circle of Lebanon where they heard a booming sound which stopped when the man threw a silver cross at the rusted iron door.

According to the story Thames Television were called in, but when they attempted to interview the man in front of the North Gate a sudden outbreak of freak weather forced them to move further down Swain's Lane.

Over the following months the mutilated bodies of foxes and cats were found in nearby Waterlow Park, an escaped mental patient was seen wandering the cemetery covered in his own blood, and graves were desecrated by the High Priest of the British Occult Society who, according to Judi Cuthbertson and Tom Randall in their 1991 book, *Permanent Londoners*, 'broke into two dozen tombs and drove stakes through the hearts of the deceased'. The High Priest later received a four-year jail term for his 'anti-Dracula activities'. The number of stories has dwindled since and there have been few fresh sightings of animal corpses or the undead.

Eastern Cemetery

The eastern section, which can be visited daily, was opened in 1854, a tunnel linking it with the western section so that coffins could be transferred discreetly. Its most famous resident is Karl Marx, who died in 1883 and whose death was commemorated a year later on its first anniversary by some 3,000 supporters, including William Morris, who journeyed to the cemetery to pay tribute. Morris was unable to get close to the grave and had to pay his respects at a nearby patch of ground where the crowd sang 'The Internationale'. Every 12 March, the day Marx died, the Marx Memorial Library holds a ceremony by the grave.

HOLLOWAY, N7, N19

His home was in the Holloway region north of London . . . a tract of suburban Sahara, where tiles and bricks were burnt, bones were boiled, carpets were beat, rubbish was shot, dogs were fought, and dust was heaped by contractors – *Our Mutual Friend*, Charles Dickens (1865)

An intensely developed grimy slice of inner suburbia caught between fashionable Islington and wealthy Highgate and known mostly for its railway lines and congested roads, Holloway was built on land owned around the time of the Norman Conquest by the Dean of St Paul's, which later passed to the St John's Priory and St Mary's Nunnery in Clerkenwell. The name first appeared in the fifteenth century in reference to the muddy hollow way, now Holloway Road, the main route through the area. Holloway grew in the mid nineteenth century following the arrival of the railways, when streets of basic brick houses were built for manual workers. Further north, by the foothills of Highgate Hill and Crouch Hill, more ambitious properties, decorated with perfunctory classical embellishments, were erected on the featureless fields for the clerical classes working in the City, who travelled there on the new railways and omnibuses, as epitomized by Charles Pooter, the hero of George and Weedon Grossmith's *Diary of a Nobody* of 1888. Due to its lack of importance, Holloway escaped severe destruction during the Second World War and has barely changed in appearance since, save for the erection of a number of council estates around the Nag's Head junction.

(i) Lower Holloway (N7)

Caledonian Road

Pentonville Prison, Caledonian Road at Wheelwright Street

> 'Jimes Potter' 'is nime was. 'E was found at seven in the morning underneaf the kitchen sink wiv 'is froat cut from ear to ear. It was the landlady's brother done it. They 'anged 'im at Pentonville – 'The Return of the Battling Billson', P. G. Wodehouse (1924)

Built in 1842 as a model prison for men between eighteen and thirty-five and based on John Haviland's Pennsylvania State Penitentiary, Pentonville initially employed a regime in which inmates were kept in solitary confinement in light, airy cells (an improvement on the overcrowding of traditional prisons), sent to the basement if they dared to make contact with other inmates, and transported to the colonies after eighteen months. The authorities deemed this system so successful that fifty prisons were built in similar fashion in England over the next decade. When Oscar Wilde spent a short time in Pentonville in 1895 after being convicted of gross indecency, friends tried to bribe the governor, J. B. Manning, by offering him £100,000 to help Wilde escape.

The poisoner Dr Crippen was hanged at Pentonville in 1910 and before his execution was visited by the librettist W. S. Gilbert, researching what became his final play, *The Hooligan*. Sir Roger Casement, the Irish patriot who was indicted for treason during the First World War after spying for the Germans, was hanged here in August 1916, his body being exhumed from the prison cemetery in 1965 and reburied in Dublin. Timothy Evans was hanged at Pentonville in March 1950 for supposedly murdering his wife, Beryl, and daughter, Jeraldine, at 10 Rillington Place, Notting Hill, an act now considered a major miscarriage of justice that aided the campaign to repeal the death sentence for murder. The real murderer was later revealed to be John Christie, Evans's landlord, who was hanged here in July 1953 by Albert Pierrepoint 'in less time than it took the ash to fall off a cigar I had left half-smoked in my room'.

► Holloway Prison, p. 338; 10 Rillington Place, p. 453.

Hilldrop Crescent

In 1910 Dr Hawley Harvey Crippen poisoned his wife, Cora, an unsuccessful music-hall star, at **No. 39** Hilldrop Crescent, off Camden Road (now replaced by council flats) for reasons unknown, then telling friends that she had died in America while visiting relatives. Suspicions were aroused when Crippen's secretary, Ethel Le Neve, was spotted wearing Cora's clothing and jewellery, and when police questioned

Crippen he claimed that Cora had eloped with a lover and that he had withheld the news out of embarrassment. The police were satisfied, but Crippen panicked and fled to the United States with Ethel. Officers searched the house but found nothing, failing to notice the loose brick leading to a coal hole where Cora Crippen's headless remains were buried. However, when police tried again they found her corpse and launched a search for Crippen. The captain of the SS *Montrose* notified them, via Marconigram wireless, that Mr and *Master* Robinson (Ethel Le Neve dressed as a boy) who were on board could be Crippen and friend. Police caught up with the absconding pair on a faster vessel and arrested them in one of the first examples of a criminal being captured with the help of radio telegraphy. Crippen was hanged at Pentonville in November 1910 and the Scottish comedian Sandy McNabb later bought the house for £100, briefly opening it as a Crippen Museum.

Holloway Road

A relentlessly traffic-choked route sloping upwards from Highbury Corner to Archway past second-hand furniture stores, corroded domes, decaying stone work, cheap cafés, the bedraggled buildings of the University of North London and the shops around the Nag's Head junction, Holloway Road is part of the ancient route north (now the A1) and in medieval times was made impassable in the rain by the hooves of animals herded down the hill from the fields of Middlesex to the Smithfield slaughterhouses, giving rise to the name *Hohl Weg*, from which comes Holloway. Shops opened alongside the cattle trail in the nineteenth century, and side roads were built, but major development did not take place until the railway linking Gospel Oak and Barking arrived in the 1840s, soon followed by the Great Northern Railway and the North London Line.

west side

Black House (1969–71), Nos. 95–99

Michael de Freitas, a.k.a. Michael Abdul Malik, or Michael X, the self-styled leader of London's black community in the 1960s, ran a number of separatist movements from this building, to which he gave the unfortunate name Black House, the same name as Oswald Mosley had given his British Union of Fascists Chelsea headquarters in the 1930s. De Freitas, who modelled himself on American black power leader Malcolm X, had been a pimp and rent collector for slum landlord Peter Rachman in Notting Hill – his excuse being that Rachman was the only west London landlord willing to house West Indians – and he enjoyed a large cult following among the fashionable white Left. (When asked what the establishment could do to tackle racism, de Freitas responded that a black man should impregnate the Queen, so that they could rear a half-caste child.)

Shortly before Black House opened the counter-culture paper *International Times* proclaimed: 'The great centre which Michael Abdul Malik will build will be white with a god-like figure like those Tibetan Buddhist temples which reflect the old vision of the winged disc, and prepare us for the new.' But much of the money to finance the project came from drug dealing and in August 1969, shortly after Black House opened, de Freitas was committed for trial at the Old Bailey for robbery and demanding money with menaces after making a business associate wear a dog collar and crawl around the building on all fours for supposedly double-crossing him. Two years later he jumped bail before his trial and fled to Trinidad, where he was joined by various associates, including Gail Benson, daughter of the Tory MP for Chatham, to form a new black power movement. After attacking a colleague and decapitating him with a cutlass de Freitas was hanged for murder.

➤ Michael X in Notting Hill, p. 458.

east side: Tollington Way to Highbury Corner

Joe Meek's studio, No. 304

In a small cramped studio converted from two bedrooms above what is now a cycle store, Joe Meek, Britain's first independent record producer, cut a number of the most successful hits of the early 1960s, including Johnny Leyton's eerie 'Johnny Remember Me' and the Tornados' instrumental 'Telstar', a tribute to the space satellite of the same name, which became the first track by a British group to top the US charts. Placing the string section in the hallway, vocal backing groups in the bathroom, and brass players on the stairs, Meek also recorded the then unknown Tom Jones and Rod Stewart, though not Marc Bolan who knocked on the door begging for the chance of a session but was rejected.

Meek, who was paranoid about rivals, particularly Phil Spector, stealing his work, would incessantly search the building for bugs and lose his temper at the slightest thing, flinging typewriters and even a speaker cabinet across the room, and once threatened drummer Mitch Mitchell (who later joined the Jimi Hendrix Experience) with a shotgun for playing the wrong rhythm, telling him: 'If you don't play it properly I'll blow your fucking head off.' Mitchell, it is believed, then played it properly. But from being one of the most powerful men in British pop in the early 1960s, Meek became unfashionable once the Beatles and other beat groups took over the charts, and he was prone to bouts of melancholy which increased when police questioned him about the so-called 'Suitcase Murder', in which a rent boy was cut up and dumped in a suitcase in a Sussex field. On 3 February 1967 Meek shot his landlady during an argument at No. 304 and then turned the gun on himself.

➤ Abbey Road studios, p. 367.

Islington Library, Holloway Road at Fieldway Crescent

The playwright Joe Orton and his lover

Kenneth Halliwell stole seventy-two books, mostly from this branch, in the late 1950s and early 1960s, pasting their own illustrations over the books' photos for humorous effect. After placing the books back on the shelves they stood around the library waiting for unsuspecting users to read their handiwork. Orton and Halliwell were eventually caught and jailed; the library keeps some of the defaced books in its archive.

Parkhurst Road
Holloway Prison, Parkhurst Road at Camden Road
Built as a House of Correction for men and women in 1849 to 1851, and used for women exclusively since 1902, Holloway was where W. T. Stead, editor of the *Pall Mall Gazette*, was jailed in 1885, during his paper's campaign against child prostitution, after buying a thirteen-year-old girl from her mother simply to show how easy it was to do so. Treated leniently, Stead was allowed to edit the paper from his cell and after his release wrote how he had 'never had a pleasanter holiday, a more charming season of repose'.

Oscar Wilde spent a couple of weeks here on remand while awaiting trial for gross indecency in 1895, his flamboyant clothes taken from him and replaced with prison issue embellished with arrows. In the early years of the twentieth century Holloway was where many suffragettes, including Sylvia Pankhurst, were jailed. When one of them, Marion Dunlop, went on hunger strike she was released, as the authorities feared she would become a martyr, and this encouraged other suffragettes to copy her. The number of women on hunger strike became so high that the prison authorities back-tracked and started to force feed the suffragettes. An internee during the First World War was Countess Constance Markievicz (Constance Gore-Booth), the Sinn Fein MP for Dublin and the first woman to win election to the House of Commons (at a time when women in Britain did not have the vote), who refused to take her seat there and was imprisoned for participating in the Easter Rising.

In March 1929 hundreds of people gathered outside the prison to witness the arrival of Lillias Arkell-Smith who, masquerading as Colonel Sir Victor Ivor Gauntlett Blyth Barker, had married in Brighton but, after failing to attend a bankruptcy hearing, had been unveiled as a woman and sentenced to nine months' imprisonment for falsely describing herself as a bachelor in a register of marriage.

In the mid-1940s Oswald Mosley, leader of the British Union of Fascists, was incarcerated in Holloway, his 'prison' conditions being a flat for him and his wife, Diana, in which they could cook their own meals and be waited on by other prisoners. But that did not suit Diana, who complained to the governor. When asked if she knew anyone in the government who could help, she replied that she knew all the Tories, beginning with Churchill, and that 'the whole lot deserve to be shot'. When it was revealed in November 1943 that Oswald and Lady Mosley were to be released there was an outcry in the press, and film companies erected rigs outside the prison to capture the event on newsreel. The authorities sidestepped reporters and photographers by releasing the Mosleys through the back gates.

It was here that Ruth Ellis became the last woman to be hanged in Britain at 9.01 a.m. on 13 July 1955, her hanging delayed by a minute after a hoax telephone call was made to the governor by someone claiming to be working for the home secretary, Gwilym Lloyd George.
➤ Old Bailey, p. 58.

Seven Sisters Road
Bank of Cyprus, Nos. 160–162
George Davis, released in 1975 from a robbery sentence after a high-profile campaign – his supporters daubed 'George Davis Is Innocent OK' graffiti throughout

London, drove through the gates of Buckingham Palace, and dug up the pitch at Headingley during the Ashes Test – was embarrassingly caught attempting to rob the Bank of Cyprus on 23 September 1977. Police, acting on a tip-off, watched the bank from a nearby property and when they approached one of the robbers threatened to shoot, grabbing an 82-year-old passer-by as a human shield; he was foiled by a member of the public who dropped his shopping bags and threw his arms around the robber, forcing him to let go. Davis, meanwhile, was sitting in a car supposedly resting between shops but suspiciously wearing a balaclava. His arrest brought the 'George Davis Is Innocent OK' campaign to an abrupt halt.

Vale Royal

An obscure side street off York Way, just north of the North London Railway line, it has been enshrined in London mythology since the 1977 publication of Aidan Dun's *Vale Royal* book of poems, championed by Iain Sinclair in *Lights Out for the Territory*, which speculates about the land north of King's Cross being converted into a city of canals and becoming the centre of the spiritual rebirth of London.

► Iain Sinclair's *Rodinsky's Room*, p. 290.

(ii) Upper Holloway (N19)

Archway Road

Begun as a tunnel in 1810 to link Holloway Road and the Great North Road through the steep Highgate Hill, it caved in prior to completion two years later, to the delight of residents who had objected to the project, but the scheme was soon resurrected, the engineer, John Rennie, being invited to submit a new design. Rennie decided to shelve the tunnel plan and cut a thoroughfare (Archway Road) through the hill, resulting in Hornsey Lane crossing the new road on a tall bridge – now popularly known as Suicide Bridge – held up by John Nash's arch (hence the name, Archway).

The road belatedly opened in 1813 but was not a success in terms of the toll money gathered until the 1830s.

Highgate Hill

A steep road with a long, eventful history and stunning views of London, it was where sometime around the year 1360 Dick Whittington, according to the well-known legend, having endured a miserable time in the City despite assurances that the streets were paved with gold, chose to leave the capital but heard in the distant peal of the bells of St Mary-le-Bow the cry: 'Turn again, Dick Whittington, thrice Lord Mayor of London', returning to the City to find a fortune awaiting him on a ship he had recently left. For the eighteenth-century commentator James Boswell, journeying into London from Scotland, Highgate Hill offered a first glimpse of the city and the writer was 'all life and joy. I gave three huzzas and went briskly on.' William Powell, the late eighteenth-century Treasury clerk who retired after winning £500 in a lottery, used to walk from his Sloane Street home to the foot of Highgate Hill every morning and after a brief pause at the bottom of the hill run towards the top without stopping until he had reached the summit. If his run were interrupted he would return to the starting point and begin again. When asked why he performed this eccentric feat Powell replied that if he stopped doing so the world would cease to exist.

south side: Archway tube to Highgate High Street

Dick Whittington stone

The stone marks the spot where Dick Whittington is meant to have sat and heard in the bells of St Mary-le-Bow a call to turn back to London. The seated cat was added in 1964.

Lauderdale House

Now a cultural centre hosting exhibitions, concerts and craft fairs, the house was built in 1580 for Richard Martin, master of the Royal Mint, on a vantage point overlooking

London, and in the mid seventeenth century came into the possession of John Ireton, brother of Cromwell's general, Henry, who was imprisoned when Charles II was restored to the throne in 1660 and banned from owning property. John Maitland, Earl of Lauderdale, Charles's Secretary of State for Scotland and the 'L' of the Cabal ministry, then took over the property. In 1670 Nell Gwynn supposedly threatened to throw the son she bore for Charles II out of an upper window if the king did not grant him a title, which made the king immediately exclaim: 'Save the Earl of Burford!'

John Wesley, the founder of Methodism, preached at Lauderdale House in 1782, and the building later became one of the many private boarding schools in Highgate. It then reverted to private use until a late-nineteenth-century resident, the Liberal MP Sir Sidney Waterlow, gave the house to the London County Council in 1889 'for the enjoyment of Londoners'.

east side
Cromwell House, No. 104
The Ghana High Commission occupies the handsome 1638 house built for Richard Sprignell, an associate of Oliver Cromwell, which was later bought by Alvaro Mendes da Costa, physician to Charles II, the first Jew to own property in London following Oliver Cromwell's decree that Jews be allowed to return to England. Early in the twentieth century Cromwell House was taken over as a convalescent home by Great Ormond Street children's hospital and was later occupied by the Montfort Missionary Society.

▶ The Jews' return to London, Jewry Street, p. 36.

STOKE NEWINGTON, N16

Quintessential village London, long popular with writers, radicals, artists and musicians despite being isolated from the centre with no tube and poor bus and rail links, Stoke Newington (which means 'new town in the wood') grew around the Romans' Ermine Street – now the A10, which includes Stoke Newington High Street and Stamford Hill. A small farming community, it began to attract wealthy merchants after the man-made New River, bringing water from Hertfordshire to the City, was cut through the fields in 1613 and in the seventeenth century Stoke Newington became a haven for dissenters and radicals who were unable to meet in the City, the best known of whom, locally, was the author Daniel Defoe, who briefly lived on Stoke Newington Church Street. By the beginning of the nineteenth century Stoke Newington was a 'misty looking village of England, where there were a vast number of gigantic and gnarled trees', according to the mystery writer Edgar Allan Poe, who was schooled locally. Its sylvan look disappeared as London became industrialized and suburbanized, and in 1821 farmland on the south side of Church Street was auctioned off for new houses. The fields west of the A10 were built over with fine houses in the 1860s, whereas east of the A10, where the housing stock was more pedestrian and cheaper to rent, immigrants moved in. Today, this is echoed in bohemian Stoke Newington village to the west and down-at-heel Stoke Newington Common to the east.

(i) Stoke Newington Common

Evering Road
Location of Jack 'The Hat' McVitie's murder, No. 97
The gangster Reggie Kray murdered Jack 'The Hat' McVitie, a bald-headed villain who always wore a hat, because he had failed to obey the Krays' order to kill an associate, in this basement flat on 28 October 1967, eighteen months after twin brother Ronnie shot dead George Cornell in the Blind Beggar pub, Whitechapel. The Krays lured McVitie to the property after urging the tenant, 'Blonde' Carol, to spend the night elsewhere, with the ruse that there was

going to be a party. When McVitie entered the room and found things were not swinging as he expected, he asked: 'Where's all the birds, where's all the booze?' Reggie Kray responded by pointing a gun at his head and firing, but the gun jammed. As McVitie tried to escape through the window, his hat fell off. He was hauled back in, held down so that he could not get away, and attacked by Kray, who picked up a carving knife and pushed it into McVitie's face below the eye, then stabbed him in the throat so severely the knife stuck to the wall and had to be wriggled around in his throat to be removed. Once McVitie was dead the Krays were faced with the problem of disposing of the body. As it would not fit into the boot of their car it was placed upright on the back seat and driven on a long tortuous route through London (to lose possible pursuers and confound potential witnesses) to a quiet street in Woolwich, and later taken to a watery grave off the coast of Sussex. The car was later reduced to the size of an Oxo cube by a friendly scrap metal merchant.

► Blind Beggar, p. 306.

(ii) Stamford Hill

Stamford Hill, the name of the A10 north of Stoke Newington and of the area around the high ground through which the road runs, is the centre of London's orthodox Jewish community, with twenty-one schools, fifty-six synagogues, and the largest population of ultra-orthodox (Hassidic) Jews outside New York and Israel. It was first colonized by Jews after the First World War, when those born in the East End of London to refugees who had fled eastern Europe in the late nineteenth century grew up and moved north, attracted by Stamford Hill's open spaces, spacious houses, greenery and river (Lea). Some of the new arrivals were White Russians (anti-communists), exiled after the Revolution, who brought their wealth with them. Others could trace their ancestry to a number of villages in Poland,

such as Lubavitch, and were followers of Israel ben Eliezer, also known as Ba'al Shem Tov, a charismatic figure who founded a mystical, ecstatic movement in the eighteenth century. They are easily recognizable, the men wearing black headwear, beards, ringlets and long black frock coats, even in summer, and the women sporting gruesome ritual wigs.

More mainstream local Jews were instrumental in the late 1950s in helping instigate the 'mod' movement, which also laid down strict rules on clothes – sharp Italian suits with narrow lapels and shirts with pointed collars – that could be bought at places such as Connick's, 55 Stoke Newington High Street, one of the few clothes shops in London which sold Levi's in small sizes, and therefore attracted custom from the teenage Marc Bolan (then Marc Feld). An article in *Town* magazine in 1962 printed photos of Stamford Hill mods, including the fifteen-year-old Feld, who told the reporter: 'You've got to be different from other kids. I mean you got to be two steps ahead. The stuff that half the haddocks you see around are wearing I was wearing years ago.' Photographs of the adolescent Bolan were taken by war photographer Don McCullin, who later worked on the Antonioni film *Blow Up*, while captions were provided by the features editor, Michael Parkinson.

Rookwood Road
Church of the Good Shepherd

> Many a time have I stood outside those barricaded *art nouveau* railings and looked up at the soaring stone spire, with great bronzed beasts at its base, and regarded that locked door with longing –
> article in the *Spectator*, John Betjeman (1956)

Built in 1892 as the Church of the Ark of the Covenant for the Agapemonites, a sect founded in Somerset in the late nineteenth century by Henry Prince, who left the Church of England claiming that the Holy Ghost had taken up residence in his body, it was the setting for a dramatic incident in

1902 when John Hugh Smyth-Piggott, Prince's successor, proclaimed his own divinity from the pulpit. A mob chased the preacher from the church into the nearby pond to ascertain whether or not he could walk on water. However, the police, indifferent to the outcome but determined to keep the peace, rescued the cleric before verification, thus saving him from either instant deification or death. The building closed as a place of worship in 1923, but was leased in 1956 to the Ancient Catholic Church, who renamed it the Church of the Good Shepherd.

➤ University Church of Christ the King, Bloomsbury, p. 83.

North-west London

CAMDEN TOWN | REGENT'S PARK, NW1

Camden Town began as a speculative development on land originally owned by Charles Pratt, 1st Earl of Camden, and became a major residential and commercial neighbourhood following the arrival of the railways in the 1830s. Regent's Park to the west developed out of Henry VIII's wish to have a hunting ground to the north of Whitehall Palace and was originally called Marylebone Park, being renamed in honour of the Prince Regent (later George IV) early in the nineteenth century.

(i) Camden Town

> Yesterday I walked for miles in that maze of poor back streets between Camden Road station and the canal. Cloudy, drizzling, not drizzling, cloudy. Canal black, with plastic cups floating in it, potato-crisp bags, Kentucky Chicken and a dead cat – *In Camden Town*, David Thomson (1983)

One of the metropolis's great centres of activity, dominated by music venues, bars, cafés and markets, Camden Town is named after the 1st Earl of Camden, who sold plots of land to the east side of what is now Camden High Street in 1791, when the only major buildings were two inns – the Black Cap (on land now occupied by the tube station) and the Old Mother Red Cap (now

the World's End). The area was dramatically altered early in the nineteenth century, as Charles Dickens outlined in *Dombey and Son*, with 'houses knocked down; streets broken through and stopped; deep pits and trenches dug in the ground; [and] enormous heaps of earth and clay thrown up', to prepare for the arrival of the London and Birmingham Railway.

As there were no local stops on the line, and the terminus was a mile south at Euston, Camden Town was unable to attract middle-class commuters and instead was colonized by Irish immigrants and covered with tightly packed houses, small shops and yards forming an intensely urban, working-class community. In the 1960s, following the growth in further education, students, attracted by the cheap rents, began to move here, their presence helping to boost the local music scene – until then purely Irish – and sustain the local markets that had opened on the land made derelict by the decline of the local railway industry.

Gradually, a youth-orientated scene grew up around the pubs of Parkway, the markets of Chalk Farm Road, and the record shops near the tube station, particularly Rock On at 2 Kentish Town Road, creating a bohemian reputation that in the 1980s attracted media companies both small (around the renovated Camden Lock area) and large (TV-am moving into Terry Farrell's corrugated metal pop art building in 1983). Since then Camden Town has grown into one of London's most sought-after areas, its market area eclipsing even Portobello Road and Petticoat Lane at weekends when tens of thousands of shoppers arrive to search for clothes old and new in Camden Market, Camden Lock Market and the Stables Market.

Albert Street

Now one of the most desirable streets in the area, thanks to its central location and smart well-maintained houses – inhabitants include the novelists Beryl Bainbridge and A. N. Wilson – Albert Street was a violent place in the 1960s, full of cheap lodging houses, according to the film director Bruce Robinson, who lived in a squat furnished with little more than an oven, light bulb and mattress. Robinson recreated the seediness for the flat shared by Withnail and Marwood in his 1986 film, *Withnail and I*. In the mid-1990s Oasis's Noel Gallagher lived at No. 83a, where he wrote 'Wonderwall', moving out in 1995 when interest in the group was at its peak.

Gloucester Crescent
A street popular in recent decades with figures from the arts, its residents have included the photographer David Bailey, the playwright Michael Frayn, the theatre director Jonathan Miller, the artist David Gentleman, the novelist Alice Thomas Ellis, the cartoonist Mark Boxer – it was home of his sixties caricatures the Stringalongs – and the jazz musician George Melly, for whom Gloucester Crescent was ideally placed, being a bracing walk across Regent's Park to the West End. Another resident, Alan Bennett, used it as the setting for his short story 'The Lady in the Van'.

Oval Road
At the northern end of Oval Road, which should have been oval-shaped to complement nearby Gloucester Crescent, lie the Camden Town catacombs, a labyrinthine expanse of tunnels and vaults, built to stable the horses used in moving railway trucks and wagons for the nearby London and Birmingham Railway in the mid nineteenth century. They were later used by Gilbey's Gin company when it was based in the Roundhouse on Chalk Farm Road.

Parkway
A busy but charming road at the centre of Camden's music scene, Parkway is home to the Jazz Café at Nos. 5–7 and at No. 94 to the Dublin Castle, one of the first pubs in Britain allowed to serve alcohol until midnight, six days a week, in the early 1970s, which led to its becoming a major music venue, where Madness secured their repu-

tation at the end of the decade. At No. 25 is the Rat and Parrot, where the scene used in the opening of the Pogues' 'A Pair of Brown Eyes' takes place. At Nos. 35–37 is London's best-stocked pet store, Palmer's, where a family of boa constrictors used to be let loose at night to deter burglars until the authorities intervened.

Chalk Farm Road
Part of the ancient route leading from the West End to the Hampstead heights, it is named after the Chalk Farm pub, whose name was a corruption of the local Chalcot's Farm.
west side: canal to Chalk Farm station
Pirate's Castle
A mock medieval castle designed by Richard Seifert and now a children's club.
Camden Lock, Chalk Farm Road at Commercial Place
One of London's most interesting markets, set in a well-preserved site surrounded by Victorian brick warehouses, chimneys and cobbles, it is named after the lock of the adjacent Regent's Canal and for much of the twentieth century was the timber yard for T. E. Dingwall's warehouse. By the 1970s the site was derelict and in 1972 craftspeople were invited to take space at low rent. Two years later a market opened, which expanded after a relaxation in the Sunday shopping laws, and now features around 100 stalls selling clothes, furniture, jewellery, gifts, books and records divided between a permanent building on Chalk Farm Road and the yards outside.
▶ Portobello Road, p. 459.
Dingwall's (1970s), Middle Yard, 35 Camden Lock Place
Dingwall's, which opened in 1973, soon became one of London's most popular night-time venues and an early home for punk. In July 1977 after a gig here by Elvis Costello and the Attractions, *Melody Maker*'s Allan Jones proclaimed: 'They played the most startling set I've experienced since Television pinned me to the deck in Glasgow. This combo is so damned

hot they could reduce the Post Office Tower to a mess of molten metal in 60 seconds.' Punk and new wave continued to dominate the bill in the 1980s but was replaced by comedy in the 1990s and Dingwall's now features a more eclectic range of acts.

▶ Roundhouse, see below.

Stables Market, opposite Hartland Road

London's biggest flea market has hundreds of stalls filling every inch of available space around the arches of the North London railway and is the best place in the capital to find retro clothes – Victorian pea jackets, twenties gowns, original Levi's – as well as oddities that are likely to appear on next year's catwalks, such is the area's popularity with designers. There are also scores of cheap noodle bars with covered seating, which help draw the largest crowds to be found anywhere in the capital at weekends.

Roundhouse, No. 99

One of London's leading rock venues in the 1960s and 1970s and now occasionally used as a theatre, the Roundhouse was originally a railway shed, designed in 1846 by Robert Dockray under the supervision of the railway engineer Robert Stephenson, built for turning locomotives on a 34-ft turntable. When the railway companies moved out in 1869, it became a storehouse for Gilbey's Gin, until falling into disuse after the Second World War.

In the early 1960s the playwright Arnold Wesker made an ambitious bid to convert the building into an arts venue for his Centre 42 organization, which he hoped would 'destroy the mystique and snobbery associated with the arts [by aiming at] the bus driver, housewife, miner and Teddy Boy', and by 1966 it was putting on unusual events such as 'The All-Night Rave Pop Op Costume Masque Drag Ball Et Al' fancy-dress party, held on 15 October 1966 to launch the underground newspaper *International Times*. As they entered the building guests were handed a sugar lump, supposedly containing acid, and inside they mingled with Swinging London luminaries such as Paul McCartney and Marianne Faith-

full, who won the best costume prize for a nun's habit that just failed to cover her behind. On stage were new groups such as the Soft Machine and Pink Floyd, the latter missing the opportunity of reaching their first worldwide audience as the reviewer from the *San Francisco Examiner* assumed that they were amateurs filling in between the major acts and failed to comment on their performance.

It was at the Roundhouse in July 1970 that the nude revue *Oh! Calcutta!*, the title a pun on '*Oh, quel cul tu as*', French for 'Oh, what an arse you have', opened, leading to immediate complaints about taxpayers' money paying for smut. In the late seventies the Roundhouse won a new lease of life as a punk venue. On 4 July 1976 a gig headlined by the Ramones was the first opportunity for a British audience to see any of the new acts from New York that were creating so much media interest, and later in the year Patti Smith played a set that became a major influence on the new music emerging from Britain. Few gigs have taken place since the early 1980s and the building is now underutilized, with no one able to find a useful role for what is probably the best medium-sized venue in the capital.

▶ Marquee I, p. 139.

Camden High Street

One of London's most energetic high streets, with a range of shops covering practically every branch of retailing, it features typical chain stores south of the tube station and shops selling leather jackets, boots and youth tribe ephemera north of the station.

east side: canal to Crowndale Road

Compendium Bookshop (1968–2000), No. 234

London's leading late-twentieth-century left-wing bookshop opened in 1968 (at No. 240), at a time when there were only two or three outlets in Britain for beat literature, obscure political pamphlets, tracts and magazines, and moved to No. 234 soon after. It closed in 2000 to widespread dismay.

Electric Ballroom, No. 184
The Electric Ballroom opened as a dance venue, the Buffalo, in 1937, catering mostly for the local Irish working class, and it was here that the American balladeer Jim Reeves pulled out of an appearance in June 1963 when the management failed to adhere to a rider in his contract stipulating that the piano be tuned. Staff left the building to deposit the ticket money safely *before* making their unfortunate announcement. A month later the teenage Van Morrison played the ballroom and stayed with his band in the flat above after the gig. In 1978 the Buffalo reopened as the Electric Ballroom and on 22 August that year Sid Vicious gave his last stage performance here, playing in a punk 'supergroup' with Rat Scabies and Glen Matlock.

Camden Palace / Music Machine, No. 1a
A grand Edwardian music hall venue, it opened in 1900 as the Camden Theatre and has since served as a cinema, BBC studio (the Goons' show was often recorded here) and the Music Machine punk/new wave venue, which stayed open until 2 a.m. six nights a week. In that incarnation it was plagued by trouble: Bob Geldof was attacked on stage at a June 1977 Boomtown Rats gig; the Human League had to play behind riot shields to protect their equipment, mostly computers, on 17 August 1978; and a twenty-year-old man was stabbed to death while talking to a friend on the stairway in January 1979. Three years later, at the height of the new romantic era, the venue reopened as the Camden Palace, hosting a narcissistic club run by Steve Strange.

(ii) Marylebone

An enclave of smart apartment blocks, offices and small shops situated around Marylebone station which is overshadowed by the main part of Marylebone to the south and St John's Wood to the north.
● Also see Marylebone in the West End, pp. 148–58.

Baker Street *Also see p. 149*
The section of Baker Street north of Marylebone Road was Upper Baker Street until 1930 and contains at No. 221 the headquarters of the Abbey National which by chance occupies an address similar to the one Arthur Conan Doyle gave his fictional detective, Sherlock Holmes (No. 221B), resulting in the building society's receiving hundreds of letters a year from Holmes devotees.
east side
Baker Street station
A station was built here for the Metropolitan Railway, the world's first underground railway, in 1863 and was later extended in several directions, first for the northern branches of the Metropolitan, and in 1906 for what became the Bakerloo Line. In autumn 1999 a statue of Sherlock Holmes, whose fictional home was on Baker Street, was installed by the Marylebone Road entrance, sixty years after it was first suggested by the writer G. K. Chesterton.

BAKERLOO LINE

The Baker Street and Waterloo underground line opened in 1906 and the name Bakerloo, coined by the *Evening News* writer 'Quex', was soon adopted by the line's owners, who were criticized by the *Railway Magazine* for appropriating 'a gutter title . . . not what we expect from a railway company'. The line was extended to Watford using existing overground track in 1917 and took over the Stanmore branch of the Metropolitan Line in 1939, but it has since contracted, losing the Watford to Harrow & Wealdstone section to British Rail and the Stanmore–Baker Street branch to the Jubilee. The Bakerloo is unpopular with commuters because it is London's slowest and noisiest line, the twisting track causing severe screeching.

Harrow & Wealdstone One hundred and twelve people were killed on 8 October 1952 when the Perth to London express smashed into the rear of a suburban train at the station.

Kenton One of the least-used stations on the network, thanks to its proximity to nearby stations on fast lines into London.

South Kenton An unnecessary station, given its proximity to North Wembley and Preston Road stations.

North Wembley Opened for steam trains in 1912.

Wembley Central Not the main station for Wembley stadium, the venue being a mile away.

Stonebridge Park In 1963 the Great Train Robbers found the train they had decided to rob in the sidings and were able to search it, which helped them with the planning for the eventual robbery. The station briefly appears in the Ealing comedy *The Man in the White Suit*.

Harlesden A station wasn't built here until seventy-five years after a line was first cut through the area.

Willesden Junction So isolated when it was built in 1866 that it was known as 'The Wilderness'. Ferdinand Lopez throws himself under a train here in Anthony Trollope's novel *The Prime Minister*.

Kensal Green The station stands at the north end of Kensal Green Cemetery, London's first commercial burial ground.

Queen's Park Named after a small, two-section park which opened in 1887 to coincide with Queen Victoria's Golden Jubilee.

Kilburn Park Named after a long-vanished park.

Maida Vale Named after a short section of the A5, whose name commemorates the 1806 Battle of Maida in Italy.

Warwick Avenue Rita Tushingham, arriving from the North of England, emerges from the station, seeking a new life and excitement in the capital in the 1965 Dick Lester film *The Knack and How to Get It*.

Paddington To entice the Bakerloo Line out to Paddington in 1913 the Great Western Railway paid a sweetener to the line's owners.

Edgware Road One of two unconnected nearby stations named Edgware Road.

Marylebone It was known as Great Central station until 1917.

Baker Street During the Second World War the prime minister, Winston Churchill, a number of secret service agents and members of the French Resistance practised pistol shooting in a range built underneath the station.

Regent's Park One of few West End tube stations that serves only one line.

Oxford Circus One of the biggest stations in the system, with five and a half miles of subways and tunnels.

Piccadilly Circus One of few tube stations on the London network without a surface building.

Charing Cross Previously two separate stations – Strand and Trafalgar Square – hence the long distances passengers must walk when changing between the Northern and Bakerloo lines.

Embankment The station was built on land reclaimed from the Thames.

Waterloo The line's original southern terminus.

Lambeth North A mostly pointless station, too close to Waterloo and Elephant & Castle to be of practical use, featuring no interchanges with other lines, and serving an under-populated neighbourhood.

Elephant & Castle An abrupt southern terminus of the line, the proposed continuation towards Camberwell having been proposed and abandoned several times.

► Metropolitan Line, p. 374.

Balcombe Street

Four IRA gunmen took hostage the elderly couple who lived at No. 22B on 6 December 1975, after police had chased them here from Scott's restaurant in Mayfair. The gunmen barricaded the occupants into the living room and phoned the police to demand a car to take them to the airport so that they could escape to Ireland, but Robert Mark, the Commissioner of the Metropolitan Police, stated on air that the only place the hostage-takers would be going to was Brixton prison and after a week the men surrendered. They were later found guilty of bombing two pubs and were given lengthy prison sentences.

Dorset Square

In 1787 Thomas Lord, a property dealer and wine supplier, leased a small field to stage a cricket match between members of the White Conduit club of Islington. The players so liked the venue that they moved here and renamed themselves the Marylebone Cricket Club (MCC), drawing up a list of rules for their own use, just as other cricket clubs had done elsewhere in the country. Healthy crowds meant Lord made a profit, which he increased by staging balloon ascents, pigeon shooting and hopping contests. When a number of cricketers complained that the ground was too small, Lord offered twenty guineas to any batsman who could smash a ball out of the playing area, but he failed to pay up in 1808 when Edward Budd duly obliged, breaking a greenhouse window. The following year Lord moved the ground half a mile further north and then to the present site in St John's Wood in 1814, the same year Dorset Square was laid out.

► Lord's, p. 369.

Melcombe Place

Marylebone station

The last of London's Victorian railway termini to be built, Marylebone opened in 1899, having been funded by Sir Edward William Watkin, a Manchester cotton magnate who was chairman of the Manchester, Sheffield and Lincolnshire Railway and the Metropolitan Railway underground line, and saw Marylebone not as a terminus, but as a stop on a line running from the north of England to France via a Channel tunnel. Watkin's grand scheme was curtailed when he suffered a stroke in 1894, and with funds running low the railway company was unable to afford an architect to design the station, which opened with only four platforms. Always less congested than other major stations, Marylebone came alive mostly on Cup Final day or before international football matches when trains left every few minutes for Wembley. It enjoyed a revival in its fortune at the end of the twentieth century.

(iii) Primrose Hill

> The fields from Islington to Marylebone / To Primrose Hill and Saint John's Wood / Were builded over with pillars of gold . . . – *Jerusalem*, William Blake (1804–20)

A gracefully built and well maintained suburb, Primrose Hill is lined with tall, grand Victorian houses and is home to one of London's most visible bohemian communities, with the writers Alan Bennett, Kazuo Ishiguro and Ian McEwan among recent inhabitants. Once part of Middlesex Forest, and covered with undergrowth until the sixteenth century, the land later came into the ownership of Eton College, but when proposals were made in 1820 to dig into the hill and create a vast cemetery which could hold 5 million corpses, a campaign to create a public park was suggested as an alternative.

In the 1830s Eton College insisted that if the London and Birmingham Railway wanted the line to run through their land it had to do so underground, and so a tunnel was built between Finchley Road and Primrose Hill Road. The public greeted it as one of the marvels of the age, and crowds flocked to admire the classical architecture framing the black hole into and out of which the trains plunged.

The hill itself, 200 ft high, has long fascinated imaginative writers and religious extremists and is the setting for an annual Druid ceremony. In the sixteenth century Ursula Sontheil, the prophetess also known as Mother Shipton, claimed that when London surrounded the hill its streets would run with blood. The painter William Blake, walking on the hill early in the nineteenth century, had a vision of the 'spiritual sun, not like a golden disc the size of a guinea, but like an innumerable company of the heavenly host crying "Holy, holy, holy" '. In H. G. Wells's *The War of the Worlds* (1898) the Martians attacking London attempt to make their headquarters on the hill. In Dodie Smith's *101 Dalmatians* (1956) the dogs run to the 'open space called Primrose Hill' after escaping from Regent's Park. Primrose Hill is also the hill referred to in the Beatles' 1967 song 'The Fool on the Hill'.

Primrose Hill and the Popish Plot

In 1678 the body of Sir Edmund Berry Godfrey, a well-known London magistrate, Protestant and friend of the diarist Samuel Pepys, was found on the hill, stabbed with his own sword. The inquest gave a verdict of wilful murder. It emerged that a few weeks previously Godfrey had been approached by two men, Dr Israel Tongue and Titus Oates, and told of a Catholic plot to massacre Protestants, overthrow the government and replace the king (Charles II) with the Catholic Duke of York (later James II). When it was revealed that the murdered Godfrey's name was almost an anagram of 'Dy'd by Rome's reveng'd fury' panic spread. A cutler who made a special Godfrey dagger with the words 'Remember the murder of Edmund Berry Godfrey' on one side and 'Remember religion' on the other sold 3,000 in one day. A Catholic silversmith named Prance later confessed that he had been hired to murder Godfrey, but what became known as the Popish Plot faded only after three years of public turmoil.

► The Gordon Riots, p. 125.

(iv) Regent's Park

London's most beautifully landscaped park – its setting so close to the heart of the metropolis being one of the capital's greatest

assets – was built on land belonging to the Abbess of Barking in the Middle Ages that was bought by Henry VIII as a hunting ground, Marylebone Park, later leased to the Duke of Portland, and eventually granted to the Crown.

In 1809 John Fordyce, the Surveyor-General, suggested the land be used for a luxurious new estate of Palladian-style properties and John Nash was hired to create the most dazzling of all London's housing estates, given the name Regent's Park in honour of the Prince Regent, who took the throne in 1820 as George IV. Nash drew up plans for fifty-six villas and classical crescents built around two circuses, set in 487 acres of parkland, linked to the Prince Regent's **Carlton House** mansion in Westminster by a new route, Regent Street. But his original quota of villas was cut by the Chancellor of the Exchequer to twenty-six, of which only eight were built, and what would have been the centrepiece, the palazzo Petit Trianon, separated from Cumberland Terrace by a stretch of water, was discarded. To make matters worse, landowners near Oxford Circus refused to sell, forcing Nash to abandon his processional route to Westminster and to insert a kink in what should have been a relentlessly straight road at the southern end of Portland Place (by All Souls' church).

During the 1820s, grand crescents, classical terraces and triumphal arches – the first being Cornwall Terrace – began to appear on what had been rough open land and Vicomte de Chateaubriand, the French ambassador to the Court of St James's, spoke in awe of how 'wide streets lined with palaces have been cut, bridges built, and walks planted with trees'. The park was fully opened to the public in 1841, and although many of the stucco crescents were bombed during the Second World War they were restored with a degree of care and attention absent from the rebuilding of other devastated parts of London.

Regent's Canal
The canal that runs through the northern end of Regent's Park by Prince Albert Road was built to allow imported goods arriving at the various London docks to reach the Midlands more easily than on the muddy roads and was incorporated into John Nash's plans for Regent's Park. But the canal, which was named after the Prince Regent and opened in 1820, was not as profitable as expected and was soon rivalled by the railways as the main local conduit for moving goods. During the twentieth century the canal was used to transport building materials and since the Second World War has become a picturesque tourist trail.

north end of Regent's Park
Macclesfield Bridge
Five barges loaded with explosives being towed along the Regent's Canal on 2 October 1874 blew up as they passed under Macclesfield Bridge, the southern extension of Avenue Road, instantly killing the crew of three, destroying the bridge and lodge-keeper's house at the park gate, blowing in the windows at nearby Townshend House, home of the Dutch painter Laurens Alma-Tadema, who was absent at the time, and damaging the tomb of the Millennial prophetess Joanna Southcott, in St John's Wood Cemetery.

Outer Circle
Zoological Gardens
London Zoo opened in 1828 after the newly formed Zoological Society bought the northern portion of Regent's Park. Decimus Burton was appointed to design the zoo buildings, many of which he created as dramatic-looking follies, and the zoo obtained its first animals from the Royal Menagerie in Windsor and the collection based at the Tower of London. When it expanded in the early twentieth century leading contemporary architects such as Berthold Lubetkin were brought in to create new pavilions for the animals, resulting in the remarkable Gorilla House (1934), built as a two-part drum with a viewing area and a public walkway and since used for koala bears, and the Penguin Pool (1935), an abstract design in reinforced concrete with long spiral ramps and rendered screen walls which allows the penguins to parade before visitors. At the outset of the Second World War chloroform was used to kill the poisonous snakes, the aquarium was drained (many of the fish were eaten), and when a bomb fell nearby in September 1940 a zebra escaped from its cage and ran off across Regent's Park, closely followed by the zoo's secretary, Professor Julian Huxley. At the end of the twentieth century a change in the public's attitude towards the caging of animals brought about a financial crisis which nearly led to the building's closure.

east side of Regent's Park

Broad Walk
The walkway running along the entire east side of the park was originally intended as the northern section of a processional route linking the Prince Regent's intended Primrose Hill palace, which was never built, to **Carlton House**, his Westminster palace.

Cambridge Gate
Named after George IV's brother Adolphus, Duke of Cambridge, and built in 1876 to 1880 to the designs of Archer and Green, it soon became home to Decimus Burton's **Colosseum**, a huge rotunda containing a panorama of London based on drawings made in 1822 by Thomas Hornor while perched in a cabin on the dome of St Paul's Cathedral. The Colosseum was meant to open in 1827, but was delayed by two years when Hornor and his backer, Rowland Stevenson, absconded after running up debts of £60,000, and after fluctuating fortunes was demolished in 1875.

Chester Terrace
A grandiose neoclassical creation, 900 ft long, abutted by triumphal arches and designed by James Burton, it was built in 1825 and named after one of George IV's

titles (Earl of Chester) but was derided by John Nash, who denounced the statues surmounting each of the terrace's columns as 'ridiculous' and ordered that the end pavilions be demolished.

Cumberland Terrace

The most magnificent of John Nash's Regent's Park terraces, constructed in 1816 with much care as the Prince Regent's palace was meant to be built opposite, it consists of three blocks that are over 250 yards long and divided by decorative arches filled with statuary, and has as its centre a large pediment decorated with Britannia and plaster reliefs representing imperial themes. Wallis Simpson was living at No. 16 in 1936 when news of her affair with Edward VIII broke, to the amazement of the public, some of whom gathered outside the twice-divorced American's flat to throw bricks at the windows, provoking her swift exit to France.

► Edward VIII at Buckingham Palace, p. 211.
south end of Regent's Park

Marylebone Road

north side: Baker Street to Albany Street
Madame Tussaud's
A perennially popular waxworks museum, founded by Marie Grosholtz (Madame Tussaud) who arrived in England from France in 1802 with thirty-five wax figures and opened a permanent exhibition on Baker Street in 1835 that moved here nearly fifty years later.

Planetarium
A star gallery which opened alongside Madame Tussaud's in 1958 and where members of the public gaze at a huge domed ceiling lit up with replicas of the constellations while listening to a tape explaining the workings of the solar system and galaxy.

west side of Regent's Park
The large three-armed lake at the west side of the park was created out of the Tyburn River by John Nash.

Clarence Terrace

A stucco terrace designed by Decimus Burton, who was obliged to scale down his original plan to have a large central block linked to the sides by an open Ionic colonnade decorated with caryatids and sarcophagi No. 2 was home from 1935 to 1952 to Elizabeth Bowen, who here wrote *The House in Paris* (1935) and two London-based novels, *The Death of the Heart* (1938) and *The Heat of the Day* (1949). In one Clarence Terrace property in the 1950s members of MI6 and the CIA planned the West's 'secret' 1,800-ft tunnel linking West Berlin's American zone and the Soviet sector, details of which were leaked to the Soviets before it was even built.

Hanover Gate

A short stretch of roadway at the west side of the park, it used to contain 𝔥𝔬𝔩𝔣𝔬𝔯𝔡 𝔥𝔬𝔲𝔰𝔢, the most expensive and elaborate of the original Regent's Park villas, designed by Decimus Burton in 1832 for the merchant James Holford, which became Regent's Park College, a Baptist school for training ministers, and was destroyed in the Second World War.

Hanover Lodge, north of Hanover Gate
Built in 1827 by Decimus Burton for Colonel Sir Robert Arbuthnot, it was home from 1832 to 1845 to Thomas Cochrane, the Earl of Dundonald, one of the most successful naval officers of the Napoleonic Wars, who was sacked in 1814 and jailed for circulating news of Napoleon's death in order to make money on the Stock Exchange. Although Cochrane was the last person sentenced to stand in the pillory, he never served the punishment, and by the time he moved to Hanover Lodge he had been cleared of fraud and reinstated into the Navy. Matthew Uzielli, the banker who financed much early railway construction work, lived at Hanover Lodge from 1846 to 1860, and in 1911 Edwin Lutyens remodelled the property for Lord Beatty. In 1926 it was bought by Alice Astor, daughter of J. J. Astor, the millionaire who perished with the *Titanic*, and when Bedford

College acquired the building in 1948 it removed Lutyens's additions. The property is now privately owned.

⊛ In the grounds stand three late-twentieth-century villas – Ionic Villa, Veneto Villa and Gothick Villa – each designed for the Crown Estate in the different period style befitting its name by Quinlan Terry, the Georgian revivalist responsible for Richmond Riverside.

Hanover Terrace
Twenty houses by Nash arranged as a unified group, their porticos linked by a continuous loggia, form Hanover Terrace, whose residents have included the play-wright Harold Pinter, who lived at No. 7 from 1968 to 1978; the composer Ralph Vaughan Williams, who composed his last symphony at No. 10, where he lived from 1953 to 1958, the last five years of his life; and the author H. G. Wells, who lived at No. 13 from 1937 to 1946 and died there.

Outer Circle
London Central Mosque, Outer Circle at Hanover Gate
The mosque has its origins in a fund set up by the Nizam of Hyderabad in the 1920s and was built from 1974 to 1977 to the designs of Frederick Gibberd on land that in 1944 had been handed to Islamic community leaders by the Crown Estate Commissioners in exchange for a site in Cairo that was used for a new Anglican cathedral.

Hertford Villa / Winfield House, north of mosque
Hertford Villa was built by Decimus Burton in 1825 for Francis Charles Seymour-Conway, the 3rd Marquess of Hertford and Envoy Extraordinary to the Court of Russia, who began the Wallace Collection of paintings and artefacts. Later it became St Dunstan's Villa, used as a training centre for blind and disabled soldiers in the First World War, and in 1934 home to Lord Rothermere, owner of the *Daily Mail*. Two years afterwards the Woolworth heiress, Barbara Hutton, acquired the lease and rebuilt the property as Winfield House. But no sooner was it

finished than the RAF at the outset of the Second World War commandeered it for storing barrage balloons. When Hutton returned in 1945 she found buckled floor-boards and broken windows, and instead of moving back donated the house to the US government, who have used it as the resi-dence for their ambassadors since 1953.
► Wallace Collection, p. 151.

Prince Albert Road
Grove House / Nuffield Lodge, south of St John's Wood High Street
Decimus Burton built the park's second mansion, Grove House, which occupies a commanding site at the north-west corner of the park, in 1823 for George Greenhough, geographer and geologist, using a circular theme for much of the design, the result being a circular entrance hall and a drawing room with a semi-circular portico. Sigis-mund Goetze produced seventeen panels depicting scenes from Ovid's *Metamorphoses* inside the house in the 1940s but they were painted over when the Nuffield Institute bought the property in 1954 and converted it to Nuffield Lodge, which is now offices.

Sussex Place
Now the London Graduate School of Business Studies, the twenty-six-house long terrace with curved wings and Corinthian columns, was designed by John Nash for the builder William Smith in a style similar to the Prince Regent's abandoned **Carlton House** mansion.
centre of Regent's Park

Inner Circle
clockwise from the north
St John's Lodge
One of Regent's Park's greatest villas, its sturdy stucco blocks massing into a power-ful frame, St John's Lodge was built in 1817 by John Raffield for Charles Augustus Tulk MP, a friend of the poet William Blake, whose work he published shortly after the latter's death, when Blake was unknown and even in his own circle uncelebrated. It was home from 1829 to 1833 to the Marquess

of Wellesley, elder brother of the Duke of
Wellington and Governor-General of India,
and in the mid nineteenth century passed to
Sir Isaac Lyon Goldsmid, the first Jewish
baronet, who founded London Docks.
In 1887 St John's Lodge became home to
the 3rd Marquess of Bute, the model for
Disraeli's Lothair in the 1870 novel of the
same name, who installed a domed circular
chapel (demolished in 1959), redecorated the
rooms with heraldic and astrological
symbols, and transformed the gardens with
terraces and 'arboured retreats' that are now
part of the park. During the First World
War the property became a hospital for
disabled soldiers and after Second World
War damage it was elaborately and pain-
stakingly restored. It was sold in 1995 to
Prince Jefri, brother of the sultan of Brunei,
for £40 million, which at the time was the
highest price ever paid for a London
domestic property.

South Villa, west of York Bridge
Only the lodge gates near York Bridge
remain of Decimus Burton's 1819 villa,
acquired by Bedford College in 1908 and
demolished in 1913.

The Holme, east of the lake
Decimus Burton planned what was the
park's first villa when he was eighteen and
built it in 1817–18 for his father, James, the
builder responsible for much of Bloomsbury and St John's Wood, incorporating
a splendid bowed drawing room featuring
Ionic pilasters that is visible from the lake.
During the Second World War the RAF
requisitioned the house, and though it was
later acquired by Bedford College it has
since reverted to being a private residence,
exchanging hands for around £50 million in
1994.

(v) Somers Town

A broken-down area of crumbling housing
estates, boarded-up shops, railway lines, gas
stations and canals south of Camden Town,
Somers Town is named after the local landowners, the Somers family, and was initially

developed as a middle-class estate around
The Polygon, a fifteen-sided building
erected in the 1780s on what is now Polygon
Road, where the feminist Mary Wollstonecraft briefly lived and the young Charles
Dickens later lodged. The rest of the scheme
foundered when the building contractors
went bankrupt, resulting in houses being
built for the working class instead. After the
London and Birmingham Railway was cut
through in the 1830s Somers Town became
a slum, the land further blighted by the
construction of the Midland Railway into
St Pancras station in the 1860s, which
rendered hundreds homeless. Attempts to
improve the area, with buildings for railway
workers, a model baths (1840), and the
St Pancras School for Mothers (1907), failed
due to the many railway lines and associated
industries, and conditions further deteriorated with Second World War bombing.

Euston Road
Built in 1756 as the New Road, London's
first by-pass, to ease the manoeuvring of
troops and allow drovers to take their cattle
to Smithfield market without having to use
Oxford Street and Holborn, it became the
setting for three of London's great railway
termini – Euston, St Pancras and King's
Cross – when Bloomsbury and Fitzrovia
landowners refused to allow the lines to
enter their land. The New Road was
renamed Euston Road in 1857 and has since
been widened and upgraded into one of
London's major traffic routes. The northern
side has been continually redeveloped and
now contains a number of large granite and
glass office blocks, while the southern side is
home to several major organizations,
including the Wellcome Trust, the Society
of Friends and Camden Council.

north side: Albany Street to York Way
**Setting for William Hogarth's *The March
of the Guards to Finchley***, Euston Road at
Hampstead Road
Hogarth's 1750 painting *The March of the
Guards to Finchley* shows a band of rough,
unshaven troops outside the long demol-

ished Adam & Eve and King's Head taverns, by what is now the junction of Euston Road and Hampstead Road, being inspected before marching north to Finchley, the hill in the background of the painting, to protect the capital during the 1745 Jacobite uprising from Bonnie Prince Charlie and the invading Scots. The inclusion of Finchley in the title stemmed from a speech made by the Duke of Cumberland, leader of the government's forces against the Jacobites, in which he mentioned that 'a camp at Finchley would prevent any little part of them who might give me the slip from giving any alarm in London'.

Hogarth filled the picture with suggestive detail: the duke's soldiers look more like a drunken rabble than a powerful unit to whom the security of the country is being trusted; a fat soldier watches a colleague kiss the milk girl, whose pail falls to the ground, the milk tipping into another soldier's hat; they in turn are being watched by a smug pastry cook who cannot see the hand reaching up to steal his pies, or the soldier urinating against the wall of the pie hut; a keg has been punctured and the contents are being drunk by a fourth soldier; and the grenadier in the centre of the picture is being simultaneously tugged by a young pregnant woman, whose basket contains a copy of 'God Save the King', and by a pregnant harridan who is threateningly brandishing rolled-up copies of Jacobite journals.

► Hogarth in Leicester Square, p. 102.

Euston Tower

Along with Centre Point and Telecom Tower, Euston Tower was built in the 1950s, at a time of intense government paranoia, as one of a number of hi-tech skyscraper office blocks equipped to shelter leading civil servants and other government personnel in the event of war. Below the blocks a network of bunkers was ready to be manned by officials if military tension increased, but the system soon became technologically obsolete and Euston Tower is now simply another London office block, albeit one in

which MI5 until recently housed its telephone network, on the seventeenth floor.

► Centre Point, p. 100.

Elizabeth Garrett Anderson Hospital (1866–1980s), No. 144

Elizabeth Garrett Anderson, who founded the hospital as a dispensary for women and children, was England's first female doctor and the only woman on the British Medical Council from 1873 to 1892. The hospital was saved from closure after a campaign in the 1980s and later moved to Huntley Street, Bloomsbury. The Euston Road site is currently being refurbished.

British Library, Euston Road at Oussulston Street

The British Library was established in 1973 to bring together the British Museum's vast collection, which includes a copy of every book published in the country, under one organization, and plans to move the library to a huge new site in St Pancras were announced soon after, with Colin St John Wilson chosen as architect. However, the project was beset by delays and it opened in 1997 £350 million over budget, with only 10 per cent more seats than in the British Museum. The critics lined up to damn the building, and Prince Charles derided it for its resemblance to 'an academy for secret police'.

The St Pancras site, formerly taken up by a goods depot, had been chosen so that the library could be linked up with a number of other strategic buildings (MI6, Buckingham Palace, Telecom Tower), connected by an underground cable network located alongside the parallel Victoria Line, which itself runs between two of the library's basement floors.

► Victoria Line, p. 247.

St Pancras station

Best known for its monumental Gothic hotel façade, one of the most exuberant expressions of Victorian architecture, the station was named after the fourteen-year-old Christian martyr killed in Rome in AD 304 and was built in 1867 on the site of scores of demolished alleyways and slum houses. Among the streets demolished was Eve Court where Dan Leno, the leading late-nineteenth-century music hall performer, was born as George Galvin in 1860. He later recalled his birthplace on stage, with the refrain: 'Ah! What is man? Wherefore does he why? Whence did he whence? Whither is he withering? Then the guard yelled out: "Leicester, Derby, Nottingham, Manchester, Liverpool." '

St Pancras's enormous iron and glass roof, spanning 240 ft, stood alone until 1873, when it was joined by George Gilbert Scott's extravagant red-brick Midland Grand Hotel, a riot of castellated fringes, dormers, pointed-arch windows and steeply pitched roofs, which incorporated 250 bedrooms and all the latest facilities – gasoliers, electric bells, lifts and rubber surfaces in the road-ways to deaden night-time sounds. The prominent journalist G. A. Sala described it as 'the most sumptuous and the best conducted hotel in the Empire', while Scott himself claimed 'that it is possibly too good for its purpose, but having been disappointed of my ardent hope of carrying out my style in the government offices [the Foreign Office], I was glad to be able to erect one building in that style in London'. (A story, probably apocryphal, tells of an American tourist staying in a nearby hotel who asked for the nearest church and having been directed to St Pancras church mistook Scott's ecclesiastical façade for a place of worship and entered, asking a porter the time of the next service, only to be told that being a Sunday it was closed.)

The hotel lost popularity after the First World War and in 1935 was converted to offices, which were used until the 1980s, since which it has lain derelict, one of the largest unused sites in the capital. However, much of the interior remains unaltered and the building is being revived in readiness for the eventual arrival of Eurostar at the adjacent station, itself the most rundown of the London railway termini.

King's Cross on film

King's Cross and St Pancras stations and the railway land to the north, with its canal, grimy yards and huge gas holders, have featured as a backdrop in a number of films, including *Chaplin* and *Richard III*, but never more so than in the 1955 Ealing comedy *The Ladykillers*, starring Alec Guinness and Peter Sellers, which is set around the King's Cross home of Mrs Wilberforce, a genteel elderly lady who lives in a house from whose steps the Gothic majesty of St Pancras station can be seen. Exterior shots of Mrs Wilberforce's house were filmed outside the **Wardonia Hotel, 48–52 Argyle Street**, just south of King's Cross and St Pancras stations, while interior scenes were filmed on **𝔉𝔯𝔢𝔡𝔢𝔯𝔦𝔠𝔨 𝔚𝔬𝔞𝔡**, off Cale-donian Road, half a mile north, where the producers built a set as close as possible to the railway lines running into King's Cross. The wages snatch was filmed at **Cheney Street**, near King's Cross station, which also features in the film, the getaway car is aban-doned on **Field Street**, a now almost obliter-ated side street to the south of King's Cross Thameslink station, while at the end of the film the villains meet their fate by the Copen-hagen Tunnel, east of **Vale Royal**.

King's Cross station (N1)

London's terminus for trains bound for Yorkshire and Scotland was built over the burial site of the first-century warrior queen Boadicea (which supposedly lies beneath either Platform 8 or 13) and was named after a monument to George IV which stood at the northern end of Gray's Inn Road from 1836 to 1845. The station was designed by Lewis Cubitt in stock brick and the plainest of styles, with none of the Gothic finery of the later St Pancras or the neoclassical piety of Euston (prior to 1960s redevelopment), as befitting the wishes of John Ruskin, who wrote in *The Seven Lamps of Architecture* in 1849: 'Better bury gold in the embankments than put in ornaments on the stations'. King's Cross opened on 14 October 1852 for the Great Northern Railway, the most powerful of the companies using London.

The station soon became associated with the romance of leaving London in the early evening and arriving in Edinburgh at midnight, ideally on the Flying Scotsman, but has long been bedevilled by accidents. In 1860 an excursion train from Manchester overshot the buffers, causing much mess but no casualties, and five years later a section of a coal train came loose and rolled down the Copenhagen tunnel into the terminus. The guard jumped off before the train hit the buffers but again, surprisingly, no one died. On 4 February 1945 two passengers were killed in a rail derailment, but the worst of all King's Cross disasters occurred below ground in the tube station concourse on 18 November 1987 when thirty-one people perished in a fire.

► Euston station, p. 358.

south side: Birkenhead Street to Bolsover Street

St Pancras (new church), east of Upper Woburn Place

The first classical revival church in London, it was built in 1819 to 1822 at great cost to replace the shabby church further north (now Old St Pancras church on Pancras Road) by Henry Inwood, who travelled to Athens where he drew the Tower of Winds and the Erechtheum, borrowing its design of columns supporting the entablature in the form of draped female figures (caryatids). Despite the expense incurred, Inwood's caryatids were too tall and had to be cut down, and the construction of the church was halted when members of the old church's congregation tried to sabotage the building work while the foundation stone was being laid.

Friends Meeting House, west of Upper Woburn Place

The Meeting House stands on land which once contained the southern gardens of Euston Square alongside a row of houses, including 181 𝔈𝔲𝔰𝔱𝔬𝔫 ℜ𝔬𝔞𝔡, where the novelist H. G. Wells lived as a student in the 1880s. When the leases were bought in the

1920s by the theatre impresario Alfred Butt, he ensured that in reselling the properties the new buyers would have no rights over the gardens. The western end of the terrace was acquired by the Society of Friends, who commissioned a new building designed in 1926 by Hubert Lidbetter, which surprisingly won RIBA's building of the year award. During a visit to London in 1931 as official spokesman for pre-independence India, Mahatma Gandhi spoke here at a reception organized by Fenner Brockway, secretary of the Independent Labour Party, telling the gathering: '[We] want freedom unadulterated for the dumb and starving millions'. He was driven after the reception to his unassuming lodgings in Bow.

► Ghandi in Bow, p. 312.

Wellcome Building, Euston Road at Gordon Street, west side

Built in 1931–2 by Septimus Warwick in the classical revival style for the laboratories of Sir Henry Wellcome, the scientist who photographed archaeological sites during the First World War, it is now the headquarters of the Wellcome Trust.

Euston Station Colonnade

The decaying hotels, run-down shops and crumbling terraces that once stood around Euston station were removed in the early 1960s when developer Joe Levy began buying up what he described as a 'derelict bloody den of disease' so that he could replace them with state-of-the-art office blocks. Levy conducted business as part of a consortium of estate agents, so that local property owners would not realize a single firm was behind the purchases and raise their prices accordingly, and he was so diligent in his dealings that by the late 1950s only one house remained occupied, the owner being a Cypriot whom Levy threatened with a council compulsory purchase order. After shaking hands on a deal for £50,000, an astronomical sum in those days, Levy revealed to the man that he needed the property so badly he would have given him a quarter of a million pounds.

Euston station

Built to serve the London and Birmingham Railway, Euston station opened on 20 July 1837 as the southern terminus of the first long-distance railway line in the world. It contained an Ionic-styled Great Hall, built in what the poet John Betjeman later described as 'palatial splendour', and its southern entrance was through a 72-ft Doric arch supported by fluted columns with the word 'Euston' etched into the stone, which was criticized by A. W. Pugin, the doyen of Gothic revival architecture, as a 'piece of Brobdingnagian absurdity'. The arch was demolished in the 1960s by British Rail, who insisted it was in the way of plans to extend the platforms, despite a campaign led by Betjeman and an outcry in the press. That the platforms were never extended led many to suggest that the demolition was pure vandalism. The early-nineteenth-century station was also destroyed and the new station that replaced it was rebuilt with no recourse either to aesthetics or practicality, containing platforms unavailable to waiting commuters, few seats for those waiting in the main concourse, an underground cab rank barely accessible to those with heavy luggage getting off trains, and a labyrinth of paths and passageways outside winding through an ugly stretch of greenery, factors which make it the least popular railway terminus in the capital.

● In 1963 the Great Train Robbers Gordon Goody and Bruce Reynolds, worried that the driver of the train they planned to rob might not co-operate, decided to steal a train so that they could practise driving it. They waited at Euston until after midnight, boarded an engine standing in a siding, and after several attempts managed to whirr it into motion. But finding the locomotive not as easy to stop as to start, they jumped off, leaving it to continue down the track unmanned.

▶ Paddington station, p. 432.

Pancras Road
Old St Pancras Cemetery

A site of Christian worship since the early seventh century, according to archaeological findings, the present church dates back to the thirteenth century although much of the building is Victorian. In its churchyard can be found the graves of Jonathan Wild, the so-called 'thief-taker general', who was hanged in 1725; the feminist Mary Wollstonecraft (died 1797); and Sir John Soane, architect of the Bank of England (1837), his grave marked by an ostentatious mausoleum designed by him for his wife, in a style which influenced Giles Gilbert Scott's red telephone kiosks. When the Midland Railway Company built a tunnel under the cemetery in the 1860s for their line into St Pancras, skulls and bones were disturbed, and after a passer-by revealed that he had seen an open coffin and locks of hair the company was forced into carrying out a reburial. One of the surveyors engaged in the work was the young Thomas Hardy, who in his poems 'The Levelled Churchyard' and 'In the Cemetery' entreats passengers who use the line to remember the 'piteous groans / Half stifled in this jumbled patch / Of wretched memorial stones'.

HAMPSTEAD, NW3

Quintessential village London, with a romantic hill and heath setting high above the metropolis, Hampstead was previously Hamestede (homestead), land which Ethelred the Unready granted to St Peter's monastery in Westminster (now Westminster Abbey) in 986. It retained its exclusivity as London expanded, thanks to its lofty position, clean air, medicinal waters, twisting winding hills, narrow streets, inaccessibility from central London and picturesque appearance, qualities which have long attracted writers (Dr Johnson, John Keats, D. H. Lawrence) and artists (John Constable, Ford Madox Brown and Stanley Spencer).

In the 1930s Hampstead briefly became home to a number of well-known figures from the arts fleeing persecution in Europe – Walter Gropius, the head of the Bauhaus; Sigmund Freud, the founder of psychoanalysis; Piet Mondrian, the Dutch painter – who brought with them the latest progressive ideas and ideologies, such as cubism, surrealism, constructivism and modernism, and made Hampstead the centre of intellectual life in Britain, a position which it maintained after the war until the qualities that made it so exclusive began to price all but the most wealthy out of the area.

(i) Belsize Park

The southernmost and lowest part of Hampstead, set around Haverstock Hill, takes its name from the French *bel assis* (beautifully situated) and became a residential area for the middle class in the nineteenth century, attracting in the 1930s avant-garde artists such as Ben Nicholson, Barbara Hepworth and Henry Moore, who congregated around Mall Studios on Tasker Road, where they were briefly joined by continental artists fleeing Nazi Europe in particular the abstract painter Piet Mondrian, who lodged at 60 Parkhill Road. In recent decades Belsize Park has lost some of its exclusive status, following the conversion of many of the houses into student bedsits and the construction of council estates to the east of Haverstock Hill; however, the streets to the west of the station retain their exclusivity.

Lawn Road
Isokon
A landmark in modernist architecture, Isokon, made of reinforced concrete and built in 1933–4 in the Bauhaus style, with reference to Le Corbusier's Pavilion Suisse in Paris, was financed by Molly and Jack Pritchard of the Venesta Plywood and Isokon furniture companies and designed by Wells Coates whose earlier architectural ambitions

had been for prefabricated houses that could be clipped to the back of a lorry on a Friday evening, taken to the countryside for the weekend, and brought back to town for Monday.

With Isokon Coates built a series of self-contained flats that were minimalist to the point of monasticity, taking up the least amount of space needed by a 'rational, modern person', calculated by Coates at 17' 2 by 15' 4, and consisting of a bedsitting area, bathroom, dressing room and all-electric kitchenette furnished with the Isokon company's furniture.

In keeping with the modernist ideology, the building incorporated communal facilities, such as a clubroom and a basement bar, Isobar, designed by the Bauhaus's Marcel Breuer, and a canteen serving meals such as kebabs, then unknown in England, made by a resident cook, Philip Harben, who later became the first TV chef.

Isokon was aimed specifically at the intelligentsia and attracted a number of artists and writers fleeing Nazi Europe, such as the Bauhaus founder Walter Gropius and the sculptor Laszlo Moholy-Nagy, as well as those closer to home looking to break away from English insularity, such as the writer Agatha Christie and the sculptor Henry Moore.

Not everyone was enamoured with the place. Cyril Connolly's *Horizon* magazine voted Isokon second in its Ugliest Building competition of 1946 and its popularity declined after the war, the developer selling it in 1968 to the *New Statesman* magazine, who tore out the bar to build more flats and sold the block to Camden Council. Somehow Isokon has survived, while continuing to deteriorate, and by the beginning of the twenty-first century was covered with graffiti and boarded-up awaiting redevelopment.
► Goldfinger's house, p. 366.

Maitland Park Road
Karl Marx died at **No. 41** in March 1883, aged sixty-five, without leaving a will. His

estate was valued at £250. His letters, notes and manuscripts passed to his patron, Friedrich Engels.

(ii) Frognal

A semi-rural idyll of hidden corners, unadopted roads and fine modernist architecture set on the hill that rises from Swiss Cottage to the Hampstead heights.

Church Row

Hampstead's best-preserved Georgian terrace, built in 1707 to meet the demand created by the success of Hampstead's chalybeate spa and barely altered since, was home to the author H. G. Wells, who lived at No. 17 from 1909 to 1912. The poet Lord Alfred Douglas, Oscar Wilde's 'Bosie', his one-time lover and ruin, moved to No. 26 in 1907 with his 'wife' after winning a libel suit against the *Daily News*, which had run an obituary calling him a degenerate, only to find he was still alive.
St John, north side, opposite Frognal Gardens

> At last we reached the wall of the churchyard, which we climbed over. With some little difficulty, for it was very dark, and the whole place seemed so strange to us, we found the Westenra tomb – *Dracula*, Bram Stoker (1897)

Hampstead's major church was designed by John Sanderson, built in 1747 to replace the medieval church of St Mary and re-orientated 100 years later to resemble St Peter's, Rome. In 1894 a group of American admirers of Keats installed a marble bust of the poet inside, and three years later Bram Stoker was probably thinking of St John when he wrote in his vampire classic, *Dracula*, of a 'lonely churchyard, away from teeming London, where the air is fresh, and the sun rises over Hampstead Hill, and where wild flowers grow of their own accord'.

Those buried in the graveyard include the artist John Constable, the architect Norman Shaw and the 1950s Labour Party leader Hugh Gaitskell.

Frognal

A winding hill leading from Finchley Road to the edge of the heath, it has long been one of London's most sought-after addresses, home to writers (Dr Johnson, Kate Greenaway and Stephen Spender), musicians (Kathleen Ferrier and Dennis Brain) and politicians (Charles de Gaulle and Ramsay MacDonald).

east side: Frognal Rise to Finchley Road
No. 66
One of London's most unusual houses, 66 Frognal was designed by Connell, Ward and Lucas in 1936 to 1938 and fulfils Le Corbusier's five points of architecture in that pilotis (slender columns) bear the weight, there is a free plan layout and façade, and it has long horizontal sliding windows and a roof garden. However, it caused such a furore that the client told the Royal Institution of British Architects: 'I can only regret that this building should offend the susceptibilities of some people and be beyond the comprehension of others.'

Frognal Way

A short unpaved road built in 1899, it contains buildings of considerable architectural interest such as Maxwell Fry's Sun House of 1935–6 – the first modernist concrete house to be built in London as opposed to the rural outskirts – which has steel balconies, slender columns and a roof terrace and shares many qualities with Le Corbusier's Villa Stein at Garches, France; No. 4, a touch of California in the windy Hampstead heights, the wall of which features a plaque of a flying monk; Shepherd's Well at No. 5, designed in 1930 by Adrian Gilbert Scott; and the Mediterranean-style Blue Tiles at No. 20, designed by R. L. Page for the entertainer Gracie Fields in the 1930s.

Maresfield Gardens

Freud Museum, No. 20
Sigmund Freud, the originator of psychoanalysis, who fled Vienna and the Nazis in 1938 when he was eighty-two, arrived in London

with little money and, after briefly living in Primrose Hill, came to Hampstead, where he charged patients between three and four guineas (about £125 in today's prices) for an hour's therapy. Here, Freud was visited by the Spanish surrealist Salvador Dalí, the novelist H. G. Wells and the Zionist leader Chaim Weizmann, and despite suffering from cancer completed a book on Moses and monotheism, in which he argued that Moses was not Jewish but Egyptian, and that the story of Moses being abandoned by his Jewish mother and reared by an Egyptian princess was a fabrication. After Freud died in September 1939 – he was cremated in Golders Green cemetery – his daughter Anna, a founder of child psychoanalysis, lived here until her death in 1982. The house is now a museum in which Sigmund Freud's study and library have been preserved as he left them, with one of his psychoanalyst's couches still in place.

► Sigmund Freud at 84 Charing Cross Road, p. 100.

Oak Hill Park

A dramatic-looking route through thick trees, lined with luxury 1960s-built apartment blocks nestling among foliage in the manner of Frank Lloyd Wright's work in the Illinois countryside, Oak Hill Park was first developed in 1851 with houses that won a Great Exhibition Award for Gentlemen's Dwellings but were mostly demolished in the 1950s and replaced by blocks such as Northwood Lodge, where Peter Sellers lived briefly in 1962 and which he described as my 'Hampstead Torture Chamber'. One of the few original properties that remains, No. 1, at the eastern end, was home in the 1930s to Sir Geoffrey Faber of the publishing firm of the same name.

Platts Lane

A sentry on anti-aircraft duty during the Second World War on Platt's Lane (previously Duval Lane, itself a corruption of Devil's Lane) was startled to see a manhole lid move and the head of the prime minister, Winston Churchill, 'suddenly appear before me out of a hole in the ground'. The PM and a team of civil servants, looking for suitably protected places for the Cabinet to meet, had come to Hampstead Heath to explore the tunnels connected to the abandoned tube station near the Bull and Bush pub on North End and had made their way along one of the tunnels for three-quarters of a mile until Churchill noticed a grille leading to a manhole and forced his way through, coming face to face with the astonished sentry.

► Cabinet War Rooms, p. 230.

Annesley Lodge, No. 8, south side
The architectural historian and local resident Nikolaus Pevsner described Annesley Lodge, designed by the modernist pioneer C. F. A. Voysey in 1896 for his father, as the 'best house in London', praising its experimental shape of two wings in an 'L' shape, long unbroken red-tiled roof with corner buttresses, and its updating of the traditional English cottage format with its white pebbledashed walls, mullioned windows and heart motifs on the front door.

(iii) Hampstead Heath

> On the top of the hill indeed, there is a very pleasant plain, called the Heath –
> A Tour Through the Whole Island of Great Britain, Daniel Defoe (1727)

The 800-acre wild heath, the best walking land in London, was formed by Ice Age glaciation, which left it with a crest of sand and gravel that is unable to sustain crops, and is probably the largest open space within the boundaries of any of the world's capitals. The heath was the site of one of the many beacons lit as part of a chain of fires to warn southern England of the approach of the Spanish Armada in 1588 and was where in 1673 the highwayman Francis Jackson was hanged on the now uprooted Gibbet Elm (near Jack Straw's Castle) and left dangling for eighteen years to dissuade his colleagues from committing further felonies. The heath was saved from development in the 1870s, thanks to the campaigns of Hampstead residents, and in the Second World War much sand was extracted to fill sandbags for civil defence use. After the war the sheep that grazed on the lands were removed and the heath has since been carefully maintained by the Corporation of London.

Hampstead Ponds, off East Heath Road
One of two sources of the River Fleet, which flows underground into central London and empties into the Thames at Blackfriars, the other being Highgate Ponds.

Inverforth House, North End Way, off Inverforth Close
A grand house redeveloped into apartments, it was built around a smaller property, The Hill, bought in 1906 by the soap magnate, Lord Leverhulme, who devised the Port Sunlight 'model village' on the Wirral, and was redesigned so that it would be invisible from the road and heath. Leverhulme also added a ballroom and art gallery and in 1926, a year after he died, the property passed to Lord Inverforth who, thirty years later, bequeathed it to Manor House Hospital. The little-known grounds, one of London's great gardens, feature Italianate 'ruins' and stone terraces with climbing plants.

Jack Straw's Castle, North End Way, opposite Spaniards Road
> We dined at Jack Straw's Castle along with a little crowd of bicyclists and others who were genially noisy – *Dracula*, Bram Stoker (1897)

The highest pub in London, built on the summit of the hill that begins in Chalk Farm, it was constructed early in the eighteenth century, taking its name from an unreliable legend that Straw, one of the leaders of the 1381 Peasants' Revolt, had taken refuge in a building that then stood on the site. In 1838 Charles Dickens invited his biographer, John Forster, to dine with him here, describing Jack Straw's Castle as 'a good 'ouse where we can have a red-hot chop with a glass of good wine', and sixty years later the pub earned a mention in

Bram Stoker's *Dracula*. Jack Straw's Castle was bombed during the Second World War – only the brick southern wall remains of the building that Dickens used – and was rebuilt in 1964 by Raymond Erith and Quinlan Terry with antiquated-looking weather-boarding, sash windows and castellated turrets. The building was renovated at the beginning of the twenty-first century.

Kenwood House
A Georgian mansion and popular tourist attraction that contains an outstanding art collection, Kenwood House is set in gorgeous landscaped grounds at the north end of Hampstead Heath near the source of the underground River Fleet. It takes its name from what was Caen Wood, named in honour of Odo, Dean of Caen in France, who owned the surrounding forest in the eleventh century, and was first built in 1616 by John Bill, printer to James I. It was rebuilt in 1694 by William Brydges, Surveyor General of the Ordnance, and remodelled in 1754 by Robert Adam, who built the second storey, the library and a bridge over the lake, describing how he saw while working 'a noble view of the City of London, Greenwich Hospital and the River Thames, the ships passing up and down'.

In 1780, when it was home to Lord Mansfield, the Lord Chief Justice, the property became a target for the Gordon Rioters, venting their fury on any building connected with members of a government planning to allow Catholics more rights, and a mob travelled north from Bloomsbury, where it had sacked Mansfield's town house, to destroy Kenwood, being stopped only by the landlord of the Spaniards Inn, who plied them with drink.

At the end of the nineteenth century the 6th Earl of Mansfield sold many of the contents and planned to demolish the mansion to build thirty villas in the grounds. But the project was abandoned when Edward Cecil Guinness, the 1st Earl of Iveagh, bought the property to house his collection of paintings, which includes

Vermeer's *The Guitar Player* (stolen in 1974, but recovered soon after) and works by Rembrandt, Gainsborough and Turner, bequeathing the property in his will to the London County Council. It is now run by English Heritage and entrance is free.
► Lord Mansfield's Bloomsbury Square property, p. 88; the Gordon Riots, p. 125.
Parliament Hill
At the southern end of the heath is Parliament Hill, at 319 ft one of the highest points in London, which was originally known as Llandin (from *Llan* sacred, *din* eminence), and was where, according to legend, St Paul once preached. The followers of Guy Fawkes came here to watch the Houses of Parliament burn down in 1605, after which it acquired the 'Parliament' prefix.
Spaniards Inn, Spaniards Road at Spaniards End

> By good chance we got a cab near the Spaniards, and drove to town – *Dracula*, Bram Stoker (1897)

One of the heath's two famous pubs (the other being Jack Straw's Castle), the Spaniards, with its alcoves, low beams and oak panels, was named either after two Spanish brothers who owned it in the seventeenth century, and killed each other in a duel, or in honour of the Spanish ambassador to the court of James II. The eighteenth-century highwayman Dick Turpin stabled his horse, Black Bess, here so that he could note the coaches worth robbing, and in June 1780 the landlord waylaid the Gordon Rioters, *en route* to destroy the Lord Chancellor's house in nearby Caen Wood (Ken Wood), plied them with drink, and sent for the army, thereby preventing the raid. John Keats heard the nightingale that inspired his poem dedicated to the bird in the pub's garden, and in Charles Dickens's *Pickwick Papers* Mrs Bardell and friends plot Mr Pickwick's downfall in the Spaniards.
● Opposite the inn, by a narrowing of the road that vexes motorists and considerably slows traffic, stands a listed eighteenth-century toll house which used to control the entrance to what was the Bishop of London's deer park.
► The Gordon Riots, p. 125.
Whitestone Pond
The pond is named after the white milestone inscribed '4½ miles from Holborn Bars' that once stood in the middle of the road but can now be found in the bushes and was where in 1588 one of a chain of beacons was lit warning of the approach of the Spanish Armada.

(iv) New End

An eighteenth-century village of pretty cottages, secluded lanes and picturesque settings tucked away between Heath Street and East Heath Road.

Hampstead High Street
A busy street dominated by boutiques, coffee bars and restaurants where at No. 42a, at the corner with Flask Walk, John Lydon squatted in the 1970s and wrote the Sex Pistols' 'God Save the Queen'.

Heath Street
The main street through Hampstead village, it winds steeply uphill from the tube station to Whitestone Pond and is lined with attractive shops, estate agents, smart restaurants and appealing pubs.
west side: Perrin's Walk to Lower Terrace
Everyman Cinema, Heath Street at Hollybush Vale, west side
Hampstead's long-running repertory cinema opened as a drill hall in 1888 and later became a theatre, making the headlines in 1922 when a planned run of Noël Coward's *The Vortex*, in which Coward himself was due to perform, was halted by the government theatre censor, the Lord Chamberlain, for promoting 'immorality'. The building became a cinema in 1933 and was London's leading venue for art house films until a change of ownership in the 1990s led to its conversion to a more mainstream cinema.

The Mount, opposite New End

A small patch of grass on an incline above Heath Street, the Mount was where the artist Ford Madox Brown, an associate of the Pre-Raphaelites, set his monumental mid-nineteenth-century painting *Work* (displayed in Manchester City Art Gallery), a vast panorama, rich in detail, imagery and incident celebrating the art of labour, which was inspired by the sight of a group of navvies digging a sewer here in 1852.

► The Pre-Raphaelites in Bloomsbury, p. 85.

Keats Grove

Originally Albion Grove, it was renamed after its most famous resident, the poet John Keats, in the nineteenth century and was depicted by George Orwell in his 1936 novel *Keep the Aspidistra Flying* as Coleridge Grove, 'a damp, shadowy secluded road [where] Coleridge was rumoured to have lived for six weeks in the summer of 1821'. Past residents include the Liberal politician Herbert Asquith (No. 12, 1877–87) and the playwright Alan Ayckbourn (No. 11a, in the 1970s).

John Keats's address (1818–20) / Keats House, south side

A small museum dedicated to John Keats, it was originally two properties, in one of which the poet lived from 1818 to 1820, when he was ill with consumption, and in the other of which lived the eighteen-year-old Fanny Brawne, with whom Keats fell in love and became engaged, only to be told to avoid spending too much time with her in case it made his condition worse. In October 1819 Keats staggered home, not drunk, as his landlord, Charles Brown, believed, but ill, made his way upstairs to lie down, and after coughing up blood asked Brown to bring him a candle which enabled him to see that the blood was bright red and therefore from an artery. Keats told Brown: 'I cannot be deceived in that colour – that drop of blood – it is my death warrant – I must die'. Although Keats went with fellow writers, the Shelleys, to Italy to recuperate, he died there in February 1821, aged twenty-

five. In 1920 the council bought the house, after public subscription had saved it from demolition, and opened it as a museum, one of the first visitors being Thomas Hardy, who was inspired to write the poem 'At a House in Hampstead', which contrasts Keats's Hampstead with that of Hardy's time. The museum contains the poet's annotated books, letters, personal possessions and lecture notes from Guy's Hospital where he did his medical training.

New End

On the north side of the road is the innovative New End Theatre, previously a mortuary, where according to rumour the body of Karl Marx, who died in Kentish Town in 1883, was laid out on a slab before being buried at Highgate Cemetery.

New End Square

Burgh House

A charming small local history museum-cum-events venue and café built for the Sewells, a Quaker family, in 1703 and home in the 1720s to William Gibbons, the man who 'proved' Hampstead's waters to be medicinal. Burgh House was taken over by the Royal East Middlesex Militia in 1858 to be an officers' mess and restored for domestic use by Thomas Grylls, the stained-glass painter who designed the rose window in Poets' Corner, Westminster Abbey, in 1884. Fifty years later, Captain George Bambridge, who was married to Rudyard Kipling's daughter, Elsie, rented the property and the elderly poet visited her here a number of times. After the war Hampstead council bought Burgh House and converted it for public use.

South Hill Park

Magdala, No. 2a, north side

The pub wall still features the bullet holes made by the gun fired by Ruth Ellis, who shot her boyfriend, David Blakely, outside the building on Easter Sunday 10 April 1955. She was convicted of his murder and was the last woman to be hanged in England (at Holloway Prison on 13 July 1955). By a remarkable coincidence the penultimate woman to be hanged, Styllou Christofi, also lived on South Hill Park.

Well Road

Built on the site of a chalybeate spa, Well Walk was home in the late nineteenth century to Karl Pearson, the statistician who coined the term 'standard deviation' and lived at No. 7, and to Flinders Petrie, the Egyptologist who in the 1880s unsuccessfully attempted to prove that the pyramids had been built with divine assistance, at No. 8. At the north-east end of the road is the Gothic monstrosity The Logs (Nos. 17–20), home in the 1960s to the comic Marty Feldman, and more recently to the singer Boy George.

Well Walk

Water containing traces of iron and, supposedly, health-giving properties was discovered in a well in the area in 1698. A Pump Room was opened and the waters were soon being bottled at the Flask Tavern on Flask Walk. The village then began marketing itself as a spa to rival Bath and Tunbridge Wells, with some success, but the waters have not been taken since the nineteenth century.

west side: New End Square to East Heath Road

Second Hampstead spa

Wells House, a block of council flats, stands on the site of the second Hampstead spa, opened in the 1730s, which the poet Alexander Pope and Dr Johnson patronized but which failed to impress Fanny Burney, who in her 1778 novel *Evelina* talks of the horrors of an evening spent there and of men 'whose appearance and language was inelegant and low-bred'. The spa closed in the nineteenth century and the room was later used for meetings, being demolished after war damage in the 1940s. A view of the spa was captured in Wedgwood for a 950-piece dinner service which is now among the exhibits of the Hermitage Museum in St Petersburg.

No. 13

No. 13 was home at the end of the nineteenth century to Henry Hyndman, one of the founders of English socialism – P. G. Wodehouse based his character Psmith on him – who is believed to have been converted to the cause in 1880 after reading Marx's *Capital* in French (it was not translated into English until 1887). Cynics claimed Hyndman was influenced more by his rejection from the Cambridge University cricket XI than by economic considerations. The poet John Masefield lived here from 1914 to 1916.

No. 27

An imposing red-brick Queen Anne-style house, it was home to the writer J. B. Priestley from 1929 to 1931 during the initial success of his novel *The Good Companions*.

'Keats's bench'

While ill with consumption in 1818 the poet John Keats was spotted sitting on a bench on Well Walk 'sobbing his dying breath into a handkerchief' by the antiquarian William Hone. The bench Keats used has since gone but its replacement is also known as 'Keats's bench'.

east side: East Heath Road to Willow Road

Klippan House, No. 50

The house, with its excessively tall Elizabethan-styled chimneys and huge size, was designed by Ewan Christian for himself in 1881 when he was an adviser to the Church Commissioners, and was where the architect George Gilbert Scott Jnr urinated on the doorstep after Christian turned down some of his designs.

First Hampstead spa, Well Walk at Gainsborough Gardens

After the discovery of medicinal waters in a local well in 1698, John Duffield opened a spa with an Assembly Room where visitors drank the iron-rich chalybeate water, played cards and listened to entertainers until their antics so annoyed residents that Duffield was served with a series of law suits, which resulted in the closure of the spa in 1719. The room was later converted to a drill hall for local volunteers and demolished in 1882.

No. 40

John Constable, the leading British land-scape artist of the early nineteenth century, lived at No. 40 from 1827 to 1834, writing to a friend that 'our little drawing room com-mands a view unsurpassed in Europe'. In the 1930s the house was occupied by the poet T. Sturge Moore, whom A. E. Housman, author of *A Shropshire Lad*, once described as a 'sheep in sheep's clothing' and who had been loosely connected with the Aesthetic Movement in the 1890s. With his wizened white beard and skull cap, Sturge Moore had become the Grand Old Man of the London poetry scene, hosting Friday night 'at-homes' where he would surround himself with young literary hope-fuls and manically recite his own verse to guests. George Orwell attended once despite his abhorrence of literary salons and brought his mother, who fell asleep.

D. H. Lawrence's address (1917), No. 32

The novelist moved to No. 32, home of the poets Dollie and Ernest Radford, during the First World War after being forced to leave Cornwall when the authorities decided, wrongly, that his wife, Frieda, was a German spy.

Wells Tavern, at Christchurch Hill

Built as the Green Man on the site of the house where the poet John Keats lived with his two brothers from 1817 to 1818, it became the Wells Tavern in 1850. The River Fleet runs under the property.

Willow Road

Erno Goldfinger's address (1939–87), south side, Nos. 1–3

A small terrace designed in the modernist style in the 1930s by the Hungarian *émigré* architect Erno Goldfinger, best known for Notting Hill's Trellick Tower, it became the National Trust's first modernist property in the 1990s, amid controversy similar to that which greeted Goldfinger's earlier decision to build it in place of some 'derelict worm-ridden cottages'. Its unusual appearance – brown brick, ribbon windows, concrete pilotis, wood, flat roof – led the politician Henry Brooke to object to what he called 'square houses', only to be told by Gold-finger, 'Only Zulus and Eskimos live in round houses.' Goldfinger and his wife, Ursula, moved into No. 2 in 1939 and rented out the adjacent units to pay for their project to turn the house into a centre for intellectual activity. The income enabled them to host exhibitions of Paul Klee and Max Ernst paintings and amass a formid-able art collection, which included works by Man Ray, Henry Moore, Max Ernst and Eduardo Paolozzi. Goldfinger died in 1987, and after Ursula passed away four years later negotiations began with the National Trust to convert the building into a museum.

► Trellick Tower, p. 446.

(v) Vale of Health

A swamp drained in 1801 by the Hampstead Water Company was given the euphemistic name 'Vale of Health' and was where Samuel Hatch, a collar-maker, built a house, 'Hatches Bottom'. Cottages and villas followed, the properties being named, rather than numbered, and a small community grew up in what is still one of the quietest and most unusual locations in the capital, accessible by car only from a barely sign-posted road off East Heath Road, containing fewer than 100 houses, no shops or pubs, and barely featured on most street atlases. (There is an indispensable local map at the East Heath Road end of the main Vale of Health road.) Past residents include the writers D. H. Lawrence (1 Byron Villas, 1917), Lady Lucy Duff Gordon ('Lucille'), couturier and *Titanic* survivor (6 Villas-on-the-Heath, 1930s), the thriller writer Edgar Wallace (Vale Lodge, 1920s) and, more recently, the actresses Janet Suzman and Judi Dench.

► Lucille and the *Titanic*, p. 174.

Spencer House

A block of flats called Spencer House stands on the site of the 𝕾𝖚𝖇𝖚𝖗𝖇𝖆𝖓 𝕳𝖔𝖙𝖊𝖑, a promi-nent-looking tavern featuring a castellated roof line and turret, built next to the Vale of

Health lake in 1863, which offered 'a commodious taproom and enclosed bowling alleys'. Being patronized mostly in summer, the hotel proved uneconomical and closed, later being used for artists' studios, and was where Stanley Spencer finished *The Resurrection: Cookham* in the 1920s.

ST JOHN'S WOOD, NW8

People . . . could, if they liked, go and live at a place with the dim, divine name of St John's Wood. I have never been to St John's Wood. I dare not – *The Napoleon of Notting Hill*, G. K. Chesterton (1904)

Built on land bought in 1312 by the Knights of St John of Jerusalem, which later passed into the hands of Eyres, City merchants and wine importers, St John's Wood was developed in the early nineteenth century from plans of 'an elevated view of the British Circus, proposed to be built by subscription between the Paddington-road and Hampstead on the freehold estate of H. S. Eyre Esq.', which were displayed by the architect John Shaw at the Royal Academy.

Whereas Regent's Park, to the east, featured large detached villas in a woodland setting, St John's Wood provided *semi-detached* villas, some of London's first, to tempt the middle classes to move away from the smoke and congestion of central London. The liberal aspirations of its earliest settlers attracted a number of political agitators taking refuge in England, and those who moved here included Karl Blind, an associate of Karl Marx; Louis Blanc, author of the phrase 'from each according to his abilities, to each according to his needs'; and Louis Kossuth, the Hungarian patriot, as well as a community of artists, the St John's Wood Group – its most famous member, Edwin Landseer, lived at **1 St John's Wood Road** from 1824 to 1873 – the most typical work of which is W. F. Yeames's

And When Did You Last See Your Father? (1876).

By the mid nineteenth century St John's Wood's veneer of respectability was being challenged by the spread of high-class brothels and of houses where politicians and aristocrats kept their mistresses. Such properties included **2 Boscobel Place, Alpha Road**, where one Frederick Cooper paid women to undress so that he could pelt them with jam tarts, and various houses on Circus Road, where the eccentric poet Algernon Charles Swinburne indulged in whipping sessions.

During the early twentieth century St John's Wood was rebuilt with stylish apartment blocks to replace the poorer housing and gradually the bohemian set moved north to Hampstead, leaving the area as the bastion of the *nouveaux riches* but also home to two internationally renowned institutions: EMI studios on Abbey Road, where the Beatles recorded almost their entire catalogue; and Lord's cricket ground to the south.

Abbey Road

An attractive, tree-lined main road, famous throughout the world for its recording studios, Abbey Road began as a footpath leading from Lisson Green to the twelfth-century Kilburn Abbey (hence the slight twist to the west at the northern end) and was improved in 1824, during the first wave of building in St John's Wood, when it was lined with spacious villas. Fifty years later members of the Free Church of Abbey Road met in the church hall to form a fund for the street's residents, the Abbey Road Building Society, which in 1944 became the Abbey National. The famous Abbey Road recording studios opened in 1931.

Abbey Road studios, No. 3

The world's most famous recording studios occupy a nine-bedroom 1872-built villa which was later converted into flats and sold in 1929 to the Gramophone Co., later EMI. It was here that in 1932 the fifteen-year-old Yehudi Menuhin recorded Elgar's *Violin*

Concerto, conducted by the composer, and over the following ten years Artur Schnabel recorded all thirty-two Beethoven piano sonatas and five concertos at Abbey Road, often slamming down the piano lid and calling a halt to proceedings while his temper cooled. Little recording was done in Britain immediately after the Second World War – the public was forced to listen to American dance band music of variable quality – but in 1950 the man who did more than anyone to enhance the studio's reputation, George Martin, joined the staff, rising swiftly to become head of EMI's Parlophone subsidiary.

In July 1958 EMI, looking to capitalize on the new American rock 'n' roll sound, hired the most professional of the new singers, Cliff Richard, who cut his first single, 'Move It', one of Britain's few credible rock records from that era, here. Four years later, on 6 June 1962, with British popular music dominated by singers who relied on the songs of others, an unusual event took place at Abbey Road when a group who wrote their own songs and played their own instruments – the Beatles – recorded their first single, 'Love Me Do'/ 'P.S. I Love You'.

The Beatles used the studios for almost their entire recorded output over the following seven years, and as rock became more sophisticated Abbey Road, with its advanced technology, capable staff and generous budgets, remained a major recording studio, being responsible for such landmark albums as Pink Floyd's *The Piper at the Gates of Dawn* (1967) and *Dark Side of the Moon* (1973), the Pretty Things' *S. F. Sorrow* (1968), Kate Bush's *Hounds of Love* (1984) and Radiohead's *The Bends* (1995).
● The famous photograph of the Beatles walking along the pedestrian crossing south of the studios that features on the cover of their *Abbey Road* album was taken by Iain MacMillan, positioned on a stepladder in the middle of the road at noon on 8 August 1969, and was the only take which showed them in step walking *away* from the studio,

to symbolize the direction in which their career was moving. A month after the album was released a Detroit student journalist claimed that McCartney had died in a car crash in 1966 and that the album sleeve was littered with clues – Lennon being the priest, Ringo the undertaker, Harrison the congregation, and McCartney, who is barefoot and out of step, the corpse – and that the number plate of the Beetle [*sic*] car on the left, LMW 281F, stands for 'Linda McCartney Widow', the '28 IF' referring to the age McCartney would have been when the album came out, had he lived.

Boundary Road
The boundary was between ancient parishes and is now that between the Borough of Camden and the City of Westminster. Here Alfred Harmsworth (later Lord Northcliffe), who founded the *Daily Mail* and *Daily Mirror*, and his brother, Harold (later Lord Rothermere), who owned the *Daily Mail* in the 1930s, were raised in the 1870s at No. 84.

Saatchi Collection, No. 98a
An unlikely setting for one of London's most progressive art galleries, given the conservative nature of nineteenth century art in St John's Wood, and the lack of any local art scene since, it was converted from an industrial workshop in 1985 and became heavily involved in promoting the work of Damien Hirst, showcasing *The Impossibility of Death in the Mind of the Living*, a tiger shark in a glass tank of formaldehyde, which earned Hirst a Turner Prize nomination, and of Tracey Emin who here exhibited *Everybody I Have Ever Slept With* (1963–95) and *My Bed*.

Grove End Road
Alma-Tadema's temple of aestheticism (1886–1912), No. 44
The Dutch painter Laurens Alma-Tadema, who designed the sets for Henry Irving's 1880 production of *Coriolanus*, reproducing the classical detail meticulously, moved into No. 44, previously the home of the French artist Jacques-Joseph (James) Tissot, after

Major matches at Lord's

27 June–1 July 1930, England *v* Australia, second Test, Donald Bradman's record double century Crowds queue overnight to see Donald Bradman, who had recently set a world record score of 425, score 254 in his first Lord's Test, leaving England bowler Gubby Allen with unenviable figures of none for 115.

21–25 June 1947, England *v* South Africa, second Test, Denis Compton's 208/Bill Edrich's 189 The first Lord's Test after the Second World War makes a slow start, but by lunch on the second day Edrich and Compton have put on 370, still a record third-wicket partnership.

24–29 June 1950, England *v* West Indies, second Test, the West Indies' first win in England The West Indies' first victory in England is celebrated by supporters such as the calypso performer Lord Beginner who comes on to the pitch at the end and performs a song written for the occasion: 'Cricket lovely cricket / At Lord's where I saw it / Yardley tried his best / But Goddard won the Test / They gave the crowd plenty fun / Second Test and West Indies won / With those little pals of mine, Ramadhin and Valentine'. The celebration procession then dances its way from Lord's to the Eros statue in Trafalgar Square.

22–26 June 1972, England *v* Australia, second Test, Bob Massie destroys England Australian fast bowler Bob Massie, who had been rejected by Northamptonshire, destroys England single-handedly in his first Test, taking 8 for 84 in the first innings and 8 for 53 in the second. Few can believe Massie's figures and accusations are made that the ball was out of shape and that he used lip salve to keep it shiny.

2–7 July 1981, England *v* Australia, second Test, Ian Botham's pair England Captain Ian Botham scores 0 twice in what turns out to be his last match in charge and his return to the pavilion is met by silence. In the next Test at Headingley Botham helps England stage the greatest comeback in the history of the game.

29 June–1 July 2000, England *v* West Indies, the Centenary Test The Friday of the 100th Lord's Test is marked by parts of all four innings taking place on the same day, the first time this has happened in Test history.

his Regent's Park house was damaged by a barge that exploded on Regent's Canal. Alma-Tadema converted No. 44 into a temple of aestheticism to rival Sir John Soane's Holborn address, with ceramics, stained glass, marble, painted wood, Roman fountains, Persian tiles, panels painted by Lord Leighton and John Singer Sargent, and an entrance hall featuring a bronze surround cast taken from the doorway of the house of Eumachia in Pompeii. The property is now divided into flats.
► The Sir John Soane Museum, Holborn, p. 123.

St John's Wood Road

Lord's, Wellington Road at St John's Wood The world's most famous cricket ground is named after Thomas Lord, a property dealer, wine supplier, and cricketer for the White Conduit Cricket Club in Islington, who in 1787 laid out a cricket pitch in Dorset Square, Marylebone, half a mile south, for what became the Marylebone Cricket Club (MCC) and moved here in 1814, hiring a flock of sheep to maintain the grass at the required length. The first match at the new Lord's took place on 22 June 1814 – the MCC beat Hertfordshire – and Lord was so pleased with the surroundings he built himself a house at the north-east corner of the ground, living there from 1816 until his death in 1832. England played Australia in the first Lord's Test Match in July 1884 and the ground has since been the setting for annual Test Matches, cup finals and other major cricketing occasions, as well as being the home of Middlesex County Cricket Club.

► The Oval, p. 394.

METROPOLITAN LINE

> The expeditions by North London trains / To dim forgotten stations – *Summoned by Bells*, John Betjeman (1960)

Following the success of the Metropolitan Railway, the world's first underground line, which opened from Paddington to Farringdon in 1863, entrepreneurs vied to extend the line north. The first new section, the Metropolitan & St John's Wood Railway, which opened as a single-track line in 1868, was not a success as the sulphurous fumes of the steam-powered vehicles greatly discomforted passengers and pickpockets thrived when the gas lamps went out.

In 1883 the new line was taken over by the Metropolitan Railway, run by Sir Edward Watkin, who envisaged the Metropolitan as part of an inner-city line from Manchester to France, via a Channel tunnel. Sir Edward extended the line in 1887 into deepest Buckinghamshire, with luxury Pullman coaches and chocolate vending machines in the carriages, but died before it was able to reach the Midlands, let alone Manchester or France.

Through a subsidiary, the Metropolitan Railway Country Estates Ltd, the company then bought up farms and estates in Northwood, Pinner and Ruislip and built smart, well-designed suburban houses rich with rustic features, coated with warm red brick, and set in luscious tree-lined settings – the epitome of the suburban dream – promoting the idea of 'living in Metroland', a term which first came into use in 1915. The Metroland dream was sold through lovingly created posters and catchy jingles ('Hearts are light, eyes are brighter / In Metroland, Metroland'), affectionately remembered by the poet John Betjeman in his famous 1971 TV special, *Metroland*: 'Child of the first war, forgotten by the second, we called you Metroland. We laid our schemes, lured by the lush brochure, down by-ways beckoned, to build at last the cottage of our dreams, a city clerk turned country-man again, and linked to the metropolis by train.' With the old Middlesex villages subsumed into the metropolis, the Metropolitan Line became one of London's best-used railway lines, even if the late-nineteenth-century luxury is no longer provided.

AMERSHAM / CHESHAM / WATFORD TO HARROW-ON-THE-HILL

> Through Amersham to Aylesbury and the Vale, / In those wet fields the railway didn't pay. / The Metro stops at Amersham today – 'Metroland', John Betjeman (1971)

Amersham At 490 ft above sea level the station is the highest in the system.

Chesham In reaching further and further north in the 1880s, the Metropolitan Line ran out of funds and instead of building the line to Aylesbury came to a halt in Chesham, where locals donated land to the Metropolitan Railway company to enable the line to reach their village.

Chalfont and Latimer One of three local Chalfonts, the others being Chalfont St Giles and Chalfont St Peter's.

Chorleywood The station is built over land that had been part of the route of the Old Berkeley Hunt.

Rickmansworth In the *Dr Who* episode 'Happy Endings' the TARDIS, disguised as a beach hut, lands on the platform at Rickmansworth station.

Watford The branch ends abruptly a mile south-west of Watford town centre as the authorities refused to allow the railway company to build through Cassiobury Park.

Croxley The upper half of the station was

designed to resemble a local suburban villa, rather than a typical tube station.

Moor Park Opened in 1910 as Sandy Lodge, for the local golf club, and later renamed Moor Park.

Northwood It opened in August 1887 when the area was still isolated. A report in *The Times* which claimed that the line was doomed to failure turned out to be unfair.

Northwood Hills Open fields until 1930, when a new suburb was planned, and named after the winning entry of a public competition.

Pinner In 1939 locals petitioned London Transport to ensure that station rebuilding work would be carried out in a manner sympathetic to the medieval character of the village. London Transport responded by abandoning the work, and so Pinner remained unmodernized.

North Harrow A prosaic name for an area known as Hooking Green when the station was built in 1915.

UXBRIDGE TO HARROW-ON-THE-HILL

Uxbridge While waiting for a train here in 1887 the librettist W. S. Gilbert noticed a poster advertising the Tower of London and dreamed up the idea of an opera set in the Tower – what became Gilbert and Sullivan's *The Yeomen of the Guard*.

Hillingdon The original station had to be demolished and rebuilt after the A40 (Western Avenue) was extended.

Ickenham When in 1905 Ickenham Parish Council asked Uxbridge Rural District Council to approach the Metropolitan Railway about building a station here, an Uxbridge councillor exclaimed: 'What! A halt out in the wilds of Ickenham!' Nevertheless, a station was built that summer.

Ruislip One of the few surviving original Metropolitan Line stations.

Ruislip Manor Opened as a halt in 1912 as part of the Ruislip Garden City scheme.

Eastcote Marathon runners in the 1908 Olympic Games passed by the station.

Rayners Lane In his 1954 poem 'The Metropolitan Railway' John Betjeman contemplates a new Metroland couple travelling 'out and on, through rural Rayner's Lane / To autumn-scented Middlesex again'. When the station opened in 1910 it was so windy and lonely locals gave it the nickname 'Pneumonia Junction'.

West Harrow Opened in 1913 in an obscure location.

HARROW-ON-THE-HILL TO ALDGATE

Harrow-on-the-Hill It was envisaged by John Betjeman as a 'rocky island' in his 1954 poem 'Harrow-on-the-Hill', in which he compares various Middlesex places to Cornwall and the surrounding sea.

Northwick Park A pointless station, built only yards from Kenton on the Bakerloo Line instead of meeting the latter at an interchange.

Preston Road Built as a two-platform halt for those using Uxendon Shooting Club, the venue for the clay pigeon shooting at the 1908 Olympic Games.

Wembley Park The main station for Wembley stadium.

Finchley Road Only two inches of concrete separate the top of the Metropolitan Line tunnel from the base of the North Star Hotel near the station.

Baker Street One of the original seven stations on the first underground line, the Metropolitan Railway.

Great Portland Street Originally Portland Road when opened as part of the first line in 1863.

Euston Square Opened as Gower Street on the original 1863 line.

King's Cross St Pancras The only station on the network with a hybrid name, a combination of the names of the two railway termini located above.

Farringdon The eastern terminus of London's first underground line, built over alleyways where cattle had been slaughtered.

Barbican The original Metropolitan Line was extended here in 1865.

Moorgate The 1865 station was rebuilt in 1890 to incorporate a headquarters for the City and South London Railway.

Liverpool Street The Metropolitan Line was extended further east to Liverpool Street in 1875.

Aldgate The eastern terminus, reached in 1876.

South-east London

SOUTHWARK, SE1

The swampy land on the south side of the Thames, where medieval builders found it difficult to lay roads, was developed at a slower rate than the north side, with none of the great buildings of Church, Crown or state that could be found north of the river. Nevertheless, Southwark is one of the oldest communities in the metropolis, where the Romans under the general Aulus Plautius built a bridge near the present-day Southwark Bridge in AD 43. In medieval times it became the home of theatres such as the Globe, with its Shakespeare associations, as well as a great coaching centre, the London terminus for vehicles journeying to the South Coast. In the nineteenth century Southwark attracted considerably more industry than the land on the opposite bank, with mills and distilleries and later engineering factories and car-making works (the first Vauxhall car plant). Second World War bombing destroyed much of the area but modern-day Southwark is still heavily industrialized (for London), its gloomy black-brick streets dominated by depots, yards and workshops.

JUBILEE LINE

London's newest underground line, extended from central London to Stratford at a cost of £3.3 billion at the end of the twentieth century, was unveiled in 1965 as the Fleet Line, running from Baker Street to Lewisham via Fleet Street. As the new tunnel from Baker Street to Charing Cross neared completion in the late seventies, the line was renamed the Jubilee, opening in 1979 and taking the Stanmore section of the Bakerloo Line north of Baker Street.

Although plans remained in place to extend the Jubilee Line east from Charing Cross to Aldwych and under Fleet Street to new stations at Ludgate Circus, Cannon Street, Fenchurch Street, Surrey Docks *en route* for either Lewisham or Thamesmead, when the newspaper industry left Fleet Street in the late 1980s the authorities decided to reroute the eastern extension to Waterloo and across Southwark and Rotherhithe to Canary Wharf, the newspapers' new home, and thence to Stratford, resulting in further delays. Later, when Bugsby's Marshes peninsula in North Greenwich was chosen for the Millennium Dome, the line was rerouted again, leading to yet further delays. The Jubilee extension eventually opened in 1999, just in time to meet government promises that the Millennium Dome section would be ready for the Millennium.

Yet despite the line's problems the stations have been hailed for their bright confident architecture, overseen by Roland Paoletti, who was given licence

to experiment, as the authorities wanted the new stations to act as beacons for the community, and who hired many leading architects such as Michael Hopkins and Norman Foster to design the ambitious new stations.

Stanmore Opened in 1932 as part of the Metropolitan Line, later transferring to the Bakerloo, and in 1979 to the Jubilee.

Canons Park Named after the canons of the medieval priory of St Bartholomew in the City, who owned the land in the fourteenth century.

Queensbury The station opened in 1932 as Kingsbury, but when a new station opened two years later half a mile south, closer to the centre of Kingsbury, it was decided to call the latter Kingsbury and this the obvious, but somewhat contrived, Queensbury.

Kingsbury The second station on the line to be called Kingsbury (see above).

Wembley Park A multi-million pound redevelopment scheme for the station was severely delayed at the beginning of the twenty-first century due to the administrative chaos surrounding the proposals for Wembley stadium.

Neasden The station serves the dull suburb that has been the butt of a thousand derogatory *Private Eye* jokes.

Dollis Hill Opened in 1909 in an area previously known as Daleson Hill and Dolly's Hill.

Willesden Green Opened as Willesden Green in 1879, became Willesden Green and Cricklewood in 1894, and reverted to Willesden Green in 1938.

Kilburn The station is situated on the Romans' Watling Street route (now the Edgware Road), about a mile north of Kilburn.

West Hampstead One of three unconnected West Hampstead stations in the vicinity.

Finchley Road It has an interchange with the fast Metropolitan Line route into the Metroland suburbs.

Swiss Cottage During the Second World War users of the station's air-raid shelter produced their own newsletter, *The Swiss Cottager*.

St John's Wood Opened in 1939 to replace two abandoned nearby stations: Marlborough Road and Lord's.

Baker Street The northern end of a new tunnel built in 1979 that allows passengers a faster alternative route to Charing Cross than that provided by the Bakerloo Line.

Bond Street There is no Bond Street as such, the name being a hybrid of Old Bond Street and New Bond Street, the latter situated more than 100 yards to the east.

Green Park The tunnel from here to Charing Cross was abandoned when the Jubilee Line extension was built at the end of the twentieth century.

Westminster The line was rerouted from Charing Cross to Westminster in the 1990s so that it ran close to 10 Downing Street and the government's Pindar bunker.

Waterloo The Jubilee Line section of the station was designed by Roland Paoletti, the architect in overall charge of the extended line's design.

Southwark Although the new station is too far away from the new Bankside developments of the Globe Theatre and Tate Modern to be useful, the station building itself is a triumph, with huge cavernous spaces and a curved wall containing 630 triangular panels of enamelled glass.

London Bridge Like Waterloo, designed by Roland Paoletti, the architect in overall charge of the Jubilee Line extension.

Bermondsey Winner of a 2001 Outstanding New Structure award from the Concrete Society but like Southwark situated in the wrong part of the area it represents.

Canada Water Incongruously sited only a few hundred yards from Surrey Quays station, and built with a huge cavern of a concourse that occupies the same space as St Paul's Cathedral.

Canary Wharf Designed by David Nelson of Norman Foster's architects' firm, it was built into a drained section of West India Dock. Above is Britain's tallest building, 1 Canada Square, which could fit sideways into the station's hall with around 100 ft to spare.

North Greenwich One of the largest London underground stations, constructed on a grand scale as part of the over-ambitious Millennium Dome project, and rendered almost useless by its closure, given the lack of a resident local population.

Canning Town Its opening, together with the new Docklands Light Railway station and revitalized North London Line, has made more accessible what used to be one of London's most isolated areas.

West Ham A station was opened here to link up with the Hammersmith & City and District lines.

Stratford Many of Britain's leading media figures and dignitaries were forced to wait here for up to three hours on New Year's Eve 1999 before being taken to the grand opening ceremony of the Millennium Dome.

▶ Bakerloo Line, p. 347

(i) Bankside

London's medieval entertainments centre, a land of theatres such as the Globe, bear- and bull-baiting pits, gaming dens and brothels, located on the south bank of the Thames opposite St Paul's, Bankside flourished until the Puritans closed the theatres in 1642 as part of a programme of moral reform. Gradually the area became industrialized, filling with wharves, warehouses and factories. Second World War bombing and the decline in manufacturing and heavy industry in the 1970s and 1980s blighted the landscape, but the building of the new Globe Theatre and the conversion of Bankside power station into the Tate Modern art gallery has brought life back to the area.

Bankside

The name of the road that runs along the Thames bank for most of the route between Blackfriars Bridge and Cannon Street rail bridge.

south side: Cannon Street railway line to Hopton Street

Shakespeare's Globe (1997–), Bankside at New Globe Walk

> The cloud-capp'd towers the gorgeous palaces / The solemn temples the great globe itself – *The Tempest*, William Shakespeare (1611)

Modelled on the nearby seventeenth-century 𝕲lobe 𝕿heatre, where Shakespeare acted, Shakespeare's Globe was the last theatre built in London in the twentieth century, an ambitious and brilliantly conceived project, devised by the late actor and film director Sam Wanamaker, that has helped revive a forgotten corner of London. Wanamaker first outlined the idea in the late 1980s, but his plans to build a theatre were constantly thwarted by Southwark Council which would not sell the land south-east of Southwark Bridge where the original 𝕲lobe stood; they denounced Shakespeare as 'elitist', and placed what they thought were enough obstacles in its way to stymie the project.

This made the Globe's supporters pursue their ideal with even greater vigour, and they built the new theatre on a different site, to the west of Southwark Bridge. Using materials faithful to the Elizabethan original, including timbering, goat's hair and water reeds, they created a galleried, circular open-air auditorium with space for hundreds to stand close to the stage. The Globe opened in 1997, four years after Wanamaker's death, with a performance of Shakespeare's *The Two Gentlemen of Verona* done, surprisingly, in modern costume, and it has since hosted performances of *Henry V*, *The Merchant of Venice* and *A Midsummer Night's Dream*, as well as works by Shakespeare's contemporaries.

As it has an open-air auditorium, the theatre is used only in the summer and attracts what is for Britain an atypical audience: raucous, restless and irreverent, good-naturedly booing villains. The surrounding building houses permanent exhibitions on Shakespeare and Elizabethan theatre.

Cardinal's Wharf

A rare surviving seventeenth-century riverside terrace for this part of London, situated immediately west of the Globe, it includes at No. 49 a house where Christopher Wren is believed to have lived while working on the reconstruction of St Paul's opposite.

Tate Modern

A spectacular art gallery built into Giles Gilbert Scott's soaring brick Bankside power station by the Swiss architects Herzog and de Meuron, who converted the shell of the building, which had been left with its huge turbines and boilers still inside after closing in 1981, making excellent use of the vast space, in time to greet the new millennium. The new Tate, which opened in May 2000, was an immediate success with the public, attracting huge and unforeseen numbers of visitors to displays arranged in four main sections by themes, rather than chronologically, or in rooms devoted to particular artists.

► Tate Britain, p. 246.

Clink Street

A narrow gloomy street of canyon-like nineteenth-century warehouses near the river, which fits the popular view of how Dickensian London looked.

south side: St Saviour's Dock to Bank End

𝔚inchester 𝔓alace

Only the fourteenth-century rose window and a tumbledown wall remain of the bishops of Winchester's London palace, which stood on this site from 1109 to 1663. Here James I of Scotland and Joan Beaufort enjoyed their wedding reception in 1424, and around 100 years later Henry VIII met his fifth wife, Catherine Howard. When the Winchester episcopacy was abolished in 1642 during the Civil War, the palace was commandeered by the Parliamentarians and used as a jail for Royalist prisoners, and

although it was returned to the Bishop of
Winchester on the Restoration of the throne
the buildings were in so poor
a condition they were barely usable and the
bishops moved out, letting the property as
apartments until the fabric of the building
deteriorated too badly. For much of their
tenure the bishops ran an unusual sideline,
licensing the local brothels and prostitutes,
known as Winchester Geese, who operated
according to the palace rule that 'No single
woman [was] to take money to lie with any
man, but she lie with him all night till the
morrow.'
▶ Priory of St John, Clerkenwell, p. 77.
Clink Prison Museum, No. 1
The prison, whose name has become a slang
term for all jails, opened *c.* 1509 within the
precincts of the Bishop of Winchester's
palace for those who misbehaved at the
theatres and brothels of Bankside. It fell into
disuse after the Civil War of the 1640s, was
burned down in the Gordon Riots of 1780
and was rebuilt as a museum in the 1990s.

Park Street

This winding street near Southwark Bridge,
with its antiquated properties, was from 1781
to 1955 the location of the **Barclay and
Perkins brewery**, visited in August 1850 by
the Austrian Field Marshal Baron von
Haynau, known for torturing prisoners,
who was attacked by a bale of hay thrown
by one of the draymen and pelted with
manure. Von Haynau fled, but was found
trying to hide in a dustbin outside the
George Inn on Bankside, and was attacked
again, finally being rescued by the river
police. The brewery merged with Courage's
in 1955 and closed in 1982. The 1998 gangster
film *Lock, Stock and Two Smoking Barrels*
was partly filmed at Nos. 13 and 15.
Rose Theatre (1587–1605), No. 56, north
side
The earliest theatre to be built locally, and
the only Elizabethan theatre in England of
which there are substantial remains, the
Rose was home to Lord Strange's company,
which included Edward Alleyn, said to be

the finest actor of his generation, who took
the lead roles here in the premières of
Marlowe's *Tamburlaine the Great* (1587),
The Jew of Malta (1589) and *Doctor Faustus*
(1589), and later founded Dulwich College.
The theatre's foundations were discovered
in 1989 and in 2001 further artefacts were
found beneath the office block that stands
on the site.
south side: Stoney Street to Sumner Street
The Anchor Inn, No. 34
Built after the Southwark fire of 1676, it was
owned 100 years later by Henry and Hester
Thrale, friends of Dr Johnson. Henry died
in 1781 leaving debts of £130,000, which
prompted Johnson, the executor of Thrale's
will, to make his famous remark about
'growing rich beyond the dreams of avarice'.
Globe Theatre (1599–1644), east of Southwark Bridge Road
> May we cram / Within this wooden O the
> very casques / That did affright the air at
> Agincourt? – *Henry V*, William Shake-
> speare (1599)

The original **Globe Theatre**, built at the end
of the sixteenth century with wood rescued
from **The Theatre** in Shoreditch, was the
setting for a number of Shakespeare
premières, including in 1599 *Henry V*, which
refers to the theatre as 'this Wooden O' in
its Prologue, *Julius Caesar* (also 1599), and
Cymbeline (1611). During the première of
Henry VIII in June 1613 cannons, which
were being used as stage props, set the
thatched roof ablaze and burned down the
theatre, as witnessed by the playwright Ben
Jonson who had just returned from Europe.
Though no one was injured, one man had
to be 'doused with pottle ale'. The Globe
was rebuilt the following year but was closed
by the Puritans in 1644.

(ii) Bermondsey

A depressed area to the south-east of
London Bridge, built on marshy land (the
name comes from Beormund's Ey – Beormund's Island), it was owned in the Middle

The Richardson gang

South London's most powerful twentieth-century gang, based around the Richardson brothers: Charlie, who had his first brush with the law in the early 1950s, being chased by the police along the Old Kent Road while driving a stolen car, and Eddie, the south London 'King of the Teds'. The brothers grew up in Camberwell in the 1940s and ran scrap metal yards locally, later branching out into 'long firms', fruit machines and, in Charlie's case, South African mining. Although less glamorous and less publicly fêted than the Krays, their east London rivals, the Richardsons were more powerful, until 1966 when they were jailed for a total of thirty-five years.

Wyndham Road, Camberwell. Charlie and Eddie Richardson were brought up in Wyndham Road, a typical south London street of working-class terraced houses, in the 1940s, were evacuated during the war and returned after hostilities ended to an area that had mostly been destroyed.

The Addington (1950s, 1960s), 33a Addington Square, Camberwell. Charlie Richardson bought a small two-storey property and yard for his burgeoning scrap metal firm in Addington Square, half a mile north of Camberwell Green, in 1951, when he was nineteen. When he moved the business to nearby New Church Road in 1957, he converted No. 33a into a drinking club and social centre for the south London underworld, open in the afternoons when pubs were legally obliged to shut, and filled the premises with exotic animals (two bears once escaped on to the streets of Camberwell). Richardson punished those who stepped out of line in his office using an old army field generator known as the 'Black Box', that had been fitted out with crank handle and leads.

The Richardsons' scrap metal firm (1957–65), 50 New Church Road, Camberwell Charlie Richardson, who saw himself as a latter-day Robin Hood, ran a semi-legitimate empire from here that involved 'reducing local crime to a dribble . . .

Ages by religious institutions including the long closed 𝕭𝖊𝖗𝖒𝖔𝖓𝖉𝖘𝖊𝖞 𝕬𝖇𝖇𝖊𝖞, and the abbeys of St Augustine, Canterbury and Battle, whose leaders built themselves luxurious properties by the river that were seats of power until the Reformation. After the opening of the nearby Surrey Docks in the early nineteenth century warehouses were built by the river, alongside which locals lived in overcrowded tenements that were demolished at the beginning of the twentieth century through the campaigning work of the local philanthropist Dr Alfred Salter. Second World War bombing hit Bermondsey, with its strong industrial base, hard, and much of the land was cleared of all pre-war buildings in the 1950s and rebuilt with crude tower blocks and barely habitable deck-access estates. Changes in economic patterns in the 1970s, in particular the closure of Surrey Docks, devastated the already depressed local economy and created a ghost town that has barely recovered, despite recent attempts at gentrification and the opening of a tube station on the Jubilee Line.

• Bermondsey occupies the parts of SE1 east of Borough High Street.

Old Kent Road

> The next morning, our money being at an end, Paddy and I set out for the spike. We went southward by the Old Kent Road –
> *Down and Out in Paris and London*, George Orwell (1933)

A road synonymous with many of the least attractive aspects of south London life – poverty, blight, decrepit housing and casual violence – it was in medieval times the major route out of Southwark into Kent (hence the name), a straight road that bypassed the wharves and docks of the

I would be enraged when local people would come and tell me of burglaries to their houses . . . We would know within hours who had done the job, give them a smack and tell them to fuck off to the West End to steal from rich people who could afford an insurance policy.' Those who disobeyed gang rules would find themselves dealt with harshly, one miscreant being bound and gagged and hung by his ankles for a few hours, a punishment idea adapted for the upside-down-gang-in-the-freezer scene in the 1979 London underworld film *The Long Good Friday*.

Shirley Ann, Queen's Road, Peckham
An illegal drinking club run in the late 1950s by the Richardsons, accessible only through a garage on Queen's Road, it was where the eventual Great Train Robbers Bruce Reynolds and Buster Edwards met, but its activities were long ignored by the police. Twenty years later the Peckham station sergeant at the time, Ken Drury, received a long jail sentence for corruption in connection with vice in Soho.

Mr Smith and the Witchdoctor, Rushey Green, Catford. A popular south London nightclub of the sixties where a major gangland fight on the night of 7 March 1966 saw Eddie Richardson (Charlie's brother), the brothers' chief ally, 'Mad' Frankie Fraser, and several others battle with the Hawards, a group planning to usurp the Richardsons' fruit machine empire. During the mêlée a gun was fired and Richard Hart, a member of the Kray gang, who was with the Hawards, was shot dead. When news of Hart's death reached the Krays they decided to exact revenge, Ronnie Kray shooting dead a Richardson acolyte, George Cornell, in the Blind Beggar pub, Whitechapel. The Richardsons' empire crashed later that year. At the subsequent trial at the Old Bailey, sentencing Eddie Richardson to ten years and Charlie Richardson to twenty-five, Mr Justice Lawton told them: 'One is ashamed to live in a society with men like you. There is no known penal system to cure you. You must be kept under lock and key.'
► Blind Beggar, p. 306.

Thames where public gallows were built to warn potential miscreants.

In 1836 James Greenacre, an Old Kent Road grocer, murdered a fifty-year-old woman and left parts of her body in various locations across south London, and when the story became public knowledge local pie-sellers renamed their meat pies 'Greenacres', to popular acclaim. Albert Chevalier's early-twentieth-century music hall song 'Wot Cher! (Knocked 'Em in the Old Kent Road)' made the road famous. Second World War bombing devastated the surrounding land, which was redeveloped with shoddy council estates, and with no tube or rail links, a poor bus service, an ever-congested roadway and only the most basic shops, Old Kent Road steadfastly refuses all attempts at improvement.

Bricklayers' Arms Station (1844–52), north side, east of Page's Walk
A number of local railway companies opened a terminus at the northern end of the Old Kent Road in 1844, naming it Bricklayers' Arms after an old coaching inn, and desperate to win passengers from London Bridge, a mile to the north, advertised the station as a 'West End terminus', despite it being nearly three miles away. Things descended into farce when the Dover Railway Company, inconvenienced by having two Bermondsey termini to deal with, began alternating the destination of the trains without warning. Passengers never knew whether their journey would end at London Bridge or Bricklayers' Arms until the last moment, to the inevitable chagrin of those meeting them. This absurdity continued until 1852 when **Bricklayers' Arms station** closed to passengers

and became a freight depot, in which guise it continued for over 100 years before being shut. The site has since been redeveloped as an industrial estate.

▶ London Bridge station, p. 381.

Thomas A Becket, No. 320, south side
A pub famous for its boxing gymnasium, the Thomas A Becket is built on the site of a medieval watering place for horses and was where Chaucer's Canterbury pilgrims drew lots to see who would begin the storytelling in *The Canterbury Tales*. Above the gym is a room where David Bowie rehearsed his *Ziggy Stardust* album in the early 1970s before taking the songs on tour.

Shad Thames

One of the best-preserved stretches of early-nineteenth-century industrial warehouses in London creates a canyon of brick whose upper floors are connected by a lattice of iron bridges. The street, whose name is a corruption of St John at Thames, has long been popular with television and film producers looking to recreate the myth of 'Dickensian London' – productions partly filmed here include *The French Lieutenant's Woman* and David Lynch's *Elephant Man* – and has recently become an enclave of cosmopolitan cool among the drabness of Bermondsey, the flats that overlook the Thames being keenly sought by the wealthy young.

Butler's Wharf, No. 36c
Butler's Wharf, the largest collection of warehouses on the Thames, and built from 1871 to 1873, was for 100 years one of the busiest sites in the capital, dealing with goods unloaded at Surrey Docks or nearby Hay's Wharf (p. 269). In 1972 traders ceased using the buildings and the space was let as studios. Those who moved in included the painter David Hockney, the film-maker Derek Jarman and the avant-garde artist Andrew Logan, at whose 1976 Valentine ball the Sex Pistols played one of their first gigs, using a set made from materials rescued from the children's department at the recently closed Biba store in Kensington and

scenery that had been used in Jarman's *Sebastiane* film. Terence Conran, founder of Habitat, bought the site in the late 1980s to redevelop it as luxury apartments, but the subsequent property crash led to the collapse of the venture. He later obtained the lease and opened a restaurant, Le Pont de la Tour, that has become particularly fashionable (Tony Blair and Bill Clinton dined there in the late 1990s). When the property market improved at the end of the twentieth century the flats were sold for exorbitant prices.

▶ Sex, King's Road, p. 409.

Design Museum, No. 28
Established by the Conran Foundation in a disused warehouse in 1989, it was the first museum in the world devoted entirely to the design of everyday objects.

(iii) The Borough

Borough comes from Burgh, a stronghold to protect a river crossing, and the area was one of the busiest in London in medieval times as well as the first metropolitan stop for immigrants from Flanders and Germany. Borough was devastated in the 'Little Fire of London' of 1676, when the Tabard inn, associated with Geoffrey Chaucer's *Canterbury Tales*, was destroyed, and after being rebuilt it became heavily commercialized. Changing economic patterns at the end of the twentieth century brought about considerable commercial decline and much dereliction.

● The Borough is the area of SE1 around Borough High Street.

Borough High Street

A road of considerable antiquity, the Roman route from Londinium to Chichester and in later centuries the main route south from London Bridge, it was one of the busiest streets in medieval London, lined with coaching inns and places of entertainment, and the site of several prisons, such as the Marshalsea, immortalized by Charles Dickens in *David Copperfield*. It was the setting for the medieval Southwark Fair, the biggest in south London, held for two weeks every September from 1462, the stalls and booths taking up every available space in the high street and side streets. The fair closed down in 1763, and around a hundred years later the coaching inns met the same fate when the railway arrived. Although Borough High Street has never recovered its importance, it retains a shabby liveliness due to the proximity of London Bridge station and nearby institutions such as Guy's Hospital. Many small medieval alleys still lead off the High Street including George Inn Yard, home of the area's oldest surviving non-religious building, the George Inn, which dates from 1676.

west side: Borough Road to London Bridge
Borough market, south of Bedale Street
The oldest fruit and vegetable market in London, dating back to 1550, Borough market's black brickwork and dark recesses evoke a period feel that has brought film-makers looking for Victorian atmosphere here decade after decade, as can be seen in Merchant Ivory's *Howards End*, the 1990s version of George Orwell's *Keep the Aspidistra Flying*, and the gangster film *Lock, Stock and Two Smoking Barrels*. Since the beginning of the 1990s Borough market, which is at its liveliest early in the morning, has attracted a cult following and a number of chic restaurants and bars, but plans to redevelop London Bridge station currently threaten its existence.
► Petticoat Lane market, p. 289.

Southwark Cathedral
The oldest building in Southwark and the oldest Gothic church in London, what is now officially the Church of St Saviour and St Mary Overie was begun in the seventh century by Mary, daughter of John Overy (John of the Ferry), who rowed people across the river to worship here, and was rebuilt by St Swithun, Bishop of Winchester, from 852 to 862. It was mentioned in the Domesday Book, rebuilt in the twelfth century, this time by Augustinian canons and, although the attached monastery was dissolved during the Reformation. St Saviour continued as a parish church, which fell into ruin by the late eighteenth century.

Parts of the building were destroyed during the rebuilding of London Bridge in 1830, and even though the leading Gothic architect A. W. N. Pugin, designer of the interior of the Houses of Parliament, described the nave as 'the vilest preaching place that ever disgraced the nineteenth century', the church survived, becoming a cathedral in 1905. Inside is the tomb of John Gower, who died in 1408 and is often described as 'the first English poet', as he wrote in English, rather than French or Latin. A carved stone screen behind the high altar of 1520, decorated with figures from Southwark's history, contains memorials to the writers Geoffrey Chaucer, John Bunyan and William Shakespeare, who may have attended services here and is commemorated with a full-size reclining alabaster effigy near a stained-glass window depicting scenes from his plays. Edmund, Shakespeare's younger brother, was buried here on 31 December 1607.
► St Paul's Cathedral, p. 61.

east side: London Bridge to Harper Road
London Bridge station, at London Bridge Street
London's first railway line, a 4-mile track resting on 978 arches, opened between Spa Road, half a mile east of London Bridge, and Greenwich in February 1836 and the following October the western terminus was rebuilt at what is now London Bridge station, the capital's oldest terminus. Over the next few decades various railway companies, including the South Eastern Railway and the London, Brighton and South Coast Railway, constructed routes to London Bridge, creating the jumble of lines that now cross south-east London, and it soon became an important station for the thousands of clerks working in the City and living in the new middle-class suburbs of Croydon, Norwood and Sydenham, a phenomenon T. S. Eliot noted in his 1922

poem *The Waste Land*. London Bridge is now one of the least loved and least attractive railway termini in the capital, with narrow and draughty platforms and poor signposting, outside which a world of dark alleyways, hidden corners and arches has become home to hundreds of garages, timber yards and workshops.

▶ King's Cross station, p. 356.

White Hart Inn, Borough High Street at White Hart Yard

Hath my sword therefore broke through London gates, that you should leave me at the White Hart in Southwark? – *Henry VI Part II*, William Shakespeare (1594)

A major coaching inn until the late nineteenth century, the northern terminus for the coaches from London to Portsmouth and Rye, the **White Hart** was where Jack Cade, the Kentish rebel, set up headquarters at the start of his unsuccessful campaign to seize control of the City of London in 1450. It was described by Charles Dickens in *The Pickwick Papers* (1837) as one of the 'great rambling, queer, old places . . . with galleries and passages and staircases, wide enough and antiquated enough to furnish materials for a hundred ghost stories', being where Mr Pickwick meets Sam Weller, the inn's boots, for the first time before taking him on as his manservant. The inn declined when the railway came to Southwark and it was demolished in 1889.

▶ Jack Cade at London Stone, p. 64.

The George, No. 77

A riot of black and white timbering, based in George Inn Yard, an alley just east of the High Street, the George is London's only remaining galleried public house and was first recorded in 1542 when it was one of nearly twenty pubs around Borough market. Rebuilt in 1620, it was destroyed by fire in 1676, rebuilt again, in a galleried style, and since 1937 has been owned by the National Trust. In Charles Dickens's *Little Dorrit* Tip Dorrit writes a begging letter to Arthur Clennam from the George. Shakespeare plays are staged in the courtyard in the summer.

Tabard, Borough High Street at Talbot Yard

In Southwark at the Tabard as I lay / Redy to wenden on my pilgrymage / To Caunterbury with ful devout corage – *The Canterbury Tales*, Geoffrey Chaucer (1387)

The most famous of the Southwark inns, thanks to its inclusion in the opening of Geoffrey Chaucer's *Canterbury Tales*, the **Tabard**, named after a knight's sleeveless jacket, was a popular gathering place for pilgrims on their way to Thomas à Becket's shrine in Canterbury Cathedral, as Chaucer related. When the pub was rebuilt in 1629 as the Talbot the landlord displayed a board outside proclaiming 'This is the inn where Sir Jeffry [*sic*] Chaucer and the nine and twenty pilgrims lay, in the journey to Canterbury, anno 1383.' The inn burned down in 1676 in the 'Little Fire of London', and though rebuilt, was demolished in 1875.

Marshalsea Prison I *(1373–1811)*, north of Mermaid Court

I visited Marshalsea Prison, a nursery of all manner of wickedness. Oh shame to men that there should be such a place, such a picture of hell upon earth! – John Wesley's journal, 3 February 1753

One of the most famous prisons of premodern London, Marshalsea's name derived from the court held by the Steward and Marshal of the King's Household, and in 1381, only eight years after opening, was destroyed by the anti-poll tax rebels. The Elizabethan explorer Walter Ralegh served a short sentence in the rebuilt prison in 1580, after being convicted of 'a fray beside the tennis court in Westminster', and in 1597 the Privy Council imprisoned the playwright Thomas Nashe and some of the actors who performed in his supposedly seditious play, *The Isle of Dogs*, in Marshalsea. By the nineteenth century the prison was mostly being used for debtors, and it closed in 1811, moving a few hundred yards south.

▶ Marshalsea II, p. 383.

King's Bench Prison (1758–1880), Borough High Street, north of Angel Place

> At last Mr Micawber's difficulties came to a crisis, and he was arrested early one morning, and carried over to the King's Bench Prison in the Borough – *David Copperfield*, Charles Dickens (1849)

Titus Oates, who was jailed at the King's Bench in 1685 for fabricating the so-called Popish Plot, a supposed widespread Catholic conspiracy which, it was feared, would lead to innocent Protestants being massacred and a Jesuit government installed, spent the first year of his confinement in irons but survived to father a child born to his prison bed-maker. In 1768 the radical politician John Wilkes, who had been charged during his absence in France with seditious libel and obscenity, was jailed at the King's Bench on his return to England, prompting demonstrations outside the prison during which supporters rent the air with the famous cry 'Wilkes and Liberty'. By the nineteenth century the prison had assumed an absurdly lax regime and outside the courtyard was filled with tailors, hatters, piano-makers and oyster-sellers. It was demolished in 1880.

► Fleet Prison, p. 56.

Marshalsea Prison II (1811–42), south of Angel Place

The final home of **Marshalsea Prison** was where Charles Dickens's father, John, was gaoled for debt in 1824. He was joined there by his wife and family, as was the custom, although the twelve-year-old Charles was spared the ordeal. After Dickens senior had been imprisoned for a few months, his mother died and he inherited £450, enough to pay off some of his creditors, and was released. Dickens remained embarrassed by his father's imprisonment throughout his life, but maintained that the latter's conduct towards his family was exemplary, and he recreated him affectionately as Wilkins Micawber in the largely autobiographical *David Copperfield* (1850). Dickens also wrote about Marshalsea in *Little Dorrit* (1857), the heroine of which is born here, 'a child of the

Marshalsea'. A section of the prison wall remains by Angel Place.

► Newgate Prison, p. 10.

St George the Martyr, Borough High Street at Long Lane

First mentioned in 1122, and at that time owned by Bermondsey Abbey, St George was rebuilt in the 1730s and again in 1897, by Basil Champneys, architect of Manchester's John Rylands Library. It is now known as the Little Dorrit church, on account of its central role in the Dickens novel of the same name, and features a window which depicts the kneeling figure of the heroine who, in the book, is baptized and married here. Outside the church in 1658 Oliver Cromwell's body was met by friends and supporters *en route* to its lying-in-state in Somerset House.

Harper Road

Horsemonger Lane Gaol (1790–1878), Harper Road at Newington Recreation Ground

The prison, which was built in the 1790s, was where the publisher and friend of Shelley, Leigh Hunt, was gaoled in 1813 for calling the Prince Regent (later George IV) a 'fat Adonis of fifty'. Charles Dickens came to the jail in 1849 to witness the hanging of a Mr and Mrs Manning, who had killed a friend for his money, and reported on it for *The Times*. The prison was closed in 1878.

(iv) Elephant and Castle

> The Elephant was not exactly a classy district. The streets were as rough and dangerous as it was possible to get without anybody actually declaring war, and even the cinema was not without its perils – *What's It All About?*, Michael Caine (1992)

A deeply unpleasant part of south-east London, dominated by traffic-choked twin roundabouts situated at the crossroads of several historically important routes, its name comes from an inn called the

Elephant and Castle, itself a corruption of the Spanish *La Infanta de Castilla*, the Spanish princess who was once engaged to Charles I. By the beginning of the twentieth century it was an area of music halls, brothels, pubs and filthy streets of closely packed houses that was one of the most lawless parts of the capital, run by gang leaders such as Charles 'Wag' McDonald of the so-called Elephant Boys.

While the men were heavily involved in racetrack protection, the women were experts at shoplifting, their leader being Aggy Hill, the 'Queen of the Forty Elephants', whose gang would descend on the West End in chauffeur-driven cars and load up while the cars waited outside (this being before the advent of parking restrictions).

The Elephant and Castle was heavily bombed in the Second World War, and for over a decade the streets lay desolate and unrepaired. Nevertheless the area gave birth to a new phenomenon – the Teddy Boy – Britain's first youth cult, made up of aggressive working-class young men staging a sartorial protest against postwar austerity by adapting American zoot suits to Savile Row's 1948 look – that of the Edwardian. The word 'Edwardian' became corrupted into 'Ted', and by the 1950s the look had changed to narrow trousers, luminous socks, brothel creeper shoes, velvet collars on overcoats and sleeked-back hair. The 'King of the Teds' was Eddie Richardson, brother of the future South London gang leader Charlie Richardson, who acquired the title not because of the quality of his drapes or the size of his quiff but by virtue of the fact that he had knocked out the reigning king, Tony Rolands, in a fight. Unlike later cults the Teds were not initially associated with a particular form of music – the infatuation with American rock 'n' roll, and rockabilly in particular, came later – and the style died out as a contemporary fashion statement in 1958 with the introduction among London's youth of Italian styles of dressing, a style that came to be described as 'mod'.

In September 1959 ambitious plans to redevelop the area with a shopping centre were unveiled by Sir Isaac Hayward, leader of the London County Council, who claimed: 'With its famous name and history of traditions the new Elephant and Castle offers opportunities one would have to go a long way to better. Here's a real chance for the South to "show them how" on the north side of the Thames.' The reality was rather different, and the new Elephant and Castle became the most derided development of its kind in the capital, a dystopia of badly lit, smelly, impenetrable tunnels leading to grim shops lying underneath a double roundabout where cars inched forward in seemingly perpetual gridlock, set alongside a housing estate that resembled an east European prison. Plans to demolish the centre and start again gathered pace at the end of the twentieth century.

Gaunt Street
Ministry of Sound, No. 103
London's best-known modern-day nightclub was opened in a disused warehouse in September 1991 by James Palumbo, son of the businessman Lord Palumbo, who after initial problems and bad publicity worked hard at establishing a cult following. Running the club with a precision rare for the nightclub world, Palumbo created a carefully executed mystique, aided by the club's official-looking 'ministry' logo, dance music compilations, clothing range, tours to other cities' clubs, website, magazine and policy of allowing entrance only selectively.
► Soho nightclubs, p. 186.

(v) North Lambeth

Lambeth you've never seen / The skies
ain't blue, the grass ain't green – 'The
Lambeth Walk', Noel Gay (1937)
Lambeth, from Loamhithe, or muddy landing place, one of few residential districts close to the political centre of the country, although lying across the Thames, is also one of the most run-down and blight-

ridden, dominated by the kind of crumbling housing estates and intimidating streets, particularly around Lambeth High Street, that would not be tolerated north of the river. Until late-eighteenth-century industrialization Lambeth was barely inhabited and the community was dominated by Lambeth Palace, the London home of the archbishops of Canterbury.

A working-class community grew to service the factories near the Thames in the eighteenth century and the area soon became overcrowded and polluted, the only variations in the landscape being the pub and the music hall. What was a lively if impoverished community was destroyed first by German bombers during the Second World War blitz and then by Lambeth Council planning officers in the 1950s and 1960s who, assuming megalomaniac dominion over the area, laid waste vast swathes of the locality so that it could be rebuilt with all areas of human activity – housing, schooling, transport, welfare, jobs – coming under the jurisdiction of the town hall. In the mid-1970s rate-capping by the Thatcher government withheld further funding and the ideal of a socialist Lambeth was wiped out, leaving a blighted, devastated land on the 'wrong' side of the river with little prospect of imminent improvement.
● North Lambeth is the part of SE1 south of Waterloo station.

Hercules Road
The postwar Ealing comedy *Passport to Pimlico* was filmed here among the Second World War rubble, Pimlico itself not being considered visually suitable, close to the address where William Blake, late-eighteenth-century artist and poet extraordinaire, lived at **13 Hercules Buildings**, a three-storey house with uninterrupted views of the Thames. There, Blake created his own alternative bible, based on the existing chapters and verses, in which Genesis and Exodus were rewritten as three books – *The Book of Urizen*, *The Book of Ahania* and *The*

Book of Los. The house was demolished in the 1920s and the site is now occupied by an austere-looking block of flats named after the artist.

Lambeth Palace Road
Lambeth Palace
London home of the archbishops of Canterbury since 1197 and one of the few surviving episcopal seats along the Thames, Lambeth Palace in medieval times was a maze of alleyways and courtyards where those in debt took sanctuary, coming out only on Sundays when they were immune from arrest. The palace was attacked during the Peasants' Revolt of 1381, when books were burned and furniture smashed, and again in 1640, when around 500 London apprentices stormed the palace on Shrove Tuesday, their annual day of lawlessness. During the anti-Catholic Gordon Riots of 1780 hundreds of demonstrators, many with drums and fifes, surrounded the palace yelling: 'No Popery', until they were beaten off by some 100 troops. In the crypt, which is the oldest surviving part of the palace, the religious reformer John Wycliffe was interrogated in 1387 for 'heretical propositions'. The palace's Morton's Tower houses the oldest free public library in the country, open only by appointment. Since 2000 the buildings and courtyards, many of which retain their medieval shape, have been open to visitors.
► Charterhouse, p. 77.

Lambeth Road
Former Bedlam / Imperial War Museum, Geraldine Mary Harmsworth Park
The museum, devoted to British conflicts of the twentieth century, was created in 1935 out of what was the Bethlehem Royal Hospital, popularly known as the Bedlam lunatic asylum, which moved to Lambeth from Moorgate in 1815 and left for Surrey in 1926. The grounds were then bought by the newspaper proprietor Lord Rothermere, who renamed them Geraldine Mary Harmsworth Park after his mother, and presented them to the council.
► Bedlam in the City, p. 21.

St George's Road
St George's Cathedral
South London's Catholic cathedral stands, ironically, on the site of St George's Fields where in 1780 Lord George Gordon's 'No Popery' rioters assembled before burning and looting central London in protest at the prospect of more rights being granted to Catholics. The large local Irish community donated money for the construction of a cathedral, and by 1839 there were sufficient funds to buy the land and hold a competition to find a suitable architect, which was won by A. W. N. Pugin, who was also responsible for the interior design of the Houses of Parliament. Unfortunately, there was not enough money to finish the building to Pugin's designs – the spire had to be abandoned – and Second World War bombing destroyed his work, although his altar frontispiece was found under the rubble and restored. Pope John Paul II celebrated mass in front of 3,000 people at St George's during his 1982 visit to Britain.
▶ Westminster Roman Catholic cathedral, p. 245.

Westminster Bridge Road
Philip Astley, a strongman and former cavalry household officer, opened a horse-riding exhibition ground in fields to the east of Westminster Bridge in 1768, attracting huge crowds. He then built 𝔄stley's 𝔄mphitheatre, which opened on the site in 1794 to stage circuses and was later described by Charles Dickens, in *Sketches By Boz*, as 'delightful, splendid and surprising'. It closed in the 1890s and was demolished soon after.
MI6 headquarters (1966–94), Century House, north side
This twenty-two-storey tower block was the unlikely home of the Secret Intelligence Service (SIS) – better known as MI6, the organization made glamorous by the antics of its most famous fictitious member, James Bond – during the last decades of the twentieth century, at a time when, officially, it did not exist. In the forecourt of the building was a petrol station staffed, inevitably, by former agents on the lookout for terrorists contemplating driving up and leaving a bomb on the premises. Meanwhile, inside the offices, agents were hatching a number of unethical plans including the toppling of Colonel Gaddafi, the Libyan leader. MI6 moved to Vauxhall Cross in 1994, and during refurbishment of the building at the end of the twentieth century workmen found a basement cell, a powerful chemical disintegrator, stronger than a shredder, and evidence that MI6 probably had its own private tube station connected to the nearby Bakerloo line.
▶ MI6 at Vauxhall Cross, p. 266.

Necropolis Railway terminus (1854–1902), No. 121, south side
In 1854 Waterloo station began operating a funeral service, the Necropolis Railway, with trains divided into carriages for the different classes (First, Second and Third) and for different shades of Christianity (Anglican and Nonconformist). Corpses that could not be accommodated in existing London cemeteries were taken to Brookwood graveyard in Woking, Surrey, passing through what the authorities hoped was scenery that would be 'comforting' to mourners – Battersea Park, Wimbledon Park, Richmond and the Surrey countryside. When Charles Bradlaugh, the Victorian free-thinker, died in 1891, having chosen to be buried at Brookwood, 5,000 mourners, none wearing black, turned up at Waterloo Necropolis station to accompany the coffin to Woking. In 1902 the Necropolis terminus moved from Waterloo station to 121 Westminster Bridge Road. The service was discontinued after the Second World War.

(vi) The South Bank

Britain's greatest concentration of arts venues can be found at the southern end of Waterloo Bridge, occupying former industrial land reclaimed for the 1951 Festival of Britain, and includes the Royal

Festival Hall, the National Theatre, the National Film Theatre and the Hayward Gallery. Despite the wealth of facilities the South Bank has been continually bedevilled by press criticism, which resulted in various schemes being outlined at the end of the twentieth century to renovate the site, including the encasing of the buildings in a glass roof designed by Richard Rogers. But by the beginning of the twenty-first century it had become apparent that the main problem facing the South Bank was not the lack of quality of its amenities but the absence of a strong and confident manage-ment, proud of this extraordinary collection of assets.

heading north from Westminster Bridge Road

County Hall

A bulky building designed by Ralph Knott in an awkward Renaissance style, County Hall was built in 1919 to 1922 for the London County Council, reformed as the Greater London Council in 1965 and abolished by the Conservative government in 1986. It has since been converted into a hotel, aquarium and museum devoted to the surrealist painter Savador Dalí.

London Eye

One of the few successes of the various millennium projects that commemorated the start of the twenty-first century, the British Airways-sponsored London Eye, a giant wheel which revolves through a complete vertical circle every forty-five minutes, was conceived in 1993 by two unknown architects – Julia Barfield and David Marks – and has won considerable praise since its opening in 2000 for the dynamic panorama of the metropolis it offers and for the elegance of its archi-tecture.

Royal Festival Hall

The permanent legacy of the 1951 Festival of Britain, and the first and most attractive of the various South Bank venues, the Royal Festival Hall was designed by London County Council architects Robert Matthew and Leslie Martin, who were influenced by the clean lines of Le Corbusier's buildings and the use of light wood associated with Scandinavian architects, and was built in only eighteen months so that it would be ready for the festival. There were immediate criticisms about the acoustics, which have barely improved since, but the hall has staged many notable concerts including Sir John Barbirolli conducting Verdi's *Requiem* and an appearance by Toscanini. The first South Bank summer music festival took place in 1968, with Jacqueline du Pré and Itzhak Perlman among the performers, and on 24 September 1969 Fairport Convention

---

Festival of Britain

To commemorate the 100th anniversary of the 1851 Great Exhibition, celebrate the achievements of Britain and rejoice in the ending of the Second World War, the government organized a Festival of Britain, held on derelict land near Waterloo. The festival was mostly held within the Dome of Discovery, a 90 ft-high self-supporting struc-ture with an aluminium roof, alongside which stood pavilions dedicated to science and the festival's most unusual structure, Skylon, a slender, cigar-shaped tower pointing to space, at that time the per-ceived setting for man's immediate progress. Although the festival was considered a success, not everyone was triumphant. The novelist Evelyn Waugh explained how 'the Government decreed a Festival. Monstrous constructions appeared on the south bank of the Thames', while the journalist Keith Waterhouse described how the festival was 'a monument to British tat; escalators which didn't work, elegant glass entrance halls stuck over with scrawled notices reading "Use other door"; the corporate italic display lettering already peeling off some of the façades'. The festival's major legacy was the Royal Festival Hall, now the oldest building of the South Banks arts complex.

► The Great Exhibition at Hyde Park, p. 427; the 1908 Franco–British Exhibition at White City, p. 464; the Millennium Dome, p. 393.

unveiled their new folk rock direction at a concert – the first following the death of drummer Martin Lamble in a car crash – in which they were supported by Nick Drake in a rare public performance. Since the 1970s the hall's programming has become increasingly eclectic, showcasing jazz, world music, rock and poetry, as well as performances by the London Philharmonic and Philharmonia orchestras, the highlight being the annual Meltdown concerts, hosted by a different celebrity each year, to showcase mostly left-field acts.

► Royal Albert Hall, p. 422.

Hayward Gallery

Named after Sir Isaac Hayward, a former leader of the London County Council, the Hayward is London's second most important gallery after the Tate Modern for showcasing contemporary works and is housed in a building typical of 1960s brutalist architecture.

National Film Theatre

Britain's leading art house cinema opened in 1952 and is home to the annual London Film Festival.

► Riverside arts centre, p. 250.

National Theatre

The National Theatre, which comprises the Cottesloe, Lyttelton and Olivier, opened in 1976, some twenty-five years after Princess (now Queen) Elizabeth laid the foundation stone, and was immediately savaged for its architecture, the work of Denys Lasdun, which critics found 'earnest, gloomy and depressing . . . like a hotel foyer at floor level and a car park at ceiling level'. There was further criticism about spending more on individual productions than most provincial companies received in grant for one year, and if that was not enough, the opening night was marred by further farce. The fanfare version of 'God Save the Queen' made the monarch shudder with horror; the chosen opening piece was an obscure work by Goldoni, rather than one of the classics of English theatre, and the great actor Laurence Olivier, who was also the National's artistic director, fell asleep while sitting next

to the Queen. Yet despite these disasters the National has been the setting for many memorable productions since, thanks to the successive artistic directors Peter Hall, Richard Eyre and Trevor Nunn.

► Sadler's Wells, p. 80.

(vii) Waterloo

A dishevelled area of grimy streets, unappealing shops and windblown council estates saved by the presence of the Old and New Vic theatres, Waterloo station and the proximity of the South Bank.

Waterloo Road

The route from Waterloo Bridge to the Elephant and Castle was built on what until the mid nineteenth century were St George's Fields, used for archery practice and popular demonstrations, where in 1768 a mob assembled in support of the demagogue John Wilkes, who had been charged (during his absence in France) with seditious libel and obscenity. Twelve years later, on 2 June 1780, thousands gathered here to march on Parliament to present a petition against laws allowing Catholics more rights, the first event in what became the Gordon Riots.

Waterloo station, west side

Waterloo opened on 11 July 1848 as Waterloo Bridge, the terminus for the London and South Western Railway, and immediately attracted wealthy passengers, as it served Southampton where the transatlantic liners docked. In its early days the station had no ticket-checking point and swarms of collectors were obliged to board trains a few yards short of the station so that they could check tickets en masse. The platform numbering system was even more chaotic and one Devonian farmer is believed to have remarked to his wife: 'No wonder the French got licked here.' The writer Jerome K. Jerome worked the confusion into his 1889 comedy *Three Men in a Boat*, whose protagonists arrive at the station to take the 11.05 to Kingston, but are unable to find their platform, obtain agreement on its location from the porters, station master or traffic superintendent, and are obliged to bribe an engine-driver to take them west.

Nearly 13,000 evacuees – children, pregnant women, hospital patients – left Waterloo in late 1939, after war had been declared with Germany, for safer accommodation in the countryside. A few months later, in May 1940, soldiers who had been evacuated from Dunkirk arrived at Waterloo dishevelled and beaten, giving Londoners their first experience of the realities of the Second World War. The station was extended in the 1990s to take Nicholas Grimshaw's Eurostar terminal and now serves some 300,000 people a day, making it Britain's busiest.
► Paddington station, p. 432.
Old Vic, east side at The Cut
One of London's oldest theatres, the Old Vic was designed by Rudolph Cabanel using stones from the Savoy Palace, by the Strand, which was being demolished, and opened in 1818 as the Royal Coburg to stage melodrama. For much of the nineteenth century it was a music hall, attracting, according to the writer Charles Kingsley, 'the beggary and rascality of London pouring in to hear their low amusement', but in 1890 it was turned into a temperance hall by the social worker Emma Cons, being converted back to a theatre in 1898 by Cons's niece, Lilian Baylis. By the early 1920s the Old Vic had become London's leading Shakespearean theatre, and in 1963, under Laurence Olivier, it became home to the National Theatre. When Olivier left in 1976, the theatre went into an artistic decline that was only partly alleviated when the Canadian Ed Mirvish bought the building in 1982 and spent £2 million on refurbishment.
► Theatre Royal, Drury Lane, p. 119.

GREENWICH, SE10

Greenwich, home of international time settings (the 0° Longitude Meridian runs through the area) and a host of world-renowned tourist attractions – the Old Royal Observatory, the National Maritime Museum, the Royal Naval College, the Cutty Sark tea clipper and Greenwich Park – began as a fishing village, Gronovic (Green Town). Humphrey, Duke of Gloucester and brother of Henry V, enclosed 200 acres of land here for a park in 1433 and built a palace alongside the river that was replaced by Christopher Wren's seamen's hospital, now home to the University of Greenwich. Alongside the hospital stands Inigo Jones's Queen's House, built for Anne of Denmark, James I's queen, the first Palladian building erected in Britain, and now part of the National Maritime Museum, while across the park on a hill stands the former Royal Observatory, where work on finding an accurate method of measuring time at sea eventually resulted in Britain becoming the home of international time settings.

(i) Greenwich Park

An immensely popular royal park, London's oldest, it was first enclosed in 1433 as the grounds for the mansion built by Humphrey, Duke of Gloucester, the younger brother of Henry V, to the north, a site now occupied by the former Royal Naval Hospital. The park was opened to the public in the eighteenth century.
Old Royal Observatory
Standing on a lofty position over Greenwich, the observatory was designed by Christopher Wren in 1675 as Charles II wanted astronomers to find a way of measuring time accurately at sea. John Flamsteed, the first Astronomer Royal, worked from sheds in the observatory garden (now Quadrant House and Sextant House), erecting a telescope on the balcony that was fixed to observe the movement of Sirius, day and

night, proving that the earth rotates at a constant speed.

In 1714 the authorities offered a lucrative prize to anyone who could construct a longitudinal watch and the winner was John Harrison (1693–1776), whose first timepiece, H1, completed in 1735, kept time at sea on the *Centurion* with considerable accuracy, despite the movement of the ship, the regular changes in the temperature and the scepticism of Isaac Newton. *Centurion* later sailed without H1, a factor which may have been instrumental in its sinking with the loss of seventy lives *en route* to the island of Juan Fernandez. Harrison was then given financial aid to construct further chronometers, resulting in H4, which won him the £20,000 prize when he was in his seventies. In 1833 Maudslay and Field installed a time-ball, the world's first public time signal, at Greenwich to allow vessels on the Thames to adjust their timepieces – it is still dropped from the top of a pole on an observatory turret at exactly one o'clock every day – and by the 1850s 98 per cent of British clocks were being set by Greenwich Mean Time.

In 1871 the world's leading nations, looking to fix a centre for international time settings, through which the 0° Meridian would be drawn on maps, called an International Geographical Congress in Antwerp, where it was suggested that Greenwich be the recognized setting. At the second congress, held in Rome in 1875, France announced it would be happy to accept Greenwich as the setting if Britain adopted the metric system. Britain agreed, but more than 120 years later the metric system has still not been fully implemented.

Even though Greenwich was given the 0° longitude setting, calculations in 1949 showed that the Greenwich meridian, rather than having a longitude of exactly 00° 00' 00", measured 00° 00' 00.417" East, an anomaly which had arisen because the seventh Astronomer Royal, George Airey, had measured 0° longitude in the 1840s in a different room of the observatory from the

one originally chosen for the task. As a consequence the Greenwich Meridian was moved 26.39 feet. The observatory moved to Herstmonceaux, Sussex, in the 1960s and the Greenwich buildings are now used by the National Maritime Museum. In the courtyard a brass strip divides east from west.

(ii) north of Greenwich Park (Greenwich town centre)

The quaint town centre with its maritime-flavoured antique shops and bookshops dates back to improvements made by Joseph Kay in 1830, when properties on King William Walk and Greenwich Church Street were given a stucco frontage.

Greenwich Church Street
St Alfege with St Peter

Nicholas Hawksmoor's only church south of the Thames is named after Aelfheah, or Alfege, an eleventh-century Archbishop of Canterbury who was kidnapped by Danes, brought to Greenwich by boat and clubbed to death with the bones of his captors' feast when he refused to allow a ransom to be paid. A church was first built *c.* 1012 and was where Henry VIII was baptized in 1491 and Thomas Tallis, remembered in Vaughan Williams' 'Fantasia on a Theme by Thomas Tallis', was organist from 1540 to 1585. The diarist Samuel Pepys worshipped here in the 1660s, and described how he enjoyed 'a good sermon, a fine church and a great company of handsome women'. The collapse of the roof of the medieval building in a storm in November 1710 led the government to introduce the Fifty New Churches Act of 1711, which resulted in the appointment of Nicholas Hawksmoor as surveyor to the Commission, and he started work on a new building in 1712. During the Second World War the crypt was used as an air-raid shelter by hundreds of locals as well as the writer George Orwell who was visiting relatives in the neighbourhood and described the stench of live bodies when the shelter was full as 'almost insupportable'.

► Hawksmoor's Christ Church Spitalfields, p. 285.

King William Walk

King William Walk, which links the river with Greenwich Park, is lined with antique stores and antiquarian bookshops displaying maritime paraphernalia.

Cutty Sark, north end

> He could not run straight against the wind because he was a sailing vessel, a tea-clipper, the *Cutty Sark – Swallows and Amazons*, Arthur Ransome (1930)

The *Cutty Sark* which is based in dry dock at the north end of King William Walk, was the fastest of the late-nineteenth-century tea-clippers. Built in Dumbarton in 1869 and named after the shirt worn by Nan, the witch in Robert Burns's 'Tam o' Shanter', it plied the tea route from China to Britain. After it was taken out of service in 1922, it was restored, and since 1954 has occupied this site, home of the nineteenth-century **Ship's Tavern**, destroyed during the Second World War. Nearby on the Thames is Sir Francis Chichester's *Gipsy Moth* (p. 271).

Park Row

Trafalgar Inn

One of London's most famous riverside inns, the Trafalgar was built in the 1770s with large bowed windows and balconies that provide splendid views of the river (and now the Millennium Dome). It was famous for whitebait dinners that attracted patrons such as the novelists Charles Dickens and Harrison Ainsworth, who gave a dinner here in 1851 to mark the release of his novel *Mervyn Clitheroe*. The pub began to lose its popularity in the twentieth century and in 1915 was converted to a seamen's hostel. It was refurbished to something approaching its original splendour, with much maritime decor, in 1965 with whitebait, caught in non-Thames waters, returned to the menu.

Romney Road

Greenwich Palace, north side

Greenwich's one-time royal connections date back to 1300, when Edward I made an offering of seven shillings at each of the holy crosses in the local Chapel of the Virgin Mary, but Greenwich's first royal building was Bella Court, which Humphrey, brother of Henry V, began constructing in 1427, equipping it with the first great privately owned library in the country, which later passed to the Bodleian Library in Oxford.

After Humphrey died, Bella Court was occupied by Margaret of Anjou, wife of Henry VI, and renamed the Palace of Placentia ('the pleasant place'). It was here that Henry VIII was born in 1491 and that his elder brother, Arthur, who died before he could assume the throne, married Catherine of Aragon in 1501.

The palace later became the summer retreat of Elizabeth I (who was born here in 1533) and was where she reinstated the Maundy ceremony of washing the feet of the poor the day before Good Friday and where the explorer and poet Walter Ralegh famously laid his cloak over a puddle for her (near the junction of Romney Road and King William Walk). James I made the palace over to his queen, Anne of Denmark, for whom Inigo Jones designed the adjacent Queen's House, but by the early seventeenth century Greenwich had gone out of fashion. Charles II drew up plans to rebuild the palace but they were abandoned due to lack of money. The remains were demolished when Wren's Royal Naval Hospital was built on the site.

► **Whitehall Palace**, p. 233.

Royal Naval Hospital and College (1696–1998) / University of Greenwich (1998–), north side

Wren's riverside masterpiece, one of the capital's most splendid sights, particularly when seen from the north bank of the Thames, was created out of Christopher Wren's abandoned work on the rebuilding of Greenwich Palace in the late seventeenth century and completed by John Vanbrugh after Wren was deposed as Surveyor General in 1716. By 1750 the hospital was bestowing relief and support to more than 1,500 pensioners, but their number declined after the Napoleonic Wars and by the mid nineteenth century many thought it incongruous that so magnificent a building was used merely as a hospital (a Captain Baillie remarked how 'Columns colonnades and friezes ill accord with bully beef and sour beer mixed with water'), resulting in the hospital closing in 1869 and being converted to the Royal Naval College. After more than a hundred years at Greenwich the college moved out in 1998 and the building was taken over by the University of Greenwich as an administration centre. The westerly parkside section, the King William Block, contains the complex's *pièce de résistance*, the Painted Hall (now open to the public), designed by James Thornhill as a dining room for the hospital pensioners, where Admiral Lord Nelson lay in state in 1805 following his death at Trafalgar.

Queen's House / National Maritime Museum, south side

When James I's queen, Anne of Denmark, expressed her dissatisfaction with Greenwich Palace as a royal residence in 1616, the king commissioned Inigo Jones to build her a house to the south. Over the next twenty years Jones created England's first Palladian villa (one where the framework was coated in white cement, rather than exposed brick), and as Anne died eighteen years before it was finished it was occupied by Charles I's queen, Henrietta Maria. By the end of the eighteenth century the house had fallen into disrepair, smugglers having set up base inside, and in 1806 it was taken over by the Royal Naval Asylum School. When the latter moved out in 1933 the property became the National Maritime Museum. In 1990 the interior was restored to its perceived 1662 appearance.

(iii) *west of Greenwich Park*

Maidenstone Hill
Jack Cade's Cavern, No. 77

The property, which can be found nearly a mile south of the main Greenwich attractions, stands above a network of caves and tunnels built into the chalk escarpment which may once have been part of a chalk mine, and were named after Jack Cade, the Kent rebel who in 1450 led an army to London and camped on Blackheath. Soon after the cavern was discovered in 1780 steps were constructed to allow access, ventilation was installed and tours were conducted by guides armed with suitably demonic stories until the lights went out one night in 1853, after which it closed down. There was an unsuccessful attempt to reopen the cavern in 1906, and when in the late 1930s the authorities selected the site for an air-raid shelter, no one could find the entrance and so a shaft was sunk at 77 Maidenstone Hill. There, a passage was found graffiti'd with names of visitors from the eighteenth century and carvings of the devil, but plans to use the cavern were abandoned due to concerns about safety, and they have remained unused since.

(iv) *North Greenwich*

> The peninsula thrives on secrecy. For as long as anyone can remember much of this land has been hidden behind tall fences. Walkers held their breath and made a wide circuit. Terrible ghosts were trapped in the ground – *London Review of Books*, Iain Sinclair (1999)

Bugsby Marshes, the peninsula to the east of the Isle of Dogs, was a blighted, polluted landscape of industrial units, wharves and gas works until it was chosen in the 1990s as the site for a new building to host the government's celebrations to greet the new millennium. The site was chosen because it was the only available large piece of land in London standing on the course of the 0° Meridian. Millions were spent on trying to decontaminate the land, rerouting the new Jubilee Line tube extension, which needed an awkward twist in what would have been a straight line from Canary Wharf to Canning Town, and building the Dome. But the venture, which opened at the end of 1999, was a spectacular disaster. Since the Dome's closure at the end of 2000, the land has lain unused while various parties negotiate over its future in the knowledge that the peninsula is too contaminated for non-industrial development.

Millennium Dome

Built at the end of the 1990s to the designs of Richard Rogers to house the official millennium celebrations, the vast hangar-like building became the setting for the single greatest financial disaster in the history of London, an exhibition centre into which £1 billion of taxpayers' money was poured to pay for a year-long show consisting of a variety of 'zones' devoted to areas of human existence that ignored the achievements of British culture from the previous millennium.

The project was beset by a series of public relations disasters from its inception. There were claims that the Dome would introduce to the world a new game, surfball, except there was no such game; details of the contents of the displays were kept a secret until the very last minute (the 'best-kept secret in the world'), but it was only when it was too late to make changes that it was realized that such a course of action had been taken because those in charge knew they would be publicly ridiculed if the exhibition details had been revealed in advance; tickets had not been sent out by Christmas, a week before the opening ceremony; and on the night itself, New Year's Eve 1999, VIP guests were kept waiting for hours at a nearby tube station before being allowed entrance, while Dome press officers denied there were any problems until they learned that newspaper editors were among those waiting.

Throughout its year as a tourist attraction visitor numbers were consistently lower than the 12 million government ministers

and Dome executives had predicted. Few people booked in advance. Many were dissuaded by the tales of horror from the opening night, by the interminable queues on the opening day, by the absence of a car park, despite the nearby motorways, and few trusted the new and then unreliable tube line to get them there. Critics were nearly unanimous in their condemnation. The novelist J. G. Ballard described the building as a 'sinister abattoir disguised as a circus tent', while Hugo Young in the *Guardian* claimed it was not an emblem of British brilliance but of a 'desperate, empty national grandiosity'.

By May the venture was bankrupt. Commissioners considered closing it down before the summer to stop the haemorrhaging of more money, but Dome executives calculated that that would be another PR disaster (rather than a triumph for the public purse) and so an injection of £229 million of public cash was given to keep the venture afloat. At the end of 2000 the Dome closed, its interior was gutted and its contents rapidly auctioned off while the computers still flickered, switched to screensaver mode. The vacant site continues to haemorrhage some £3 million pounds a month in security costs while the authorities considered its future.

► British Library, p. 355.

KENNINGTON, SE11

Kyning-tun, the 'place of the king', was an occasional home to royalty until the flat open land of Kennington Common (now Kennington Park) became popular with holidaying workers, preachers and protestors, and by the mid nineteenth century thousands were gathering regularly on the Common to take part in political demonstrations. On 10 April 1848, the year of revolution across Europe but not England, 150,000 people were present at one of the best attended of the various Chartist meetings taking place at the time. The

Major sporting events at the Oval

The world's first football international, 5 March 1870 England draw 1–1 against a Scottish Representative XI.

The first FA Cup Final, 16 March 1872 Wanderers beat the Royal Engineers 1–0 in the first FA Cup Final and as winners are given a bye until the following year's final, and they are allowed the choice of venue, favouritism which was swiftly expunged.

The 'Ashes' Test, 28–29 August 1882 England, needing only 85 in their second innings to beat Australia, lose by 7 runs. The following day the *Sporting Times* carries a mock obituary: 'In Affectionate Remembrance of ENGLISH CRICKET which died at the Oval on 29th August, 1882. Deeply lamented by a large circle of Sorrowing Friends and Acquaintances, RIP. NB – The body will be cremated and the Ashes taken to Australia.' Since then the regular Test series between England and Australia has been known as the Ashes.

England v Australia, fifth Test, Hutton's record innings, 21–24 August 1938 Len Hutton and Maurice Leyland establish a second wicket stand of 382 as Hutton sets a new world runs record of 364, a score which remains unbeaten in England until the 1990s. England declare at 903 for 7 and Australia, with Don Bradman injured, lose by an innings and 579 runs.

England v Australia, fifth Test, England regain the Ashes, 15–19 August 1953 The Ashes return to England for the first time in twenty years thanks to Laker and Lock's devastating bowling and a powerful batting order featuring Len Hutton, Bill Edrich, Denis Compton and Trevor Bailey. It is the first time since 1926 that England have beaten Australia at home.

England v Australia, fifth Test, 10–16 August 1972 Australia win by five wickets in the only test to be played over six days, with both Chappell brothers, Ian and Greg, scoring centuries for the visitors.

England v South Africa, third Test, Devon Malcolm's 9 for 57, 18–21 August 1994 Malcolm, the bespectacled West Indian-born fast bowler known as 'The Destroyer', rips through South Africa with remarkable bowling figures, spurred on, it is alleged, by being hit on his helmet earlier in the Test.

► Lord's, p. 369.

---

authorities, fearing insurrection, hired extra special constables and stationed 5,000 troops at strategic points across the capital, including Hyde Park, the Tower and the Bank of England to ward off the mob. The royal family and a number of landowners fled London, but after the Chartist leader, Feargus O'Connor, agreed to the authorities' demand that the crowd should not accompany the Chartists to Whitehall to deliver their radical petition, the events passed off relatively peacefully. Kennington was heavily bombed in the Second World War and later rebuilt with disregard for aesthetics, although a few elegant Georgian terraces remain to the west of the tube station and attract MPs as residents due to their proximity to the House of Commons.

Kennington Oval

The Oval

South London's major sporting arena came into being in 1844 when the Montpelier Cricket Club, founded in 1796 in Walworth and looking for a new ground, chose the site of a Kennington market garden owned by the Duchy of Cornwall that stood alongside the meandering River Effra. At a dinner held at the Horns public house on Kennington Road on 2 August 1845 Montpelier members formed the Surrey County Cricket Club and as the Players of Surrey they played their first game at the new ground, which they called the Oval, against the Gentlemen of Surrey on 21 August 1845.

Originally, the Oval had no clubhouse, and the pitch, which consisted of 10,000 squares of turf cut from Tooting Common, was of poor quality, so when the duchy gave the club notice to quit in 1854 a new site was identified in Brixton. However, the threat of eviction was lifted by the intervention of the Prince Consort, and as facilities improved, other sports, including tennis and football, began to be played here. The 1870s witnessed a series of historic matches at the ground, including the world's first football international in 1870, and the first FA Cup Final in 1872, and in 1878 spectator areas, which consisted solely of unsheltered banks of earth arranged in tiers, were added for the first ever visit by an Australian cricket team, an event watched by 20,000 spectators. The ground was used as a prisoner-of-war camp in the 1940s, but has continued to be home to Surrey County Cricket Club and a regular Test venue for cricket matches since, despite being disfigured by unattractive extensions and the 'official' renaming of

the ground first to the Foster's Oval and later to the AMP Oval.

Lambeth Walk

Once crammed with market stalls and a boisterous working-class community, Lambeth Walk was celebrated in song in the 1937 musical *Me and My Girl* with a number that became so popular internationally that the Italian dictator, Benito Mussolini, ordered a London girl to go to Milan to teach it to him. Ironically, Lambeth Walk was destroyed in the Second World War and was redeveloped in the precinct style with overhead walkways that hastened its descent into a postwar slum. It is now lined with boarded-up shops, abandoned pubs, graffiti'd concrete walls, run-down council flats and few signs of life.

► Robin Hood Gardens, Poplar, p. 318.

South-west London

BELGRAVIA, SW1

Belgravia, the flower boxes, and the awnings over doors, and the front walls painted different shades of cream. The gracious living in red with huge green squares outside the windows – *Absolute Beginners*, Colin MacInnes (1958)

An ostentatiously wealthy district dominated by stucco-clad nineteenth-century properties, Belgravia was developed after Lord Grosvenor paid £30,000 in the 1820s for what was then known as the Five Fields – a swamp through which the River Westbourne flowed and 'a place where robbers lie in wait', as Addison wrote in the *Tatler* – and obtained an Act of Parliament to drain, clear and raise the land. Grosvenor hired Thomas Cubitt, the first master-builder to use a permanent workforce of craftsmen, to build an estate and Cubitt in turn hired architects such as George Basevi, who also designed Cambridge's Fitzwilliam Museum, to create what he called Belgravia, named in honour of the Grosvenors' Belgrave estate in Leicestershire. Graceful terraces, well-appointed villas and handsome squares filled the streets but, though luxurious and much sought after, the new estate had a rigidity and intensity that caused the Conservative politician and novelist Benjamin Disraeli to comment: 'the Belgrave district is as monotonous as Marylebone, and is so contrived as to be at the same time insipid and tawdry'. Being the suburb closest to the royal palaces and buildings of government, Belgravia soon attracted wealthy residents and embassies, particularly around Belgrave Square, Eaton Square and Chester Square, and has remained among the most desirable addresses in inner London.

• Belgravia is the part of sw1 west of the railway line into Victoria.

(i) The Cadogan Estate

An estate of some 4,000 flats, 700 houses and 300 shops built in a flamboyant Flemish style with much red brick, the Cadogan Estate, which lies either side of Sloane Street, is owned by the Cadogan family, hence the use of the name for several streets, and is home to several of Britain's most celebrated stores, particularly Harrods. In 1975 Peter York coined the name 'Sloane Ranger' in the magazine *Harpers and Queen* to describe the kind of wealthy local socialite who in the 1920s would have been called a 'Bright Young Thing' and in the 1960s an 'International Jet-setter', whose embodiment was the late Princess of Wales.

Brompton Road

Harrods, Nos. 87–135

London's most prestigious, and Europe's largest, department store, its motto *omnia, omnibus, ubique* ('everything for everyone everywhere'), opened as a small grocery store, run by Henry Harrod in Stepney, in 1835, moved to Eastcheap in the City, and then to Belgravia in 1849. It expanded through the efforts of Richard Burbridge, who left Whiteley's on Westbourne Grove, then London's greatest department store, where he had been head of provisions, and transformed Harrods into a worthy rival. In 1901 Stevens and Munt began work on the store's grandiose baroque frontage, and they installed Britain's first escalator, at the top of which was an attendant equipped with *sal volatile* and brandy to resuscitate those troubled by moving stairs. The House of Fraser group acquired Harrods in 1959, selling it to the Fayed brothers in 1985. In 2000 Harrods lost its royal warrant, probably because of Mohamed Al-Fayed's criticism of the authorities' alleged role in the death of his son, Dodi, in the crash that also killed the Princess of Wales.

► Whiteleys, p. 435.

Lennox Gardens

Middlesex County Cricket Club headquarters (1872–6)

The Middlesex club, founded in 1850, moved to the Cadogan Estate in 1872 to play in a field that two years previously had been a market garden and was described in that

year's *Wisden* as 'grand and quick and one
of the truest playing grounds in England'.
As there was a skating rink close by for
'ladies who had been presented at Court',
batsmen were warned not to hit the ball too
hard to square leg in case they hit a lady
skater. Following an argument about
finances Middlesex left for St John's Wood,
and after the ground closed in 1886 most of
the fields were built over, although a small
patch of grass between the two sections of
road remains.
▶ Lord's, p. 369.

Pont Street
Named after a bridge over the now
culverted Westbourne River, Pont Street
was developed from 1805, with gabled red-
brick houses that were derided by the upper
classes but sought after by those with social
aspirations and were later given the name
'Pont Street Dutch' by the cartoonist Osbert
Lancaster, a term that came into general use
to describe similar properties everywhere.
In one such Pont Street property in 1965
Michael Holingshead, a disciple of the LSD
guru Dr Timothy Leary, who had assumed
his name in honour of the imagination's
supposed 'third eye', or 'hole in the head',
opened the World Psychedelic Centre.
Clearing the building of everyday furnishings, which he replaced with 'sympathetic'
objects such as wood, flowers, fruit, cheese
and incense, he organized a soundtrack that
included music by Ravi Shankar, John Cage
and Bach (Beatles tracks not then being
hallucinogenically suitable and Pink Floyd
not existing), and held Britain's first acid
trip using the first batch of LSD to be
imported into the country (it was not then
illegal), which had been impregnated in
grapes. When news of Holingshead's activities spread, the newspapers began a hostile
campaign of publicity against this new
risqué hedonism, the *Evening Standard*
leading with 'The Drug That Could
Threaten London', which explained that
'LSD, one of the most powerful drugs
known to man, produces hallucinations

[and] can cause temporary insanity . . . just
half an ounce could knock out London.'

Sloane Square
A major south-west London junction and
meeting place, which acts as a buffer
between Chelsea and Belgravia, the land was
the traditional site of the maypole and was
where the Chelsea Volunteers drilled. Sloane
Square was laid out in 1771 and later lined
with houses designed by Henry Holland. By
the twentieth century it had become
completely commercialized. It is now best
known for the Royal Court Theatre and the
Peter Jones department store.
east side
Sloane Square station
Opened in 1864 on the Metropolitan District
Railway (now the District Line), Sloane
Square was until the 1990s one of only two
stations on the network with a platform bar
(the other being Liverpool Street); this one
was known as the Drink Under the River as
the River Westbourne runs above the lines
in a pipe clearly visible from the platforms.
Two bombs fell on the station in 1940 when
two trains were at the platforms and an
unknown number of people were killed.
Royal Court Theatre
Long one of the most progressive theatres in
London, the Royal Court dates back to the
1870s, when a Dissenters' chapel on the
south side of the square was converted into
a theatre. It was taken over in 1904 by
Harley Granville-Barker who produced
eleven plays here for George Bernard Shaw,
including the premières of *Major Barbara*,
Heartbreak House and *Candida*. At the first
night of the latter in 1905 the audience
demanded the appearance of the author and
cheered uproariously when the manager,
J. E. Vedrenne, came on stage. With some
difficulty Vedrenne convinced the audience
that he was not Shaw, who had just left the
building to take the tube home, whereupon
some of the audience ran into the station
only to find Shaw's train pulling out and the
playwright waving to them as it sped off.
In the 1930s the Royal Court briefly

became a cinema, but it was converted back to a theatre in 1952 following bomb damage and was bought by George Devine who made it London's most talked-about theatre after premièring John Osborne's *Look Back in Anger* in May 1956. The set included a kitchen sink, a prop that soon gave its name to the genre of working-class productions with a vaguely northern, socialist feel. Although the arch critic Kenneth Tynan hailed *Look Back in Anger* as the 'best young play of its decade', takings were low until the theatre's publicity department answered a journalist's question by describing Osborne as a 'very angry young man', a term that became a convenient hook to sell the production.

In 1965 the Royal Court challenged the Lord Chamberlain's prerogative to censor plays, after his department had cut entire scenes from Edward Bond's *Saved*, by converting the theatre into a private club to show the unexpurgated work. Prosecution followed, none the less, and the theatre was fined, but when Bond's *Early Morning* was performed here three years later the second performance was described as a free 'critics' dress rehearsal', thereby circumventing the law, and within a few months Parliament had expunged the Lord Chamberlain's powers. In 1972 the Royal Court staged *Owners*, the first of many Caryl Churchill works, and challenging productions continued, mostly under Max Stafford-Clark, until the 1990s when the theatre shut for £26 million of refurbishment, reopening in 2002.
▶ Theatre Royal, Drury Lane, p. 119.

west side
Peter Jones
A perennially popular department store, its founder was a Welsh draper's assistant who opened a shop in Hackney in 1868 and later moved, first to Southampton Row, Bloomsbury, and then to Draycott Avenue, Chelsea. After a wall between his two shops collapsed, with fatal results, Peter Jones walked bareheaded at the funeral of the victim, and despite opposition he reopened his store here in 1877, with much success.

After Jones died in 1905 the store was beset by financial problems until a buyer emerged in the shape of John Lewis, who walked from his Oxford Street store to Sloane Square with twenty £1,000 banknotes in his pockets to buy the company. The current building, designed by Slater, Crabtree and Moberly in the 1930s, embodies some of the best ideas from the modernist architecture of the period, in particular the glass curtain wall, the first seen in Britain, which was modelled on Erich Mendelsohn's Shocken store in Chemnitz.
▶ John Lewis, p. 138.

Sloane Street
The major traffic route from Knightsbridge to Sloane Square, Sloane Street was created by Henry Holland in 1780 and lined with elegant houses designed with fanlights, of which only No. 123 remains. It is now London's most prestigious shopping street, linking Harrods and Harvey Nichols at its northern end with Peter Jones and King's Road at the southern end, and is home to several major fashion labels in between.
Cadogan Hotel, Sloane Street at Pavilion Street, west side
The aesthete, wit and writer Oscar Wilde was found by police drinking hock and seltzer in Room 118 of the Cadogan Hotel in April 1895 and was arrested without putting up any resistance on charges of gross indecency, having failed to take advantage of the few hours' grace that the authorities had unofficially given him so that he could flee the country. The adjacent Pont Street home of the actress Lillie Langtry, in which she installed a machine that printed out up-to-the-minute racing results, is now incorporated into the Cadogan.
Holy Trinity, Sloane Street at Sloane Square, east side
A major church of the Arts and Crafts movement, designed for the Earl of Cadogan by John Dando Sedding, a friend of William Morris, in 1890, it led Norman Shaw, the leading suburban architect of the period, to exclaim: 'What arches! What surprises!',

when he first saw it. In the mid-1970s the poet John Betjeman led a successful campaign against the threat of closure of the church, which he described as 'the Cathedral of the Arts and Crafts' (its nave is wider than St Paul's), and which he had previously celebrated in his 1940s poem 'Holy Trinity, Sloane Street'.

(ii) Upper Belgravia

The eastern, non-Chelsea section of King's Road divides Upper Belgravia (to the north) from Lower Belgravia (to the south).

Belgrave Mews West
Star, No. 6
Showbiz people and aristocrats who lived locally, such as Lord Lucan, who vanished in 1974, drank in this up-market pub in the 1960s alongside the West End gang leader Billy Hill, the Great Train Robber Bruce Reynolds and the lesser-known Nobby Clarke, who fell foul of the law when an associate, 'Little Caesar', was heard running from the scene of a crime shouting: 'Wait for me, Nobby Clarke of Number 18 Garven Road, Fulham'. (Clarke was once entering a shop, surprisingly, by unlocking the door with a key, when a man approached and asked him what he was doing. 'What does it look like?', replied Clarke. 'I'm the manager and I'm not locking up', to which the man replied, 'Oh, that's odd because *I'm* the manager and I'm locking up.') The jewel thief Peter Scott announced in the Star one night in May 1960 that he was going to steal the jewellery of the actress Sophia Loren, who was staying in London at the time. Posing as a journalist he found out the actress's temporary London address, staged the robbery, and seized some clothes and a briefcase containing cash and jewellery worth £200,000, a record haul for the time. After committing the theft Scott returned to the Star where he made more money selling items of Loren's lingerie than he did selling her gems.

▶ Planning of the Great Train Robbery, p. 425.

Belgrave Square
Hearts just as pure and fair, May beat in Belgrave Square, As in the lowly air, Of Seven Dials – *Iolanthe*, W. S. Gilbert (1882)

The centrepiece of the area, at the mercy of speeding traffic desperately trying to avoid Victoria, Belgrave Square was begun by Thomas Cubitt in 1825 and lined with immense stucco properties that soon became favoured by the aristocracy. With the decline of service in the twentieth century the houses became unmanageable and a number were converted into embassies, such as the Syrian at No. 8, Portuguese (No. 11) and Turkish (No. 43).

No. 5, north side
No. 5 was the home from 1935 to 1958 of Henry 'Chips' Channon, who wrote the best-known social diary of the era and whose gatherings, held in a dining room modelled on that of Amalienburg Palace in Munich, were so exclusive that when the celebrated novelist Somerset Maugham was invited he told Channon it was the apogee of his career.

Downshire House, No. 24, south-west corner
A four-storey ornate terraced house built by Henry Kendall for Thomas Read Kemp, developer of Brighton's Kemp Town, it was in the early twentieth century home to Lord Pirrie, owner of the Harland and Wolff shipyard, and was where at a dinner in 1907 he and the businessman J. Bruce Ismay planned the construction of two new ships for the cross-Atlantic run – the *Olympic* and the *Titanic*. The building is now part of the Spanish Embassy.

Eaton Square
A luxurious but grimly austere square, which is really two long parallel streets set either side of the eastern end of King's Road, it was built from 1826 to 1855 by Thomas Cubitt and named after Eaton Hall in Cheshire, the country seat of the local landowners, the Grosvenors. Past residents include the American philanthropist George

Peabody, who built well-planned estates for the working class in the nineteenth century and lived at No. 80 in the 1860s, and Raymond Chandler, the American detective writer, who stayed at No. 116 for several months in 1955, explaining to guests at lunch one day that he was just a 'beat-up pulp writer' who ranked 'slightly above a mulatto' in the USA. *Upstairs Downstairs*, the 1970s TV costume drama about life among a rich family and their servants in the early decades of the twentieth century, was set here.

No. 1, east side

Bob Boothby, the Tory peer who lived here from 1946 to 1986, threw parties attended by the gangster Ronnie Kray and the Labour politician and spy Tom Driberg where 'rough but compliant East End lads were served up like so many canapés', according to the latter's biographer, Francis Wheen. When the *Sunday Mirror* ran an article in 1965 entitled 'The Peer and the Gangster' Kray and Boothby were furious, even though the story mentioned no names, and Boothby contacted Driberg, who in turn sought help from the prime minister, Harold Wilson. Following encouragement from the latter's QC, Arnold Goodman, Boothby sued and was awarded £40,000 compensation.

► The Krays' Bethnal Green headquarters, p. 310.

Knightsbridge

The name comes from the story of two knights who, according to legend, once staged a duel on the bridge that spanned the now-culverted River Westbourne, close to the modern-day No. 58.

north side, SW1 boundary to Hyde Park Corner

Mandarin Oriental Hyde Park Hotel, No. 66

Built by Archer and Green in 1882 on the site of the 𝔉𝔬𝔵 𝔞𝔫𝔡 𝔅𝔲𝔩𝔩 pub, whose sign had been painted by Joshua Reynolds, it was originally a luxurious apartment block. After a fire in 1904 it was converted into a hotel that

in the 1920s was favoured by the silent screen film star Rudolph Valentino.

French Embassy, No. 58

A once grand property, built in 1844 by Thomas Cubitt on the site of a leper hospital, it was bought the following year by the railway entrepreneur George Hudson, MP for Sunderland and former Lord Mayor of York, who ran his companies with a disdain for corporate law, issuing more than the authorized number of shares, selling new issues at inflated prices, and misappropriating £600,000 of shareholders' money – misdeeds which went undetected for years. Although Hudson escaped arrest for debt, through the immunity of being an MP, he was forced to move to humbler accommodation in Pimlico and then left for France, where he lived in poverty. On returning to England in 1865 to stand as MP for Whitby, Hudson was challenged by his creditors and imprisoned in York Castle for the duration of the election. The house was later sold to the French government for its embassy.

south side: Hyde Park Corner to Knightsbridge Green

Spaghetti House (1970s), No. 77

Three gunmen held up nine members of staff in a much-publicized burglary at the restaurant on 28 September 1975, claiming that they represented the Black Liberation Front and demanding the release of allies from prison and use of an aircraft so that they could escape abroad. When the police discovered that the prisoners the gunmen wanted released were not actually in custody, the gunmen gave themselves up. At the subsequent trial at the Old Bailey their leader, Franklin Davies, when asked to plead, exclaimed: 'We've been pleading for five hundred years,' while an associate cried: 'This isn't a trial but a lynching party.' Davies received twenty-one years.

Harvey Nichols, Nos. 109–125

London's most glamorous store was built on the site of the 𝔚𝔬𝔯𝔩𝔡'𝔰 𝔈𝔫𝔡 𝔗𝔞𝔳𝔢𝔯𝔫, where the diarist Samuel Pepys ate a 'mess of cream, was merry and tarried late', and was

opened in 1813 as a draper's shop by
Benjamin Harvey, later merging with the
nearby Nichols store, and first being
recorded as Harvey Nichols in 1859. The
new store thrived as the neighbourhood
prospered, being rebuilt with a grand
frontage in the 1880s, and its current chic
status dates back to a 1991 takeover by
Dickson Poon, the previous owners being
Burton's.
▶ Harrods, p. 397.

Wilton Crescent
The northern approach to Belgrave Square,
it was designed by Seth Smith around a
grassed area decorated with classical embellishments.
Lord Mountbatten's address (1959–68),
No. 2
No. 2 Wilton Crescent, 1960s home of Louis
Mountbatten, Britain's post-Second World
War army chief, was the setting in May 1968
for a bizarre plan, hatched by Cecil Harmsworth King, chairman of *Mirror* group newspapers, to stage a coup to replace Harold
Wilson's ruling Labour government by a
'Government of National Emergency',
which would be run by a team of patriotic
politicians and capable businessmen, such
as himself.

King did not go to see Mountbatten
himself, but sent his assistant, Hugh
Cudlipp, also a *Mirror* executive, and the
two men discussed the liberalization of
laws on abortion and homosexuality under
Wilson and the huge number of letters
sent to the Queen complaining about the
lowering of standards. Although Mountbatten, who had recently retired as Chief of
the Defence Staff, was disillusioned with
the government, he felt uneasy about the
proposal and sought the advice of his confi-
dant, Solly Zuckerman, who, ironically, was
also Wilson's scientific adviser. Zuckerman
denounced the *Mirror* chairman for 'rank
treachery' and walked out.

As the journalist David Leigh explained in
The Wilson Plot, the coup got as far as iden-
tifying the Shetland Isles as a home for 'inter-

nees', and King used the *Mirror* to wage a
war of words against Wilson until he
himself was removed from his position that
spring by angry newspaper executives. Later
that year Mountbatten sold the property to
the Republic of Singapore who wanted the
building for its embassy.
▶ *Daily Mirror*, p. 5.

(iii) Lower Belgravia

Chester Square
According to one survey, by the early
twenty-first century Chester Square had
become the richest street in Europe, the
combined wealth of the residents, such as
the musical impresario Andrew Lloyd
Webber and the former Tory prime minister
Margaret Thatcher, being some £20 billion.
In June 1965 the film-maker David Larcher
invited the Beatles to a dinner party in his
Chester Square basement flat so that they
could meet the American beat poet Allen
Ginsberg. When John Lennon and George
Harrison arrived with their wives, they were
greeted at the front door by Ginsberg
himself, drunk, wearing nothing but a pair
of underpants on his head and a 'No
Waiting' sign dangling from his penis,
which prompted Lennon, ever the gentleman, to exclaim: 'You don't do that in front
of the birds.'
north side
Mary Shelley, author of *Frankenstein*,
moved to No. 24 in 1846, twenty-five years
after the death of her husband, the poet
Percy Bysshe Shelley. The leading Victorian
poet Matthew Arnold lived at No. 2 from
1858 to 1868.
Guy Burgess's address (1935–40), No. 38
Guy Burgess, the Foreign Office official who
famously defected to the Soviets in 1951,
moved into the top-floor flat in 1935 after
his Cambridge friend Victor Rothschild
secured him a job as an investment adviser
in the family's powerful banking firm.
Burgess hid his communist beliefs by displaying fascist tendencies (then considered
mildly fashionable) in public and decorated

his flat with splashes of patriotic red, white and blue.

east side

The Dutch government was based at No. 77, Queen Wilhelmina's London home, during the Nazi occupation of Holland in the Second World War.

south side

The British government ran the Second World War Joint Broadcasting Committee at No. 71, organizing propaganda which could be broadcast to Germany to combat the pro-Nazi bulletins aired by William Joyce, the notorious 'Lord Haw Haw'. Margaret Thatcher moved into No. 73 in 1990 after resigning as prime minister.

Lower Belgrave Street

Lord Lucan's address (1970s), No. 46
Richard John Bingham, the 7th Earl of Lucan, disappeared from society, never to be seen again in public, following the murder of the family nanny and an attack on his wife, Veronica, Lady Lucan, at 46 Lower Belgrave Street on 7 November 1974. The drama unfolded when Lady Lucan, wondering why the nanny, Sandra Rivett, who had gone downstairs to make a cup of tea, was so long in returning, went down to the darkened basement and was grabbed around the throat by a gloved hand and hit on the head by, she claimed, her husband, who admitted that he had killed the nanny mistakenly thinking it was her. Lady Lucan saved her own life, she later explained, by reasoning with the peer while she nursed her wounds, and as soon as Lucan had left the house she fled in her nightclothes and ran into the nearby Plumber's Arms pub shouting: 'Murder, there's been a murder. He's in the house . . . my children . . . he murdered the nanny', her head wet with rain and blood.

Police searched No. 46 and found Rivett's body and a weapon, a 9-in. section of piping. Later that night the peer phoned his mother, the Dowager Countess Lucan, to tell her that a 'terrible catastrophe' had taken place. Two days after the murder

police discovered that Lucan had posted letters to two friends, one of which, to the jockey Bill Shand Kydd, read: 'Dear Bill . . . the circumstantial evidence against me is strong . . . I will lie doggo for a while . . .' Speculation soon mounted that Lucan had fled Britain, even though he had left his passport behind. Over the next few years there were regular supposed sightings of the peer, but he has never officially been discovered and in his absence was found guilty of murder by a coroner's jury.

BRIXTON, SW2, SW9

A cosmopolitan but notoriously violent area, first recorded in 1067 as Brixistane ('Brixi's stone'), it was developed as a suburban retreat for City merchants following the opening of Brixton station in 1862. This saw the market gardens, meadows and brickfields replaced with streets of densely packed houses for clerks and artisans, and after the Second World War Brixton became home to a large proportion of the 492 West Indian immigrants who came to Britain on the *Empire Windrush*.

As the 1950s proceeded other West Indians, attracted by advertisements placed in Caribbean newspapers promising well-paid jobs with London Transport or the National Health Service, began to move to Britain and settle in Brixton where they had friends and relatives, who had themselves met with hostility from local landlords who had placed signs proclaiming: 'No Blacks, No Irish, No Dogs' in their windows. The arrival of black immigrants predictably led to an exodus of the established white lower middle class from their rented properties and this left the housing stock ripe for squatters, a phenomenon which increased in 1971 after the arrival of the tube eradicated Brixton's quiet village feel.

By the end of the decade what had been a dull, uneventful petit-bourgeois community, epitomized by its most famous native, John Major, who went on to be Tory

The Brixton riots

On three occasions – 1981, 1985 and 1995 – Brixton has witnessed considerable unrest as simmering local tension, mostly caused by policing methods, has boiled over into serious violence.

The first Brixton riots, 10–13 April 1981

Early in 1981 plainclothes police stop nearly 1,000 people (mostly black) in Brixton on suspicion ('sus') that they have committed or are about to commit a crime, arresting 118 people in one six-day burst. Although the police try to justify the operation by citing a 138 per cent increase in local crime between 1976 and 1980, compared with 38 per cent across London as a whole, they ruin their case by using the operation as an excuse to indulge in racial harassment that causes much resentment locally, resulting in the first Brixton riots.

● Friday 10 April 1981. Two police officers on foot patrol stop a black youth who is being chased by a group of black men along **Kellett Road**, near the Ritzy cinema. He has been stabbed in the back and is bleeding profusely, but the youth, who assumes he is being arrested, refuses to explain his injuries. As he tries to flee a crowd forms and jostles the officers, helping him take refuge in a nearby house and later putting him into a taxi. When the police stop the taxi and try to call an ambulance a crowd gathers and there are shouts of 'look they're killing him . . . we will look after our own'.

Sporadic confrontations between black youths and the police take place.

● Saturday 11 April. The morning starts off calmly, with shoppers packing the streets, but rumours spread that the injured youth has died in hospital, fuelling tension. At 3.30 p.m. officers spot a man on **Atlantic Road** placing something in his socks and, assuming it is drugs, stop him. He explains that he is a mini-cab driver and is putting his takings there for safekeeping, but police search the vehicle and a crowd gathers, deciding that the officers' actions are provocative. The man is arrested for obstruction, but when news spreads that he has been punched in the stomach violence breaks out. The police charge to clear the road and at around 6.30 p.m. petrol bombs are thrown, a police car is set alight and a police van stoned. As reinforcements arrive the crowd flees, looting shops. The police, who have no riot gear, protect themselves from attack using dustbin lids, but by 7 p.m. there is rioting throughout Brixton. At 7.40 p.m. a fire engine turntable is set alight on **Railton Road** and later a mob hijacks a No. 37 bus, robs the conductor of his takings, and drives it at police, finding the way blocked by vehicles abandoned by other rioters. The police gain the upper hand after 9 p.m., but nearly 300 officers and sixty-five civilians are injured and 145 properties damaged in the worst disturbances witnessed in London since the 1780 Gordon Riots.

prime minister in the 1990s, had begun to fracture. The first generation of children born locally to West Indian immigrants met hostility and racism in school and when they left without suitable qualifications found few jobs available. Many left home, and not wishing to move out of the area, took up places in the local squats, where their refusal to conform to the established social codes and to respect (white) authority provoked hostility from the police.

During the 1970s increasingly draconian policing led to growing social tension, which exploded in the riots of the 1980s and 1990s that left much of Brixton destroyed. More recently, the demography of Brixton has changed again as white liberals, attracted by the diverse cultural and racial mix of the area, have moved in, opening café bars, delis and chic shops near the station and frequenting night-time venues such as the Roxy cinema, Fridge, Telegraph and Brixton

● Sunday 12 April. The Metropolitan Police Commissioner blames 'outside agitators' for the violence as home secretary Willie Whitelaw tours Brixton to taunts of '*Sieg heil!*' and 'Why haven't you been here before?' At night gangs assemble and rioting erupts, although not as fierce as the previous day's, with around 122 officers injured and sixty-one police vehicles and twenty-eight private vehicles damaged or destroyed.

● Monday 13 April. There is more violence and looting at night along **Railton Road**. The prime minister, Margaret Thatcher, rubbishes suggestions that unemployment and racism lie beneath the Brixton disturbances: 'Nothing, but nothing, justifies what happened,' she says, and rejects calls for increasing investment in the area with the claim 'Money cannot buy either trust or racial harmony.' Lord Scarman, who is in charge of the inquiry into the disturbances, finds that the riots were spontaneous and that there was no premeditated plan by outside agitators to destroy the area.

The second Brixton riots, 28 September 1985 Four years later Brixton erupts again as police officers and youths, mostly black, clash following a police raid on **22 Normandy Road**, home of a black man, Michael Groce, who is wanted for illegal possession of a shotgun. During the raid Groce's mother, Cherry, is wounded by an officer, who later explains how he 'shot the first black shape I saw', and is permanently paralysed. A few hours later 300 youths

attack **Brixton police station**, at 367 Brixton Road, with bricks, stones and petrol bombs. During eight hours of mayhem the mob ransacks a Texaco petrol station and firebombs high street shops. The police charge the crowd at midnight but it is not until 2.30 a.m. that the fighting subsides, with forty-three civilians and ten police officers injured and 230 people, over half of whom are white, arrested. The following day the area is flooded with riot police to prevent further trouble.

The third Brixton riots, 13 December 1995 The third and most recent riots, supposedly organized by men with mobiles to outflank the police, occurred after the death in police custody of a young black man, Wayne Douglas, at **Brixton police station**.

On Wednesday 13 December a peaceful protest outside the station turns nasty after one public speaker describes the police as killers and an hour later scuffles break out during a march along Brixton Road. The first bottle is thrown at 8 p.m. near the **Ritzy Cinema** and during running battles between the police and masked youths shops are attacked and cars are set alight. The **Dogstar** pub (formerly the Atlantic), at 389 Coldharbour Lane, which was refurbished with a £200,000 grant and aimed at an upmarket white clientele after being burned down during the 1981 riots, is singled out for attack.

► Notting Hill race riots, pp. 448–9.

Academy, but without managing to rid the area of its lawless character.

Electric Avenue
Opened in 1888 as one of the first shopping streets lit by electricity – hence its name – with glazed canopies to protect shoppers from the weather, it was given an international reputation with the success of Eddy Grant's 1981 hit single, 'Electric Avenue', a statement of support for the riot-

torn area. It was here on Saturday 17 April 1999 that David Copeland, a lone psychopath with extremist political views, left a bomb taped to the inside of a sports bag which was spotted by street traders who called the police. The bomb exploded at 5.25 p.m., just as officers arrived, injuring fifty people. Copeland later planted two more bombs in other parts of London.

► Copeland's Brick Lane bomb, p. 284; Copeland's Soho bomb, p. 199.

Gresham Road

Brixton Mosque, No. 1, north side

Two of those who worshipped here in the 1990s were Richard Reid, the so-called 'shoe bomber', who tried to blow up an American Airlines plane in December 2001 by setting alight explosives hidden in his shoe, and Zacarias Moussaoui, the alleged Al-Qaeda supporter who was detained by the American authorities shortly before the September 11 attacks and became popularly known as the 'twentieth hijacker'.

Jebb Avenue

Brixton Prison

The Surrey House of Correction, built here in 1820, was converted to a military prison in 1882 and became Brixton Prison, for everyday criminals, in 1897. When in 1921 George Lansbury and twenty-four other Poplar Labour councillors were jailed at Brixton after refusing to cut grants to the local poor, thousands of supporters besieged the building and Lansbury addressed the crowd through the grille of his prison cell. The councillors also held meetings in Lansbury's cell and on one occasion in the governor's office.

In 1940, at the start of the Second World War, scores of Jewish refugees who had fled Hitler's Germany were held in Brixton alongside a number of fascists, detained under Regulation 18B, who taunted the Jews mercilessly, to the indifference of the prison officers. The 89-year-old Lord (Bertrand) Russell spent a week in Brixton in 1961 after he and members of the Campaign for Nuclear Disarmament refused to be bound over for a year. Six years later the Rolling Stones' Mick Jagger was incarcerated here for one night on a drugs charge, having been convicted to set an example, rather than as a just punishment for a heinous crime. *The Times* railed against his plight in a famous editorial on 1 July 1967 entitled 'Who Breaks a Butterfly on a Wheel?', a line taken from Alexander Pope's *Epistle to Dr Arbuthnot*. Jagger spent his short time in jail constructively, writing the songs '2,000

Light Years from Home' and 'We Love You' on Her Majesty's notepaper, and later told reporters that the jail was no worse than a Minnesota hotel room.

On 16 December 1980 the IRA bombmaker Gerard Tuite, the suspected armed robber Stanley Thompson and the security van hijacker extraordinaire James Moody escaped from Brixton using tools which relatives had brought in secreted in food. Thompson had gone to a lot of trouble for nothing, as he had escaped while the jury was out during his trial and when it reconvened it found him not guilty. Moody was later shot dead in the Royal Hotel, Hackney, by a mystery gunman.

► Holloway Prison, p. 338.

CHELSEA, SW3, SW10

A land of idyllic streets, luxurious houses, artists' studios and riverside walks, its name derived from either Ceoles-ige ('place of ships'), Chesil ('a gravel bank'), or Celchyth ('a chalk wharf'), Chelsea grew as a fishing village where, according to a local historian in 1829: 'salmon, trout, pike, carp, roach, dace, perch, chub, barbell, smelt, gudgeon and of flounders there are numbers in this river, the roach and dace being sold to Jews for the purpose of making false pearls'. Away from the river, which was the village's best transport route into London until the nineteenth century, Chelsea was known for its gardens of cherries, plums, peaches and apricots, becoming fashionable with the king and court during the Restoration period when the King's Road, now Chelsea's most famous street, was built as a private royal route to Westminster.

In the nineteenth century rows of brick houses were erected around its oldest road, Old Church Street, and Cheyne Walk, which became popular with artists such as James Whistler, who came to capture the light, the best in London, and take in the riverside views nearby. With the growth of London Chelsea became an exclusive residential area, thanks to its pleasant riverside setting and bijou houses, all the more desirable for being so rare in the capital, the main road, King's Road, attracting clothes shops, nightclubs and pubs patronized by a raffish, bohemian crowd.

By the 1960s Chelsea had begun to rival Soho as the hippest area in London, the so-called Chelsea Set including the photographer David Bailey, the clothes designer Mary Quant and the Rolling Stones, and in the following decade punk rock developed around the King's Road boutique run by Vivienne Westwood and Malcolm McLaren. Since then Chelsea has remained wealthy but has lost its bohemian/avant garde crowd to Camden Town, Notting Hill, Spitalfields and Brixton.

(i) north of King's Road

Cale Street

Hung On You (1960s), No. 22

A typical Chelsea boutique of the 1960s, where the Beatles were regular customers, it was run by Jane and Michael Rainey, whom Jon Savage described in his punk history, *England's Dreaming*, as 'one of the original aristocratic Chelsea stylists . . . who believed in clothes worn not in a uniformity of caste or taste but in a riotous confusion of colours, eras and nationalities'. It featured a façade that had the front end of a car stuck in the window, a technique much copied since, and moved to 430 King's Road in 1967.

► Hung On You, King's Road, p. 409.

Fulham Road

One of the longest roads in south-west London, stretching nearly 3 miles from Fulham Palace in the west to Brompton Cross at the edge of the Exhibition Road museum land in the east, its route is marked by scores of well-stocked shops and smart restaurants.

north side (SW6)

Chelsea Football Club, Fulham Road at the West London Railway

The only major English football club without a nineteenth-century history, Chelsea were formed in 1905 by the Mears Brothers, who had bought the freehold of the land on the Fulham–Chelsea boundary to build what they hoped would be the finest sporting arena in the country, but having no team to play there approached nearby Fulham Football Club to move in.

When Fulham rejected their offer the Mears decided to form a new club from scratch, considering various names, including Kensington and even London, before eventually opting for Chelsea, even though the stadium was technically in Fulham. A number of established players signed for the new club, including the highly rated 22-stone Sheffield United goalkeeper, Willie 'Fatty' Foulke, and after stern canvassing in the bar of Covent Garden's Tavistock Hotel, the Mears brothers scrambled enough votes to join the newly extended Football League at the start of the 1905–6 season, making Chelsea the only team ever to enter the League without having kicked a ball.

Archibald Leitch built an impressive 5,000-seater grandstand for the new ground, Stamford Bridge, using earth excavated during the construction of the Piccadilly Line for the banking, and it was considered so good that it was used for the FA Cup Final until Wembley was built. In November 1945 Stamford Bridge was the setting for one of the strangest football matches ever seen in Britain when Chelsea played the touring Moscow Dynamos team at a time when games between English and European clubs were a rarity. Crowds began arriving soon after breakfast and the ground had to be shut an hour before the afternoon kick-off, with perhaps 100,000 inside, many having climbed over walls and gates to gain entrance. Before the kick-off each Soviet player, their shirts emblazoned with an ornate letter 'D', came on the field bearing a bunch of flowers, but though the press had dismissed Moscow Dynamos as enthusiastic amateurs, they were considerably fitter than the Londoners, if naïve tactically, and drew 3–3.

Chelsea won the League Championship for the only time in 1955 and in 1972 recorded what is still the highest ever aggregate total in European cup football, beating Luxembourg's Jeunesse Hautcharage in the European Cup Winners' Cup 21–0 over two games, the scorelines helped by the fact that one of the Jeunesse players wore glasses and another had only one arm. Soon after though, the Chelsea board made the first of several ill-considered decisions, including the building of a new £2 million stand, which crippled the club financially, leading to a decline that culminated in relegation from the First Division in 1975.
In the early eighties David Mears sold his holding to the property speculators Marler Estates, thus ending the family's seventy-five-year connection with the club, and further relegation ensued before revival under Ruud Gullit, Gianluca Vialli and Claudio Ranieri saw Chelsea begin their second most successful spell with three Cup Final appearances towards the end of the millennium and the winning of the European Cup Winners' Cup in 1998.

➤ Arsenal Football Club, p. 331.

south side: Brompton Road to Sydney Street
Habitat, No. 77
Terence Conran opened the first Habitat store at No. 77 on 11 May 1964 – he chose the name by going through the thesaurus to find alternative words for 'house' – to sell high-quality continental household wares, including Italian furniture, kitchen units made from Swedish pine, and office chairs from Finland, in a store hung with signs urging customers: 'Don't just sit there . . . sit there ergonomically'. Conran was warned that as the shop was not located on a major bus route it would never succeed, but Habitat, with its bright, simple and clean look, was soon lauded in the style magazines as a welcome reaction against 1950s austerity, and Conran's ideas revolutionized

domestic design. The store moved to the renovated Michelin Building nearby in November 1987.
Michelin Building, No. 81, south side
A memorable art deco building, designed by François Espinasse from 1909 to 1911 for the Michelin tyre company, its reinforced concrete walls, then rarely found, are covered in white tiles coloured with motifs relating the early story of automobiles and images of Bibendum, the Michelin Man. It now contains shops, offices and Terence Conran's Bibendum restaurant.

(ii) King's Road

King's Road
One of London's most glamorous and popular routes, King's Road, which cuts through the heart of Chelsea, was synonymous with what *Time* magazine described in the 1960s as 'Swinging London' when the street was renowned for its clothes shops, nightclubs and cafés. It was built in the late seventeenth century as a private road between Hampton Court and Westminster for Charles II, at a time when there was no thoroughfare linking Chelsea and central London, and until 1830, only those who had a pass stamped 'The King's Private Roads' could use it.

Once King's Road had opened to the public appealing houses were built and shops sprang up, and by the early twentieth century King's Road had become a major London thoroughfare. But it was not until 1955, when Mary Quant opened Bazaar, the country's first boutique, at No. 138a, that King's Road began to be associated with the fashion industry. Bazaar was soon joined by other stores selling outrageous clothes, and by the mid-1960s King's Road had become the stamping ground for London's hippest crowd – Terence Stamp, Vidal Sassoon, David Hemmings, Michael Caine, Twiggy, David Bailey – making their way from the Chelsea Potter pub to Le Rêve restaurant or from the Markham Arms to the Dell' Aretusa nightclub, while at weekends crowds of hippies, beatniks and freaks would stroll along the road, visiting Gandalf's Garden bric-a-brac shop or the I Was Lord Kitchener's Valet clothes store looking for Regency jackets, tie-dye shirts and boots.

The following decade the hedonism of the late sixties gave way to a post-party malaise, but at No. 430 Vivienne Westwood and Malcolm McLaren opened their Let It Rock boutique, aka Sex, aka Seditionaries, where not only the next generation's outrageous fashion was sold but its most notorious rock band, the Sex Pistols, was formed. In the early 1980s King's Road remained a fashion parade ground, with Mohican-haired punks, who would occasionally pose for tourists' cameras, lining the route, but later that decade many of the independent shops were driven out by high rents and were replaced by bars, restaurants and chain stores. Though King's Road remains a magnet for tourists and shoppers and has retained its energy and excitement into the twenty-first century, it has been upstaged as a bastion of the unusual by Camden Town and Portobello Road.

north side: Chelsea Creek to Sloane Square
Granny Takes A Trip (1960s), No. 488
One of the best-known King's Road boutiques, Granny Takes A Trip featured blackened windows, a car emerging from the front wall, a mural painted by Mickey Finn, who later joined Tyrannosaurus Rex, and an upstairs flat occupied by the writer Salman Rushdie. It was run by Nigel Waymouth, one of the pioneers of disposable clothing, who sold kaftans, velvet trousers and satin jackets in a suffocating atmosphere of incense and patchouli oil to rock stars such as Mick Jagger, Keith Richards, Syd Barrett and Jimi Hendrix, who stocked up on most of his flamboyant wardrobe here in October 1966.

World's End, No. 430
British punk rock was born in the 1970s in the outrageous clothes shop run by Vivienne Westwood and Malcolm McLaren at 430 King's Road, first used for selling clothes in 1967, when Michael Rainey moved his

Hung On You boutique from Cale Street here. Two years later it was taken over by Trevor Miles and Tommy Roberts, who reopened it as a fifties Hollywood pastiche, Mr Freedom, and in 1971 Malcolm McLaren, an ex-film student, and his partner, Vivienne Westwood, moved into the empty flat above the shop. By November they had taken over the premises, renaming it Let It Rock, in homage to Teddy Boy culture, and had begun selling period records, winkle-picker shoes and drape jackets designed by Westwood, attracting a clientele of teddy boys and the occasional rock star – David Bowie, Roxy Music, Marc Bolan – looking for chic revivalist gear. In the spring of 1972 McLaren and Westwood spotted the slogan 'Too Fast To Live Too Young To Die' on a biker's jacket and changed the shop's name accordingly, attracting new customers such as the film director Ken Russell, who asked Westwood and McLaren to provide the clothes for his film *Mahler*, some of the costumes for which – leather, swastikas, fishnet tights – exhibited ideas later manifest in punk fashion. In April 1974 they refurbished the interior again, this time to look like a womb, gave the store a new name, Sex, 'specialists in rubberwear, glamour-wear and stagewear', and decorated it with slogans such as the French philosopher Rousseau's 'Craft must have clothes but Truth loves to go naked'.

After McLaren visited New York also in 1974 he began selling torn T-shirts and clothes decorated with safety-pins and nurturing ideas for forming an unmusical rock band, with a singer looking like Hitler 'talking about his mum in incestuous phrases'. McLaren recruited the fledgling group members from a bunch of youths, all called John, who hung out at the shop and included John Wardle (later Jah Wobble, bass player extraordinaire and well-known William Blake promoter), John Beverly (later Sid Vicious), who occasionally helped out in the store wearing a padlock over his crotch, and John Lydon (aka Johnny Rotten), who wore a Pink Floyd T-shirt with the words 'I hate' scrawled over the group's logo. McLaren was so impressed with Lydon's surly attitude that he suggested the latter join his new band, which became the Sex Pistols, as singer.

In 1976 Sex was renamed Seditionaries, its brilliant white decor setting off provocative photos of the Second World War bombing of Dresden and featuring a hole punched in the ceiling to resemble bomb damage, designed by Ben Kelly, who later created Manchester's Hacienda club and Dry Bar. But the following year, when the Pistols brought the new King's Road look to national recognition, other designers took up punk fashion and 430 King's Road became one of many places, rather than the only place, to buy such clothes. The store was reborn in the 1980s as the avant-garde clothes store World's End, part of what had by then become the Vivienne Westwood empire, and is identifiable by its backward-moving clock above the awning.

Bluebird Garages, No. 350
Europe's largest motor garage for much of the twentieth century, built by Robert Sharp for the Bluebird company in 1924 in reinforced concrete clad in white faience, it was converted by Terence Conran into a shopping centre in the mid-1990s.

Registry Office, No. 250
A venue for celebrity weddings until 1968, it was where the playwright John Osborne married Mary Ure, who had starred in his groundbreaking play *Look Back in Anger*, in 1956, telling reporters: 'We both have the strongest possible objection to marrying in church – we loathe all clergymen.'

The Pheasantry, No. 152
A stylish café bar-cum-nightclub, built into a flamboyantly designed but much-altered 1769 property, the Pheasantry took its name from the pheasants the owner Samuel Baker sold here from 1864 to 1878. In 1916 the Russian ballet dancer Princess Serafina Astafieva, great-niece of Leo Tolstoy, converted it into a dancing academy, her students later including Alicia Markova and Margot Fonteyn, and in 1932 the basement

became the Pheasantry club, favoured by actors and artists. When the club closed the building was converted into luxury apartments whose tenants included Martin Sharp, the illustrator who co-edited the underground magazine *Oz* and wrote the lyrics to Cream's 'Tales of Brave Ulysses', the epitome of the psychedelic rock sound that encapsulated the era, and Eric Clapton, then Cream's guitarist. (On one occasion Clapton narrowly escaped arrest on drugs charges by fleeing out of the back of the building as Norman Pilcher, a detective who had a talent for arresting rock stars, buzzed the intercom, shouted 'postman, special delivery' and burst in.) When the building was threatened with demolition in 1969 all manner of fanciful tales were told about the Pheasantry's history, in a desperate bid to save the property, including one that claimed Nell Gwynn, Charles II's mistress, had lived here, and after protracted negotiations it was saved.

Bazaar (1950s, 1960s), No. 138a
Mary Quant opened King's Road's first boutique here in 1955 – a 'tough time when girls wore white gloves', according to the writer Angela Carter – allowing customers the hitherto unknown pleasure of wandering at will through the shop without being harangued by tape measure-wielding assistants. Bazaar's success inspired Quant to design her own clothes, what she termed, 'The Look', which was epitomized by the floppy hat, skinny-rib sweater and miniskirt with white boots and was worn by middle-class girls who refused to conform to their parents' expectations and came to be known semi-disparagingly as 'dolly birds'. In the basement below the shop was a restaurant run by Quant's husband, Alexander Plunkett-Greene, who had once appeared at Quaglino's, the fashionable St James's restaurant, in a suit with no shirt and a row of buttons painted on his chest.
➤ Carnaby Street, p. 189.

No. 120
Thomas Crapper, royal plumber, ran his toilet production company at No. 120 from

1907 to 1966, advertising his goods with the slogan 'a certain flush with every pull'.

Peter Jones

See Sloane Square.

south side: Sloane Square to Chelsea Creek

Former Duke of York's Headquarters

Built in a powerful classical style by John Sanders in 1801 to 1803 on the site of Chelsea House, the eighteenth-century residence of the Cadogans, the building, named after George III's second son, was originally the Royal Military Asylum school, where soldiers' orphans were educated, and from 1909 until the end of the twentieth century was used by the Territorial Army. Roger Bannister and Christopher Chattaway practised for what became Bannister's record-breaking four-minute mile race in the grounds in the early 1950s. In 2000 the site was sold for £66 million to be redeveloped for shops, offices and housing.

British Union of Fascists headquarters / Black House (1933–5), west junction King's Road / Cheltenham Terrace

Oswald Mosley, leader of the British Union of Fascists, converted what had been the Whitelands Teacher Training College into the party's new headquarters, Black House, named after the colour of the shirts its members wore, in 1933, decorating the exterior of the building with posters proclaiming 'For King and Country' and equipping it inside with a gym for boxing and judo, a mess, canteen, social centre, dormitories and cellars where miscreants could be disciplined. Mosley spent a tenth of his personal fortune on Black House, supplemented by donations from the Italian dictator, Benito Mussolini, and for three years the building resounded to the noise of heel-clicking and arm-swishing (Blackshirts would salute even when answering the phone).

Meanwhile, the party's anti-Bolshevik, anti-organized labour stance won support from influential establishment figures such as Lord Rothermere, owner of the *Daily Mail*, who in an article on 8 January 1934

entitled 'Hurrah for the Blackshirts', claimed that Mosley would bring Britain 'up to date, [for] at these next vital elections Britain's survival as a great power will depend on the existence of a well-organized party of the Right ready to take over responsibility for national affairs with the same direct purpose and energy of method as Mussolini and Hitler have displayed'. But Rothermere and many others withdrew their support after violence marred a BUF rally at Kensington Olympia on 7 June 1934 – Mosley, predictably, blamed Jewish hecklers – and by 1935 the British Union of Fascists' overt anti-Semitism had led to a decline in donations, forcing Mosley to sell the lease of the building. It was subsequently pulled down to make way for flats.

▶ The Battle of Cable Street, p. 279.

Chelsea Drug Store (1960s), No. 49

A sprawling 1960s shopping centre with a restaurant, disco and boutiques, modelled on Le Drugstore in Paris, it was mentioned in the Rolling Stones' 1969 song 'You Can't Always Get What You Want' and its existence so annoyed the residents of nearby Royal Avenue that they urged the council to protect them from 'rubbish, noise and hippies'. The venture closed in the 1970s and the premises are now a branch of McDonald's.

▶ Mick Jagger in Cheyne Walk, p. 418.

I Was Lord Kitchener's Valet (1960s), No. 65

One of the most famous 1960s King's Road boutiques, its quasi-military touches inspired a number of rock groups, including the Beatles, who personified the look on the sleeve of their 1967 *Sergeant Pepper's Lonely Hearts Club Band* album.

Chelsea Potter, Nos. 117–119

A pub patronized in the 1960s by celebrities such as the actors Michael Caine and Terence Stamp, its premises were raided in 1968 by police looking for the Great Train Robber Bruce Reynolds, who, having returned to the UK after being on the run for five years, phoned an associate and arranged to meet at the Chelsea Potter that night. The police didn't realize that 'Chelsea

Potter' was code for Sloane Square tube station and the raid proved fruitless.
► The planning of the Great Train Robbery, p. 425.

Apple Tailoring (1960s), No. 161
The less famous of the two Apple boutiques opened here on 23 May 1968, selling what the company called civil and theatrical clothes, and closed soon after *without* the stock being given away, unlike at the better-known store at 94 Baker Street.
► Apple, Baker Street, p. 149.

Chelsea Old Town Hall, Nos. 165–179, King's Road at Chelsea Manor Street
Judy Garland married her fifth husband, Mickey Deans, at the Registry Office in Chelsea Old Town Hall on 15 March 1969. Only fifty or so of the hundreds of invited guests turned up and Garland argued with reporters outside the building after the ceremony. A few months later she was dead from an accidental overdose of sleeping tablets.

No. 181
Chelsea Arts Club was founded at No. 181 in March 1891, its first secretary being the painter James McNeill Whistler, by then in his late fifties, who always dressed in full-length frock coat with white duck trousers, even in summer. A regular patron was the painter Philip Wilson Steer, who would go to the club every night in mortal dread of catching a cold, close all the doors and windows, play chess and walk home carrying a box of fifty cigarettes. Steer even refused to attend formal dinners because of the supposed risks involved in changing into evening dress. The club moved to 143 Old Church Street in 1902.

World's End Estate
An extensive housing estate of ungainly brick-clad tower blocks to the east of Edith Grove, it is named after the World's End pub at 459 King's Road, and was built from 1966 to 1978 on the site of a number of traditional streets, thereby spoiling the architectural consistency of the area. Though billed as a symbol of progress at the time, World's End has become a sink estate, plagued by crime and squalor.

(iii) Chelsea village

Between King's Road and the Thames lies one of the most visually splendid quarters of the capital, a village of exquisite streets, gaily painted cottages and elegant houses, closer in spirit to a Mediterranean town than to suburban London. Before the growth of the capital it was isolated enough to give rise to its own bohemian community, its principal characters being, at various times, the early-nineteenth-century publisher and poet Leigh Hunt, who described how the 'air of the neighbouring river is so refreshing', the Victorian philosopher Thomas Carlyle, who complained about the absence of hills, the late-nineteenth-century artist James Whistler and the writer and wit Oscar Wilde. Despite being subsumed into the rest of Chelsea, the village has retained its exclusivity, attracting twentieth-century residents such as the actors Judy Garland, Laurence Olivier and Vivien Leigh and the writers Antonia White and Anita Brookner.

Cheyne Row
A short turning built in 1708, known chiefly for Carlyle's House at No. 24 and used in the filming of Jules Verne's *Around the World in Eighty Days*, which starred David Niven, in the summer of 1955.

Carlyle's House, No. 24
One of few writers' houses in London to have been preserved as a museum, it was home from 1834 to 1881 to Thomas Carlyle, historian, philosopher and critic, who originally meant to stay only for a year, thought Chelsea 'very dirty and confused in some places' and spent much of his time wandering around the streets, often with the poet Alfred Lord Tennyson, denouncing the government and complaining about the 'acrid putrescence' of the neighbouring houses and the 'black jumble' of the suburbs. Working in the attic, which was soundproofed from distracting neighbour-

hood noise, Carlyle wrote his renowned history of the French Revolution. The manuscript was used by John Stuart Mill's maid to light the fire after he had lent it to the philosopher. Having spent a number of years researching and writing the work, Carlyle no longer had much interest in the subject, but after Mill gave him £200 for the inconvenience he rewrote it. Carlyle died here in 1881 and the house was converted into a museum in 1896, preserving many original furnishings and mementoes, including a piano on which Chopin once played.

► Keats House, p. 364.

Glebe Place

A delightful dog-leg-shaped street built on land owned by the Chelsea Rectory and beloved of artists and writers, it contains an eclectic mixture of follies (No. 50), gingerbread cottages and creeper-covered houses, in one of which in 1991 the householder created a roof garden containing minarets resembling those of the Brighton Royal Pavilion, 800 potted plants and speakers which played bird songs. At No. 51 is White Cottage, believed to be the oldest building in Chelsea, which according to local lore may have been Henry VIII's hunting lodge, and at No. 49 Charles Rennie Mackintosh, the celebrated Scottish architect, was resident during the First World War, having moved from Suffolk, where he had been accused of being a German spy. At No. 35 is Philip Webb's best-preserved London house, built in the Arts and Crafts style in 1868 to 1871 for the artist George Boyce, the interior of which was used in the film *Withnail and I* as the home of Withnail's lascivious gay uncle, Monty.

Oakley Street

Oakley Street was the first London street to be planted with trees, thanks to the eccentric late-nineteenth-century barrister-architect-scientist Dr John Samuel Phené, who lived at No. 2 in the so-called 𝕲𝖎𝖓𝖌𝖊𝖗=𝖇𝖗𝖊𝖆𝖉 𝕮𝖆𝖘𝖙𝖑𝖊, a five-floor house decorated with rococo effects and baroque carvings

based on the designs of the family's ancestral home in the Loire valley, which contained a dining room filled with models of ancient American and Asian temples. Because Phené never completed work on the building, or ever lived in the property, preferring to stay at 32 Oakley Street, opposite, the legend arose that it was a memorial to his bride-to-be, who had died on their wedding day, causing him to abandon England and travel the world voraciously collecting *objets d'art* and interesting junk. Phené did however spend much time in the garden, which he filled with monstrous classical statues and ornaments, and a mortuary for dead cats. He uncovered parts of an underground passage which connected the property with the medieval riverside mansion of 𝕾𝖍𝖗𝖊𝖜𝖘𝖇𝖚𝖗𝖞 𝕳𝖔𝖚𝖘𝖊 on Cheyne Walk and with Henry VIII's nearby manor house (p. 418). Phené's property was demolished in 1917 and the site is now occupied by a large Arts-and-Crafts house whose ground floor displays Charles Rennie Mackintosh-style touches.

Oakley Street has also been home to Jane Wilde, mother of Oscar, an Irish patriot who wrote poems under the pseudonym Speranza, who lived at No. 87, where Wilde took refuge during his trial at the Old Bailey in 1895; Robert F. Scott, the ill-fated polar explorer (No. 5, 1905–8); and the reggae musician Bob Marley (No. 42 in 1977).

Old Church Street

A long narrow road, it is the oldest in the area and the only one to run from the river as far north as Fulham Road.

John Betjeman's address (1917–24), No. 53, west side

The poet moved from his beloved Highgate to Chelsea when he was eleven, in 1917, later describing No. 53 as being in Chelsea's 'slummy end' in his autobiographical work of 1960, *Summoned by Bells*.

Sound Techniques Ltd (1960s, 1970s),
No. 46a, east side
Now private apartments, in the 1960s the
building contained one of London's major
recording studios, Sound Techniques – 'a
big sort of greenhouse place [where] the
coffee machine didn't always work, and you
had to watch out for the wires and things on
the floor', according to Jethro Tull's Ian
Anderson. The studios were used by the
vanguard of the British rock underground,
such as AMM whose *Music for a Continuous
Performance*, recorded here in June 1966,
featured Cornelius Cardew playing piano,
cello and transistor radio. Others who
recorded here include Pink Floyd, who cut
their first two singles, 'Arnold Layne' and
'See Emily Play', at Sound Techniques in
1967; Tyrannosaurus Rex, featuring Marc
Bolan; the Incredible String Band; and Nick
Drake, whose three esoteric albums of loneliness and isolation – *Five Leaves Left* (1969),
Bryter Later (1970) and *Pink Moon* (1972) –
are now among the most fêted works from
the era.
➤ Abbey Road studios, p. 367.

Radnor Walk
Quorum (1960s), No. 52
Ossie Clark, the clothes designer extraordinaire, who, according to Vivienne
Westwood's assistant, Bella Freud, could
cut into cloth without a pattern, opened a
boutique at No. 5 with Alice Pollock in 1965
after returning to London from America.
His op art-influenced hot pants, maxi coats,
snakeskin trousers and jackets attracted
custom from Raquel Welch, Elizabeth
Taylor, Twiggy, and the Rolling Stones
Mick Jagger and Brian Jones. Clark sold
the shop in 1968.

Royal Avenue
The approach to Wren's Royal Hospital
from King's Road was intended to be part of
a mile-and-a-half processional walk from
Kensington Palace, but only 100 yards of the
route was built.

Royal Hospital Road
Chelsea Royal Hospital, Royal Hospital
Road at West Road
One of Christopher Wren's greatest achievements, the hospital, founded by Charles II,
was built from 1682 to 1694 as a home for
discharged soldiers, in the style of Paris's
L'Hôtel Royal des Invalides, with shallow
steps to make walking easier for elderly
limbs and a colonnade so that the men
could enjoy the fresh air but keep dry. It is
still used as an almshouse for around 450
retired soldiers – the red-coated Chelsea
Pensioners – who give up their pension
when they join in exchange for free board,
lodging and clothing, and who can be
publicly seen on alternate weekends at the
Chelsea football ground. Every June, on
Oak Apple Day, Charles II's statue in the
grounds is decorated with oak branches,
while the Pensioners parade in uniforms
covered in oak leaves before saying three
cheers for their founder. The National Army
Museum is located in the grounds, and to
the east, in Ranelagh Gardens, the annual
Chelsea Flower Show has taken place since
1913.
➤ Wren's Royal Naval Hospital, Greenwich,
p. 391.

Swan Walk
Chelsea Physic Garden
The second oldest garden in England,
created in 1673 by the Society of Apothecaries for the study of plants used in medicine, it is home to England's first cedar trees
as well as the largest olive tree and the oldest
rock garden in the country, the latter
created from blocks of lava brought back
from Iceland in 1772. When the gardens ran
short of funds in the 1730s Hans Sloane, the
physician and botanist whose collection
later formed the basis of the British
Museum's first exhibits, and who had
studied botany here, stepped in with a
rescue plan and presented the Physic
Garden to the Apothecaries Society on
condition that fifty plants be given to the
Royal Society every year.

Tite Street

One of Chelsea's most famous streets, many of its houses built with studios for artists, it took its name from William Tite MP, the member of the Metropolitan Board of Works responsible for building Chelsea Embankment in the 1870s, and at the end of the nineteenth century briefly rivalled Cheyne Walk as the most fashionable address in Chelsea.

west side: Chelsea Embankment to Tedworth Square

Oscar Wilde's address (1881), No. 44
When the architect E. W. Godwin submitted to the Board of Works a design for remodelling the house which Oscar Wilde shared with the artist Frank Miles, a friend from Oxford who introduced various Japanese flowers to England, they took one look at the plans and exclaimed in horror: 'It's worse than Whistler's [the adjacent No. 46, Tower House]!', before turning it down. Godwin, obliged to rethink his ideas, moaned about 'retired farmers and cheesemongers [sitting] in judgement on my work', but complied with their request, toning down some of the effects but producing a shockingly asymmetrical façade with a great expanse of brick and unusual-shaped balconies.

Oscar Wilde's address (1884–95), No. 34
Wilde bought the property (then No. 16) in 1884 when he married Constance Lloyd, at the time he was coming into public recognition as a self-styled 'Professor of Aesthetics', wit and art critic, and hired the architect E. W. Godwin to redesign the house with much use of white: white for the front door, hall and stairs, 'different shades of white', according to Wilde, for the dining room; buttercup yellow for the drawing room walls; and blue with painted dragons and peacock feathers for the ceiling.

Wilde did his writing at a desk that had once belonged to the Scottish philosopher and long-term Chelsea resident Thomas Carlyle, in a room painted not white, but primrose, there producing the fairy tale *The Happy Prince* (1888), the novel *The Picture of Dorian Gray* (1891), and the plays *Lady Windermere's Fan* (1892), *A Woman of No Importance* (1893), *An Ideal Husband* (1895) and *The Importance of Being Earnest* (also 1895). After Wilde was convicted of gross indecency in 1895 (ironically, the judge lived only a few doors away) looters broke in and stole his possessions, and a little while later the house and its contents were sold for a pittance to help pay off court costs.

► Oscar Wilde's downfall, p. 167.

(iv) Cheyne Walk

Cheyne Walk

A riverside street of considerable historical importance and period charm, lined with the finest Jacobean and Queen Anne properties, it was named after the Cheyne family, lords of the Chelsea manor in the late seventeenth century, and was washed every day by the high tide until the embankment was built in the late nineteenth century. Because of its sweeping views and, for London, excellent clear light, Cheyne Walk has attracted several painters, including J. M. W. Turner and James Whistler. Other well-known residents have included George Eliot, the composer Ralph Vaughan Williams, the Rolling Stones Keith Richards and Mick Jagger, and more recently the celebrity cook Jane Asher and the footballer George Best.

north side: Cremorne Road to Chelsea Embankment

J. M. W. Turner's address (1846–52), No. 119
The artist J. M. W. Turner moved to the property, then 6 Davis Place, in 1846, when he was in his seventies. He spent the last six years of his life here living incognito as 'Mr Booth' (locals thought he was a retired admiral) to avoid the public glare and built a gallery on the roof of the cottage so that he could watch the sunsets. Turner's last words on his deathbed on 19 December 1851 were 'The sun is God', which some have interpreted as the more devout 'the Son is God'. The young Ian Fleming moved here with his

mother in 1923, when he was fifteen, and was still living here in his late twenties, by which time he had become a stockbroker, as it was a convenient *pied à terre* for a man about town.

▶ William Hogarth in Leicester Square, p. 102.

Hilaire Belloc's address (1900–1905), No. 104

The French-born essayist, who became a British citizen two years after moving here, had the area's first telephone installed, its number being KEN(sington) 1724. He left Cheyne Walk after being elected Liberal MP for Salford at the 1906 general election.

No. 101

Home from 1863 to 1866 of the American-born painter James Whistler – whom the art historian James Laver claimed 'no educated person can walk along the bank of the Thames at nightfall without thinking of' – who specialized in painting the new buildings and structures of the industrialized city, such as its wharves and warehouses. Here, Whistler painted *Nocturne: Blue and Silver – Cremorne Lights* (1872), a view from Battersea Bridge of the Battersea factories and Chelsea's **Cremorne Pleasure Gardens**, and *Nocturne in Black and Gold: The Falling Rocket* (1875), inspired by the fireworks in the Pleasure Gardens, which led John Ruskin, the great art critic who felt that art ought to have a moral message, to comment that he 'never expected to hear a coxcomb ask 200 guineas for flinging a pot of paint in the public's face'. Whistler sued for libel and won a farthing's damages but was made bankrupt on account of the huge legal costs.

Lindsey House, Nos. 96–100

Nos. 96–100 form Lindsey House, the only remaining seventeenth-century aristocratic property in Chelsea, built in 1674 by the 3rd Earl of Lindsey, Lord Chamberlain to Charles II, on the site of a farmhouse that was once part of Thomas More's estate and later home to Count Zinzendorf, leader of the Moravian church. It is now divided into separate properties.

No. 100

Home of Robert Bourne, the property developer who was involved in the long-term plans for the Millennium Dome site and donated money to the Conservative Party and the Labour Party in the 1990s.

No. 98

From 1808 to 1825 No. 98 was occupied by the engineer Marc Brunel, who was responsible for the first tunnel under the Thames (now part of the East London Line), and his son, Isambard Kingdom Brunel, who went on to become chief engineer for the Great Western Railway and design Paddington station.

James Whistler's address (1866–79) / Paul Channon's address (1970s), No. 96

It was at No. 96 that the American-born painter James Whistler painted the famous picture of his mother that hangs in the Louvre and worked on a portrait of the writer Thomas Carlyle, who sat for the artist while he painted the face but was replaced by someone with the same figure wearing the same clothes for the rest of the portrait.

In the 1970s No. 96 was home to the millionaire Tory MP Paul Channon and was where members of the British government, including Willie Whitelaw, the Northern Ireland secretary, secretly met members of the IRA on 7 July 1972 at a time when the government were regularly insisting in the media that ministers would 'never talk to terrorists'.

The Irish delegation comprised the two best-known nationalists of modern times, Martin McGuinness, who was then twenty-two and on the run from the authorities and who only agreed to participate if his safety could be guaranteed, and Gerry Adams, who was released from prison to take part. Their journey from Ulster to England would have graced a spy film. They and four others met in Londonderry, were transported in a blacked-out van to a field, from where a helicopter took them to Aldergrove airport, near Belfast. When the party stepped off the helicopter a British soldier saluted them, though it is not clear whether he was acknowledging their status in the Republican movement or had mistaken them for military personnel. In Belfast they transferred to an RAF plane, which landed in a military field, probably Northolt, and was met by a fleet of limousines carrying members of the Special Branch, from where the delegation was transported to Cheyne Walk.

Around the negotiating table the Irish delegates listed their demands: that the British government recognize the right of Irish self-determination, that the troops be withdrawn by 1 January 1975, and that all prisoners be granted an amnesty, all of which were rejected. Whitelaw later recalled in his memoirs that the meeting was a 'non-event. The IRA leaders simply made impossible demands which I told them the British government would never concede.'

Elizabeth Gaskell's birthplace (1810), No. 93

A month after the novelist was born here as Elizabeth Stevenson on 29 September 1810, her mother died and she was sent to an aunt in Knutsford, Cheshire, where she grew up.

Belle Vue House, No. 92

Built in 1771 and possibly designed by Robert Adam for John Hatchett, a cabinet maker, No. 92 was home in the 1960s to the Conservative MP Patrick Wall, who founded the right-wing 92 Committee pressure group at a dinner party here in 1964 to 'keep the Conservative Party conservative'. When Margaret Thatcher won the 1979 general election six of its members were made ministers, including, most famously, Norman Tebbitt. In the 1990s the property became home, ironically, to the 'champagne socialists' the Folletts: Ken, the blockbuster novelist, and Barbara, who was responsible in the mid-1990s for the sartorial make-over of several Labour Party MPs, particularly Robin Cook, whom she encouraged to dress in 'earth colours', and who herself was elected a Labour MP in 1997.

Thomas More's manor house, Cheyne Walk at Danvers Street, west side

Life in the manor house of Thomas More, Speaker of the House of Commons, who built a 34-acre estate here in 1523, was run with the strictest discipline. The sexes were segregated, all members of the household were obliged to attend prayers, and heretics were tied to trees and flogged. In 1529, following the dismissal of Cardinal Wolsey, More became Lord Chancellor, but he resigned three years later when Henry declared himself, rather than the Pope, head of the English Church. When More was committed to the Tower in 1534 for incurring the wrath of the King, his estates were confiscated.

Crosby Hall, Cheyne Walk at Danvers Street, west side

The hall, built from 1466 to 1475, originally stood near Bishopsgate in the City, where it was home to Richard III before he became king, and later to Thomas More, the ill-fated sixteenth-century Lord Chancellor (see above). It was moved here in 1907 to be used as a hostel for the British Federation of University Women, and changed hands in the 1990s, when it was refurbished according to Tudor specifications.

Chelsea Old Church (All Saints), Cheyne Walk at Old Church Street

> The clock of Chelsea Old Church ground out grudgingly the hour of ten – *Murphy*, Samuel Beckett (1938)

The oldest building in the area, Chelsea Old Church is believed to have Saxon origins dating back to 789, although the first documentary evidence comes from the mid twelfth century. A number of writers have had associations with the church, particularly Thomas More who attended services in the sixteenth century, sang in the choir, and is commemorated with a huge seated statue outside the building, a Thomas More chapel in which he worshipped and a tomb designed by him. The church was heavily bombed in the Second World War, but the disaster, ironically, helped to preserve its history, as ancient monuments were found in the rubble and restored.

► Church of the Good Shepherd, p. 341.

Carlyle Mansions, Cheyne Walk at Lawrence Street, east side

Three writers – Henry James, T. S. Eliot and Ian Fleming – had flats in this luxury block overlooking the river early in the twentieth century. James, who moved into No. 21 in January 1913, found 'this Chelsea perch . . . just the thing for me'. A hypochondriac, he once compared constipation to terminal cancer, which he never contracted, and eventually collapsed with a stroke, gasping: 'it's the beast in the jungle, and it's sprung'. T. S. Eliot lived in monastic austerity, with a bare light bulb and a crucifix over the bed, the latter his sole concession to decoration, and Ian Fleming had a flat two floors above Eliot in the early 1950s, around the time that he was planning his first Bond novel, *Casino Royale*, which he wrote in Jamaica in 1952.

The King's Head and Eight Bells, No. 50

Now a restaurant, the pub was popular with the 1930s Chelsea in-crowd, what biographer Humphrey Carpenter dubbed the 'Brideshead Generation', and a favourite of Dylan Thomas who, one night here in 1934, explained to the novelist Pamela Hansford Johnson that his criteria for being a poet were drinking, being tubercular and being fat. The former pub is George Smiley's local in John le Carré's spy books.

Mick Jagger's address (1967–78), No. 48

A Queen Anne town house built in 1711, it was bought for £40,000 in 1967 by the Rolling Stones singer, who moved in with Marianne Faithfull and was shortly afterwards visited by a young Richard Branson, then editor of *Student* magazine, for an interview. Neither party had much to say, and when Branson asked Jagger: 'Do you like giving interviews?', he simply replied: 'No.' Branson then asked him: 'Why did you ask *Student* to interview you?' and the singer responded: 'I don't know. I've got no idea. I don't usually give interviews. I mean hardly ever.' Police found Jagger and Faithfull in possession of a quarter-ounce of cannabis when they raided the house in

May 1969 and the courts fined Jagger £200 but cleared Faithfull.

Henry VIII's manor house, Nos. 19–26

In 1536 Henry VIII built a manor house on the site and made himself Lord of the Manor of Chelsea. His wish was that the house should pass to his queen, Jane Seymour, but she died in 1537, nine days after bearing him a male heir (the future Edward VI). Six years later he gave the house to Catherine Parr, his sixth wife, as a wedding present. Sir Hans Sloane, who owned much of Chelsea in the early eighteenth century, bought the property in 1712 to house his vast array of antiquities and curios, which after his 1782 death formed the bulk of the British Museum's first collection. Although the house was demolished in the 1780s, traces of the brickwork and gardens remain at the end of the alleyway under the arch at No. 24, in what for London is a remarkably peaceful and verdant setting.

Don Saltero's, No. 18

John Salter, valet to Sir Hans Sloane, the founder of the British Museum, opened a coffee house, **Don Saltero's**, on Lawrence Street in 1695 and moved it here in 1717, by which time he had acquired his former master's penchant for collecting curios, filling the establishment with an assortment of arcana that included a petrified crab from China, pieces of the 'True Cross', William the Conqueror's Flaming Sword, the Pope's 'infallible candle', a necklace supposedly made of Job's tears, Henry VIII's coat of mail and, most treasured of all, 'Pontius Pilate's wife's chamber-maid's sister's hat'. It was all rubbish, of course, but many of the leading writers of the day, including Oliver Goldsmith, Laurence Sterne, Fanny Burney and Richard Steele, would drop by to marvel at the wonder of it all, or just to watch Saltero pull out customers' troublesome teeth. One visitor in 1725 was Benjamin Franklin, the American politician and scientist, who was then working in London as a printer, and who on leaving

Saltero's swam back to central London. After Salter died his daughter converted the property into a museum and in 1799 sold the stock for £50. **No. 18** then became a tavern and was demolished in 1876.

No. 17

The author Naomi Mitchison, an expert on African affairs, lived here from 1919 to 1923.

Queen's House (Dante Gabriel Rossetti's address (1862–82)), No. 16

Dante Gabriel Rossetti, the Pre-Raphaelite painter and poet, moved into No. 16, a 1719-built property designed by John Witt into which the river would trickle at high tide, while mourning the death of his wife, Elizabeth Siddal in 1862, and converted it into a temple to Aestheticism where, as one visitor explained, the only modern possession was a box of Bryant and May's safety matches. The house also became home to a number of poets (his brother, Michael, George Meredith and Algernon Swinburne), and a menagerie of exotic animals that included a raven, a jackdaw, owls, lizards, an opossum that came in at night to sleep on Rossetti's table, a zebra, a donkey, an armadillo, a kangaroo, a racoon that killed the kangaroo, a wombat that ate a guest's hat and led Rossetti to exclaim: 'Oh poor wombat! It is so indigestible', a white bull with eyes supposedly like those of William Morris's wife, some dormice that Rossetti tried to wake by prodding them until a visitor remarked: 'They can't. They're dead, and I believe they've been dead for some days', and peacocks that caused such problems that to this day the authorities have banned Cheyne Walk residents from keeping such birds.

▶ Birth of the Pre-Raphaelites, p. 85.

No. 14

While living here in the early twentieth century and working on his *Principles of Mathematics*, Bertrand Russell established his famous paradox, which says that some sets, such as the set of all teacups, are not members of themselves, while other sets, such as the set of all non-teacups, are members of themselves, a proposition that went on to influence much of the thinking involving logic, set theory and philosophy.

George Eliot's address and deathsite (1880), No. 4

An exquisitely designed 1718-built house with a hooded doorway and Corinthian pilasters, it was occupied in the 1830s by the Irish artist Daniel Maclise, who was caught here in bed with his mistress, a Lady Sykes, by her husband. In 1880 the novelist George Eliot moved to No. 4 Cheyne Walk after marrying John Cross, twenty years her junior, and enduring an unsuccessful honeymoon in Venice, during which he had tried to commit suicide by drowning in a canal and had been rescued by gondoliers. When Eliot moved in she announced, somewhat optimistically: 'I find myself in a new climate here, the London air and this particular house being so warm', but she died a few weeks later from kidney trouble.

Keith Richards's address (1969–78), No. 3 / River House

Richards moved into No. 3 in 1969 with his then girlfriend, Anita Pallenberg, and a year later installed a shrine to Jimi Hendrix, who had recently died. In June 1973 the property was raided by the drugs squad and Richards and Pallenberg were caught with an assortment of illegal substances, including heroin, cannabis and mandrax, as well as a revolver and ammunition. The guitarist was convicted and fined £275 at Soho's Great Marlborough Street magistrates court. A year later, future Sex Pistol Steve Jones burgled the house and took a colour TV.

EARL'S COURT, SW5

A small square-shaped area between Hammersmith and South Kensington, almost entirely covered with tall, imposing terraced houses, Earl's Court is spoiled by its overriding shabbiness, incessant traffic, bad pubs, cheap restaurants and run-down shops. It is home to one of the capital's most transient populations due to the presence of a large number of foreign students, particularly Australians. Earl's Court's aristocratic name derives from the Earls of Warwick and Holland, former lords of the manor, whose court house was situated locally, and it grew after a station was built for the Metropolitan District Railway in 1869. The area attained much of its present-day look in the 1880s with the construction of grand houses that were originally home to large families and were looked after by servants, but following the decline in service during the twentieth century many of the properties were converted to cheap hotels and hostels.

Earl's Court has long been associated with male homosexuality. It was notoriously described as being 'famous for male perverts' by Brian Leary, counsel for the prosecution during the 1971 *Oz* obscenity trial, and was brought to international attention in 1977 with the release of the Stranglers' song 'Hanging Around' from their debut album which refers to the hustlers big and burly down Earl's Court Road and the leather-clad revellers in the sweaty steamy Coleherne, the macho gay bar at 261 Old Brompton Road.

Warwick Road
Earl's Court Exhibition Hall

The area's best-known amenity, regular home of the Boat Show and the Motor Show and one of London's largest buildings, was built in the 1930s to the designs of C. Howard Crane as the largest reinforced concrete building in Europe and rests on sixty bridges spanning the railway lines below. It opened in September 1937 with the Chocolate and Confectionery exhibition and in 1951 featured the world middleweight title bout between Randolph Turpin, son of the first black man to settle in Warwickshire, and Sugar Ray Robinson, who had previously lost only one fight, but was beaten by Turpin on points. Since the 1970s Earl's

Court has been one of Britain's most prestigious rock venues, despite the fact that the sound of even the biggest groups tends to get lost in the huge cavernous spaces. David Bowie unveiled his Aladdin Sane persona here in 1973 before a record 18,000 audience – an event marred by fighting in the auditorium, fans dancing naked and urinating in the aisles – and a few weeks later Pink Floyd played the recently released *Dark Side of the Moon* album in its entirety, greeting concert-goers with Second World War style spotlights outside the venue. At the edge of the venue lies the West London Railway, which opened to public indifference in 1844 – 'going from nowhere to nowhere', the local paper said.

➤ Olympia, p. 466.

SOUTH KENSINGTON, SW7

South Kensington exudes wealth and importance thanks to its colleges, museums, stucco villas, hotels, smart apartment blocks and, at its north-eastern corner, the charming mews and alleys of Knightsbridge village, one of London's most desirable residential quarters.

(i) north of Cromwell Road

London's greatest concentration of museums and cultural buildings – the Natural History Museum, Science Museum, Victoria and Albert Museum and Royal Albert Hall – can be found between Hyde Park and Cromwell Road, their existence a legacy of the 1851 Great Exhibition held in Hyde Park, the profits from which were directed, thanks to Prince Albert, towards creating a cultural and educational quarter where art and science could be promoted. The first development was the South Kensington Museum (later the Victoria and Albert Museum) which opened in 1856, the Natural History Museum followed in 1881, and the Science Museum building opened on the present site in 1913.

Brompton Road
The London Oratory of St Philip Neri
The first large Catholic church to be built in London following the Catholic Emancipation Act of 1829, the Oratory is the London headquarters of the Catholic Oratorian order, founded by Renaissance saint Filippo Neri in the sixteenth century, which Cardinal Newman introduced to London in 1848. The church was designed in the 1880s not in the then fashionable Gothic manner but in a baroque style modelled by Herbert Gribble on the order's mother church, the Chiesa Nuova in Rome, to impress those who 'had no opportunity of going to Italy'. During the 1980s the KGB had a dead letter box (a safe place where they could leave secret documents and messages) in a recess behind a column by the altar.

Ennismore Gardens Mews
At the outset of their acting careers in the late 1950s the actors Terence Stamp and Michael Caine moved into a mews flat at 12 Ennismore Gardens where, according to Stamp's autobiography, *Coming Attractions*, a typical morning would begin with Caine announcing: 'Right, it's a shiny, upper-middle-class day. You have first bath; I'll make some breakfast. Then we'll stroll to Harrods and mingle with the other idle classes. You can cruise the pet shop and I'll see what new books they've got. Then we'll cut through the parks to Leicester Square and read all the papers in the library. At lunchtime we'll nip into that gaff in Whitcomb Street before the luncheon voucher lot get loose.'

Exhibition Road
Laid out in 1856 on land owned by the 5th Earl of Harrington, the road was meant to be at the centre of an international exhibition scheduled to be held in 1861, ten years after the highly successful 1851 Great Exhibition, but the events were delayed for a year when Prince Albert, who had been heavily involved originally, died. When the exhibition took place in 1862 it was a flop. Queen Victoria failed to attend, visitor numbers were considerably lower than in 1851, and there were no profits. The prefabricated buildings which had been erected here for the exhibition were swiftly demolished and in their place came various museums, and a number of grand Italianate villas, designed by Charles James Freake, a friend of the Prince of Wales, of which only Nos. 69–72 remain.

west side: Cromwell Road to Kensington Gore

Natural History Museum
Alfred Waterhouse, master of the secular Gothic grand statement, created this monumental block between 1873 and 1881 in the style of a thirteenth-century Flemish cloth hall, as with his contemporaneous Manchester Town Hall. His first public building in London, it was not universally admired, the historian W. J. Loftie claiming its design was 'in defiance of all the rules of proportion laid down by the architects of the last generation and equally in defiance of all the rules of taste'. Nevertheless, the museum has weathered well and now ranks as a prime example of Victorian civic pride, ideal for its vast collection of specimens from the animal kingdom (past and present), minerals and maps.

Science Museum
The Science Museum had its origins in the South Kensington Museum, which opened opposite in 1856, receiving its first collection of scientific instruments in 1874 and the Patent Office's stock of models, which included Stephenson's Rocket of 1829 and Arkwright's original textile machinery, in 1884. By 1909 the authorities had decided that the collection had grown to a sufficient extent to be categorized and Richard Allison was hired to create a new museum on the present site, a building that Edward Jones and Christopher Woodward have described as being like an Edwardian office block outside and a department store inside. The museum has continued to expand since opening in 1913 and now contains some 300,000 objects, covering the entire history of western science, technology and medicine.

Imperial College of Science, Technology and Medicine
Established in 1907 from a number of local institutions, and affiliated to the University of London a year later, Imperial College soon attracted the greatest names in science teaching including T. H. Huxley, known as 'Darwin's bulldog' for his robust defence of the evolutionist. At the outset of the Second World War it was the setting for the government's early work on nuclear weapons, at a time when it was feared that Germany, then the most scientifically advanced country in the world, had the technology to make an atomic bomb.

east side
Victoria and Albert Museum
Britain's major museum for the arts and design had its origins in the Museum of Ornamental Art, which moved from Pall Mall's Marlborough House to South Kensington to take up room in William Cubitt's 'Brompton Boilers' buildings in 1857. Sir Henry Cole, the museum's first director, amassed its huge collection of furniture, tapestries, pottery, porcelain, jewellery, glass, china and medals which, along with the Gherardini collection of sculpture models, John Sheepshanks's British paintings, Raphael's Cartoons and the contents of the India Museum, stretch over 100 galleries, being so uncategorizable that the museum has defied logical definition since. The British Galleries were revamped at a cost of £31 million at the beginning of the twenty-first century and in recent years there has been considerable debate over the merits of a planned £30 million extension in the form of an unusual, multi-faced abstract shape designed by Daniel Liebeskind.
► British Museum, p. 89.

Kensington Gore
A short stretch of the main Kensington Road, it is named after the **Kensington Gore mansion**, built in 1750, which was occupied from 1808 to 1821 by the slavery abolitionist William Wilberforce. Bought in 1836 by Lady Blessington, it was where she estab-lished a literary salon that was visited by Benjamin Disraeli, Louis Napoleon and the Duke of Wellington, who was amused by the house's talking crow's shrieks of 'Up boys and at 'em'. The house was converted to a restaurant for the 1851 Great Exhibition in Hyde Park and demolished in the 1870s.

south side: Exhibition Road to Queen's Gate
Royal Geographical Society
Built from 1873 to 1875 by Norman Shaw for William Lowther MP, its rural appearance and asymmetry were an incongruous sight for an inner London suburb at that time. Lowther's son, James, Speaker of the House of Commons, sold the property to the Royal Geographical Society in 1912.

Royal Albert Hall
Britain's most famous concert hall, setting for the annual promenade concerts (the Proms), came into being, like much of South Kensington, through the success of the 1851 Great Exhibition, held nearby in Hyde Park, but was bedevilled in its early years by abandoned plans and untimely deaths. The foundation stone was laid in May 1867 by Queen Victoria, who announced that the building would be called the Royal Albert Hall, rather than the Hall of Arts and Sciences, as previously mooted, after her late husband, Prince Albert. The queen was too overcome with emotion, however, to conduct the ceremony at the opening concert, on 29 March 1871, after hearing the Austrian composer Anton Bruckner play the organ, and her place was taken by Edward, Prince of Wales.

There were problems with the hall's acoustics from the beginning: the 'Amens' during the opening prayers reverberated so strongly that the conductor joked that any work receiving its première at the Royal Albert Hall was immediately assured of a second performance, but major concerts soon began taking place. In 1877 Richard Wagner conducted eight times during a festival of his music; in 1906 a 9,000 record attendance heard the first ever gramophone concert; and in 1918 the choral version of Blake's

'Jerusalem', composed by Hubert Parry, was given its first performance to celebrate the granting of the vote to women.

On 11 June 1965 some 7,000 people attended the Poets of the World/Poets of Our Time Festival, featuring Adrian Mitchell, Stevie Smith, the American beat poet Lawrence Ferlinghetti, who called for an 'international fucking exchange', and Allen Ginsberg, who topped the bill, but in his drunken state ruined his own performance with a slipshod reading. In the front row sat a group of certified schizophrenics who had been allowed out of hospital for the evening, and caused some chaos during the performances, while backstage Jeff Nuttall, author of one of the era's major sociological works, *Bomb Culture*, and the avant-garde artist John Latham paraded through the corridors tarred and feathered in pages torn out of books as a statement about the printed word. Latham had also painted himself blue, but having forgotten to leave his nose or mouth clear passed out and was thrown into a dressing-room bath where he came to and was joined by Nuttall, the two men washing the muck off each other until a commissionaire entered the room to investigate the source of the commotion and found two men seemingly *in flagrante delicto* at a time when such behaviour could result in a prison sentence.

In 1968 mushroom shapes were hung from the roof to improve the acoustics, and refurbishments took place following a centenary appeal in 1971, the same year that Steeleye Span manager Tony Secunda threw the night's takings, around £8,000, over the balcony on to the heads of bemused and soon to be slightly richer punters. In recent years the hall has witnessed performances by the Bolshoi Ballet and the Kirov Opera, the month-long annual concerts by Eric Clapton, and the first Sumo tournament ever held outside Japan, but it is best known for the annual Prom concerts, which moved from the bombed Queen's Hall near Oxford Circus in 1941. At the end of the twentieth century a major refurbishment programme was begun.

► Covent Garden Opera House, p. 109.

Royal College of Art

The college was created as the School of Design in 1837 to provide British industry with trained designers and after a variety of addresses came to Kensington Gore in 1961 when the current building, by H. T. Cadbury-Brown and Sir Hugh Casson, believed by many to be one of the worst eyesores in the capital, was erected.

Albert Hall Mansions

Albert Hall Mansions, designed in 1879 by Norman Shaw, was the capital's first block of flats to be built in red brick with tall Dutch gables, a style subsequently imitated throughout the wealthy parts of the capital.

Prince's Gate

A peeling stucco terrace set back from Knightsbridge, it was built as an entrance to Hyde Park and opened by Edward, Prince of Wales, in 1848.

Iranian Embassy (1980s), No. 27, south side
The setting for a dramatic siege from 30 April to 5 May 1980 by gunmen demanding autonomy for the Khuzestan province of Iran and the release of ninety-nine political prisoners. The siege was captured live on television and proceeded amid enormous media attention. The prime minister, Margaret Thatcher, stipulated that there would be no surrender to terrorism. On the sixth day the gunmen threatened to kill the hostages one by one unless their demands were met and at 7.10 p.m., half an hour after shots were heard and the body of an Iranian diplomat was pushed out of the front door, the SAS stormed the building, freed the hostages and killed five gunmen. Twenty-four of the twenty-six hostages were rescued unharmed.

(ii) south of Cromwell Road

A shapeless area of ostentatious houses and tree-lined streets, it lacks the sophistication of neighbouring Kensington, or the warmth of Chelsea and Fulham, and is spoiled by the traffic of the A4 and the high proportion of hotels.

Cromwell Place

Francis Bacon's studio (1940s), No. 7
Few London houses have played a role as central to the history of British art as 7 Cromwell Place, near South Kensington station, where the Pre-Raphaelite John Millais lived in the 1860s, using as his studio a room that is now the boardroom of the Art Fund charity, and which was later occupied by the photographer E. O. Hoppé (in 1912), the ballet photographer Gordon Anthony (in 1936), and in the 1940s by Francis Bacon, who painted the windows black. When not working on his paintings, Bacon ran an illegal gambling club, bringing back a succession of rough-looking men whom he had met in Soho pubs and who, on being told that he was a painter, would occasionally ask him to do a painting and decorating job for them.
▶ Francis Bacon in Reece Mews, South Kensington, p. 425.

Gloucester Road

No. 79
John George Haigh, the acid bath murderer of the 1940s, killed his first victim, an acquaintance called William McSwan, in his workshop at 79 Gloucester Road in September 1944, disposing of the body in acid and pouring the remains down the drain. Haigh kept in contact with McSwan's parents, writing them letters which suggested their son was still alive but had disappeared to avoid joining the army, and a year later invited Mr and Mrs McSwan to the workshop to show off some contraptions he had been working on. When they arrived he shot them and, wearing a full-length leather apron and gas mask, immersed their bodies in acid. He then posed as their son to claim his share of their £5,600 estate. After carrying out further murders Haigh became too arrogant and was tracked down by the police. He was convicted of murder and hanged.

Harrington Road

Russian Tea Rooms (mid twentieth century), No. 50
Nikolai Volkov, a naval attaché at the Russian embassy in London in 1917, opened a caff at No. 50 that soon became the meeting place of the extreme nationalist Right Club, an organization run by Captain Archibald Ramsay, MP for Peebles. Its aim was to 'oppose and expose the activities of organized Jewry', for Ramsay believed Jews responsible for communism, capitalism, the Masons and the Vatican. In May 1940 Anna, the Volkovs' daughter, was arrested here on espionage charges – an event watched, supposedly, by the eleven-year-old Len Deighton, whose mother worked here at the time. He went on to write a series of well-received espionage thrillers.

Queen's Gate

A relentlessly straight road, it was known as Albert's Road until 1859 and was lined with luxurious family homes designed in an Italianate style by Norman Shaw, among others, which have either been demolished for college buildings or converted to embassies and expensive hotels.
Onslow Court Hotel (Jury's), Nos. 109–113, south of Cromwell Road
John George Haigh, the suave and charming acid bath murderer of the 1940s, lived in Room 404 while planning his last murder, that of Olive Durand-Deacon, a fellow guest who had expressed enthusiasm for his ideas for manufacturing stick-on fingernails. Haigh invited Mrs Durand-Deacon to his workshop in Crawley, Sussex, and there he shot her in the back and then dissolved her body in acid. When those staying at the hotel began to miss her, Haigh offered to go to the police station, but there an officer recognized him as a convicted fraudster and took him in for questioning. A police pathologist went to his Crawley workshop and noticed human gallstones in a pile of rubble (they do not dissolve in acid) and a set of dentures which Mrs Durand-Deacon's dentist later identified as hers. Haigh

admitted his crimes and explained that he had a fascination for blood dating back to his childhood and that he killed to satisfy his craving rather than for profit. His plea of insanity was not accepted, and he was hanged in August 1949.

➤ 10 Rillington Place, pp. 454–5.

Reece Mews
Francis Bacon's address and studio (1961–92), No. 7
Bacon, Britain's most celebrated twentieth-century artist, who once claimed that he had had an epiphany to rank alongside William Blake's vision of angels in Peckham, namely the sight of a dog-turd on the pavement which made him realize that 'There it is. This is what life is like', lived at 7 Reece Mews in conditions which the journalist Mick Brown described as 'almost monastic simplicity'. His small sitting room was reached by a narrow set of stairs with a rope for a banister and contained only a bed, table, battered sofa and four bare light bulbs. Bacon's studio, where he worked on his disturbing visions of alienation and paranoia, was in contrast to his sparse quarters a confusion of artists' ephemera and impedimenta. There he created works such as the triptych *Crucifixion* (1965), based around a distorted headless being immersed in a pool of blood, in the third section of which a swastika armband is wrapped around the same figure, by now more recognizable as a sleek blond-haired Aryan, and *May–June 1973* which was sold for £3.53 million at Sotheby's, New York, in 1989 making Bacon the world's highest-selling living artist. Three years later he left the property for a tryst in Spain, where he died of a heart attack, aged eighty-two. For six years after his death the studio and its contents remained undisturbed except for the gathering dust, until a team of archaeologists

and conservators from Dublin arrived to transport the contents to Ireland for reassembly in a museum.

➤ David Hockney in Notting Hill, p. 462.

Selwood Terrace
A short turning connecting Onslow Gardens and Fulham Road, it was where Charles Dickens briefly lived (at No. 11) in 1836 so that he could qualify to be married at the nearby church of St Luke's.

Anglesea Arms, No. 15
Bruce Reynolds, an antique dealer, and an associate known only as 'Geordie' began planning what became the 1963 Great Train Robbery, one of the most famous crimes of late-twentieth-century Britain, at the Anglesea Arms after conversation turned to the subject of a train carrying South African gold from Southampton Docks to London. After staking out the train in Weybridge in the early hours one morning, they abandoned the plan and instead turned their attention to the Glasgow–London mail train, assembling an eighteen-strong gang that included motor racing driver Roy James, former boxer Buster Edwards, Ronnie Biggs and Gordon Goody, who had tattoos saying 'Hello Ireland' on one arm and 'Dear Mother' on the other. The Great Train Robbers stopped the London–Glasgow mail train at Bridego Bridge, Buckinghamshire, on 8 August 1963, seizing 120 mailbags and a haul of £2,631,684 (around £40 million in today's prices), then a world record for a robbery, but despite the assiduous preparations things soon began to go wrong and most of the gang were rounded up, receiving some of the stiffest sentences ever meted out for robbery. Reynolds, who remained on the run for five years and was only caught after police staged a huge international manhunt, received twenty-five years.

West London

BAYSWATER, W2

A cosmopolitan and once fashionable district, Bayswater, the name a corruption of Bayards' Water, a former well in Hyde Park, was one of the first suburbs to be colonized by wealthy Londoners moving west to escape the squalor of the City and West End. It was formally developed at the beginning of the nineteenth century when Samuel Pepys Cockerell built stucco houses in crescents and squares overlooking Hyde Park and became one of the most desirable addresses in London. It has gradually declined in status, mainly due to the commercialization around Paddington station, although there are still pockets of opulence near Hyde Park with expensive hotels, luxury offices and mews that date back to the great era of stabling.

(i) Hyde Park

The largest stretch of open land in inner London, and the largest of the royal parks, Hyde Park was created in 1536 when Henry VIII seized land roamed by wild bulls and boar that belonged to Westminster Abbey to use as a deer park, and it was opened to the public by James I early in the seventeenth century. The Parliamentarians, under Oliver Cromwell, took it over for military use during the Civil War and Cromwell, driving a carriage through the park in September 1654, was thrown to the ground when his horses bolted, but remained unhurt even though the pistol in his pocket fired. It was Cromwell's second lucky escape in Hyde Park: an assassin once stalked him, but never got the opportunity to attack.

Charles II took possession of the park after the restoration of the throne in 1660 and enclosed it for the first time. It became fashionable in the eighteenth century once the wealthy had moved away from the City and had begun to live locally. Decimus Burton was hired to add classical furnishings in the 1820s, which resulted in new carriage drives and the Grecian lodges and screen at Hyde Park Corner, and in 1851 the Great Exhibition, now seen as the embodiment of Victorian confidence, was held at the southern border of the park (roughly opposite Ennismore Gardens) from 1 May to 11 October. The first of its kind in the world, the exhibition was the brainchild of Prince Albert, Victoria's consort, who wanted to draw attention to Great Britain as a world industrial power,

Hyde Park glossary

Achilles statue When Westmacott's statue of Achilles, its head modelled on that of the Duke of Wellington, was unveiled there was an outcry about the penis – not believed necessarily to have been modelled on that of the duke – which was immediately covered with a fig leaf to protect the sensibilities of passers-by.

Apsley Gate A classical screen copied from the Parthenon, built to the west of Apsley House by Decimus Burton in 1825.

The Broad Walk In 1954 elm trees on the walk, west of Park Lane, were felled to leave a strip 25 yards on each side of the path, large enough to take a Hawker Siddeley 748 twin-engine plane capable of carrying fifty-two people for 500 miles, that could be used as an emergency air strip for the royal family should they need to escape London in an emergency.

Cumberland Gate Named after the Duke of Cumberland, brother of George IV, the gate can be found at the north-east corner of the park by Marble Arch, and was where in the summer of 1821 riots broke out when the funeral cortège of Queen Caroline, estranged wife of George IV, tried to pass through. Magistrates ordered troops to open fire and two people were killed.

Hudson Memorial To the north-east of the bridge over the Serpentine stands a memorial to W. H. Hudson, author of *Birds of London* (1898), the book that influenced the park authorities into taking an interest in its wildlife, partly designed by Jacob Epstein and featuring Rima, the spirit of the forest from Hudson's *Green Mansions*.

Unfortunately the stone sides of the memorial are too deep to allow birds to drink from it.

The Long Water Formed in the 1720s from damming the River Westbourne and now a wildlife sanctuary.

Reformers' Tree A circular mosaic in the north-east corner of the park marks the site of a tree that was burned down in 1866 after the police refused to allow supporters of the Reform League to hold a rally. The mosaic was unveiled by the Labour politician Tony Benn in 2000.

Rotten Row William III built a new illuminated path, the Route des Rois or Route of Kings (later corrupted to Rotten Row), to connect Kensington Palace with St James's, after discovering that the existing walk was plagued by thieves and footpads. Lined with 300 oil lamps, it became the first artificially lit highway in the country.

The Serpentine Created from the damming of the River Westbourne in the 1720s, it was where Harriet Westbrook, wife of the poet Shelley, drowned herself in 1816.

Speaker's Corner Since 1872 members of the public have been allowed to speak without prior arrangement on practically any subject at this designated spot in the north-east corner of the park, set up after violence marred a Reform League march in Hyde Park in 1866. Those who have spoken here include Karl Marx, Friedrich Engels, Lenin, the suffragette campaigners the Pankhursts, the Trinidadian historian C. L. R. James and the black nationalist Marcus Garvey.

► Regent's Park, p. 350.

and it was held in a vast greenhouse of iron, glass and wood, designed by Joseph Paxton, the Duke of Devonshire's gardener, which earned the nickname Crystal Palace from a cartoon in *Punch*.

Inside the Crystal Palace some 6 million people saw railway engines, sewing machines, model working-class houses ventilated by a rudimentary system of air conditioning, a kite-drawn carriage for travelling on windy days, rare jewels including the Koh-i-Noor diamond, the latest in technology and pavilions representing different countries (at a time when most people had never left England). Toilets were installed especially for the occasion – hundreds of thousands of people experienced a sit-down flushing convenience for the first time – and refreshments were supplied by Schweppes, who sold a million bath buns (no alcohol was allowed). After the exhibition closed the structure was emptied and the building dismantled and rebuilt in Sydenham, south-east London, where it gave its name to the area and the local football club. Of the exhibition's £186,437 profit £5,000 went to Paxton and the rest went towards founding the museums on and around Exhibition Road in South Kensington. In 1885 W. S. Gilbert, librettist of the Gilbert and Sullivan operas, found inspiration for *The Mikado* after visiting a Japanese village of dwellings, tea-houses and temple in the park and watching demonstrations of wood-carving, fencing, dancing and wrestling.

In 1920 Winston Churchill, then war secretary, was driving through the park with Sir Basil Thompson, head of Special Branch, discussing the discovery of Churchill's name on an IRA hit-list, when Thompson noticed a man loitering by some bushes. Churchill gripped his pistol and growled: 'If they want trouble, they can bloody well have it,' but Thompson decided not to stop. 'Drive like the devil!', he bellowed at the chauffeur, and the car continued its route without incident. In 1936 the Jarrow hunger marchers ended their long trek from the north-east in the park, and two years later, when a crowd spotted the Nazi sympathizer Unity Mitford at a Labour Party rally here, they attempted, unsuccessfully, to throw her in the Serpentine, whereupon she told them: 'I am looking forward to becoming a German citizen as soon as possible.'

On 7 June 1969 150,000 gathered here to see the debut of Blind Faith, the short-lived supergroup formed by Eric Clapton and Stevie Winwood, an event which prompted the Rolling Stones to play a concert, their first live show for two years, in the park on 5 July 1969. The group were going to introduce Mick Taylor as Brian Jones's replacement on guitar at the gig, but on 2 July Jones was found dead at his Sussex farm and the concert was turned into a memorial to the guitarist, at which Mick Jagger, wearing a white dress and sporting a wooden cross and dog collar, read from Shelley's 'Adonais' ('Peace, peace, he is not dead, he doth not sleep, he hath awakened from a dream of life') He released thousands of mainly dead butterflies into the air. After the concert the Stones were berated for the amateurishness of their set, which was put down to Jones's death, and the plaudits went to Family and the barely known King Crimson, who were playing one of their first shows. Subsequent concerts in the park have failed to capture the public imagination.

The park continues to be used as a last stop for political demonstrations that start at Trafalgar Square and in recent decades has seen Ban the Bomb marchers, miners' strike supporters, anti-poll tax demonstrators and pro-countryside lobbyists.

(ii) Kensington Gardens

> Then the Divine Vision like a silent Sun appear'd above / Albion's dark rocks: setting behind the Gardens of Kensington / On Tyburn's River, in clouds of blood – *Jerusalem*, William Blake (1804)

Kensington Gardens, the stretch of parkland west of the Long Water and the Serpentine, was originally the grounds of Nottingham House, converted into Kensington Palace by William III in 1689, and first opened (on Sundays only) in 1733. Servants in livery were excluded and a strict dress code banning silk neckties and breeches without boots was enforced, but relaxed in 1820 to allow all 'respectably dressed persons'. The number of people using Kensington Gardens increased considerably after the 1997 death of Princess Diana, who occasionally lived in Kensington Palace (see p. 441).

Kensington Gardens glossary

Albert Memorial Now seen as typical of Victorian excess, the memorial to Prince Albert, in the form of a shrine housing John Foley's statue, was designed by George Gilbert Scott, built from 1863 to 1875, and inlaid with mosaics, statues and marble figures. During the Second World War anti-aircraft guns in Hyde Park accidentally shot off the orb and cross at the apex and in the 1980s £11.2 million worth of cleaning and restoration work took place, during which the memorial's detractors claimed the scaffolding that encased the work was more visually exciting than the memorial itself.

The Broad Walk It marks the boundary between Kensington and Bayswater and runs the length of the park from Kensington Road to Bayswater Road.

The Fountains Until 1795 the site, opposite Lancaster Gate station, was known as Bayard's or Baynard's Watering Place, named after Ralph Baynardus, a Norman baron. The name was later corrupted to Bayswater and ascribed to the area to the north.

Kensington Palace See p. 441.

Peter Pan statue George Frampton's sculpture on the west side of the Long Water was installed on the evening of 3 April 1912 as a fully completed work because J. M. Barrie, Peter Pan's creator, wanted children to believe it had appeared as if by magic. The novelist and artist Wyndham Lewis later denounced the statue as 'the sickly and dismal spirit of that terrible book'.

Powder magazine It was used to store ammunition to defend London until Winston Churchill feared that German agents in London might destroy the building and had it closed.

Round Pond It was here in 1904 that the playwright J. M. Barrie, walking his dog, met Jack Llewellyn Davies, the

(iii) Little Venice

> Her one rich wish is to write a book about / A Venetian mother's problems on a barge in Little Venice – 'Chateau in Virginia Waters', Tyrannosaurus Rex (1968)

A small picturesque harbour area north of the Westway, where the Paddington branch of the Grand Union Canal meets the main canal, its name may have come from remarks made by Lord Byron and repeated by the poet Robert Browning, who lived locally, but was not commonly used until the 1950s. An island in the middle of the canal is known as Browning's Island, as the poet is believed to have planted trees on it, while the streets to the north, such as Maida Avenue, are among the most pleasant to be found in this part of London with elegant villas decorated with arches, urns and balustrades.

(iv) Paddington

Paddington is named after Padda, an Anglo-Saxon chieftain who lived in the vicinity, and after the Norman Conquest the land came into the possession of the Abbot of Westminster until it was seized by Henry VIII for his sixth wife, Catherine Parr, in the 1540s. Henry's son, Edward VI, returned the estate to the Church and the Bishops of London remained landlords (except during the Commonwealth) until the area's rural identity and role as a market garden for central London withered away, first by the opening of an extension of the Grand Junction Canal in 1801, and then by the building of Paddington railway station in 1838. Second World War bombing led to much blight, a sharp decrease in the population and an unsavoury identity; Christine Keeler, the call-girl caught up in the 1960s Profumo Affair, claimed that in the early fifties Paddington succeeded Soho as the capital boy who became the inspiration for Peter Pan.

Queen Anne's Alcove One of the gardens' first furnishings, the alcove was designed by Christopher Wren in 1705, originally located to the south of Kensington Palace, and moved here in 1867 after becoming a haunt of prostitutes.

Queen's Temple A small Palladian structure with three arches, it was designed by William Kent and is located in the middle of the gardens, a few hundred yards west of the bridge that separates the Long Water from the Serpentine.

Serpentine Gallery The building opened as a tea pavilion in 1934 and was converted into a gallery in 1970. In 1994 Damien Hirst's *Separated from the Flock*, a lamb preserved in formaldehyde in a glass tank, was exhibited here and vandalized with black ink by Mark Bridger, who told police that his 'positive contribution' might add value to the work.

of the British underworld, and the area around the station remains one of London's worst red-light districts. Redevelopment in the 1960s, particularly the construction of the Westway motorway, wiped out much of Paddington, and by the beginning of the twenty-first century major changes were being planned for the disused canal basin near the station.

Harrow Road

One of London's longest roads, Harrow Road began as a horse track and in Paddington is eclipsed by the Westway, which runs above it on a bridge.

Paddington police station
Ealing Studios' *The Blue Lamp* (1949), one of the first so-called British 'cop' films, was set in and around Paddington Green police station, shot at various west London locations, including White City stadium, that are mostly now unrecognizable given the extensive redevelopment of the area, and mixes Crown Documentary pictures with vignettes of force life sympathetic to the

constabulary but unconvincing in characterization. The film is best known for introducing the character of George Dixon, the ever reliable community 'bobby', played by Jack Warner, who later featured in the long-running TV show *Dixon of Dock Green*, despite being killed by a villain (played by Dirk Bogarde) in the film.

▶ King's Cross on film, p. 356.

Lancaster Gate

The grand centrepiece of Bayswater, Lancaster Gate was designed by Sancton Wood in an unusual cross shape in 1857 and is based around Christ Church, designed by F. & H. Francis, which closed in 1978 and has since been ingeniously converted into flats. The Lancaster Gate house in the Henry James novel *The Wings of a Dove* is based on No. 56, the late-nineteenth-century home of Pearl Craigie, who wrote for the Aesthetic Movement's *Yellow Book* and was part of the family that owned Carter's Little Liver Pills. The Football Association was based at No. 16 until the end of the twentieth century, when it moved to Soho Square.

Columbia Hotel, No. 95
Haile Selassie, the best known of the post-colonial black African leaders of the twentieth century, who was originally named Lij Makonnen but took the title Ras Tafari ('prince, nobleman' in Amharic) after his 1930 coronation, and claimed to be descended from King Solomon and the Queen of Sheba, used the hotel as his Second World War headquarters until 1941 when he was reinstated as Ethiopian emperor. Selassie later became the spiritual leader of the Jamaican Rastafarian movement.

Leinster Gardens

Nos. 23–24 are dummy houses, built to blend in with surrounding property, which have 5-ft thick false windows and contain behind their façade machinery built to take exhaust from the steam-powered Metropolitan Railway extension of 1868 (now the Circle Line).

Paddington Green

The only remaining green space in the area and the first site to be developed locally, it was where the first London vehicle described as an 'omnibus' ran in July 1829, its route being Paddington to Bank. The setting was later commemorated in the music hall song 'Pretty Polly Perkins of Paddington Green', which begins with the confessions of a 'broken-hearted milkman, in grief arrayed / Through keeping of the company of a young servant maid / Who lived on board and wages the house to keep clean / In a gentleman's family near Paddington Green'.

Praed Street

William Praed was an eighteenth-century banker and MP for St Ives who was one of the main promoters of the Grand Junction Canal in 1793.

north side: Eastbourne Terrace to Edgware Road

Paddington station

Opened on June 1838 for the Great Western Railway, the station, now considered to be London's most handsome railway terminus, was originally a simple wooden building north of Bishop's Bridge Road and was rebuilt in the 1840s by Matthew Wyatt and Isambard Kingdom Brunel. Paddington was part of Brunel's grand vision of a route from London to New York via Bristol, where people would board his liner, the *Great Western*, and journey across the Atlantic in fifteen days. In 1863 the western terminus of the Metropolitan Railway, the world's first underground line, was constructed by Paddington station and, though the various rail services using the station brought huge changes to the area, Paddington was still rural in 1868 when Edward, Prince of Wales (the future Edward VII), took part in a hunt in Buckingham-shire that took him through Harrow and Wormwood Scrubs to Paddington where he cornered a deer in the goods yard, killing it in front of railway workers, before making off on his horse into nearby Hyde Park.

● In Michael Bond's Paddington Bear stories the teddy bear is found at Pad-dington station, having travelled from Peru with just a jar of marmalade and his hat.

▶ Liverpool Street station, p. 19.

St Mary's Hospital

Alexander Fleming discovered the germ-killing properties of penicillin at St Mary's Hospital on 3 September 1928 by accident while looking for a chemical that could stop bacterial infection. Noticing that some of the bacteria around the mould in a Petri dish he was about to wash had been killed, Fleming and his team took a sample and found that it came from the penicillium family. Later in Oxford they injected it into diseased mice and when the mice showed signs of recuperation they tried the experi-ments on humans, with successful results. Research on bacteria, funded by the Rocke-feller Foundation in the United States, continued during the Second World War, and Fleming's Praed Street laboratory (now a museum), reeking of cigarette smoke and lysol, and cluttered with papers and Petri dishes, received regular visits from journalists and curious members of the public.

▶ St Bartholomew's Hospital, p. 9.

(v) Tyburnia

The oldest part of Bayswater, Tyburnia, the mostly elegant estate to the north-west of the site of the 𝕿𝖞𝖇𝖚𝖗𝖓 𝖊𝖝𝖊𝖈𝖚𝖙𝖎𝖔𝖓 𝖙𝖗𝖊𝖊, and also known as the Hyde Park Estate, was designed by Samuel Pepys Cockerell and built from 1807 to 1815 around Connaught Place, attracting wealthy middle-class resi-dents such as the Victorian novelist William Makepeace Thackeray, who moved into 18 Albion Street, off Bayswater Road, in 1836, and George Smith, publisher of the Brontës, who entertained the sisters at his home at 𝕹𝖔. 𝟐𝟔 Bishop's Bridge Road. The area declined following the commercialization of the streets nearest Paddington station and when the leases ran out in the 1930s many wealthy residents left for other areas, particularly Hampstead and Chelsea, the houses they vacated being converted into offices or replaced by shops and hotels. Near Bayswater Road streets such as Hyde Park Gardens and Hyde Park Street retain their period flavour but nearer the station there are a number of hotels of varying standard.

Bayswater Road

The main road running through Bayswater was originally known as The Way to Uxbridge and was where in 1861 the American George Train, whom Jules Verne later used as the model for Phileas Fogg in *Around the World in Eighty Days*, established London's first tram service, a line unpopular with cab drivers, who complained vociferously to the authorities when their wheels began to bump against tracks jutting out of the ground.

north side: Albion Street to Edgware Road
Hyde Park Place, Bayswater Road between Albion Street and Stanhope Place
Laurence Sterne, author of the great comic novel *Tristram Shandy*, was buried in a now disused graveyard here in 1768, his body being removed a few days later by body-snatchers who dug up the corpse and sold it for dissection. Sterne was recognized on the slab, however, and his body was returned to the graveyard, but in 1969, when the site was redeveloped for flats, the coffin was opened and two heads were found inside. After the authorities examined contemporary paintings, the correct one was placed back in the coffin and sent for reburial in Coxwold, Yorkshire. Charles Dickens lived at 𝔑𝔬. 5 𝔥𝔶𝔡𝔢 𝔓𝔞𝔯𝔨 𝔓𝔩𝔞𝔠𝔢 in January 1870 and there began his last novel, the unfinished *Mystery of Edwin Drood*, dying later that year in Kent.

Tyburn Convent, No. 12
The convent is home to a nineteenth-century order whose members, according to the custom of St Benedict, dedicate their lives to the Sacred Heart by the perpetual adoration of the Holy Sacrament. After being driven from its home in Montmartre (the Mount of Martyrs), in Paris, in 1901, the order moved to this location near Tyburn (the Hill of Martyrs). In the crypt chapel a replica of the Tyburn Tree used for hangings (see below) can be seen on request alongside a number of relics of the martyrs hanged at Tyburn.

𝔗𝔶𝔟𝔲𝔯𝔫 (1388–1783), Oxford Street at Edgware Road
Gallows were erected by the Tyburn stream on the 11-ft 'Tyburn Tree', which could hold eight people simultaneously, in 1388, and here the condemned would be hanged by a rope connected to a cart that would move off leaving the victim dangling. Friends and relatives would often pull on the body to bring on death quickly and alleviate the suffering. Sometimes, though, a pardon would arrive just in time. In 1447 five men who had been placed on the gallows were lucky enough to win a reprieve while still alive and were cut down but were stripped by the hangman, who was traditionally allowed to keep the clothes of victims and refused to part with the garments, despite the pleas of the men, who were obliged to walk home naked. A would-be victim who underwent an even more remarkable revival was William Duell, hanged at Tyburn in 1740, whose 'corpse' was sent to an anatomy class and there started showing signs of life, sitting up and speaking to the surgeon, who promptly arranged for him to be sent back to prison.

As the condemned went to the gallows they would be approached by authors seeking their approval to publish material already written as 'last confessions' or memoirs. The condemned would then advertise the forthcoming work to the crowds before being executed. Executions at Tyburn were among the most eagerly awaited social occasions in the London calendar. There was spectator seating and many celebrities came along to view the events, including Samuel Pepys, who described in his diary entry for 21 January 1664 how he 'got for a shilling to stand upon the wheel of a cart, in great pain, about an hour before the execution was done'; and Dr Johnson's biographer, James Boswell, who exclaimed after witnessing the hanging of the high-wayman Paul Lewis in May 1763: 'I was most terribly shocked, and thrown into a very deep melancholy.' The biggest crowd ever recorded at Tyburn was to see the execution of Dr William Dodd, hanged in 1777 for forging the Earl of Chesterfield's signature on a £4,250 bond. Pressure from Mayfair residents resulted in the removal of executions in 1783 to Newgate, where the population was not so wealthy.

► Newgate Prison, p. 10.

Hyde Park Crescent

Used as a residential area by US servicemen in the Second World War and since rebuilt into flats.

St John

Richard Branson, whose first venture, *Student* magazine, was based in the church crypt in the 1960s, was visited by two plain-clothed policemen in November 1969 and warned that the magazine might have viol-ated the Indecent Advertisements Act (1889) and the Venereal Disease Act (1917) by publishing remedies for the latter. Branson ignored the warnings, and a month later the police returned to St John's to arrest and charge him, leading to a court case in which he was defended by John Mortimer (creator of *Rumpole of the Bailey*) who pointed out that every public lavatory contained a notice offering advice to those suffering from VD and if Branson was guilty, then so was the government. Branson was convicted, none the less, and fined £7, so Mortimer told journalists outside the court that the government would now have to be prosecuted for breaking its own law. The legislation was amended soon after and the home secretary, Reginald Maudling, sent Branson an apology. On the third Sunday in September every year riders gather outside St John, according to a tradition that began in 1868 as a protest against the closure of a number of stables

during redevelopment, and ride through the area.

► Virgin Records, p. 460.

(vi) Westbourne Park

A mansion known as **Westbourne Park** or **Westbourne Place** stood on Lord's Hill Bridge, by what is now Royal Oak station, before the building of the Great Western Railway in the 1830s.

Chepstow Road

A major traffic route at the western end of Bayswater, it was where Peter Rachman, the 1950s slum landlord whose rogue practices led to a tightening of the letting laws in the 1960s, owned a brothel (at No. 58). The road is featured in the 1966 Lewis Gilbert comedy *Alfie*, whose hero, played by Michael Caine, briefly lives here in a flat with Annie, played by Jane Asher. *Alfie*'s director, Lewis Gilbert, filmed the scenes at night until police complained that the lights were causing problems for motorists.

► Peter Rachman's slum empire, pp. 435, 462.

Hereford Road

Location of Marconi's first patented wire-less experiment, No. 71, north of West-bourne Grove

Guglielmo Marconi made the first British wireless at No. 71 in 1896, two years after sending radio waves two miles across Bologna, Italy. He gave his first demon-stration of the wireless on the roof of the General Post Office on St Martin's-le-Grand, in the City, on 22 July 1896, and later exhibited his invention on Salisbury Plain.

Queensway

Now a thriving shopping street with a variety of restaurants, it was originally Black Lion Lane, which the young Princess Victoria (later Queen) used when living at Kensington Palace, and was renamed Queen's Road in the 1830s, soon after she took the throne, becoming Queensway during Edward VII's reign. Until the liberalization of the Sunday shopping laws in the 1980s Queensway was one of the few streets busy with shoppers at unusual hours of the weekend. It is now best known for Whiteleys, an American-style mall on the site of the former department store of the same name, once London's largest, and which originally stood in Westbourne Grove.

Westbourne Grove

Bayswater's first major shopping street, it was developed in the mid nineteenth century but soon became known as Bankrupt Avenue because of the closure of many businesses. Things improved when William Whiteley's shop at No. 43 grew into London's major department store at the end of the nineteenth century, but declined after Whiteleys moved to nearby Queensway in 1911, four years after the store's owner, William Whiteley, was murdered by his own estranged son on the premises. In the 1950s the street became home to members of the newly arrived West Indian community and during the 1958 race riots was a major flashpoint for fighting between immigrants and local white youths. No. 189 was briefly the headquarters of the neo-fascist Union of British Freedom.

south side: Queensway to Chepstow Place
Whiteleys (1863–1911), No. 43
London's leading late-nineteenth-century department store was opened in 1863 by William Whiteley, who wanted to cater for every need – 'from a pin to an elephant at short notice' – and helped by the opening of the nearby underground station, Queen's Road grew quickly, taking over fifteen neighbouring premises within ten years. Styling itself as the 'Universal Provider', Whiteleys sold clothes, furniture and stationery, provided a hairdressing service, an estate agency and house-decorating, and attracted members of Queen Victoria's court. But it was not universally popular. Local butchers burned effigies of Whiteley on Guy Fawkes Night 1876, after he opened a meat counter, and the store suffered a number of arson attacks. On 24 January 1907 the founder met

a tragic end, murdered in his office above the store by his long-lost son, Horace Rayner, in whose pockets was found a note that read: 'To all whom it may concern William Whiteley is my father and has brought upon himself and me a double fatality by reason of his own refusal of a request perfectly reasonable R.I.P.' It transpired that nearly thirty years previously Whiteley and a friend, George Rayner, had spent a weekend in Brighton with two girls, one of whom later gave birth to a boy, Horace, whom she brought up with Rayner. When the boy grew up Rayner told him: 'Anytime you're in trouble, go and see your real father, William Whiteley', but when Horace did so a bemused Whiteley, by then seventy-five, suggested he went abroad, resulting in Horace producing a gun, shooting Whiteley dead and injuring himself. He was tried at the Old Bailey but acquitted, following a wave of public sympathy for a son wronged by his rich father. The store moved to Queen's Road, now Queensway, in 1911.

Peter Rachman's office (1950s), Nos. 91–93, west corner with Monmouth Road
Peter Rachman, London's most notorious post-war landlord, based his property empire here in the 1950s, letting out barely habitable flats across west London to vulnerable tenants with little regard for the law or common decency. Born in Lvov, Poland, in 1919, Rachman came to London as a refugee during the Second World War – he claimed fancifully that he had had his testicles removed at Auschwitz – and took a job with a Notting Hill estate agency, launching his property letting business from a phone box in Bayswater. He would buy houses for a few thousand pounds, divide them into as many flats as possible, and rent them out as 'furnished', with little more than a rotten mattress and a broken chair. Rachman would then increase the rent, and if the tenant complained would use various unscrupulous means to force them to leave, such as moving into the adjoining flat friends who would host all-night parties,

disconnecting the supply of water or electricity, or damaging the lavatories, a practice which usually had the desired effect. In 1959 Rachman was brought before the Rent Tribunal and his practices exposed, and he subsequently pulled out of the area. On 14 July 1963 the *Sunday People* ran a feature describing how Rachman had 'built up an empire based on vice and drugs, violence and blackmail, extortion and slum landlordism, the like of which this country has never seen', but by that time Rachman was dead.

► Rachman in Powis Square, p. 462.

HAMMERSMITH, W6

A bustling community occupying a bend in the Thames, dominated by a motorway flyover and served by three underground lines, Hammersmith grew as a small isolated village where the willows by the river supported a trade in basket-making. As it grew into a prosperous riverside suburb commercialization increased, destroying the peacefulness of the setting. In recent decades Hammersmith has taken on the appearance of a downtown American city, with tall, hi-tech corporate headquarters for firms such as Coca-Cola, large hotels, and a smart shopping mall connected to the tube, its most unusual feature being Ralph Erskine's Ark, a glass and steel office block by the A4, built from 1988 to 1991 in the style of the biblical ark.

● For riverside sites, see River Thames, p. 25.

HAMMERSMITH & CITY LINE

The line grew as an extension to the Metropolitan Railway, London's first underground line. The name Hammersmith & City Line was first adopted in 1868, when Hammersmith station opened, was later dropped in favour of Metropolitan Line, but was revived in the 1980s to differentiate the Hammersmith to Barking section of the Metropolitan Line from the various branches north of Baker Street.

Hammersmith The western terminus of the line, opened in 1868.
Goldhawk Road Opened on 31 March 1914 the day after a nearby inconveniently located station closed.
Shepherd's Bush An earlier station of the same name, a little further to the south, was used from 1864 until 1914, when it was replaced by the current one.
Latimer Road The 1958 Notting Hill race riots began with a domestic dispute between a Swedish woman and her West Indian husband outside the station.
Ladbroke Grove Originally known as Notting Hill when first opened in 1864, it became Ladbroke Grove in 1938 after a variety of name changes.
Westbourne Park Originally used by trains of the Great Western Railway.
Royal Oak Little more than a halt by the Great Western Railway a few hundred yards west of Paddington, it is named after the nearby Royal Oak tavern (now the Railway Tap) and when first opened in 1871 could only be entered via a wooden plank over the Westbourne River.
Paddington Originally Bishop's Road, it was the western terminus of London's first underground line, the Metropolitan Railway, and opened on 9 January 1863.
Edgware Road One of the first stations built for the first ever line, opened in 1863.
Baker Street It was rebuilt as London Underground's flagship station with offices and a block of flats between 1911 and 1933.
Great Portland Street Opened as Portland Road on the first underground line in January 1863.
Euston Square Originally Gower Street, and also one of the first seven stations.
King's Cross The original station was situated a few hundred yards to the east of the present site and its disused platforms can still be seen from some trains.
Farringdon Chosen for the eastern

terminus of London's first underground line due to the proximity of Smithfield meat market.

Barbican The Dynamiters, an anarchist terror group, took revenge for the seven-year sentence given to one of their members by leaving a bomb at this station (then Aldersgate) in April 1897 that killed one man. The station became Barbican in 1968.

Moorgate Named Moorgate Street when first opened on this line, in 1875.

Liverpool Street One of only two stations on the network (the other being Sloane Square) which until recently had a platform bar.

Aldgate East A connection from here to Shadwell on the East London Line (the St Mary's Curve) was closed in 1939.

Whitechapel Under the Hammersmith & City tracks is the East London Line that connects Brick Lane with New Cross.

Stepney Green The station is situated in Globe Town, Stepney Green being a pleasant street some distance away.

Mile End Where the line meets the Central Line, conveniently allowing commuters to change without negotiating corridors and escalators.

Bow Road A spur from here to Stratford remains closed even though its reopening would considerably improve transport through East London.

Bromley-by-Bow A station now stranded in an industrial wasteland by the thunderous motorway leading to the Blackwall Tunnel.

West Ham Until recently an isolated station, but now linked with the North London Railway and the Jubilee Line extension.

Plaistow A listed building which originally opened for the London, Tilbury and Southend Railway in 1854.

Upton Park The station for West Ham Football Club.

East Ham The first station opened here on the London, Tilbury and Southend rail line in 1858.

Barking Though the eastern terminus of the line, Barking is also an ordinary stop on the District Line and stands at the junction of two rail routes into Fenchurch Street.

KENSINGTON, W8

A Saxon tribe, the Cynesige, established a fortified village, or 'tun', in the area in the eighth century and the land later passed to the De Vere family who sold the northern section, the manor of Knotting Barns, an area of garden nurseries and orchards, in 1488, relinquishing ownership of the rest of Kensington at the end of the sixteenth century. John Bowack described Kensington as a town 'standing in a wholesome Air, not above three miles from London, resorted to by Persons of Quality and Citizens' in his 1705 *Antiquities of Middlesex*. By then the area had started to attain an exclusive air, thanks to the joint monarchs, William III and Mary Stuart, who had moved their court to Nottingham House (now Kensington Palace) in 1690 and had brought with them a large number of attendants. Kensington has since maintained its status as one of London's most desirable suburbs, was created a Royal Borough in 1901, and continues to attract wealthy residents and high-class shops, thanks to the lack of local industry.

(i) Campden Hill

Baptist Hicks acquired an estate west of Hyde Park known as the Racks, which was dotted with brickfields, in a game of cards in 1616 and took the title Viscount Campden when he was granted a peerage, renaming his villa **Campden House**. Wealthy merchants began moving into the area in the eighteenth century, but of the grand villas that were built few survive, the best known being Thorpe Lodge, now part of Holland Park School. Elsewhere, the smaller properties were most attractive, with Italianate flourishes and stucco cladding, in luscious green settings and gently sloping avenues, resulting in Campden Hill becoming one of the most sought-after areas in the capital, popular with well-paid professionals, retired military personnel and politicians.

⬤ Campden Hill is the area between Holland Park and Kensington Church Street.

Airlie Gardens
Thorpe Lodge
Now part of Holland Park school, Thorpe Lodge is a rare surviving original Campden Hill mansion, home in the early twentieth century to Montagu Norman, the occult-loving Nazi-sympathizer who was Governor of the Bank of England between the wars, gave Hitler credit, arranged for the rearmament of Nazi Germany, and is believed to have managed the 'Hitler Project', a plan to bankroll Hitler's rise to power as a counter against the Soviets. Norman entertained Hjalmar Schacht, the Nazis' Minister of Finance and President of the Reichsbank, at Airlie Lodge, attended Schacht's son's christening. When the Nazis overran Czechoslovakia in September 1938 and applied through the Bank of England for the release of £6,000,000-worth of Czech gold, Norman complied. After the Second World War Norman resigned from the Bank of England and founded the British National Association for Mental Health, which was initially based here.

► Bank of England, p. 22.

Holland Walk
A footpath to the east of Holland Park, leading from Holland Park Avenue to Kensington High Street, Holland Walk is now considered to be one of the most delightful promenades in west London but was described in the *Kensington Gazette* in the nineteenth century as 'a dark sink hole' which wives and daughters were warned not to use.

Holland House
Two wings remain of Holland House, the only surviving E-plan Jacobean manor house near central London, built in 1599 as Cope's Castle by Sir Walter Cope whose ghost, carrying its disconnected head, is said to haunt the house. At the end of the eighteenth century the house became renowned for its literary salons which were attended at various times by the writers Walter Scott, William Wordsworth, Lord Byron (who at one party in 1812 first met Lady Caroline Lamb) and later by Alexandre Dumas, the French author of *The Three Musketeers*, who would consume a bottle of Château-d' Yquem with his breakfast.

When the earl died childless in 1859, Lady Holland saved the family line by making a distant relative, the 5th Earl of Ilchester, whose wife is said to have been the inspiration for Aunt Dahlia in P. G. Wodehouse's Jeeves stories, the new owner of the title. On 27 September 1940 Holland House was badly bombed and the roof of the library was destroyed, but because the walls were relatively undamaged passers-by were able to wander at will through the debris, examining the books on the library shelves before repair work began. Partial restoration took place during the 1950s when the east wing was rebuilt as a youth hostel and the Garden Ballroom as a café. The Orangery and the Ice House (the former dairy) are now used for exhibitions.

► Kenwood House, p. 362.

Kensington Church Street
When the funeral cortège of Queen Caroline, wife of George IV, passed along Kensington Church Street in summer 1821 the crowd took the opportunity to demonstrate against the unpopular King, who they believed had acted in an unnecessarily nasty manner to the Queen. The mob overturned vehicles and threw other obstacles across the road, forcing the cortège to turn back and make for Hyde Park, where troops fired on the crowd and killed two people, provoking further rioting. Kensington Church Street,

the main link between Notting Hill and Kensington, is now an exclusive shopping enclave, particularly good for designer clothes and antiques.

St Mary Abbot's, Kensington Church Street at Kensington High Street, west side
George Gilbert Scott's church, which has the tallest spire in London at 278 ft, stands on the site of a twelfth-century church which Godfrey de Vere, the local landowner, donated to the Abbey of Abingdon after the abbots helped cure his sick son. The church was demolished in 1683, save for the tower, so that it could be rebuilt in a fitting manner for William III, who had recently taken residence in Nottingham House (now Kensington Palace), but after it was rebuilt again in 1772 the Bishop of London claimed it was the ugliest church in the diocese, not to say one of the most dangerous, given its bulging walls and dry rot. George Gilbert Scott, who also built the Foreign Office building and the hotel fronting St Pancras station, was responsible for the fourth church on the site, built in 1869 to 1872, the nave roof of which was destroyed by a Second World War bomb and later rebuilt.

(ii) Kensington Palace

Kensington Palace Gardens
London's most expensive houses can be found to the west of Kensington Palace on Kensington Palace Gardens, built as Queen's Road in 1841 and lined with luxurious mansions that had to be Italianate in design and could not be bought for less than £3,000, according to the rules of the development. Only the wealthiest individuals were able to afford its properties, and many of them are now embassies, including the Lebanese at No. 21, the Kuwaiti (No. 22), the Slovakian (No. 25) and the Czech (No. 26).
west side: Palace Green to Notting Hill Gate
No. 15a
Built by the Victorian country house designer David Brandon in 1852 to 1854 it was until recently home to the Nigerian

High Commission and then went on sale at £35 million.
Soviet Embassy (1945–90), No. 18
A Charles Barry-designed mansion in which Julius Reuter, founder of the Reuters news agency, lived from 1867 to 1899, and which Lionel Rothschild, the natural historian, bought in July 1927, it became the Soviet Union's Embassy in 1945. As the Cold War intensified, No. 18 was continually filmed by MI5 from the upstairs room of the house opposite or from cars parked in the road that were repainted and renumbered every few months.

While preparing for a visit from Soviet leader Nikita Khrushchev in April 1956, KGB chief Ivan Serov naively decided to meet the British press on the steps of the embassy. He faced an onslaught from journalists who posed questions such as: 'Mr Serov, is it true that you were responsible for butchering Estonians?' and the next day the tabloids ran headlines such as: 'Serov, Butcher Lies', 'The Butcher Is Here Giving Orders!'

In the autumn of 1957 a number of journalists received invitations, purportedly from the Soviet ambassador, to a reception at the Embassy to celebrate the fortieth anniversary of the October Revolution. The invitations were decorated with red blobs, meant to symbolize drops of blood, emanating from the sickle on the Soviet crest and were accompanied by a note that explained: 'Our reasons for approaching you are not based on any special animosity to the Soviet Ambassador . . . [but] his invitation is issued in the name of a Government which, in the years since the war, has been responsible for more collective human misery and oppression than any other single agency in world affairs.' The bogus invitations were the work of the Czech satirist and former commando Josef Josten, who in 1976 produced 250,000 bogus pound notes to mark the visit to Britain of the Soviet propaganda chief Boris Ponomarev; they so alarmed the Bank of England that the Counterfeit Currency Squad was called in.

In 1994 the art collector Nasser David Khalili bought No. 18 and the neighbouring No. 19 for £40 million and converted them into one mansion, at the cost of a further £40 million, using marble from the same Agra quarry that was used in building the Taj Mahal. Seven years later he put the combined block on sale for £65 million, at the time the highest price ever placed on a London property.

► Lenin in Bloomsbury, p. 84.

No. 24
A Moorish extravaganza built in 1845 by Owen Jones which is now the Saudi ambassador's residence.

east side: Notting Hill Gate to Palace Green
No. 5
A Soviet Consulate in the 1960s, it was here on 23 December 1962, according to some theories, that Hugh Gaitskell, the Labour Party leader, was fatally poisoned as 'punishment' for hounding communists out of the Labour Party. Gaitskell had visited the building to obtain a visa for a visit to the USSR and was given tea and biscuits while he waited. A week later he complained of feeling unwell and was taken to Middlesex Hospital where, asked about his recent diet, he told his doctor that he had had some refreshments at the consulate; by 18 January he was dead from heart and kidney failure. According to Peter Wright, the secret agent who later wrote *Spycatcher*, the biscuits may have contained hydralazine, a drug that produces the symptoms of *lupus disseminata erythematosis*, a tropical disease rare in Britain – even rarer in someone who has not visited the tropics – and not usually seen in men over forty (Gaitskell was fifty-six), which induces heart and kidney failure and which had already been proposed as a method of assassination in a Soviet journal.

'**The Cage**', No. 8
Built by Owen Jones in the 1850s, and later owned by the art collector Lord Duveen of Millbank, who also had a suite at Claridge's, **No. 8** was used during the Second World War as the headquarters of the War Crimes Investigation Unit interrogation centre known as 'The Cage', where German prisoners of war who had been close to the upper echelons of the Nazi Party, or those who had specialist knowledge of the V1 and V2 rockets that were bombarding London, were questioned. The prisoners, whose number included a small proportion of stool pigeons, usually German or Austrian Jews, who, it was hoped, would be accepted as genuine Nazis, were kept in cells with floors of solid concrete and windows covered with barbed wire. There were no furnishings that could be used by a prisoner to hang himself, and each cell door had a 'Judas hole' to enable the guards, who moved noiselessly around the complex, to spy on the inmates without being heard or seen.

Those who were kept here included Franz von Werra, the only German to escape from Britain and return home, and SS Colonel Alfred Naujocks, the man who boasted he had started the Second World War by leading the raid on the Gleiwitz Radio Station near the Polish border on 31 August 1939 which Hitler blamed on the Poles and gave him the excuse to invade Poland. Although the prisoners were under no obligation to answer any questions other than to give their name, rank and number, the inmates, according to one of the interrogators, the Earl of Listowel, were 'anxious to talk about their homes, their work as civilians, indeed the whole of their lives before they were caught by the Wehrmacht'. **No. 8** was later demolished and replaced by a Richard Seifert-designed block of flats.

No. 13
Built from 1851 to 1854 for the Earl of Harrington, who owned most of South Kensington, it was bought in 1930 for the Russian ambassador, to the distaste of Lionel Rothschild, who lived opposite and was upset at having a communist as a neighbour. It is now the Russian Federation's Embassy.

Palace Green

A short stretch of road south of Kensington Palace Gardens leading to Kensington High Street, Palace Green was built in the 1850s on what had been Kensington Palace's kitchen garden and now contains a number of embassies, including the Israeli at No. 2, which in the 1860s was the last address of the novelist William Makepeace Thackeray.

Palace Avenue

Kensington Palace

> I went to Kensington, which King William III has bought off Lord Nottingham, and altered, but was yet a patched building, but with the garden however it is a very sweete villa, having to it the Park and a straight new way through this park – *Diary*, John Evelyn (1690)

A popular tourist attraction on account of its associations with Diana, the late Princess of Wales, Kensington Palace began as Nottingham House, built by Sir George Coppin in the seventeenth century, which was later acquired by Sir Heneage Finch, Speaker of the House of Commons, and in 1689 by William III, looking for somewhere away from 'the smoak of London' to ease his chronic asthma, who paid 18,000 guineas for the property.

The king commissioned Christopher Wren to redesign the house but Wren, obliged to down tools at St Paul's, showed little interest in the work and redesigned the building with little decoration. After Mary Stuart, William's queen, died, William abandoned plans to move to Hampton Court and stayed in Kensington. Riding through Hampton Court Park in 1702 he fell from his horse, Sorrel and broke his collar bone. He returned to Kensington Palace to recuperate, but lay down by an open window and caught a chill, which turned to pneumonia, and died.

Anne, Mary's sister, who took the throne when William died and was nicknamed 'Brandy Nan' due to her fondness for alcohol, commissioned much work on the gardens, hiring Nicholas Hawksmoor to build an Orangery. On her deathbed at the palace in 1714, crippled with gout, Anne pressed the Lord Treasurer's wand into his hands with the words 'For God's sake use it for the good of my people.' The succession remained Protestant through George, elector of Hanover, a distant cousin of Anne, who spoke no English and whose first visit to the country was to assume the throne. George moved into the palace with his mistress, whom he appointed Duchess of Kendal, banished his own son, Prince George, from the court, but invited a bizarre collection of companions including Jory the Dwarf, who was so badly behaved he had to be locked in the east wing, and Peter the Wild Boy, found in the forest near Hamelin, who roamed the Kensington Palace grounds on all fours and outlived the king by nearly sixty years.

George II was the last monarch to live in Kensington Palace and his consort, Caroline, who discovered a cache of Holbein paintings secreted in a drawer, died in the palace in 1737 after failing to cure a hernia with snake-root. Just as George II's father had removed him from the house, George banished his own son, Frederick, and later, when he was told while playing cards that Frederick was dead, he retorted: 'Dead is he! Why, they told me he was better', and returned to his game.

After George died in the palace in 1760 – he fell off the toilet and smashed his head on a cabinet – his successor, George III (his grandson), uprooted the court to Buckingham House (now Buckingham Palace), and Kensington Palace fell into disrepair, standing empty for some sixty years, after which it became home to a succession of royals, including in the 1980s Prince Charles and Princess Diana. Floral tributes brought here by people following the death of the Princess on 31 August 1997 grew into the largest collection of flowers ever seen in London. It is now the London home of Prince and Princess Michael of Kent and the Duke and Duchess of Gloucester.

➤ St James's Palace, p. 209.

(iii) Kensington Court

Leigh Hunt, the nineteenth-century publisher who first introduced the works of Shelley and Keats to the public, coined the phrase the 'old court suburb' for the area south of what is now Kensington High Street, which grew after William III made nearby Nottingham House the royal seat of Kensington Palace.

Abingdon Road
Biba's (1964–6), No. 87
Barbara Hulanicki began Biba's in 1963 as a mail-order business, naming it after the nickname of her sister, Biruta, and it came to public attention when the *Daily Mirror* featured one of its pink gingham dresses in a fashion spread later that year. Pop stars and television compères soon began buying Biba clothes, and in 1964 Hulanicki opened the shop on Abingdon Road which became London's most outrageous and fashionable sixties clothes shop. As she explained in her autobiography, she was determined Biba's would not be another 'Can I help you, madam?' store so she had the walls painted navy blue and the windows hung with plum and navy curtains, furnished it with old bronze lamps and an antique Dutch wardrobe and festooned the floor with palms and ostrich feathers. There was no sign over the door and even though when it rained 'it stank of wet wool and the floor would be awash,' as Hulanicki later said, it was soon being patronized by glamorous twenty-year-old girls teetering around on what were described as 'asparagus legs', their emaciated appearance blamed on the lack of nourishing protein they received when they were babies due to rationing, but whose skeletal frames proved ideal for Biba's op-art dresses. Major success for the shop came about after the TV presenter Cathy McGowan wore Biba clothes on air, and cash-flow problems were further eased when the flamboyant singers Sonny and Cher arrived in a limousine and bought out practically the entire stock. Biba's

moved to a succession of bigger premises in 1966.
► Biba's (1973–5), p. 443.

Kensington High Street
The main east–west route through the area, Kensington High Street grew after William III created Kensington Palace in 1689, its first building of note being the Goat public house of 1695, which has since been rebuilt, and from its inception was clogged with traffic. The publisher Leigh Hunt wrote in 1851 that 'what with waiting for an omnibus and its stoppages when I got in, I found myself at a quarter to four just arrived at Knightsbridge when I ought to have been at Temple Bar'. As the century proceeded Kensington High Street became west London's major shopping centre, a status it has enjoyed since through stores such as Barker's (opened by John Barker in 1870), Derry & Toms (now Marks & Spencer), Ponting's, to the west of the tube station (since replaced by Boots), and the cultish Kensington Market which closed in 1999.
south side: Kensington Court to Addison Bridge
The Goat Tavern, No. 3
John George Haigh, the so-called acid bath murderer of the 1940s, picked up his first victim, an acquaintance called William McSwan, in the Goat tavern in 1944, and after a few drinks took him back to his workshop at 79 Gloucester Road and killed him. Haigh murdered probably nine people in all, and then dissolved the bodies in acid. He was executed at Wandsworth Prison in 1949.
► Haigh in Gloucester Road, p. 424.
Barker's, Nos. 63–97, between Young Street and Derry Street
John Barker, a departmental manager at Whiteleys, London's biggest late-nineteenth-century department store, opened Barker's here in 1870 when Whiteleys owner, William Whiteley, refused him a partnership, and within twenty years owned twenty-eight shops in Kensington, employing over 1,000 people. In 1907 Barker bought out neighbour and rival Ponting's,

and won election to Parliament as MP for Penryn and Falmouth, but his first setback came in November 1912 when a fire broke out in the food hall and twenty people died after jumping from an upper window to escape the flames. Nevertheless, Barker's enthusiasm for empire building remained undiminished. He erected temporary premises on open land on the north side of the road and later linked the new building with the rebuilt main store by a subway under the High Street. In 1919, five years after Barker died, the shop merged with Derry & Toms, which meant that the entire frontage from Wright's Lane to Young Street belonged to the same company. In 1957 the firm was taken over by the House of Fraser, who closed the branch on the north side of the road, sold the western side of the store to rivals, and in the 1980s leased the upper floors to Associated Newspapers, owners of the *Daily Mail* and *Evening Standard*.

Derry & Toms (1861–1973) / Biba's (1973–5), Nos. 103–105

Joseph Toms opened a 'Toy and Fancy Repository' in 1861 and after going into partnership with Charles Derry in 1869 expanded the shop into one of the most fashionable in Kensington. The store never recovered from the economic downturn brought about by the First World War and it merged with Barker's. The premises were rebuilt to incorporate a sixth-floor restaurant, the Beaux Arts Rainbow Room, and a Spanish-style roof garden with stream, flamingos, arches and follies. When Derry and Toms closed in January 1973 Biba's, the ultra-chic boutique, moved into what *The Times* described as 'five floors of incredibilia' to sell its outré clothes. Biba's also held occasional rock concerts in the shop, including two rare London dates on 26 and 27 November 1973 by the New York Dolls, whose outrageously camp clothes and visceral rock 'n' roll impressed even the cynical Biba's crowd and led to an *Old Grey Whistle Test* appearance that left the show's conservative presenter, Bob Harris, foaming

at the mouth, lambasting them as 'mock rock'. Biba's closed in November 1975 after running into financial difficulties and the site is now occupied by Marks and Spencer.

Kensington Square

Thomas Young, a woodcarver, planned the square as a speculative development in 1685, when Kensington was an unassuming village outside London, but failed to recoup his costs and landed in debtors' prison. Things improved after William III bought nearby Nottingham House and converted it into Kensington Palace, as court personnel such as Adam Linsey, William III's Groom of the Bedchamber, moved here. But when George III left Kensington for St James's in 1760 Kensington Square became less fashionable with the upper classes and instead attracted intellectuals such as the philosopher John Stuart Mill and the artist Edward Burne Jones. By the end of the nineteenth century the growth of the shops along nearby Kensington High Street had begun to encroach into the square, with Barker's stabling horses at one corner and buying up houses on the north side. In 1946 Kensington Council declared the square to have little architectural or historical interest but voted against its demolition. Now a conservation area, it is too close to the High Street to be a desirable residential address.

Pembroke Gardens
No. 31

Ernest Oldham, a low-rank, poorly paid Foreign Office clerk who lived on Pembroke Gardens, to the west of Earl's Court Road, in the 1930s, on a visit to Paris on official business presented himself at the Soviet Embassy as 'Mr Scott', offering to sell government secret documents in his possession. He was refused but left the package on his chair. When embassy staff examined Oldham's material they found to their surprise that the contents were valuable but had no idea how to repay him. The problem was solved by Soviet agent Hans Galleni, a.k.a. Dmitri Bystrlyotov, who journeyed to London, where it was likely the

English 'Mr Scott' lived, wandered into a police station and spun a highly unlikely story about how he and his sister had been involved in a car crash in Paris which had been witnessed by an Englishman whose name and address they had unfortunately lost, but who worked at the Foreign Office. The duty sergeant, eager to assist, phoned the Foreign Office, and gave Galleni the names and addresses of the four FO personnel who had been in Paris that weekend. Galleni visited each in turn until he caught a glimpse of Oldham walking along Pembroke Gardens. Realizing this was indeed his man he approached him and thrust an envelope containing £2,000 into his hand. Oldham soon became a full-time agent for the Soviets but the relationship soured when, racked with guilt, he resigned his Foreign Office post. In September 1933 the KGB sent their agents to Pembroke Gardens and murdered Oldham in his flat.

NORTH KENSINGTON, W10

A medieval land of market gardens and hayfields owned by Westminster Abbey, it grew after the construction of the Grand Junction Canal in 1801 and the arrival of the railways in the 1830s, and because of its remoteness from fashionable parts of London attracted cheaply built houses, let out to poor families. The area's social problems were aggravated by Second World War bombing and, although some of the worst housing was demolished soon after, the opportunity to improve the area was lost when the authorities replaced the slums of brick-built houses and the streets on which they were located with slums of tower blocks and deck-access flats on culs-de-sac and landscaped grounds. The influx of poor West Indians to North Kensington in the mid-1950s increased social tension and led to sporadic outbreaks of violence from white working-class youth, exploding into the race riots of August 1958.

Once the West Indian community established roots in the area racial tension eased, but conditions have failed to improve in line with neighbouring Notting Hill, and North Kensington has remained an impoverished community, dominated by districts of supreme ugliness and blight.

The Westway

The Westway, like Angkor Wat, the ancient temple city in Cambodia, is a stone dream that will never awake. As you hurtle along this concrete deck you become a citizen of a virtual city-state borne on a rush of radial tyres – J. G. Ballard (1999)

The Westway, London's best-known motorway, which runs above roof level for two miles between White City and Edgware Road, was constructed in the mid-1960s at a cost of £33 million. Hundreds of homes had to be demolished and streets were left as stumps either side of the new road, but many of the residents living only a few yards away received no compensation. Opposition to the road grew as completion neared and when Conservative minister Michael Heseltine opened the Westway on 18 July 1970 he was greeted by protestors armed with placards proclaiming: 'Get us out of hell! Rehouse us now.'

Amusing graffiti was soon to be daubed on the concrete supports and stanchions, one of the first instances being a Situationist take on William Blake's 'The road of excess leads to the Palace of Wisdom' redrawn as 'The Road of Excess leads to the Palace of Willesden'. That was later followed by an existentialist warning, clearly visible from the nearby tube line until recently, which read: 'Same thing day after day – tube – work – diner [sic] – work – tube – armchair – TV – sleep – tube – work – how much more can you take – one in ten go mad – one in five cracks up.'

Film-makers, writers and rock bands have long enjoyed a love–hate relationship with the road. One of the best cinematic uses was in Christopher Petit's *Radio On* (1979), a rare English road movie, which blends arresting images of the road and the locale with a sharp soundtrack, while J. G. Ballard's *Concrete Island* (1973) relates the story of a car crash on the Westway that leaves the driver unable to flag down assistance from passing vehicles. The road has featured on scores of album covers since appearing on the back of Nick Drake's 1970 album *Bryter Later*, and after the Clash, whose records were initially promoted as 'the Sound of the Westway', sang about driving up and down the Westway, in and out of the lanes on 'London's Burning', in 1977, punk groups were keen to mention the Westway to boost their credibility as purveyors of gritty urban realism.

(i) west of Ladbroke Grove (North Pole)

The unusual name of the locality, which is dominated by Kensal Green Cemetery, various railway lines, the Grand Union Canal and terraced housing of dubious quality, derives from the North Pole Tavern at 13–15 North Pole Road, near Wormwood Scrubs, and has been reinforced in recent decades by the naming of the local railway depot 'North Pole International'. The 1950s author Colin MacInnes kept the name's consonants but reworked the vowels to come up with 'Napoli' in describing the area ('the residential doss-house of our city . . . one massive slum crawling with rats and rubbish') for his 1959 novel, *Absolute Beginners*, partly set locally during the 1958 race riots when, according to MacInnes, 'Napoli was like a prison or concentration camp: inside, blue murder, outside, buses and evening papers and hurrying home to sausages and mash and tea.'

Freston Road

In October 1977 a group of squatters living in Freston Road, near Latimer Road tube station, who were threatened with eviction to make way for a new factory, announced that they had seceded from the UK, formed themselves into the 'Free and Independent Republic of Frestonia', and appealed to the United Nations to send a peacekeeping force to prevent council bailiffs evicting them. Having adopted the motto *Nos sumus una familia* ('We are one family'), all Frestonia residents took the surname Bramley to ensure that the Greater London Council would be obliged to rehouse them together, if it succeeded in evicting them. As events unfolded the national media took much interest, the *Daily Mail* carrying a report from 'Our Foreign Correspondent in Frestonia' and coachloads of tourists visiting Frestonia had their passports stamped. A National Film Theatre of Frestonia opened in the People's Hall, the first showing being inevitably *Passport to Pimlico*, the Ealing comedy about the inner London district which declares independence from Britain, and after a public inquiry a Frestonia of houses and craft workshops, using money donated by a 'foreign' government, Great Britain, via the Notting Hill Housing Trust, was established.

▶ *Passport to Pimlico*, p. 245.

Harrow Road

Kensal Green Cemetery, between Harrow Road and the Grand Union Canal

> For there is good news yet to hear and fine things to be seen / Before we go to paradise by way of Kensal Green – 'The Rolling English Road', G. K. Chesterton (1914)

Filled with stone monuments of angels and sphinxes, catacombs and mausoleums, and roamed by one of the most varied collections of wildlife to be found in London, Kensal Green is officially the General Cemetery of All Souls, the capital's first major burial ground, founded in 1832. Faced with the problem of overcrowded, unsanitary graves, the authorities had engaged in a building programme in the London suburbs that resulted in cemeteries in Norwood, Highgate, Nunhead, Abney Park, Tower Hamlets and Brompton, as well as here.

Built to the designs of George Frederick

Carden, a barrister who had visited Paris and wanted to create a London version of Paris's Père-Lachaise cemetery, Kensal Green holds the graves of many famous people, including the Duke of Sussex, sixth son of George III, who died in 1843 and had expressed the wish to be buried in Kensal Green after witnessing embarrassing royal behaviour at the funeral of William IV in Windsor; Fergus O'Connor, the nineteenth-century Chartist leader, who died from senile dementia in 1855 in a dirty Notting Hill lodging house and whose funeral was attended by 50,000 mourners; Isambard Kingdom Brunel, buried alongside the Great Western Railway, which he built (1859); John Barbirolli, Director of Music of the Hallé Orchestra (1970); and Ossie Clark, the clothes designer (1996).
➤ Highgate Cemetery, p. 334.

(ii) east of Ladbroke Grove (Golborne Town)

Houses were built on the northernmost section of the Kensington estate after the Grand Junction Canal was cut through in 1801 and industrialization increased following the building of various railways locally in the mid nineteenth century. In 1860 fights broke out between residents and Irish immigrants prompted by the question 'Who are you for? The Pope or Garibaldi?', an oblique reference to whether the Church or state should have ultimate authority, and a hundred years later the area regularly witnessed racial violence as locals chose West Indian immigrants as scapegoats for their own poor social conditions. In recent decades more immigrants, mostly Portuguese, Lebanese and Moroccan, have arrived, bringing their own unique cultural flavours to the area, particularly along Golborne Road.

Golborne Road

Going the other way is Golborne Road. You can see right along it to where it hooks on to Portobello. Same crowd

shifting. Or not. Slumming trustafarians in their Goa chic and blonde dreds. Slumming trustafarians in Gucci slingbacks and Versace wraps. Arab men, Portuguese men, drinking coffee, smoking Marlboros
– *The Crumple Zone*, Nick Barlay (2000)
A ramshackle street east of Portobello Road, Golborne Road in recent decades has become one of the most exciting spots in London, thanks to its junk shops, ad hoc street stalls of cheap ephemera and cosmopolitan population – Moroccan, Portuguese, Lebanese – who fill the cafés and cake shops and provide the nearest thing London has to a continental outdoor culture. At the eastern end of the street is the Trellick Tower, London's best-known residential tower block.

Trellick Tower, Golborne Road at Elkstone Road, south side
A sleek and beautifully proportioned thirty-one storey tower block, once the tallest in England, seen at its best from the nearby Westway or Great Western Railway, it was erected between 1966 and 1973 and designed by Erno Goldfinger, the egotistical Hungarian *émigré* said to be the model for Ian Fleming's Goldfinger in the James Bond books. He put considerable thought into his vision of homogeneous high-rise community, providing maisonettes on three levels – access was therefore required only every three floors – separating services from the living areas in a different wing according to the template laid down by Le Corbusier in his Unité d'Habitation in Marseilles, and installing timber-framed double-glazed windows which could be turned inside out to facilitate cleaning, sliding doors within the flats that allowed unrestrained use of space, and balconies finished with cedar cladding, facing south-west to catch as much light as possible. On site were shops, a doctor's surgery, a nursery and an old people's club.

Despite all this the popular press vilified the tower, and the local council's policy of using the block as a sink estate for low-income families meant that it was soon plagued by the usual social blight of vandalism, urine-infested lifts, graffiti and litter, and it became known as the 'tower of terror'. Things changed in the mid-1980s after a new residents' association was formed and chaired by Lee Boland who had once met Goldfinger in the lift and berated him for failing to provide broom cupboards. Money was spent on rehabilitating the property and single professional people started to move in, attracted by the stunning views and lively architecture, resulting in Trellick Tower being reborn as a fashionable address.

► Goldfinger's house, Hampstead, p. 366.

Southam Street

One of the poorest side streets in London in the 1950s, described by Colin MacInnes in his novel *Absolute Beginners* as a 'rotting slum of sharp, horrible vivacity', it attracted further notoriety on 16 May a year later when Kelso Cochrane, an Antiguan carpenter, was surrounded by six white men outside the Earl of Warwick pub at the corner with Golborne Road (now the Golborne House), then a stronghold of the fascist Union Movement. They taunted Cochrane with cries of 'Hey! Jim Crow!' (a reference to the 'Jim Crow' laws of the southern US states which barred blacks from jobs and public places), attacked him with a knife, and left him to bleed to death. Three days later *The Times* reported an interview with a local youth 'with sideburns two inches long and a pencil slim tie' who, asked what he felt about the murder, replied: 'One less of the blacks, that's the way I look at it. We've got too many of them around here.' Others were of the opinion that blacks drove around in cars that were 'too big' and lived in houses that were 'too big', whilst, paradoxically, simultaneously claiming that they 'lowered the tone of the neighbourhood'. No one was ever apprehended for the crime but a local youth later revealed he had been approached by a fascist organization to kill a black man – any black man – for £200. Hoping to feed off local discontent, Oswald

Mosley, former leader of the British Union of Fascists, stood as Union Movement candidate for the local parliamentary constituency in October 1959 when billboards on Southam Street were plastered with pictures of Mosley emblazoned with the message: 'He Is Coming', that were swiftly defaced with the quip 'Lucky Old Him'. A scene of children playing on a bomb site on Southam Street features in the Ealing cops and robbers thriller *The Blue Lamp*, a clip of which was later sampled by Donald Cammell and Nicholas Roeg for their celebrated 1970 film *Performance* (p. 452).

NOTTING HILL, W11

> There has never been anything in the world absolutely like Notting Hill. There will never be anything quite like it to the crack of doom . . . And God loves it as he must surely love anything which is itself unreplaceable – *The Napoleon of Notting Hill*, G. K. Chesterton (1904)

Now London's most fashionable and modish area, a magnet since the early 1960s for writers, actors, rock stars, journalists, designers and film-makers and seen as the embodiment of all things bohemian (a title previously held by Soho), Notting Hill grew during the nineteenth century as a slum and after the Second World War attracted poor West Indian immigrants, unable to afford the rents in more popular parts of London.

The new inhabitants soon found themselves at the mercy of a council which for a while refused to collect rubbish in streets where black people lived and of unscrupulous landlords such as Peter Rachman who would overfill the properties and forgo repairs. Throughout the area there was a culture clash between the West Indian immigrants, who were used to a mainly outdoor, noisy, night-time lifestyle, the indigenous, staid, petit bourgeois white population, and the more volatile working-class locals, which erupted at the end of the summer of 1958 in the Notting Hill race riots, the most intense

The 1958 Notting Hill race riots

The race riots, two weeks of mayhem in August 1958 barely paralleled in London history, were the culmination of a summer of simmering violence that saw white gangs, partly out of malice and partly spurred on by the inflammatory speeches of Oswald Mosley's neo-fascist Union Movement, roaming the streets of North Kensington and Notting Hill wrecking West Indian shops and looking for suitable victims.

Friday 15 August 1958 Charles Appio, a West Indian, about to enter Ladbroke Grove station, steps aside to let a group of white youths pass, but is grabbed and beaten up. Three white men are arrested, but the police fail to prosecute.

Saturday 23 White Teddy Boys roam Notting Hill randomly attacking anyone with black skin.

Sunday 24 The police stop groups of young whites in their cars, suspecting that they are planning violence, and find nine youths in one vehicle with a boot full of weapons, including iron bars, railings and table legs.

Friday 29 What becomes the first day of rioting begins after a domestic dispute between a Swedish woman, Majbritt Morrison, and her West Indian husband, Raymond, outside Latimer Road station gets out of hand, and leads to fighting between local white youths, blacks and the police.

Saturday 30 Tension, already high, builds up during the day in pubs such as the Kensington Park Hotel (139 Ladbroke Grove) where gangs sing 'Bye Bye Blackbird, Keep Britain White'. Majbritt Morrison, involved in the previous night's argument outside Latimer Road station, is spotted on Bramley Road, taunted with cries of 'black man's trollop' and attacked with milk bottles and lumps of wood. When she gets to her home in Bard Road she finds smoke pouring out of the house, which has been torched by mistake, and shouts: 'Is it blood you're after? Go on, kill me,' at which point she is attacked with an iron bar. Morrison is arrested – for her own safety – and held until the early hours. Meanwhile, a mob gathers outside a blues party on Blechynden Road, near Latimer Road tube station, and smashes its way inside screaming: 'Kill the niggers! Keep Britain white.'

Sunday 31 Around a hundred white youths congregate outside Latimer Road tube station armed with crowbars and knives, randomly attacking black people. Disappointed with the small number of potential victims they turn on the police with cries of 'Coppers are nigger lovers!'

Monday 1 September The worst day of violence yet occurs after Jeffrey Hamm, a leading associate of the fascist demagogue Oswald Mosley, speaks to some 700 supporters outside Latimer Road station, igniting the crowd with inflammatory statements: 'The government is to blame for allowing black people into Britain in the first place. Look what they've done to Notting Hill – they've turned it into a brothel.' A cry goes up from the crowd, 'Kill the niggers', and as the mob makes off women lean out of windows shouting: 'Go on boys, get yourselves some blacks.'

outbreak of violence seen in London during the twentieth century.

After the riots community leaders helped ease tension through such bodies as the Notting Hill Housing Trust, which took advantage of the 1965 Rent Act giving tenants more protection against rogue landlords. Also around this time musicians, writers, artists and political activists – mostly white began moving to Notting Hill, attracted by its reputation as an area constantly on the edge and by its large black population. Yet by the mid-1980s many parts of Notting Hill had become priced out of the range of all but the wealthiest and had turned it into one of London's status symbol areas, a position maintained since, despite the loss of credibility with the release of the

Before long white gangs, nearly 600 strong, are roaming the area armed with broken bottles, chair legs, iron bars, whips and petrol bombs, which they throw into houses believed to contain black inhabitants. In one of the worst incidents 26-year-old African student Seymour Manning, who has travelled down from Derby to visit friends in Notting Hill, gets out at Latimer Road tube station, seemingly unaware of the danger, walks along Bramley Road, and a minute or two later runs at great speed back to the station closely followed by three attackers.

Tuesday 2 A strange calm descends on an area described by the *Manchester Guardian* as like something out of an American Deep South movie: 'Notting Hill does not know what has hit it. Among the faces, some of them distorted, some merely curious that congregate along the pavements there lies an appalling pleasure with self. They are waiting for something to happen and too many of them will be stirred to gratification when it does.' At dusk hundreds of whites gather around Powis Square chanting: 'We want a nigger.'

Wednesday 3 The riots are over, but Notting Hill and North Kensington are a sea of broken glass and debris, with traces of blood everywhere.

Friday 5 Norman Manley, the white prime minister of Jamaica, visits Notting Hill. Stopping in the street to talk to a black man, he is told by the police to move on.

▶ The Brixton riots, p. 404.

twee 1999 Hugh Grant–Julia Roberts romantic comedy *Notting Hill*, set and filmed in the area.

Ladbroke Grove

This is now honeyed London for the rich . . . and there are more stars than beggars. For example? Van Morrison in a big over-coat is hurrying towards somewhere in a nervous mood. 'With Your Tongue Down My Throat', Hanif Kureishi (1987)

One of London's longest roads, running two miles north–south from Kensal Green to Holland Park Avenue, Ladbroke Grove, often used as a synonym for the area, was named after Sir Robert Ladbroke, a banker, who acquired the land in 1750. Sir Robert's heir, Richard Weller, built an estate of sumptuous villas, rich with baroque detail, around Lansdowne Crescent and Stanley Crescent, and the surrounding crescents were lined with spacious imposing stucco houses featuring communal gardens.

After the Second World War Ladbroke Grove became something of a promised land for London's bohemian intelligentsia, partly out of feelings of guilt for the treatment black immigrants had received from the local white working class and partly out of a belief that to be truly hip one had to adopt black culture and mannerisms. As Mike Phillips explained in *Notting Hill in the '60s*: 'For some the Grove was a testing ground in which they lived wild and free, uninhibited by laws and respectability'. One such figure was the reclusive singer–songwriter Nick Drake, who in the early 1970s spent time in a house on Ladbroke Grove that had been taken over by drug addicts, sitting and saying nothing, and returned to the house in 1974 racked by advanced paranoia and depression, to ask one of the residents: 'You remember me. You remember how I was. Tell me how I was. I used to have a brain. I used to be somebody. What happened to me? What happened to me?' He died three days later of an overdose of antidepressants.

Ladbroke Grove has seen little change, physically, in recent years and remains one of London's most fascinating and compelling roads, not least because of the demographic changes that can be glimpsed from walking its redoubtable length.

The Notting Hill Carnival
In the aftermath of the 1958 Notting Hill riots there was an outburst of black pride in the area. Various organizations were founded, including Baron Baker's United Africa–Asia League and Frances Ezzrecco's Coloured People's Progressive Association, with its motto 'United We Stand; Divided We're Lumbered', while Amy Dashwood-Garvey, Marcus Garvey's widow, opened an office for the Association for the Advancement of Coloured People. From these groups emerged the idea of a Notting Hill carnival, now Europe's largest street parade, its performers, singers, sound systems and food stalls filling the local streets every August Bank Holiday weekend.

1959 The first 'Notting Hill' Carnival takes place not in Notting Hill, but at St Pancras Town Hall, organized by Trinidadians living in Notting Hill to coincide with the Caribbean festival taking place back home.

1965 The first of the modern-day carnivals takes place in April, rather than August, and consists of a donkey cart, clown and jugglers and one man, Russell Henderson, parading a steel drum around his neck along Tavistock Road, Portobello Road and a few neighbouring streets, followed by a fire engine. Seven thousand people attend and the police arrest a pantomime horse.

1969 A float organized by the Situationist group King Mob features a 'Miss Notting Hill' – a girl with a needle stuck in her arm out of which pours ketchup as a send-up of society's preoccupation with drugs.

1974 By now the carnival is attracting crowds of 100,000, thanks largely to the efforts of Alex Pascal, presenter of the BBC's *Black London* radio show.

1976 The event, attended by a crowd of some 250,000, is spoiled by insensitive policing, with officers goading the most likely troublemakers into causing a fracas. At the end of the carnival youths throw cans at the police, who protect themselves with dustbin lids and charge across Ladbroke Grove, while those who flee overturn skips, loot off-licences, and burn cars. There are sixty arrests and 450 people are injured.

1981 The police use the carnival to test out new methods of crowd control, such as the deployment of snatch squads to arrest troublemakers.

1987 The worst riots since 1976 occur as the carnival is blighted by indiscriminate violence: an electrician is knifed to death, a man prowls the streets armed with a broken cider bottle which he shoves into people's faces, cars are set alight and skips overturned. Eventually, 1,000 officers in full riot gear charge the crowd and the violence is dispelled.

1990 By now the carnival is being remarketed as a hip event for fashionable whites. An Association for a People's Carnival is formed to combat the trend.

1997 William Hague, the leader of the Conservative Party, is photographed at the carnival disingenuously wearing a baseball cap and drinking from a coconut. The crowd reaches 2 million, two-thirds of whom are white.

2001 The carnival has become so popular the authorities consider moving it away from Notting Hill to a large open site such as Hyde Park or Wormwood Scrubs. No longer a purely Trinidadian, or even West Indian, affair, it now includes contributions from Bangladesh, the Philippines, Bulgaria, Russia, Brazil, Afghanistan and Kurdistan.

(i) Notting Dale

A slum peopled mostly by Irish immigrants and known variously as the Potteries, on account of the kilns and brick works, and the Piggeries, after Samuel Lake moved his pig farm here from Tottenham Court Road in 1818, covered the area in the nineteenth century and was described by Charles Dickens as 'a plague spot scarcely equalled in insalubrity by any other part of London'. By 1830 there were 3,000 pigs and 1,000

Notting Hill music

West Indian immigrants arriving in Notting Hill in the early 1950s and finding themselves barred from nightclubs and pubs had little option but to make their own entertainment, mostly weekend blues parties, gathering in houses where Caribbean sounds were played and alcohol was sold (illegally) to cover the cost of hosting the function and supplying the goat curry. As the technology for playing records became more sophisticated, the blues parties began to feature ever more elaborate sound systems, that were taken on tours of different houses by flamboyant showmen such as Duke Vin the Tickler and Count Suckle, both of whom were based around Ladbroke Grove in the early 1960s.

West Indian immigrants also set up a number of record labels and, as Caribbean music began to be dominated by reggae in the 1970s, they were instrumental in introducing the music to London. Island remixed Bob Marley's songs to make them more palatable to the general rock audience and Virgin established the Front Line subsidiary for unadulterated 'roots rock reggae'. But local reggae groups such as Aswad, known initially as the 'Lions of Ladbroke Grove', were unable to make the same headway and because the local scene never discovered an artist to rival the leading West Indian performers it gradually lost impetus, with reggae becoming little other than a clubbing alternative to soul, funk and rap.

Meanwhile, a white Notting Hill rock scene developed in the late sixties, the best-known group being Hawkwind, who played free festivals, led anarchist lifestyles, and made few concessions to the rock industry. Hawkwind's gigs pushed the boundaries of what was then deemed acceptable, featuring a naked dancer (played in the 1990s by Samantha Fox) and a naked drummer. Members of the group, who used to hand out condoms and controversial literature during the gigs, were busted for drugs sixty-eight times in thirty-six months around the beginning of the seventies.

Later in the decade Notting Hill became home to three of Britain's leading record labels: Virgin, originally an experimental label, built around the phenomenal success of Mike Oldfield; Island, purveyors of progressive rock and home of the most impressive roster of the era's music including Fairport Convention, Traffic, King Crimson, Nick Drake, Cat Stevens, Free, John Martyn and Jethro Tull; and later Rough Trade, which opened as a shop on Kensington Park Road in 1976 and made the transition from retailer to provider in 1978, setting up a label which broke new ground in English music, thanks to left field acts such as the Slits, the Pop Group, Cabaret Voltaire and Subway Sect, most of whom lived locally. Notting Hill retained its leading role as a centre for avant-garde music throughout the 1980s, as Rough Trade blossomed from enthusiastic tyro to major player, but by the end of the decade with the demise of the organization, the area lost its elevated status in music circles as other areas, inspired by Notting Hill's lead, began to make their own advances.
► Rough Trade, p. 458.

people, but when the authorities tried to rid the area of the animals locals greeted them with bricks made from the pigs' stools. Things reached their nadir in 1849 with an outbreak of cholera, but after Charles Dickens highlighted the problems in his magazine, *Household Words*, the area was cleaned up, churches in Kensington proper, further south, helping with religious services in mission halls and establishing a school and a temperance society.

In 1958 the Notting Hill race riots brought unwelcome attention to the area, but over the next two decades things became relatively peaceful, marred only by the occasional outbreak of violence at the

Notting Hill on film

From the earliest days of British film Notting Hill was popular with location managers as it was one of the nearest areas to the Gaumont studios in Shepherd's Bush and the Ealing studios where many British films were made. In Ealing's 1949 cops and robbers thriller *The Blue Lamp*, which introduced to the public the character of George Dixon (of Dock Green), a car chase takes place along St Mark's Road, Bramley Road, Freston Road and Ladbroke Grove. The seedy bedsit of Bryan Forbes's *The L-Shaped Room* (1962) was a house on St Luke's Road, just south of Westbourne Park tube. In *The Italian Job*, the ever-popular 1968 crime caper, Charlie Croker (played by Michael Caine) lives in a mews house off Portobello Road. Two years later the seedy side of Notting Hill featured heavily in Richard Fleischer's chilling *10 Rillington Place* about the real-life murders at that address. There are also Notting Hill scenes in *The Lavender Hill Mob* (1951), *Quadrophenia* (1979), *Sid & Nancy* (1984) and *Absolute Beginners* (1986), among others. However, the area is mostly associated with two films, Donald Cammell and Nicholas Roeg's bleak psychological drama *Performance* (1970) and the wispy Roger Michell romantic comedy *Notting Hill* (1999).

Performance (Donald Cammell/Nicholas Roeg, 1970)

Gangster Chas (James Fox) goes on the run from fellow crooks and while waiting for a train at Waterloo station overhears a conversation between a rock musician and his mother about a flat in Powis Square, Notting Hill, he has vacated that is also home to Turner, a reclusive rock star (played by Mick Jagger). Chas decides that the flat would make an ideal bolthole and hails a cab to Powis Square, getting out to the strains of Ry Cooder's 'Powis Square' theme as a hippy girl comes out of Nos. 23–24 holding a milk bottle and a cauliflower. On the doorstep of No. 25 (depicted as No. 81 in

the film) Chas walks past a Mars Bar – a jokey reference to the item found inside Marianne Faithfull during the infamous Rolling Stones drugs bust in 1967 – bluffs his way inside (interior shots were filmed mostly at 23 Lowndes Square, Belgravia, and at an unknown property on Hyde Park Gate) where, fuelled by the fashionable drugs of the day, the main protagonists engage in exotic sex, swap identities and participate in tortuous mind games, after which the merged Chas/Turner is driven away from Powis Square in a Rolls-Royce. Warner Brothers executives were shocked when they saw the takes. The sex scenes between Jagger and Anita Pallenberg didn't look faked; there were scenes in which Jagger was sharing a bath with Pallenberg and another woman, Michele Breton; and the violence was deemed to be too realistic (the film's 'Dialogue Consultant and Technical Adviser', David Litvinoff, was an associate of the recently jailed Kray twins on whom the film's villains were obviously modelled). Warners called a halt and it took the producers some time to convince them to proceed. Consequently it was two years before the film, by then heavily cut, was released. Reviewers have since called *Performance* a masterpiece of British cinema and Marianne Faithfull has proclaimed it to be 'truly our Picture of Dorian Gray'.

Notting Hill (Roger Michell, 1999)

The lightest of romantic comedies, roundly condemned for showing a w11 shorn of all its character, edge and black faces, *Notting Hill* was billed as a 'sort of but not really' sequel to *Four Weddings and a Funeral*, which also starred Hugh Grant. Much of the film was shot locally, but things did not always go according to plan. One night, with roads roped off and the camera crew preparing for action, the loud strains of Bruckner's 7th Symphony came booming from an upstairs window. Film-makers remonstrated with the resident to turn down the music, to no avail, and eventually

Julia Roberts was obliged to go and plead with the man. This seemed to work and the music was turned off, but as filming began it returned, louder than ever. 'You said you'd turn it down,' the producer called up. 'I will,' replied the man, 'when the movement is finished.' Despite the film's shortcomings its success sent large numbers of tourists to Notting Hill in search of the local sites portrayed in the film. These include:

Nicholl's Antique Arcade, 142 Portobello Road. Setting for the bookshop owned by William Thacker, played by Hugh Grant, where he encounters world-famous film star Anna Scott (Julia Roberts).

The Travel Bookshop, 13–15 Blenheim Crescent. The inspiration for Thacker's shop and where scriptwriter Richard Curtis, researching the film, learned the art of bookselling.

Coronet Cinema, 103 Notting Hill Gate. Where Thacker and Scott go on their first date.

Communal Gardens, Rosmead Road, off Ladbroke Grove. A residents-only garden where the couple climb in for a kiss on a bench.

280 Westbourne Park Road. Thacker's home, from where he emerges out of the 'blue door' to be greeted by paparazzi. The film's scriptwriter, Richard Curtis, owned the property and after *Notting Hill*'s release sold it to Caroline Freud for £1.2 million. By late 1999 Freud was so annoyed at being besieged by fans of the film that she put up the door for sale and it went at an auction for £5,750. The next day graffiti, 'blue door R.I.P.', appeared on the adjacent wall and foreign tourists, not realizing that the door from the film had been removed, kept knocking, assuming it had simply been painted over.

Portfolio, 105 Golborne Road. The card shop which featured as the restaurant where Thacker and friends discuss his decision to end his affair with Scott.

Zen Garden, 31–35 Craven Hill Gardens, Bayswater. Anouska Hempel's hotel where the couple marry.

annual Notting Hill carnival. After the villas were split into flats they became popular with writers, rock musicians and others in the arts until in the 1980s some of the properties were converted back to family homes by incoming professionals.

● Notting Dale is the area south of the Westway, west of Ladbroke Grove.

Bartle Road
10 Rillington Place
No. 10 Rillington Place, a shabby three-storey terraced house overlooking the railway line, became the most infamous address in London in the early 1950s thanks to the killing spree carried out by John Christie, who lived here between 1943 and 1953 and killed at least eight women, including his wife.

Blenheim Crescent
One of a number of crescents radiating from the centre of Ladbroke Estate, Blenheim Crescent was built in 1841 with roomy Italianate stucco-clad houses of several storeys and was a desirable address before the Second World War, declining in status in the 1950s when the houses were broken up into poorly maintained flats.

Marc Bolan's address (1968–70), No. 57 Bolan and his wife, June, moved to what the singer's biographer, Mark Paytress, described as 'the heart of the capital's freak community' in 1968, soon after the formation of his first major group, Tyrannosaurus Rex, a mostly acoustic duo playing a blend of folk, English whimsy and space rock. The flat was sparsely furnished, with little more than a two-ring cooker, and there was a shared bathroom. Nevertheless Bolan found the room to create what he optimistically called 'Toadstool Studios', a ringed-off section of the one room, soundproofed with egg cartons, where he wrote songs for Tyrannosaurus Rex's first two albums. The Bolans moved out when he became successful at the beginning of the 1970s.

Christie's victims
Victim one, Ruth Fuerst, August 1943

John Christie, a wartime special constable who had an officious, zealous manner that earned him the nickname the 'Himmler of Rillington Place', strangled student nurse and part-time prostitute Ruth Fuerst during sex, while his wife was on holiday. A few minutes later a telegram arrived informing him that his wife would soon be returning home with her brother. He buried the body under the floorboards though he let his brother-in-law stay the night in the room, retrieving the corpse after he had left. Before reburying Fuerst in the yard Christie shaved off her pubic hair, placing it in a tin he eventually used for storing the pubic hairs of all his victims. Fuerst's disappearance was blamed on an air raid.

Victim two, Muriel Eady, October 1944

A year after murdering Fuerst, Christie killed Muriel Eady, a 32-year-old workmate, when she made the mistake of responding to his invitations to visit 10 Rillington Place for a cure for her catarrh. While making Eady a cup of tea Christie rigged up a glass jar containing Friar's Balsam, pierced two holes through the lid and inserted them into rubber tubing connected to the gas mains. Eady buried her head under a towel to breathe in the mixture, whereupon Christie turned on the mains. When she was poisoned by the carbon monoxide fumes he carried her to his bed, sexually assaulted her and strangled her. He then buried the body in the back yard and used her thighbone to hold up the rickety fence. Her disappearance was also blamed on German V2s.

Victims three and four, Beryl and Jeraldine Evans, 8 November 1949

In May 1948 Timothy Evans, a Welsh simpleton, and his pregnant wife, Beryl, moved into the top-floor flat at 10 Rillington Place, and that October Beryl gave birth to a girl, Jeraldine. A few months later she fell pregnant again and Evans made inquiries about getting an abortion (then illegal), which Christie offered to perform himself. While Evans was at work Christie told Beryl to lie down and then attacked and killed her, leaving her on the bed. Christie later explained to Evans that complications during the operation had led to Beryl's death but that he could not go to the police immediately as he might be prosecuted for manslaughter – poor reward for selflessly performing a home abortion – with Evans viewed as an accomplice.

Christie disposed of Beryl's body in the washhouse, promising to take care of the baby by placing her with 'a nice couple' in east Acton, but a few days later the child was killed, strangled either by Christie or, as some believe, by a distraught Evans. Christie encouraged Evans to go to Wales and think things over, but a few days later, panic-stricken, Evans went into a police station and announced: 'I want to give myself up. I have disposed of my wife and have put her down the drain.' Police went to 10 Rillington Place where three officers lifted the manhole cover but found nothing down the drain. Accused of lying, Evans admitted that he had done so 'to protect a man called Christie'. The police returned to the house

Hippodrome Place

A 140-acre racecourse, advertised in the *Sporting Magazine* as 'an emporium even more extensive and attractive than Ascot or Epsom', opened in 1840 on a large patch of land to the north-west of Notting Hill Gate, and was attended by racegoers described by the *Sunday Times* as 'a more filthy or disgusting crew than we have the misfortune to encounter . . . with a coarseness and obscenity of language as repulsive to every feeling of manhood as to every sense of common decency'. The venture was a financial failure as the ground consisted of heavy clay which made racing unsuitable, and it closed in 1841.

and found the two bodies, but Christie, the ex-policeman, was never suspected of the murders and Evans, persuaded to confess to them, was hanged.

Victim five, Ethel Christie, 14 December 1952

After Evans's hanging Christie's murderous tendencies remained dormant for a few years. By the end of December 1952, however, he was becoming increasingly agitated with his wife, who had begun complaining incessantly about the presence of black people in the neighbourhood and taunting him about his impotence, and on 14 December 1952 he strangled her in bed, burying her under the floorboards.

Victim six, Kathleen Maloney, January 1953

Christie picked up the drunken Kathleen Maloney, an occasional prostitute, in the Westminster Arms on Praed Street, took her back to Rillington Place and gassed her. He then strangled her, had sexual intercourse with the dead body, made himself a cup of tea and went to bed. The following day he buried Maloney in an alcove in the house.

Victim seven, Rita Nelson, January 1953

A few days later Christie murdered another prostitute, Rita Nelson, whom he enticed back to the house on the pretext of being able to help her with an abortion. He gassed her, strangled her, had sexual intercourse with the corpse and buried her in the alcove alongside Maloney.

Lansdowne Crescent

The western half of Richard Weller's grand circus, the centrepiece of his Ladbroke Estate, built in the 1860s.

Site of Jimi Hendrix's death, Samarkand Hotel, No. 22

Jimi Hendrix died in the Samarkand Hotel (now private apartments) on Friday 18

Victim eight, Hectorina Maclennan, 6 March 1953

Christie's last victim was a 26-year-old Scottish girl who had come to look at a room at 10 Rillington Place. Christie attacked her, gassed her and then had sexual intercourse with the body. As with the two previous victims he placed the corpse in the alcove.

After murdering Maclennan Christie moved out and sublet the undesirable residence, which had eight corpses secreted in various places. On 24 March 1953, a few days after Christie had left, one of the new tenants, Beresford Brown, engaged in DIY repairs, shone his torch into the alcove where Christie had buried his three most recent victims and saw the bodies. Hysterical, he called the police, who uncovered the remaining corpses. Now the police realized that Christie was the culprit and launched a nationwide search, and he was spotted in Putney a week later. Christie was convicted of the various murders at the Old Bailey where, three years previously, Timothy Evans had been sentenced to death for a crime he had not committed. Like Evans he was hanged at Pentonville.

In his book *10 Rillington Place* (1961), Ludovic Kennedy argued that Evans was wrongly hanged and launched the campaign that led to a posthumous pardon for the Welshman. Rillington Place, which had been renamed Ruston Close in the late 1950s, was demolished in the 1970s and rebuilt as Bartle Road. There is no longer a property at No. 10, just a garden between the modern-day Nos. 9 and 11.

September 1970. He had returned to the room rented by his girlfriend, Monika Danneman, at around 3 a.m., eaten a tuna sandwich and taken a sleeping tablet. When he woke up at about 7 a.m. he spoke to Danneman, but fell asleep again. A few hours later Danneman found she could not wake the guitarist and noticed that he had

been sick and had taken a number of pills.
She called an ambulance, which took him
to St Mary Abbot's Hospital in Kensington
where he was pronounced dead. Although
a doctor at the hospital claimed Hendrix
had drunk so much red wine that he had
drowned trying to regurgitate it, the official
reason given at the time was 'inhalation of
vomit due to barbiturate intoxication', later
changed to an open verdict.

Princedale Road

A pleasant street of charming small houses
and offices, leading north from Holland
Park Avenue, it was the setting for much
political and counter-culture activity in the
first decades after the Second World War.
Colin Jordan ran the White Defence League,
an avowedly racist organization which advocated keeping Britain white at a time of
growing black immigration, from No. 74
in the 1950s. Caroline Coon opened Release,
Britain's first drugs awareness organization,
at No. 70 in the 1960s, and around the same
time *Oz*, the counter-culture magazine, was
based here.

Oz (1960s, 1970s), No. 52

Oz, the irreverent underground magazine,
founded in Australia on April Fools' Day
1963 by Richard Neville, Richard Walsh and
Martin Sharp, was relaunched in Britain in
February 1967 and caught the rebellious
flavour of the times by encouraging readers
to 'Turn On, Tune In and Drop Dead'. It
ran articles on the novelist Colin MacInnes;
the black activist Michael X; *Private Eye*,
which was criticized for having too many
writs; the burgeoning flower power movement; drugs; the Beatles' *Sergeant Pepper* LP;
and alternative theatre, but unlike its main
rival, *International Times*, was mostly a
hedonistic affair. It had no socialist manifesto, little awareness of progressive social
issues (male writers had their names printed
in full, while female contributors were
identified solely by their first name) and,
although it published Germaine Greer's
ground-breaking feminist essay, 'The Politics of Female Sexuality', in 1970, it ruined

the effect by labelling the issue containing
the piece 'Cunt Power Oz'.

Early in 1970 Neville called for 'any
readers who are under 18 to come and edit
the April issue'. Those who responded
included Peter Popham (later of the *Independent*), Deyan Sudjic (who went on to
become the *Guardian*'s architecture correspondent) and Charles Shaar Murray (an
influential journalist on the *New Musical
Express* during its 1970s heyday), who produced an issue with a cover containing
images of naked black girls. That led to
officers from the Vice Squad raiding the
premises and the editors – Felix Dennis, Jim
Anderson and Richard Neville – being
charged with publishing an obscene magazine. The trial that followed was the longest
obscenity trial ever held in Britain, and after
the three were convicted in August 1971 of
various obscenity charges they were sent to
Wormwood Scrubs.

More than twenty years later the judge
who sentenced them, Mr Justice Argyle,
told the *Spectator* that behind *Oz* lay 'a
conspiracy of criminals who were selling
[the magazine] together with soft drugs at
the entrance to state schools and youth
clubs'. Dennis sued, won an apology and
£10,000 in damages which he donated to
charity.

(ii) Kensington Park

The centre of what is now fashionable W11
and one of the liveliest areas in London,
Kensington Park was given its name in the
1840s by developers desperate to attract
wealthy residents and was covered thirty
years later with elegant spacious houses
coated in cream stucco, at its southern end,
and closely packed terraced houses in stock
brick further north. It was these houses that
were at the centre of the slum empire run by
Peter Rachman in the 1950s and were later
colonized by the kind of white liberals now
often described by the slightly disparaging
neologism 'trustafarian'.

All Saints Road

Built from 1852 to 1861 on land which belonged to Porto Bello Farm and named after All Saints church on Talbot Road, All Saints Road became a street of shabby shops and pokey flats in the early 1950s, attracting West Indian immigrants looking for cheap accommodation. By the 1970s it had become a haunt of anarchists, muggers and hard-selling ganja dealers who would accost passers-by to sample their wares and stage indiscriminate robberies, during which doors would be broken down and people beaten up in hallways; victims were beaten even harder if they did not have 'enough' money on them. Things began to improve by the end of the 1980s during the general gentrification of w11, when crime moved north of the Westway towards Harlesden, and All Saints Road has since become an attractive street of record shops, cafés, restaurants and presentable flats.

east side: Tavistock Crescent to Westbourne Park Road

No. 18

Previously the Apollo pub, it became the hub of local West Indian nightlife in the 1960s, after the landlord lifted the colour bar but was closed down by police in 1982, having become a centre for drug dealing. It later reopened as Metamorphosis recording studios.

No. 8

Frank Critchlow opened the Mangrove Restaurant here in 1968 and it soon became an unofficial advice centre and meeting place for the local black community, visited by dignitaries such as the singer Sammy Davis Jnr and the historian C. L. R. James, and a fashionable hangout for white bohemians. When drug dealers began frequenting the Mangrove in 1969 it became a target of police raids, and in the summer of 1970 officers used the excuse that food had been served after 11 p.m. to prosecute Critchlow. There were local demonstrations against police harassment but officers raided the restaurant again and arrested nine regulars, who became known as the Mangrove Nine, their number including Darcus Awonsu, now Darcus Howe, the Brixton community leader.

Critchlow made a name for himself during the fifty-five-day trial by replying to the judge's claim that he had thirty-five years of experience: 'We have had 400 years of colonial experience'. Five of the nine were found guilty on minor drugs charges; Critchlow was acquitted. Over the next decade or so, there were fifty more raids on the Mangrove and several more prosecutions, with Critchlow again being acquitted. Finally, on 20 May 1988, two decades of confrontation came to a head when a squad of forty-eight officers descended on the Mangrove and arrested Critchlow for drugs offences. He was remanded in Wormwood Scrubs for six weeks, but when the case came to court the judge threw it out and it later transpired that police had planted the drugs. Critchlow sued for false imprisonment and was awarded £50,000 by the High Court. The restaurant went bankrupt in 1991, briefly reopened as Mas Café, and is now shut again. Opposite stands the Mangrove Information Centre.

Blenheim Crescent *Also see p. 453*

The eastern end of Blenheim Crescent is Notting Hill's best road for bookshops with Books for Cooks at No. 4, Garden Books (No. 11) and the Travel Bookshop, inspiration for William Thacker's bookshop in the film *Notting Hill* (No. 15).

Totobag's (1950s–1970s), No. 9, south side
Totobag's café, one of the area's first important West Indian meeting places, where men played dominoes, cards and ludo, was also patronized by white liberals, including Sarah Churchill, daughter of Winston, who would turn up in a chauffeur-driven Rolls-Royce. During the 1958 riots it was besieged by a white mob that was taunted from an upstairs window by one of the regulars, Baron Baker, who mockingly shouted at them: 'Get back to where you come from.' As the siege went on for some hours, those trapped inside resorted to drastic measures,

such as the throwing of Molotov cocktails out of the windows on to their attackers, which brought the swift arrival of the police who arrested six blacks and three whites for causing an affray.

Colville Terrace

The eastern continuation of Elgin Crescent, it was where landlords crammed West Indian immigrants into crumbling villas in the 1950s resulting in the street having the highest population density in the UK outside Glasgow.

Michael de Freitas's address (early 1960s), No. 24

Michael de Freitas, the self-styled leader of Notting Hill's black community in the 1960s, worked as a pimp when he first arrived from Trinidad in the mid-1950s, briefly appeared in the news after trying to smuggle a Yugoslav girl into Britain, and gained notoriety in criminal circles after carrying to the getaway car a gang leader who fainted during an armed robbery in Reading. He also played a leading role in organizing resistance to attacks from white groups during the 1958 Notting Hill race riots. Two years later De Freitas became a rent collector for the rogue landlord Peter Rachman after the latter caught him burgling his Monmouth Road office, but eventually he turned on Rachman, helping his tenants win rent reductions.

De Freitas converted to Islam in 1965 and took the name Michael Abdul Malik, but after reading an article in the *Sunday Times* about Malcolm X, the American Black Power leader, and another former pimp, whom he once briefly met in an Earl's Court restaurant, changed it to Michael X. De Freitas helped organize the first Notting Hill carnivals and in 1966 took boxer Cassius Clay around the area before his fight with Henry Cooper. Clay later gave him his blood-spattered shorts with the greeting: 'Here's the blood of an Englishman for you.'

In 1967 X became the first person to be prosecuted under the Race Relations Act, for using the term 'white monkeys' and publicly urging the shooting of any white man seen with a black girl, and was jailed for nine months. Yet he retained popularity with the largely white underground scene that congregated around Notting Hill and rock groups were keen to hire his RAAS (Racial Adjustment Action Society) organization to provide 'security' for various gigs. At the end of the sixties X opened a Centre in Holloway Road, but in 1971 he left for Trinidad, where he was hanged for murder.
► Michael X's Black Centre, Holloway Road, p. 337.

Kensington Park Road

A long, skewed road running parallel to Portobello Road, it takes in the spacious villas of the Ladbroke Estate, with their exquisite cream-coloured stucco, at its southern end and small, intimate shops further north. In the 1950s the road was a major meeting place for local fascists who held street meetings outside the synagogue at No. 206.

Rough Trade (1976–85), No. 202, east side
Inspired by Lawrence Ferlinghetti's City Lights alternative bookshop in San Francisco, Geoff Travis opened the Rough Trade record shop at No. 202 in February 1976, filling the racks with hardcore Jamaican reggae and obscure American punk rock, which had a small fanatical cult following in the UK. When British groups began making records in the punk idiom, Rough Trade became a major meeting place for fanzine writers, rock journalists, hangers-on and the bands themselves, who would bring in copies of their records and pin the sleeves on the wall gallery next to their rivals' efforts.

Musicians soon began asking Travis for help in getting a record cut and he came to the conclusion that he should release them himself, setting up the Rough Trade record label in 1978. Early releases covered a huge range of styles: the whimsical English eccentricity of Swell Maps; the slapstick of the Monochrome Set; the brutal onslaught of Stiff Little Fingers; and the deadpan satire of

Cabaret Voltaire, who used cut-and-paste techniques that mixed electronics, dub reggae, avant-garde classical ideas and noise samples in a style that is now widespread even in the mainstream, but was then revolutionary.

Travis and colleagues conducted business as a co-operative that he described as 'pro-feminist, pro-humanitarian, anti-fascist, anti-authoritarian' – unlike the practice of most record labels, female acts were not shunted to the side or paraded as novelties but, in the case of the Raincoats, Delta 5, Essential Logic, Kleenex and Slits, pushed as central to the label's image – and by the mid-eighties Rough Trade had set up a national independent record distribution network that helped establish Joy Division, New Order and Depeche Mode, and had signed the Smiths who, along with New Order, became one of the leading British groups of the era.

But things did not remain buoyant for long and rapid expansion, combined with lax business control, led to cash flow problems. When the independent distribution network collapsed, so did the Rough Trade label, which passed through various unsympathetic owners before eventually returning to Travis's hands during the 1990s. The shop, protected under a separate franchise, moved in 1985 to Talbot Road, where it has continued to thrive, with branches opening in Covent Garden and Tokyo.

Notting Hill Gate

Notting Hill Gate, the main east–west road at the southern end of w11, is named after the tollgate that was situated at the Pembridge Road corner from 1769 to 1864. It offers little indication of the wealth of interest that can be found in the streets on either side, being a shabby mix of Victorian shops, many now owned by the Music and Video Exchange chain, built into the front gardens of the terraced houses, and crude 1960s precinct-style blocks on the south side.

Pharmacy, No. 150, north side
Briefly the most fashionable restaurant in London at the end of the twentieth century, Pharmacy, the brainchild of the shock artist Damien Hirst, the PR guru Matthew Freud and superchef Marco Pierre White, opened on 15 January 1998, its medical decor, inspired by Peter Savile's cover for the New Order single 'Fine Time', featuring oversized medicine cabinets and walls decorated with pictures of pills and capsules. The opening-night party was attended by the most famous names from Notting Hill's bohemian past, including the actress Anita Pallenberg and the chanteuse Marianne Faithfull, and those who began patronizing the restaurant included other local celebrities such as Damon Albarn, Kate Moss and Helen Fielding. Pharmacy was unable to maintain its elevated position, though, and, with mounting losses, was sold to a restaurant group at the end of the year. It reopened in September 2001 with a party ignored by celebrities and the public.

Portobello Road

All along the gutter rickety stalls and barrows were piled high with rags, torn jerseys, mismatched shoes, chipped china, bent tin trays, three-legged furniture and unfunctioning appliances from the early days of electricity – *An Open Book*, Monica Dickens (1978)

One of London's most famous street markets, along with Petticoat Lane, and the centre of the capital's antique trade, Portobello Road began as a country lane linking Kensal Green and Kensington Palace alongside a farm, Barley Shotts, which was situated between modern-day Chesterton Road and Oxford Gardens, and was renamed 'Portobello' in the mid eighteenth century in honour of Admiral Vernon's capture of Puerto Bello in the Gulf of Mexico from the Spanish in 1739. The route later took the name Portobello Lane and a market was opened by gypsies trading horses in the 1870s, the first licences being handed to stallholders in 1929. Antique traders arrived after the Second World War, following the closure of Caledonian market in Holloway, and business boomed as public interest in nostalgia increased. Portobello Road is now one of the most crowded weekend spots in the capital, its enduring popularity explained by the quality of the goods on offer, its winding length, which provides an unexpected visual treat at every turn, and the picturesque nature of its compact, gaily painted houses south of West-bourne Grove.

▶ Petticoat Lane, p. 289.

west side: Pembridge Road to the Westway
No. 115
June Aylward opened Portobello Road's first antique store at No. 115 in 1950.

Virgin Records (1973–85), 2–4 Vernon Yard at 117 Portobello Road
Following the success of his Virgin record shops in the early 1970s Richard Branson founded a record company in 1973 with four releases including *The Faust Tapes* by the German group Faust, an amalgam of guitar noises, tape loops and histrionic effects which was banned from the album charts on account of its 49 pence price tag, and *Tubular Bells*, written and recorded in almost its entirety by Mike Oldfield, a prodigious twenty-year-old multi-instrumentalist. *Tubular Bells* was cut from 2,300 different recordings, eventually topped the British and American charts, was featured in *The Exorcist* film and remains one of the artistic cornerstones of progressive rock.

Branson's attempts to replicate Oldfield's success did not initially work. A bid to sign 10cc, then at their peak, foundered, as did over-ambitious moves to enrol the Who and Pink Floyd, while the Rolling Stones decided that Virgin were too small. By the start of 1977, with punk having replaced prog rock as the sound of the era, Virgin was desperate to find a major new commercial act and approached the newly formed and unsigned Dire Straits, whom a talent scout had heard on a radio session, with a view to signing a deal. The two parties negotiated over dinner

at a nearby Greek restaurant and before the bill arrived a waiter brought to the table a platter covered with a silver lid which he removed with a flourish to reveal ten joints – one for each of the assembled throng. The following day Dire Straits' management phoned to tell Virgin that the band had chosen to sign for Phonogram instead. No reason for rejecting Virgin was given, and Branson remained mystified at the group's decision until he learned ten years later that Dire Straits had thought Virgin were trying to ply them with drugs to soften them up before presenting them with the contracts. In fact the joints had come courtesy of the waiter, whose generosity could be said to have cost the label some £500 million in sales.

Soon Virgin did achieve notable success, however, signing the Sex Pistols in 1977 when no other established label in the country would touch them after their ignom-inious departures from EMI and A&M, and setting up a reggae offshoot, Front Line Records, which for many whites was an introduction to reggae with a heavier production sound and more arcane lyrics than the bowdlerized Bob Marley & the Wailers' offerings available from Island Records. Virgin emerged from the punk/new wave era on a strong footing, signing PiL, the Human League, XTC, Japan and Culture Club, and by the mid-eighties the label had outgrown Vernon Yard and its former small-scale independent status and established itself as one of Britain's biggest labels, inspiring Branson to begin building his multi-faceted business empire.

Electric Cinema, No. 191
One of the oldest purpose-built cinemas in the country, the Electric Cinema is decor-ated with furnishings typical of the Edwar-dian period, including ornate plaster work, a mosaic floor, swags of fruits, vegetables and flowers, and has a cream faience tiled exterior. It opened in 1911 with a screening of a film of Shakespeare's *Henry VIII* recorded at Her Majesty's Theatre, Hay-market, and during the First World War

locals, suspecting that the German manager was signalling to overhead Zeppelins, stoned the cinema. In the 1960s the Electric Cinema became an art-house venue, and the policy of showing esoteric films continued until 1983, when the premises were sold and the new owners began screening first runs. Repertory films were later reintroduced, however, and in 1992 the celebrated Spanish director Pedro Almodóvar, spotted watching an all-nighter of his own films and urged to give a short speech, rambled on at length in incomprehensible Spanglish, finishing off by declaring: 'I love New York' to bemused patrons. The cinema closed down in the 1990s but reopened in 2001.

east side: Westway to Pembridge Road
Market Bar (Former Golden Cross), No. 240, north-east junction with Lancaster Road
In his 1989 novel *London Fields* Martin Amis depicted the pub, then the Golden Cross, as the Black Cross, a den of 'TV, darts and pimball [*sic*]' and haunt of Keith Talent, 'an obsessive tail-chaser of the type that was meant to have died out years ago'. In the 1990s the building was gentrified and reopened as the Market Bar to cater for the new moneyed 1990s Notting Hill crowd under the stewardship of John Leyton, the former actor and singer who starred in *The Great Escape* and recorded the atmospheric single 'Johnny Remember Me' for Joe Meek in the 1960s.
▶ Joe Meek's studio, p. 337.
George Orwell's address (1927–8), No. 22
After resigning his commission in the Burmese police force, Orwell (then Eric Blair) moved to London, finding lodgings with an old acquaintance, the poet Ruth Pitter, who, on finding out that he wanted to be a writer, told him that he had left it too late and had no income to fall back on. Her scepticism was reinforced when she looked at his verse, which she thought naive and amateurish, later recalling how 'we used to laugh till we cried at some of the bits he showed us'. Nevertheless Blair pressed on with his ambitions and chose to experience

life as a tramp in the slum areas of east London with the idea of collecting research for a book on the subject – which became *Down and Out in Paris and London* (1933).

Powis Gardens
All Saints Hall
In autumn 1966 the newly formed Pink Floyd played some of their earliest concerts in a now-demolished church hall, just south of Westbourne Park Road as part of the London Free School's Light and Sound Workshop. Joel and Toni Brown, associates of Dr Timothy Leary, the prime mover of the sixties counter-culture, put on a light show, probably for the first time at a rock concert in Britain, projecting slides on to the bodies of the musicians as they played. When the Browns returned to America the gig's promoters, Peter Jenner and Andrew King, having little idea how to put on a similar show, made a trip to British Home Stores, where they bought some spotlights. At the next gig they used everyday household switches to operate the spotlights through coloured Perspex nailed on to wood and stretched condoms across the projector to create unusual effects. Pink Floyd later took their show to the UFO club on Tottenham Court Road. Hawkwind, who became the epitome of Notting Hill rock in the 1970s, made their first appearance at the hall on 29 August 1969, though not on the bill, after gatecrashing the stage and announcing they would be the first band on.
▶ **UFO club**, p. 148.

Powis Square
By then long decayed into one of the seediest spots in west London, Powis Square was a haunt of pimps and prostitutes in the 1950s and became the setting for some of the worst violence that befell the area during the 1958 race riots. A BBC reporter, Commander George Villiers, recorded his reactions to the violence as it took place around him: 'Today, as an Englishman, I have been made to feel ashamed of British justice.' When approached by a policeman, who

asked him if he had any weapons on him, Villiers replied: 'Yes, my weapons are pen and paper,' handing his fountain pen to the bemused officer before being thrown into a Black Maria.

In June 1959 the West London Rent Tribunal found flats at Nos. 31, 32, 44 and 45 Powis Square owned by Peter Rachman, the landlord who came to be associated with London's worst slum landlordism, 'scruffy, dirty and unfit for human habitation'. But tenants who had been due to appear before the tribunal to complain about Rachman withdrew their appeals after being intimidated by him and his associates. In the 1960s the Situationist group King Mob planned to open up the fenced-off area within the square as an ad hoc children's playground, a plan that was by far the least contentious of the group's various eccentric and unrealized aims, which included blowing up Wordsworth's Lake District cottage and hanging the Holland Park peacocks. External shots of No. 25 were included in the cult Donald Cammel/Nicholas Roeg film *Performance* (see Notting Hill on film, p. 452).

Powis Terrace

Peter Rachman, the slum landlord, bought his first properties, Nos. 1–16 Powis Terrace, for £20,000 in the early 1950s, installing a Nigerian landlord who was obliged to find him £300 a week in rent. Although there was room for around 200 people in the houses there were soon 1,200 living there, the rent being collected by agents who visited the flats accompanied by a wrestler and an Alsatian. Powis Terrace was a major flashpoint during the 1958 Notting Hill race riots, but a decade later was at the centre of the local bohemian culture, John Hopkins's London Free School being based at No. 26a.
London Free School (1960s), No. 26a, west side
John Hopkins, a photo-journalist who was one of the main figures in the 1960s London counter-culture and helped set up *International Times*, launched the London Free School where anybody who had anything to

teach could run a class in 1965. John Michell, now connected with *Fortean Times*, who owned the property, lectured on UFOs and other mysterious business, and the school also helped organize the first proper Notting Hill Carnival in 1964 and stage early gigs by Pink Floyd at the nearby All Saints Hall (see above) in 1966. That year, Hopkins, having heard a tape of the newly formed Velvet Underground, made an audacious attempt to become the group's manager, phoning contacts in New York and eventually getting through to the band's John Cale, who explained that a 'Mr Warhol' was looking after their affairs. The London Free School closed in 1967.
► **UFO club**, p. 148.
David Hockney's studio (1960–77), No. 17, east side
Before moving to California the artist David Hockney lived on Powis Terrace where, as Roy Strong noted in his diary, there was 'every sign that gentility had long since fled', and used to throw Saturday afternoon tea parties which Andy Warhol attended on a couple of occasions. Of the various pieces Hockney created here the best known is probably *Domestic Scene, Notting Hill* (1963), which shows a seated figure, modelled on the clothes designer Ossie Clark, who had been at the Royal College of Art at the same time as Hockney, and a naked man, Mo McDermott, Hockney's regular model and assistant, placed in a two-dimensional space with no floors or walls.
► Francis Bacon, p. 424 and p. 425.

SHEPHERD'S BUSH, W12

A vibrant but charmless district of Victorian terraced houses, partly gentrified in recent years, Shepherd's Bush takes its name from the local shepherds who rested their flocks on Shepherd's Bush Common, the centre of the district, and was commercialized following the arrival of the railways in the mid nineteenth century, the population rising from around 10,000 to 250,000 soon after.

The area has been associated with film and television production since the earliest days: many of Britain's first films were made at the Lime Grove studios early in the twentieth century, and BBC Television has been based in Wood Lane, White City, since the late 1950s.

(i) Wormwood Scrubs

The open land at the north of Shepherd's Bush was first recorded in 1189 as Wormholt Scrubs ('holt' meaning wood) and due to the soil's unsuitability for growing crops remained common land, where locals kept cattle and pigs by two streams, Stamford Brook and Counters Creek. At the beginning of the twentieth century Wormwood Scrubs became an important testing ground for early attempts at aviation and during the two world wars was used for training soldiers and testing weapons.

Braybrook Street

On 16 August 1966 Harry Roberts and two accomplices shot three unarmed policemen sitting in a car on Braybrook Street, close to Wormwood Scrubs prison, after one of the officers, a Sergeant Head, who thought Roberts's car might be used in an escape attempt, approached the vehicle and mentioned the absence of a tax disc on the windscreen. Roberts, worried that the policeman would search the car and find the gun he had secreted, shot Head, and when a second officer, DC Wombwell, ran back to the police car to take cover, Roberts chased him and shot him in the face. The gunman then ordered an accomplice, John Duddy, to shoot the third officer, PC Fox, as the latter tried to flee, but as the villains sped off a passer-by, who had witnessed the shooting and assumed there had been a jailbreak, took down their registration number. The third member of the gang, John Witney, was arrested and during questioning he implicated Duddy and Roberts, who went on the run for ninety days, camping out in the Hertfordshire woods until being spotted by a schoolboy. While the drama unfolded, the provocative chant 'Harry Roberts is our friend, he shoots coppers' could be heard on football terraces throughout Britain. Roberts was later jailed for thirty years.

Du Cane Road
Wormwood Scrubs Prison

Britain's most famous prison, its reputation based more on its descriptive name than on the harshness of its conditions, was designed by Edmund Du Cane, after whom the nearby road is named, and built in 1873 as a replacement for Millbank Penitentiary, Westminster. It was commandeered during the Second World War by the government for storing twenty-six cans of heavy water, needed for research on what Britain hoped would be the first atomic bomb, which had been brought to London by two scientists escaping from France. The Scrubs remained a prison during the Second World War, inmates including the composers Ivor Novello, jailed for altering documents relating to his Rolls-Royce, and Michael Tippett, a conscientious objector. The Scrubs was also the temporary home of MI5 and used as a prisoner-of-war camp where POWs, shown newsreel footage of the findings made by the Allies at the Nazi concentration camps, dismissed the pictures as propaganda designed to shame the German people.

Britain's three most notorious twentieth-century gangsters – Charlie Richardson and Ronnie and Reggie Kray – all served time in the Scrubs in the 1950s. Richardson, aged fourteen, was put into a cell on his own so that he would not be raped by an older inmate, while the Krays spent a month here after attacking a policeman on Bethnal Green Road. The playwright Joe Orton spent six months in the prison in 1962 after being prosecuted for stealing books from Islington libraries, but the spy George Blake, sentenced to a record forty-two years in 1961, was sprung from the prison in 1966. He was driven off in a waiting car to make the short journey to 28 Highlever Road, North Kensington, where he holed up before being whisked off to Moscow.

Rolling Stones guitarist Keith Richards begun a year-long sentence in the prison in June 1967 after a drugs bust, but a successful appeal set him free after one night (during which inmates asked him repeatedly if he wanted any hash). Another Rolling Stone, Brian Jones, spent a night here that October for possessing cannabis; his nine-month sentence commuted, this time, on the recommendation of a psychiatrist, who claimed that Jones was 'an extremely frightened young man'. The editors of the irreverent counter-culture publication *Oz* – Richard Neville, Jim Anderson and Felix Dennis – served only three days of their various sentences in the Scrubs in the early seventies before being released to be taken, according to a story that Dennis later told author Jonathan Green, to an office in an Inn of Court, where Lord Widgery, the Lord Chief Justice of England, told them that he had spoken to the prime minister (Harold Wilson) and arranged a deal for their release on the condition that they did no further work on the magazine. His parting words to the three were, supposedly: 'Now get out and leave those sherry glasses behind you.'

In 1979 IRA prisoners staged a rooftop protest over visiting rights, and there were riots the same year regarding overcrowding, hygiene, sanitation and the quality of prison facilities, a popular gripe being the toothpaste, which 'ripped your mouth to shreds'. During the 1980s £30 million-worth of improvements were carried out in the aftermath of riots, hostage-taking and other violent disturbances.

► Pentonville Prison, p. 335.

(ii) White City

What began as a nickname coined to describe the white stucco-clad buildings erected for the local 1908 𝔉𝔯𝔞𝔫𝔠𝔬–𝔅𝔯𝔦𝔱𝔦𝔰𝔥 𝔈𝔵𝔥𝔦𝔟𝔦𝔱𝔦𝔬𝔫 soon came into widespread usage for the local stadium, which hosted that year's Olympic Games, the nearby 1930s council estate, a tube station, BBC Television Centre, and for the grimy surrounding district.

Commonwealth Avenue
White City estate

A 50-acre council estate of unrelenting dreariness, White City was begun in 1938 on land that had been used for the 1908 𝔉𝔯𝔞𝔫𝔠𝔬–𝔅𝔯𝔦𝔱𝔦𝔰𝔥 𝔈𝔵𝔥𝔦𝔟𝔦𝔱𝔦𝔬𝔫. Both the roads and the tower blocks were given names connected with the exhibition and the

---

1908 𝔉𝔯𝔞𝔫𝔠𝔬–𝔅𝔯𝔦𝔱𝔦𝔰𝔥 𝔈𝔵𝔥𝔦𝔟𝔦𝔱𝔦𝔬𝔫

For the 1908 𝔉𝔯𝔞𝔫𝔠𝔬–𝔅𝔯𝔦𝔱𝔦𝔰𝔥 𝔈𝔵𝔥𝔦𝔟𝔦𝔱𝔦𝔬𝔫 Britain, France and the countries of the British Empire constructed exhibition halls and pavilions that included a Canadian Palace, a Ceylon Tea House, a Scenic Railway, a Franco–British Pavilion, a Palace of Music and an Irish Village, on 200 acres of semi-rural wasteland south of Wormwood Scrubs. A number of mud huts were built, off Wood Lane, in which around 150 Senegalese lived for four months simulating native conditions (without the native weather). The exhibition continued until that October after which the site was handed back to the owners, the Kiralfy family, hosting a variety of exhibitions until the 1930s, when Hammersmith Council announced that the land would be used for new housing, which is now the White City estate.

---

empire – Commonwealth Avenue, Australia Road, India Way, South Africa Road et al. Although the architects received praise for separating the kitchens from the living area and for including bathrooms, tenants claimed they preferred a traditional 'parlour' and were unimpressed with the monotonous grid-like layout of the estate. By the 1970s a sizeable portion of White City had become derelict. It still awaits suitable redevelopment, if not outright demolition.

Wood Lane

A long bleak road of unrelenting ugliness alongside the thunderous M41 crossed by the equally noisy Westway and lined with shoddy municipal houses close to Wormwood Scrubs, it is also home to several ungainly BBC studios and office blocks.

west side: Uxbridge Road to Scrubs Lane
BBC Television Centre

The BBC bought the site, which had been occupied by the Court of Honour during the 1908 Franco–British Exhibition, in 1949 to build its main television studios, whose first programme was broadcast here on 29 June 1960. The studios have since been used to make many of the BBC's best-known shows including *Blue Peter*, *That's Life* and *Top of the Pops*.

White City Stadium, west side, south of Westway

The 68,000-seater White City stadium, mostly used for greyhound racing, had its heyday during the 1908 Olympic Games that had been scheduled to take place in Rome and were hurriedly transferred to London when Mount Vesuvius erupted in 1906.

The rearranged Games were marred by various rows and mishaps. The Russians insisted that competitors from Finland, then under Russian rule, paraded under the Russian flag, which led to considerable ill-feeling and the Finns marching without any flag; the organizers initially forgot to provide US and Swedish flags, and when some were found, Martin Sheridan, the eventual discus champion, refused to dip the flag as he passed in front of the king, Edward VII, announcing: 'This flag dips to no earthly king'; the Americans pulled out of the tug-of-war after a team from the Liverpool police force arrived with steel spikes in their boots; and British officials decided to re-run the 400 yards final after their athlete was supposedly pushed off the track, resulting in the American competitor refusing to take part and the British runner, Wyndham Halswelle, running by himself to take gold.

The tournament's biggest drama involved the marathon, run between Windsor Castle and White City, at the end of which the leader, Dorando Pietri, an Italian pastry shop owner, ran the wrong way when he entered the stadium, was corrected by officials, with whom he argued, and collapsed as he was helped over the line. He was then disqualified for receiving aid, a decision which led to arguments and fighting in the stands, lasting an hour.

Britain enjoyed its most successful Games in 1908, winning 145 medals, of which fifty-six were gold, but success was due more to gamesmanship than sporting prowess. The host country supplied all the officials, outlawed sports such as rowing at which it was not likely to win, included events that nobody else practised, such as small-bore rifle shooting, and spread the Games from April to October so that participants from other countries would have to return home. After the Games finished the stadium was used for the Coronation Exhibition of 1911, marking George V's accession to the throne, and the Latin British Exhibition of 1912, and after the First World War it was leased to the Greyhound Racing Association. White City also occasionally hosted football: Queens Park Rangers used it as their home ground from 1931 to 1933 and Uruguay played France here during the 1966 World Cup. It was demolished in 1985 and replaced by BBC radio headquarters.
► The Oval, p. 394.

(iii) Shepherd's Bush Common

Shepherd's Bush Green
Shepherds Bush Empire

A three-tiered theatre designed by Frank Matcham for Oswald Stoll, it opened in 1903 and was a music hall for fifty years. The BBC bought it in 1953 to convert into a studio that came to be used for recording *Juke Box Jury*, *The Generation Game*, *Wogan*, *Crackerjack!* and *The Old Grey Whistle Test*. In the mid-1990s the Empire was reopened as a rock venue with occasional stand-up comedy nights.

Lime Grove
𝔅𝔅ℭ 𝔏𝔦𝔪𝔢 𝔊𝔯𝔬𝔳𝔢 𝔖𝔱𝔲𝔡𝔦𝔬𝔰

London's second most important film studios, after Ealing, opened in 1913. Alfred Hitchcock filmed scenes here for *The Man Who Knew Too Much*, including the 'Albert Hall' sequence, in which a diplomat is about to be assassinated, and an ingenious version of John Buchan's *The Thirty-Nine Steps* in which Hitchcock even managed to improve Buchan's dynamic plot, adding characters such as Mr Memory, who answers questions from the audience on a range of topics but not on the nature of the mysterious thirty-nine steps themselves. During the Second World War filming continued – the biggest success was Carol Reed's version of H. G. Wells's *Kipps* – but Rank went into decline and at the end of the forties the studios were bought by the BBC who, in 1953, used them for recording the first family 'soap', *The Grove Family*. The first *Grandstand* was broadcast from here in 1958 and countless episodes of *Dr Who* and *Blue Peter* were later made at Lime Grove. At the end of the twentieth century the studios were demolished and replaced by a homeless persons' hostel.

WEST KENSINGTON, W14

Separated from Kensington proper by Holland Park and the West London Railway, West Kensington is a jumble of seedy hotels, once grand terraced houses now broken up into depressing flats, and roaring roads, particularly Talgarth Road/ West Cromwell Road, notorious for its Rolex watch thieves who seize their booty from the arms of drivers through the open windows of their cars. Nearer Holland Park there are some of the most magnificent properties in London, grand villas mostly designed for the area's late-nineteenth-century artistic community.

(i) around Olympia

Addison Road

Addison Road, the first road to connect Holland Park Avenue and Kensington High Street, was built in 1823 with a twist around the ponds at the southern end known as the Moats, and soon after was built up with houses that veer from the unassuming to the spectacular. No. 8, constructed in the early years of the twentieth century for Ernest Debenham, the store owner, is a riot of rococo detailing.

The Debenham House, No. 8, east side
London's most ostentatious and flamboyant twentieth-century private property was designed by Halsey Ricardo in 1905 to 1907 for Ernest Debenham, the West End store owner, with a dynamic mix of Arts and Crafts, classical and Byzantine styles that included an exterior of blue and green glazed bricks, which Ricardo believed would offer protection from the London climate, and an interior featuring peacock blue tiles by William de Morgan that were surplus from the Tsar of Russia's yacht. There were also motifs of fish, peacocks and eagles (the work of Ricardo's associates in the Art Workers' Guild) and a vast hall exquisitely decorated with mosaics, marble and veined stone with Byzantine arches, signs of the Zodiac and Greek gods. Debenham, who rarely spent time here, installed a telephone connected to West End theatres so that he and his family could enjoy shows, audibly if not visually. The house was used in the 1968 Joseph Losey film *Secret Ceremony*, starring Mia Farrow and Robert Mitchum, and at the end of the twentieth century was occupied by the Richmond Fellowship for Mental Welfare and Rehabilitation until it went on sale for £20 million.
► Debenhams, p. 138.

Hammersmith Road
Olympia, east of Blythe Road
A huge exhibition centre, best known for the *Daily Mail* Ideal Home Exhibition, it opened as the National Agricultural Hall in

1884 and became Olympia two years later. Early events held here were mostly circus or grand extravaganzas, such as the *Venice in London* show, featuring replicas of the Grand Canal, which lasted for most of 1891, and the first British Aero Show, in 1909, with eleven exhibits, including seven biplanes and two monoplanes, but there were also sports events. On 11 May 1922 Ted 'Kid' Lewis, the British middleweight and welterweight champion, fought Georges Carpentier for the world light-heavyweight championship in a contest marred by a bizarre incident in the first round. The referee made some comment to Lewis, who dropped his guard to listen, was sent reeling to the canvas by Carpentier's right hand, and was then counted out none the less.

On 8 June 1934 the British Union of Fascists held their first major rally at Olympia, an event which they hoped would be attended by middle-class voters as well as the usual working-class foot soldiers who mostly made up their attendance figures. There were also 2,000 opponents, who had spread out inside the hall and were heckling party leader Oswald Mosley, and many of them were beaten up by BUF supporters. Two protestors then climbed a gantry and began walking along a narrow ledge high above the auditorium while the crowd below held its breath. The following day a furore in the newspapers and the House of Commons led members of the establishment who had previously been receptive to Mosley, such as Lord Rothermere, owner of the *Daily Mail*, to withdraw their backing. ▸ Earl's Court, p. 420.

Holland Park Road
A road at the centre of the late Victorian artists' community of West Kensington that features a number of outstanding houses including No. 10 which was built for the portrait painter James Shannon around the original farmhouse of Holland Farm.
Leighton House, No. 12, north side
A large red-brick Italianate villa with a restrained exterior but decorated to the

highest standards within, Leighton House, now a museum, was designed by George Aitchison between 1865 and 1879 and was originally home to Frederic Leighton, the charismatic late-nineteenth-century classical painter who was first exhibited at the Royal Academy in 1855, when he was twenty-five, and later became its President. An avid art collector, Leighton acquired works by Constable, Corot and Delacroix, and during his travels became a keen Arabist, which led him to build an Arabian hall, based on the twelfth-century Muslim palace of La Zisa in Palermo, Sicily, as the centrepiece of the property. Leighton House now contains paintings by Leighton, Edward Burne-Jones, John Millais and their contemporaries.

Melbury Road
Architecturally the most interesting road in west London, owing to the properties created for the artists who moved here in the mid nineteenth century.
north side: Addison Road to Kensington High Street
Tower House, No. 29
A medieval fantasy of exquisite and eccentric design, Tower House, built from 1876 to 1881, is a monumental folly designed for himself in a fifteenth-century French Gothic style by the architect William Burges, a fanatical medievalist. Each room is based on a different theme from nature – the hall's is Time, the drawing room's Love, the library's the Liberal Arts – and there are rooms devoted to the Sea, Animals, Stars and signs of the Zodiac. The bronze entrance hall has a representation of the Four Ages of Man and a mosaic floor devoted to Theseus and the Minotaur, which contains a trace of the Cretan maze; there are literary themes in the library, with ceiling paintings of the lawgivers Luther, Justinian and Moses; a fireplace featuring the parts of speech watched over by Mistress Grammar – Pronouns blowing trumpets, Queen Verb followed by her pages, plus the Articles and Nouns carrying Adjectives – and stained-glass windows decorated with the muses of

Poetry, Music and Architecture; the dining room is based on Chaucer's House of Fame; the drawing-room fireplace features a carving of the Garden of Hesperides; the Music Room is dedicated to the Fortunes and Misfortunes of Love; what was Burges's bedroom contains intricately painted butterflies and a chimneypiece in silver and gold decorated with mermaids; and in the garden are trees that were once part of Holland Park and a terrace with a mosaic pavement and marble seats. Nevertheless the work was unfinished, as Burges died in 1881, only three years after moving in. In 1969 the house was bought by the actor Richard Harris and four years later Led Zeppelin's Jimmy Page purchased it from Harris for £350,000, outbidding David Bowie. Page invited the cult film maker Kenneth Anger to use the basement to apply the finishing touches to his film *Lucifer Rising*, which Anger did until he tired of living in what he called Page's 'evil fantasy house'.

► Dr Phené's Gingerbread Castle, p. 413.

Woodside, No. 31

An English country mansion stranded in deepest West Kensington, Woodside was built in 1875 by Norman Shaw, the pioneer of the red-brick suburban house, for the painter Luke Fildes, who, in comparing the property to No. 8 (which Shaw built for Fildes's friend and rival Marcus Stone), boasted: 'It is by a long way the most superior house of the lot. I consider it knocks Stone's to bits.' Once a year Fildes hosted 'Show Sunday', on which much of the London art world came to socialize, and he would count the visitors by dropping a coffee bean into a brass bowl as each one entered the house. Woodside is now the home of the film director Michael Winner.

south side: Kensington High Street to Addison Road

No. 22

Benjamin Britten, the composer, lived in this sumptuous block of flats from 1948 to 1953 and here wrote the operas *Billy Budd* and *Gloriana*.

Holman Hunt's address (early twentieth century) / MI6 headquarters 1923–4,
No. 18

It was to No. 18 that William Holman Hunt, the Pre-Raphaelite painter best known for *The Light of the World* in St Paul's Cathedral, had the carcass of a horse delivered, so that he could paint the animal accurately. Here the young Virginia Woolf had 'lessons in the art of behaviour from Mrs Holman Hunt [Edith Waugh] and found old Holman Hunt himself dressed in a long Jaeger dressing gown, holding forth to a large gathering about the ideas which had inspired him'. In 1923 MI6 moved briefly to Melbury Road, driven out of central London by lack of funds, but within a year had raised enough money to return to Westminster. The property has since been converted into flats.

► MI6, p. 266.

No. 8

Norman Shaw built the house with tall windows in the Queen Anne style in 1875–6 for the illustrator Marcus Stone, who upset neighbours by incorporating three gates – one for family members and friends, one for models and one for servants. The film director Michael Powell, who lived here from 1951 to 1971, shot scenes for his 1960 film *Peeping Tom* inside.

Kingfisher House, No. 6

Kingfisher House, a bland block of flats, stands on the site once occupied by the earliest property in the area, 𝕷𝖎𝖙𝖙𝖑𝖊 𝕳𝖔𝖑𝖑𝖆𝖓𝖉 𝕳𝖔𝖚𝖘𝖊, home in the mid nineteenth century to the Prinsep family, who used it for hosting art salons. The Prinseps once offered a room to the artist G. F. Watts, who was recuperating from an illness and thanked them by staying for thirty years. In the 1870s the widowed Lady Holland, owner of the surrounding estate, sold the land to allow Melbury Road to be built, and Watts hired the architect Frederick Pepys Cockerell to build him a house large enough to hold his huge sculptures. (It was demolished in 1963.)

(ii) around West Kensington station

Beaumont Crescent

Marcus Garvey's address (1935–40), No. 2
The leading figure in the rise of black consciousness during the mid twentieth century, Marcus Garvey, often referred to as the 'Black Moses', was born in Jamaica and worked in social reform and the newspaper industry until he read Booker T. Washington's *Up from Slavery*, a book that advocated black self-help, and led him to campaign vigorously for black self-determination. In 1914 Garvey founded the Universal Negro Improvement Association – motto 'One God, One Aim, One Destiny' – which advocated repatriation from America to Africa on his Black Star Shipping Line, but the venture was not a commercial success and he was charged with fraud, possibly on false evidence concocted by the FBI, and sentenced to five years in jail. After serving two years Garvey was deported as an undesirable alien and returned to Jamaica where he became involved in politics, leaving in 1935 to move to London, where he died (at No. 2 Beaumont Crescent) of pneumonia on 10 June 1940, in virtual obscurity. In the 1970s Garvey became a household word in (white) music circles thanks to the championing of his cause by reggae acts such as Burning Spear.
▶ Notting Hill music, p. 451.

Gunterstone Road

No. 11
On arriving in Britain from New York for the first time in September 1966 Jimi Hendrix, accompanied by his mentor, Animals bassist Chas Chandler, was brought from Heathrow Airport to 11 Gunterstone Road, home of British R&B singer Zoot Money and his band, who lived in the various flats into which the property had been divided. Hendrix had spent the previous six years touring noisy, seedy American bars playing with local groups before graduating on to major tours as backing guitarist for the Isley Brothers and Little Richard, but he was unknown in Britain. At No. 11 Hendrix began jamming with Money's guitarist Andy Summers (later of the Police), and those listening were stunned into speechlessness at Hendrix's virtuoso technique and his exuberant style. Ronni Money, Zoot's wife, rushed upstairs to urge the tenant Kathy Etchingham to come downstairs because 'Chas has just brought this guy back from America and he looks like the Wild Man of Borneo.' When Etchingham entered the room Hendrix displayed a different side of his technique, leaning over her, kissing her ear and whispering, 'I think you're beautiful.' Over the next few days the unknown guitarist was taken round central London's most popular nightspots, beginning with the Scotch of St James, off Pall Mall, where he was introduced to the major players on the rock scene and fulfilled his main wish – to meet his idol, Eric Clapton. When Clapton, then revered as Britain's most talented rock guitarist, heard Hendrix play he turned to Chandler and whispered 'He's *that* good?'

Select Bibliography

Ackroyd, Peter, *Blake*, London: Sinclair Stevenson, 1995

Alderman, Geoffrey, *Modern British Jewry*, Oxford: Clarendon Press, 1992

Ali, Tariq, *Street Fighting Years*, London: Collins, 1987

Barker, Felix and Silvester-Carr, Denise, *Crime and Scandal: The Black Plaque Guide to London*, London: Constable, 1987

Barnes, Richard (compiler), *Mods!*, London: Plexus, 1979

Barson, Susie and Saint, Andrew, *A Farewell to Fleet Street*, London: Historic Buildings and Monuments Commission for England, 1988

Beckett, Francis, *Enemy Within: The Rise and Fall of the British Communist Party*, London: John Murray, 1995

Beckman, Morris, *The 43 Group*, London: Centerprise, 1992

Berkeley, Roy, *A Spy's London*, London: Leo Cooper, 1994

Bermant, Chaim, *London's East End: Point of Arrival*, New York: Macmillan, 1975

——, *The Cousinhood*, London: Eyre and Spottiswoode, 1971

Bignell, John, *Chelsea Seen from 1860 to 1980*, London: Studio B, 1978

Blake, Robert, *The Conservative Party from Peel to Major*, London: Arrow, 1998

Bolitho, Henry, *No. 10 Downing Street 1660–1900*, London: Hutchinson, 1957

Boston, Ray, *The Essential Fleet Street: Its History and Influence*, London: Blandford, 1990

Brandreth, Gyles, *The Funniest Man on Earth: The Story of Dan Leno*, London: Hamish Hamilton, 1977

Campbell, Duncan, *The Underworld*, London: BBC Books, 1994

Coleridge, Nicholas, *Paper Tigers*, London: William Heinemann, 1993

Cross, Colin, *The Fascists in Britain*, London: Barrie and Rockliff, 1961

Dorril, Stephen, *MI6: Fifty Years of Special Operations*, London: Fourth Estate, 2000

Downes, Kerry, *Hawksmoor*, London: Thames and Hudson, 1970

Eatwell, Roger, *Fascism: A History*, London: Chatto and Windus, 1995

Edmonds, Mark, *Inside Soho*, London: Robert Nicholson, 1988

Edwards, Dennis and Pigram, Ron, *London's Underground Suburbs*, London: Baton Transport, 1986

Ellmers, Chris and Werner, Alex, *London's Lost Riverscape*, London: Viking, 1988

Farson, Daniel, *Gilbert and George: A Portrait*, London: HarperCollins, 1999

——, *Limehouse Days*, London: Michael Joseph, 1991

——, *Soho in the Fifties*, London: Michael Joseph, 1987

Foot, M. R. D., *SOE, An Outline History of the Special Operations Executive 1940–46*, London: Mandarin, 1984

Foot, M. R. D. and Langley, J. M., *MI9: Escape and Evasion 1939–45*, London: Futura, 1979

Fountain, Nigel, *The London Alternative Press 1966–74*, New York and London: Routledge, 1988

Fraser, Frankie and Morton, James, *Mad Frank and Friends*, London: Little Brown, 1998

——, *Mad Frank: Memoirs of a Life of Crime*, London: Little Brown, 1994

Fraser-Smith, Charles, *The Secret War of Charles Fraser-Smith*, London: Michael Joseph, 1981

Fryer, Peter, *Staying Power: The History of Black People in Britain*, London: Pluto, 1984

Giuseppi, John, *The Bank of England: A History from Its Foundation in 1694*, London: Evans Brothers Ltd, 1966

Glover, Stephen, *Paper Dreams*, London: Jonathan Cape, 1993

Gordon, Elizabeth, *Prehistoric London: Its Mounds and Circles*, London: Elliot Stock, 1914

Graham-Dixon, Andrew, *A History of British Art*, London: BBC Books, 1996

Green, Jonathan, *All Dressed Up: The Sixties and the Counter-Culture*, London: Jonathan Cape, 1998

Green, Jonathan (editor), *Days in the Life*, London: Heinemann, 1988

Harrison, J. F. C., *The Second Coming: Popular Millenarianism 1780–1850*, London and Henley: Routledge and Kegan Paul, 1979

Hayter, Peter (editor), *Great Tests Recalled*, London: Bloomsbury, 1990

Hibbert, Christopher, *King Mob: The Story of Lord George Gordon and the Riots of 1780*, London: Longman's, 1958

Hill, Christopher, *The World of the Muggletonians: Christopher Hill, Barry Reay and William Lamont*, London: Temple Smith, 1983

Howse, Derek, *Greenwich Time and the Discovery of the Longitude*, Oxford: Oxford University Press, 1980

Humphries, Steve and Taylor, John, *The Making of Modern London 1945–85*, London: Sidgwick & Jackson, 1986

Hunt, James D., *Gandhi in London*, New Delhi and London: Promilla and Co, 1978

Hyde, H. Montgomery, *The Atom Bomb Spies*, London: Hamish Hamilton, 1980

Itzin, Catherine, *Stages in the Revolution: Political Theatre in Britain Since 1968*, London: Methuen, 1968

Jenkins, Simon, *Newspapers: The Power and the Money*, London: Faber and Faber, 1979

Jones, R. V., *Most Secret War*, Ware: Wordsworth Editions, 1998

Katz, David S., *The Jews in the History of England*, Oxford: Clarendon Press, 1994

Kelland, Gilbert, *Crime in London*, London: Grafton, 1996

Laurie, Peter, *Beneath the City Streets: A Private Inquiry into the Nuclear Preoccupations of Government*, London: Penguin, 1970

Lawrence, David, *Underground Architecture*, Harrow: Capital Transport, 1994

Leigh, David, *The Wilson Plot: The Intelligence Services and the Discrediting of a Prime Minister 1945–76*, London: Heinemann, 1988

Litvinoff, Emanuel, *Journey through a Small Planet*, London: Michael Joseph, 1972

Lucas, Norman, *Britain's Gangland*, London: W. H. Allen, 1969

Marks, Leo, *Silk and Cyanide*, London: HarperCollins, 1999

McAuley, Ian, *Guide to Ethnic London*, London: Immel, 1987

Mellor, David, *The Sixties Art Scene in London*, London: Phaidon, 1993

Morton, James, *East End Gangland*, London: Little Brown, 2000

——, *Gangland*, Volume 2, London: Little Brown, 1994

——, *Gangland, London's Underworld*, London: Little Brown, 1993

Mosley, Oswald, *My Life*, London: Thomas Nelson and Sons, 1968

Nicholson, John, *The Great Liberty Riot of 1780*, London: Bozo, 1985

Nuttall, Jeff, *Bomb Culture*, London: MacGibbon and Kee, 1968

Palmer, Alan, *The East End: Four Centuries of London Life*, London: John Murray, 1989

Pearce, Brian and Woodhouse, Michael, *A*

History of Communism in Britain,
London: Bookmarks, 1995

Pearson, John, *The Profession of Violence,*
London: Grafton Books, 1985

Pendreigh, Brian, *On Location: The Film
Fan's Guide to Britain and Ireland,*
Edinburgh and London: Mainstream,
1995

Pentlow, Mike and Rowe, Marsha, *Characters of Fitzrovia,* London: Chatto and
Windus, 2001

Perry, Maria, *Mayfair Madams,* London:
André Deutsch, 1999

Perry, Roland, *The Fifth Man,* London: Sidgwick and Jackson, 1994

Phillips, Mike and Phillips, Trevor, *Windrush: The Irresistible Rise of Multi-Racial
Britain,* London: HarperCollins, 1998

Piper, David, *Artists' London,* London:
Weidenfeld and Nicolson, 1982

Pudney, John, *John Wesley and His World,*
London: Thames and Hudson, 1978

Ramsey, Winston G. (editor), *The East End,
Then and Now,* London: After the Battle,
1997

Reynolds, Bruce, *The Autobiography of a
Thief,* London: Bantam, 1995

Rice, Jonathan, *One Hundred Lord's Tests:
A Celebration of the Home of Cricket,*
London: Methuen, 2001

Richards, Huw, *The Bloody Circus: The
Daily Herald and the Left,* London: Pluto
Press, 1997

Richardson, Charlie, *My Manor,* London:
Sidgwick and Jackson, 1991

Richardson, John, *Camden Town and Primrose Hill Past,* London: Historical Publications, 1991

Rowbotham, Sheila, *Promise of a Dream,*
London: Penguin Press, 2000

Savage, John, *England's Dreaming: Sex
Pistols and Punk Rock,* London: Faber and
Faber, 1991

Scobie, Edward, *Black Britannia,* Chicago:
Johnson Publishing Company, 1972

Scott, Harold, *The Early Doors: Origins of
the Music Hall,* London: Ivor Nicholson
and Watson, 1946

Seldon, Anthony, *10 Downing Street: The
Illustrated History,* London: Harper-
Collins, 1999

Service, Robert, *Lenin: A Biography,*
London: Macmillan, 2000

Sinclair, Iain, *Lights out for the Territory,*
London: Granta, 1997

Sinclair, Iain and Lichtenstein, Rachel,
Rodinsky's Room, London: Granta, 1999

Summers, Judith, *Soho: A History of
London's Most Colourful Neighbourhood,*
London: Bloomsbury, 1989

Tames, Richard, *St John's Wood and Maida
Vale Past,* London: Historical Publications, 1998

——, *Bloomsbury Past: A Visual History,*
London: Historical Publications, 1993

Taylor, S. J., *The Great Outsiders: Northcliffe,
Rothermere and the Daily Mail,* London:
Weidenfeld and Nicolson, 1996

Trease, Geoffrey, *Samuel Pepys and His
World,* London: Thames and Hudson,
1972

Trench, Richard and Hillman, Ellis, *London
under London,* London: John Murray,
1984

Uglow, Jenny, *Hogarth: A Life and a World,*
London: Faber and Faber, 1997

Watkins, Alan, *A Short Walk down Fleet
Street,* London: Duckworth, 2000

Watson, Isobel, *Hackney and Stoke
Newington Past,* London: Historical Publications, 1990

Weale, Adrian, *Renegades: Hitler's
Englishmen,* London: Weidenfeld and
Nicolson, 1994

Weightman, Gavin and Humphries, Steve,
The Making of Modern London 1815–1914,
London: Sidgwick and Jackson, 1983

West, Nigel, *MI5 British Security Services
Operations 1909–45,* London: The Bodley
Head, 1981

Wheen, Francis, *Karl Marx,* London: Fourth
Estate, 1999

Wintour, Charles, *The Rise and Fall of Fleet
Street,* London: Hutchinson, 1989

Ziegler, Philip, *London at War 1939–1945,*
London: Sinclair Stevenson, 1995

Index